Four Psychologies Applied to Education

Freudian • Behavioral
Humanistic • Transpersonal

Four Psychologies Applied to Education:

Freudian • Behavioral
Humanistic • Transpersonal

Edited by THOMAS B. ROBERTS

Schenkman Publishing Company

HALSTED PRESS DIVISION
JOHN WILEY AND SONS
New York   London   Sydney   Toronto

Copyright © 1975
Schenkman Publishing Company, Inc.
Cambridge, Massachusetts 02138

Distributed solely by Halsted Press, a division
of John Wiley & Sons, Inc., New York.

Library of Congress Cataloging in Publication Data

Roberts, Thomas B.   comp.
    Four psychologies applied to education: Freudian,
behavioral, humanistic, transpersonal.

    "A Halsted Press book."
    1. Educational psychology—Addresses, essays,
lectures.   I. Title. [DNLM: 1. Psychology, Applied—
Psychology, Educational. LB1051 R647f]
LB1055.R52   370.15'08   74-9729
ISBN 0-470-72586-9
ISBN 0-470-72588-5

F (?)

ACKNOWLEDGEMENTS

According to the philosopher Nastrudin, causation is an endless succession of intertwined events. So are the inputs into an author and his book. Some are people. Some are places. Some are planned and searched for. The best are serendipitous. Those I'd particularly like to thank are my students in Education 302 and Education 501 at Northern Illinois University; your reading and comments on these articles and others have been a primary basis for selection of this book's contents.

Thank you especially to my colleagues, students, and friends who have brought my attention to many of these articles that I otherwise would have missed. Your leads are directly responsible for several of these articles, and your curiosity and encouragement have helped me keep working on this.

A special thanks goes to the authors and publishers of these articles and to those who gave their permission, but whose good works I have had to exclude because of space limitations. And part of the intertwined succession of events would include their students, their subjects, their secretaries, and on and on. The secretaries in the Williston education office over the last three years have worked hard on this book, as they have on their other work too.

Finally, there are some special places and events which have energized my body, refreshed my mind, and cleaned my spirit. This book is dedicated to Thor's Woods in Iceland, a rainbow in the Grand Canyon, a New Year's Eve shooting star, the fragrance of sagebrush in the moonlight, and Moose Gulch days.

TBR
DeKalb, Illinois

CONTENTS

PART TWO: BEHAVIORAL PSYCHOLOGY

PART THREE: HUMANISTIC PSYCHOLOGY

PART FOUR: TRANSPERSONAL PSYCHOLOGY

EDITOR'S HELLO

We humans are fascinating creatures. The more I experience my own actions and the more I see the actions of others, the more I am intrigued. The more I'm intrigued, the more questions I ask. And every answer raises more questions than it solves. How do we do what we do, and why? What are we capable of that we still don't know about? How can we learn to do more, to do it better, and to learn it faster? Can we teach others to achieve these abilities more efficiently than we have learned them? This book is a progress report on these questions.

The authors whose works are printed here are also people who have asked these questions, and their writings are partial answers. These articles are some of my favorite answers, but they only begin to solve the questions. Every writer here will raise more questions than he answers, which is good. Learning *should* raise more questions than it answers. The ideas in this book are only one kind of answer—the psychological kind. The other studies of man have their sorts of specialized questions and specialized answers, too. The scope of this book is to present ideas from within the realm of educational psychology. I selected the articles for teachers, other educators, and for parents who are especially curious about how the questions above apply to children and in what ways we can improve children's learning. If you are among this professional and parental audience, I expect this book will give you some useful ideas. For your own good? Yes. But more than that, for your students and children. I hope you will make them the indirect but major beneficiaries of this collection of ideas and techniques.

There is a triple arrangement of articles in this book. Most obviously, the four sections—Freudian, behavioral, humanistic, and transpersonal psychologies—are presented with some of their applications to education. What I have to say about each psychology is contained in the introduction to each section. Also, each article has a comment or two preceding it.

A second way the book is organized is by a series of topics. They include developmental psychology, creativity, curriculum, teacher education, and more. Each of the four major sections shows how its psychology approaches these topics, although articles on each topic do not always appear in the same part of each section. I anticipate that this book will be useful to students and faculty members in psychology and education who want to compare, contrast, or combine different psychological approaches. Each of these psychologies asks different questions, makes different assumptions, and studies different human actions. Can you build a psychology that encompasses them all? A complete psychology would account for all human behavior. We have a long way to go.

1

The order within sections is arranged for "learnability." In my own learning and teaching, I've found that starting with a conceptual framework, e.g., a chapter on theory or an intellectual background, did little to make things clear and frequently contributed to making them foggier in my mind. Although that may be a logical way to present information, it is not a pedagogical, or optimum learning, way. A mass of abstractions with no concrete examples succeeded only in allowing the haze of intellectual abstractions to drift over the ground of practical specifics. So, I've started the readings in each section with several specific examples of the educational applications of their respective psychologies. The introductions to the sections, on the other hand, present an overall view of their psychologies. People who like to taste specific examples before learning general ideas may want to read the introductions as summaries, after they have finished the readings of a section. Those whose learning style is compatible with pre-organized learning may want to start with the introductions.

After an example or two, the more theoretical articles appear. With a knowledge of some specifics to keep in mind, the abstract articles should be clearer and can be seen in the light of the specific examples. More educational applications follow the theoretical articles; then each section moves back and forth between specific applications and general theory. Another organization for "learnability" is that the easier-to-understand articles are the first ones in each section, so that there is also a movement (particularly in the first half of each section) from the more basic concepts of each psychology to the more complex ones. I expect that by the time someone reads through a section, he'll have a good grasp of the underlying psychology as well as its educational applications.

What can we humans learn? How can we teach it to others? This book is for you who ask, knowing these questions will never be completely answered. These readings are especially for my fellow teachers who want some ideas of how to use psychology to improve their classrooms. Human behavior is fascinating, and the articles in this book are some of the best I've found. I hope they answer some of your questions and raise many more.

PART ONE

Freudian Psychology

INTRODUCTION
THE EDITOR

In understanding how Freudian psychology can be applied to education it is helpful to keep in mind the times and background of Sigmund Freud as a person. The nineteenth century was very much a century of biology. Pasteurization, vaccination, and antisepsis were giant strides in the practice of medicine and public health. Graham (of cracker fame) and others developed the field of dietetics and founded the basis for modern dietary practices. Darwin's theory of evolution provoked a furor in philosophy and social theory, as well as biology. While it can be fallacious to judge current ideas only on the basis of their origin almost a century ago, it is enlightening to keep this factor in mind in the case of Freudian psychology. Freud and his ideas developed as he experienced more; likewise, his followers have changed and developed their own variations on his ideas. The following overall summary is generally true of most Freudians, but by no means always true for all of them.

UNDERLYING PREMISES OF FREUDIAN THOUGHT

Biological orientation. Freud saw human behavior in biological terms, and he hoped and expected that some day our actions could be understood in terms of our physiology, especially our nervous system. This reduction of psychology to biology was a natural assumption for someone whose education took place in the century of biology. Furthermore, Darwin's recently published ideas were permeating scientific and social thought. One of Darwin's implications was that man is part of evolution, and as such, shares many traits with other animals. With this idea Darwin paved the way for Freud, who based his psychology on the assumption that human motivation could be understood to a large extent (not entirely) in terms of animal-like, physiological drives. Thus, when Freud said that biological energy was the basis of human behavior, as it was in animals, Darwin's previous linking of man with animals made Freud's idea more palpable. When Freud said that pleasure was organically-based, e.g., in the mouth, anus, and genitals, and when he emphasized the role of sexual drives in human motivation, his ideas fit in with the intellectual climate of the times with its interest in the survival of the fittest both personally and socially. When Freud interpreted child development as a sequence of stages based on anatomy, his ideas made sense to people who were then beginning to look at the idea that human ontogeny (the growth of one person) recapitulates human phylogeny (the evolution of mankind as a species). Several of the articles in this section show this biological bias; this is strongly evident in "Readings from *Normal Adolescence*," which exemplifies the Freudian assumption that psychology is rooted in biology.

Curing. Freud was a doctor. As such he was interested in diagnosing and curing illness. His psychology was predominantly built and revised by his seeing patients. As a result, Freudian psychology and educational practices derived from it still are concerned with psychological illness, either curing or preventing it. In "Excerpts from *Fantasy and Feeling In Education*" Richard Jones discriminates between therapy and education. A teacher, he says, should be more concerned with preventing psychological problems and with increasing mental health than he should be concerned with therapy. This is a valuable distinction for educators to keep in mind and to have ready in case concerned parents confusedly think that teachers are trying to practice therapy, a skill we are unprepared for. In distinguishing between education and therapy, Jones represents a view held by some younger Freudians. Tenenbaum's article "School Grades and Group Therapy" and Bower's "An In-Service Program in Mental Health" show that the therapeutic model is not entirely outdated, however.

Psychological determinism. A common belief in Freud's times, although not universally held, was that mankind's actions were the product of will or decisions. From that point of view man was aware of his reasons for doing whatever he did, and he was seen as entirely responsible for himself. While he could be the victim of circumstances, in some cases, and have to act with conflicting wishes, decision-making was seen as basically a rational process with economic and social inputs into his choices. Freud said that there was another type of determinism, psychological determinism. Our behavior, according to him, was not the result of current economic or social situations or of the use of reason, but was a result of psychological forces. For example, the Oedipus Complex, in which a boy desires to possess his mother and kill his father, or the Electra Complex, the girl's counterpart, are seen as basic to human nature. The importance of economic, social, or familial experiences is how these influence the psychological make-up of the person, which in turn influences his behavior. In one sense Freud said that these psychological processes intervene between the past and the present, so that in order to understand current behavior and to control our future behavior we must know both how the human psyche acts and what the past and current influences on it are. Freud believed not only that human behavior was determined, but also that it was frequently over-determined; that is, there is a large number of influences into our behavior. Any one of them would be enough to cause us to act as we do. In Tyler's and Grossman's articles we see examples of how knowledge of a psychological process is useful in understanding a student's behavior. In schools we frequently see students acting toward teachers or other adults as if they were acting toward their parents, regardless of how appropriate or inappropriate their actions are. Knowledge of transference helps us understand what otherwise could be puzzling, confusing, or worrisome behavior. A teenager's love for a teacher or hate for a teacher could be a transference of the Oedipus or the Electra Complex, and have practically no realistic basis. In fact, to a young person who is just beginning to make these transferences, a teacher may often be a psychologically "safe target" for these feelings because the teacher is older, married, or otherwise unreachable. The idolization of entertainment and sports stars is another example. Political, economic, and social events are influences on psychological processes and are transformed by psychological processes; thus, if we are to understand human behavior, we must know about these general psychological processes as well as the particular history of an individual's life. Freud agreed that human behavior is directed toward goals, but he added that some of these goals were not socially acceptable and remained unconscious, hidden, or camouflaged.

MAJOR IDEAS IN FREUDIAN PSYCHOLOGY

The Unconscious. As indicated in the paragraph just above, our behavior is interpreted not as fully rational, but as being more complex than has previously been thought. In a time when reasoning was seen as a conscious, deliberate process, it was a radical idea to say that there were reasons of which people weren't aware. Freud didn't invent the idea of the unconscious, but he used and developed it more than anyone else. The role of the unconscious in human behavior is a primary concept of Freudian psychology. In fact, if there is any one question that is most characteristic of Freudian thought, it is, "What part does the unconscious play?" Most Freudian thought branches out from this question, and in each of the articles in this section this question is either implicitly or explicitly stated in some form. The unconscious is not a biological organ. It can't be found by dissection. It is a name for a collection of processes, and calling it by the shorthand name of "the unconscious" as if it were an object is merely simpler than saying "the unconscious processes." The unconscious is a memory storage, an organizer of psychic energy, a switching system, and the master control of our behavior. At first it seems that this tyranny of the unconscious limits our freedom and that Freudian psychology could lead to a misanthropic view of human nature and to a hopelessness for improving society or ourselves. These conclusions come from an incomplete understanding of Freudian theory. While the unconscious and its drives for immediate gratification are always there, therapy and education give us ways to rechannel these energies into socially useful activities and toward individual growth, rather than psychological fatalism. Psychological laws, like physical or chemical laws, are part of reality. When we know them, we can act in accordance with them and use them for our benefit.

Since the unconscious (what we aren't aware of) is such an important influence on us and is so powerful, two of the goals of education are to become aware of our unconscious and to use its vast abilities in beneficial ways. In "Excerpts from *Fantasy and Feeling in Education*" Jones says that if we can learn to tap this resource in a constructive way, we can have creative learning; while if we let the energy get misdirected, we develop anxiety and may need therapy. One of our jobs as teachers, then, is to teach people to use the unconscious rather than let it use us. The psychological energy is there. It is up to us to use it well. Weisskopf and Kubie see the unconscious as a vast and nearly untapped psychological resource.

Personality structure. Freudians describe personality structure very much as if it were a group of three people linked to each other in many and complicated ways. Here too, the names of the parts do not refer to actual biological objects, but are shorthand names for groups of processes and relationships. The id is the lusty infant who wants immediate gratification. Physical pleasure is what the id is after, and it will use the libido (sexual energy) to get what it wants. The id's typical remark in the personality dialog is, "Gimmie. I want it. Now!" Because of its animalistic anti-social nature, the rest of the personality and society have kept the id mostly unconscious. It still influences us, but unconsciously. This is one of the more interesting explanations of childhood amnesia (our inability to remember much about our early childhood); our infancy and early childhood were so dominated by the id, that we have repressed it into our unconscious so as not to feel anxiety and guilt about that stage of our development.

The super-ego is the conscience. *Should* and *shame* are the staples of its vocabulary, and its favorite line is, "You should be ashamed of yourself!"

While the id is predominantly unconscious, the super-ego is partly conscious and partly unconscious. The unconscious part contains the remonstrations and rules we were taught, "Don't do that. Don't play with . . . Nasty! Nice people don't . . ." The super-ego is judgmental.

Between the id and the super-ego lives the hero and executive of the Freudian personality structure, the ego. Not only is he caught between the id and the super-ego and forced to moderate their conflicting pressures, he also is the one who is most aware of outside, social reality. Thus, his line to the others is, "Now, let's be realistic about this." As is probably apparent, a major task of education is to help students develop a strong ego. This should not be confused with the self-centeredness of someone who is "egotistical." The ego generally straddles the conscious and the unconscious. In a healthy personality he is the manager and can call the shots without being overpowered by the id or the super-ego. Each of the three parts has a genius all of its own. The ego's armamentum includes his "ego defenses." Sublimation, for example, is the redirection of socially unacceptable impulses into acceptable channels: "Don't play in the toilet, dear. Why don't you go out and play in the sandbox?" A large part of our work as teachers is to provide socially acceptable outlets for otherwise destructive desires. In "The Latency Period" Anna Freud describes some of the typical ploys the ego uses to juggle the id, the super-ego, and reality.

Infantile sexuality. This is one of the most controversial Freudian ideas and is a topic of disagreement among the various branches of Freudian psychology. True to the biological origins of Freudian psychology, the main point of the idea of infantile sexuality is that infants and children feel pleasure when various parts of their body are stimulated, just as adults do. This basic physiological pleasure moves from one part of the anatomy to another as the child matures. In youngest infancy it is the mouth, and various theories of breast vs. bottle and demand vs. schedule feeding are derived from this assumption. In the second and third years of life as the child learns to control his bowels, the anus becomes important as he finds that he can control his parents' reactions by controlling his bowel movements. The anus which had previously been only a source of pleasure, starts to become a way of interacting with the world. This, of course, is an origin of various approaches to toilet training. The phallic phase occurs when the child discovers that the genitals can give pleasure too, and that he also can cause certain kinds of reactions in his parents or other adults by displaying them. After a "latent period" of several years around the age of seven, children go through puberty and on to adolescence and adulthood, the mature genital stage.

It is helpful to remember that these various Freudian ideas are not acting separately from each other. Here we can see the biological orientation with its emphasis on bodily pleasure and an organ-centered way of understanding human behavior. If these various stages are resolved satisfactorily, then the person doesn't need therapy, but the need for curing may result if the wrong actions are done to him at these various critical points. Our development is set in its general course by these stages, but each person's individual life gives infinite variations on the broad developmental scheme. If most people don't remember these stages, or if they seem shocking, that is because we have repressed them into our unconsciouses because they are anxiety-provoking or make us feel guilty. They are still there influencing our ids and super-egos. Many of our actions, values, and goals result from our egos' attempts to integrate all this and keep us functioning in the world. Freudian psychology is a system of interacting ideas; to do it justice and to use the ideas in our everyday teaching, we should not try to oversimplify the ideas or use them independently of one another.

Genetic approach. This does not have to do with chromosomes and genes, but is the idea that adult personality has its genesis in childhood experiences. This is why Freudians emphasize childhood so much in their therapy and education. Perhaps more than any other psychology, Freudian psychology stresses the importance of childhood education, especially early childhood education. This is also why Freudian therapy reaches back for childhood memories.

The four stages of development mentioned above (oral, anal, phallic, and genital) are the foundations of adult personality, and in order to understand an adult one must know how a person experienced these stages. The stage-theory of growth is one of the most accepted ideas in our culture. "He's only going through a stage," or "It's just a phase she's passing through," are examples of the extent to which the idea of developmental stages has permeated our thinking. This idea, of course, is not limited to Freudians, but many of our other approaches to developmental psychology are built on this popular concept. Erikson gives a variation of this approach in his article "Youth and the Life Cycle," and Roberts uses a humanistic derivative of the stage theory in "Developing Thoughts on Developmental Psychology and Moral Development."

SUMMARY

As the psychology which is most dominant in our culture, outside of academia, Freudian psychology provides the major psychological way we think about ourselves and our culture. People who use these ideas and assumptions, however, frequently don't realize the origin of the concepts they are using. A fuller knowledge of Freudian psychology, including its branches, can lead to even more useful ideas and insights into why we act as we do. The articles in this section show many educational applications of Freudian psychology to education. The books and articles the authors cite can take you further into understanding Freudian psychology and on to its educational applications. In many cases other writings by the authors and the books and journals these articles were selected from will prove interesting for further reading. Listed below are selected references which I have found most helpful.

REFERENCES

Freud, Sigmund, *New Introductory Lectures on Psycho-analysis*, W. W. Norton, 1933.

Hall, Calvin, *A Primer of Freudian Psychology*, New American Library, New York, 1954.

Holt, Robert R., "Sigmund Freud," pp. 1–12, Vol. 6, *International Encyclopedia of the Social Sciences*, The Macmillan Co. and The Free Press, New York, 1968.

Munroe, Ruth L., "The Basic Concepts of Psychoanalysis," pp. 26–68, *Schools of Psychoanalytic Thought*, Holt, Rinehart, and Winston, New York, 1967.

Pearson, Gerald Hamilton Jeffrey, *Psychoanalysis and the Education of the Child*, W. W. Norton, N.Y. 1954.

Psychoanalytic Study of the Child, Yearbook, International Universities Press, New York, 1945+.

A WORD OF INTRODUCTION *

A. S. Neill

Personal Happiness Brings Social Health. In a few words Neill captures the essence of Freudian psychology: "Freud showed that every neurosis is founded on sex repression; I said, 'I'll have a school in which there will be no sex repression.'" Cure inner neuroses for society's health. The medicines are love, trust, freedom, and responsibility. Change what is going on inside a person (his feelings and thoughts), and he will change his behavior toward himself and toward others, because outer behaviors are manifestations of inner states. Did you know that Neill didn't write *Summerhill*? It is a compilation from the other books he has written, edited by Harold Hart. It is one of the most loved, controversial, and exciting books in educational psychology. In fact, *Summerhill* often works in a Freudian way on its readers. They become more accepting, loving, understanding, and tolerant toward themselves as they read the book and, consequently, start acting in healthier ways toward their children, their students, and the rest of society. Read it. You'll know and experience a lot of Freudian psychology while reading it, and you'll probably be psychologically healthier and happier too. Just what Neill would want.

In psychology, no man knows very much. The inner forces of human life are still largely hidden from us.

Since Freud's genius made it alive, psychology has gone far; but it is still a new science, mapping out the coast of an unknown continent. Fifty years hence, psychologists will very likely smile at our ignorance of today.

Since I left education and took up child psychology, I have had all sorts of children to deal with—incendiaries, thieves, liars, bed-wetters, and bad-tempered children. Years of intensive work in child training has convinced me that I know comparatively little of the forces that motivate life. I am convinced, however, that parents who have had to deal with only their own children know much less than I do.

It is because I believe that a difficult child is nearly always made difficult by wrong treatment at home that I dare address parents.

What is the province of psychology? I suggest the word *curing*. But what kind of curing? I do not want to be cured of my habit of choosing the colors orange and black; nor do I want to be cured of smoking; nor of my liking for a bottle of beer. No teacher has the right to cure a child of making noises on a drum. The only curing that should be practiced is the curing of unhappiness.

*From A. S. Neill, *Summerhill: A Radical Approach to Child Rearing* (New York: Hart Publishing Company, 1960), pp. xxiii–xxiv, by permission of the publisher. A former public school teacher, A. S. Neill founded Summerhill School and was its headmaster until his death at age eighty-nine.

The difficult child is the child who is unhappy. He is at war with himself; and in consequence, he is at war with the world.

The difficult adult is in the same boat. No happy man ever disturbed a meeting, or preached a war, or lynched a Negro. No happy woman ever nagged her husband or her children. No happy man ever committed a murder or a theft. No happy employer ever frightened his employees.

All crimes, all hatreds, all wars can be reduced to unhappiness. This book is an attempt to show how unhappiness arises, how it ruins human lives, and how children can be reared so that much of this unhappiness will never arise.

More than that, this book is the story of a place—Summerhill—where children's unhappiness is cured and, more important, where children are reared in happiness.

SUMMERHILL: A FOLLOW-UP STUDY OF ITS STUDENTS *

But How Do They Fit Into Society? What _does_ happen to Summerhill students? After experiencing freedom and responsibility, how _do_ they adjust to a society with limited freedom and responsibility, and to public schools in a repressive society? By interviewing Summerhillians, Bernstein answers these and other questions that parents and teachers ask. Note that this article is rich in details of their lives, home, and work. Bernstein demonstrates the Freudian assumption that these areas indicate psychological health too. They are clinical or case details, not merely description. What do these details imply about the people? Neill says that the aim of life is to find happiness, and happiness is interest. Learning is not so important as personality and character. A successful school is measured, not by the incomes or power of its graduates, but by their _joie de vivre_, personality, and character. Using these criteria, as well as the traditional economic and vocational ones, Bernstein reports on Neill's example of Freudian education.

One December evening in 1964 I sat by my fireside after putting down the book _Summerhill_ (1960), and was impressed that there might be a school where children were happy and came to love both learning and life.

Early next morning as I wrote addition problems on the blackboard for my 7–10 year-olds with learning problems, I suddenly found myself letting Charlie finish a story that he was inspired to complete, even though it was a period assigned to arithmetic; and later on letting Frank work in his arithmetic workbook during a writing period. When Charlie had finished at least three times as much writing as he had ever accomplished in a single period, and after I observed the sudden smile and interest in Frank's usually bland, expressionless face, thoughts came to me with new intensity about this strange school in England .where children could always choose their activities, and were never forced to go to a lesson or to do any work.

In the faculty lunchroom we talked of the philosophy of education which allowed a child to discover his own ways of finding self-fulfillment (through knowing what he wants, working for it, and getting it).

Taking a second cup of coffee, Mrs. Tuttle, who had taught at our small, private New England school for many years, passed me the sugar. "But if no work is required, how can a child learn any responsibility at all?"

*From Dr. Emmanuel Bernstein, "Summerhill: A Follow-up Study of Its Students," _Journal of Humanistic Psychology_ 8, no.2 (Fall, 1968): 123–136, by permission of the author and publisher. Dr. Bernstein is Principal Psychologist at Raybrook State Rehabilitation Center and Director of Adirondack Counseling. He is the author of the forthcoming book _Living and Teaching with Freedom_.

I smiled, "Yes. What happens to them after they leave this little paradise?"

Thinking of his teen-age students still struggling with fundamental grammar, Bert Woodward remarked, "Still, wouldn't our results be better if students were taught as their need arose?"

"But many would never learn to write at all," argued another faculty member.

"Remember Frank Jones?" asked Mr. Woodward.

"What about him?" Mrs. Tuttle groaned.

"He dropped by to see me last month. Well, he became so interested in TV repair work that he taught himself to read excerpts from his TV repair books—owns his own business, even though he never graduated from high school."

"Well, what do you know. Shows what a little self-motivation can do," observed Mrs. Harrow.

The next day, still curious about this allegedly free approach, I said to Miss Nickles, my jolly assistant, "How about a Summerhill day?"

"Sure, why not?" she said while muttering "Oh! brother!" less audibly.

After lunch I briefly explained the Summerhill philosophy to my class. These ten boys and girls were here because of learning problems. Although they had average or above average intelligence, many were still struggling with first and second grade books.

"How would you like a Summerhill afternoon?" I found myself saying. A few minutes later, when the cheers subsided, Mike laughed, "Are you kidding?" throwing a paper glider into the air. I refrained from ordering him to pick it up and forced a pleasant smile. The Summerhill afternoon had begun.

"What should we do?" asked Betty.

"Anything you want," I said hesitantly, "We're here to help you if you want us." My assistant and I sat down and waited.

Several looked lost, a few began drawing with pen and crayon, another set up water colors, Mary was reading, Charlie and Billy were involved in their arithmetic workbooks, and Frank was writing a story. However, by the end of a half-hour two crises had occurred. Eight year old Jeffrey, his brown eyes large with excitement, had apparently regressed to an early stage of babyhood and was jumping up and down flailing his arms wildly.

"Jeffrey," I strongly advised, "Stop that!"

"I thought you said we could do anything."

I groped for words. "I did, uh, that is—within reason."

In the meantime, Irene, a usually shy little girl, put her arms around Mike, who enjoyed the reputation of being the best fighter in our class. He stared in surprise and horror as she gently stroked his hair and kissed him affectionately on the cheek. Then, from beneath his desk, he weakly called "Help, Mr. Bernstein, help!" while Irene giggled from above. I suggested to Irene that she might try a more constructive activity. This was the beginning of our "modified Summerhill approach."

During the following weeks, I talked more of Summerhill. Questions kept recurring, such as "How can one brought up in such a permissive environment adjust to the realities of a job, marriage, parenthood? . . . Can he face obligations? . . . Will he do some things he does not wish to do?" It was only my 7–12 year-old students who fully and unconditionally endorsed the Summerhill idea.

During the winter, I corresponded with Summerhillians, questioning whether any follow-up study of Summerhill students had ever been attempted. I learned that only one person had tried, sending by mail questionnaires, but he had difficulty obtaining names (even though he was teaching at Summerhill at the time) because the school has never kept records in its forty-five years of existence. He had received only a few replies. Despite these discouraging reports, I decided to spend my summer vacation in England, to see the school and to meet former Summerhill students. I hoped to learn how they felt about themselves and their Summerhill experience.

On June 16 I arrived in London and caught an early morning train for Summerhill School. In the dining car, I asked the waiter, "Have you ever heard of a school called Summerhill?"

"I saw scenes from the school on television last week," he said. I told him about my proposed survey.

"Where," I asked (hopefully opening my notebook), "do you suppose one might find these former students of the school?"

As the train began slowing down blowing its characteristic yodel at the approach to a crossing, he answered.

"It would be lots quicker if you went to the prisons, if you don't mind my saying so."

I dropped my notebook.

By the end of the summer, I was to find that the Summerhillian was certainly not a rebel. Later that day, Neill was to tell me that he was struck by the lack of rebelliousness in the products of his school. More significantly, a majority of the former students, whom I was later to interview, spontaneously mentioned only one characteristic of the "Summerhillian": *tolerance!* No, the prisons would be one of the last places to look.

Two persons and I descended at the Leiston, Suffolk station, and soon I walked down the school's tree-arched driveway. A boy shot by me on a bicycle followed by another. Elementary-aged children were running around, paying no attention to me or to each other. I passed some of the acres of fields in which children roamed freely, climbing trees and building private shacks. Next to a sunny corner of the main building, there was a huge, old, maroon sofa, with the stuffings coming out, upon which was seated a small girl of eight, who was concentrating on taking more of the stuffings out, in the morning sunlight.

When I entered the large, vacant hall of the main building, I was shocked to find a series of bulletin boards completely filled with page after page of single-spaced typed rules with accompanying penalties. One fifteen year-old boy told me, "There are more rules in a free school than anywhere else, even though we make them all for ourselves."

That evening I attended the weekly meeting wherein the children air all inter-personal and school problems, making new rules and abolishing old ones. The hall with the bulletin boards was then filled with children, sitting ten deep on the floor, up the stairway, filling every available inch of space. I can still see A. S. Neill's tall, slightly stooped figure, his head bowed as was his habit, as he slowly waded through his children, occasionally taking his large pipe from his mouth to exchange a word with one. The loud talking and shouting suddenly stopped as Neill took his place, near the center, sitting down on the old, chipped-green kitchen chair that awaited him. A boy of twelve opened the meeting. The oldest and youngest argued about bedtime hours; complaints against too many visitors making some teen-age boys feel like "zoo animals on display" were discussed in relationship to an enterprising dormitory group who were charging one shilling admission to see their rooms; the committee to investigate stealing was abolished. Perhaps ten new rules were established and just as many liquidated or revised, all by "ayes" and "nayes," after which the chairman would solemnly announce "carried" or "not carried."

Afterwards, Neill and I stood talking in the hallway. I asked him what happened to the children after they left the school, as a general rule. "They go into the arts," he said in his soft Scottish.

At the end of my survey, I was to find that this did not seem to be the case. The only occupations which included more than two of those interviewed were housewife, and secretary. Occupations were as varied as their personalities. "Is there such a thing as a Summerhill personality?" I asked.

"They come out well-balanced and sincere," Neill said. But then he admitted being a bit tired of talking about Summerhill these days. After all, he was in his eighties!

Walking through the dark 10 p.m. drizzle beneath the canopy of trees, I tried to gather my thoughts and feelings. The happiest school in the world? Yes! For some. That afternoon, I had wandered into a tiny room filled with music from a spontaneous jam session with teen-agers playing a piano, several guitars, a harmonica: some seven and eight year-olds leaned against chair-back or piano, staring seriously into space with vacant looks of intoxication while several of their contemporaries amused themselves by tipping each other over backwards as they sat deep within the security of the old over-stuffed chairs. A girl of eight with a sapphire dress that almost matched her eyes had begun to dance the twist with one of the other little girls, her light blonde curls thrown back, face aglow with laughter. Someone whispered in her ear. She stopped dancing, and the blue eyes filled with tears. Her parents had arrived a week early to take her home. Several little children and one teen-age girl quickly surrounded her, trying to comfort her as she slowly left. I remembered this little girl telling me of her activities at the school: music, dancing, writing, reading, acting, painting, and her boyfriend. But for others the outlook did not seem so optimistic. Summerhill could also be a lonely place, with too little stimulation or direction. One group of teen-age boys told me that they had been bored, and as a result their lives had become centered around their tape recorders. I remembered a dark, thin boy with horn-rimmed glasses, staring blankly out of a window, and a sad, petite red-headed girl sitting alone on the front steps.

Back in London, I began my follow-up study in earnest. Officers of the Summerhill Society gave me a few names, and these persons gave me more, and so on. Purchasing an old motor scooter and a large map of the London area gave me maximum mobility, and I began visiting one household of former students after another. By the end of the summer I had seen fifty, twenty-nine men and twenty-one women, between the ages of nineteen and fifty-two. Within the first week I had been invited to use the household of three Summerhillians as my headquarters, an invitation I gladly accepted and found I was at once made a member of the family. But this was typical of the hospitality of all fifty former students whom I interviewed: that meant most of those presently living in the London area, according to the consensus. I was almost always invited to tea, dinner, and even for weekends.

In the weeks that followed, I was to have my initial impressions of Summerhill clarified. Indeed, there were students who found the school ideal, and others whose needs were not met by the school. Final analysis showed that ten former Summerhill students (according to their feelings and my observation) had benefited most. They felt strongly that Summerhill had given them confidence, maturity, and had enabled them to find a way of life that led to fulfillment. Typical of their statements were: "It helped me to grow out of the need to play continuously." . . . "It got the hate out of me, somehow." . . . "It led me to explore and be curious about all things." They talked of the free environment that enabled them to develop as they were, into more complete personalities, through following their natural bent. These were the more communicative people who usually had had definite ideas and direction before they came to Summerhill.

Seven of those interviewed felt that Summerhill had not helped them to grow, but instead had led to their finding more difficulty in life than they might have otherwise experienced. Most of these complained of the academic side being de-emphasized and the lack of good teachers really involved with their subjects or with the children, and most complained of the lack of protection against bullies. Typical of their statements were; "It made me lose the little self-confidence I had." . . . "I think it gave me the habit of not following through, giving up too easily." These were apparently the more dependent shy persons.

Thus, the gregarious aggressive people (both as children and as adults today) seemed to benefit the most; while the school seemed to have a negative effect on the more withdrawn, quiet ones. There were a few exceptions: occasionally Summerhill triumphed by suggestion to some shy pupils the pleasant rewards of becoming more gregarious.

For my first interview I arrived promptly at the appointed hour of four. Soon I was sitting with Paul and his parents having tea in the living room of their home near central London. He was a soft-spoken 20-year-old with a huge crop of blonde hair, who had attended Summerhill from 6–16 years old. "The classes were rather humdrum," he told me, "but before we left all of our group passed the 11+ exam to enter other schools, with above-average grades." He went on, "You know, I think one can stay at Summerhill too long. It was easy to be led astray by new students who did little or no studying." He had gone to trade school for two years and was now making furniture in his own home. He showed me an unfinished sample of his work.

"That's beautiful," I said as his mother came in from the kitchen, admiring it with me but reminding him that he had procrastinated in finishing it.

"This is an attitude that I think one can easily pick up at Summerhill," he said with a smile.

When I returned to the States, I remembered Paul's comments when compiling my conclusion. Those in the survey who stayed longest at Summerhill were, by far, the group who had the most difficult and tenacious adjustment problems. Four of the fourteen who spent over ten years at Summerhill were definitely unsettled and having personal and job problems. Still, half of this group considered themselves and were (from my observations) presently adjusted with regard to work and personal life. Not a bad showing for the results of the freest philosophy of education in the world.

That evening I was having cocktails on the patio with Irene, a former Summerhill student and her husband, a child psychiatrist, having left a drawing room with rich tones of Persian rugs and paintings on the walls that almost demanded slow progress to the cool outdoors. Their two children were calling to us from their bedroom window above the patio. The Doctor told them that it was time for bed, and quiet. "That's all now," added mother as the younger child interrupted her. "My husband and I do not always agree on all child-raising techniques," she told me, "but we compromise and are consistent." The oldest boy, then 5 years old, had run downstairs and was already on the patio in his pajamas crawling into his mother's lap where he received a hug. In one hand he had a knight on a horse which he had formed from clay. He showed it to me, and both parents praised his artistic creations. He said good night, kissing his parents and waving to me. "You can see one thing!" said Irene, "Summerhill children aren't afraid of their parents!"

Irene's statement was confirmed by the eleven parents interviewed, all of whose children certainly seemed comfortable with their parents. Without exception, parents who had experienced Summerhill as a student were raising their children in a self-directive way, and their interrelationship was warm: the children, happy and spontaneous.

Further evidence of the relationship between Summerhillians and their children came into focus in my visit with Connie, a 27-year-old housewife, who had left Summerhill at the age of 14 (due to financial difficulties of her parents).

Connie and her husband had been living a number of years in one of the "mansions," which often meant an entire block of one gigantic mass of apartments. I stopped my scooter for the fourth time in search of the apartment, scanning the five stories of windows and some balconies with elderly couples sipping tea. At last the correct faded number on the door came into focus, and I unstrapped the box of Black Magic chocolates for my hosts (I had been invited for supper as well as the afternoon). Connie lived on the ground floor. Her tall slender figure was striking in the dark doorway. She led me down the long, narrow hallway past bedrooms to her kitchen, with a brunette pony-tail of hair bouncing from her back to her shoulder as she would turn to talk. Her 2 and 3½-year-old daughters ran in to ask her for help in setting up a play tea party in the back yard. "Yes, honey. Just one moment," she said, as one little girl smiled at me, and the other shyly watched us all as she sucked her thumb. Connie disappeared into the yard holding the hand of one daughter, and allowing the other to cling to her skirt. Shortly she reappeared and poured me some raspberry liquid similar to "Kool-Aid" and talked vivaciously of how every child should have the opportunity to live in the country, climbing trees and building huts in the open. I asked whether she would consider sending her own children to Summerhill. "No, indeed," she said, "I'm enjoying them too much to send them anywhere!"

Of the eleven parents interviewed, most never sent their own children, and for Connie's reason. They wanted their children with them. Three parents had sent their children to Summerhill, but had taken them out before the age of 13, almost wholly due to their convictions that not enough emphasis was placed upon the academic side and that there should be more fine teaching and good equipment than Summerhill provided.

Connie then showed me the children's room, a light, airy one with colorful murals of animals playing on the walls (painted by her husband, who was a window decorator). The little girls ran into the room, and immediately began jumping up and down on their neatly made beds before pulling the mattresses to the floor to engage in more complicated acrobatics. I noticed that Connie did not blink an eyelash, but calmly brought up the subject of discipline. "I believe in giving children as much freedom as possible," she said, "but I have had great conflicts. For example, I don't believe in hitting children, but I have lost my temper, and pushed them a bit or yelled. Then I felt terribly guilty afterwards."

Incidentally, most of the parents expressed conflicting feelings about discipline, similar to Connie's, and all but two had experienced a sense of guilt when they had punished their children. Most parents, however, had never used corporal punishment.

We left the children playing on the mattresses and resumed our conversation over the rest of our drinks. I asked Connie about her adjustment to the regular state school when she left Summerhill, and she smiled. "This was a peculiar thing," she said, "I loved the way learning was presented! It was something new and fresh! And, you know, it was strange: I couldn't understand why all the other children stopped working when the teacher left the room." She went on to tell of her astonishment at the fear other children had of the teacher and the principal. To her, the teacher was an instrument to gain what she wished to know, and she was full of questions. Later that evening, her mother visited and exclaimed, "The teachers and headmasters couldn't get over it! They all said that she soaked up knowledge like a sponge!"

Perhaps the most striking direction in which the statistics later pointed, showed up when I tallied the responses of children who had left before they were teen-agers, and then returned to the regular public schools. Of those six, all of whom had spent at least three years at Summerhill (and left before they were 12 years old), all but one were enthusiastic about how the school had not only helped them, but actually prepared them for working well with their studies. Five felt that, after leaving Summerhill there were no adjustment problems to the ordinary local schools, but instead they found themselves enthusiastic about having learning presented in an organized way. Although usually "behind," they were easily able to catch up to the other children, learning the required academic skills within the first year.

The one exception to this record of successful adjustment, interestingly enough, was Connie's brother, who arrived with his mother for spaghetti dinner. Henry attended Summerhill from 7–12 years old, and was the only person I came across who ever ran away from Summerhill. He did not adjust to the local school when he left, either. He said that he was somewhat immobilized by the sudden rigid discipline, and tended to stay in the background, fearing to ask questions. He was now a thin, shy, 24-year old. It was difficult for me to talk with him, either at the supper table or later on in the living room, for his mother always answered for him, even to the extent of interrupting him if he began a statement. He felt that he had lost two years when he entered the regular school, and that it was only through his own sheer effort and determination that he was now in his first year of post-graduate physics at London University.

Connie and her husband were the ones who brought me to Gill and Jane's home. They had both gone to Summerhill and were now raising a happy little girl, who was watching her father paint a mammoth gourd when I met him in their little backyard near central London. Gill was now an art teacher and artist, still fascinated with his craft. At Summerhill for six years, leaving in 1948, he had attended no lessons for the first three years, but instead had painted from dawn to dusk in the art room. In his painting he had helpful criticism and real encouragement from certain gifted members of the Summerhill staff. Gill's parents had chosen this school because of their belief in freedom (the reason most Summerhillians and their parents had stated for sending their children, according to final results of the survey). Gill had gone to Polytechnic for three terms after Summerhill and then passed the Oxford examinations. In their attractive dinette we had supper consisting of cold cuts, cheese, biscuits, black ripe olives, pickles, and salad, along with good French red wine. Everything about their home was well-ordered. The walls of every room displayed fine paintings, several of them his own. Upon entering the living room, Gill turned on a wall light, which he had made from lollypop sticks, which sounds disastrous, but in reality was intriguing and distinctly attractive. The various shades of brightly colored translucent papers accentuated the intricate geometric design. I noticed the large variety of paintings: impressionistic, modern, and classic. I was gazing upon them from what I thought was a low, modern day bed until Jane, Gill's wife, leaning down to pass me a cup of tea, mentioned that I was seated on box springs and a mattress, which oftentimes doubled for sleeping arrangements for guests. Jane said, "I feel Summerhill saved my life. I was a nervous child and probably ready for a breakdown when I left a strict girls' boarding school at 12 years old to enter Summerhill. Naturally I went wild with the new freedom at first, playing outdoors continually and never opening a book, but I gradually settled down in a few months. For the first time in my life, I was enjoying comfortable, matter-of-fact relationships with boys."

We talked well into the night, and the two had almost nothing but praise for their Summerhill experiences. "Once you have decided what you want, you will do it fully," Gill said with conviction shortly before we said good-by in the cold midnight air.

Their approving comments were typical of the group, as a whole. Viewing the positive attitudes towards Summerhill, five items were mentioned more than any others. Leading the list were, 1) fostering a healthy attitude towards sex and relationship with one's opposite sex, 2) enabling one to have a natural confidence and ease with authority figures, and, 3) providing an environment in which children could develop naturally, staying with their own interests and abilities. Then equally important, 4) allowing them to grow out of the need to play continuously and then to settle comfortably into academic or more serious pursuits and, 5) helping them to understand their own children better and raise them in a wholesome way.

The majority of Summerhillians had only one major complaint against the school: the lack of academic opportunity and inspiration along with the lack of inspired teachers. I discovered that the school attracted a variety of teachers. Some would go padding about in sandals and growing long beards, content that nobody was coming to their classes, whereas others would run about the school grounds plucking children out of trees and trying to lure them to their class! One former student told me that he first learned to read and write in German because he liked the German teacher so well.

In spite of the complaints that Summerhill was academically weak, of the fifty persons interviewed, ten passed the examinations necessary to enter a university. Eight had graduated. Four did feel, however, that they lost two or more years cramming to pass these examinations. Perhaps there were enough inspired teachers who loved and understood children, after all.

"Corky" Corkhill was one of the few teachers whose former students unanimously claimed as having meant a good deal to them. I interviewed one of his former students in London later that week who talked with much affection about "Corky" and how he made science come alive for him. He was now a noted zoologist who had just come back from a government job in Nigeria, pioneering on a snail disease problem. Corky, now in his 70's, had taught at Summerhill for 30 years, and now lived with his wife some 100 miles Northeast of London where I was invited to visit. 'Corky' met me at the door with a smile, his large, tanned, gnarled hand strongly grasping mine. He was a tall, lean, now slightly bent man with a soft voice, and an easy-going manner. There was compassion in Corky's lined face as he talked of some troubled children he had helped.

Their son dropped by to show them his latest color slides. He was in his early 40's and grew up at Summerhill, leaving in 1939 at the age of 17. He was a calm, self-assured person with a quiet sense of humor like his father's. As he flashed a slide of the patio in his new ranch-style home showing his two children and wife, he mentioned that his interest in photography had begun at Summerhill. Later, he said that he had rarely attended classes at the school, but instead had spent most of his time taking Neill's car apart and doing things with his hands which required manual dexterity. After Summerhill, he served a three year apparenticeship in skilled metal work; then worked for the same company until three years ago when he opened his own highly profitable repair business in his home.

I was invited for supper. There were vegetables freshly picked by my hosts from their backyard, while Corky identified some birds which landed at their feeding station. The Corkhills were vegetarians, "Partly by choice," added Corky with a slight smile, "and partly from economic necessity." The $15 per week salary (which was sometimes less) while at Summerhill had allowed no room for saving. Now they were living from a government pension. After supper, Corky roared off with me on the scooter, although he had never ridden one before, and he led me to more Summerhillians who lived nearby. Before I left, the Corkhills gave me a long list of former students and walked out to the street with me, waving until I was out of sight.

My next stop was to be with a country doctor who lived some 70 miles south in a little town. It was a rare, sunny day with bright blue sky broken with cotton-bright cumulus clouds, and the whole journey was over narrow country roads, wheat waving high over my head at times, thatched roofs dotting the countryside, walls and houses to the very edge of the road, and friendly tweedy people in hamlets where it was easy to "pass the time of day" as well as ask directions.

Dr. Fortune's home was just off the main street, and although his home looked modest from the outside, several new additions including a spectacular living room with two entire walls of glass looking out on a spacious, tree-shaded lawn gave a different picture from the inside. His practice was thriving as there were no other doctors in any of the surrounding villages. After a warm welcome, and some good English Scotch I went with him to deliver camping equipment to his teen-age son who was camping with a friend in a nearby field; and then accompanied him on his medical rounds, visiting several families in the surrounding areas. He spoke warmly with those he met, and seemed like a good doctor—one who was aware of their emotional needs—and he talked of them as persons with problems about which he expressed deep feeling. We had supper with his wife, his other teen-age son, and a teen-age French girl who had come to learn English, paying her way with some light household tasks. There was a comfortable atmosphere about this home, too: a free and easy kind of inter-personal relationship, which I was to find in most Summerhill homes. The children retired to the television room, and Dr. Fortune and I talked of his experience at the school. He had gone to Summerhill at the age of 13 and continuously studied, mostly on his own, and easily passed his examinations for university entrance in 1928 when he was 16 years old. The doctor summed up his feelings about the school as we stood by my scooter the next morning. "The freedom was a wonderful thing. It was a good experience for me." He put his hand out and gave mine a warm grip. "But I must say there was very little direction from adults. I taught myself what I knew I should know. Well, see you again, I hope."

My next stop was in a small suburb of London, Dr. Fortune's brother's home. He told me that their mother had so believed in freedom that she set up housekeeping near Summerhill in the daytime. John Fortune had attended Summerhill from the age of 9 to 16, passed university entrance examinations with little difficulty, and was now an electrical engineer.

Now in his spacious white-walled living room, we sipped sherry while his 11-year-old daughter and 13-year-old son joined Mary, his wife, and me in a conversation. John said with conviction, "Summerhill is good for children up to about the age of ten. After that it's too weak, academically." I asked his daughter what she thought of her school this year.

"I go to a Quaker boarding school," she said with a smile and added laughingly, "I don't think Summerhill would have agreed with *me*. It sounds a little too loose and unorganized!" We all talked jokingly and seriously about Summerhill for about an hour before having lunch. The atmosphere was relaxed and seemed habitually jovial in this family.

Throughout my visits I was to find Summerhill homes filled with warmth and responsive understanding: they were happy, communicative families. The philosophy of Summerhill certainly seemed to make for warm satisfying parent-child relationships.

My last glimpse of such a Summerhill home came a few days before my departure. Ron George not only invited me to spend Sunday at his home, but also invited another Summerhillian and her husband. Ron had attended Summerhill from the ages of 6 to 16 and was now a lawyer, with offices in two of the larger communities in Kent. He was tall, striking, in his early 40's, with a shock of white hair, a tanned strong-looking face, and a warming smile. He escorted me through the floor-to-ceiling glass doors of the living room onto the patio where his nine year-old boy greeted me with the same winning welcome. The late morning sunlight was just the right temperature for comfort without excessive heat, and we stretched out on the low wall, which separated the patio from the large back lawn. "I had some happy times at that school," he said, "and some never wanted to leave the little paradise."

"Was there an adjustment problem for you, after you left?" I asked.

"Not for me," he said, raising his face towards the sky. "I joined the R.A.F. I wanted to fly, and so I put up with what I knew I had to, and I flew." He felt that there were some years with better teachers than others, "and a couple of consistently good ones, like 'Corky.' " The sun was getting warmer. I accepted his invitation for one of those deliciously flat, full-bodied, hearty glasses of English beer.

To add to the pleasure of that bright day, I was to see one of the warmest family and inter-family relationships I had ever witnessed. Fran and Theodore Shaw with their daughter, Robin, arrived and I began to see an almost indescribable warmth and intensity of communication between these people as they drank, dined, played, or merely sat together. Ron and Theodore began playing a combination of cricket and baseball, with no rules, while Robin leaned against her mother, who slipped an arm around her daughter, exchanging a few words. Ron and his younger son wrestled; now Ron said, "That's enough," in a firm but gentle tone. Every now and then the boy would put an arm around the back of his father, who might be sipping a drink, absorbed in conversation on the patio. Still, this token of affection would be immediately returned with an arm or hand thrown or placed on the boy's shoulder.

As we sat on the patio chatting, Mrs. George asked Fran, "How is your course coming?" Fran was taking a course in working with handicapped children, a field which held growing interest for her.

"Have you ever been a teacher?" I asked.

"No, after Summerhill, I was a secretary for a few years until I married, but I have been active in volunteer work at the hospital near our home." Fran, now in her late thirties, had attended Summerhill from 6 to 16-years old. She was an attractive, self-assured person with definite charm. Fran claimed that she had no adjustment problems after leaving.

The survey, as a whole, was to reveal that 15 former students denied any adjustment problems after leaving, 7 of whom stated that their adjustment was made easier as a result of their Summerhill experience. Fifteen admitted to problems in adjusting after leaving, which they attributed, at least partially, to having attended the school: 7 of these had attended Summerhill for over 10 years.

The Shaws, Georges, and I took a drive that afternoon to visit Neill George (named in honor of A. S. Neill). He was now 18, and preparing to enter a university to become a lawyer. I met this poised, handsome lad between sets in the tennis tournament in which he was playing. He told me, "I hardly opened at book at Summerhill, especially at first. Guess I learned to hate learning at the strict ordinary school and that's why Dad sent me." At the end of his third year at Summerhill, it was his own decision to go back to the regular school in his neighborhood. "I was ready to learn," he said.

I left the Georges and the Shaws with the happy feeling one has when he has come from a visit with a serene and wholesome family. But this was typical of my visits with the 49 other Summerhillians.

There had been a Sadler-Wells ballet dancer with top billing, enjoying a distinguished career all over the world (he remembered having learned his first steps and a darting Nijinski leap at Summerhill); a quiet, thoughtful musician absorbed in his work of both playing piano and composing; a young teacher who left her high school position because the system left too little room for children to experience freedom and self-direction (she was now a successful recreation worker); secretaries; truck drivers; sales clerks; students. There were 34 different occupations. The only line of endeavor in which more than two were engaged was that of "housewife" which claimed six.

The impact of what the summer had meant suddenly struck me; I stopped short just before boarding the bus which would take me to the plane at London Airport. High above on the spectators balcony stood nobody but Summerhillians waving goodbye, a whole row of them. Yes, there had been much friendship involved. So much warmth had been given this inquiring American.

As the plane droned through the night, I looked over my notes and thought of the praise and complaints heaped upon Summerhill by its former students. My feelings were mainly positive. Almost all of its former students were working; raising responsive children; enjoying life. And the group who returned to the regular state schools were so enthusiastic about learning that they caught up with others within a year! Yes, freedom was especially important for the younger child.

Back in New England, I found myself wondering, "But what was lacking in Summerhill's completely free approach?" In my Boston apartment, I put my notes on lesson ideas down as it suddenly came to me. Neill has said that the goal of good education should be "happiness." And he has said happiness is "interest." This is where Summerhill's philosophy could be improved: A child cannot be interested in anything until he *succeeds*: then he can find satisfaction in anything—even arithmetic and reading!

This year, I watched my class with new perception. I noticed that Charlie had learned to enjoy arithmetic, but Frank just wanted to draw. It was with new confidence that I told Frank, "That picture is good. I have a question to ask you. How high is our school building?"

"A thousand feet? A hundred feet?" guessed Frank.

"How long is this room?"

"Fifty feet? A hundred feet?" Another guess for Frank.

Others in the classroom began wondering and rulers began to appear from their desks. The room was measured, and at recess, Frank and a friend were climbing down the fire escape to measure the height of our building (25 yards, which needed to be changed into feet).

"How many feet in 25 yards?" Frank asked me.

"Well to answer that, let me show you what division is all about."

"Awww," said Frank with a grimace, "Can't I draw?"

"After you think about some division," I directed.

I wondered what Neill would say if he were observing. I could hear him saying, "This is certainly not a Summerhill classroom." But if he came back a half-hour later he would find Frank busily finishing his drawing; and Charlie still at work with arithmetic. He would also see three boys working at reading, taking turns following a second grade text; Harold and Jeffrey giving each other spelling words; and two writing a story, while Jimmy prepared a test tube for one of his scientific experiments.

"Close," I pictured Neill saying, rubbing his forehead.

An hour later, he might have overheard me telling Jimmy, "Your experiments are improving, but now how about writing them up with the date, your procedure and the results?"

"Do I have to?"

"It's an order," I said with a smile which was halfheartedly returned.

Jimmy struggled with his writing, but the next week he began to see the importance of recording what day the mold began to grow in his test tube with yeast and sugar, and how it became fuzzy and changed from day-to-day. He almost had begun to enjoy writing. Would Neill say, "But he is not self-directed. He is writing for *you*," or would he see a child learning new satisfactions with new horizons opening for him? I would hope the latter, for compromising with Summerhill is surely possible.

REFERENCES

Neill, A. S. *Summerhill*. London: Hart, 1960.

BIBLIOGRAPHY

Aiken, W. Thirty schools tell their story. In *Adventure in American education*, Vol. 5, New York: Harper, 1943.

Bernstein, E. Summerhill after 50 years, the first follow-up. *The New Era*, Vol. 48, 2, 1967.

The Free Schools of Leicestershire County. *Christian Science Monitor*, May 14, 1966.

Featherstone, J. Teaching children to think: school for children. *New Republic*, Aug. 19, Sept. 2, Sept. 9, 1967.

Lane, H. *Talks to parents and teachers*. London: Allen & Unwin, 1928.

Redefer, F. L. The eight year study—eight years later. Unpublished doctoral dissertation, Teachers College, Columbia University, 1952.

HOW TO TEACH FEAR *

Donald J. Rogers

Are Schools Fear Factories? Rogers, like Neill, is concerned about fear in education; his focus, however, is on that fear which arises from social pressures rather than from sexual repression. How much of this social fear is the result of one's own imagination? How might we overcome this fear in ourselves, and how can we keep from passing it on to our colleagues and students? Rogers suggests self-acceptance, a positive self-concept, and an enjoyable learning atmosphere. For ways to implement these, see the articles by Jersild and Bower later in this section. If schools are large contributors to the amount of fear in our society, does this fear influence our psychological processes and reappear in the way we treat ourselves and others?

Despite a variety of programs to teach reading more efficiently, despite an assortment of approaches to make mathematics more meaningful, and despite a wealth of materials to render every topic from Afro-American history to ecology more relevant, the subject we may be teaching most effectively in our schools is fear. Fear pervades our school systems from the local school board to the classroom teacher. Everyone suffers in this apprehensive atmosphere, but the children are the most tragic victims because they are the most innocent and the most vulnerable.

It is often said that in the USA achievement is highly valued. A man's worth is judged, not by what he is but by what he does, not by his human qualities but by what he can accomplish in society. American businessmen have long felt the pressure to produce results. Now this same pressure is beginning to weigh heavily on our children.

From the news media, parents learn of reports on achievement tests—reports that compare scores. City schools are pitted against private schools, progressive schools against traditional schools. Despite some recent misgivings, the slogan, "To get a good job, get a good education," still influences the attitude of the American public toward learning. Understandably, then, parents worry. Are their children learning? What are they supposed to learn? Are they accumulating enough information in school to compete successfully in an ever shrinking job market? Out of the pressure to achieve grows the fear that the schools are not making the children accomplish enough. And out of this fear grows the demand for accountability, the insistence that the school system be held responsible for the children's progress or their lack of it.

From Donald J. Rogers, "How to Teach Fear," *Elementary School Journal* 72, no. 8 (May, 1972): 391–395, by permission of the author and publisher. The author is at Mark Twain Elementary School, Northlake, Illinois.

As the pressure for concrete, statistical evidence of progress mounts, the tension within the school system increases. School board members worry. How much criticism will be heaped on their heads? Will they be re-elected to their positions of power and influence in the community? School administrators, the superintendent, and the principals worry. They fear charges of incompetence or mismanagement. Teachers worry, especially teachers not on tenure. They feel insecure about their positions. These fears may take various forms, depending on one's position in the system, but all the fears seem to come down to one common fear—the fear that someone will think the schools are not making the children produce, not making them work hard enough, not keeping them in line. As a result, the children are the dubious benefactors of all this anxiety.

FEAR WEARS MANY MASKS

Day to day, these fears and pressures may appear in subtle guises. The principal may crack down on disorderly lines on the playground, or on noise in the school hallways, or on activity-filled classrooms, once rated as creative but now frowned on as simply messy. In the classrooms, teachers are a bit less patient with repetitious questions, or shout a bit more in an exasperated attempt to keep the class in order, or abandon innovative projects that might make the room look chaotic. Sound educational rationale can always be marshalled to justify such actions; but often the justifications offered are simply the by-products of fear—fear that the school may "look bad" to a school board member, an administrator, or a parent.

FEAR DISTRACTS

Fear in the school system may influence the daily routine, but there are other hazards too. The school may become concerned mainly with presenting an orderly, businesslike image rather than with treating learning problems realistically and effectively. The major question becomes: "Who is at fault for the child's low achievement" not "What is the child's learning problem, and what can be done about it?" Teachers may become more concerned about talking with parents diplomatically rather than frankly. Likewise, parents may hesitate to admit their children's academic weaknesses or limitations for fear of being blamed for not preparing them better for school. While teachers and parents are distracted by their fears, the child's learning problems go undiagnosed and untreated.

Worst of all, fear in the school system is likely to produce fear in the children. As Bonaro W. Overstreet has put it: "Because the world is full of worried adults, it is bound to be full of uneasy infants and children; for the prevailing moods and attitudes of the care-taking adult constitute the most important single factor in the child's climate of emotional growth" (1: 40). Reflecting on the school environment, the Indian philosopher

Jiddu Krishnamurti has come to these conclusions: "If children are to be free from fear ... the educator himself must have no fear. But that is the difficulty: to find teachers who are not themselves the prey of some kind of fear.... A teacher who is fearful obviously cannot convey the deep significance of being without fear. Like goodness, fear is contagious. If the educator himself is secretly afraid, he will pass that fear on to his students, although its contamination may not be immediately seen" (2: 105). Simply put, then, fear in ourselves breeds fear in others.

FOR LEARNING—FREEDOM FROM FEAR

If we see that fear exists in our school systems and that fear is an obstacle to learning, the question arises: What can we do to free ourselves of fear? What is needed for all involved in the education of children is a change of consciousness. What is needed is the realization that a healthy psychological atmosphere, one free of fear, is more conducive to real learning than stress on achievement. As things stand now, there is a dangerous tension between man's mental and emotional needs and the stress American society lays on ambition, competition, and success (1: 114). What is needed is the realization that mental and emotional maturity are basic goals for education—more important than expertise in any strictly academic discipline. We come to the conclusion, then, that the greatest obstacle to maturity is the kind of emphasis on academic achievement which produces fear by requiring the child to prove his own personal worth (1: 116).

FOR LEARNING—SELF-ACCEPTANCE

Perhaps the most important action educators can take to reduce fear in our school systems is to teach people simply to like and to accept themselves (1: 145). One way to encourage self-acceptance is to help people take realistic attitudes toward their limitations (1: 149). A positive self-concept can best be created in "an atmosphere where errors and shortcomings are treated as real but not as disastrous; where they are treated as something to *grow beyond* rather than as something over which to brood" (1: 150).

How would such a change of consciousness affect our school systems? In such an atmosphere the parents would seek to discover their child's strengths and weaknesses, potentials and limitations, likes and dislikes. Their purpose would not be to find fault with school personnel but to encourage the child's strengths and remedy his weaknesses. The school board and the administration would seek to create an atmosphere in which teachers would feel free to experiment with materials and methods designed to make learning an enjoyable experience rather than a scramble to cover a mass of information as soon before achievement tests as possible.

WHAT CAN TEACHERS DO?

Ultimately, however, the task of freeing our schools and our children from fear rests with the individual teacher. How might this task be accomplished? Krishnamurti offers a radical suggestion: "Suppose, for example, that a teacher is afraid of public opinion; he sees the absurdity of his fear, and yet he cannot go beyond it. What is he to do? He can at least acknowledge it to himself, and can help his students to understand fear by bringing out his own psychological reaction and openly talking it over with them. This honest and sincere approach will greatly encourage the students to be equally open and direct with themselves and with the teacher" (2:105).

If this approach seems too extreme, teachers could work at creating therapeutic situations in their classrooms. Through role-playing, children could learn to act out their fears and come to a better understanding of them. In creating such situations, the teachers themselves might finally come to understand that humanistic values cannot be commanded into existence through rules and punishments (1: 153). For "when we move in on people's private lives and problems in a mood of 'righteous' exasperation, we simply drive them further into those self-centering emotions of fear and hostility by which they are already burdened in their approach to life" (1: 139).

VALUES—A BULWARK

Wise teachers will learn to help children develop their own values. Wise teachers will help by creating situations in the classroom to which the children can respond emotionally rather than by preaching to them moralistically. As difficult as the task of freeing people from fear may be, especially in school systems where it is already firmly entrenched, fear must not contaminate the classroom if the children are to be spared.

The importance of eliminating fear from human relationships extends beyond the classroom. Fear separates the individual from reality (1: 104); it narrows thinking and inhibits initiative (2: 105). "Fear," Bonaro Overstreet writes, "cannot be looked upon as a private affair. From the point of view of our total society and its ideals, every fear that keeps an individual *self-centered* means waste and danger: the waste of his capacities for loving and learning; danger to all whom he variously tries to use as means to his own emotional ends" (1: 105).

GROWING UP TRUSTING

Are American parents wrong in expecting results from their schools? No, but they may be wrong about the results they expect. Overstreet writes: "What children need more than anything else, for their own good and the good of their society, is the privilege of growing up with parents and teachers whose interpersonal relations are not distorted by fear. As this realization grows, we see that every influence that helps grown-ups to a happier, more informed, more fulfilling adult experience is an influence for child education and child welfare. The specific curriculum—whether that of home 'socializing' or classroom training—is incidental compared to the all-important problem of helping children grow up trusting themselves and liking life: which they can never do except as the adults around them make it contagiously possible" (1: 110).

The formula for teaching fear, then, is simple—create an atmosphere in which achievement is valued over personal worth, in which blame is more common than understanding, and in which the opinion of others is more important than the opinion of self. The formula for teaching self-acceptance is also simple—create an atmosphere in which freedom is valued over force, in which realistic evaluation is more common than scape-goating, and in which psychological maturity is more important than pedantry. From this kind of education parents may reasonably expect children who are free from fear.

REFERENCES

1. Bonarc W. Overstreet. *Understanding Fear in Ourselves and Others.* London: Collier-Macmillan Ltd., 1951.

2. J. Krishnamurti. *Education and the Significance of Life.* Edited by Mary Lutyens. New York: Harper and Row, 1953.

PSYCHOANALYSIS AND THE FUTURE OF EDUCATION

Goodwin Watson

Dare We Take the Freudian Plunge? Can We Afford Not To? The challenge Watson gave in 1957 remains fresh today. While some of his ideas have been tried, many of his concepts have not yet been adopted on a large scale. How many of us teachers have had instruction on how to develop rapport with our students, and how many see this as an important prerequisite to educating them? Can we use artistic and symbolic expressions to convey what cannot be explicitly taught by precise words? Are we afraid to link our verbal teachings to the unconscious processes which stand behind them? It is less personally threatening for teachers, educational psychologists, and researchers to limit ourselves to observable, external, behavior. But does that attitude keep us from confronting the stronger forces of internal psychology and keep us from developing an education that includes the internal as well as the external?

It is remarkable that the discipline of psychoanalysis, which over a half century has revealed so much about the dynamics of child life, should have had so little direct impact upon education. Two well-recommended textbooks in educational psychology, both published in 1956, were lying on my desk as I began this article. In the index of one, written by a professor in an excellent college for teachers, neither "psychoanalysis" nor "Freud" is listed. Of the 700 pages in the other, only 4 are given to the theories of psychoanalysis. These conclude with the revealing sentence: "Many people rebel, for instance, when asked to believe that the child has a very elaborate sexual life; that each of our separate urges has a drive and intelligence of its own; or that ideas actually reside, as such, in a subconscious." This author, although teaching educational psychology in one of our best-known universities, apparently has never felt impelled to read enough psychoanalytic literature to achieve a clear grasp of its basic concepts. Contrast the sentence quoted above—too typical of what is being given most teachers in training, even today—with Ernest Jones's masterful two-sentence summary of Freud's discoveries:

"The images of the innocent babe or unfolding plant have been replaced by more sympathetic and living ones of creatures pathetically struggling, 'with no language but a cry,' to achieve the self-control and inner security that civilized man has so far attempted in vain to attain. And the infant is urged to accomplish in five years of life what civilized adults have only imperfectly accomplished in a period ten thousand times as long."[1]

*From Goodwin Watson, "Psychoanalysis and the Future of Education," *Teachers College Record* 58, no. 5 (February, 1957): 241–247 by permission of the author. Goodwin Watson is Professor Emeritus, Teachers College, Columbia University. He now is associate director of the Union for Research and Experimentation in Higher Education, Yellow Springs, Ohio.

Freud's influence has filtered into teacher education by indirection. Resistance has been reduced by dilution. The present writer's study[2] of textbooks in educational psychology published during the decade 1920–29 showed an average of only 4 pages describing some kinds of unconscious factors in motivation; those published since 1950 show a tenfold increase in attention, with an average of 46 pages per textbook on this topic. The general field of mental hygiene was allotted only 7 pages in the average text a generation ago; the average today is 53 pages on mental hygiene. Teachers using the 1956 text which does not refer to Freud will nevertheless be taught something about "rationalization," "displaced hostility," "self–punishment," "repression," "projection," "regression," "fantasy," and "compulsiveness." Teachers are undoubtedly being exhorted to study the causes of emotionally disturbed behavior, but few are yet being given the necessary tools and training.

It is tempting now to predict that the barriers are at last giving way and that education is on the verge of a rapid assimilation of the essential insights of psychoanalysis. But the realism so carefully cultivated in psychoanalytic training makes us skeptical. In a recent review of the relation of psychoanalysis to the social sciences[3] we find the observation that, while it is now "fashionable" in social psychology textbooks to acknowledge Freud as having been a genius contributing most significant and fundamental insights, one actually finds in the work of social psychologists little close attention to psychoanalytic formulations. In the study of education, also, Freud is praised more freely than he once was, but there is still little use of psychoanalytic concepts in guiding practice or defining research. This technique of substituting verbal deference for genuine acceptance is not unfamiliar to observers with psychoanalytic orientation. Resistance is hardy and resourceful.

Given more favorable consideration and enough time, six lines of development of psychoanalytic theories in education can be foreseen.

CONCEPTION OF CONFLICT IN LEARNING

Most academic learning theory has been naively one-sided. A popular view of the mind as a blank tablet of wax upon which experience engraves its impressions still persists. The child is still seen by many parents and some curriculum makers as a more or less passive receptacle for subject matter.

The more scientific theories of conditioning and stimulus response still view learning as an almost unresisting conformity along easily determined paths, with the energies coming from outside the system. It is true that E. L. Thorndike formulated a law of "readiness," but this referred to the readiness of a specific neural connection (for example, sufficient myelinization; not in refractory phase) or an expectancy "set," rather than to central personality determinants. Even Gestalt theory, while crediting the learner with a far more complex and organized perceptual and cognitive structure, failed to achieve a dynamic interpretation.

Out of psychoanalytic therapy stems an insight which may be expected eventually to bring considerable comfort as well as guidance to discouraged teachers. Nothing is clearer during therapy—which is, after all, an important kind of teaching—than that the patient resists evidence which disturbs hard-won complacency or arouses fresh anxiety. One of Freud's first discoveries was that the neurotic who seems to want to get better, still opposes attempts to help him. Quite normal children, adolescents, and adults also experience learning as a conflict between a desire to hold onto the more or less satisfactory ways of the past and a need to meet the upsetting demands of the new. When educators have developed a theory of learning which takes due account of resistance, a more dynamic and insightful pedagogy may emerge.

An interesting battle seems in prospect between those advocates of "progressive education" who have thought of all learning as properly made pleasant and those even more progressive—closer to Dewey's insight—who achieve the psychoanalytic view of what it costs a complex system to undergo marked readjustment and reorganization. One substantial gain will be clearer recognition that resistance to learning does not necessarily imply stupidity or incorrigible meanness. We may expect from teachers a more patient and sympathetic understanding of the learning conflict, resembling that which good therapists give their patients.

TRANSFERENCE (PARATAXIS) A CENTRAL FACTOR IN LEARNING

In psychoanalytic therapy the emotional relationship which the patient experiences toward the therapist is an essential factor in overcoming resistance and achieving insight into unconscious projection. The parallel, of course, is to be found in the pupil's relationship to the teacher. Educators have long recognized, in a general way, that the feeling of pupils toward the teacher has some importance. Parents commonly inquire, after the first day of school, "How do you *like* your teacher?" As the contributions of psychoanalysis are assimilated, education may be expected to show more discriminating attention to the nature and source of the pupil–teacher feeling. Redl has proposed ten categories of "central-person" role, most of which correspond to possible teacher–pupil relationships. A teacher may be, for example, a direct love object, a strict superego figure, an ego ideal, or an ego-helper. Almost regardless of what the teacher intends to be, each pupil will at first project upon his teacher a role which arises out of the experience of that child with other significant adults. This distorted personal perception (which Sullivan has called "parataxis") inevitably affects the child's reaction to whatever the teacher may be trying to convey. Whether the pupil learns, and what he learns, depend in large measure on a variable factor which pedagogy has blithely taken for granted.

It is, of course, difficult to work out techniques for discerning and responding to the shifting emotional perceptions of a score or more of pupils reacting simultaneously to a teacher. Still, recent progress in sociometrics encourages the hope that instruments may be devised which will help teachers become aware of far more than meets the naked eye. Psychoanalysis is moving toward more group therapy, and the position of the group therapist is closer to that of the teacher. Each, to follow the changing transference patterns, needs the aid of new techniques such as the role-inventory being developed by Bach at the Institute of Group Psychotherapy in Bedford Hills, California.

At the same time, the principal reliance of psychoanalytic therapists, whether in individual or group treatment sessions, is upon minimizing behavior which would justify, and hence conceal, the predispositions of the patients. This affectively neutral role—neither seductive nor rejecting, giving little praise and little scolding—is much more common in therapy than in teaching. Therapists have been aware, as teachers generally have not, that an overactive role may hamper discovery of the role the pupil is projecting. Of even more importance in education is the fact that the pupil who learns on his own responsibility, and not primarily to win approval or to escape disapproval from the teacher, is better prepared for independent learning outside and beyond the schools. Both therapists and teachers want their clients to outgrow emotional dependence and to achieve a mature self-reliance which is less easily won if the therapist or teacher is over-directive.

UTILIZATION OF INTRA-GROUP FEELINGS

The progress of psychoanalytic practice from dyads to larger groups has brought increased attention to member–member relationships as a source of constructive learning and therapy. When psychoanalysis dealt only with the progress of a single patient in his relationships with the therapist, teachers who tried to apply psychoanalytic insights found themselves thinking mainly about conferences outside class with a single pupil or a single parent. While this was often helpful, it neglected—as we now are beginning to realize—an immense resource in the class itself. In group psychotherapy, the affections, jealousies, suspicions, and aggressive attacks of one member directed toward other members are the principal subjects of attention. Everyone must "listen with the third ear." The very limited range of constructs which each member has carried into all interpersonal relations—his stereotyped perception of other people—becomes apparent as he again and again uses his few key patterns in reacting to other members of the group. Group members commonly perceive this kind of limitation in the social perceptions of others before recognizing it in themselves. In this and many other ways, group members become enlightening and wholesome influences upon one another. As psychoanalysts become more competent in the constructive management and interpretation of inter-personal relations within groups, they will be able to contribute far more which teachers and other group leaders can carry over for direct application.

Not only the therapist but also the group members themselves grow in their ability to discern and to clarify the feelings of others. For all the talk in education about improving human relations, fostering cooperation, and developing communication skills, very little has yet been done to enable pupils to react sensitively and constructively to the feelings of other pupils. If we can foresee classrooms in which teachers will comment about as often to clarify feelings as to expound subject matter, we can also hope for graduates who, in home life and on boards and committees, will be better able to respond wisely to the feelings of their co-workers.

EMOTIONAL COMMUNICATION

Schools have traditionally been very much concerned with what Suzanne Langer has called "discursive thought" and denotative symbols. Pupils have been taught to define words precisely, to operate mathematical processes correctly, to reason logically, and to weigh evidence objectively. This is all very important, but it neglects some of the oldest and most fundamental processes of the mind, those which Langer has called "presentational" or "expressive." Beneath the superficial, rational, and technological mechanisms of our civilization lie stirrings of another sort. Biologically grounded, they antecede the patterns of any particular culture. Fromm has referred to the unconscious symbolism of dreams and fantasy as "the Forgotten Language." Schools are now busy teaching many languages: ancient Latin, modern French or Spanish, the vocabulary of each science, the symbols and formulae of mathematics. Some day the Forgotten Language may reappear in schools and be recognized as more vital than any of the denotative systems. The poetry of Blake or Yeats, impressionistic art, modern dance or music all convey much that is not made explicit in words. Most education in primitive societies centered about presentational symbols such as myths of creation, legends of heroes, symbolic dances, religious rituals, magic rites, totems, and taboos. Given a curriculum composed so largely of "facts," we may impoverish the learner's experience and foster a shallow form of competence.

What we foresee is certainly not a return to the primitive but a new synthesis. Northrup, in his *Meeting of East and West*, voices the hope for a culture which will some day combine the technological achievements of Western industrial society with some of the mystical insights and philosophical depth characteristic of the spiritual leaders of Hinduism and Buddhism. The communication between mother and nursing baby, or between two parents who have lost their child, is not less vital because it has nothing to do with spelling, reading, writing, pronunciation, enunciation, syntax, or grammar. Are schools inherently limited to the cultivation of only verbal communion?

DIFFERENTIATION OF SELF FROM ROLE

Professor Lionel Trilling, in the Freud Anniversary Lecture of 1955 before the New York Psychoanalytic Institute and Society,[4] acclaimed "Freud's emphasis on biology as a *liberating* idea." He notes how, "entranced by all that the idea of culture and the study of culture can tell us about the nature of man, we have been inclined to assign to culture an almost exclusive part in man's fate." Much modern literature and the various philosophies of existentialism join psychoanalysis in recognizing inevitable conflicts between self and culture. It has been the recent fashion to say that Freud unhappily conceived the culture and its enforcing superego as too alien to the self. Yet there is a hard truth for education in Freud's perception of some irreducible difference between the demands of the organism and those of socialization. "Pessimistic this new period of psychoanalytical thought may be," concludes Trilling, "yet when we think of the growing power of culture to control us by seduction or coercion, we must be glad and not sorry that some part of our fate comes from outside the culture." Teachers along with therapists may well increase their respect for the non-conformist. The late Robert Lindner's *Prescription for Rebellion*[5] speaks with an angry voice but gives impressive evidence of concern that "adjustment" should not mean passive acquiescence. Perhaps "rebel" is not the best word for the life-affirming character, but as education assimilates psychoanalytic insights, schools will be increasingly concerned that pupils should develop the attitudes and behavior which Lindner called "aware, identified, skeptical, responsible, employed, and tense." ("Tension" has become a bad word in mental hygiene, but Lindner uses it to designate discontent with the gap between what is and what might better be.)

We all live in social systems, occupying many "positions" for which certain role behavior is prescribed. Inevitably we take on many characteristics from these roles. But there remains a central core of what Erikson called "identity," resisting too great diffusion into socially prescribed roles. Good education in the world of tomorrow will be increasingly concerned to conserve and to strengthen that firm inner selfhood.

PREPARATION OF PSYCHOANALYTICALLY ORIENTED TEACHERS

If, as urged in the five earlier propositions, education in the future is to be based on a dynamic theory of new learning struggling against resistance; fully aware of transference responses in pupils toward the teacher and toward other pupils; centering upon feelings and emotional communication; liberating creative selves from entanglement in conformity to role-expectations, then clearly teachers need a kind of training more like that given to other therapists. To urge teachers to meet emotional needs without giving those teachers appropriate specialized training brings two dangers. One would be that teachers would again feel frustrated by one more educational "ideal" which does not correspond to any practical skills they have been taught. Even more serious is the other possibility—that eager teachers without adequate preparation might plunge in anyhow and flounder about in a maze of symbolism, interpretation, and relationships, succeeding only in making many bad matters worse.

The first step may well be recognition of group psychotherapy for those teachers who want the deeper insight into themselves and others which such experience usually contributes. In a large graduate course on "Education and Personality" offered at Teachers College, Columbia University, provision has been made in recent years for some students to substitute participation in therapy groups for other types of course requirement. The results have been very encouraging. Participants have reported that they gained more than they commonly did in other courses. If the preparation of a teacher is supposed to be packed into four college years with four or five courses carried each term, then it would not be excessive to permit one course meeting five hours a week throughout one year to be devoted to group psychotherapy. Because the focus is on actual emotional relationships and problems, the learning is far more vital and personal than in most lecture, textbook, or laboratory courses. An increasing number of teachers may be expected to go on for individual psychoanalysis in order to increase their awareness of formerly unconscious dynamic factors in themselves. Another constructive step would be to recognize personal analysis as at least the equivalent of more course credits or "travel" for in-service salary increments.

As psychoanalytic insight diffuses more effectively into education, more teachers will find themselves wrestling with the kind of problem which Dr. Leonard Kornberg has discussed so brilliantly.[6] He conceives teaching as the organization of interpersonal interactions in groups of three or more (the dyad is a different case) to convey meanings that meet personal needs and purposes. As he phrases it, "individual tutoring is 'therapy' and [all] forms of group treatment are 'teaching.'"

REFERENCES

1. Ernest Jones, *Sigmund Freud: Four Centenary Addresses* (New York, Basic Books, 1956), p. 145.

2. Goodwin Watson, "Educational Psychology: General Theory," *Review of Educational Research*, June, 1956, XXVI:241–46.

3. C. S. Hall and G. Lindzey, "Psychoanalytic Theory and Its Applications in the Social Sciences." In *Handbook of Social Psychology*, G. Lindzey, ed. (Cambridge, Mass., 1954), Ch. IV.

4. Lionel Trilling, *Freud and the Crisis of Our Culture* (Boston, The Beacon Press, 1955).

5. Robert Lindner, *Prescription for Rebellion* (New York, Rinehart, 1952).

6. Leonard Kornberg. *A Class for Disturbed Children* (New York, Bureau of Publications, Teachers College, Columbia University, 1955).

SCHOOL GRADES AND GROUP THERAPY *

Samuel Tenebaum

A Stronger Ego Cures Weak Grades. Here is a clear example both of the curative emphasis in Freudian psychology and of the use of groups that Watson mentioned in the previous article. Tenenbaum sees low grades and academic probation as visible manifestations of underlying psychological problems. To cure the low grades, he alleviates the deeper problems they stem from—anxieties, fears, guilt, and weak self-images. He also shows the Freudian emphasis on intra-family dynamics, particularly with parents, as a major source of problems. He asks, "Are grades a symptom of the whole functioning person, who and what he is, and not primarily a matter of intelligence?" If so, hadn't we better educate the whole functioning person? Judged by its results, his group "therapy" is actually a kind of "education."

There are no lazy people. There are frightened people, anxious people, bored people who have found no meaning in life and hence no meaning in the activities necessary for life. And there are people who have unrealistic notions of who they are and what they are. They, too, are crippled for realistic living. As for students, what keeps them from their work for the most part is fear of failure, terrible self-demands, low self-esteem, inability—intellectually or emotionally—to cope with the tasks set before them. In our culture, students find it more acceptable and more respectable to plead disinterest and laziness, rather than lack of capacity and intelligence, and this is the way most students and parents prefer to explain failure.

In the main, young people who have school problems are immobilized by their fears. When a child is doing poorly at school, teachers are wont to attribute it to indolence and laziness; rarely to his fears, his hang ups or his great desire to please his parents, all of which may be debilitating and self-defeating.

There were a number of education major students at Long Island University who had been on probation semester after semester. Before expelling them, the then Dean of the Division of Education, and the adviser of the Educational Counseling Service thought that as a last chance, they ought to be given the opportunity of having a group therapy experience. I was asked if I would like to take over the group and I accepted, having advocated such group experiences, not only for students in academic difficulties, but for all our students for many years.

*From Samuel Tenenbaum, "School Grades and Group Therapy," *Mental Hygiene* 54, no. 4 (October, 1970): 525–529, by permission of Jeanne Tenenbaum. Samuel Tenenbaum was Professor of Counselling and Guidance at Long Island University and author of the book *Why Men Hate*.

About 15 students were originally assigned to the group. Six came once or twice and never came back. I was left with a group of nine, six of whom came regularly and three irregularly.

In my private practice I seldom experience a cancellation. The thought that students who did not pay a fee would reject the chance for a therapeutic experience was something I could not contemplate without a severe blow to my self-esteem. But this was my own problem and I never communicated this to the group. I held firmly to the belief (and I still do) that it was for each student to decide whether he wanted to attend or not; and if a member stayed away, I interpreted it to mean that he wasn't profiting and it was, then, a reflection on me and not on him. Every absence made me feel very uneasy and guilty.

From the outset I never asked students to work or study harder, for I assumed that the thought had occurred to them; or if not, someone else had told them of the need. Never once did I bring up the matter of grades unless they did. I did try to listen, to be sensitive to them as they expressed their grief, worry and often despair. As I listened I often wished that faculty members could be present and hear these anguished communications, so that they could understand what a grade means.

Although students could attend at most ten sessions of one hour and a quarter, not one of the nine failed a single course, not only during the semester in which they participated in the group experience but also in the semester that followed. Where hitherto their records had been filled with Fs, Ds and Cs, after their group experience there were several As, B+s, Bs and C+s.

Prior to their group experience, grades C+ and higher for these students came to 24.7%; after the group experience it rose sharply to 65.0%. Before the group experience, grade C and below came to 76.3%; after, it was 34.5%. In all their previous school experience, these students had failed 10.4% of their courses. After their group experience, they did not experience a single failure or F grade for the entire academic year. As for the D grade, there was a sharp drop, from 31.2% to 9.6%. Even for the gentlemanly pass, the C grade, there was also a drop from 28.9% before to 22.5% after. These percentage deficits in C and lower grades were made up by the sharply upward movement to grades above C after the students became involved with the group.

In their prior years at Long Island (two had attended the university six semesters and seven, four semesters), these students made altogether one A, which was 0.5% of all their grades. In the semester concurrent with and the semester following their group experience, they made eight As, representing 8.6% of all their grades. Before their group experience, their B+ grades came to 2.3%, after, 10.6%; their B grades before, 9.8%, after, 25.8%; C+ 10.4% before, after 17.1%. After the group experience, their grades rose markedly from the lower end to the higher end of the grading scale.

During the semester of the group meetings, I asked the students to write brief reactions to each session and several of those are quoted here.

At the start, they found talking difficult; and their communication was random and desultory. They could not understand how plain, ordinary talk could help them with their grades. All were reluctant to reveal their probationary status and their silences were long and severe.

These are two typical early reactions:

> I noticed today that we, as a group, have a lot in common as to why we are on probation, but that our fears of being with strangers prevent our really coming out with the true facts of our problem. . . . I am sure if someone starts, others will follow.

> I don't see how anyone can really be helped. . . . and there are many things I won't say because there are other people in the room.

One member took to the process immediately:

> After leaving the first session I felt as if a great burden was lifted from my shoulders because for the first time in my life I could speak freely of the personal problems which I have been faced with in the last few years. . . . For the first time in a long while I didn't feel any anxiety about being in a classroom.

Mostly, however, they did not know how to articulate feelings; and they resented having to make the effort. This was a hard stage for them and for me. Wrote one member: *"If it seems that I don't participate as much as the others, it's just that I get very upset telling my problems. . . . I hope at future meetings it won't bother me as much to tell my problems."*

Gradually, they talked less and less about school and grades and sought each other out for support and comfort. Bound as they were by a common grief—the pain and the hurt and the shame of their probationary status—the group slowly began to jell and assume a close, in-group quality.

> I was happy during this session because I felt that we are learning different facets of each other's personalities. I felt in the past our lives started and ended with classes and that we had no other lives outside of school. During the hour we spoke of ourselves socially.

It is amazing to what extent parents figure as a disturbing influence to the members of the group; how, instead of helping them, they fill them with disturbing emotions, so that the tasks in connection with school do not become a personal student involvement but a way to win parental approval and an honorable and respected position in the family. For these students, school represents nothing but a vehicle to get grades sufficiently high so that parents will think well of them. For the openly rebellious, a struggle may develop between student and parents. The parents will badger their offspring: "Have you studied enough?" "What grades did you get on your examination?" "Have you done your homework?" The educational experience becomes subsidiary to parental needs and demands. In such instances, there may be acrimony and bitterness and sometimes despair, not because of what goes on at school and what school represents, but at what goes on at home. Here are typical student reactions:

> I was very glad to see that I'm not the only one with "mother problems."

> One thing we have in common is meddling parents. I am not saying this is the cause of our probation status, but it may very well be one of the causes.

The parents took the responsibility of the school task away from their children. Further, no matter how they rebelled and how bitter the acrimony, these students took it for granted that their parents were right and that they were worthless. Although this did not make them better able to cope with the school situation, it did make them feel guilty and inadequate. These feelings, in my judgment, only accentuated students' anxieties and made them less able to meet school demands. In the group sessions, students began to perceive how parents figured in the school situation, and to understand better the nature of their parental relationships. One student writes:

> I realize that my mother will never be pleased. That is something I never realized. I'm sure this ... will help me ... now and in the future. For if I keep listening to her, I may find I'm living for her rather than for me.

Although the matter of grades and probation was always present, the discussions soon went far afield of grades. They included their whole persons; how they struggled, how they failed, also, how they triumphed. In my opinion, this proved to be the most valuable part of the experience since it helped them gain realistic insights into their own difficulties and their own persons.

> I feel that much was accomplished in (our last session) in that the meeting really brought me to thinking why I got marks as I did ... The family situations described (by others) were somewhat like my own so I was helped in that area as well. ... Though I don't fully understand why I've been so erratic in my work, I know that it has been at least 90% of my own doing and I aim to better myself.

In the final stage, they were a united group, working in unison, understanding one another, better aware of their own feelings and their own problems, more realistic about what needed to be done. Below is one reaction articulating this new awareness of self, these new insights and new resolutions.

> I truly believe that our open-mindedness about our individual problems has helped us to achieve our success. If we can continue to verbalize about ourselves,

then surely we can allay our fears about school. . . . Of course, we have to work and study, but I feel that by talking, half the battle to get off and stay off probation is won.

I asked for a final reaction as to how they viewed their experience and requested that they send me their final grades. These were mailed to me after their final examinations and long after the group had broken up. I wish there was sufficient space to quote these communications verbatim. One in particular sums up the many reactions:

. . . it was a very good feeling to know that there were others in the same category as myself; and that there was a person, such as yourself, who seemed to take an honest interest in each individual. I feel that now that I am off probation, I will stay off.

DISCUSSION

At first the group members did not know how to talk and were reluctant to talk. Each member of the group thought that "being on probation" was unique to him and each carried this burden for the most part secretly and in shame. When they discovered that all in the group were on probation, it had an exciting, liberating effect. Eventually, their common problem served as a bond and a tie to unite them.

I want to emphasize that in none of the sessions did I bring up the matter of their grades; in no instance did I make them feel that I wanted them to get higher grades, or that I was in any way involved with their grades.

Although the group members' probationary status was always present, once they revealed themselves as persons, they discussed grades from a deeper and more significant point of view. Grades became linked with their anxieties, their hopes, their weaknesses, their failures, their parents, etc., etc.

In the group, the members received regard, encouragement, support, affection. Their ego strength increased, their self-respect rose, and as one of the outcomes, I believe, they were able to confront their school situation in a healthier and more intelligent way. They were able to view themselves and their problems more insightfully, more realistically. One spoke of anxieties so great that she could scarcely live through an examination. Others spoke of frightening instructors who marked you down for anything and everything so one couldn't think. My heart went out to these unfortunates, as they tried so hard to make themselves small and inconspicuous in class, fearful of being called on. Others spoke of personal situations which they faced that kept them so distraught that they were immobilized from doing anything. "I got started studying and then my mother got after me and we had the worst fight in a month and I couldn't study, and she said I was no good and I would never be good." The tears rolled down her eyes. "I couldn't study. . . and I couldn't sleep that night."

The group experience made the members more articulate. Before they were silent in class—outsiders. As they became more aware of their feelings and better able to articulate them, several managed to develop more personal relationships with some of their instructors and, best of all, a number became more active as class participants. These began to feel like persons and act as persons, not nonentities.

When I discovered that the group members made even higher grades in the following semester than they did while they were undergoing the group experience, I was puzzled until the thought occurred to me that they did not have the full force of whatever is therapeutic in a group until the following semester; and that this could account for the difference.

Although they were doing unsatisfactory school work, it appears that every member of the group had the requisite intelligence to perform the academic tasks set before them. In fact, several became, after the group experience, not only successfully functioning students but superior students. The question arises: On what exactly does academic success and failure hinge? Are grades a symptom of the whole functioning person, who and what he is, and not primarily a matter of intelligence which hitherto was regarded as the main and only component. If yes, what are these other factors? Further, if these students had not undergone the group experience, what would have happened to them? How would their lives have been changed? This is a matter not to be taken lightly. In our society, college graduation is the union card for valuable rights and prerequisites, vocational, social and even marital. Would they have righted themselves on their own or would they have been expelled as academic failures with all its inherent emotional and psychological trauma, very often lifelong.

This is not a statistical study. It is rather an account of nine persons, each one apart and separate, who participated in a group experience. Although we can conjecture, I do not believe that at this stage we know exactly what happens to the members in a group of this kind; how a group affects each in it; and how each in it affects the group.

The hope is that with time, with further study and inquiry, the process will be better understood and therefore better controlled, and hence, we will be more able to replicate outcomes. Even with our present knowledge, we have every reason to believe that when a group works, it can be highly salubrious and therapeutic, in ways which we have not nearly plumbed.

EXCERPTS FROM *FANTASY AND FEELING IN EDUCATION**

Richard M. Jones

Beyond Curing. In these selections Jones shows the Freudian interest in the unconscious as it expresses itself through imagination and emotions, but instead of seeing educators' jobs as trying to cure illness or solve psychological problems, he departs from most Freudians by saying teachers should educate peoples' imaginations and fantasizing for their own growth beyond merely curing. In *Fantasy and Feeling in Education* Jones shows some ways teachers can involve students' emotions to increase both cognitive and affective learning, especially in elementary and secondary social studies.

Psychoanalysis had done some sniffing in schoolhouses prior to Sputnik. This consisted largely in the setting up of clinical enclaves in schools. Sometimes by way of the front door, through which it was sought to practice preventive psychiatry, i.e., to diagnose mental disorder early and to render treatment on the spot. Sometimes by way of the back door, through which a range of objectives were pursued, from improved social adjustment to the conducting of less boring English classes. Both were essentially grafting operations. That is to say, neither approach aspired to bring psychodynamic principles and methods to bear on the educative process itself. Schools happen to be where the children are, where one can get at them for a variety of right purposes which need not be directly relevant to formal education. Certainly it is as advisable to use schools as places to prevent schizophrenia and to better the resolutions of family conflicts as it is to use them as places to prevent poliomyelitis and to instill good driving habits.

There are now a small minority of school systems whose staffs include a cadre of teachers and counselors skilled and practiced in the clinical arts of diagnosis and referral, and with whom normal children have learned to consult in times of healthy emotional crisis. There are also a small minority of school systems whose openness to the mental health professions has been abused. Through the front door, to take the most disreputable case, by psychiatrists in search of the most lucrative referrals; and through the back door, by teachers who view themselves as psychiatrists and who find children handy objects on which to practice self-deception. In between, there are many well meaning and well trained members of the teaching and clinical professions who can count among

*From Richard M. Jones, *Fantasy and Feeling in Education* (New York: Harper & Row, 1968), pp. 5–7, 77, 85–86, 174–176, 182–184, 243–244, by permission of the author. Richard M. Jones is Professor of Psychology, The Evergreen State College, Olympia, Washington. He is the author of *The New Psychology of Dreaming* (New York: Grune and Stratton, 1970).

their better professional moments the time they learned to respect each other. But the respect of teachers for clinicians is usually superimposed upon a fundamental mistrust. A variety of causes are at work here: differences in status, disparities of income, outright snobbishness, and so on. The primary cause, however, is the clinician's characteristic lack of involvement in the teacher's realm of expertise, the educative process. For a clinician to exercise his skills, the pupil must be converted into a patient, however temporarily. He or his parents must be prepared to view certain behavior or certain attitudes as sick, whatever the euphemisms used against stigmata. Otherwise it might not be seen as appropriate to consult a doctor. Some teachers, recognizing the values of the clinician's objectives, and impressed by the delicacies of his skills, become practiced at lending a hand in the conversion process. But clinicians in schools are part-time help; they treat and leave. There is almost never occasion for professional exchange, for the teacher to enlist the help of the clinician in the instructional process, which to any honest observer would be as recognizably valuable and as impressive in the delicacies of skill required.

In developing *instructional* methods of cultivating emotion and imagery, should we model our efforts after the more polished and practiced methods of psychotherapy? The answer I want to give to this question, and it will take some explaining, is: yes, provided we are very careful to reverse everything.

A therapist's first concern is anxiety. A teacher's first concern is learning, i.e., *human* learning, i.e., creative thought (some purists will reject the equation but much more evidence suggests it than disputes it). As we have seen, anxiety and creative thought are related as the two poles of a continuum. Their interrelations should be born in mind, but they should not be mistaken, one for the other. It follows that a therapist's methods seek to reduce aloneness and helplessness, and that a teacher's methods seek to increase the polar opposites: community and mastery. These interrelations can be schematized so:

$$(\text{imagination} + \text{aloneness} + \text{helplessness}) = \text{anxiety} \leftarrow \text{psychotherapy}$$
$$\text{instruction} \rightarrow (\text{imagination} + \text{community} + \text{mastery}) = \text{creative learning}$$

It says that imagination plus aloneness plus helplessness produces anxiety, which may be relieved by psychotherapy. And that instruction may lead to imagination plus community plus mastery, which produces creative learning.

Be reminded, however, that invoking the imagination is only the first step in the direction of creative learning. There remains the question, to be put to any comprehensive theory of instruction, of *how* to cultivate and deploy aroused imaginations, and their attendant emotions, in the interest of increased mastery of subject matter. Educational—not clinical—research must answer this question. Merely to state it properly has required a rather long way around the considerable advances made by clinical research in its closely related spheres of interest. The advantages that accrue to correctly stated questions come immediately into view, however, for we are now free to modify, adapt, refine, or even to copy the methods used by psychotherapists, because we have now more clearly defined the respective means and ends. If, as teachers, we employ the therapist's methods as means to the end of reducing anxiety, we are merely doing psychotherapy with students. Sometimes beneficial, but discourteous in being uninvited. If we employ these methods as ends in themselves, we embark on a course of ineffectual psychotherapy—not as risky as some fear, because being uninvited it is not likely to be followed. But, in any event, this is not a course of instruction. If, however, we can see ways to employ such methods, or the modifications of such methods, as means to the ends of instructing creative learning, we open new vistas in pedagogy. If the students indirectly acquire greater insight, and thus reduce their anxieties as a secondary gain, so much the better. But that is their business. Our business, at the beginning, and again at the end, is the subject matter of the social sciences and the humanities: our species, where we came from, where we are, where we may be going—using as our touchstone what the students can imagine, share, and use of their special acquaintance with these subjects, which is theirs by virtue of quite literally being first-hand specimens of the subject matter.

TOWARD A COMPLETE THEORY OF INSTRUCTION

The rationale for cultivating emotions in schoolrooms is thus the reverse of the rationale for cultivating emotions in clinics. In clinics, issues which are known to be emotionally charged are raised for the purpose of creating conditions under which emotions can come to be controlled and expressed. In schoolrooms, conditions are created which invite expression of controlled emotions for the purpose of imbuing curricular issues with personal significance. The power of emotion to generate interest and involvement in subject matters which would otherwise find children uninterested and uninvolved lies in their deep personal familiarity—such familiarity being a consequence of emotion having been integral to every phase of personal development from infancy on. The value of emotional involvement in the learning process thus lies in its potential for aiding assimilation of new or remote experiences in idiomatically illuminating ways.

This potential is carried by more than merely associative connections. The emotions are intimately interrelated with certain symbolic functions known to be central to creative thinking. The symbolic functions which regulate all human experience have been classified into three systems: conscious, unconscious, and preconscious. Conscious symbolic processes are predominantly verbal, thrive on repetition, and serve primarily the communication of ideas. Unconscious symbolic processes are pre-dominantly nonverbal, also thrive on repetition, and serve primarily to *prevent* communication by disrupting connections between conscious symbols and their referents. Unconscious symbolic processes are ultimately traceable to childhood experiences in which attempted communication led to situations of being alone and helpless with *pre*conscious experiences. Preconscious symbolic processes are predominantly analogical and there-fore serve primarily to diversify the relations between conscious symbols and their referents. These is why the preconscious has become the focus of so much theorizing among investigators concerned with "creative thinking"—especially its so-called "incubative" and "illuminative" phases.

Human mentality would not be possible without both the conscious and the preconscious processes—and their interaction. So we cannot be accused of taking a perjorative view of the conscious system if we note, with Kubie, that in most instances it consists of a biased sampling of the "preconscious stream." For example, I wish to concentrate at this moment on communicating in English a rather fine distinction pertaining to human mental functioning. I can very palpably sense the rush of enteroceptive, exteroceptive and proprioceptive activity just below the threshold of consciousness. I am sure that a polygraph would indicate at this moment that I am in a state of emotional arousal. Yet, I am not aware of experiencing any particular emotion; rather I am aware only of concen-trating on a line of thought. That is, I am automatically ruling out any emotion or attendant image which might divert me from my chosen line of conscious thought. In other words, I am biasing my sample of pre-conscious mentation for the sake of communicating something I already know. If, on the other hand, I should conclude that I am not as much in command of what I know as I thought I was, or that to communicate effectively I must refresh it, see it from another angle, or relate it in this instance to some otherwise disparate thought, then it would be clear what I should do: go for a walk, take a swim, play tennis, read a novel, or entertain some fantasies that would probably not bear reporting. That is, I should need to stop concentrating in the hope that a less biased sample of my preconscious vagaries would supply what was lacking.

In a sense, then, we often choose to be unimaginative in order to be effectively conventional, and we do so by remaining aloof from the collateral and emotional references which orbit preconsciously around our conscious lines of thought. This is obviously all to the good; nothing less than civilization depends upon it. The trouble comes when the vague sense of choice wanes and we find ourselves being unimaginative for no very good purpose. I need hardly add that people are as frequently miseducated into this dilemma as they are not educated out of it. This, because most teachers—I should say most teaching methods—place a tacit premium on remaining aloof from emotional references in subject matters not only when there is a good reason for doing so but also when there is not.

I think it important to have included these latter speculations because of what I have found to be a typical first error made by many teachers who become persuaded that psychoanalytic principles can improve their teaching skills. Not content to lead their students to confront emotionally charged issues, they rush to *interpret* them in ways that are all too readily available in psychoanalytic case histories, overlooking that these are insight-oriented, not outsight-oriented, and therefore run contrary to the manifest purposes of teaching. Imagine the impact on my moment of creative outsight concerning the Kalahari Bushmen, for example, had someone interpreted my momentary loss for words as reflecting a mental block rooted in early ambivalences on the toilet! Remember, however, that the interpretation would probably have been valid, its rudeness residing not in remoteness from truth but in remoteness from relevance.

We may at this juncture seek to clarify a point of typical obscurity along the topographical dimension of psychoanalytic theory, namely the distinction between unconscious and preconscious symbolization. Freud successfully precluded our venturing fruitlessly into notions of differential cortical locations in these matters. But when he came to formulate the more general distinction between the primary (metaphorical) and secondary (literal) symbolic processes he did not say in so many words how he conceived it to coexist with his earlier tripartite formulation of conscious, preconscious, and unconscious symbolization. Kubie gave the clarification: in both preconscious and unconscious symbolization the primary process is dominant, but the former seeks conscious reception, elaboration, and communication, whereas the latter is refractory to consciousness and appears to "seek" deception and miscommunication.

However, in his enthusiasm to trace creative behavior to preconscious symbolization and neurotic behavior to unconscious symbolization, Kubie allows another misconception, one that can be particularly misleading to teachers who usually can only effect commerce with either of these potentials through conscious channels: the notion that the difference is fundamentally intra-psychic or "in the head." Thus creative persons have more preconscious symbols at their disposal and neurotic persons are afflicted by more unconscious symbols. There is some psychological truth in this way of putting the matter, but it is a truth of little service to teachers whose concerns are less with what is already in students' heads as with what they can help the students make of it.

The truth of the matter, let us call it the operational truth, is that the primary process is rendered preconscious in its functioning by the *psychosocial conditions* which define it and give it value. These conditions are the same that we emphasized earlier: (1) the subject matter should be significant and believable (or make-believable) and (2) the approach to the subject matter should be such that *all* emotions and images are welcomed and sought after and assumed to be ultimately relevant to the educative process—not shunned and belittled or assumed to be threatening to children. When these conditions obtain, neurotic persons are capable of creative behavior; when they do not obtain, creative persons are capable of neurotic behavior. The fluid condition, in other words, which our previous considerations of community-aloneness and mastery-helplessness antici- pated.

Moreover, these are conditions which find their impetus less in a teacher's method than in her attitudes, for they are less subject to permission or arrangement than they are to authorization. Finally, for all their predetermining effects on non-conscious processes, they are con- ditions which begin and end in consciousness.

I have taken pains to present the emergent problems, and to suggest tentative approaches to their solution, in exclusively pedagogical terms, so as to invite *teachers* to see promise in accepting the challenges involved. For, let there be no mistake about it: it will be neither Bruner, nor Kubie, nor I, nor all the curriculum coordinators and psychological consultants currently at work, or in training, or yet to be born, who will do ultimate justice to these challenges; it will be *teachers*, working alone and in small informal task forces, who will do the job—and, more often than not, with precious little reward for their efforts, save the intrinsic satisfaction of being more competent teachers.

SOME COMMENTS CONCERNING THE ROLE OF EDUCATION IN THE "CREATION OF CREATION"*

Edith A. Weisskopf

Mining the Unconscious. There is more to thinking than logic and reason, and there is more to knowing than recalling facts. Weisskopf challenges us to teach non-reasoning abilities and non-factual memory, for these are the basis of creativity. Where do these powers lie? According to Freudians, they lie in the unconscious. Our education usually concentrates on *conscious* thinking and *conscious* knowledge, rather than exploring the unconscious for its larger stores of facts and its powerful unconscious thinking processes. Instead of spending all our efforts on the first and fourth stages of creativity (fact-gathering and verification), she says, we can and should put some of our efforts into the middle stages (incubation and illumination). Weisskopf's article dovetails nicely with Koestler's in the transpersonal section. Both hint at ways to expand our creative intellectual abilities by tapping into unexploited realms of our behavior. Weisskopf and the Freudians stress this as tapping the unconscious, while Koestler and transpersonal psychologists concentrate on using altered states of consciousness as methods of tapping these mental reserves.

Most people would agree that it is one of the main aims of education to encourage the development of creative abilities. Therefore, educators are forced to concern themselves with the following question: What are the conditions which enhance the formation of creative thought? The literature in psychology and related fields contains a considerable amount of information about creative thought and the conditions of its growth. This information is based on general impression, on the analysis of biographical data, on introspective statements of creative thinkers, or on experimental research. In spite of the diversity of its origin the literature shows a considerable amount of agreement as to some of the conditions enhancing creativity. Thus, one would expect educators to use techniques in their intellectual work similar to the techniques which are thought to create a fertile soil for the growth of new ideas.

Strangely enough this is not often the case. It is the objective of this paper to discuss some specific aspects of the well-known fact that the mental attitude during intellectual work encouraged by our schools is in many respects diametrically opposed to the mental attitude which is thought to stimulate creativity.[7,18]

Most educators in their oral or written admonitions to their pupils stress the importance of industry. Yet, if we scan through the literature on

*From Edith Weisskopf, "Some Comments on the Role of Education in the 'Creation of Creation,'" *Journal of Educational Psychology* 42 (March, 1951): 185–189, by permission of the author. Edith Weisskopf-Joelson is Professor of Psychology at the University of Georgia, Athens, Georgia.

creativity, we find statements such as the following: " . . . though without industry great intellectual work cannot be done, yet mere industry may prevent creation"[18] (p. 149). Educators emphatically stress the first part of this statement when teaching students, but are, with few exceptions (e.g.[10]), reluctant even to mention the second part. The constant activity enforced by many educators does not give young people the leisure which is an essential prerequisite for intellectual or artistic creation.[7,18]

We teach our pupils the importance of regular study habits. Why do we ignore statements such as the following? "The advantage of regular habits during the student years is great; but the optimum point at which the curve of that advantage cuts the curve of the advantage of fresh initiative is different for those whose professional work will be intellectual origination, and for those of different powers and aims"[18] (p. 297). If pupils would use the explicit admonitions received from their teachers as their only source of knowledge on study techniques, it would never occur to them that regular study habits could be anything but advantageous.

We try to instill a critical attitude towards intellectual matters in our students, but Hutchinson quotes a scientist saying: "It is surprising how fertile the mind becomes when not interrupted, or restricted by criticism in the free and often fantastic expression of its ideas"[6] (p. 32).

Our school system stresses the importance of intellectual objectivity and the liabilities of one-sidedness. Thus, " . . . students often start their careers with some intense enthusiasm, then learn in college how narrow and 'immature' it is, how much can be said on the other side, and how many other good ways of doing things exist. They gradually acquire a spirit of mellow tolerance and scholarly insight, but lose the creative impulse"[11] (p. 301).

It is challenging to examine in this connection suggestions made by psychiatrists or clinical psychologists on the mental attitude which leads to optimal results in producing insight and understanding with regard to their patients' problems. Freud, for example, makes the following recommendations on treatment techniques: "All conscious exertion is to be withheld from the capacity for attention . . . "[2] (p. 324). "One has simply to listen and not to trouble to keep in mind anything in particular" (p. 325). "It is not a good thing to formulate a case scientifically while treatment is proceeding, to reconstruct its development, anticipate its progress, and take notes from time to time of the condition at the moment, as scientific interest would require" (p. 326–7). " . . . the most successful cases are those in which one proceeds, as it were, aimlessly, and allows oneself to be overtaken by any surprises, always presenting to them an open mind, free from expectation" (p. 327). Reik also emphasizes the liabilities of continuous sharp attention and the benefits of inattentive states: " . . . training in attention may succeed "too well," so that the child is shut off from a whole flood of freely emerging associations and ideas"[17] (p. 165). "The concentration of attention involves a setting up of inhibitions, so that keen observation of particular things corresponds to the ignoring of others. Withdrawal of certain contents from consciousness is no less a part of attention than the appearance of others at the center. It is open to questions which part is the more significant to the essence and action of attention, the illumination of particular objects, the bestowal of intensive interest upon them, or its diversion away from others" (p. 164). "Not until I cast off the customary restraint of voluntary attention was I able to get hold of the hidden psychical data. Not until I left the firm and broad high road did I reach the goal along side paths. The secret meaning escaped my conscious, active attention, and was not found until I had become 'inattentive' in the popular meaning of the word, that is, until I gave myself up to unconscious ideas of the goal" (p. 169).

If a student would show a mental attitude towards his school work similar to the one advocated by these clinicians, he would elicit the serious criticism of his teachers. The objection may be raised that intellectual work of the academic type is basically different from the achieving of insight into the personality problems of a neurotic patient, and that it, therefore, requires a different mental attitude. Quite true. Yet the literature on creative thought suggests that Freud's admonitions may prove useful in any situation where insight is required. Moreover, Maier and Luchins show that the arriving at solutions of various kinds of problems is facilitated by such 'loosening' instructions as "Do not be a creature of habit and stay in a rut," "Keep your mind open for new meanings," "The solution pattern appears suddenly. You cannot force it"[9] (p. 147), or "Don't be blind"[8] (p. 2).

Thus, educators may find it profitable to advocate a passive, inattentive attitude to their students not as a permanent condition but as a stimulating technique during specific phases of their intellectual work. As Bateson states " . . . the advances in scientific thought come from a *combination of loose and strict thinking*, and this combination is the most precious tool of science"[1] (p. 55).

At this point I expect some readers to voice objections. "Industry, regular study habits, a critical, controlled attitude, are necessary attributes of successful intellectual work," they will say. "The creative individuals who found that relaxation, irregular habits, and temporary abandonment of criticism and control enhance creativity have spent years of strenuous preparation during which they exercised all the virtues advocated by traditional educators." Quite true. Yet the question remains unanswered why, among the four stages of the creative process, namely, preparation, incubation, illumination, and verification[3-7,12-16,18] we prepare children for the first and last stage only, and completely ignore the other two stages.[18] Only one possible cause of this educational bias will be suggested in this paper.

The process of insight and illumination appears to be directed by unconscious forces to a higher degree than the process of preparation and verification. Just as lightning represents the sudden explosive merging of positive and negative electricity, intellectual insight may represent the sudden merging of conscious content accumulated during the stage of preparation with unconscious, repressed material.[5,6] Thus, it may be the denial of this repressed material which causes educators to deny the process of illumination. In other words, we do not want to accept the fact that intellectual activity takes part of its energy supply from the big reservoir of unacceptable impulses called the Id, that the material carefully and rationally accumulated during the period of preparation has to become imbued with Id-impulses in order to be brought to life. We falsely admonish our students to exert control in order to keep these impulses repressed instead of teaching them to make their impulses subservient to intellectual activity.

Just as we often deceive small children about the nature of biological creation, we deceive older children by pretending that intellectual creation is unemotional. Thus, by de-emotionalizing intellectuality and by keeping the 'sweet secret' of intellectual creation from youth, we suffocate intellectual creativity.

BIBLIOGRAPHY

G. Bateson. "Experiments in thinking about observed ethnological material," *Phil. Sci.*, 1941, 8, 53–68.

S. Freud. *Collected Papers*, London: Hogarth Press, 1949. Volume II

H. von Helmholtz. *Vorträge und Reden*, Braunschweig: F. Vierweg & Sohn, 1903.

E. D. Hutchinson. "Materials for the study of creative thinking," *Psych. Bull*, 1931, 28, 392–410.

————. "Varieties of insight in humans," *Psychiatry*, 1939, 2, 323–332.

————. "The nature of insight," *Psychiatry*, 1941, 4, 31–43.

————. "The phenomenon of insight in relation to education," Psychiatry, 1942, 5, 499–507.

A. S. Luchins. "Mechanization in problem solving. The effect of *Einstellung*," *Psychol. Monogr.*, 1942, 54, No. 248.

N. R. F. Maier. "An aspect of human reasoning," *British J. Psychol.*, 1933, 24, 144–155.

R. L. Munroe. *Teaching the Individual*, New York: Columbia University Press, 1942.

T. Munro. "Creative ability in art and its educational fostering," *Yearb. Nat. Soc. Stud. Educ.*, 1941, 40, 289–322.

C. Patrick. "Creative thought in poets," *Arch. Psychol.*, 1935, 26, No. 178.

————. "Creative thought in artists," *J. Psychol.*, 1937, 4, 35–73.

————. "Scientific thought," *J. of Psychol.*, 1938, 5, 55–83.

————. "Whole and part relationship in creative thought," *Am. J. Psychol.*, 1941, 54, 128–131.

H. Poincaré. *Science et Méthode*. Paris: Flammarion, 1918.

Th. Reik. *Listening with the Third Ear*. New York: Farrer, Straus, and Co., 1949.

G. Wallas. *The Art of Thought*. New York: Harcourt Brace and Co., 1926.

CURRICULUM DEVELOPMENT
FROM A PSYCHOANALYTIC PERSPECTIVE[*]

Louise L. Tyler

Freudian Objectives. Although Freudian psychology has influenced many bits and pieces of educational practice, Tyler suggests that it become a major influence on education in an organized, systematic way, rather than just an incidental consideration in curriculum planning. The five goals of education which she derives from psychoanalytic psychology are helpful ones for teachers and curriculum workers. How does your overall school curriculum meet these goals? Do your own courses and individual units meet the criteria she suggests? Can you make your courses measure-up to the content and objectives she lists? Like Neill and Rogers, Tyler points out the importance of the school "atmosphere" too, and like them, she says that an "open" or "free" atmosphere does *not* mean *completely* permissive, but should include supportive constraints. Chaos is not freedom.

INTRODUCTION

Psychoanalytic theory has been in existence for a half-century, yet no attempt has been made to utilize it in any systematic way for curriculum development or for understanding curricular effectiveness. This article is an attempt to suggest the contribution that psychoanalytic theory can make to curriculum development.

Prior to dealing with the central focus of this article it is useful to make some general comments about the relevance of psychoanalysis to education as well as some of its limits.[1]

Psychoanalysis is viewed as a theory of personality development, as a form of therapy, and a technical procedure for investigating mental processes. Much of psychoanalytic writing has focused on man's internal behavior, i.e., his thoughts and feelings, whereas much of what has been written in education has focused on man's external (overt) behavior. Specifically, a most influential movement in curriculum has concerned itself with behavioral objectives. A slogan "Help stamp out non-behavioral objectives" has even been coined. Behavioral objectives are statements of the ends of education and they are to be overt and measurable. Recently, however, in education there has developed interest in relating external behavior with internal behavior. Consequently, education may find psychoanalytic concepts of development and behavior very useful. Likewise, psychoanalysis is expressing interest in man's external behavior. Anna

*From Louise L. Tyler, "Curriculum Development From a Psychoanalytic Perspective," *Educational Forum* 36 (January, 1972): 173–179, by permission of the author and Kappa Delta Pi, An Honor Society in Education, owners of the copyright. Louise Tyler is Associate Professor at the School of Education, U.C.L.A.

Freud[2] in *Normality and Pathology in Childhood* discusses the importance of linking surface observations (external behavior) with layers of the mind (inner). It is likely that education and psychoanalysis will both profit from this communication.

However, education cannot find in psychoanalysis or any science the values upon which to base decisions. Psychoanalysis cannot give moral direction to education. What psychoanalysis can do is contribute to an understanding of how values develop and influence behavior. Another limitation is that in psychoanalysis, while its theory is mainly based on data obtained from individuals in a clinical situation, the substantive propositions that result are generally not applicable to particular individuals without a great deal of supplementary information. A third limitation is that much of what occurs in school is in a group setting, whereas most of the theory has been formulated as a consequence of a doctor to patient relationship. If these limitations are kept in mind, it is possible that education can use what is emerging from the field as a body of lore and some hypotheses which will help in understanding and improving education.

There is no agreement in the field as to a definition of what is meant by the term curriculum. This author assumes that curriculum making is an art based upon science. An art presupposes ends and consequently a major concern has to do with ends (objectives). An art also presupposes means, consequently the matters of content and instructional approaches are pertinent. This article will deal with objectives, content, and instructional approaches.

OBJECTIVES

All societies educate their children. In more developed societies a formal school system is developed so that the youth are able to learn most efficiently. That there is a relationship between a particular society and its school system is obvious, but what the nature of its specific relationship should be may be a matter of disagreement. This writer makes two assumptions: (1) that the function of the school is to provide an educational program that develops the potentialities of all members of the society and (2) that while a very subtle balance exists and is necessary between man's requirements and society's demands, man's requirements have priority over the demands of a particular society.

There are five goals that underlie an entire program of schooling which can be formulated from psychoanalytic notions. A first goal is that of individuals developing an attitude toward self, toward other individuals and the world which can be characterized by terms such as hopeful, will-power, purposeful, competent, faithful, loving, caring, and wise. These are the characteristics which Erikson has formulated for Julian Huxley's *Humanist Frame*. These are the strengths which emerge from a favorable ratio for each of the psycho-social stages. To state them as Erikson does,[3] they appear as follows:

Basic Trust *vs.* Basic Mistrust: Drive and Hope
Autonomy *vs.* Shame and Doubt: Self-Control and Willpower
Initiative *vs.* Guilt: Direction and Purpose
Industry *vs.* Inferiority: Method and Competence
Identity *vs.* Role Confusion: Devotion and Fidelity
Intimacy *vs.* Isolation: Affiliation and Love
Generativity *vs.* Stagnation: Production and Care
Ego Integrity *vs.* Despair: Renunciation and Wisdom

While these characteristics or "basic virtues" will differ in their manifestations at various stages, they are foreshadowed earlier than they appear, i.e., direction and purpose (virtues of initiative *vs.* guilt) are present in some form during the basic trust *vs.* mistrust stage.

These emerging strengths constitute a healthy personality and are essential for a happy productive life. It is not only psychoanalysts who are concerned with a healthy personality characterized by hope, competence, devotion, and wisdom, but any humanist or educator.

A second goal is the facilitation of ego development. This is a goal which is inferred primarily from the theory of personality development postulated by psychoanalysts. A strong ego is a pervasive concern of the entire program of schooling, and makes it possible for an individual to govern himself while still meeting his own interests and those of the group. A strong ego is able to organize perceptions, delays discharge of energies, regulates tension between the id and superego and the id and reality. This goal is viewed as desirable by other than the psychoanalysts. Many educators discuss the importance of knowing the world as it is, or "telling it like it is." Without a strong ego, this is not likely.

A third goal is the facilitation of thinking, which is inferred from some of the ideas of analytic therapy as well as from a notion about how the ego grows and develops. According to analysts, an aim of analysis is to free the individual from his neurosis so that he can decide *intelligently* (italics mine) about his own destiny. Bettelheim[4] elaborates in an article about adolescents,

> The adolescent can master his problems somehow through intellectualization which, at the same time gives him the prestige and strength of ego that he badly needs ... Thinking strengthens the adolescent's ego, while action usually weakens it by defeat because he cannot yet act successfully with regard to his most pressing problems.

Thinking as a goal of education receives a great deal of attention from educators. It is spoken of in various ways; for example, to develop the intellect, to develop cognitive skills, or problem-solving skills. There is no disagreement in this field that thinking is an important attribute to develop in students if they are to have happy, useful lives.

A fourth goal is to develop some understanding of self and the relationship that exists between self and others. This is a goal derived from some general beliefs held by psychoanalysts about the necessity of understanding self. Not only analysts, but philosophers long before were urging "Know thyself." Self-knowledge is an essential ingredient to maturity. It is essential to understand oneself in order to understand the world.

Finally, the fifth general goal is the development of the imagining, feeling, playing, fancying qualities of mind. This is a goal which is inferred from notions presented by L. Kubie[5] in *Neurotic Distortion of the Creative Process*. Here Kubie outlines the importance of *cogito* in creativity. *Cogito* is the shaking-together, a pre-conscious process and is a necessary aspect of creativity. According to Kubie, it is by the process of free association, in which man puts seemingly unrelated ideas together in new patterns and combinations, that creativity is aided. There is no need to elaborate upon the necessity of developing creative persons.

In addition to these general goals for all individuals, it is possible to formulate some particular objectives for learners at the various stages of their development. Some age-specific objectives will be indicated for children three to seven years of age.

Three to Seven Years of Age. Many of the objectives which are formulated for this age emerge primarily from Erikson's conception of a healthy personality. Such objectives as to trust self and others; to be able to hold on and let go; to be purposeful; to accept boy and girl roles, stem directly from Erikson's sense of trust, autonomy, and initiative. (These objectives can be elaborated more fully if they are to function as a basis for developing instructional materials.) In addition to these behaviors, which seem to be primarily concerned with feelings, there are a number of objectives which pertain to the environment, both physical and social. A young child must have knowledge of parents, teachers, policemen, schools, buildings, trees, birds, books, music, toys. In addition, skills of listening and speaking must be developing. Finally, the importance of developing the physical is not to be overlooked or minimized. A child's physical behavior is an essential aspect of his total functioning. Such skills as running, skipping, bicycling are to be developed. Psychomotor skills, however manifested, reveal many attitudes of trust, control, and purpose. A distrustful, fearful child can avoid and limit his physical development.

While these objectives have been discussed in a serial form, they are all related. At times a specific objective may be central; at other times peripheral. For example, in a nursery school a teacher may focus on helping a child develop skill in using the jungle gym; at the same time she is facilitating his development of trust in his own body, as well as trust of her as she helps him. Saying it in another way, a child's physical development can be the basis from which the desirable attitudes of trust emerge.

CONTENT

Formulation of objectives from psychoanalysis is a difficult task and subject to doubt by psychoanalysts. When it comes to discussion of appropriate content from psychoanalysis, it turns out after long discussion by psychoanalysts that psychoanalytic concepts cannot be taught. In spite of these negative reactions some content will be indicated and the basis for the selection of content will be advanced. The effectiveness of this approach must be subject to empirical verification.

General Topics. There are five content areas which can underlie a program. These are 1) Self 2) Relationships to Groups 3) Relationships to Authority 4) Values 5) Problems: Violence, Drugs, Alienation.

Briefly, psychoanalysis contributes many significant ideas to understanding 1) self and 5) problems of violence, drugs, and alienation. Psychoanalytic insights about the importance of the quality of the maternal relationships, about aggression and sibling rivalry are basic to understanding individual behavior and consequently self, as well as our relationships to groups, to authority, and to matters of alienation, violence, drug use. In the matter of values, psychoanalysis can give much insight into what psychological mechanisms underlie a great deal of social and political behavior, e.g., what lies beneath value positions such as fascism, communism, racism, *apartheid*.

Ages Three to Seven Topics. There are six topics which can be explored during this age span. Our School; Helpers; Groups; Friends; Self; Problems. These topics have been arranged on a continuum of outer to inner, that is, from looking at *Our School*, which is quite external and would be descriptively treated, to topics such as *Self* and *Problems*: Isolation, which would be about the child's own feelings of anger, fear, rivalry, and problems of isolation and fighting.

My general conception of this period of time is that the child is leaving home and can have happy expectations as well as fears of what is to come. The environment should be need fulfilling and comforting. Teachers and materials are to be such that they help open up the environment of the outer and inner worlds. Teachers are to help pupils learn; this may be difficult and painful at times but they are not to be mothers or fathers or therapists. Policemen help keep law and order and sometimes they must restrain persons. Even children must know that sometimes adults restrain them for their own good. Some of the attitudes and ideas, then, that would be communicated are that teachers are helpful and understanding and help us learn, that it is natural to feel frightened when first in school; that friends help you carry out a desired task, that it is good to share toys; that it is all right to communicate our feelings (both friendly and unfriendly) to friends and teachers.

MEDIA AND INSTRUCTIONAL APPROACHES

If means are not effective, it is of no avail that objectives are significant or that content is relevant. Inadequacies of textbooks, films, and other instructional materials are well known, a common illustration being the upper-middle-class bias of readers. Also well documented is the difficulty teachers have had in utilizing discovery modes of instruction when they themselves have been educated in a traditional pattern. And lastly, even though a school has rationally adopted a permissive, accepting philosophy, it is infrequent that this adopted philosophy is made functional throughout the school setting.

These same difficulties beset the developer of a curriculum based upon psychoanalytic notions. If anything, the difficulties are greater because few materials are available and the instructional approaches have not been conceptualized, nor have implications for the setting been suggested. However, tentative formulations can be made.

Two aspects of the setting which can be described are the atmosphere of the school and the relationships which permeate the setting. In this article only atmosphere will be discussed.

Atmosphere. There has been much discussion about the kind of atmosphere desirable in a school or in individual classrooms. Terms such as permissive, accepting, open are frequently used to describe the desired atmosphere. These terms are also used to characterize the atmosphere and behavior of the analyst. Analysts are supposed to be accepting, understanding, and permissive with patients. However, there is a general structure which underlies the openness, acceptance, and permissiveness which also sets a tone. This is a structure of regular appointments, certain routines for both analyst and patient, and certain rules to appropriate behavior in the treatment hour.

It would seem that the implications for schools and individual classrooms or teaching situations should be characterized by acceptance, permissiveness, and openness. However, all experienced teachers know that this can be the road to chaos, particularly in some difficult situations and at times in the best of situations. Even if the statement to the group is that you can *say* anything you want and do anything you want, children are not able to cope with what may be directed at them or what they hear directed at the teacher and, incidentally, the teacher may not either.

Rather than draw all of our implications from a model of adult therapy, it is useful to look at child analysis. Anna Freud comments:

> . . . under the pressure of the unconscious, the child acts instead of talking, and this unfortunately introduces limits into the analytic situation. While the freedom of verbal association accompanied by restraint of motility is literally limitless, the same principle cannot be adhered to as soon as motor action in or outside the transference comes into question. Where the child endangers his own or the analyst's safety, severely damages property or tries to seduce or enforce seduction, the child analyst cannot help interfering, in spite of the greatest forbearance and the best intentions to the opposite, and even though the most vital material emerges in this manner. Words, thoughts, and fantasies equal dreams in their lack of impact on reality, while actions belong in a different category. It is no help to promise child patients that they can let all restraints go in the analytic hour and, parallel to the license to talk given in adult analysis—

'do as they want.' The child will soon convince the analyst . . . that the promise cannot be kept. . . . What children overwhelmingly act out in the transference are therefore their aggressions, or the aggressive side of their pregenitality which prompts them to attack, hit, kick, spit, and provoke the analyst.[6]

It is obvious that acceptance, permissiveness, and openness must be set in a general structure of some constraints which are supportive.

Verbalization by teachers and staff are essential for communication of the constraints of the schooling situation. External controls must be firmly established if non-primitive self-control is to be established.

Such comments as the following are examples of verbal constraints:

"At this school we don't let children hurt each other."

"There are rules to protect you, and keep you safe."

"No, you can't. The teachers here don't let children hit each other."[7]

Learning Opportunities. Films, texts, slides, discussion, field trips, role-playing, charts, maps all can be thought of in light of two concepts that have psychological ramifications: interpersonal relationships and activity. Most of the learning opportunities utilized in schools eliminate interpersonal communication on any other than a superficial level of direction-giving and answer-giving. The textbook is the focus of most classroom instruction and its use eliminates interpersonal communications of a significant nature. Secondly, most of the learning opportunities engender passivity. Students are not active intellectually or behaviorally. A textbook, film, filmstrip usually gives at best a prepackaged description of the problem, ways of solving the problem, and solutions. The student who is accustomed to "prepackaged" descriptions, explanations, and solutions loses the capacity to produce them for himself. In other words, his passivity has been constricting his development; his "activity" is greatly shaped by the environment.

The implications are apparent—to facilitate the development and utilization of learning opportunities predicated upon interpersonal communication and necessitating activity. Easier said than done. First, learning opportunities which primarily consist of interpersonal components should be utilized. Two examples would be role-playing and small group discussion, which can be about the group's relationships themselves or about any ideas that the group thinks are important. In addition, the interpersonal milieu which surrounds the utilization of texts, films, and workbooks must be expanded time-wise and also must be looked at in the light of its possible psychological meaning. For example, in an early primary situation, a child and a teacher are sitting together and the child is composing a short story. The child can't spell a particular word and the teacher tells him. The child learns that the teacher takes time, listens, and is helpful and knowledgeable. Numerous examples can be given of what not to do because of unfortunate implicit meanings. An example is the teacher who asks a student to summarize what a particular author is saying, who listens attentively, and then when the student is finished says, "Yes, excellent as far as you've gone, but didn't you overlook the author's major point which was . . ." The meaning for the student can be "Yes, I can do some things, but I don't get the major ideas."

With regard to activity, students should be developing their own instructional materials; students should be writing their own texts and developing their own films. There are instances in the literature where students have developed their own readers—the use of the "experience chart" in reading is a good illustration.

REFERENCES

1. Joseph Goldstein, "Psychoanalysis and Jurisprudence," in *The Psychoanalytic Study of the Child*, Vol. XXIII (New York: International Press, 1968).

2. Anna Freud, *Normality and Pathology in Childhood* (New York: International Universities Press, 1965), pp. 10– 24.

3. Erik Erikson, *Childhood and Society*, 2nd Ed. (New York: W. W. Norton & Co., 1963), p. 274.

4. Bruno Bettelheim, "The Social Studies Teacher and the Emotional Needs of Adolescents," *School Review*, 56, 585–592 (1948).

5. L. Kubie, *Neurotic Distortion of the Creative Process* (Lawrence, Kansas: University of Kansas Press, 1958).

6. Anna Freud, *op. cit.*, p. 30.

7. Robert A. Furman and Anny Katan (eds.), *The Therapeutic Nursery School* (New York: International Universities Press, 1969), pp. 49–52.

FREUD AND THE CLASSROOM*

Bruce D. Grossman

Whose Flak Are You Catching? Why do students react to you the way they do? This is an important and sometimes bewildering question. At times their behavior seems entirely unrealistic, and you may ask, "What did I do to cause that?" Grossman points out that your students may be reacting, not to you and what you do, but to their parents. Because your role as a teacher resembles a parent's role in many ways, students may transfer their feelings about their parents to you, and then react to that transference, not to you as a person. Do you know of teachers who act unrealistically toward principals? Have you run across administrators who are anxiously afraid of school board members or people who have a habit of criticizing any authority? Transference doesn't end with childhood.

Freud has been criticized as having been too much concerned with biological forces and too little concerned with environmental forces, such as interpersonal relationships. Undoubtedly, as a pioneer on a trail which was to lead to invaluable discoveries in the fields of social science and medicine, Freud was struck by the more obvious phenomena: those which contrasted most sharply with what was known at the time of his scientific travels. These phenomena tended to be biological in nature. Then, too, Freud understandably was influenced in a biological direction by the then contemporary discoveries of Darwin and by his own training in physiology and medicine.

However, it would be unfair to Freud to suggest that he was unaware of the role played by environmental forces in the child's development. For example, he must be duly credited with the discovery that the actual basis for the cures effected by his colleagues Charcot and Breurer, through hypnosis, were actually attributable to the relationship between the therapist and the patient, and could be accomplished on that basis alone—that is, without hypnosis. He later studied this phenomenon as *transference*, which we shall discuss in detail below.

Freud was also the first social scientist to give serious attention to the early relationship between parents and children. His theory of psychosexual development has an obvious biological, universal orientation, but at the same time does not discount the importance of the quality of the parent-child relationship, particularly in the resolution of the Oedipal conflict and in the process of what he termed *identification*, which is the second of Freud's more interpersonally oriented concepts to be discussed below.

*From Bruce D. Grossman, "Freud and the Classroom," *Educational Forum* 33, no. 4 (May, 1969): 491–496, by permission of the author. Bruce D. Grossman is Associate Professor at Hofstra University, Hempstead, New York.

Identification and transference are two aspects of Freud's general psychoanalytic theory which specifically focus on the child's relationship to authority, and it is primarily on this basis that I have chosen to demonstrate the relevance of psychoanalytic theory to actual classroom practice. The material here does not always prove to be a perfect fit in its new application, but the reader should be reminded that such an attempted fitting of a model from one discipline to another for heuristic purposes is in the best tradition of science.

TRANSFERENCE

Transference as a psychoanalytic concept has both a general and a specific meaning. In general terms it refers to the transference of feelings originally directed toward parents and parental surrogates to other persons with whom an individual comes into contact later on in life. Specifically, it refers to the tendency of patients to react to the psychoanalyst as if he were one or more significant figures from the past. Freud felt that such a reaction, the transference neurosis, was vital to the therapeutic process, and that without it a genuine cure could not take place. He made a deliberate attempt to encourage transference by remaining a relatively neutral figure during the analysis so that the patient could better imagine him to be a parent or a brother, etc. He sat behind the patient where he could not be seen to further the possibility of being "mistaken" for another.

A primary reason offered for the effectiveness of the transference process in psychoanalytic treatment is the emotional relationship thereby established between patient and therapist. In a situation where the intensity and genuineness of feeling are paramount, transference provides patient and therapist with an important point of contact. It matters little that that emotion is misdirected; that the analyst is not the real evoker of the response, but merely serves as a stimulus for its rearousal. The effectiveness of transference is furthered by the fact that the feelings aroused in the patient are conjured up from the past and expressed perhaps for the first time in the permissive atmosphere of the therapeutic environment. Once the feelings have been expressed in this way the patient is better able to examine them and often to realize that while they have had a neurotic hold on him, they need not do so any longer when they are under conscious control. In most cases the patients are relieved to find that the feelings they have harbored are no longer valid, if they ever were. In most cases the circumstances are likely to have changed a good deal since these feelings were first aroused in early childhood.

How does this phenomenon apply to the teaching situation and how might it be utilized there?

Transference has most directly to do with the relationship between the teacher and pupil. The teacher represents for most children, especially younger ones, a substitute or surrogate parent. The possibility of this identification increases as the role of teacher and parents overlap, as is the case in contemporary American culture. Parents carry the educative role into the home, helping with assignments brought from school, exposing children to new experiences, and generally being more involved in and cognizant of the educative process than most parents have been traditionally. Similarly, teachers assume what have been more traditionally parental assignments in their concern for the extra-educational socialization activities and general "total development" of the child. Other conditions, including the authority of the teacher as well as her nurturant attitude, make the transference process in the school situation quite possible and understandable.

Part of the nature of transference is that it is for the most part unconscious, that is, the child is likely to be unaware of his confusion between parent and teacher. Being unconscious, transference is also likely to be "unreasonable"; not very logical, nor even realistic. This presents its problems, as when a teacher is subjected to accusations such as "You don't care about me" or "You never let me do what I want to," which come as a surprise because they actually represent feelings stored up about parents. On the other hand, this "case of mistaken identity" may also have great value if used as it is used in psychotherapy; to allow the child to get his feelings out into the open and then to learn, at least, that these feelings are not realistic in the present situation, and that the teacher in actuality may be a very different person than the stereotype "parent figure" the child is projecting.

Maybe the real parents or whomever else the child has the teacher confused with are not as projected either. It is not the task of the teacher to explore this in any detail, but the corrective experience regarding authority figures in schools may have the effect of clearing up the child's vision of adults generally. The give-away for the transference neurosis, as for any neurotic action, is (1) the inappropriateness and (2) the excessiveness of the response. The teacher may be limiting the child in some relatively mild way (e.g., not allowing him to get a drink of water), but the overreaction of the child in response to this limit would reveal the likelihood of a transference phenomenon. For example, the child with a serious deprivation problem may view the above situation as a traumatic instance of the teacher's nongiving and react to it on the same level as earlier deprivations (real or imagined) suffered at the hands of her parents.

There are no universal prescriptions for the utilization of transference in a therapeutic way, except at a very general, global level. In each case the goal may be quite similar, but the means of reaching it must necessarily be tailored to the individual and to the situation in question. The goal is first to help the child identify the feelings expressed in his attitude toward the teacher and then to help him assess the degree to which these feelings are appropriate to their relationship and how they affect it.

The feeling or attitude involved in transference need not be unpleasant. On the contrary, Freud capitalized on what he termed "positive transference." The child who has a positive attitude about the teacher or who is fond of her may be more receptive to the learning process, while the child who mistakes the relationship with the teacher for the more intimate parent-child relationship, who demands and offers a great deal of affection and attention is usually not responding realistically, nor able to get the most out of the learning process because of the intensity of his needs for love and attention.

Increasing the child's knowledge of himself and helping him to improve his ability to respond realistically to others, whether peers or teachers, is a worthwhile goal for the teacher. This may be done without insisting that the child examine the original source of his feelings. The latter is better left to the therapist's office.

IDENTIFICATION

Closely related to transference is the process called identification. Instead of confusing a contemporary person with someone from the past, identification consists of confusing oneself with another. As described by Freud, this phenomenon first occurs in the parent-child relationship when the child "incorporates" characteristic qualities of the parents. The psychoanalysts distinguish this from "learning" or imitation of specific gestures, attitudes, etc. Identification is a more inclusive and global acceptance of the identity of parents or other significant figures. Identification may also be distinguished from an initial failure to separate oneself from others, such as in infancy or in the case of symbiotic psychosis.

A genuine identification does not take place until what Freud terms the *phallic period* of development when the child is four to six years of age. The basis for identification in the traditional Freudian scheme may be divided into two principal types— *defensive* and *anaclitic*. The crisis which occurs for the child during the phallic period emphasizes the defensive aspects of identification. Fearing attack from the father for amorous feelings toward the mother (Oedipal conflict), the boy makes an identification with father and is thereby eliminated from competition with him; but rather enjoys his protection and vicariously, his conquests. The situation for girls is of course somewhat different, but in this case as well, the vulnerability of the child and fear of attack ultimately lead to identifying with the like-sexed parents for reasons of protection. Anna Freud has given a good deal of attention to this phenomenon in what she has termed "Identification with the Aggressor."[1]

Anaclitic identification or what more recently has been called "developmental identification" takes place on the basis of the affectionate relationship between parent and child.[2] In a desire to avoid the loss of the loved one, the child internalizes the parent's characteristics to be assured of their ever-presence. This form of identification is more consistent with the common sense notion of emulating someone whom you admire, but like defensive identification is described by the psychoanalysts as a rather inclusive adoption of another's attitudes, behaviors, etc. In the traditional analytic framework, what I have called here a positive identification may also serve the very important function of converting libidinal energy from the Id, the more primitive part of personality, to the Ego, the more reality based, adaptive part of personality.[3]

According to Freud, resolution of the Oedipal conflict through identification results in the development of the superego or conscience. The superego, as characterized by him, is generally severe and restrictive, limiting the individual's actions by the arousal of guilt anxiety. While the superego is the internalization of prohibitions and other forms of negative sanctions, the positive moral purpose of the individual is guided by the *ego-ideal*. It is the latter, more forward looking aspect of the identification process as described by Freud, which has particular significance for the teaching situation.

Much of Freud's conceptualization of personality is *defensive* in nature, and identification is certainly no exception. Modern theorists have tended to place less emphasis on the defensive motive in development, but one would have to be looking at the world through rose-colored glasses to deny that feelings of vulnerability and fear of inevitable attack, whether unconscious or otherwise, are a fact of childhood. A study of normal children by Morgan and Gaier, for example, suggests that children are apt to exaggerate punishments they receive from their parents for misdemeanors. The teacher as the parent substitute, figure of authority, and disciplinarian is likely to be a source of threat to the child, realistic or not.[4] This threat and the general awesomeness of the teacher's role may be minimized. The modern trend for both teachers and parents is to be less of an authority figure, but to a young child particularly, the teacher who controls so much of one's fate and who is inevitably in the position of reminding the child of the need to restrict a variety of natural impulses is certainly a potential target for defensive identification.

Freud warned parents against being overly restrictive with children out of guilt at having failed to live up to their own parent's prescriptions. Teachers are naturally subject to the same guilt as parents and are likely to react in the same restrictive way. It behooves the teacher to make a conscious effort to avoid making prohibitive demands upon a child with which he cannot reasonably comply. Otherwise the child will be forced to break the rule and to suffer the guilt and fear of reprisal that result.

The child's tendency to identify with the teacher on a defensive basis is a function of what he brings to the situation in the form of familial experiences, as well as a function of what the teacher supplies in the form of classroom environment. The teacher serves as an available identification model which in most instances is meant to be emulated. The teacher presumably has acquired skills and attitudes which she expects the child to share. Punishments, threats, and other forms of prohibitions are among the devices available to accomplish the teaching goal.

The compliant, fearful child is one type of student. This child's anxiety has led him to seek the teacher's approval in the best way he knows how;

by responding often, by offering to help, by following the rules, and by trying to get others to do the same. While this child's cooperativeness may be a boon to a teacher in certain respects, it is likely to limit the child's imaginative and active pursuit of knowledge. The child who identifies out of fear has little choice in the matter—he must comply or suffer the pangs of anxiety. He cannot be original for fear of reprisal. Even more important, such a child is likely to harbor unconscious feelings which differ remarkably from his outward guise. For example, he is likely to resent the very compliance which he cannot seem to avoid. The discrepancy between his unconscious feelings and his conscious behavior is an unhealthy one, psychodynamically. It places a great strain on the child's psychic resources to keep from becoming aware of his true feelings and places him in a precarious position in terms of mental health.

Identification on a more positive basis is clearly the more desirable alternative. We spoke earlier about Freud's concept of the ego-ideal, which represents qualities of another admired by an individual and to which he aspires. Being an ego mechanism this type of identification is more of a conscious phenomenon than identification based on fear. This makes it subject to reason and gives it a more deliberate quality which is, of course, desirable. The ego-ideal is an internalization of an image which may never be actually recreated by the individual, but it serves as a source of inspiration and direction in his goal-directed behavior. The teacher not only presents to the child the prohibitions and other restrictions demanded by society, she also presents opportunities for growth and a model for some directions in which this growth might occur.

Positive identification is fostered by the teacher's rapport with the child and by the feeling conveyed to the child of the teacher's encouragement and support for his emotional and intellectual growth. In this situation the child is made to feel that he does have a choice, and it is because he does that he elects to emulate the qualities in his teacher which he admires. The teacher who is herself fearful of new knowledge and new directions and who must rely rather exclusively on authority in teaching cannot provide the conditions or the model for a positive identification. On the other hand, the teacher who is secure enough and adventuresome enough to be open to new experience herself is more likely to be able to convey an intellectual, inquiring model to her students. Such a teacher is also likely to be able to accept the uniqueness of each child and in turn provide a classroom atmosphere which would foster a positive identification.

REFERENCES

[1] Anna Freud, *The Ego and Mechanisms of Defense* (New York: International Universities Press, 1946).

[2] U. Bronfenbrenner, "The Changing American Child," *Merrill-Palmer Quarterly*, 7:73–84 (1961).

[3] Charles Brenner, *An Elementary Textbook of Psychoanalysis* (New York: Doubleday, 1955).

[4] P. Morgan and D. Gaier, "Types of Reactions in Punishment Situations in the Mother-Child Relationship," *Child Development*, 28:161–166 (1957).

YOUTH AND THE LIFE CYCLE *

Erik H. Erikson

Age-Stage and Growth Phase. One of the strongest points of Freudian psychology is its emphasis on childhood stages. This has permeated our thinking in statements such as, "It's just a stage he's going through." There are many Freudian and non-Freudian theories of stages, and in this article we see Erikson's well-known variation on this Freudian theme. Typical of Freudian approaches, Erikson assumes that the earlier stages are foundations for the latter stages. Strengths or weaknesses in earlier stages influence later stages, and many problems of children and adults stem from earlier childhood problems which were never resolved at the appropriate stage. For an opposite view of child development, Baer's article in the next section presents a behavioral approach to childhood. A humanistic approach that does use stages is presented in "Developing Thoughts on Developmental Psychology." Freudian developmental psychology frequently concerns itself with how a child adapts to basic drives for physiological pleasure: other behaviors are, then, interpreted as substitute or devious ways to obtain these basic good feelings. For example, in "Excerpts from *The Natural Mind*," in the transpersonal section, Weil posits another human drive that the Freudians would try to "explain away" by seeing it as a substitute for sexual (pleasurable) gratification; while Weil says it is another basic biological desire.

Question: *Are there any points about your concepts of psychosocial development which you would now like to stress in the light of what you have heard about how they have been interpreted during the past decade in the training of professional persons and through them of parents and future parents?*

Yes, I am grateful for the opportunity of making a few observations on the reception of these concepts. You emphasize their influence on teaching in various fields; let me pick out a few misunderstandings.

I should confess to you here how it all started. It was on a drive in the countryside with Mrs. Erikson that I became a bit expansive, telling her about a kind of ground plan in the human life cycle, which I seemed to discern in life histories. After a while she began to write, urging me just to go on; she had found my "plan" immediately convincing. Afterwards, a number of audiences of different professional backgrounds had that same sense of conviction—so much so that I (and others) became somewhat

*From Erik H. Erikson, "Youth and the Life Cycle," *Children* 7, no.2 (March–April, 1960): 43–49, by permission of the author. "An Epigenetic Chart" reprinted from Erik H. Erikson, *Childhood and Society* 2nd ed. rev. (New York: W. W. Norton & Co., 1963), p. 273, by permission of the publisher. Erik Erikson is Professor Emeritus of Harvard University. He is author of the recent book *Dimensions of the New Identity* and of the forthcoming books *The Child's Toys and the Old Man's Reasons* and *Life History and History*.

uneasy: after all, these psychosocial signposts are hardly *concepts* yet, even if the whole plan represents a valid *conception*, one which suggests a great deal of work.

What Mrs. Erikson and I subsequently offered to the White House Conference of 1950 was a kind of worksheet, which has, indeed, been used by others as well as myself in scientific investigation, and well integrated in a few textbooks.[1] But its "convincingness" has also led to oversimplifications. Let me tell you about a few.

There has been a tendency here and there to turn the eight stages into a sort of rosary of achievement, a device for counting the fruits of each stage—trust, autonomy, initiative, and so forth—as though each were achieved as a permanent trait. People of this bent are apt to leave out the negative counterparts of each stage, as if the healthy personality had permanently conquered these hazards. The fact is that the healthy personality must reconquer them continuously in the same way that the body's metabolism resists decay. All that we learn are certain fundamental means and mechanisms for retaining and regaining mastery. Life is a sequence not only of developmental but also of accidental crises. It is hardest to take when both types of crisis coincide.

In each crisis, under favorable conditions, the positive is likely to outbalance the negative, and each reintegration builds strength for the next crisis. But the negative is always with us to some degree in the form of a measure of infantile anxiety, fear of abandonment—a residue of immaturity carried throughout life, which is perhaps the price man has to pay for a childhood long enough to permit him to be the learning and the teaching animal, and thus to achieve his particular mastery of reality.

You may be interested to know that further clinical research has indicated that our dream life often depicts a recovery of mastery along the lines of these stages. Moreover, nurses have observed that any adult who undergoes serious surgery has to repeat the battle with these nemeses in the process of recovery. A person moves up and down the scale of maturity, but if his ego has gained a positive balance during his developmental crises the downward movements will be less devastating than if the balance, at one stage or another, was in the negative.

Of all the positive aspects mentioned, trust seems to have been the most convincing—so convincing, in fact, that some discussions never reach a consideration of the other stages. I don't mean to detract from the obvious importance of trust as the foundation of the development of a healthy personality. A basic sense of trust in living as such, developed in infancy through the reciprocal relationship of child and mother, is essential to winning the positive fruits of all the succeeding crises in the life cycle: maybe this is what Christmas, with its Madonna images, conveys to us. Yet, it is the nature of human life that each succeeding crisis takes place within a widened social radius where an ever-larger number of significant persons have a bearing on the outcome. There is in childhood, first, the maternal person, then the parental combination, then the basic family and other instructing adults. Youth demands "confirmation" from strangers who hold to a design of life; and later, the adult needs challenges from mates and partners, and even from his growing children and expanding works, in order to continue to grow himself. And all of these relationships must be imbedded in an "ethos," a cultural order, to guide the individual's course.

In our one-family culture (supported by pediatricians and psychiatrists who exclusively emphasize the mother-child relationship) we tend to lose sight of the fact that other people besides parents are important to youth. Too often we ask only where a given youth came from and what he once was, and not also where he was going, and who was ready to receive him and his intentions and his specific gifts. Thus we have movements to punish parents for the transgressions of their children, ignoring all the other persons and environmental factors that entered into the production of a young person's unacceptable behavior and failed to offer support to his positive search.

Another way in which the life cycle theory has been oversimplified is in the omission of stages which do not fit into the preconceived ideas of the person who is adopting or adapting the theory. Thus a large organization devoted to parenthood distributed a list of the stages but omitted *integrity vs. despair*—the problem of senescence. This is too easy a way to dispose of grandparents; it robs life of an inescapable final step; and, of course, it defeats this whole conception of an intrinsic order in the life cycle.

This kind of omission ignores the "cogwheeling" of infantile and adult stages—the fact that each further stage of growth in a given individual is not only dependent upon the relatively successful completion of his own previous stages, but also on the completion of the subsequent stages in those other individuals with whom he interacts and whom he accepts as models.

Finally, I should point to the fact that what my psychoanalytic colleagues warned me of most energetically has, on occasion, come to pass: even sincere workers have chosen to ignore my emphasis on the intrinsic relation of the psychosocial to the psychosexual stages which form the basis of much of Freud's work.

All of these misuses, however, may be to a large extent the fault of my choice of words. The use of simple, familiar words like "trust" and "mistrust" apparently leads people to assume that they know "by feel" what the theory is all about. Perhaps this semantic problem would have been avoided if I had used Latin terms, which call for definitions.

I may point out, however, that I originally suggested my terms as a basis for discussions—discussions led by people who have an idea of the interrelatedness of all aspects of human development. For the eight stages of psychosocial development are, in fact, inextricably entwined in and derived from the various stages of psychosexual development that were described by Freud, as well as from the child's stages of physical, motor, and cognitive development. Each type of development affects the other and is affected by it. Thus, I feel that discussants would do well to study each key word in its origins, in its usage in various periods and regions, and in other languages. Simple words that touch upon universal human values have their counterpart in every living language, and can become vehicles of understanding at international conferences.

Incidentally, I made up one new word because I thought it was needed. To me, "generativity" described the chief characteristic of the mature adult. It was turned into a comfortable, if inaccurate, homespun word before it ever left the Fact-Finding Committee of 1950. I had deliberately chosen "generativity" rather than "parenthood," or "creativity," because these narrowed the matter down to a biological and an artistic issue instead of describing the deep absorption in guiding the young or in helping to create a new world for the young, which is a mark of maturity in parents and nonparents, working people and "creative" people alike.

Enough of this fault-finding! But it *is* interesting to see what can happen to new ideas; and you *did* ask me.

Question: *During the past 10 years you have been treating and studying mentally ill young people at a public clinic in a low-income area in Pittsburgh and at a private, comparatively expensive, mental hospital in the Berkshires. Have you found any common denominator in the disturbances of these patients—from such opposite walks of life—that would seem to point to any special difficulty harassing the young people of our land today?*

Since 1950, I have concentrated on the life histories of sick young people in late adolescence and early adulthood primarily in order to study one of the crises magnified, as it were, with the clinical microscope. I think that our initial formulations of the identity crisis have been clinically validated and much refined.[2]

Many of these sick young people in their late teens and early twenties had failed during their adolescence to win out in the struggle against identity confusion. They were suffering so seriously from a feeling of being (or, indeed, wanting to be) "nobody" that they were withdrawing from reality, and in some cases even attempting to withdraw from life itself: in other words, they were regressing to a position where trust had to be reinstated. Their malaise proved to be related to the same sense of diffuseness which drives other young adults to incessant and sometimes delinquent activity—an effort to show the world, including themselves, that they are "somebody" even if deep down they do not believe it.

In the meantime, of course, the identity issue has been taken up by many writers and by some magazines, almost in the form of a slogan. We are prone to think that we have cornered an issue when we have found a name for it, and to have resolved it when we have found something to blame. So now we blame "the changing world."

Actually, there is no reason why youth should not participate with enthusiasm in radical change; young people are freer for change than we are. The bewildering thing for them must be that we now complain about change, having eagerly caused it ourselves with inventions and discoveries; that we seem to have played at change rather than to have planned it. If we had the courage of our inventions, if we would grow into the world we have helped to create, and would give youth co-responsibility in it, I think that all the potential power of the identity crisis would serve a better world than we can now envisage.

Let me say a word about identity, or rather about what it is not. The young person seeking an identity does not go around saying, even to himself, "Who am I?" as an editorial in a national magazine suggested last year's college graduates were doing on their way home. Nor does the person with a secure sense of identity usually stop to think or to brag about the fact that he has this priceless possession, and of what it consists. He simply feels and acts predominantly in tune with himself, his capacities, and his opportunities; and he has the inner means and finds the outer ways to recover from experiences which impair this feeling. He knows where he fits (or knowingly prefers not to fit) into present conditions and developments.

This sense of a coincidence between inner resources, traditional values, and opportunities of action is derived from a fusion of slowly grown, unconscious personality processes—and contemporary social forces. It has its earliest beginnings in the infant's first feelings of affirmation by maternal recognition and is nurtured on the quality and consistency of the parental style of upbringing. Thus identity is in a sense an outgrowth of all the earlier stages; but the crucial period for its development to maturity comes with the adolescent crisis.

Every adolescent is apt to go through some serious struggle at one time or another. The crises of earlier stages may return in some form as he seeks to free himself from the alignments of childhood because of both his own eagerness for adulthood and the pressures of society. For a while he may distrust what he once trusted implicitly; may be ashamed of his body, and doubtful of his future. He experiments, looking for affirmation and recognition from his friends and from the adults who mean most to him. Unconsciously, he revamps his repertory of childhood identifications, reviving some and repudiating others. He goes in for extremes—total commitments and total repudiations. His struggle is to make sense out of what has gone before in relation to what he now perceives the world to be, in an effort to find a persistent sameness in himself and a persistent sharing of some kind of essential character with others.

Far from considering this process to be a kind of maturational malaise, a morbid egocentricity of which adolescents must be "cured," we must recognize in it the search for new values, the willingness to serve loyalties which prove to be "true" (in any number of spiritual, scientific, technical, political, philosophical, and personal meanings of "truth") and thus a prime force in cultural rejuvenation.

The strengths a young person finds in adults at this time—their willingness to let him experiment, their eagerness to confirm him at his best, their consistency in correcting his excesses, and the guidance they give him—will codetermine whether or not he eventually makes order out of necessary inner confusion and applies himself to the correction of disordered conditions. He needs freedom to choose, but not so much freedom that he cannot, in fact, make a choice.

In some adolescents, in some cultures, in some historical epochs this crisis is minimal; in others it holds real perils for both the individual and society. Some individuals, particularly those with a weak preparation in their preceding developmental crises, succumb to it with the formation of neuroses and psychoses. Others try to resolve it through adherence—often temporary—to radical kinds of religious, political, artistic, or criminal ideologies.

A few fight the battle alone and, after a prolonged period of agony characterized by erratic mood swings and unpredictable and apparently dangerous behavior, become the spokesmen of new directions. Their sense of impending danger forces them to mobilize their capacities to new ways of thinking and doing which have meaning, at the same time, for themselves and their times. In my book "Young Man Luther"[3] I have tried to show how identity is related to ideology and how the identity struggle of one intense young genius produced a new person, a new faith, a new kind of man, and a new era.

I think I chose to write about Luther and his time because there are many analogies between our time and his, although today the problems which beset all historical crises are global and, as it were, semifinal in character. Today, throughout the world, the increasing pace of technological change has encroached upon traditional group solidarities and on their ability to transmit a sense of cosmic wholeness and technological planfulness to the young.

To me one of the most disturbing aspects of our technological culture is the imbalance between passive stimulation and active outlet in the pleasures that are sanctioned for young people. With the passing of the western frontier and the accelerated appearance of automatic gadgets, young people have become increasingly occupied with passive pursuits which require little participation of mind or body—being conveyed rapidly through space by machines and watching violent fantasies at the movies or on television—without the possibility of matching the passive experience with active pursuits. When an adolescent substitutes passivity for the adventure and activity which his muscular development and sexual drives require, there is always the danger of explosion—and I think that this accounts for much of the explosive, unexpected, and delinquent acts on the part of even our "nice" young people.

This is probably why "Westerns," always on the borderline of the criminal and the lawful, capture the passive imagination of a youth which has traditionally substituted identification with the rugged individualist—the pioneer who ventures into the unknown—for commitment to a political ideology; and which now finds itself confronted with increasing demands for standardization, uniformity, and conformity to the rituals of a status-convention. While the national prototype has historically been based on readiness for change, the range of possibilities of what one might choose to be and of opportunities to make a change have narrowed. To this has been added most recently the rude shaking of the once "eternal" image of our Nation's superiority in productivity and technical ingenuity through the appearance of Sputnik and its successors.

Thus one might say the complexity of the adolescent state and the confusion of the times meet head on.

However, I believe that the "confusion" derives from a hypocritical denial of our true position, both in regard to obvious dangers and true resources. When youth is permitted to see its place in a crisis, it will, out of its very inner dangers, gain the strength to meet the demands of the time.

Clinical experience with young people has, it is true, verified that combination of inner and outer dangers which explains aggravated identity crises. On the other hand, it has convinced me and my colleagues, even in hospital work, of the surprising resources which young people can muster if their social responsibilities are called upon in a total environment of psychological understanding.

Question: *Does this kind of confusion have anything to do with juvenile delinquency?*

I would not want to add here to the many claims concerning distinct and isolated causes of juvenile delinquency. But I would like to stress one contributing factor: the confused attitudes of adults—both laymen and professionals—towards the young people whom we, with a mixture of condescension and fear, call teenagers.

Except perhaps in some rare instances of congenital defects resulting in a low capacity to comprehend values, juvenile delinquents are made, not born; and we adults make them. Here, I am not referring to their parents exclusively. True, many parents, because of their own personalities and backgrounds, are not able to give their children a chance for a favorable resolution of the identity crisis. Nor am I referring to the failure of society at large to correct those blights on the social scene—such as overcrowded slums and inequality of opportunities for minority groups—which make it impossible for tens of thousands of young people to envisage an identity in line with the prevailing success-and-status ideology.

Rather I am referring to the attitudes of adults—in the press, in court, and in some professional and social institutions—which push the delinquent young person into a "negative identity," a prideful and stubborn acceptance of himself as a juvenile delinquent—and this at a time when his experimentation with available roles will make him exquisitely vulnerable (although he may not admit or even know it) to the opinions of the representatives of society. When a young person is adjudicated as a potential criminal because he has taken a girl for a ride in somebody else's car (which he intended to abandon, not to appropriate), he may well decide, half consciously, of course, but none the less with finality, that to have any real identity at all he must be what he obviously *can* be—a delinquent. The scolding of young people in public for the indiscretions they have committed, with the expectation that they show remorse, often ignores all the factors in their histories that force them into a delinquent kind of experimentation. It is certainly no help toward a positive identity formation.

In his insistence on holding on to an active identity, even if it is temporarily a "negative" one from the point of view of society, the delinquent is sometimes potentially healthier than the young person who withdraws into a neurotic or a psychotic state. Some delinquents, perhaps, in their determination to be themselves at all costs and under terrible conditions have more strength and a greater potential for contributing to the richness of the national life than do many excessively conforming or neurotically defeatist members of their generation, who have given up youth's prerogatives to dream and to dare. We must study this problem until we can overcome the kind of outraged bewilderment which makes the adult world seem untrustworthy to youth and hence may seem to justify the choice of a delinquent identity.

Actually, transitory delinquency, as well as other forms of antisocial or asocial behavior, often may be what I have called a *psychosocial moratorium*[2]—a period of delay in the assumption of adult commitment. Some youths need a period of relaxed expectations, of guidance to the various possibilities for positive identification through opportunities to participate in adult work, or even of introspection and experimentation—none of which can be replaced by either moralistic punishment or condescending forgiveness.

Question: *The theme of the 1960 White House Conference on Children and Youth charges the Conference with studying and understanding "the values and ideals of our society" in its efforts "to promote opportunities for children and youth to realize their full potential for a creative life in freedom and dignity." On the basis of the scheme which you presented to us in 1950, could you add a word about how these values, once identified, can be transmitted in a way that will insure their incorporation into the value systems of the young?*

Like every other aspect of maturity the virtues which we expect in a civilized human being grow in stages as the child develops from an infant to an adult. What is expected of a child at any time must be related to his total maturation and level of ego-strength, which are related to his motor, cognitive, psychosexual, and psychosocial stages. You can't expect total obedience from a 2-year-old who must test a growing sense of autonomy, nor total truth from a 4-year-old involved in the creative but often guilt-ridden fantasies of the oedipal stage.

It would be in line with the course of other historical crises if in our Nation today a certain sense of moral weakness were producing a kind of frantic wish to enforce moral strength in our youth with punitive or purely exhortative measures.

Today, a sense of crisis has been aggravated by the long cold war and the sudden revelation of the technical strength of a supposedly "backward" rival. We are wondering whether we have made our children strong enough for living in such an unpredictably dangerous world. Some people, who suddenly realize that they have not been responsible guardians of all the Nation's young, now wonder whether they should have beaten moral strength into them or preached certain absolute values more adamantly.

No period, however, can afford to go back on its advances in values and in knowledge, and I trust that the 1960 White House Conference will find a way to integrate our knowledge of personality development with our national values, necessities, and resources. What we need is not a plan whereby relatively irresponsible adults can enforce morality in their children, but rather national insistence on a more *responsible* morality on the part of adults, paired with an *informed* attitude toward the *development* of moral values in children. Values can only be fostered gradually by adults who have a clear conception of what to expect and what not to expect of the child as, at each stage, he comes to understand new segments of reality and of himself, and who are firm about what they are sure they *may* expect.

It must be admitted that psychiatry has added relatively little to the understanding of morality, except perhaps by delineating the great dangers of moralistic attitudes and measures which convince the child only of the adult's greater executive power, not of his actual moral power or true superiority. To this whole question, I can, on the basis of my own work, only indicate that the psychosocial stages discussed in 1950 seem to open up the possibility of studying the way in which in each stage of growth the healthy child's developmental drives dispose him toward a certain set of qualities which are the necessary fundaments of a responsible character: in *infancy*, hope and drive; in *early childhood*, will and control; in the *play age*, purpose and direction; in the *school age*, skill and method; and in *adolescence*, devotion and fidelity. The development of these basic qualities in children, however, depends on the corresponding development in adults of qualities related to: in *young adulthood*, love, work, and affiliation; in *adulthood*, care, parenthood, and production; and in *old age*, "wisdom" and responsible renunciation.

Now I have given you another set of nice words, throwing to the winds my own warning regarding the way they can be misunderstood and misused. Let me point out, therefore, that I consider these basic virtues in line with our advancing psychoanalytic ego-psychology, on the one hand, and without advancing knowledge of psychosocial evolution, on the other, and that the conception behind this list can only be studied in the context of advancing science. I will discuss this further in a forthcoming publication,[4] but I mention it now because I thought I owed you a reference to the way in which my contribution of 1950 has gradually led me in the direction of the great problem of the anchoring of virtue in human nature as it has evolved in our universe.

We ought to regard the breaking of a child's spirit—by cruel punishment, by senseless spoiling, by persistent hypocrisy—as a sin against humanity. Yet today we have back-to-the-woodshed movements. Last year in the legislature of one of our greatest States a bill was introduced to allow corporal punishment in the public schools and was lauded by part of the press. This gave the Soviets a chance to declare publicly against corporal punishment, implying that they are not sufficiently scared by their own youth to go back on certain considered principles in the rearing of the young. Actually, I think that we stand with the rest of the civilized world on the principle that if adult man reconsiders his moral position in the light of historical fact, and in the light of his most advanced knowledge of human nature, he can afford, in relation to his children, to rely on a forbearance which step by step will bring the best *out* of them.

The 1960 White House Conference comes just in time.

The Eight Stages of the Life Cycle of Man

"Personality," Erikson has written, "can be said to develop according to steps predetermined in the human organism's readiness to be driven toward, to be aware of, and to interact with a widening social radius, beginning with a dim image of a mother and ending with an image of mankind. . . ." Following are the steps he has identified in man's psychosocial development, and the special crises they bring. In presenting them, he has emphasized that while the struggle between the negatives and positives in each crisis must be fought through successfully if the next developmental stage is to be reached, no victory is completely or forever won.

I. Infancy: Trust *vs.* Mistrust. The first "task" of the infant is to develop "the cornerstone of a healthy personality," a basic sense of trust—in himself and in his environment. This comes from a feeling of inner goodness derived from "the mutual regulation of his receptive capacities with the maternal techniques of provision"[5]—a quality of care that transmits a sense of trustworthiness and meaning. The danger, most acute in the second half of the first year, is that discontinuities in care may increase a natural sense of loss, as the child gradually recognizes his separateness from his mother, to a basic sense of mistrust that may last through life.

II. Early Childhood: Autonomy *vs.* Shame and Doubt. With muscular maturation the child experiments with holding on and letting go and begins to attach enormous values to his autonomous will. The danger here is the development of a deep sense of shame and doubt if he is deprived of the opportunity to learn to develop his will as he learns his "duty," and therefore learns to expect defeat in any battle of wills with those who are bigger and stronger.

III. Play Age: Initiative *vs.* Guilt. In this stage the child's imagination is greatly expanded because of his increased ability to move around freely and to communicate. It is an age of intrusive activity, avid curiosity, and consuming fantasies which lead to feelings of guilt and anxiety. It is also the stage of the establishment of conscience. If this tendency to feel guilty is "overburdened by all-too-eager adults" the child may develop a deep-seated conviction that he is essentially bad, with a resultant stifling of initiative or a conversion of his moralism to vindictiveness.

IV. School Age: Industry *vs.* Inferiority. The long period of sexual latency before puberty is the age when the child wants to learn how to do and make things with others. In learning to accept instruction and to win recognition by producing "things" he opens the way for the capacity of work enjoyment. The danger in this period is the development of a sense of inadequacy and inferiority in a child who does not receive recognition for his efforts.

V. Adolescence: Identity *vs.* Identity Diffusion. The physiological revolution that comes with puberty—rapid body growth and sexual maturity—forces the young person to question "all sameness and continuities relied on earlier" and to "refight many of the earlier battles." The development task is to integrate childhood identifications "with the basic biological drives, native endowment, and the opportunities offered in social roles." The danger is that identity diffusion, temporarily unavoidable in this period of physical and psychological upheaval, may result in a permanent inability to "take hold" or, because of youth's tendency to total commitment, in the fixation in the young person of a negative identity, a devoted attempt to become what parents, class, or community do not want him to be.

VI. Young Adulthood: Intimacy *vs.* Isolation. Only as a young person begins to feel more secure in his identity is he able to establish intimacy with himself (with his inner life) and with others, both in friendships and eventually in a love-based mutually satisfying sexual relationship with a member of the opposite sex. A person who cannot enter wholly into an intimate relationship because of the fear of losing his identity may develop a deep sense of isolation.

VII. Adulthood: Generativity *vs.* Self-absorption. Out of the intimacies of adulthood grows generativity—the mature person's interest in establishing and guiding the next generation. The lack of this results in self-absorption and frequently in a "pervading sense of stagnation and interpersonal impoverishment."

VIII. Senescence: Integrity *vs.* Disgust. The person who has achieved a satisfying intimacy with other human beings and who has adapted to the triumphs and disappointments of his generative activities as parent and coworker reaches the end of life with a certain ego integrity—an acceptance of his own responsibility for what his life is and was and of its place in the flow of history. Without this "accrued ego integration" there is despair, usually marked by a display of displeasure and disgust.

AN EPIGENETIC CHART

		1	2	3	4	5	6	7	8
VIII	Maturity								Ego Integrity vs. Despair
VII	Adulthood							Genera-tivity vs. Stagnation	
VI	Young Adulthood						Intimacy vs. Isolation		
V	Puberty and Adolescence					Identity vs. Role Confusion			
IV	Latency				Industry vs. Inferiority				
III	Locomotor-Genital			Initiative vs. Guilt					
II	Muscular-Anal		Autonomy vs. Shame, Doubt						
I	Oral Sensory	Basic Trust vs. Mistrust							

REFERENCES

[1] Stone, L. Joseph; Church Joseph: Childhood and adolescence; a psychology of the growing person. Random House, New York, 1957.

[2] Erikson, Erik H.: The problem of ego identity. *Journal of American Psychoanalytic Association*, April 1956.

[3] _____: Young man Luther. W. W. Norton & Co., New York, 1958.

[4] _____: The roots of virtue. *In* The humanist frame, Sir Julian Huxley, ed. Harper & Bros., New York (in preparation).

[5] _____: Growth and crises of the "healthy personality." *In* Symposium on the healthy personality, supplement II; Problems of infancy and childhood. M. J. E. Senn, ed. Josiah Macy, Jr., Foundation, New York, 1950.

THE LATENCY PERIOD *

Anna Freud

Some Basic Freudian Concepts. Sigmund Freud's daughter Anna has specialized in child psychology. The article is a translated transcript of one of four talks she gave to teachers in "horts," which are similar to day-care centers. This article presents many basic Freudian concepts as they pertain to children and includes childhood examples. When reading this, it's helpful to think of other instances of these ideas from one's teaching and one's own childhood. Notice the Freudian emphasis on curing and preventing illness, rather than on positive mental health. We also see the importance of interpreting family relationships as children experience them, whether or not this is how an adult would do so. In this talk the author gives examples from childhood of defense mechanisms. These are fun to try to spot in your students and in yourself.

I have now during two lectures kept you far removed from the sphere of your own particular interests. I have engaged your attention for the emotional condition and the development of the instincts of the tiny child—a subject, indeed, which you most likely think could only have practical significance for mothers, nurses and, at the most, for the kindergarten teachers. I should not like you to think, on account of my choice of material, that I underestimate the problems which arise in your work with older children. But my object was to bring before you in the course of these lectures many of the fundamental ideas of psychoanalysis, and, in order to develop them vividly for you, I required some very definite material which only the first years of childhood can supply.

Let us examine what you have already learned from the things you have now heard concerning the theory of psychoanalysis, in order that I may ultimately justify the roundabout ways into which I have led you. From the very beginning I asserted that human beings are acquainted with only a fragment of their own inner life, and know nothing about a great many of the feelings and thoughts which go on within them—that is to say, that all these things happen unconsciously, without their awareness. You might reply that therefore we ought to be modest. In the vast mass of stimuli pressing upon man from within and without, which he receives and elaborates, it is not at all possible to retain everything in consciousness; it should suffice if one knows the most important things. But the example of the big gap in memory in which the childhood years are hidden must shake this conception. We have seen that the importance of any event is by no means a guarantee of its permanence in our memory; indeed, on the contrary, it is just the most significant impressions that regularly escape

*From Anna Freud, *Psychoanalysis for Parents and Teachers* (Buchanan, New York: Emerson Books, Inc.), pp. 64–91, by permission of the author and publisher. A daughter of Sigmund Freud, the author has specialized in the applications of psychoanalysis to children.

recollection. At the same time experience shows that this forgotten part of the inner world has the curious characteristic of retaining its dynamic force when it disappears from memory. It exercises a decisive influence on the child's life, shapes his relations to the people around him and reveals itself in his daily conduct. This twofold characteristic of the experiences of childhood, so contrary to all your expectations, its disappearance into the void while retaining all its power to influence, has given you a good idea of the conception of the *unconscious* in psychoanalysis.

You have, in addition, learned how the forgetting of important impressions may arise. The child would probably be inclined to remember clearly his first very highly valued desires and the satisfaction of the impulses so dearly treasured. He responds to an external pressure when he turns away from them, pushes them aside with a great expenditure of energy and refuses to know anything more about them. We say, then, that he has *repressed* them.

You have further realized that education has not yet accepted the fact of the child's accomplishment of this act of repression. It obviously fears that the characteristics pushed on one side with so much difficulty might at a favorable opportunity emerge again from the depths. It is, therefore, not content to break the child of a habit which it regards as bad, but it strives to put every obstacle in the way of its re-emergence. Thus there arises the reversal of the original feelings and characteristics in the manner I have already described to you.

Let us assume that a little child of about two years has the desire to put his excreta in his mouth. He learns through the pressure of education not only to reject such an action which he now knows as dirty and to renounce his original desire, but also to feel disgust for it. He gets now a feeling of nausea in connection with his excrement and a desire to vomit, obviously the answer to the original wish to put something into his mouth. To use his mouth for such an action becomes quite impossible for him owing to this feeling of repulsion. Psychoanalysis calls such a later acquired attribute, which has arisen from a conflict and as a reaction against an infantile impulse, a *reaction-formation*. When later on we discover in a child an unusually strong sense of sympathy, an unusual modesty or a feeling of nausea which is easily aroused, we may conclude that in his earliest years he had been specially cruel, shameless, or dirty in his habits. It is essential that this reaction should be strong in order to prevent a relapse into his earlier habits.

But this reversal to the exact opposite in the shape of a reaction-formation is only one of the ways in which the child can discard an attribute. Another way is to transform an undesirable activity into a more desirable one. I have already given you an example of this kind. The little child who has enjoyed playing about with his own excreta need not completely forego this pleasure in order to escape blame from his teacher. He can seek a substitute for this pleasure, finding, for example, in games with sand and water a substitute for his preoccupation with urine and feces, and, according to the opportunities given him, he builds things in a sand heap or digs in the garden or makes canals, just as little girls learn to wash their dolls' clothes.

The pleasure in smearing things is, as we have already indicated, continued in the use of paints and colored chalks. In each of these social and often useful activities, thoroughly approved by adults, the child enjoys some portion of the pleasure originally experienced. To this refinement of an impulse and its diversion to an aim estimated by education as of higher value, psychoanalysis has given the name of *sublimation*.

You have, however, been able to gather from the two previous lectures something more than merely the definition of some of the fundamental ideas of psychoanalysis. You have learned that there are ideas and idea-complexes which, through their becoming definitely associated together, play a dominant role in the emotional life of the child. They dominate certain years of life, then they are repressed and are no longer to be discovered in the consciousness of the adult without further investigation. The relation of the little child to his parents is an example of such an association of ideas. Psychoanalysis, as you have already heard, discovers behind this relationship the same motives and desires which inspired the deeds of King Oedipus, and has given the name of the *Oedipus complex* to it. Another such complex of ideas is to be seen in the effect of the threats which education employs to make the child submit to its wishes. As the purport of these threats—even if they are only hinted at—is to cut off an important part of the child's body—his hand, or tongue, or his penis—psychoanalysis has named this complex the *castration complex*.

Furthermore, in my first talk, you became acquainted with the fact that the way in which the child experiences these earliest complexes, especially his relation to his parents, becomes the pattern for all his later experiences. There is in him a compulsion to repeat in later life the pattern of his earlier love and hate, rebellion and submission, disloyalty and loyalty. It is not a matter of indifference for the child's later life that he has an inward urge to choose his love-relations, his friends and even his professional career so that he obtains almost a repetition of his repressed childhood's experiences. We say, as you saw in the example of the relation of the school child to his teachers, that the child *transfers* his emotional attitude toward an earlier figure on to a person in the present. It is obvious that the child must very often reinterpret or misunderstand the real, actual situation, and has to distort it in all sorts of ways in order to make such an emotional transference at all possible.

Finally, you found in my description of the childish instinctual development a confirmation of the assertion so often heard that psychoanalysis extends the conception of the sexual beyond the hitherto customary limits. It designates as sexual a series of childish activities which had formerly been regarded as completely harmless and far removed from anything sexual. Psychoanalysis, in opposition to all the teaching you have ever known, asserts that the sexual instincts of man do not suddenly awaken between the thirteenth and fifteenth year, i.e. at puberty, but operate from the outset of the child's development, change gradually from one form to another, progress from one stage to another, until at last adult sexual life is achieved as the final result of this long series of developments. The energy with which the sexual instincts function in all these phases is in its nature always the same, and only different in degree at different periods.

Psychoanalysis calls this sexual energy *libido*. The theory of the development of the childish impulses is the most important part of the new psychoanalytic science, and at the same time it is this theory that from the outset has made enemies for psychoanalysis. Very likely this has been the reason why so many of you have hitherto held yourselves scrupulously aloof from analytic theories.

I think you may be content with this summary of the theoretical knowledge which you have hitherto possessed of psychoanalysis. You have become acquainted with a number of the most important fundamental ideas of psychoanalysis and with its customary terminology. You have met with the idea of the *unconscious, repression, reaction-formation, sublimation, transference,* the *Oedipus complex* and the *castration complex,* the *libido* and the theory of *infantile sexuality*. Perhaps these conceptions, but recently worked out, will help us very much in our further task, that of investigating the next period in the child's life.

We will now continue the account of the child from the point where we left off in our last discussion. This was at his fifth or sixth year, at that period when the child is entrusted to the public educational institutions and consequently claims all your interest.

Let us, in the light of the knowledge we have now acquired, examine the complaint made by teachers in the kindergarten and the school that the little children come to them as already finished human beings. We can now fully confirm the teachers in the accuracy of this impression, from our own knowledge of the inner situation of the child. The little child, by the time he comes to the school or kindergarten for the first time, has already had a host of profound emotional experiences. He has suffered a curtailment of his original egoism through love of a particular person; he has experienced a violent desire for the possession of this beloved person; and he has defended his rights by death-wishes directed against others and by outbreaks of jealousy. In his relation to his father he has become acquainted with feelings of respect and admiration, tormenting feelings of competition with a stronger rival, the feeling of impotence and the depressing effect of a disappointment in love. He has, moreover, already passed through a complicated instinct-development and has learned how hard it is to be obliged to confront conflicting forces in his own personality.

Under the pressure of education he has suffered terrible fears and anxiety, and accomplished enormous changes within himself. Burdened with this past, the child is indeed anything but a blank sheet. The transformation which has taken place within him is verily amazing. Out of the creature so like an animal, so dependent on others, and to those around him almost intolerable, a more or less reasonable human being has been evolved. The school child who enters the classroom is consequently prepared to find that he is there only one among many, and from this time onward he cannot count on any privileged position. He has learned something of social adaptation. Instead of continually seeking to gratify his desires, as formerly, he is now prepared to do what is required of him and to confine his pleasures to the times allowed for them. His interest in seeing everything and finding out the intimate mysteries of his environment has now been transformed into a thirst for knowledge and a love of learning. In place of the revelations and explanations which he longed for earlier he is now prepared to obtain a knowledge of letters and numbers.

Those of you who are workers at the Infant Horts will probably think that I am describing the good behavior of the child in too glowing colors, just as in my last talk with you I painted his naughtiness too black. You feel you have not met such good children. But you must not forget that the Children's Horts, as they are conducted today, only receive cases in which the earliest education of the children, owing to some internal or external circumstances, has not been entirely satisfactory. On the other hand, the teachers in the ordinary schools will recognize many of their pupils in my description and will not accuse me of exaggeration.

This might be, indeed, a splendid proof of the practical possibilities and the enormous influence of education. The parents to whom, speaking generally, must be ascribed the credit for the earliest education, have every right to be somewhat proud if they have succeeded in making out of the crying, troublesome, and dirty infant a well-behaved school child. There are not many spheres in this world where similar transformations are accomplished.

But we should still more unreservedly admire the work which the parents have performed if two considerations were not forced upon us in judging its results. One of these considerations arises from observation. Whoever has had the opportunity of being much with three-to-four-year-old children, or of playing with them, is amazed at the wealth of their fantasy, the extent of their vision, the lucidity of their minds and the inflexible logic of their questions and conclusions. Yet the very same children, when of school age, appear to the adult in close contact with them rather silly, superficial, and somewhat uninteresting. We ask with astonishment whatever has become of the child's shrewdness and originality! Psychoanalysis reveals to us that these gifts of the little child have not been able to hold their own against the demands which have been made upon him; after the expiration of his fifth year they are as good as vanished. Obviously, to bring up "good" children is not without its dangers. The repressions which are required to achieve this result, the reaction-formations and the sublimations which have to be built up, are paid for at a quite definite cost. The originality of the child, together with a great deal of his energy and his talents, are sacrificed to being "good." If the older children, compared with the little child, strike us as dull and inactive the impression is absolutely correct. The limitations which are placed upon their thinking, and the obstacles put in the way of their original activities, result in dullness and incapacity to act.

But if in this connection parents have little cause to be very proud of their success, in another direction likewise it is somewhat doubtful if they deserve much credit. That is to say, we have no guarantee at all whether the good behavior of the older child is the product of education or simply the consequence of having reached a certain period of development. We have still no essential data whereby to decide what would happen if little children were allowed to develop by themselves. We do not know whether they would grow up like little savages or whether, without any external help, they would pass through a series of modifications. It is quite certain that education influences the child tremendously in various directions, but the question remains unanswered as to what would happen if the adults round a child refrained from interfering with him in any way.

An important experiment to elucidate this problem was made from the psychoanalytic standpoint, but unfortunately it was not completed. The Russian analyst, Mme. Vera Schmidt, founded in Moscow in 1921 a children's home for thirty children from one to five years old. The name, the Children's Home Laboratory, which she gave to it characterized this institute as a kind of scientific experimental station. Mme. Schmidt's object was to surround this little group of children with scientifically trained teachers employed to observe quietly the various emotional and instinctual manifestations of the children; and, though the teachers would help and stimulate, they were to interfere as little as possible with the changes that were taking place in the children. By such means it would gradually be established whether the various phases which follow one another in the child's first years arise spontaneously and then disappear without any direct educational influence, and also whether the child, without being forced, would abandon his pleasure-activities and the sources of pleasure after a certain period and exchange them for new ones.

Mme. Vera Schmidt's Children's Home Laboratory, on account of external difficulties, was not long enough established to complete this new kind of educational experiment, except in the case of one child. The question, therefore, of how much credit for the changes in the child is to be ascribed exclusively to the earliest education remains unsolved until it becomes possible to undertake again a similar experiment under more favorable circumstances.

But whether this phenomenon is to be ascribed to the training of the parents or simply to be regarded as the necessary characteristic of that particular stage of life, observation in any case teaches us that in the fifth or sixth year the overwhelming force of the infantile instinct slowly dies down. The culminating point in the child's violent emotional mani-festations and insistent instinctual desires has already been passed by his fourth or fifth year, and the child gradually arrives at a kind of peace. It appears as if he had taken a great leap to become completely grown-up, just as the animal develops from birth to maturity without a break, and thereby cuts off all possibility of change. But with the child the case is otherwise. In his fifth or sixth year he suddenly comes to a standstill in his instinctual development without, however, having brought it to any definite conclusion. He loses the interest in the gratification of his instincts which so surprised us at first in the little child. He now for the first time begins to be like the picture of the "good" child which until now has only existed in the wish-fantasy of the grownups.

But the instincts which had hitherto caused the child to seek satisfaction in all kinds of ways have not ceased to exist; they are only less noticeable outwardly. They are latent, dormant, and only to awaken again after a period of years with renewed vigor. Adolescence, which has so long been regarded as the period when sexual feeling has its beginning, is thus merely a second edition of a development now indeed completed, but which began at birth and came to a standstill at the end of the first period of childhood. If we follow the growth of a child from this first period of childhood, through this quiet time—the *latency period* as it is named in psychoanalysis—to the stage of puberty, we shall find that the child once more experiences, in a new edition, all the old difficulties which had lain dormant. The emotional situation which had caused him special conflicts as a little child, such as the rivalry with his father or the peculiarly difficult repression of a forbidden pleasure (the love of dirt, perhaps), will burst forth again, creating extraordinary difficulty. Thus the earliest period of the child's life often shows, even in the minutest details, far-reaching similarities with the period of adolescence. And yet in the calmer latency period the child resembles in many respects a sensible, sedate adult.

Here again, from time immemorial, education has acted as if it had been guided by a good psychological understanding of the child's inner situation. It utilizes the latency period, in which the child is no longer exclusively engrossed with his inner conflicts and is less disturbed by his instincts, to begin the training of his intellect. Teachers in the schools have from the beginning of time behaved as if they understood that the child at this period is the more capable of learning the less subject he is to his instincts, and consequently they have punished most severely and pursued pitilessly the child at school who makes manifest his instinctual desires or seeks pleasure satisfaction.

Here the tasks of the school and the Hort diverge. The object of the school is above all else instruction—that is to say, the development of the mind, the imparting of new ideas and of knowledge and the arousing of mental capacity. The training in the Children's Hort, on the contrary, has the task of supplementing that training of the impulses which has probably not been completed in the child's infancy. The educators there know they have only a limited time at their disposal; they know that the sexual instinct, which bursts forth anew in puberty and overwhelms the child with its force, marks also the end of his educability. The success or failure of this later education in many cases determines whether it is possible at this later period to establish from the outside a reasonable agreement between the child's ego, the urge of his impulses, and the demands of society.

You will want to know finally how the possibilities of education in infancy and in the latency period stand in relation to one another. Is there a difference between the attitude of the little child to his parents and that of the older child to his teachers and tutors? Does the teacher simply inherit the role of the parents, and must he play the part of the father and mother, and, as they do, work with threats of castration, fear of the loss of love and manifestations of tenderness? When we think of the difficulties which the child has to endure at the height of his Oedipus complex we are right to be alarmed at the idea of similar conflicts, many times multiplied, to be suffered in the intercourse between the class and its teacher. It is not possible to imagine a teacher playing the part of a mother successfully in a large Children's Hort, and doing justice to the claims of each individual child without arousing outbreaks of jealousy on all sides. It must be equally difficult for the teacher, as father of so many, to remain continually the object of fear, the goal of all these insurgent tendencies, and yet at the same time the personal friend of each.

But we forget that the child's emotional situation also has in the meantime altered; his relations to his parents no longer assume the old form. As the childish instincts begin to weaken at this stage of life, the passionate feelings which have hitherto dominated the relation of the child to his father and mother also weaken. Here again we cannot say if this change simply corresponds to a new phase of development upon which the child enters at this age, or whether the child's passionate love-demands gradually succumb to the many unavoidable disillusionments and privations caused by the parents. In any case, the relation between the child and his parents becomes calmer, less passionate, and loses its exclusiveness. The child begins to see his parents in a more reasonable light, to correct his overestimate of his father, whom up to now he has regarded as omnipotent, and to see things in their true perspective. The love of his mother, which in his earliest childhood is almost adult love, passionately desirous and insatiable, now gives place to a tenderness which makes fewer claims and is more critical. At the same time the child tries to get a certain amount of freedom from his parents, and seeks independently of them new objects for his love and admiration. A process of detachment now begins which continues throughout the whole of the latency period. It is a sign of satisfactory development if, on the termination of puberty, the dependence on the beloved beings of childhood's days has come to an end. The sexual instinct at this period, after having come successfully through all the intervening phases, now reaches the adult genital stage, and should be combined with the love of another who does not belong to his own family.

But this detachment of the child from the earliest and most important of his love objects only succeeds on one very definite condition. It is as if the parents said: You can certainly go away, but you must take us with you. That is to say, the influence of the parents does not end with removal from them and not even with the abatement of feeling for them. Their influence simply changes from a direct to an indirect one. We know that the little child obeys his father's or mother's orders only when he is in their immediate environment and has to fear a direct reprimand from them or their personal interference. Left alone, he follows without scruple his own wishes. But after his second or third year his behavior alters. He is now well aware, even when the person in authority has left the room, of what is permitted and what forbidden, and can regulate his actions accordingly. We say that besides the forces that influence him from without he has also developed an inner force which determines his behavior.

Among psychoanalysts there exists no doubt as to the origin of this inner voice, or conscience, as it is generally designated. It is the continuation of the voice of the parents which is now operative from within instead of, as formerly, from without. The child has absorbed, as it were, a part of his father or mother, or rather the orders and prohibitions which he has constantly received from them, and made these an essential part of his being. In the course of growth this intensified parental part of him assumes ever more and more the role of the parents in the material world, demanding and forbidding certain things. It now continues from within the education of the child who has already become independent of his actual parents. The child gives to this part of his being which has come originally from without a very special place of honor in his own ego, regards it as an ideal, and is prepared to submit to it, often indeed more slavishly, than in his younger days he had submitted to his actual parents.

The poor ego of the child must henceforth strive to fulfill the demands of this ideal—the *superego*, as psychoanalysis names it. When the child does not obey it, he begins to "feel" his dissatisfaction as "inner dissatisfaction," and the sense of satisfaction when he acts in accordance with the will of this superego as "inner satisfaction." Thus the old relation between the child and the parents continues within the child, and the severity or mildness with which the parents have treated the child is reflected in the attitude of the superego to the ego.

Here, looking backward we can say: The price which the child has paid for detaching himself from his parents is their incorporation in his own personality. The success of this incorporation is at the same time also the measure of the permanent success of education.

Our question concerning the differences between the possibility of education in the earliest period of childhood and in the latency period is now no longer difficult to answer.

The earliest educators and the little child are opposed to each other like two hostile factions. The parents want something that the child does not want; the child wants what the parents do not want. The child pursues his aims with a wholly undivided passion; nothing remains to the parents but threats and the employment of force. Here one point of view is diametrically opposed to the other. The fact that the victory is nearly always won by the parents is only to be ascribed to their superior physical strength.

The situation is quite otherwise in the latency period. The child that now confronts the educator is no longer an undivided simple being. He is, as we have learned, divided within himself. Even if his ego occasionally still pursues its earlier aims, his superego, the successor to his parents, is on the side of the educators. It is now that the wisdom of the adults determines the extent of educational possibilities. The educator acts mistakenly when he treats the child as if the latter were still his absolute enemy, and by so doing he deprives himself of a great advantage. He merely requires to recognize the cleavage that has arisen in the child and to adapt himself to it. If he succeeds in winning the superego to his side and allying with it then two are working against one. He will have no more trouble in influencing the child in any way he wishes.

Our question regarding the relations between the teacher and the class or group is now also easier to answer. We see from what has already been said that the teacher inherits more than merely the child's Oedipus complex. As long as the teacher has the guidance of a group of children under his control he assumes for each one of them the role of his superego, and in this way acquires the right to the child's submission. If he were just the father of each child, then all the unsolved conflicts of early childhood would take place around him, and moreover his group would be torn asunder by jealousies. If he does succeed in becoming the universal superego, the ideal of all, then compulsory submission changes into voluntary submission, and the children of his group are combined under him into one united whole.

EXCERPTS FROM *NORMAL ADOLESCENCE* *

Committee on Adolescence,
Group for the Advancement of Psychiatry

Popsicles, Mudpies, and B-B Guns. These excerpts clearly illustrate the importance Freudians place on physiological drives and on how people adjust
themselves and their drives to society. They see libido, or sexual energy, as
the major motivating force in humans. With infants and young children (as we
saw in Anna Freud's talk) the drive for pleasure may be centered around their
mouths and anus. With adolescents, however, genital sex takes over. Instead of
wanting people to try to block off this libidinous energy and thus divert it to
guilt, anxiety, fear, or neuroses and psychoses, Freudians try to teach people
to accept their bodies and energies. It is a job of teachers and parents to
give this powerful sexual energy socially and individually acceptable ways of
expressing itself—sublimation.

BEGINNING AND ENDING OF ADOLESCENCE

The Onset. Adolescence begins with puberty. As the changes at puberty
occur, there are corresponding changes in personality, not all of them
necessarily displayed in overt behavior. There is considerable variation in
the manner in which individuals cope with the events of puberty. For
example, girls may deal with menstruation in very different ways. A girl
may attempt to deny to herself that it has happened, and as a result she
will evidence no anxiety or other overt reaction to the menstrual flow.
Another girl may deal with it in the same basic way but reveal an increase
in tomboyish behavior; she denies that menstruation has happened and
behaves as though she were not becoming a woman. And still another girl
may welcome menstruation as a clear sign of sexual maturity.

Even though a girl has denied her menarche as well as other signs of
puberty, and her overt behavior has remained unchanged, she nevertheless
will have entered adolescence. On the other hand, when the onset of
puberty is delayed into the middle or late teens, the understandable
concern with the delay in physical development is not an adolescent
problem, according to our definition of the onset of adolescence.

The Phases. Adolescence can be divided into two major phases. The first
phase is initiated by an increase in the strength of the instinctual forces.
The child suddenly experiences strong erotic and aggressive impulses that
seem to come from nowhere and clamor for expression. A boy who has
been indifferent to observing his sister's undergarments lying about the

*Excerpts from *Normal Adolescence* (Copyright 1968 by Group for the Advancement of
Psychiatry) by Committee on Adolescence, Group for the Advancement of Psychiatry are reprinted
by permission of Charles Scribner's Sons.

house now begins to have sexual fantasies and feelings which result in pleasure, guilt, shame, and confusion. And he furthermore feels that he dare not tell anyone about this. His emotional equilibrium is upset, as evidenced by the repeated breakthrough of these impulses (for example, peeking on his sister in her bedroom or reaching out to touch her body), or by the harshness and extremity of the means employed to control them (for example, intense waves of guilt and self-condemnation). In his conflictual struggle a boy might pick a fight with his sister, go to church and confess, masturbate, or suffer in silent anguish—or do all of these things. The ego is continually threatened and often is temporarily overwhelmed. In its attempt to re-establish equilibrium and maintain control it must expend excessive energy, sometimes paying the price of rigidity, loss of spontaneity, and inhibition of intellectual abilities. These latter factors may account for "the seventh- or eighth-grade slump" described by educators.

The first phase of adolescence usually ends in the middle teens and is followed by a second phase in which the balance of power between the ego and id shifts in favor of the ego. The factors causing this shift are by no means clear, but several possible explanations can be offered. (1) There may be an improved regularization and stabilization of the underlying hormonal and biological processes. (2) The fear and panic that accompany the beginning of puberty may diminish considerably as the still developing ego gains mastery over the new impulses, feels less threatened, and begins to function more effectively. An example of this would be the shift from the tantrums and outbursts of the early teens to the later attempts to use logic and rational argument to achieve one's goals. (3) A major shift in love interest normally takes place. Dating has begun, and the youngster gives up the former closeness to the parents, directing both dependency needs and sexual feelings toward the boy friend or girl friend. This shift, even though at first still colored by unconscious incestuous motives, nevertheless diminishes intrapsychic conflict and is a most important step toward the eventual choice of a marital partner. (4) The ego begins to utilize its increased capacity for the highest forms of abstract thinking, newly provided at this time apparently by the further biologic maturation. As part of his coping behavior, the teenager can begin to reason and argue, for example, about the validity of God and religion or the advantages of celibacy or of free love in an ideal society. Thus he can start to deal with the instinctual drives in fantasy and thought rather than by either impulsive action or excessive inhibition.

The observation that the adolescent in his middle or late teens begins to concern himself in a very personal and often intense way with such philosophic questions as the meaning of life and death, with religion, and with political and social issues, also lends support to the division of adolescence into two phases. At the same time this observation correlates with the fact that the adolescent at this age generally is much more amenable to reason and discussion and to psychotherapy or psychoanalysis than is the younger adolescent. The older adolescent is not nearly so frightened of his sexual and aggressive drives, and may be quite willing or even eager to join the analyst in the task of helping himself. The ego has gained a different orientation toward the id forces, and the adolescent can begin to use his faculties of self-observation and self-evaluation and his intellectual abilities in seeking to understand himself. Although there is greater psychological stability in the second phase of adolescence, the disequilibrium nevertheless continues. Consequently the opportunity for inner change continues, but now with the help of thoughtful reflection and planned experimentation.

One of the unique characteristics of adolescence, in both phases, is the recurrent alternation of episodes of disturbed behavior with periods of relative quiescence. These episodes have the qualities both of rebellion and experiment. There are times when the instinctual drives and needs gain ascendancy over the ego and superego controls. As a result there is often a temporary and essentially normal outburst of more primitive behavior. Presently the instinctual drives are again brought under control, the tensions relieved, and the balance of forces restored. During the resulting period of quiescence there is the opportunity for working over what has happened, and the ego gains additional strength through the mastery of the new experience.

These episodes and the ensuing periods of calm may last only a few minutes or hours, or may extend over a period of months. An episode of brief duration is illustrated by a reaction in a 15-year-old boy who normally was very shy and afraid to reveal his feelings. He had been attracted to a girl for some time, and under the influence of feelings of warmth and excitement at a New Year's Eve party he confessed to her that he loved her. When she did not take his statement seriously, he felt hurt, became morose, and vowed that he would never again love any girl. The next day, however, he realized that the girl could not have been expected to think he was serious and he then decided to ask her for a date.

An episode of longer duration is exemplified by the experience of an 18-year-old girl who on her own initiative went on a summer-long European trip, her first prolonged separation from her parents. Under what were very free and unsupervised circumstances, she yielded to her impulses and joined the other girls of her group in "wild" behavior which included drinking to the point of intoxication. She had sexual relations with a man whom she hardly knew and felt quite guilty and remorseful. Upon returning home she announced that she had decided to spend the next summer vacation with her family. During the school year she had a steady boy friend and behaved very conservatively, steering clear of both alcohol and sex. Off and on throughout the year she reflected on the experiences of her summer in Europe. As her guilt feelings lessened she came to recognize a cause-and-effect relationship between what had been an excessive conformity and dependency and her exaggerated, rebellious behavior of the previous summer. By the end of the following summer vacation she was able to assume responsibility for herself, her standards, and her behavior in a quite mature way.

The Offset. Adolescence comes to an end when the psychological disequilibrium of the second phase is replaced by a relatively stable equilibrium. Adolescence as a stage of development ends at this point regardless of whether the patterns which crystallize into the final equilibrium are adaptive or maladaptive. From the viewpoint of personality structure, the adolescent will have achieved a reasonable balance between the ego, id, and superego. Ideally, the superego facilitates adaptation to social reality without excessive prohibition of the instinctual needs, and the ego is able to control the instinctual drives while still having ready access to their energy and creative potential.

The adolescent struggle may also be resolved, however, by pathological means. Some individuals pass through these years with a minimum of upheaval. They maintain a status quo in which the id is dominated by a rigid ego-superego alliance, this in turn sometimes being supported by excessively controlling parents. Such youngsters are often considered to be "very good" and may be held up to other teenagers as the ideal model. They have not experienced the constructive changes which normally occur in adolescence. Though adult in years, they are emotionally immature.

Other individuals experience what has been described as "protracted" adolescence. The offset is markedly delayed because the conflicts and behavior typical of adolescence persist and become "a way of life." Protracted adolescence usually does terminate, but in some cases it continues indefinitely.

In many instances, the offset of adolescence may come about through the establishment of a neurosis, a character disorder, or a borderline psychotic disorder. The equilibrium thus achieved, while sometimes quite stable, is easily threatened and much psychic energy may be required to maintain it. The consequence of such illnesses is a decreased flexibility, adaptability, and productivity. Adolescence, nevertheless, is over.

It must be emphasized that the shift from disequilibrium to equilibrium as marking the transition between adolescence and adulthood is only a relative distinction. The balance between intrapsychic forces may seldom again be as unstable as in adolescence, but neither will it ever be completely stable. The normal state is not one of stasis but of dynamic tension which permits spontaneity, creativity, and flexibility in coping with the challenges to be faced in adult life.

The physiological changes of puberty which initiate adolescence stabilize somewhere in the mid-teens. This usually occurs long before there is an equivalent balancing out of the emotional and psychological responses. It may be said, then, that adolescence as a stage of human development has a biological onset and a psychological offset.

MASTURBATION

Masturbation becomes a central concern in early adolescence, generally more so for boys than for girls. However, those adolescent girls who do masturbate regularly are prone to feel as much guilt and anxiety as do boys. Girls may be more secretive than boys because of greater feelings of shame, but children of both sexes feel intensely conflicted about masturbation, both consciously and unconsciously. Our culture has been rife with rumor regarding the harmful consequences of masturbation, and these rumors are given credibility by parental attitudes which on the whole have been disapproving and prohibitive of sexuality. In addition, children generate their own fears and false ideas about masturbation. With the increase in masturbatory activity which begins at puberty, the old fantasies from earlier stages of development are revived to complicate the new, age-appropriate fantasies and intensify the conflict and guilt feelings.

The revived incestuous feelings and the associated fear of retaliatory castration tend to cause a hypochondriacal preoccupation with the genitalia. Adolescent boys are much concerned with the discharge of seminal fluid and construct their own fantasies about its significance. They watch anxiously for signs of damage following masturbatory activity. The discharge of seminal fluid following ejaculation may not be understood as a normal phenomenon, or its leakage in association with sexual excitement may be taken as a sign that "something is wrong with the valves inside the penis." Ejaculation may be perceived as an irreparable draining of virility, a using up of one's finite masculinity and reproductive capacity. If the sexual and aggressive urges are confusingly intertwined, the ejaculate may even be regarded as a dangerous and destructive poison. The normal pubertal increase in the size of the penis and testicles sometimes is falsely attributed to too much "handling" of these organs, and is regarded as evidence of damage. The opposite belief that the genitals are too small and will never reach full masculine size also may be attributed to masturbation. The ultimate consequence of damage from masturbation often is conceived to be a premature loss of sexual potency. Girls similarly imagine all kinds of dire consequences from masturbation. Among them are premature sterility, defective genitalia, and loss of value as a marriage partner. Normal vaginal discharge may be regarded with great concern as a proof of having harmed oneself.

As was suggested above, sexual and aggressive elements can be confusingly admixed in masturbatory fantasies. Thus sexual fantasies can be tinged with violence, and aggressive fantasies can cause sexual excitement. This admixture or fusion accounts in large measure for the relative, and sometimes complete, absence of tenderness as a component in the sexual play and fantasies during early adolescence.

All of the various imagined consequences of masturbation can be seen to stem from the fear of castration. This fear is reinforced by the carry-over from early childhood of the belief that parents are all-knowing. There is the concern that forbidden sexual activity will in some way become known to the world. The adolescent worries that his shameful secret is revealed by his acne, by the bulge of a spontaneous erection, a shiftiness of his eyes, or his staying too long in the bathroom. He fears that he is being silently condemned, and his expectation of derision and humiliation helps explain the excessive embarrassment, self-consciousness, withdrawal, and self-depreciation so often observed in early adolescents. On the other hand, guilt and fear can be denied and defended by behavior such as exhibitionistic dress and excessive forwardness, and by boastfulness to one's peers of masturbatory prowess.

All this notwithstanding, masturbation is an essentially normal activity. It is a normal response to increased sexual development, and is necessary to the control and integration of new urges and to the working out of new relationships through trial acting in fantasy. It serves as a means of experimenting with new biological capacities, a reassurance against castration anxiety simply because the organ is still there and functioning, and a temporary retreat from the increased problems in relationships with people. It may also be used for relieving tensions both sexual and non-sexual in origin. Either excessive masturbation or complete abstention from it can be symptomatic of underlying psychopathology deserving of evaluation, but masturbation in itself is not a cause of primary mental disorder. Yet, even when youngsters have been told about the normal nature of masturbation, their fantasies, feelings, and worries about self-harm may cause them considerable distress.

The way in which the adolescent experiments with orgasm as the climax to masturbation illustrates how masturbation can serve normal development. The adolescent learns that sexual excitement and engorgement and erection of the penis or the clitoris can be initiated at will, and that orgastic climax with the ensuing predictable subsidence of tension can be quickly brought about or repeatedly deferred by the manner of masturbation. This contributes to a developing sense of mastery over the sexual impulses and the new sexual capacities, and helps the adolescent prepare for heterosexual relationships. In the male the prominence of the erection, the forcefulness of the ejaculation, and the tangibility of the ejaculate may also foster acceptance of the masculine, aggressive role in relationships with girls.

ADOLESCENT LOVE AND THE ROLE OF COITUS

In late adolescence the task shifts from seeking and finding one's sexual identity to exploring it in all its implications. Falling in love, now, for the first time, involves feeling a truly intense concern for one's beloved. In the experience of first love, the partner is of paramount importance, this in spite of the fact that first love relationships usually are not long-lasting. Now a quality of tender affection makes its appearance alongside the sexual feelings. In contrast to the self-centered sexual preoccupations and activities of early adolescence, the adolescent now moves toward a shared sexual experience. Mature sexual behavior comprising both tender and sexual feelings for the loved person begins to be demonstrated. Whereas to others the emotions and attitudes of the adolescent who is in love appear sometimes to be exaggerated to the point of caricature, to the adolescent they are exquisitely real.

As has been stated, the impetus of puberty is primarily sexual. The pressure toward sexual relations is imperative and ultimately and almost invariably will prevail. The normal male or female youth becomes biologically ready for coitus, thinks about it, and in due time desires it. Yet for the most part our Western culture (at least in its "official" attitude) disapproves of sexual intercourse outside of marriage. Also, the goal our culture sets for adults—achievement of a firm sexual identity and the union of tender and sexual love in relationships with the marriage partner—is difficult to attain without sexual experience and experimentation during the years of late adolescence.

Our Puritan heritage has burdened us with a set of taboos and prohibitions which historically may have been appropriate but today seem inappropriate in light of modern understanding and medical scientific advance. In all probability, the forces that originally produced these prohibitions were concerns about venereal disease, illegitimate pregnancy and its destructive impact on the family, and other social values and structures such as property rights and hereditary titles. And underlying these forces were others such as intrafamilial rivalries and the fear of the younger generation which resulted in the need to keep it "down."

But despite the prevailing ethic, the question is: Should adolescents, at an appropriate age, be allowed or perhaps even encouraged to engage in sexual intercourse before marriage? More than that, does such experience foster healthy psychological development and successful adulthood or not?

These are crucial questions. Insofar as our society is concerned with fostering optimum human development and functioning, it needs to face this issue and be willing to consider the effect of sexual relations during adolescence on total development.

Two major and opposing points of view present themselves in our culture. One position regards the sexual mores as outdated. Now that medical science can prevent accidental or unwanted pregnancy, and can provide adequate protection from and treatment for venereal disease, why should the prohibitions be preserved? The argument is that teenagers are biologically, psychologically, and socially ready for sexual intercourse and moreover need this experience to consolidate their sexual identity, sense of self, and pattern of relationships with others. Besides, so vital an aspect of marriage and adult pleasure and love deserves experience and practice. Furthermore, the choice of marital partner and performance as a mate can be arrived at much more intelligently if the sexual factor can be evaluated from the standpoint of personal experience rather than hearsay, forbidden and hedged about by mystery and danger. According to this view, then, it follows that late adolescents, if they act responsibly, should be free to seek coital experience with a variety of partners; that the pleasure-seeking aspect of this kind of behavior should be sanctioned, but with an emphasis on learning and growth; and that protection against pregnancy and possible venereal disease be provided as a matter of course.

The opposing viewpoint differs sharply. Coitus is by no means just another form of pleasure. If its serious and important implications for mature adult relationships are to be fulfilled, it needs some of the prohibitions which our culture has evolved. Above all, it should be concerned with the development of tenderness and affection in heterosexual patterns. Abandonment to sensation-seeking with a variety of partners is no guarantee of growth. Instead, might it not tend to fixate a person on a pleasure-seeking level, delaying development toward mature sexual functioning? This position, while agreeing that to delay sexual experience is stressful, believes that such delay is necessary for full social development. Sexual intercourse is an activity of adulthood, and to turn to it prematurely will by no means ensure the development of sexual and emotional maturity. Moreover, the still present cultural realities are a part of the adolescent's conscience. Youngsters have internalized the cultural prohibitions against premarital sexual relations, and permitting or encouraging them to act in violation of the presumed "norms" will inevitably lead to guilt and serious internal conflicts.

These concerns are for the most part overstated, deriving more from fear of sexual impulses and guilt over sexuality than from careful observation and study. An understanding of the interrelationship between familial-subcultural value systems and individual development makes it clear that the answer to the question under discussion, while it can be generalized, finally has to be formulated in terms of the maturity of a given adolescent boy or girl. The average 13-year-old who is just beginning to feel the effects of puberty is very different from the average 18- or 19-year-old who has established dating patterns and who may already be firmly settled on the road to adult identity. There would probably be fair agreement that coitus in the early teens usually would be "rushing things," and could be dangerous, not only because it might interfere with orderly, sequential development but because of the lack of sufficient maturity to understand and act upon factors such as responsibility to the sexual partner and the possibility of pregnancy. There would be much less of a consensus that the same considerations apply in late adolescence.

Of further significance in any rational consideration of adolescent sexual behavior is the fact that all adolescents do not develop at the same rate. Some 18-year-olds may not be at all ready, developmentally, for sexual intercourse, and may need the help of various cultural attitudes and institutions to reinforce the postponement. Such young people might do well, for example, to go to a non-coeducational college, at least for the first year or two. On the other hand, a 17-year-old or perhaps even younger adolescent from a different family or subcultural background, or because of a constitutionally determined difference in rate of maturation, might well be ready for the experience of sexual relations. Adolescent group pressures may operate to the detriment of some youngsters because the group does not make allowance for differing degrees of individual maturation. In some adolescent groups there is considerable pressure to engage in intercourse in order to be fully accepted by the group. Some members of such groups will pretend to be involved in sexual exploits and thus protect both their status and their mental and emotional equilibrium. But others try to comply, prematurely for themselves, with serious emotional or practical consequences.

Nowadays words like "chastity" and "purity" are heard relatively infrequently in discussions of teenage behavior. Undoubtedly this is related to the widespread cultural acceptance of sex play among adolescents in the form of necking, petting, or "making out"—that is, heterosexual activity short of intercourse, and usually short of orgasm. It also represents a decided shift away from the ideals prevalent in earlier times. Our society seems to be drifting further and further away from the older concepts of morality to some new although still dimly perceived ordering of sex life.

THE GIFTED CHILD* **

Carl G. Jung

Social Adjustment, Not Enriched Classes. In this article Jung considers
aesthetic, physical, moral, and social giftedness as well as intellectual
giftedness. Although many aspects of his work are more transpersonal than
Freudian, in this article he shows a Freudian flavor in a number of ways: his
use of an actual case of one person; his interest in self-knowledge; his desire
to see how the various kinds of human behavior relate to each other; his stress
on the importance of early family influences and of fitting into society; and
his use of the Freudian ideas of ego and of defense mechanisms in explaining
giftednesses and its ramifications.

When I visited the United States for the first time, I was much astonished
to see that there were no barriers at the railway crossings and no pro-
tective hedges alongside the railway track. In the remoter districts the line
was actually used as a foot-path. When I voiced my astonishment about
this, I was informed, "Only an idiot could fail to see that trains pass along
the line at forty to a hundred miles an hour!" Another thing that struck
me was that nothing is *verboten*; instead, one is merely "not allowed" to
do something, or one is politely requested: "Please don't——."

These impressions, and others like them, reduced themselves to the
discovery that in America civic life appeals to the intelligence and expects
an intelligent response, whereas in Europe it plans for stupidity. America
fosters and looks forward to intelligence; Europe looks back to see
whether the dumb ones are also coming along. What is worse, Europe
takes evil intentions for granted and is forever crying that bossy and
officious "Verboten!" into our ears, whereas America addresses herself to
people's common sense and goodwill.

Involuntarily I found my thoughts drifting back to my school-days, and
there I saw the European prejudice embodied in certain of my teachers. I
was not, as a twelve-year-old schoolboy, by any means drowsy or stupid,
but often I felt uncommonly bored when the teacher had to busy himself
with the slowcoaches. I had the good fortune to possess a genial Latin
master who, during the exercises, used to send me to fetch books from
the university library, and in these I browsed with delight as I dawdled

*From *The Collected Works of C. G. Jung*, ed. by G. Adler, M. Fordham, W. McGuire and H.
Read, trans. by R. F. C. Hull, Bollingen Series XX, vol. 17, *The Development of Personality* (copy-
right 1954 by Bollingen Foundation), pp. 125–135; reprinted by permission of Princeton University
Press.

**This was first delivered at the annual meeting of the Basel School Council, in December,
1942. It was published as "Der Begabte" in the *Schweizer Erziehungs-Rundschau*, XVI (1943): 1,
and in *Psychologie and Erziehung* (Zurich, 1946), from which the present translation is made.—
Editors.

back by the longest possible route. Boredom, however, was by no means the worst of my experiences. Once, among the numerous and not exactly stimulating themes for an essay, we were given something really interesting. I set to work very seriously and polished my sentences with the greatest care. In happy anticipation of having written the best, or at least one of the better essays, I handed mine in to the teacher. When giving them back he always used to discuss the best essay first, and then the others in order of merit. All the others came before mine, and when the last, feeblest effort was about to be discussed, the teacher inflated himself in a manner that boded disaster, and pronounced the following words: "Jung's essay is by far the best, but he has composed it frivolously and dashed it off without taking any trouble. Therefore it merits no attention whatever." "That is not true," I cried, "I've never put so much work into any essay as I did into this." "That's a lie!" he shouted. "Look at Smith Minor"—the boy who had produced the worst essay—"*he* took trouble over his. He will get on in life, but you won't, no, not you—for in life you can't get away with cleverness and humbug." I was silent. From that moment I never did a stroke of work during German lessons.

This mishap lies more than a half a century behind me, and I have no doubt that there have been many changes and improvements in the school since then. But, at the time, it obsessed my thoughts and left me with a feeling of bitterness, though this naturally gave place to better understanding as my experience of life increased. I came to realize that my teacher's attitude was after all based on the noble precept of helping the weak and eradicating the bad. But, as so often happens with such precepts, they are apt to be elevated to soulless principles which do not bear thinking about further, so that a lamentable caricature of goodness results: one helps the weak and fights against the bad, but at the same time one runs the risk of putting the gifted child in a back place, as though being ahead of one's fellows were something scandalous and improper. The average person distrusts and readily suspects anything that his intelligence cannot grasp. *Il est trop intelligent*—reason enough for the blackest suspicion! In one of his novels Paul Bourget describes an exquisite scene in the antechamber of some Minister, which serves as the perfect paradigm. A middle-class couple offer this criticism of a celebrated scholar, with whom of course they are not acquainted: "Il doit être de la police secrète, il a l'air si méchant."

I trust you will forgive me for having dwelt so long on autobiographical details. Nevertheless this *Wahrheit* without the *Dichtung* is not just an isolated instance; it is something that happens all too often. The gifted schoolchild faces us with an important task which we cannot ignore, despite that worthy maxim about helping the less gifted. In a country as small as Switzerland we cannot afford, however charitable our aspirations may be, to overlook these much-needed gifted children. Even today we seem to proceed somewhat diffidently in this matter. Not long ago I heard of the following case: An intelligent little girl in one of the lower forms at primary school suddenly became a bad pupil, much to the astonishment of her parents. The things the child said out of school sounded so comical that her parents got the impression that the children were treated like idiots and were being stultified artificially. So the mother went to see the Principal about it and discovered that the teacher had been trained to cope with defectives and had formerly looked after backward children. Obviously she did not know the first thing about normal ones. Luckily the damage was caught in time, so that the child could be passed on to a normal teacher under whom she soon picked up again.

The problem of the gifted child is not at all simple, because he is not distinguished merely by the fact of being a good pupil. Occasionally he is the exact opposite. He may even be notoriously absent-minded, have his head full of other things, be indolent, slovenly, inattentive, badly behaved, self-willed, or evoke the impression of being half asleep. From external observation alone it is sometimes difficult to distinguish the gifted child from a mental defective.

Nor should we forget that gifted children are not always precocious, but may on the contrary develop slowly, so that the gift remains latent for a long time. The giftedness can then be spotted only with difficulty. On the other hand too much goodwill and optimism on the part of the teacher can imagine talents that later turn out to be blanks, as in the biography which says: "No signs of genius were observable up to his fortieth year—nor indeed afterwards."

Sometimes the only thing that helps in diagnosing a gift is careful observation of the child's individuality both in school and at home, which alone enables us to see what is primary disposition and what is secondary reaction. In the gifted child inattentiveness, absent-mindedness, and day-dreaming may prove to be a secondary defence against outside influences, in order that the interior fantasy processes may be pursued undisturbed. Admittedly the mere existence of lively fantasies or peculiar interests is no proof of special gifts, as the same predominance of aimless fantasies and abnormal interests may also be found in the previous history of neurotics and psychotics. What does reveal the gift, however, is the *nature* of these fantasies. For this one must be able to distinguish an intelligent fantasy from a stupid one. A good criterion of judgment is the originality, consistency, intensity, and subtlety of the fantasy structure, as well as the latent possibility of its realization. One must also consider how far the fantasy extends into the child's actual life, for instance in the form of hobbies systematically pursued and other interests. Another important indication is the degree and quality of his interest in general. One some-times makes surprising discoveries where problem children are concerned, such as a voracious and apparently indiscriminate reading of books, done mostly in the forbidden hours after bedtime, or else some unusual practical accomplishment. All these signs can only be understood by one who takes the trouble to inquire into the reasons for the child's problems, and who is not content merely to pick on the bad qualities. A certain knowledge of psychology—by which I mean common sense and experience—is therefore a desirable requisite in a teacher.

The psychic disposition of the gifted child always moves in violent contrasts. That is to say, it is extremely rare for the gift to affect all regions of the psyche uniformly. The general rule is that one or the other region will be so little developed as to entitle us to speak of a defect. Above all the degree of maturity differs enormously. In the region of the gift abnormal precocity may prevail, while outside that region the mental attainment may be below normal for a child of that age. Occasionally this gives rise to a misleading picture: one thinks one is dealing with a rather undeveloped and mentally backward child and, in consequence, fails to credit him with any ability above the normal. Or it may be that a precocious intellect is not accompanied by a corresponding development of verbal facility, so that the child is driven to express himself in a seemingly confused or unintelligible way. In such cases only a careful inquiry into the why and wherefore, and a conscientious deliberation of the answers, can save the teacher from false judgments. But there are also cases where the gift applies to some aptitude not affected by schoolwork at all. This is particularly true of certain practical accomplishments. I myself remember boys who distinguished themselves at school by their remarkable stupidity, but who were highly efficient at the peasant trades of their parents.

While I am on this subject I must not omit to point out that very erroneous views used to be held at one time concerning the gift for mathematics. It was believed that the capacity for logical and abstract thought was, so to speak, incarnate in mathematics and that this was therefore the best discipline if one wanted to think logically. But the mathematical gift, like the musical gift to which it is biologically related, is identical neither with logic nor with intellect, although it makes use of them just as all philosophy and science do. One can be musical without possessing a scrap of intellect, and in the same way astounding feats of calculation can be performed by imbeciles. Mathematical sense can be inculcated as little as can musical sense, for it is a specific gift.

The gifted child is faced with complications not only in the intellectual but in the moral sphere, that is, in the province of feeling. The prevarication, lying, and other moral laxities so common in grown-ups can easily become a distressing problem for the morally gifted child. It is just as easy for an adult to disregard moral criticism that springs from feeling, as it is to overlook or underestimate intellectual sensitivity and precocity. The gifts of the heart are not quite so obvious or so impressive as intellectual and technical endowments, and, just as the latter demand special understanding from the teacher, so these other gifts often make the even greater demand that he himself should be educated. For the day will inevitably come when what the educator teaches by word of mouth no longer works, but only what he is. Every educator—and I use the term in its widest sense—should constantly ask himself whether he is actually fulfilling his teachings in his own person and in his own life, to the best of his knowledge and with a clear conscience. Psychotherapy has taught us that in the final reckoning it is not knowledge, not technical skill, that has a curative effect, but the personality of the doctor. And it is the same with education: it presupposes self-education.

In saying this I have no wish to set myself up as a judge over the pedagogues; on the contrary, with my many years as active teacher and educator, I must count myself as one of them and await judgment or condemnation with the rest. It is only on the basis of my experience in treating human beings that I venture to draw your attention to the profound practical significance of this fundamental educational truth.

There are, besides the gifts of the head, also those of the heart, which are no whit less important, although they may easily be overlooked because in such cases the head is often the weaker organ. And yet people of this kind sometimes contribute more to the well-being of society, and are more valuable, than those with other talents. But, like all gifts, talented feeling has two sides to it. A high degree of empathy, especially noticeable in girls, can adapt itself to the teacher so skilfully as to arouse the impression of a special talent, and moreover on the evidence of no mean achievements. But as soon as the personal influence ceases, the gift fizzles out. It was nothing but an enthusiastic episode conjured into existence through empathy, flaring up like a straw fire and leaving the ashes of disappointment behind.

The education of gifted children makes considerable demands upon the intellectual, psychological, moral, and artistic capacities of the educator, demands which, it may be, no teacher can reasonably be expected to fulfill. He would have to be something of a genius himself if he were to do justice to the gift of genius among any of his pupils.

Fortunately, however, many gifts seem to have a peculiar ability to take care of themselves, and the closer a gifted child comes to being a genius the more his creative capacity—as the very word "genius" implies—acts like a personality far in advance of his years, one might even say like a divine daemon who not only needs no educating, but against whom it is more necessary to protect the child. Great gifts are the fairest, and often the most dangerous, fruits on the tree of humanity. They hang on the weakest branches, which easily break. In most cases, as I have already suggested, the gift develops in inverse ratio to the maturation of the personality as a whole, and often one has the impression that a creative personality grows at the expense of the human being. Sometimes, indeed, there is such a discrepancy between the genius and his human qualities that one has to ask oneself whether a little less talent might not have been better. What after all is great intellect beside moral inferiority? There are not a few gifted persons whose usefulness is paralysed, not to say perverted, by their human shortcomings. A gift is not an absolute value, or rather, it is such a value only when the rest of the personality keeps pace with it, so that the talent can be applied usefully. Creative powers can just as easily turn out to be destructive. It rests solely with the moral personality whether they apply themselves to good things or to bad. And if this is lacking, no teacher can supply it or take its place.

The narrow margin between a gift and its pathological variant makes the problem of educating such children much more difficult. Not only is the gift almost invariably compensated by some inferiority in another sphere, but occasionally it is coupled with a morbid defect. In such cases it is almost impossible to determine whether it is the gift or the psychopathic constitution that predominates.

For all these reasons I would hardly like to say whether it would be of advantage to educate particularly gifted pupils in separate classes, as has been proposed.[1] I at least would not care to be the expert upon whom devolved the selection of suitable pupils. Although it would be an enormous help to the gifted ones, we have still to consider the fact that these same pupils do not always come up to the level of their gifts in other respects, human as well as mental. Segregated in a special class, the gifted child would be in danger of developing into a one-sided product. In a normal class, on the other hand, although he might be bored with the subject in which he excelled, the other subjects would serve to remind him of his backwardness, and this would have a useful and much-needed moral effect. For all gifts have the moral disadvantage of causing in their possessor a feeling of superiority and hence an inflation which needs to be compensated by a corresponding humility. But since gifted children are very often spoilt, they come to expect exceptional treatment. My old teacher was well aware of this, and that is why he delivered his moral "knock-out," from which I failed at the time to draw the necessary conclusions. Since then I have learnt to see that my teacher was an instrument of fate. He was the first to give me a taste of the hard truth that the gifts of the gods have two sides, a bright and a dark. To rush ahead is to invite blows, and if you don't get them from the teacher, you will get them from fate, and generally from both. The gifted child will do well to accustom himself early to the fact that any excellence puts him in an exceptional position and exposes him to a great many risks, the chief of which is an exaggerated self-confidence. Against this the only protection is humility and obedience, and even these do not always work.

It therefore seems to me better to educate the gifted child along with the other children in a normal class, and not to underline his exceptional position by transferring him to a special class. When all is said and done, school is a part of the great world and contains in miniature all those factors which the child will encounter in later life and with which he will have to come to terms. Some at least of this necessary adaptation can and should be learnt at school. Occasional clashes are not a catastrophe. Misunderstanding is fatal only when chronic, or when the child's sensitivity is unusually acute and there is no possibility of finding another teacher. That often brings favourable results, but only when the cause of the trouble really does lie with the teacher. This is by no means the rule, for in many cases the teacher has to suffer for the ruin wrought by the child's upbringing at home. Far too often parents who were unable to fulfill their own ambitions embody them in their gifted child, whom they either pamper or else whip up into a showpiece, sometimes very much to his detriment in later years, as is sufficiently evident from the lives of certain infant prodigies.

A powerful talent, and especially the Danaän gift of genius, is a fateful factor that throws its shadow early before. The genius will come through despite everything, for there is something absolute and indomitable in his nature. The so-called "misunderstood genius" is a rather doubtful phenomenon. Generally he turns out to be a good-for-nothing who is forever seeking a soothing explanation of himself. Once, in my professional capacity, I was forced to confront a "genius" of this type with the alternative: "Or perhaps you are nothing but a lazy hound?" It was not long before we found ourselves in whole-hearted agreement on this point. Talent, on the other hand, can either be hampered, crippled, and perverted, or fostered, developed, and improved. The genius is as rare a bird as the phoenix, an apparition not to be counted upon. Consciously or unconsciously, genius is something that by God's grace is there from the start, in full strength. But talent is a statistical regularity and does not always have a dynamism to match. Like genius, it is exceedingly diverse in its forms, giving rise to individual differentiations which the educator ought not to overlook; for a differentiated personality, or one capable of differentiation, is of the utmost value to the community. The levelling down of the masses through suppression of the aristocratic or hierarchical structure natural to a comunity is bound, sooner or later, to lead to disaster. For, when everything outstanding is levelled down, the signposts are lost, and the longing to be led becomes an urgent necessity. Human leadership being fallible, the leader himself has always been, and always will be, subject to the great symbolical principles, even as the individual cannot give his life point and meaning unless he puts his ego at the service of a spiritual authority superordinate to man. The need to do this arises from the fact that the ego never constitutes the whole of a man, but only the conscious part of him. The unconscious part, of unlimited extent, alone can complete him and make him a real totality.

Biologically speaking, the gifted person is a deviation from the mean, and in so far as Lao-tzu's remark that "high stands on low" is one of the eternal verities, this deviation takes place simultaneously in the heights and depths of the same individual. This produces a tension of opposites in him, which in its turn tempers and intensifies his personality. Like the still waters, the gifted child runs deep. His danger lies not only in deviating from the norm, however favourable this may appear to be, but even more in that inner polarity which predisposes to conflict. Therefore, instead of segregation in special classes, the personal interest and attention of the teacher are likely to be more beneficial. Although the institution of a trained school psychiatrist is thoroughly to be recommended and need not be a mere concession to the craze for what is technically right, I would say, in the light of my own experience, that an understanding heart is everything in a teacher, and cannot be esteemed highly enough. One looks back with appreciation to the brilliant teachers, but with gratitude to those who touched our human feelings. The curriculum is so much necessary raw material, but warmth is the vital element for the growing plant and for the soul of the child.

Because there are, among the other pupils, gifted and highly strung natures which ought not to be hemmed in and stifled, the school curriculum should for that very reason never wander too far from the humanities into over-specialized fields. The coming generation should at least be shown the doors that lead to the many different departments of life and the mind. And it seems to me especially important for any broad-based culture to have a regard for history in the widest sense of the word. Important as it is to pay attention to what is practical and useful, and to consider the future, that backward glance at the past is just as important. Culture means continuity, not a tearing up of roots through "progress." For the gifted child in particular, a balanced education is essential as a measure of psychic hygiene. As I have said, his gift is one-sided and is almost always offset by some childish immaturity in other regions of the psyche. Childhood, however, is a state of the past. Just as the developing embryo recapitulates, in a sense, our phylogenetic history, so the child-psyche relives "the lesson of earlier humanity," as Nietzche called it. The child lives in a pre-rational and above all in a pre-scientific world, the world of the men who existed before us. Our roots lie in that world and every child grows from those roots. Maturity bears him away from his roots and immaturity binds him to them. Knowledge of the universal origins builds the bridge between the lost and abandoned world of the past and the still largely inconceivable world of the future. How should we lay hold of the future, how should we assimilate it, unless we are in possession of the human experience which the past has bequeathed to us? Dispossessed of this, we are without root and without perspective, defenceless dupes of whatever novelties the future may bring. A purely technical and practical education is no safeguard against delusion and has nothing to oppose the counterfeit. It lacks the culture whose innermost law is the continuity of history, the long procession of man's more than individual consciousness. This continuity which reconciles all opposites also heals the conflicts that threaten the gifted child.

Anything new should always be questioned and tested with caution, for it may very easily turn out to be only a new disease. That is why true progress is impossible without mature judgment. But a well-balanced judgment requires a firm standpoint, and this in turn can only rest on a sound knowledge of what has been. The man who is unconscious of the historical context and lets slip his link with the past is in constant danger of succumbing to the crazes and delusions engendered by all novelties. It is the tragedy of all innovators that they empty out the baby with the bath-water. Though the mania for novelty is not, thank heavens, the national vice of the Swiss, we live nevertheless in a wider world that is being shaken by strange fevers of renewal. In face of this frightening and grandiose spectacle, steadiness is demanded of our young men as never before, firstly for the stability of our country, and secondly for the sake of European civilization, which has nothing to gain if the achievements of the Christian past are wiped out.

The gifted ones, however, are the torch-bearers, chosen for that high office by nature herself.

NOTES

[1] [By and large, children in Switzerland are taught in classes composed of pupils belonging to the same age group. There is no attempt to separate them according to their ability as is usual in Great Britain.—Editors.]

THE FORGOTTEN MAN OF EDUCATION *

Lawrence S. Kubie

The Unconscious, The Deep Wellspring of Behavior. Thoughts, feelings, purposes, goals, and behavior: these give meaning to our lives and our education. But these are *not* the starting point of living or of education. These are controlled by unconscious forces, according to Kubie, and if we are to be psychologically free from this tyranny of the unconscious, we must understand ourselves. This self-knowledge in depth can free ourselves and our culture to grow psychologically, culturally, and socially. Kubie shows the classic Freudian posi- tion that it is the unconscious that really counts, and if we are going to make any basic advances, it must be at this deeper level; other changes are merely super- ficial rearrangements of our surface thoughts, motivations, feelings, and actions.

Every discipline has its tools, and each such tool has its own inherent errors. The finest microscope produces an image not of facts but of facts embedded in a setting of obscuring artifacts which the microscope itself creates. The first thing that the young microscopist is taught is how to distinguish the one from the other. A discipline comes of age and a student of that discipline reaches maturity when it becomes possible to recognize, estimate, and allow for the errors of their tools. This is true for physics, chemistry, physiology, the social sciences, the humanities, history, literature, and the arts. Within its own field each of these disciplines is meticulously self-critical about the sources of error which reside in its special instruments.

Yet there is one instrument which every discipline uses without checking its errors, tacitly assuming that the instrument is error-free. This, of course, is the human psychological apparatus. As a result of the failure to consider the sources of error in the human being himself, when our academic disciplines assemble together in our great education institutions they re-enforce the tacit, fallacious assumption that man can understand the world that lies outside of himself without concurrently understanding himself. Actually, each man is his own microscope with his own idio- syncrasies, to which he alone can penetrate. Therefore we cannot perceive the outside world without distorting our very perceptions unless we search out individually the sources of error which lie hidden within. This is precisely what every mature discipline does in its own field: yet it is what no discipline does for the broad concept of education as a whole.

As we view the world around us, and as we look and listen and think and feel and interact with our fellow man and his works and his history, we view all such external realities through a cloud of distorting projections

*From Lawrence S. Kubie, "The Forgotten Man of Education," *Harvard Alumni Bulletin* 56 (1954): 349–353, by permission of the author. Dr. Kubie is Clinical Professor of Psychiatry at the University of Maryland. His book *Neurotic Distortion of the Creative Process* concerns education and creativity.

of our own unconscious problems. It is a scene observed as through the wavering convection currents over a hot fire. This is why it is impossible to produce scholars, who in the true sense of the word are wise men, if they know nothing about themselves. Without self-knowledge in depth, the master of any field will be a child in human wisdom and human culture. Even the seemingly objective data of his own field at the same time represent projections of his own unresolved problems in dreamlike symbolic disguises: and as long as he knows nothing of his own inner nature, his apparent knowledge merely disguises his spiritual confusion.

What I am saying is nothing that has not been said many times since Socrates: namely, that man must know himself. What modern psychiatry adds to this ancient adage is that self-knowledge if it is to be useful and effective must comprise more than superficial self-description. It must include an understanding of unconscious as well as conscious levels of psychological processes. Yet such self-knowledge, which requires the mastery of intricate new tools of psychological exploration, is wholly overlooked throughout the entire scheme of "modern" education, from the kindergarten to the highest levels of academic training.

This deepening of our self-knowledge is in turn intimately dependent on the nature of symbolic thinking. Learning depends upon a progressive mastery of the many processes of symbolic thought. Symbols, however, are not all alike. They fall into three groups. There is the realistic form of symbolic thinking in which we are fully aware of the relationship of the symbols of language to that which they represent. Here the function of the symbol is to communicate the hard core, the bare bones, of thoughts and purposes. Secondly, there is the symbol whose relationship to its root is figurative and allegorical. The purpose of this second form of symbolic thinking is to communicate by inference all of the nuances of thought and feeling, all of the collateral references which cluster around the central core of meaning. This is the symbolic language of creative thinking whether in art or science. In technical jargon, the first is called conscious, and the second preconscious. Third, there is the symbolic process in which the relationship between the symbol and what it represents has been buried or distorted, so that the symbol becomes a disguised and disguising representative of unconscious levels of psychological processes. Here the function of the symbolic process is not to communicate but to hide. This is the unconscious symbolic process of the dream and of psychological illness.

Yet all three always operate together, with the consequence that every single thing we ever do or say or think or feel is a composite product of them all. Consequently when a scientist is studying atomic energy or a biological process or the chemical properties of some isotope, when a sociologist studies the structure of government and society, when a historian studies the development of events, or an economist the play of economic forces, when a classicist studies an ancient tongue, or a musicologist the intricacies of musical composition, when a theologian studies theology, each deals with his subject on all three of these levels at once. On the conscious level he deals with them as realities. On the preconscious level he deals with their allegorical and emotional import, direct and indirect. On the unconscious level, without realizing it, he uses his special competence and knowledge as an opportunity to express the unconscious, conflict-laden, and confused levels of his own spirit, using the language of his specialty as a vehicle for the projection outward of his internal struggles. Since this happens without his knowledge, it is a process which can take over his creative thinking in his own field, distorting and perverting it to save his unconscious needs and purposes.

The result is a structure of unconscious compromises which may render great intellectual brilliance as futile and as impotent as are any other symptomatic products of the neurotic process. It is for this reason that we can no longer tolerate with complacency the fact that art and science and every other cultural activity are hybrids, born of an unhealthy fusion of that which is finest and that which is sickest in human nature. It is a further consequence that the greater the role played by the unconscious components of symbolic thought, the wider must become the gap between erudition and wisdom. A scholar may be erudite on conscious and preconscious levels, yet so obtuse about the play of unconscious forces in his own life, that he cannot tell when he is using realistically and creatively the subject of which he is a master, or when he is using it like the inkblot on a Rorschach card. Education for wisdom must close this gap, by providing insight which penetrates into those areas of human life in which unconscious forces have always hitherto played the preponderant role.

This is the challenge which psychoanalytic psychiatry brings to the goals and techniques of education. At first thought the suggestion seems simple, a mere extension of the ancient Socratic admonition to "Know Thyself," making it read "Know Thyself in Depth." Yet these two added words, "in depth," will demand one of the most difficult cultural steps which civilized man has ever taken: a step which is essential if the man of the future is to be saved from man's present fate. And what has been that fate? It has been that in spite of a growing knowledge of the world around him he has repeated like an automaton the errors of his past; and that furthermore he has repeated these old errors in forms which become increasingly destructive and catastrophic as he becomes more educated. Whether his erudition has been in history, art, literature, the sciences, religion, or the total paraphernalia of modern culture, this has been the limiting factor in our Culture of Doom.

This automaticity of conduct which is governed predominantly by our unconscious psychological mechanisms is dependent directly upon their remaining inaccessible. Therefore if "self-knowledge in depth" ever becomes the goal of a new concept of education and if it becomes a part of the equipment which education brings to the cultured man it will make it possible for man to attain freedom from his ancient slavery to those repetitive psychological processes over which at present he has no control.

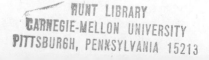

In his *Personal Record* Joseph Conrad describes himself as a knight in shining armor mounted on a magnificent horse. The picture was quite flattering until on looking more closely, he noticed that little knaves were running by the head of the horse and holding onto the bridle. Thereupon he realized that he did not know who was guiding that horse; the knight on the horse's back, or the knaves running by its head. This is the image of the educated man of today. He is a noble figure on a noble charger, magnificently armed. But the knaves who trot unheeded by the horse's head, with their hands on the reins, are guiding that horse far more than is the pretentious figure of culture astride the horse's back.

Like infinity, self-knowledge is an ideal which can be approached but never reached. Therefore, like education, it is a process which is never finished, a point of continuous and never-ending journey. It is relative and not absolute. Consequently, the achievement of self-knowledge is a process which goes on throughout life, demanding constant vigilance; and because it requires a continuous struggle, true self-knowledge never becomes an occasion for smug complacency.

The man who knows himself in depth does not look down his nose at the rest of the world from a perch on Mt. Olympus. Rather will he acknowledge with proper humility the impossibility of knowing himself fully, and the importance of struggling constantly against the lure of insidious, seductive illusions about himself. Nor on the other hand will he be incessantly preoccupied with his own conscious and unconscious motivations. Instead the more fully he approaches self-awareness, the more coherent and integrated become the various levels of his personality.

As a result, self-knowledge brings with it the right to trust his impulses and his intuitions. He may continue to watch himself out of the corner of his eye with vigilant self-skepticism, but he will give the center of his attention to his job and to the world around him. Thus, self-knowledge brings freedom and spontaneity to the most creative alliance of the human spirit, the alliance between conscious and preconscious processes: and it brings this spiritual liberation by freeing us from the internal blocking and distortion which occur when conscious and preconscious processes are opposed by an irreconcilable unconscious. Thus my vision of the educated man of the future is not an unreal fantasy of an individual out of whom all of the salty seasoning of preconscious and unconscious processes will have been dissolved, like a smoked ham which has soaked too long. It is rather of a man whose creative processes are relatively freed of the burden of unconscious internal conflicts.

In turn, however, this does not mean that to become educated a man must be psychoanalyzed. It means rather that new procedures must be introduced into the pattern of education which will make therapeutic analyses necessary only for those in whom the educational process has failed. The positive goal of this vital aspect of education is to shrink the dark empire in which unconscious forces have in the past played the preponderant role, and to broaden those areas of life in which conscious and preconscious processes will play the dominant role.

It is one thing, however, to describe self-knowledge in depth as the ultimate goal for culture and education. To achieve it is another. I will not presume here to write out a prescription on how this can be done. In dealing with any individual patient we know that without too much difficulty the psychiatrist can trace the interweaving patterns of complex, conscious, preconscious, and unconscious forces which have shaped an entire life. Yet many weeks, months, and even years of additional work may be required to communicate the analyst's insight to the patient himself. If the communication of insight to a single individual presents such formidable problems, we should not be surprised that the communication of insight to successive generations will require the development of basically new techniques of education, techniques which will have to start in the nursery and continue into old age, techniques which will have to circumvent adroitly the unconscious opposition of the oldsters among us who lack these insights and who feel personally threatened by them. Thus a new and critical version of the ancient battle between the generations is surely in the making.

Yet I believe that the whole future of human culture depends upon our solving this problem of how to introduce into education processes which will in essence be both preventive and curative. They will be preventive in the sense that they will limit and guide the fateful dichotomy which occurs early in life between conscious and preconscious processes on the one hand, and the inaccessible unconscious on the other. It will have to be curative as well, because we cannot expect prevention ever to work perfectly. Consequently we shall always have to build into the concepts and techniques of education certain types of therapeutic experiences, both for groups and for individuals, which will be designed to reintegrate unconscious with conscious and preconscious processes. Even to attempt this will require that we overcome not only the individual resistances and prejudices to which I have just referred, but also the entrenched opposition of many existing social, cultural, religious, and educational institutions. This is no small order: and I would hesitate to offer the challenge, if I did not have so deep a conviction that all of our vaunted culture and education, as we have known them in the past, have failed mankind completely.

Some may feel these views to be unduly pessimistic. Yet I believe that these criticisms of our educational processes are rooted in optimism, and pursue an optimistic ideal. It is not pessimism to face the fact of past failure, if our purpose in studying our failures is to learn how not to fail in the future. It was neither pessimism nor a morbid fascination with death which led medicine to the autopsy table, but rather courage, optimism, spiritual humility, and a determination to avoid the endless repetition of past error. Mankind's reward is scientific medicine; and we must now face the failure of education with the same combination of humility and determination. Because education has failed mankind in the past, it does not follow that it must necessarily continue to fail, unless we cling obstinately and defensively to methods which have already been tried without success.

Yet the tendency to prescribe more of the old medicines is deep in us. For instance, when I read that a new college president declares that what we need in education is a greater emphasis on religion, I confess that my heart sinks. This is not because he singled out religion. I have the same sinking feeling when some one says that what we need is more of the humanities, or when Hutchins and Adler call for more of the "great" books by "great" thinkers out of the past, or when a classicist calls for more of the classics, or a mathematician for more mathematics, or a chemist for more chemistry.

It is not a pretty spectacle, nor a reassuring measure of the maturity of educators, when in the face of our general cultural failure each cultural specialist cries out for larger doses of his own specific remedy. Such spiritual arrogance and obstinacy, whether from the pulpit or from the laboratory, should have no place in the deliberations of educated men. Indeed, it is a symptom of the very illness I am stressing, namely, that our educational system produces men of erudition with little wisdom or maturity; with the consequence that every cultural discipline is led by human beings who spend their time defending their vested interests in their own special fields. In this respect, the great washed have little on the great unwashed.

It is important to understand that scientists, including psychiatrists, are not immune to these frailties; and that they are equally true for all of those who carry the banners of culture. It is an old story of youthful idealism, of young confidence that the way to the good life is in their hands, then of a gradual disillusionment which usually is masked by a paradoxical defensiveness and a refusal to face the limitations of existing methods, turning instead in anger against anyone who is honest and skeptical enough to challenge his particular road to salvation.

All of us want to go on educating as we have in the past, making at the most only trivial curricular changes. But what mankind actually needs is a cultural stride of far grander dimensions. A little more or less of science, or of history, or of sociology, or of the classics, or of languages whether ancient or modern (for man can be as foolish in five languages as in one), or of philosophy or theology, or in the history of any of these: None of these gives to man the power to change or grow. Having devoted a lifetime to mastering some erudite discipline, and having thereby become a pew-holder in a towering cathedral with a limited seating capacity (to plagiarize Robert Nathan and *The Bishop's Wife*), it is indeed difficult for any of us to say, "This technique of mine which I have mastered at such great cost is just not enough." Instead we say, "Give the patient more of my medicine. More of the same is what he needs. Pour it down his throat. It may not have worked in the past: but more of it will surely cure him in the future."

These words are an expression of the human frailties which the artist, writer, historian, scientist, and theologian share equally with the least "cultured" man in the community. Every one of us is guilty of this—the scientists, the technologists, the classicists, the romanticists, the humanists, the musicians, the writers, the sculptors, and the dramatists. And especially is it true of the theologians of every sect and variety, because they give to this arrogance a divine sanction, in which I am sure that the Divinity would have no part. All say "Believe in me," "Believe in my way," "Believe in my special field." Few among us have the courage to say: "Do not believe at all. What I advocate is at best a working hypothesis to be rigorously and skeptically tested, but never believed. I ask for no credulity or faith. My challenge is to the courage and dignity of doubting, and to the duty of testing and experimenting. Man is Man not by virtue of believing, but by virtue of challenging belief. Let believing be the starting point for an investigation, but never its end." Just once in my life have I been privileged to hear a great religious teacher say from his pulpit, "It is the search for truth which is religion: and as soon as any religion believes that it has found the truth, it ceases to be religious."

Those who represent the world of the mind and of the spirit must acquire the humility which led medicine to study its defeats at the autopsy table. This was a unique moment in human culture. We need now to apply the same self-scrutiny to all of culture. And as we do this, let us stop to remind ourselves that when a patient dies, the doctor does not blame the patient: he blames himself. But when humanity fails, the artists and the writers scold, and the theologian thunders angry denunciations of human deficiencies, when they should be turning a pitiless scrutiny on themselves, their beliefs, and their techniques.

What then must education achieve? It must make it possible for human beings themselves to change. That is the next necessary goal of education. We would find it hard to prove that even the greatest works of art, of literature, of music, of philosophy, of religion have freed the hearts of men. Yet until we have found out how to make it possible for man himself to change, we have no right to revere our culture as though it were a creative and moving force in the Divine Comedy. Until what we call culture, whether with a small "c" or a capital "K," can free man from the domination of his own unconscious, it is no culture. An education which gives man only sophistication, taste, historical perspective, manners, erudite parlor conversation, and knowledge of how to use and control the forces of nature is a fraud on the human spirit, no matter what inflated pretensions and claims it makes.

It is we, the educated and the educators, who have failed mankind, not mankind which has failed us. Science and art and philosophy and religion and learning have failed; just as it is medicine which has failed when a patient dies, not the corpse. This charge is not made lightly; nor is it to be brushed aside in facile self-defense. The next goal of education is nothing less than a progressive freeing of man—not merely from external tyrannies of nature and of other men, but from internal enslavement by his own unconscious automatic mechanisms. Therefore, all of education and all of art and culture must contribute to this. It has long been recognized that in spite of technological progress, and in spite of art, literature, religion, and scholarly learning, the heart of man has not changed. This is both a challenge and a rebuke to our complacent acceptance of this bitter and devastating commentary on culture. My answer is based on the conviction that it is possible to break through the sonic barrier between conscious and unconscious processes, and thereby to bring to man for the first time in human history the opportunity to evolve beyond his enslaved past. That is why this thesis can claim for itself a realistic spiritual optimism.

Toward this goal a first step will be a deeper study of those early crises in human development, when the symbolic process begins to splinter into conscious, preconscious, and unconscious systems. The purpose of such a study of infancy would be to illuminate the origins of the repressive processes which produce these cleavages, since it is these which must be guided and controlled. As its second goal such a study would aim at the reintegration of unconscious with preconscious and conscious processes: something which has to be done not merely once, but repeatedly throughout the entire process of growth, from infancy through childhood, puberty, adolescence, and on into adult years. Just as the battle for political freedom must be won over and over again, so too in every life the battle for internal psychological freedom must be fought and won again and again, if men are to achieve and retain freedom from the tyranny of their own unconscious processes, the freedom to understand the forces which determine their thoughts, feelings, purposes, goals, and behavior. This freedom is the fifth and ultimate human freedom; and like every other freedom, it demands eternal vigilance.

At present, except in a few experiments (like those which are made in a few pioneering institutions, such as Goddard College) education is making no effort to meet this challenge. At present a farmer is given more training for raising stock than all of our institutions of lower or higher learning offer to men and women for raising the children whose lives they will make and break.

I would not give the impression that I believe that this is all there is to education. But what I do believe is that without this at its heart education, culture, literature, art, science, and religion are all hollow frauds. Without this, education has sold humanity down the river—back into slavery. And I believe that this will continue to be true until we rescue from his present oblivion this forgotten man of education.

I want to repeat that self-knowledge in depth is not all there is to wisdom, but that it makes maturity and wisdom possible; and what is even more important, it frees us from the tyranny of those rigid compulsive mechanisms which have made impossible our psychological evolution.

Without self-knowledge in depth, we can have dreams but not art, we can have the neurotic raw material of literature, but not mature literature. Without it we have no adults, but only aging children armed with words, paints, clay, and atomic weapons, none of which they understand. It is this which makes a mockery of the pretentious claims of education, of religion, of the arts, and of science. Self-knowledge is the Forgotten Man of our entire educational system and indeed of human culture in general. Without self-knowledge it is possible to be erudite, but never wise. My challenge to all of us is to have the humility to face this failure, and the determination to do something effective about it before it is too late.

UNDERSTANDING OTHERS
THROUGH FACING OURSELVES *

Arthur Jersild

The Self Is Door To The World. When I know something about myself, I can understand that thing in others. A major purpose of education is to teach students to know more about the world, including other people, and to be able to act appropriately in the world and with other people. We often claim to do this by teaching the "content" of subject matter, but that content came from the feelings and thoughts of other people. If we are to understand the subject matter content, say the Freudians, then we should try to recognize these thoughts and feelings in ourselves. What starts off as self-knowledge, ends up as knowledge of the world. Jersild's books *When Teachers Face Themselves* and *In Search of Self* provide more ways this view has been applied to teachers and education. The door to inner-knowledge opens outward too.

In the school there are countless opportunities for helping the child in his search to find himself. In school the child can discover his aptitudes and abilities. He can be helped to face some of his inner difficulties and to realize that there are limits to what he can do. His attitudes regarding his worth as a person may be affected in important ways since life at school is heavily invested with praise and blame, pride and shame, acceptance and rejection, success and failure.

Everything that enters into the relationship between a teacher and the child has or might have a significant bearing on what a child thinks about himself and how he feels about himself. Everything that transpires in a teacher's dealings with a child might also help the teacher to learn something about himself for his functioning as teacher is to a large extent a projection of what he is.

In order to have insight into the child's strivings and the problems and issues he is coping with the teacher must strive to face the same issues within his own life. These issues are largely emotional in nature and the endeavor to understand oneself and others has a deep emotional meaning. It calls for more than intellectual cleverness and academic competence.

To appreciate another's feelings one must seek to recognize and understand one's own. To be able to sympathize with the child who is hostile (and all children are, more or less) the teacher must face his own hostile tendencies and try to accept the implication of his anger as it occurs, say, in his annoyance with his pupils, his impatience with himself, his feuds

*From Arthur T. Jersild, "Understanding Others Through Facing Ourselves," *Childhood Education* 30, no. 9 (May, 1954): 411–414, by permission of the author and publisher. Arthur T. Jersild is Professor Emeritus of Teachers College, Columbia University. He is the author of *When Teachers Face Themselves* and *In Search of Self*.

with other teachers, his complaints against parents or school authorities or others on whom he fixes his ire.

He must be prepared to examine and seek to realize the significance of his feelings of being abused, his devices for avoiding responsibility for himself by blaming others. The more a person can face some of the ramifications of his own anger and make some allowance for his tendency to become angry, the more sensitive he can be to the hurts, frustrations, and anxieties involved in another person's anger.

Similarly, to realize the turmoil another is undergoing a person must try to examine his own fears and anxieties. To do so may be more painful and threatening at the moment than to keep pretending they don't exist, but unless he can seek to fathom his fears as these appear in his phobias, squeamishness, fear of misfortune, timidity, uncertainties, fear of making mistakes, and fear of what others may think of him, his ability to perceive that others are frightened will be quite limited.

Unless a person is prepared to take at least a little note of his own anxieties he is likely to be uncomprehending when children helplessly express theirs. He may even be harsh when children's anxieties break through in such signs as inability to learn, unwillingness to try for fear of making mistakes, impertinence, inattentiveness, restlessness, irritability, unreasonableness, and countless other symptoms which indicate that a child is uneasy and at odds with himself.

To perceive the significance of problems in the lives of others one must be able, at least to some degree, to recognize and face the implications of corresponding problems in one's own life:

One must undertake to face, for example, one's irrational attitudes toward authority as they might appear in a tendency to be servile or rebellious toward people who have power or higher rank.

One must face the possibility that unresolved conflicts regarding sex might make one appear to be unconcerned or unduly fearful or prudish or harsh in one's attitudes regarding the sexual behavior of others.

One needs also to examine the possibility that one's demands upon others are tied to impossible requirements of goodness, brilliance, and perfection which one places upon oneself.

It is possible that one's complacent attitude regarding the damage competitiveness inflicts on some children may be linked to a tendency within oneself to seek competitive triumph over others. Again, one may have a tendency to pity oneself, to feel sorry for bearing so hard a lot, and being so little appreciated by others and thus have trouble in perceiving how desperately someone else might wish to be understood and appreciated.

A person's wisdom as he looks outward upon others can only be as deep as the wisdom he possesses as he looks inward upon himself. The farther a teacher goes in understanding himself and others the more deeply he can realize the common humanity he shares with others, even with those whom he dislikes. The more genuinely he is involved in his own struggle to understand and to face the problems of life the more he can realize this kinship with others whether they be younger or older, or like him or unlike him in education, wealth, race, religion, social status, or professional rank.

CAN IT BE A PART OF EDUCATION?

How does one achieve understanding of self? This is a crucial question in the preparation of teachers. It cannot be answered by the usual courses of study, methods, and lesson plans in our teacher-education programs. These may be valuable for other purposes, but knowledge of self requires a different kind of personal involvement than the usual academic course encourages or demands.

One broad principle is this: *To gain in knowledge of self one must have the courage to seek it and the humility to accept what one may find.* If one has such courage and humility one can draw upon many sources in everyday life.

One can learn from experience of life's joys and tragedies. One can profit from self-inquiry into what it might mean that one was so elated or impressed or prejudiced or angry or frightened or depressed after this or that happening. One can learn from seeing a motion picture portrayal of people with emotional tendencies that hold up a mirror to oneself. One can learn from asking why one is inclined to gloat or to inflict pain or to resist so strongly or to yield so meekly. Even to hear a recording of one's voice at a time when one has been expressing grievances, worries, or self-reproach may be a revelation.

A valuable help in self-examination which may be mainly intellectual but might also strike at a deep emotional level is the reading of books written by compassionate people who have made some progress in their own painful struggle to know themselves.

LOOKING AT OUR OWN OBJECTIVITY

The method of "participant observation" offers a promising means of taking a look at oneself. One records what one hears and sees and what one's feelings are as one listens in on a discussion or visits a class and then, preferably with help and through comparison with records kept by other observers, one examines this record. The examination may show that what one notices and fails to notice is determined by habits of thought one usually takes for granted, and that the emotional effect of what one witnesses tells a great deal about one's prejudices. What one perceives "objectively" may be, to a large degree, a projection of one's own subjective state and thus tell more about oneself than about the people whom one observes.

This broad principle also holds: Just as it is within an interpersonal setting that one acquires most of the attitudes involved in one's view of oneself so it is likely that *it is only in an interpersonal setting that a person can be helped to come to grips with some of the meanings of these attitudes.*

A relationship that can promote knowledge of self prevails when one seeks private therapy or joins with others in a group therapy situation. It exists also, to some degree, whenever one enters into any situation with people, in any walk of life, who can help one to gain perspective on oneself.

In a group setting a person may be helped to hear an echo of his anger or to catch a glimpse of the impressions his fears make on others. The way others express themselves or respond to him may help him to face in a new and self-revealing light some of the evidences of shame, self-effacement, anxiety, vindictiveness, and other outcroppings of deep-seated attitudes of which ordinarily he is not aware. Likewise, to witness a mimicking of his conduct by a child or by a role-playing peer may throw a little gleam of light on unrecognized conflicts.

It is in a setting of joint and common work and airing of self with other people that some of the richest possibilities for self-examination can be found. In the teaching profession we have hardly begun to explore and tap the resources for growth in knowledge of self which people might gain from one another. The committee meetings, staff meetings, seminars, discussion groups, panels, and other enterprises teachers take part in may serve many good purposes but usually they do not serve this purpose. Indeed, they often proceed as though they were intended to defeat the purpose of self-discovery for even when the participants are dominated by emotion they usually make a pretense of dealing with the issue in a reasonable way. When acrimony and anxiety creep in, as often happens, the appearance of being involved in a logical discussion is usually maintained.

Feelings might be aired in a revealing and growth-producing way if people could help one another to learn to be free to come out from behind the curtain that commonly conceals their emotions from others and from themselves. The writer believes that future developments of vast importance in education will come from plowing this fertile field. Some work in this area already is going on through role playing, group dynamics, and the like. These activities can be revealing and show the way to further possibilities even when they deal with relatively surface material, as often they do.

A couple of summers ago a workshop attended by teachers from schools in many sections of the United States dealt with the school's responsibility for promoting self-understanding. The members recommended that experiences designed to promote knowledge of self should be a part of every teacher-education program. Experience equivalent to what a person might obtain from group therapy under the leadership of a professionally trained psychotherapist was recommended as an example of what each prospective teacher should have. Such a recommendation is really not far-fetched when viewed in the light of the budget of time and money now invested in the training of teachers.

The exact recommendation is less important than the issue raised. The courage to face this issue is the important thing, and it must be faced if teachers are to realize their potentialities for finding themselves in their profession and for helping others in their search. Knowledge of self can be gained through many avenues and it is not something that is acquired once and for all, like mastery of the multiplication table. Even those who are quite blind to themselves have a little of it, and the capacity to acquire more. One of the outstanding marks of those who have achieved the deepest knowledge is that they still are seeking. No one procedure alone will give the answer since the search for selfhood, when genuine, is pursued through all channels of experience as long as a person lives.

AN INSERVICE PROGRAM FOR MENTAL HEALTH *

Libbie B. Bower

You Can Learn To Be Understanding. Understanding, acceptance, and sensitivity aren't just "gifts" that some people have and others don't. They can be learned. In this article Bower presents some ideas of how they can be learned. To a Freudian, knowledge of others starts with knowledge of oneself; as we learn to be sensitive to ourselves, we learn to accept and understand ourselves. Introspection, thus, is a way of obtaining knowledge of oneself that may be generalizable to others. As Jersild explained, the more we know about ourselves, the more we know about other people, and Bower presents ways to increase teachers' self-understanding. Teachers, inservice planners, and teacher educators who want more information on these seminars and workshops may want to check the bibliographic items.

Self-understanding plays an important part in understanding and helping others. Yet little has been done to develop leadership and techniques to acquaint teachers with this area (beyond academic courses). Learning about one's self is a delicate problem. But educators who are the *significant others* (next to parents) in the lives of children, are increasingly aware of the importance of the psychological aspects of their work and strive to deepen their self-understanding.

Over a period of a half dozen years, the Massachusetts Association for Mental Health has proceeded in an empirical way to develop programs in line with current trends both in education and psychiatry, trends which have shifted the focus of mental hygiene away from thinking of it in terms of maladjustment to a preventive program.

This program was set up on varying levels of complexity. The goal was to help teachers achieve not only an optimal level of professional functioning but also to sharpen their awareness of the preventive aspects of their role as classroom teachers. Through courses in mental health, seminars in individual and group psychology, and inservice mental health workshops, a design for teacher-training has evolved using techniques and methods from the fields of dynamic psychiatry, social psychology, education, and other disciplines.

COURSES IN MENTAL HEALTH

A course, such as "Children's Emotions Reflected in Classroom Behavior," offered a dynamic approach to understanding human behavior. Such a course was presented at the invitation of local school systems in a

*From Libbie B. Bower, "An Inservice Program for Mental Health," *Childhood Education* 30, no. 9 (May, 1954): 419–422, by permission of the author. Dr. Bower was formerly Program Director of the Massachusetts Association for Mental Health.

dozen townships in the state. It was sponsored by Boston University-Harvard Extension Service and Tufts University, and carried graduate and undergraduate credit. The leader was trained in analytic psychiatry with experience in teaching and working with children.

The objective of the course was to see to what extent the *feelings, thinking,* and *actions* of teachers could be influenced. It was hoped that through such an experience teachers would not be overwhelmed by some of the behavior problems in the classroom, that they would develop greater self-confidence to deal with them and in the end would not only do a better job with their children but also would be more comfortable in what they did. It was important that the teacher become aware of how he was affecting the situations because of his own point of view. Instead of regarding interpersonal relationships as "correct" or "incorrect," understanding was directed toward discovering the reasons behind the behavior, toward the understanding that behavior is caused. There were 15 two-hour sessions—the 30 hour period divided as follows: 1/3 to 1/2 devoted to didactic lectures; 1/3 to 1/2 devoted to discussion of material presented; and 1/3 devoted to free discussion, interaction within the group, and discussion of the assignments.

The didactic lectures were planned in such a way as to present the genetic development of personality from the psychoanalytic point of view. The concept of the unconscious and its influence upon personality development was brought in.

In the material presented, the policy was not to introduce any new terms—medical, psychiatric, psychoanalytic or otherwise—unless absolutely indispensable for clarity, and then the terms were carefully defined. It was felt that presenting a new vocabulary would be confusing and perhaps become an obstacle to real understanding of the material.

The setting the leader encouraged was the easy relaxed atmosphere which allowed many situations to develop which were similar to situations one might expect to occur in the usual classroom—such as boisterous conversations which would delay the beginning of the class, delays in returning from the five-minute recess between hours, conversations by small cliques which would disturb the rest of the group. These situations were deliberately encouraged and were used during discussion periods to determine their meaning and best methods of handling them since this kind of behavior by implication is often typical of classroom behavior.

The most positive evidence that something happened and that the attitudes of the teachers changed is revealed by the striking contrast in attitudes and language used in the two case studies, one of which was presented after the first few sessions and one presented toward the end of the course. The first case study usually indicated a puzzled, sometimes hostile attitude toward a child, who is "bad," "spoiled," "trouble-maker," "lazy." During the first few sessions there was a great deal of anxiety displayed when the various ways in which the teacher revealed his unconscious through his own writing was discussed. The second case study displayed more feeling and understanding, and even though conclusions might be entirely erroneous, revealed an attempt to see what is behind the overt behavior that is troubling the teacher and the child.

INSERVICE MENTAL HEALTH WORKSHOP

The mental health inservice workshop for teachers, representing another level of teaching, developed out of Inter-Agency Committee meetings with the state departments of education, public health, mental health, Boston University School of Education, Massachusetts Society for Social Hygiene, and our Association. Representatives of these agencies working as a team and cooperating with local teacher associations helped design the structure, procedure, and content of these workshops. The pattern of the workshop varied with the needs, interests, and problems of the school personnel working together toward a common goal, such as, for example, *accepting children*. This requires successful intercommunication of understanding attitudes, feelings, and information.

The preplanning phases were cooperatively talked through with the result that when the workshop commenced, the stage was set for the recruitment of evaluation, resource, public relations, and social committees and their responsibilities, as well as the selection and inventory of problems of concern to the teachers.

The workshop continues to be problem centered. It does not deal with theoretical or intellectual concepts. The workshop provides a way of working together to bring about a new quality of participation and acceptance, of understanding the leadership role and problem-solving. Teachers are encouraged to share experiences around common concerns. They are helped to see the commonality of problems and to broaden their perspective. Teachers who come for "answers" grow to see that there are no "pat" answers for handling behavioral manifestations that seem difficult.

Resources for general assemblies such as provocative films, pamphlets, case conferences with the local mental health clinic staff, selection of key people with special skills and knowledge, as well as techniques such as role playing, sociograms, evaluation and observer's feed-back, help to sharpen teachers' understanding about themselves, group interaction and on-the-job problems.

SEMINARS

The seminars concern themselves with feelings rather than intellectual concepts of mental health principles. The goal is new awareness of oneself and new capacity to respond to this new understanding. The announcement states "These seminars deal primarily with problems which participants present from their own experiences at work. The situations which develop within the seminars are utilized as far as proves possible to further self-understanding and understanding of others. Although the approach utilized by the seminar leader resembles in some ways what takes place in psychiatric treatment, this seminar is essentially an educational experience and is not offered as a substitute for such treatment."

The seminar leaders' training must be such that they are aware of unconscious processes and understand their place in group interaction. It was agreed that it would be practical to include only psychiatrists with psychoanalytic background and experience. The leader's task was to handle resistances and group tensions, forces working against group growth and cohesion. His task also was to encourage work toward movement for growth and change through interpretation of material presented, thus making use of skills peculiar to his training.

The leader recognizes the worth of each group member, accepts him where he is in his development, and helps him, by his attitude, to more competent functioning. Group members come to know other members, feel free to express themselves more openly in relation to their own experiences and feelings. A group member may talk about failure—other group members sharing such an experience, with support from the leader, participate in the discussion and together they create a climate of permissiveness and acceptance which has educational and therapeutic effects.

It becomes apparent that in the group learning situation there are forces at play which facilitate relative freedom with which members are able to talk about their feelings. When members of groups support one another they encourage members to grow and develop to get new understandings. The help derived from discussion of personal problems may be referred to as a process of clarification and enhances self-understanding and the understanding of others with the chief purpose of improving the group member's functioning level on the job. The seminar approach with an experienced clinician as leader offers an opportunity to deepen an educator's psychological understanding of himself, his students, and his colleagues in a way which could be more meaningful than other more academic approaches like some college courses and lectures. It offers the possibility of dealing constructively with some of the minor subjective anxieties and conflicts of "normal" individuals who are fulfilling important functions in the community.

EDUCATION AND GROUP DYNAMICS

Three types of experiments in teacher training designed to help one learn about and accept himself and others have been briefly described. The method in all three is educational help based on concepts of the dynamics of the group process. Social science has reinforced the common belief that group experiences go a long way in shaping personality development. Controlled studies are adding clearer notions of how group association operates to influence the way people think and behave. Group members presenting problems close to the everyday life of people profit not only from contact with the leader but from interaction with each other. A final answer will have to await basic and action research.

BIBLIOGRAPHY

Berman, Leo. "Psychoanalysis and Group Psychotherapy," *The Psychoanalytic Review*, Vol. 37, April 1950.

Bower, Libbie B. "Education Placed in a New Perspective: Helping Educators Understand Themselves." *Educational Leadership*, March 1950.

——. "A Massachusetts Teacher Workshop in Mental Health." *Understanding the Child*, Vol. 22, October 1953.

Weinreb, Joseph. "Report of an Experience in the Application of Dynamic Psychiatry in Education," *Mental Hygiene*, Vol. 37, April 1953.

PART TWO

Behavioral Psychology

INTRODUCTION
THE EDITOR

Behavioral educational psychology is the predominant educational psychology in America today. In fact, when they talk about their specialty, professors of "educational psychology" usually omit the word "behavioral," they take it so much for granted. Behaviorism is nearly *the* academic psychology, and in many universities non-behaviorists often have hard times being hired, and are looked at as anti-scientific heretics or unfortunate examples of mis-conditioning. Behaviorists have recently further secured their positions by being declared the officially established educational psychology. Like the officially established churches in other nations, they have the rights of influencing practice and winning monetary and political support. These political successes by the behavioral sect of educational psychologists are most frequently evidenced in the statewide adoptions of behavioral objectives in "competency-based" programs, and in legislated accountability can also be seen in funding policies of governmental agencies and in grant-allocation of foundations. "The New World of Accountability" and "Behavioral Objectives? YES!" show this combination of educational evangelism and political proselytizing in action. Why is behaviorism so successful? What does it do that other psychologies don't? The articles in this section give some examples of behavioral techniques in education, and they justify some of behaviorism's successes.

The word "behavior" refers to almost all human activity, excluding, of course, many basic biochemical and physiological processes. The exact line of demarcation between what is and what isn't learned, controllable behavior is an open question which is being re-explored. Apparently we can learn to control many physiological activities that previously were thought to be outside the realm of learning. The article "The Ins and Outs of Mind-Body Energy" in the transpersonal section illustrates this, as does "The Learning of Visceral and Glandular Responses," by Neal Miller. Since almost everything we do is "behavior," this psychology is a broad-based approach to human activity, which tries to explain our behavior by a few simple principles. The word "behavior" should not be confused with our everyday language use of the word as in, "How did Johnny behave today?" meaning "Did he do as he was told?" or "Did he cause trouble?" While behaviorists are concerned with these activities too, the word "behavior" includes more than "discipline," "conduct," or the classic "deportment." Since almost all human behavior is seen as the result of learning, behaviorism is a psychology which is naturally compatible with educators, who naturally tend to see things in terms of learning.

There are two principles which are especially helpful in understanding the ways behavioral psychology contributes to educational practices: 1) People learn what they are rewarded for learning; 2) Be clear about what you are doing. Like Newton's Laws of Motion, however, they are simple in principle but become complex in practice. The purpose of this introduction to behavioral psychology is to give some background for understanding behavioral educational psychology and to introduce some of the common behavioral ideas and terminology so that the articles in this section will make more sense. For more complete treatments of behavioral educational psychology, the authors of the articles in this section and the journals and books they are taken from will be good sources, as will the references at the end of this introduction.

CLARITY

If there is any one ability that especially separates us from other animals, it is our ability to think. The behaviorists' desire for clarity calls on that human ability, and the behaviorists' ways of thinking about learning helps us be clear about our educational goals, the relative success of different classroom activities, and our judgment of those activities. Thinking clearly about what we are doing is an integral part of doing it. After all, if we are to teach, then we need a clear idea of just what we are teaching. We also need to know how successful we've been so that we can know when we are improving or have selected a new classroom exercise that teaches more than an older one. The more accurately we can measure what our students have learned, the more accurately we can improve our teaching. This is Smith's theme in the appropriately titled "Educational Objectives and the Systematic Improvement of Instruction." We can best tell whether we've done the right thing only when we can see the results of what we've done.

This is really what behavioral objectives are all about, to let us see the results of our actions. Whether one calls them instructional objectives, behavioral objectives, performance criteria, or any other similar name, the main thrust is to be clear about what we're teaching. And the way to be clear is to have results we can clearly see. The words "visible objectives" catch much of the meaning of "behavioral objectives" and its cognate relations. To know what we have done, we must see the results, and since we are interested in teaching things to students, then we want to look at the students' visible behavior. Thus, visible objectives are always written in terms of what the student does, not what we as classroom teachers do. After the visible objectives are written, then the teacher plans her classroom experiences so that the students reach those goals. Thus, writing a lesson plan follows stating the visible objectives. Gagné and Popham, two of the main spokesmen for behavioral objectives, describe the methods of writing behavioral objectives and how we can use them to clarify our goals in teaching, to improve our results, and to select the most appropriate learning experiences based on how well our teaching techniques have brought us our intended results.

REINFORCEMENT

The main idea in behavioral psychology applied to education is that of reinforcement. A reinforcement is a consequence of an action *that makes that action more likely to be repeated.* People who don't understand this sometimes make the mistake of saying, "Behaviorism doesn't work. I reinforced him, but nothing happened." Something isn't a reinforcement unless it works, i.e., unless it changes behavior. What these people mean is that they *intended* to reinforce the behavior they wanted, but that actually they didn't. "Reinforcement" is similar to the word "reward." The idea is simple, but the variations of kinds and techniques are sometimes surprising and complex. This points out one of the complexities: Whether or not something is reinforcing depends on the person, and it may vary from time to time for the same person. One cannot simply list objects, activities, feelings, or relationships that always are or are not reinforcers. The proof of a reinforcement is in the behavioral pudding: Did his subsequent behavior change?

There are many ways of classifying reinforcements, and the categories are not exclusive. The *intrinsic/extrinsic* distinction is based on whether the behavior is reinforcing itself or whether it is reinforcing because of subsequent rewards that are not an integral part of the behavior. For example, pride of achievement, satisfaction of curiosity, the joy of learning, aesthetic pleasure, and many aspects of sex and other bodily feelings are enjoyable in themselves, not because they lead to an extrinsic reward.

In the intrinsic case the activity (behavior) is its own reward. We often hope that our students will become intrinsically motivated to learn, but our use of compulsory attendance, grades, and other extrinsic reinforcements shows that we recognize that this remains a hope.

A second way of classifying reinforcements is *positive/negative*. In both cases the reinforcement makes it more likely that the behavior will recur, in the positive case because it is pleasurable or enjoyed, and in the negative case becuase it stops a situation that the person doesn't like. The teacher's smile, a word of appreciation, esteem from classmates, a sense of accomplishment, are all likely to function as positive reinforcers; they are likely to make the person's action occur again. "The Effects of Adult Social Reinforcement on Child Behavior" shows how very rewarding attention can be. Frequently we unintentionally reinforce behavior we don't want to. In "Behavioral Management of School Phobia" we see an example of a girl who was unintentionally reinforced for staying home from school. The distinction between what we *intend* to reinforce and what we actually *do* reinforce is an important one for teachers and parents. I have seen parents and teachers pay attention to their children only to scold, reprimand, break-up fights, etc. A child brought up in such a family or school soon learns how to get adults' attention. The rule for developing good behavior is: Catch them being good (and reward it).

Negative reinforcement also makes behavior more likely to recur because the student gets rewarded for his actions by escaping from an unpleasant, anxiety-filled, or guilty situation. For example, a child who gets an upset stomach and is excused from school on a day he has a test is rewarded for his sickness by escaping from the exam. In "The Learning of Visceral and Glandular Responses" Neal Miller suggests that we may teach people many of their diseases. Another example of negative reinforcement in schools is to reward students for getting all the spelling words right on Thursday by allowing them not to take the Friday test. In this case their correct spelling is rewarded by escaping the tension of the Friday quiz.

A third useful way to categorize reinforcements is whether they are *self-administered, social* (coming from someone else), or *impersonal*. In "Behavioral Self-Control: Power to the Person" Mahoney and Thoreson show one way to teach people how to develop behavioral skills for their own, intrinsic purposes. Unfortunately, behaviorists have the reputation of trying to control others. The Mahoney-Thoreson article shows a new thrust in behaviorism: Every person his own controller. The person who controls his own reinforcements is the truly independent person. Behavioral self-control is one way of achieving independence. It depends on selecting activities that are intrinsically rewarding and on controlling one's own extrinsic rewards.

One of the historical roots of behavioral psychology involved an attempt to find rules of behavior that applied to other organisms as well as to humans. In order to study this in other animals, researchers had to use reinforcements that they could control. These, of course, were extrinsic rewards, or basic physiological rewards such as food, water, or sex, which the experimenters could still control. It would be hard, for example, to carry out an experiment which used a rat's intrinsic rewards, the rodent counterpart of a person's intrinsic "feeling of achievement." The habit of using extrinsic rewards supplied by the experimenter generalized to the study of humans. As a consequence most behavioral studies of humans have used experimenter-controlled rewards rather than subject-controlled rewards. Most of the studies in this section show experimenter-controlled extrinsic rewards rather than subject-controlled extrinsic or intrinsic rewards. This emphasis on the external control of rewards has resulted in a view of the teacher as reward-controller and of teaching as the proper selection, timing, and sequencing of rewards. The articles, "Instructing Beginning Teachers in Reinforcement Procedures" and "Doing Your Own Thing with Precision" conceive of teaching this way.

The behavioral underemphasis on intrinsic rewards and self-rewarding may also be due to neglecting the fact that a major difference between humans and other species is that we have a highly developed symbol system, including our languages. Among other things, these symbols are sometimes reinforcers. These symbolic reinforcements allow us to learn and maintain all sorts of behavior that would be difficult to learn and to keep going without the use of symbols. Our ability to "talk to ourselves" in thinking gives us rewards—the ability to reward ourselves in thoughts. For example, when we have acted according to our moral principles, we can verbally reward ourselves for "doing the right thing." When we have been patriotic, we can intrinsically reward ourselves by feeling good about it. When we have acted on a religious principle in spite of possible quick reward for not doing so, we can temporarily reward ourselves with the idea that justice will prevail and our reward will come later. Our ability to use language gives us a whole repertoire of reinforcements not available to other animals. We can carry these reinforcements around with us "in our heads," and this realm of subject-controlled symbolic reinforcements allows us to develop behaviors which non-symbolizing animals cannot. The article "The Effect of Self-Recording on the Classroom Behavior of Two Eighth Grade Students," is a case in which the teacher and a behavioral counselor show a student how to increase her studying by symbolically rewarding herself by writing "+" marks on a piece of paper. Once this behavior is established, they are ready to teach her to think of the plus marks, instead of writing them down. When she has internalized the system of rewarding herself, then she has learned more self-control.

Social reinforcement means reinforcement coming from another person such as attention, compliments, a smile, answering questions, talking, or any other pleasant interaction. As is obvious from this list, many of our daily interactions with people can be reinforcing; although we may not think of them as reinforcements at the time. Another of the complexities of behavioral psychology comes when we consider that a person has many social relationships going at once. While we as teachers may want to reinforce a student's work in class, if we single him out for attention, his peers may withhold their friendship (withholding a stronger reinforcement). A behavioral way of looking at the peer-orientation of adolescence, for example, is to see that the strongest reinforcers are his friends, not his mother, father, or teacher. While educationally-oriented behavioral psychologists are becoming aware of the interpersonal influences in a classroom, their purer brethren who are less interested in classroom applications often miss the behavioral importance of having other people around. Much behavioral research was done with only one rat, pigeon, or other animal in a cage, or sometimes with a lone human. Classrooms have only one student in them infrequently. While one may obtain cleaner data by controlling social influences, experimental cleanliness is not next to educational relevance. A more educationally accurate experiment would have 20 or 30 rats in a cage. Now that some teachers have so successfully simulated the experimental cage in their classrooms, the reciprocal step of simulating a classroom in a psychology laboratory may provide the next scientific breakthrough.

Objects, tokens, or pay as reinforcement constitute another type of reward. These impersonal objects are often overemphasized when working with people, probably because their use is so easy with animals that behavioral psychologists have simply transferred their learning with animals to learning with humans. They are, of course, important, but for humans they are also usually experienced as mixed with social rewards. A raise in pay is enjoyable because we can buy more things than we could without it, but it also is frequently associated with a feeling that the boss "thinks I'm doing a good job." Tokens, objects, and pay may also elicit feelings of approval from the person controlling the reinforcements as well as have a value in themselves. One of the most frequent objections to the use of object reinforcers or to social reinforcers is that people should do the action "because it is the right thing to do." It would be nice if we could all work for the intrinsic rewards, but even in that case, we are doing it because of the rewards. Furthermore, if our job as teachers and parents is to teach children to do what is right and to learn, then aren't we shirking our job to refuse to do it to the best of our ability? Since behavior results from reinforcement, we are abdicating our responsibility to the random reinforcements of the world instead of taking on the responsibility of teaching what we admire. Some of the common moral objections to the use of reinforcements are answered in "A Note About Resistance and Opposition." Reinforcement is the most important idea in behavioral psychology as it's applied to education. When Freudians think about human behavior, they immediately ask, "Where does the unconscious come in?" When behaviorists plan education, when they explain why someone acts as he does, and when they learn how to teach, the question they ask is "What behavior is being reinforced?" If they are trying to account for someone's actions, they ask, "How is he being reinforced for that behavior?" or "How was he reinforced for it in the past?"

The rules of using reinforcement are:

1. Choose an appropriate reinforcement. (If it doesn't work, you'll have to choose another).
2. The reinforcement should come after the behavior. Grandma's Law: First you eat your vegetables, then you can have dessert.
3. The reinforcement should come as soon after the behavior as possible. Teachers who don't return student papers at all or who delay a long time are committing professional misconduct.
4. Many small rewards work better than a few big ones, especially for shaping.

There are other variations on the idea of reinforcement. *Punishment* is the opposite of positive reinforcement. Many people confuse it with negative reinforcement. In negative reinforcement a person is rewarded by escaping from an unpleasant situation, e.g., wandering around the room may be a way of escaping from facing an exam or from doing difficult and unrewarding work. As a consequence of getting up and wandering around the room, the student lowers his anxiety about the class material. In punishment, on the other hand, a student's action leads to a consequence that he doesn't like. For example, "If you wander around the room, you cannot go out for recess." These are two peculiarities that teachers have to look out for with punishment. First, what the teacher thinks is punishment may have elements of reward in it. In "Producing and Eliminating Disruptive Behavior" the authors found that increased disapproval by the teacher brought about increases in disruptive behavior. And in "An Analysis of the Reinforcing Function of 'Sit Down' Commands," the more the teacher said, "Sit down," the more standing up increased. This brings up the second problem with using punishment: it is reinforcing to the teacher in the short run. Usually, there is an immediate cessation of the punished behavior. The teacher has the class' attention, and the room is quiet. This reaction is reinforcing the teacher's use of punishment. However, the obedience usually is short-lived, and the student acts up again. The short-run effect is to reinforce the use of punishment, and the long-run effect is to increase the undesired actions. The teacher is negatively reinforced by ending a situation she doesn't like (the student wandering around the room), and the student is negatively reinforced by escaping from a situation he doesn't like (sitting at his desk doing unrewarding work). This frustrating back-and-forth dance can go on indefinitely.

Can you imagine a parent who would say to his child who was learning to talk, "You made a mistake. Don't you try to talk again until you can do it right."? If that happened to all of us, we'd probably never learn to talk. What most parents naturally do is reinforce their children for every little improvement as they learn to talk. First, perhaps any sound, then those sounds which are most like words, then only well-formed words, and so forth. This is the process of *shaping*. Although the final goal is in mind, it is usually necessary to teach the behavior we want by rewarding each little step along the way. This is where real teaching talent comes in, knowing which step to reinforce and when to move to the next step. In "The Effects of Adult Social Reinforcement on Child Behavior" and in "Instructing Beginning Teachers in Reinforcement Procedures Which Improve Classroom Control," we see examples of shaping behavior.

What happens when behavior isn't reinforced or isn't punished? After a while it will become less and less frequent. This is *extinction*. Have you heard the advice, "Just ignore him,"? That's extinction. Extinction is often hard to do because it requires not reacting to things that we usually react to. But once extinction is started, it is important to continue it. Otherwise you end up teaching the child that he has to persist in order to get attention, and persistence gets reinforced. Extinction is especially useful when a teacher suspects that his "punishment" actually is rewarding in the long run because of the attention his students receive from him and/or their friends. It is also particularly useful when combined with positive reinforcement for the desired behavior.

A special kind of extinction is called *desensitization*. In "The Behavior Therapist in the Schools" Mordock and Phillips describe how some teachers had to be desensitized to disruptive student behaviors in order to extinguish them. Like shaping, desensitization is done by little steps. The person starts out desensitizing himself to something that bothers him a little, e.g., whispering. Then a step at a time, he works on to bigger things, e.g., making faces, then switching the lights on and off. Learning to tolerate a situation is another way of thinking about desensitization. It is particularly useful for unrealistic fears or other instances of habitually reacting to things which one would like to learn how to ignore.

Reinforcement of various types, shaping, punishment, extinction, and desensitization are specific ways to teach people things. The use of any of these or combinations of them is known as *behavior modification*. We do not have the choice of deciding not to use behavior modification, for everything we do to another person, or don't do, effects what he does. If we decide to reward some behavior, even if only by a smile, a "thank you," by answering a question, or by turning toward the person, we are rewarding him. And if we choose to ignore the student, we are extinguishing his action, or teaching him that he will be rewarded later if he is persistent. *There is no way not to use behavior modification.* The question comes down to whether we will use it intelligently or let the reinforcements fall where they may and hope they follow socially responsible behavior.

REFERENCES

CRM Books, *Educational Psychology: A Contemporary View*, Chapter 8, "Principles of Learning," pp. 147–165; Chapter 10, "Motivation and the Management of Learning," pp. 185–203, Del Mar, California, 1973.

Journal of Applied Behavior Analysis.

Miller, Neal, "The Learning of Visceral and Glandular Responses," *Science*, No. 163, pp. 434–453, 1969.

Patterson, G. R. and M. E. Gullion, *Living With Children*, Research Press, Champaign, Illinois, 1971.

Skinner, B. F., *The Technology of Teaching*, Appleton-Century-Crofts, New York, 1968.

Thomas, D. R., W. C. Becker, and M. Armstrong, "The Production and Elimination of Disruptive Classroom Behavior by Systematically Varying Teacher's Behavior," *Journal of Applied Behavior Analysis*, Vol. 1, pp. 35–46, 1968.

Ulrich, R., T. Stachnik, and J. Mabry (eds.), *Control of Human Behavior*, Scott, Foresman, Glenview, Illinois, 1966.

EFFECTS OF ADULT SOCIAL REINFORCEMENT ON CHILD BEHAVIOR* **

Florence R. Harris, Montrose M. Wolf, and Donald M. Baer

Accentuate the Positive. These examples of behavioral shaping show clearly that a wide variety of behaviors can be increased by rewarding them and that it's possible to teach unwanted behaviors by unknowingly rewarding them. Frequently, for example, a stern word from a teacher or parent seems to act as a punishment at first when the undesired behavior stops, but in the long run it is a reinforcement. The child learns that he will get rewarding attention in the form of a reprimand. To turn the situation around, it is necessary to reward the desired actions.

There is general agreement among educators that one of the primary functions of a nursery school is to foster in each child social behaviors that contribute toward more pleasant and productive living for all. However, there is no similar consensus as to precisely how this objective is to be attained. Many writers subscribe to practices based on a combination of psychoanalytic theory and client-centered therapy principles, usually referred to as a mental hygiene approach. Yet there are considerable variation and vagueness in procedures recommended, particularly those dealing with such problem behaviors as the child's hitting people, breaking valuable things, or withdrawing from both people and things. Read (1955), for example, recommends accepting the child's feelings, verbalizing them for him, and draining them off through vigorous activities. Landreth (1942) advises keeping adult contacts with the child at a minimum based on his needs, backing up verbal suggestions by an implicit assumption that the suggestion will be carried out and, when in doubt, doing nothing unless the child's physical safety is involved. In addition to some of the above precepts, Taylor (1954) counsels parents and teachers to support both desirable and undesirable behaviors and to give nonemotional punishment. According to Standing (1959), Montessori advocates that teachers pursue a process of nonintervention, following careful preparation of a specified environment aimed at "canalizing the energy" and developing "inner command." Nonintervention does not preclude the "minimum dose" of instruction and correction.

Using some combination of such guidance precepts, teachers have reported success in helping some nursery school children who showed

*From Florence R. Harris, Montrose M. Wolf, and Donald M. Baer, "Effects of Adult Social Reinforcement on Child Behavior," *Young Children* 20, no. 1 (October, 1964): 8–17, by permission of the author and publisher. Florence Harris was formerly the Director of the Developmental Psychology Laboratory Preschool at the University of Washington.

**These studies were supported in part by research grants from the National Institute of Mental Health (MH-02208-07) and the University of Washington Graduate School Research Fund (11-1873). The authors are also indebted to Sidney W. Bijou for his general counsel and assistance.

problem behaviors; but sometimes adherence to the same teaching principles has not been helpful in modifying the behavior of concern. Indeed, it is usually not at all clear what conditions and principles may or may not have been operative. All of these precepts have in common the adult behaviors of approaching and attending to a child. Therefore, it seemed to the staff of the Laboratory Preschool at the University of Washington that a first step in developing possible explicit criteria for judging when and when not to attend was to study the precise effects that adult attention can have on some problem behaviors.

This paper presents an account of the procedures and results of five such studies. Two groups of normal nursery school children provided the subjects studied. One group enrolled twelve three-year-olds and the other, sixteen four-year-olds. The two teachers of the younger group and the three teachers of the older group conducted the studies as they carried out their regular teaching duties. The general methodology of these studies was developed in the course of dealing with a particularly pressing problem behavior shown by one child at the beginning of the school year. It is worth considering this case before describing the procedures which evolved from it.

The study dealt with a three-year-old girl who had regressed to an excessive amount of crawling (Harris, Johnston, Kelley, and Wolf, 1964). By "excessive" is meant that after three weeks of school she was spending most of her morning crawling or in a crouched position with her face hidden. The parents reported that for some months the behavior had been occurring whenever they took her to visit or when friends came to their home. The teachers had used the conventional techniques, as outlined above, for building the child's "security."

Observations recorded in the third week at school showed, however, that more than 80% of the child's time was spent in off-feet positions. The records also showed that the crawling behavior frequently drew the attention of teachers. On-feet behaviors, such as standing and walking, which occurred infrequently, seldom drew such notice.

A program was instituted in which the teachers no longer attended to the child whenever she was crawling or crouching, but gave her continuous warm attention as long as she was engaging in behavior in which she was standing, running, or walking. Initially the only upright behaviors that the teachers were able to attend to occurred when the child pulled herself almost to her feet in order to hang up or take down her coat from her locker, and when she pulled herself up to wash her hands in the wash basin. Within a week of the initiation of the new attention-giving procedure, the child acquired a close-to-normal pattern of on-feet behavior.

In order to see whether the change from off- to on-feet behavior was related to the differential attention given by the teachers, they reversed their procedure, making attention once again contingent only upon crawling and other off-feet behavior. They waited for occasions of such off-feet behavior to "reinforce" with attention, while not attending to any on-feet behavior. By the second day the child had reverted to her old pattern of play and locomotion. The observational records showed the child was off her feet 80% of the class session.

To see whether on-feet behavior could be re-established, the teachers again reversed their procedure, giving attention to the child only when she was engaging in behaviors involving upright positions. On-feet behavior rose markedly during the first session. By the fourth day, the child again spent about 62% of the time on her feet.

Once the child was not spending the greater portion of her day crawling about, she quickly became a well-integrated member of the group. Evidently she already had well-developed social play skills.

As a result of this demonstration that either walking or crawling could be maintained and that the child's responses depended largely upon the teachers' attending behaviors, the teachers began a series of further experimental analyses of the relationship between teacher attention and nursery school child behavior.

PROCEDURES

A specified set of procedures common to the next studies was followed. First, a child showing problem behavior was selected and records were secured. An observer recorded all of the child's behavior, the environmental conditions under which it occurred, and its immediate consequences under conventional teacher guidance. This was done throughout the 2½-hour school session, daily, and for several days. The records gave detailed pictures of the behavior under study. In each case, it became apparent that the problem behavior almost always succeeded in attracting adult attention.

As soon as these records, technically termed "baseline" records, of the typical behavior of the child and teachers were obtained, teachers instituted a program of systematically giving differential attention to the child. When the undesired behavior occurred, they did not in any way attend to him, but remained absorbed in one of the many necessary activities of teachers with other children or with equipment. If the behavior occurred while a teacher was attending to the child, she at once turned to another child or task in a matter-of-fact and non-rejecting manner. Concurrently, teachers gave immediate attention to other behaviors of the child which were considered to be more desirable than the problem behavior. The net effect of these procedures was that the child could gain a great deal of adult attention if he refrained from engaging in "problem behavior." If under this regime of differential attention the problem behavior diminished to a stable low level at which it was no longer considered a problem, a second procedure was inaugurated to check out the functional relationship between changes in the child's behavior and the guidance procedures followed.

The second procedure was simply to reverse the first procedure. That is, when the problem behavior occurred, the teacher went immediately to the child and gave him her full, solicitous attention. If the behavior stopped, she turned to other children and tasks, remaining thus occupied until the behavior recurred. In effect, one sure way for the child to secure adult attention was to exhibit the problem behavior. This procedure was used to secure reasonably reliable information on whether the teachers' special program had indeed brought about the changes noted in the child's behavior. If adult attention was the critical factor in maintaining the behavior, the problem behavior should recur in stable form under these conditions. If it did so, this was evidence that adult attention was, technically speaking, a positive social reinforcer for the child's behavior.

The final stage of the study was, of course, to return to procedures in which attention was given at once and continuously for behaviors considered desirable. Concurrently, adult attention was again withheld or withdrawn as an immediate consequence of the problem behavior. As the problem disappeared and appropriate behaviors increased, the intense program of differential adult attention was gradually diminished until the child was receiving attention at times and in amounts normal for the teachers in the group. However, attention was given only on occasions of desirable behavior, and never (or very seldom) for the undesirable behavior.

CRYING AND WHINING

Following the above procedures, a study was conducted on a four-year-old boy who cried a great deal after mild frustrations (Hart, Allen, Buell, Harris, and Wolf, 1964). This child averaged about eight full-fledged crying episodes each school morning. The baseline observations showed that this crying behavior consistently brought attention from the teachers, in the form of going to him and showing solicitous concern. During the following days, this behavior was simply ignored. (The only exceptions to this were to have been incidents in which the child had hurt himself considerably and was judged to have genuine grounds for crying. Naturally, his hurts were to be attended to. Such incidents, however, did not occur.) Ten days of ignoring the outcries, but giving approving attention for verbal and self-help behaviors, produced a steady weakening of the crying response to a nearly zero level. In the final five days of the interval, only one crying response was recorded. The number of crying episodes on successive days is graphed in cumulative form in Fig. 1. (page 000)

During the next ten days, crying was again reinforced whenever it occurred, the teachers attending to the boy on these occasions without fail. At first, it was necessary to give attention for mere grimaces that might follow a bump. The daily crying episodes quickly rose to a rate almost as high as formerly. A second ten-day period of ignoring the outcries again produced a quick weakening of the response to a near-zero level, as is apparent in the figure. Crying remained at this low level thereafter, according to the informal judgment of the teachers.

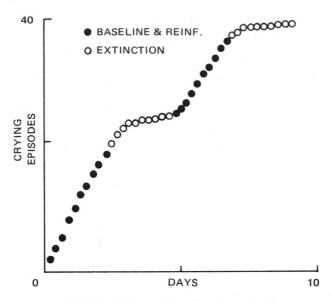

Fig. 1. Cumulative record of the daily number of crying episodes.

The same procedures were used in another study of "operant crying" of a four-year-old boy, with the same general results.

ISOLATE PLAY

Two studies involved children who exhibited markedly solitary play behavior. Extremely little of their morning at nursery school was spent in any interaction with other children. Instead, these children typically played alone in a quiet area of the school room or the play yard, or interacted only with the teachers. For present purposes, both of these response patterns will be called "isolate play." Systematic observation showed that isolate play usually attracted or maintained the attention of a teacher, whereas social play with other children did so comparatively seldom.

A plan was initiated in which the teacher was to attend regularly if the child approached other children and interacted with them. On the other hand, the teacher was not to attend to the child so long as he engaged in solitary play. To begin with, attention was given when the child merely stood nearby, watching other children; then, when he played beside another child; and finally, only when he interacted with the other child. Teachers had to take special precautions that their attending behaviors did not result in drawing the child away from children and into interaction solely with the teacher. Two techniques were found particularly effective. The teacher directed her looks and comments to the other child or children, including the subject only as a participant in the play project. For example, "That's a big building you three boys are making; Bill and Tom and Jim (subject) are all working hard." Accessory materials were also kept at hand so that the teacher could bring a relevant item for the subject to add to the play: "Here's another plate for your tea party, Ann." In both isolate cases this new routine for giving adult attention produced the desired result: Isolate play declined markedly in strength while social play increased two- or threefold.

After about a week of the above procedure, the consequences of nonisolate and isolate play were reversed. The teachers no longer attended to the child's interactions with other children, but instead gave continuous attention to the child when he was alone. Within a week, or less, isolate play became the dominant form of activity in both cases.

The former contingencies were then reinstated: The teachers attended to social interactions by the child, and ignored isolate play as completely as they could. Again, isolate play declined sharply while social interaction increased as before. The results of one of these studies (Allen, Hart, Buell, Harris, and Wolf, 1964) are summarized in Fig. 2.

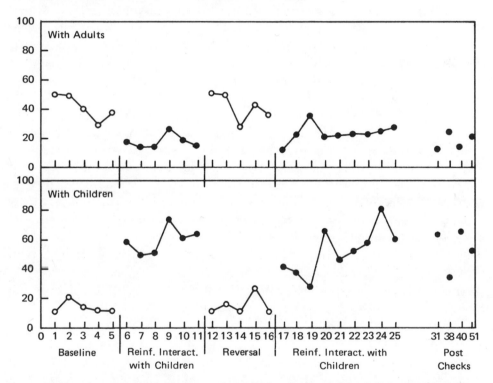

Fig. 2. Daily percentages of time spent in social interaction with adults and with children during approximately two hours of each morning session.

Figure 2 shows the changes in behavior of a 4½-year-old girl under the different guidance conditions. The graph shows the percentage of play time that she spent in interaction with other children and the percentage of time spent with an adult. The remainder of her time was spent alone. It is apparent that only about 15% of this child's play time was spent in social play as long as the teachers attended primarily to her solitary play. But interacting behaviors rose to about 60% of total play time when the

teachers attended only to her social play. At the same time, her interactions solely with teachers, not being reinforced, fell from their usual
40% of the child's playtime to about 20%. These were considered
reasonable percentages for this nursery school child. During Days 17
through 25 the schedule of adult reinforcement of social play was
gradually reduced to the usual amount of attention, given at the usual
irregular intervals. Nevertheless, the social behavior maintained its strength,
evidently becoming largely self-maintaining.

After Day 25, the teachers took care not to attend too often to the
child when she was alone, but otherwise planned no special contingencies
for attending. Four checks were made at later dates to see if the pattern
of social behavior persisted. It is apparent (Fig. 2, Post Checks) that the
change was durable, at least until Day 51. Further checks were not
possible because of the termination of the school year.

A parallel study, of a three-year-old isolate boy (Johnston, Kelley,
Harris, Wolf, and Baer, unpub.) yielded similar results showing the same
pattern of rapid behavioral change in response to changing contingencies
for adult attention. In the case of this boy, postchecks were made on
three days during the early months of the school following the summer
vacation period. The data showed that on those days his interaction with
children averaged 55% of his play time. Apparently his social play was
well established. Teachers reported that throughout the remainder of the
year he continued to develop ease and skills in playing with his peers.

The immediate shifts in these children's play behavior may be partly
due to the fact that they had already developed skills readily adapted to
play with peers at school. Similar studies in progress are showing that, for
some children, development of social play behaviors may require much
longer periods of reinforcement.

EXCESSIVE PASSIVITY

A fifth case (Johnston, Kelley, Harris, and Wolf, unpub.) involved a boy
noted for his thoroughgoing lack of any sort of vigorous play activity. The
teachers reported that this child consistently stood quietly about the play
yard while other children ran, rode tricycles, and climbed on special
climbing frames, trees, fences, and playhouses. Teachers also reported that
they frequently attempted to encourage him, through suggestions or
invitations, to engage in the more vigorous forms of play available.
Teachers expressed concern over his apparent lack of strength and motor
skills. It was decided to select a particular form of active play to attempt
to strengthen. A wooden frame with ladders and platforms, called a
climbing frame, was chosen as the vehicle for establishing this activity. The
teachers attended at first to the child's mere proximity to the frame. As
he came closer, they progressed to attending only to his touching it,
climbing up a little, and finally to extensive climbing. Technically, this was
reinforcement of successive approximations to climbing behavior. Fig. 3

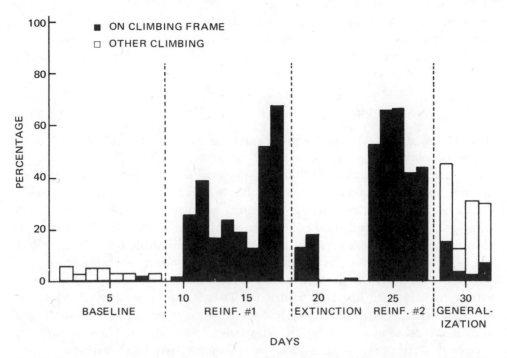

Fig. 3. Daily percentages of time spent in using a climbing-frame apparatus. Open bars indicate time spent in climbing on other equipment.

shows the results of nine days of this procedure, compared to a baseline of the preceding nine days. In this figure, black bars represent climbing on the climbing frame, and white bars represent climbing on any other equipment in the play yard. The height of the bars shows the percentage of the child's play time spent in such activities. It is clear that during the baseline period less than 10% of the child's time was spent in any sort of climbing activity, but that during the course of reinforcement with pleased adult attention for climbing on the frame, this behavior greatly increased, finally exceeding 50% of the child's morning. (Climbing on other objects was not scored during this period.) There then followed five days during which the teachers ignored any climbing on the frame, but attended to all other appropriate activities. The rate of climbing on the frame promptly fell virtually to zero, though the child climbed on other apparatus and was consistently given attention for this. Another five days of reinforcement of the use of the climbing frame immediately restored the climbing-frame behavior to a high stable level, always in excess of 40% of the boy's play time. After this, the teachers began an intermittent program of reinforcement for climbing on any other suitable objects, as well as vigorous active play of all sorts, in an effort to generalize the increased vigorous activity. Frame-climbing weakened considerably, being largely replaced by other climbing activities, which were now scored again as data. Activities such as tricycle-riding and running were not systematically recorded due to difficulties in reliably scoring them. It is clear from the data obtained, however, that climbing activities were thoroughly generalized by this final procedure. Checks made the following school year in another play yard indicated that vigorous climbing had become a stable part of his behavior repertoire.

SUMMARY AND DISCUSSION

The above studies systematically examined effects of adult attention on some problem behaviors of normal preschool children. The findings in each case clearly indicated that for these children adult attention was a strong positive reinforcer. That is, the behavior which was immediately followed by a teacher's giving the child attention rose rapidly to a high rate, and the rate fell markedly when adult attention was withheld from that behavior and concurrently given to an incompatible behavior. While it seems reasonable that for most young children adult attention may be a positive reinforcer, it is also conceivable that for some children adult attention may be a negative reinforcer. That is, the rate of a behavior may decrease when it is immediately followed by the attention of an adult, and rise again as soon as the adult withdraws. Actually, for a few children observed at the preschool, it has been thought that adult attention was a negative reinforcer. This seemed to be true, for instance, in the case of the climbing-frame child. Before the study was initiated, the teachers spent several weeks attempting to make themselves positively reinforcing to the child. This they did by staying at a little distance from him and avoiding attending directly to him until he came to them for something. At first, his approaches were only for routine help, such as buttoning his coat. On each of these occasions they took care to be smilingly friendly and helpful. In time, he began making approaches of other kinds, for instance, to show a toy. Finally, when a teacher approached him and commented with interest on what he was doing, he continued his play instead of stopping, hitting out, or running off. However, since his play remained lethargic and sedentary, it was decided that special measures were necessary to help him progress more rapidly. It was the use and effects of these special measures that constituted the study. Clearly, however, adult attention must be or become positively reinforcing to a child before it can be successfully used to help him achieve more desirably effective behaviors.

Studies such as those reported here seem to imply that teachers may help many children rapidly through systematic programming of their adult social reinforcements. However, further research in this area seems necessary. Some of our own studies now in progress suggest that guidance on the basis of reinforcement principles may perhaps bring rapidly into use only behaviors which are already available within the repertory of the child. If the desired behavior requires skills not yet in the child's repertory, then the process of developing those skills from such behaviors as the child has may require weeks or months. For example, a four-year-old child who could verbalize but who very rarely spoke was helped to speak freely within several days. On the other hand, a child of the same age who had never verbalized required a lengthy shaping process that involved reinforcing first any vocalization, and then gradually more appropriate sounds and combinations of sounds. The latter study was still incomplete at the close of a year of work. The time required to develop social behaviors in isolate children has likewise varied considerably, presumably for the same reason.

Although the teachers conducted the studies in the course of carrying out their regular teaching duties, personnel in excess of the usual number were necessary. The laboratory school was staffed with one teacher to no more than six children, making it possible to assign to one teacher the role of principal "reinforcer teacher" in a study. The teacher was responsible for giving the child immediate attention whenever he behaved in specified ways. In addition, observers were hired and trained to record the behavior of each child studied. Each observer kept a record in ten-second intervals of his subject's behavior throughout each morning at school. Only with such staffing could reinforcement contingencies be precisely and consistently administered and their effects recorded.

Unless the effects are recorded, it is easy to make incorrect judgments about them. Two instances illustrate such fallibility. A boy in the laboratory preschool frequently pinched adults. Attempts by the teachers to ignore the behavior proved ineffective, since the pinches were hard enough to produce at least an involuntary startle. Teachers next decided to try to develop a substitute behavior. The selected patting as a logical substitute. Whenever the child reached toward a teacher, she attempted to forestall a pinch by saying, "Pat, Davey," sometimes adding, "Not pinch," and then strongly approving his patting, when it occurred. Patting behavior increased rapidly to a high level. The teachers agreed that they had indeed succeeded in reducing the pinching behavior through substituting patting. Then they were shown the recorded data. It showed clearly that although patting behavior was indeed high, pinching behavior continued at the previous level. Apparently, the teachers were so focused on the rise in patting behavior that, without the objective data, they would have erroneously concluded that development of a substitute behavior was in this case a successful technique. A second example illustrates a different, but equally undesirable, kind of erroneous assumption. A preschool child who had to wear glasses (Wolf, Risley, and Mees, 1964) developed a pattern of throwing them two or three times per day. Since this proved expensive, it was decided that the attendants should put him in his room for ten minutes following each glasses-throw. When the attendants were asked a few days later how the procedure was working, they said that the glasses-throwing has not diminished at all. A check of the records, however, showed that there was actually a marked decrease. The throwing dropped to zero within five days. Presumably, the additional effort involved in carrying out the procedure had given the attendants an exaggerated impression of the rate of the behavior. Recorded data, therefore, seem essential to accurate objective assessments of what has occurred.

The findings in the studies presented here accord generally with results of laboratory research on social development reviewed in this journal by Horowitz (1963). The importance of social reinforcement was also noted by Bandura (1963) in his investigations of imitation. Gallwey (1964) has replicated the study of an isolate child discussed here, with results "clearly confirmatory of the effectiveness of the technique." Further studies in school situations that can combine the function of research with that of service seem highly desirable.

REFERENCES

Allen, K. Eileen, Hart, Betty M., Buell, Joan S., Harris, Florence R., & Wolf, M. M. Effects of social reinforcement on isolate behavior of a nursery school child. *Child. Develop.*, 1964, 35, 511–518.

Bandura, Albert. The role of imitation in personality development. *J. Nursery Ed.*, 1963, 18, 207–215.

Gallwey, Mary, Director of the Nursery School, Washington State University, Pullman, Wash., 1964. Personal communication.

Harris, Florence R., Johnston, Margaret K., Kelley, C. Susan, & Wolf, M. M. Effects of positive social reinforcement on regressed crawling of a nursery school child. *J. Ed. Psychol.*, 1964, 55, 35–41.

Hart, Betty M., Allen, K. Eileen, Buell, John S., Harris, Florence R., & Wolf, M. M. Effects of social reinforcement on operant crying. *J. Exp. Child Psychol.* In press.

Horowitz, Frances Degen. Social reinforcement effects on child behavior. *J. Nursery Ed.*, 1963, 18, 276–284.

Johnston, Margaret K., Kelley, C. Susan, Harris, Florence R., Wolf, M. M., & Baer, D. M. Effects of positive social reinforcement on isolate behavior of a nursery school child. Unpublished manuscript.

Johnston, Margaret K., Kelley, C. Susan, Harris, Florence R., & Wolf, M. M. An application of reinforcement principles to development of motor skills of a young child. Unpublished manuscript.

Landreth, Catherine. *Education of the Young Child.* New York: Wiley, 1942.

Read, Katherine H. *The Nursery School* (2nd ed.). Philadelphia: Saunders, 1955.

Standing, E. M. *Maria Montessori, Her Life and Work.* Fresno: American Library Guild, 1959.

Taylor, Katherine W. *Parents Cooperative Nursery Schools.* New York: Teachers College, Columbia University, 1954.

Wolf, Montrose M., Risley, T. R., & Mees, H. L. Application of operant conditioning procedures to the behavior problems of an autistic child. *Behav. Res. Ther.*, 1964, 1, 305–312.

AN AGE-IRRELEVANT CONCEPT OF DEVELOPMENT *

Donald M. Baer

Development Is Learning. Baer's position on child development strongly contrasts with the Freudian approach described by Anna Freud, Erik Erikson, and the Committee on Adolescence. While they see child behavior in terms of a sequence of naturally occurring biological states which interact with the child's social environment, Baer sees child development in terms of how the child was reinforced. To Baer, developmental or "age" differences in children are primarily due to the differences in how they were reinforced; thus, developmental problems turn out to be learning problems. Instead of waiting and hoping that nature will take its course with haphazard reinforcement, it is up to teachers and parents to plan learning experiences in which the child will be rewarded for the right actions.

It seems clear that the great majority of developmental psychologists study children. Many of this majority study children almost exclusively. Thus one meaning of developmental psychology may be, quite simply, *child psychology*: the behavioral characteristics of children, the processes responsible for these characteristics, and their future consequences. Of course, most psychologists characterize themselves and their journals by the processes they study, rather than their usual experimental subject. Thus we have physiological, sensory, perceptual, and clinical psychology, rather than monkey, rat, pigeon, or ambulatory-schizophrenic psychology. However, this need not be an important objection to the concept of child psychology.

The equation of developmental psychology with child psychology has other problems. The most striking of these is the heterogeneity of children, such that a child psychology derived from the study of infants will be quite different in many ways than that derived from ten-year-olds. One solution to the possibly unmanageable diversity of child psychology is to concentrate on a particular sub-child psychology, on the grounds, perhaps, of the intrinsic fascination of this type, or more prosaically, its availability.

There is another way to respond to the apparently unmanageable diversity of child psychology. Any diversity can be managed if it can be catalogued in a systematic manner, and if the cataloging system itself is not too diverse. Child psychologists have noted that the age of the child is exactly such a cataloging device. It is a simple linear dimension, based

*From Donald M. Baer, "An Age-Irrelevant Concept of Development," *Merrill-Palmer Quarterly of Behavior and Development* 16, no. 3 (1970): 238–245, by permission of the author. Donald M. Baer is Professor of Human Development at the University of Kansas.

exclusively upon time. Time is an operationally definable concept. A technology has been aimed at its precise definition for some centuries. However, child psychology has rarely required this sort of accuracy. It has found it more than sufficient simply to note the daily sunsets and mediate their succession with a calendar, to produce a useful concept of age.

The basic virtue of age, however, is that it really does manage the diversity of child behavior. It organizes the differences between infants and ten-year-olds by laying them out ten points away from one another on a scale of years. More important than that, it makes the ten-year-old look like he belongs in the same textbook with the infant, simply by presenting the behavior of one-year-olds, two-year-olds, three-year-olds, and all other children of intermediate age, *in order*. An ordering by age, it appears, is at the same time an ordering on many other dimensions of behavior: elaboration, precision, complexity, strength, amount, variety, and internal organization.

Consequently, a new psychology emerges: *age psychology* replaces, or subsumes, child psychology. The age-cataloging psychologist does not restrict himself to the study of a single sub-type of child so as to avoid diversity. His essential technique is the ordering of that diversity, and the more diversity, the better his chance to note its orderliness. He studies children only because they represent a condition of the organism in which a great deal of behavior does in fact vary in an orderly way. Typically, as age increases beyond childhood, behavior change becomes less thoroughly ordered by it, and the interest of the age psychologist wanes correspondingly. Late in life, age change may again take on a powerful function in correlating with behavior change; thus a developmental psychology, concerning this time of senescence, again is possible. Furthermore, the target of the age psychologist is that period in *any* organism when age change orders behavior change. Thus he may study young monkeys rather than young children, and still speak to a warmly receptive Society for Research in Child Development.

The research design of the age psychologist consequently has a single distinctive feature: the age of his subjects is an organizing variable in his studies. What worries me is that my own studies do not include age as an independent variable. Even so, I feel strongly that they are developmental studies. They use environmental variation, they achieve a certain control over behavior, and they are aimed *exactly* at developmental change—but they do not include age as a variable.

Let me begin to defend the developmental character of my own studies by pointing to someone else's instead. In 1958, Wendell Jeffrey published a report which greatly clarified my own partially formulated ideas about development. (However, let it be clear that Jeffrey cannot be blamed for any errors I commit in response to his design.) His study (1958) was concerned with mediational processes in children. As a case in point, he had examined the ability of four-year-old children to discriminate left from right. The left-right discrimination was embodied in two stimulus cards, each a picture of a stick figure pointing either to its left or to its right. The child was asked to learn that the figure pointing off to the left was called "Jack"; the one pointing off to the right, "Jill." The left-right difference was the only stimulus dimension distinguishing the cards. The children were shown these cards in a random order and were reinforced for correct naming. It seems clear that older Ss, say seven-year-olds, could have learned this task quite readily. Jeffrey's four-year-olds, however, did not; as a group, the largely remained at chance levels of guessing, even after 80 trials. Thus, it begins to qualify as developmental research: an age difference could organize a major difference in the response of children to a given teaching technique. All that is missing is the actual testing of some seven-year-olds.

Jeffrey, however, continued with the four-year-olds who did not learn to discriminate left from right—Jack from Jill. He presented them with a slightly different problem to learn. Showing them the same cards while they were seated at a table, he asked them not to name the cards, but instead to make a distinctive motor response to each figure. In response to the card pointing off to their left, the children were to reach out to their left and touch a pushbutton mounted on the left side of the table-top. In response to the card pointing off to their right, the children were to reach out to their right and touch a pushbutton mounted on the right side of the table-top. The four-year-olds who had failed to make different *verbal* responses to the figures now quickly learned to make different *reaching* responses to them.

I think it worthwhile to point out that this phase of the study was not developmental research according to the criterion of age. The children were still four years old. All that had been shown was that with these techniques, these four-year-olds could discriminate particular motor responses to certain stimuli but could not discriminate particular verbal responses to them.

After the children had learned the correct reaching response to each of the stick figures, they were once again returned to the original naming problem. But now most of the children learned the discrimination quite readily.

Let me assume that control groups of four-year-olds who were given some innocuous activity during a break between two sessions with the Jack and Jill problem would still have failed to learn the discrimination during the second session. Let me also assume that a certain self-selection by Jeffrey's subjects did not alter the outcome of the study in any significant way. Those are not the kinds of design characteristics which I want to discuss. What I want to emphasize is that by the end of the study, the four-year-olds apparently had *developed.* They were not older than at the beginning, but their Jack and Jill learning behavior had become functionally like that of seven-year-olds. Jeffrey may well have shown us an effective developmental mechanism. The first part of his study had suggested that if a four-year-old who cannot solve the left-right problem is simply allowed to grow three years older, he will probably be able to solve it then. What is it that happens during those years? Obviously, various processes of development go on; but the demonstration of an age difference is not thereby the demonstration of one or more of these developmental processes. On the other hand, the second and third parts of Jeffrey's study point to exactly an environmental process which *can* produce that delightful ability of a seven-year-old to tell his Jack from his Jill.

It may be asked: is that what happens during the three years? Do four-year-olds begin to discriminate motor responses to stimuli differing on various left-right dimensions, such that about three years later the Jack and Jill problem will be one they can easily mediate with some already existing part of their repertoire? I don't know, of course. What Jeffrey's study tells us is that such a mechanism is a demonstrated possibility. It is not merely logical; it is feasible.

In my opinion, Jeffrey's design is the essence of developmental research: it describes a *possible process* of development. In my opinion, it is the process of development, not merely the *outcome* of development, which should be our subject matter.

Consequently, I have one more suggestion to make about Jeffrey's design. The "missing" part of it should not be considered essential to its status as developmental research. That missing part was the demonstration that seven-year-olds could learn the left-right discrimination quite readily. With this study, restricted entirely to four-year-olds, it seems to me that we know exactly as much about a developmental process relevant to left-right discrimination as we could learn from a larger design including seven-year-olds. The age difference is irrelevant to the developmental process displayed in the study. The only children in whom we know that this process operated are the four-year-olds of the study. Seven-year-olds are an essentially mysterious group; we do not know what process gives them their ability to make left-right discriminations. Hence the developmental aspects of the study, as I see them, are restricted to the actual study, in which age was *not* a variable.

Let me move to a different study, which also combines developmental and non-developmental aspects. In this case, I am referring to an unpublished study by Jill McCleave, conducted at the University of Washington a few years ago as her senior honors thesis. I advised her, and did do on the assumption that development is largely an age-irrelevant concept.

Jill studied a single child. He was enrolled in the University's Laboratory Preschool, and was a much-studied boy. During most of his early years, he had suffered from cataracts. In addition to a good deal of visual deprivation, he had developed tantrum and self-destructive behaviors which were so severe that they effectively overcame all efforts of his parents to control and teach him. Montrose Wolf, Todd Risley, and Haydon Mees undertook the extinction of his tantrum and other destructive behaviors:

and trained his parents in certain techniques of maintaining and extending these repertoires (1965). The child was then enrolled in preschool, largely to build and elaborate a repertoire of social interaction with other children—a class of behaviors which, initially, he lacked almost completely. While he was there, it seemed reasonable to do something about the effects of his early visual deprivation, so that he might be able to learn to read when he entered the public school's special education system the next year. Jill McCleave took on that project. Essentially, she meant to develop discriminations of small, complex visual stimuli, eventually culminating in letter recognition. She used a variety of reinforcers, ranging from social to ice cream, choosing whatever worked well at the time.

Much of this training went along quite smoothly. Some of it went so well that I would not insist on calling it developmental research. If it needs a systematic label, it could be called the discrimination of differentiated verbal operants to visual stimuli by differential reinforcement, or, in simpler terms, calling an "A" and "A" and not a "V," calling a "Y" a "Y" and not an "X," and the like. When I was a boy, we called that learning. Subsequently, I have found that reinforcement, punishment, extinction, discrimination, and differentiation are better defined terms. However, one may use "learning" as an inclusive term to refer to any combination of the previously mentioned processes which produce behavior change.

Jill McCleave found that most of the letters were quickly learned by the boy. That is, she set up reinforcement and extinction contingencies for the verbal responses he might make to various letters. For the most part, these contingencies produced their usual effects, and the correct verbal response soon was attached only to the corresponding letter. That could be called development. But it is also called the discrimination of differentiated verbal operants to visual stimuli through differential reinforcement, or learning; and still another label seems the last thing that anyone would need.

However, in a few instances, the reinforcement and extinction contingencies did *not* produce the expected effect. The letter "C," for example, could be chosen from a group of letters when asked for, but was as likely to be put down backward as forward. The boy did not discriminate a forward C from a backward C, even when differentially reinforced for doing so. Similarly, he had trouble with a few other letters, and the classic confusion between lower case "b" and "d," and "p" and "q," seemed very likely in his future reading. To avoid this, Jill resorted to techniques other than the standard learning procedures she had used so far, and the outcome appeals to me as another example of clearly developmental research.

First, she began showing the boy displays of five letters at a time. Four of the letters were forward C's, and the fifth was a backward C. He was asked to choose the letter that was different. The position of the backward C among the four ordinary C's varied randomly from trial to trial, of course. Under these conditions, despite differential reinforcement, the boy repeatedly failed to discriminate forward C's from backward C's. He showed a similar failure to discriminate a few other letters in their forward and backward orientations. Yet, at the same time, he was quickly mastering all other letters of the alphabet in this type of problem, and so his specific failures could not be attributed to a general ineffectiveness of the learning techniques being used. Consequently, Jill had to try something else.

She introduced displays in which the backward C was appreciably larger than the forward C's. The boy immediately achieved perfect discrimination. Therefore, on successive presentations, randomly varying the position of the backward C, Jill had its size shrink until it was the same size as the ordinary C's. The boy continued to discriminate perfectly until the last stage, when all C's were the same size; he then reverted to his usual chance level. Jill had to try something else again.

She introduced displays containing four ordinary C's and an "O." A "C," of course, is simply an "O" with a gap in its perimeter on the right side. However, the boy could discriminate C's from O's, and immediately reached perfect performance. Now, Jill began to degrade the O in the direction of a backward C: she presented displays in which a very small gap was opened on the left side of the O. That made it a backward C, but one which was very like an O. The boy continued to discriminate perfectly. As the presentations proceeded, the gap in the O-like backward C gradually opened and became the standard backward C. Nevertheless, the boy's discrimination remained perfect. Thus, at the end of one session of these trials, he was performing a problem at which he had consistently failed for many previous sessions. Now Jill examined him again on the other letters which previously he had failed to discriminate in their forward or backward orientations. All of them were immediately discriminated, without any special techniques of training being applied to them. Perhaps some pattern of visual inspection of small forms was developed in the "C" exercise which generalized to the other problems. At any rate, this is another example of what I am calling developmental research.

Now, I can better generalize this age-irrelevant concept of development, and perhaps I can contrast it to learning at the same time. I argued previously that the mere demonstration of a behavior change over time was unsatisfyingly mysterious to me. I wanted to know the process which produced the change, not just its outcome or its typical calendar schedule. Learning procedures, in their considerable variety, are exactly behavior-changing processes. But they need not be called developmental processes for two reasons. One is that they already have names which are considerably more precise than "learning" and tremendously more precise than "development." The other is that a particular learning procedure may not produce its expected effect in an organism, *unless it occurs at the right time.* Jeffrey's study and McCleave's study both showed just that. But both studies also showed that the "right time" was not an age, but a point in a sequence of experiences. Both studies also used nothing but learning procedures: patterns of reinforcement, punishment, extinction, differentiation, and discrimination, in general. Such procedures take time to produce their effects, *but they do not take much time*. Consequently, even sequences of these procedures will not take much time. In my opinion, they rarely will take enough time to require calendar-sized units for their application. At least, they will not require much time if they are applied promptly, one after another, in the effective sequence. Consequently, age has no relevance to development; sequence, or *program*, has.

The natural environment should not be expected to apply a correct sequence of learning procedures to the typical organism in the quickest possible order. The natural environment very likely exposes an organism to a great variety of learning procedures, almost constantly. Within its pattern of presentation, many correct sequences no doubt are imbedded—as are many *more* incorrect sequences. Natural sequencing thus is often inefficient sequencing. Jeffrey's four-year-olds required only about half an hour to become functionally similar to seven-year-olds in a particular left-right problem, when their instructor knew what he was about. It is illuminating that natural sequencing takes something approaching three years. If such findings are general, it would indicate that the age-based concept of development reflects two things: very poor programming by nature, and a thorough ignorance of how to do better in the age-cataloging psychologist. That ignorance, I think, is not likely to be improved by institutionalizing nature's bad programming into an age-based concept of development. If I am right, a great deal of that aging is a thorough waste of time.

This age-irrelevant concept of development hence is simply a sequence-relevant, or sequence-dependent, concept of learning. Both Freud and Piaget make heavy use of the same idea, but in two tremendously different ways. Both seem to rely upon sequential processes which are unrealistically slow, in my opinion. Those lazy successions of their stages simply do not remind me of the changes that are seen in organisms whose environments press them toward development. This is especially true when the organism's environment is under constant experimental analysis by an investigator who *knows* that it need not take this long. Freud and Piaget also do not seem to envision any reasonable *variety* of effective environmental sequences. It seems to me implicit in modern behavioral technology that there must be quite some number of environmental programs, or sequences, which will bring an organism to any specified developmental outcome. This is a very happy characteristic, I suggest, if it is a correct one. It allows for alternative programs of instruction when a particular one is not possible; thus it suggests that behaviorally, it is rarely too late—or too early— for a good outcome.

Looking back over this argument, it must be apparent that it derives from the typically quick effects produced by learning procedures, such that even programs or sequences of them will not require enough time to justify measurement in terms of age. I am sure it is clear that I rely upon learning mechanisms because they are the ones that I know something about. If there are other important and unavoidable mechanisms of behavior change which intrinsically require much more time to produce their effects, then my argument fails to that extent. Learning technology, as I know it, is comprehensive, powerful, flexible, and readily amenable to experimental study and to practical application. Consequently, it seems thoroughly reasonable to build a concept of development squarely upon that technology. The concept that results—to summarize it for the final time—is that to produce certain behavioral changes, the procedures of learning technology, which ordinarily work in isolation, in this case may be effective only if applied in a correct sequence to a well-chosen series of behaviors. There must be many such sequences for any specified behavioral outcome; and the sequences are not intrinsically lengthy in time. Thus, development is behavior change which requires programming; and programming requires time, but not enough of it to call it age. That, I think, is exactly what Sidney Bijou and I had in mind when, in our first volume of a book called *Child Development* (1961), we defined development as "progressive changes in the way an organism's behavior interacts with the environment" (p. 1). Development in this argument is based upon learning, but is slightly super-ordinate to learning, as a concept. If anyone feels that the programming of learning procedures is so slightly super-ordinate to the learning procedures themselves that it does not deserve the status of a separate concept, that will not distress me at all. And if anyone should suggest that programming is, in fact, *sub*ordinate to the concept of learning, again I shall not be disturbed. Perhaps that is why the program for this symposium suggests that I will present a *learning* concept, in contrast to Eugene Gollin's presentation of a *developmental* concept.

REFERENCES

Bijou, S. W. & Baer, D. M. *Child Development*. Vol. I, New York: Appleton-Century-Crofts, 1961.

Jeffrey, W. E. Variables in early discrimination learning: I. Motor responses in the training of left-right discrimination. *Child Development*, 1958, 29, 269–275.

Kessen, W. Research design in the study of developmental problems. Chapter 2 in P. H. Mussen (Ed.), *Handbook of Research Methods in Child Development*. New York: Wiley, 1960.

Wolf, M. M., Risley, T. R., & Mees, H. Application of operant conditioning procedures to the behavior problems of an autistic child. *Behav. Res. Ther.*, 1964, 1, 305–312.

BEHAVIORAL SELF-CONTROL:
POWER TO THE PERSON *

Michael J. Mahoney and Carl E. Thoresen

Control Thyself. Why do some people persist in erroneously thinking that behavioral psychologists are out to manipulate other people against their wills and that they primarily want control over others? These are favorite charges by people who have only shallow knowledge of behavioral psychology. The goal which knowledge is used for depends on the person using it, and the ways that laws of human activity are used are similar to the ways that chemical and biological laws are used. When we know them, we can use them, and their use depends on the decisions and desires of the people who use them. Just as we have employed knowledge of chemistry, physics, and biology to give us more control over our world and ourselves, we can use psychological knowledge that way too. When somebody learns behavioral principles, he can use them to implement his own decisions better and to reach more of his own goals. Perhaps one reason behavioral psychologists give the impression of being manipulators is that they too often judge their success by their ability to change others. In this article, Mahoney and Thoresen show that teaching people to achieve their own goals through applying behavioral principles can also be a behavioral goal.

How many times have you set out to stop smoking, lose weight, restrain your temper, or improve your relations with another person? Like most people, you may have admonished yourself to exercise some will power and really make a go of it. But then, after some brief and minor progress, your resolution fell victim to forgetfulness, loss of motivation, or any of the other popular excuses for unsuccessful self-control. Frustrated and beaten, you may have decided that your habit wasn't so bad after all—not all smokers develop cancer—or that you are "naturally" inclined toward obesity, temperamental behavior, or the like. You may even have decided that you simply don't have what it takes, namely the "will power," to master your vices. All too many efforts at self regulation follow this pattern.

The notion of self-control is often associated with the ideals of freedom and self-improvement. A free person is one who guides and directs his own actions. He is the master of himself and his immediate environment. Moreover, we value self-control because of its role in the survival of our society and culture. One measure of a "civilized" society is the degree to which its inhabitants direct, maintain, and coordinate their activities with-

*From Michael J. Mahoney and Carl E. Thoresen, "Behavioral Self-Control: Power to the Person," *Educational Researcher* (October, 1972), pp. 5–7, by permission of the authors. Carl Thoreson and Michael Mahoney are connected with the Center for Research and Development in Teaching, Stanford University. They are the authors of *Behavioral Self-Control* (Holt, Rinehart & Winston, 1974).

out external coercion. If more individuals could develop effective self-management skills, the need for professional helpers and the number of passive, "you help me" patients might be sharply diminished.

The term "self-control" has meant different things to different people. Its most popular synonym, by far, has been "will power"—a vaguely defined inner force. Other definitions have emphasized personality traits or supernatural forces. One of the oldest examples of effective self-control was reported by Homer in describing the travels of Odysseus. To manage the bewitching effects of the Sirens, Odysseus had his oarsmen fill their ears with beeswax. To manage himself he commanded his men to tie him to the mast after warning them not to release him under any circumstances. Instead of beseeching the gods for aid or admonishing himself to exercise his will power, Odysseus altered some important environmental factors.

Vague notions and mysticism, have dominated our perspectives on self-control. Unable to fully understand how some individuals have been able to demonstrate self-control in the face of very trying circumstances, we have called their capacity "will power," or have attributed their behavior to the influence of some supernatural entity or hitherto hidden personality trait. This way of thinking about the problem has retarded understanding and discouraged research by its circularity. The person who demonstrates self-control by resisting a major temptation, such as the heavy smoker who quits cold turkey, is often described as having will power. How do we know he has will power? Well, he quit smoking, didn't he? Observing a self-regulative behavior, inferring will power, and then using the latter to "explain" the former is an all too frequent journey in discussions of self-control. It does not take us beyond the behavior to be explained. If John's unsuccessful attempt to lose weight can be attributed to his lack of will power, then we need not look any further for causes (or solutions). The question is whether conceiving of self-control as the exercise of will is useful in understanding and self-regulatory processes. To date, the consensus among people who have studied self-control is that the volitional approach has seriously impaired the collection and interpretation of knowledge about self-management.

What are the alternatives to the Will Power party? If we had listened to Homer many centuries ago, perhaps our efforts toward understanding self-control would not have gone so far astray. The key to Odysseus's success was in recognizing that self-control is integrally bound up with immediate environmental considerations. During the past decade we have again learned that an individual's ability to control his own actions is a function of his knowledge of and control over situational factors. A rapidly expanding body of evidence indicates that effective, durable methods of self-regulation can be established if attention is given to the significant relationships between the person and his environment. Indeed, preliminary studies have pointed toward the possibility of creating a "technology" of behavioral self-control—a set of procedures that the individual can learn to use in directing and managing his own internal and external actions (Thoresen & Mahoney, in press).

The acquisition of these self-control skills is dependent on the person's ability to identify patterns and causes in the behaviors to be regulated—to pick out cues or events that frequently precede overeating, for example, or to notice the consequences that often follow smoking. The Greek maxim "Know thyself" might be paraphrased as "Know thy controlling variables." Beyond this, a person must know how he can alter the factors that influence his actions in order to bring about the changes he desires. In effect he must become a scientist investigating himself. He begins by observing what goes on, recording and analyzing personal data; he learns to use certain techniques to change specific things, such as thought patterns or his surroundings; and finally he examines the data about himself to see whether the desired change has occurred.

The assessment part of this model is worth discussing further, since people are not accustomed to being systematic about observing their own actions. Attending to the everyday situations where the problem behavior occurs is crucial. What happens, for example, just before Carol, the incessant smoker, reaches for another cigarette? The "antecedents" or prior events include what Carol is thinking, what she is saying to herself, and perhaps what she is imagining. Prior events also include the physical and social setting: two friends, a cup of coffee, an ashtray on the table. The immediate consequences of having that cigarette also demand careful observation, in terms of internal reactions as well as the actions of others. Examining the ABCs—the Antecedents of a Behavior and its Consequences—helps reveal what may be controlling the behavior.

Behavioral self-control generally involves three factors—the specification of a behavior, the identification of antecedent cues and environmental consequences, and the alteration of some of the antecedents and/or consequences. But how does one do it? Preliminary research has shown three major approaches (Thoresen & Mahoney, in press). At least one of them has been present in every successful self-control attempt thus far reported.

BECOMING AWARE

The first strategy is simply self-observation. This means that the person attends to his own actions and records their occurrence in order to check up on himself and evaluate his progress. As mentioned earlier, few people are in the habit of carefully monitoring their own behavior. The use of golf counters, diaries, or wall charts can encourage accurate self-observation. The individual who records his own behavior not only becomes more aware of himself but also receives both immediate and cumulative feedback on what he is (or is not) doing. For example, a weight chart in the bathroom might show trends in weight gain or weight loss (such as large increases around weekends and holidays) and it might point up gradual changes that would otherwise go unnoticed. Self-recorded data may also provide significant information on the rate of occurrence of a behavior, its eliciting cues, and its consequences. Recording devices like those mentioned above help make objective self-evaluation possible: if my personal data indicate that I am changing in a desired direction, then I have good reason to feel positive about myself.

The research evidence on self-observation seems to indicate that desired behaviors can often be increased simply by being recorded. The implications of the data on self-observation of undesired behaviors are not yet clear. In a recent study, an adolescent girl concerned with doing better schoolwork in a history class was asked to observe and record her studying in class (Broden, Hall, & Mitts, 1971). In one week this procedure alone increased her studying in class from about 30 percent of the available time to over 80 percent, an increase that continued after the self-observation procedure had been gradually phased out. Self-observation in this study and others can be viewed as a kind of behavioral sensitivity training. The systematic recording of a particular action—in this case, studying or not studying—sensitizes the person to himself. Although further research is needed to determine the most effective types of self-observation for specific kinds of behavior, we may tentatively conclude, that the systematic recording of one's own behavior can sometimes have a dramatic effect on that behavior.

ALTERING THE ENVIRONMENT

The second self-control strategy might be labeled environmental planning. This involves changing one's environment so that either the cues preceding a behavior or the immediate consequences of it are changed. Odysseus changed his environment, for example, by altering the antecedent cues for his men and by arranging for his own behavior to be controlled when temptation arose. Often, environmental planning involves eliminating or avoiding situations in which a choice is necessary. Avoiding cigarette machines, buying only dietetic snacks, and carrying only minimal amounts of money are effective ways of controlling smoking, overeating, and overspending. Other strategies rely on rearranging environmental cues. Obesity is often affected by social and physical cues that prompt eating in the absence of physiological hunger. Thus, many people eat to avoid waste (particularly in restaurants) or because a clock tells them to eat. Environmental cues such as a television set, a cookie jar, or a kitchen can also elicit eating behavior. Stuart (1967), in an early study on behavioral self-control of overeating, showed that individuals trained to detect and alter maladaptive eating cues significantly reduced their weight. This success was attained by such strategies as restricting eating to a specific and novel room, making food cues less salient around the home, and gradually slowing the pace of eating.

This finding has since been shown to be highly consistent and applicable to behaviors other than overeating. Upper and Meredith (1970), for example, have reported a successful study on smoking reduction. They trained smokers to break longstanding, cue-elicited smoking patterns by altering the physical cues to smoke. A smoker was asked to record his initial daily smoking rate. The average time between cigarettes was then computed, and the person was asked to wear a small portable timer. Initially, the timer was set to buzz whenever the average inter-cigarette time elapsed. The smoker was instructed to smoke only after the timer buzzed. By establishing this new environmental cue to smoke, previous cueing situations, such as the completion of a meal, a conversation with a friend, or a stress experience, were displaced. Gradually, the interval between cigarettes was increased until the frequency of smoking was greatly reduced.

These and other studies have shown that altering the environment can help the person modify chronic and resistant behavior problems.

ALTERING THE CONSEQUENCES OF BEHAVIOR

The third self-control strategy might be labeled behavioral programming. Here the individual concentrates on altering the consequences of his behavior rather than its eliciting cues. Self-reward and self-punishment, are common examples of self-administered therapeutic techniques. Both internal and external events can be used as consequences in this programming. For example, self-praise, self-criticism, and pleasant or unpleasant mental imagery might be used as self-administered internal consequences for an act. External consequences might include special privileges (e.g., allowing oneself to watch a favorite television program) and/or tangible rewards (e.g., clothing, a hobby item, etc.). Private contracts ("If I do this, then I get that") are common in individual programming.

An illustration of this approach is provided by a case history of a schizophrenic young man whose problem behavior involved frequent obsessive thoughts about being physically unattractive, stupid, and brain damaged (Mahoney, 1971). After he had assessed the initial frequency of these maladaptive thoughts through self-observation, the man was instructed to punish himself by snapping a heavy-gauge rubber band against his wrist whenever he engaged in obsessional thoughts. When the frequency of these thoughts had been drastically reduced, positive self-thoughts were established and gradually increased by using a cueing procedure paired with self-reward. To "prime" these thoughts, the man was asked to write down three positive things about himself on small cards attached to his cigarette package. Whenever he reached for a cigarette he was instructed to read a positive self-statement and then reward himself with a cigarette. A "wild card" alternated with the other three and required a spontaneous, original positive self-thought.

The man soon began to generate complimentary self-thoughts without prior cueing and in the absence of smoking stimuli. Gradual fading of the treatment techniques allowed the young man to resume a normal and adaptive life without lengthy hospitalization or extended therapy. Several other studies have shown that individual programming strategies can be effective in modifying both private and observable behavior patterns.

An expanding body of literature is currently adding to our knowledge of self-control phenomena. New trends in therapy include the use of imaginal consequences (e.g., imaginary rewards and punishments), the self-control of thoughts and feelings, and the use of self-instructions. These trends point up an intriguing aspect of the area of self-control—that it may well provide grounds for a rapprochement between behavioristic and humanistic approaches to psychology (Thoresen, 1972). Research involving behavioral analyses of self-esteem, for example, seems to have incorporated both the empirical rationale and the personal relevance that have traditionally characterized two disparate factions of psychology. The term "behavioral humanism" would seem to characterize many self-control endeavors. Continuing research will enlarge our understanding of how behavioral principles can be applied to self-control. To this end, self-control researchers might appropriately adopt the slogan "Power to the Person!"

REFERENCES

Broden, M., Hall, R. V., & Mitts, B. The effect of self-recording on the classroom behavior of two eighth grade students. *Journal of Applied Behavior Analysis*, 1971, *4*, 191–200.

Mahoney, M. J. The self-management of covert behaviors: A case study. *Behavior Therapy*, 1971, *2*, 575–78.

Stuart, R. B. Behavioral control over eating. *Behavior Research and Therapy*, 1967, *5*, 357–65.

Thoresen, C. E. *Behavioral humanism*. R&D Memorandum No. 88. Stanford, Calif.: Stanford Center for Research and Development in Teaching, 1972.

Thoresen, C. E., & Mahoney, M. J. *Behavioral self-control*. New York: Holt, Rinehart & Winston, in press.

Upper, D., & Meredith, L. A stimulus-control approach to the modification of smoking behavior. *Proceedings of the 78th American Psychological Association Convention*, 1970, *5*, 739–40.

THE EFFECT OF SELF-RECORDING
ON THE CLASSROOM BEHAVIOR OF TWO
EIGHTH-GRADE STUDENTS*

Marcia Broden, R. Vance Hall, and Brenda Mitts

Teaching Self-Control. "With 28 kids in the room, I can't spend all my time passing out rewards and making behavior graphs. I'm supposed to teach, at least some of the time." Here is an excellent example of teaching students behavioral self-control instead of relying on control by the teacher. Some teachers I know who have tried this with younger children report it works well with them too. They say that drawing happy faces or sad faces works better than +'s and −'s. Notice which of these two examples works, the one that calls attention to the desired behavior and rewards it, not the one that points out mistakes. Do you mark the answers that are *right* on your students' papers, instead of the wrong ones?

The effects of self-recording on classroom behavior of two junior high school students was investigated. In the first experiment, study behavior of an eighth-grade girl in history class was recorded. Following baseline observations her counselor provided slips for the girl to record whether or not she studied in class. This resulted in an increase in study. When slips were withdrawn, study decreased and then increased once self-recording was reinstated. After teacher praise for study was increased, self-recording was discontinued without significant losses in study behavior. In the final phase, increased praise was also withdrawn and study remained at a high level. In the second experiment, the number of talk outs emitted by an eighth-grade boy were recorded during math period. Following baseline, slips for recording talk outs were issued for the first half of the period, for the second half, and then for the entire period. Talk outs decreased when self-recording was in effect and increased again when self-recording was discontinued. When self-recording was reinstituted in the final phase there was a slight, though not significant decrease in talking out when compared to the baseline condition.

Helping a student acquire appropriate study behaviors has probably been a problem since schools began. Various techniques, including counseling, special classes, and use of the leather strap have been tried. Very often these approaches have been ineffective and parents, teachers, and students have resigned themselves to a year of problems and frustration.

Since the 1960s, a concerted effort has been exerted to apply systematically behavior modification principles in the public school classroom. A number of studies have shown that giving attention for a behavior

*From Marcia Broden, R. Vance Hall, and Brenda Mitts, "The Effects of Self-Recording on the Classroom Behavior of Two Eighth-Grade Students," *Journal of Applied Behavior Analysis* 4, no. 3 (Fall, 1971): 191–199, by permission of the authors. Dr. Broden is a Research Associate with the Bureau of Child Research, University of Kansas.

immediately after it occurred caused this behavior to increase in strength, while consistently ignoring a behavior frequently resulted in a decrease in strength. Hall and Broden (1968), Hall, Lund, and Jackson (1968), and Thomas, Becker, and Armstrong (1968) successfully used this technique to affect study behavior in the classroom by having teachers attend only to study or non-disruptive behaviors while ignoring non-study or disruptive ones. Hall, Fox, Willard, Goldsmith, Emerson, Owen, Davis, and Porcia (1970) used teacher attention, feedback, praise, and other available reinforcers to control disputing and talking-out behaviors in various classrooms.

The use of behavior modification principles was expanded to include varied techniques by other experimenters. Madsen, Becker, and Thomas (1968) assessed the effect of rules as well as ignoring and praising behaviors. Peer control of arithmetic and spelling scores was demonstrated in a study by Evans and Oswalt (1968). Barrish, Saunders, and Wolf (1968) used a loss of classroom privileges to reduce out-of-seat and talking-out behaviors in a fourth grade class. Hall, Panyan, Rabon, and Broden (1968) showed that teacher attention, a study game, and loss of time for a between-period break were effective in increasing an entire class study behavior.

McKenzie, Clark, Wolf, Kothera, and Benson (1968) used a token system backed by privileges and allowances to increase academic performance in a special education classroom. Broden, Hall, Dunlap, and Clark (1970) increased study behavior in a junior high special education class using a point system in which points were redeemable for privileges available in the class and school. They demonstrated that while praise was effective in modifying behaviors, praise coupled with points issued contingently for acceptable behaviors seemed more effective at the junior high level.

Each of the methods listed, while successful, involved a relatively systematic effort on the part of the teacher to initiate the behavior change or to monitor and reinforce the desired behaviors. None of these studies dealt with the problem of what to do with a student in a room where the teacher does not want to or "cannot" work with a specific student. Such situations are often found in secondary level classrooms where teacher lectures are a primary form of instruction.

The method used in the present study was self-recording. It was initially an effort to assess whether a subject's recording of his own behavior would help increase or decrease its occurrence, and whether someone not in the classroom could modify classroom behavior. It was also an attempt to assess a procedure whereby self-recording could be withdrawn with no significant decrease in study once higher study rates had been established.

EXPERIMENT I

Subject and Setting. Liza was an eighth-grade girl enrolled in history class at Bonner Springs Junior High, Bonner Springs, Kansas. She was doing poorly in history (her grade was a D–) and had told the counselor she was interested in doing better in school. The counselor set up weekly counseling sessions with Liza but found that according to the teacher and to Liza, just talking over a problem had not carried over into the class setting.

Liza's history class met daily immediately after lunch for 40 min. The teacher, a young man, stood near the front of the room throughout most of the period. Liza sat toward the back of the room. Classes were primarily lecture sessions in which the teacher talked as he stood in the front of the class. There was some class discussion when the teacher interspersed questions within the lecture.

The counselor and the experimenter had approached the teacher about giving increased attention to Liza for study. The teacher expressed a willingness to cooperate but felt that due to the lecture format of the class and the amount of material he had to cover each day he could not consistently attend to Liza for studying. For this reason it was decided to use self-recording with the counselor as the agent for initiating and carrying out the experimental procedures.

Observation. An observer entered the classroom during a 5-min break before the class and took a seat at the back of the room. She observed for 30 min of the 40-min session, beginning when the bell rang to signify the start of class. She left during a break at the end of the class session. Pupil behaviors were recorded at the end of each 10 sec of observation. Teacher attention to Liza was recorded whenever it occurred. Liza was not told that she was being observed.

Pupil behaviors were dichotomized into study and non-study behaviors. "Study" was defined as attending to a teacher-assigned task and meant that when it was appropriate, Liza should be facing the teacher, writing down lecture notes, facing a child who was responding to a teacher question, or reciting when called upon by the teacher. "Non-study" behaviors meant that Liza was out of her seat without permission, talking out without being recognized by the teacher, facing the window, fingering non-academic objects such as her makeup, comb, purse, or working on an assignment for another class.

Data were recorded on sheets composed of double rows of squares with each square representing the passage of 10 sec of time. (See Hall, *et al.*, 1968). The top row was used to record teacher attention which was recorded whenever the teacher called on or spoke to Liza. The bottom row was used to record Liza's study or non-study behaviors.

Reliability checks were made at least once during each phase of the study. During these checks, another observer made simultaneous and independent observations. After the observation the sheets were compared and scored interval by interval for the number of intervals of agreement. The total number of intervals of agreement were divided by the total number of intervals observed and this figure was multiplied by 100 to obtain a percentage figure. Agreement of the records for this study ranged from 87 to 96% for study behavior and 100% for teacher attention.

Method. *Baseline.* Baseline data were recorded for seven days before experimental procedures began. The counselor saw the subject twice during this time for a weekly conference (a procedure followed before recording data and continued throughout the study).

Self-Recording$_1$. On the eighth day of observation, the counselor met the subject in conference and gave her a slip containing three rows of 10 squares (See Fig. 1) and directed her to record her study behavior "when she thought of it" during her history class sessions. Some aspects of study behavior were discussed at this time, including a definition of what constituted studying.

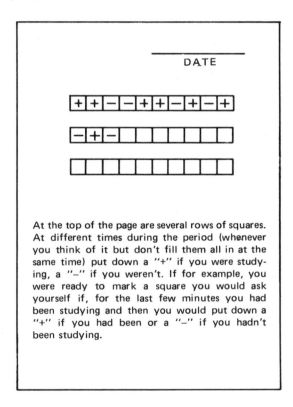

Fig. 1. Sample of self-recording sheet used by Liza.

Liza was instructed to take the slip to class each day and to record a "+" in the square if she was studying or had been doing so for the last few minutes, and a "−" if she was not studying at the time she thought to record. Sometime before the end of the school day she was to turn it in to the counselor. The slips were available each day from the counselor and could be obtained during breaks between classes. At the weekly pupil-counselor conference, the self-recording slips were discussed and the counselor praised Liza's reports of study behavior emphasizing the days when the percent of plus marks was high.

Baseline₂. Slips were not issued for five days (Days 14 through 18). When, on the second day of Baseline₂ Liza requested one, the counselor stated that she was out of slips and would tell her when she got more.

Self-Recording₂. Slips were once again handed to the subject by the counselor at some time before history period and Liza was instructed to record her study and non-study behavior.

Self-Recording Plus Praise. The teacher was asked to attend to Liza "whenever he could" and to praise her for study whenever possible. Slips for self-recording continued to be available to Liza and counselor praise continued to be issued for plus marks on the self-recording slips during the weekly conference.

Praise Only. No slips were issued to Liza. Teacher attention continued at a higher rate than during Baseline.

Baseline₃. Increased teacher attention was withdrawn.

Results. *Baseline.* Figure 2 presents a record of Liza's study behavior and of teacher verbal attention. During baseline conditions, Liza had a low rate of study (30%) despite two conferences with the counselor and promises to "really try." The mean rate of teacher attention was two times per session.

Self-Recording₁. During the Self-Recording₁ phase, when Liza began to record her classroom behavior, a significant change in study behavior was noted. It increased to 78% and remained at that approximate level for the next six days. Teacher attention remained at a mean level of two times per session.

Baseline₂. On the fourteenth day of observation, Liza was told by the counselor that no more recording slips were available. The first day under these conditions the rate of study was 70%. It then dropped to an average of 27% for the next four days. Teacher attention averaged 2.5 times per session.

Self-Recording₂. When recording slips were again issued to Liza her study rate increased to an average of 80%. However, when on two days no slips were issued (Days 20 and 27) the rate declined to 30% and 22% respectively. During this phase, the teacher gave Liza attention approximately 1.7 times per class session.

Self-Recording Plus Praise. On Day 30, the teacher was again asked to praise Liza or give her increased attention when she studied. At this point the teacher agreed to do so because Liza was now engaging in a higher

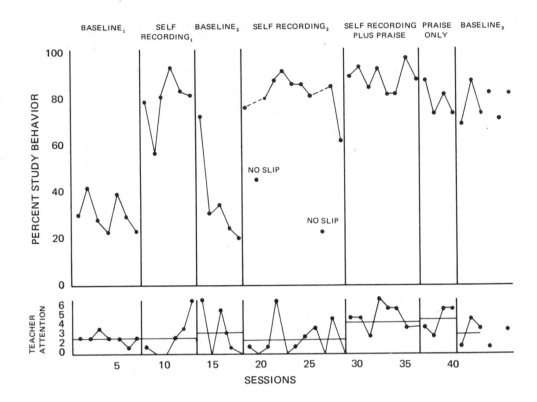

Fig. 2. A record of Liza's study behavior and/or teacher attention for study during: *Baseline*—before experimental procedures; *Self-recording₁*—Liza recorded study or non-study on slips provided by counselor; *Baseline₂*— Self-recording slips withdrawn; *Self-Recording₂*—Self-recording slips reinstated; *Self-Recording Plus Praise*—Self-recording slips continued and teacher praise for study increased; *Praise Only*—Increased teacher praise maintained and self-recording withdrawn. *Baseline₂*—Teacher praise decreased to baseline levels.

rate of study and he felt it would be easy and justifiable to do so. In this phase, teacher attention increased to 3.5 times per session. Liza continued to carry slips to class, sometimes filling them out and sometimes not. Under these conditions study increased to 88%.

Praise Only. On Day 38 the Praise Only phase was begun and slips discontinued. Teacher attention was observed to be at a mean rate of 3.7 times per session. Liza's study rate averaged 77%.

Baseline₃. The teacher was then asked to decrease the amount of attention to Liza. During this Baseline₃ phase, no marked decrease in study rate was evident, though there was some decline. The first three joined points of the Baseline₃ phase represent consecutive days following the Praise Only phase. The three separated points represent post check days with approximately one-week intervals between observations, which further indicates increased study was being maintained.

Subject's Record Vs. Observer's Record. Table I presents the levels of

Table 1. A record of percent of study recorded by the observer and by Liza during self-recording phases of Exp. I.

EXPERIMENTAL PHASE		OBSERVER	LIZA
SELF-RECORDING$_1$		78%	80%
		54%	70%
		79%	– –
		92%	63%
		82%	79%
		80%	90%
	MEAN	78%	76%
SELF-RECORDING$_2$		75%	60%
		PROBE "A"	
		78%	100%
		87%	80%
		90%	FORGOT
		84%	FORGOT
		84%	FORGOT
		79%	75%
		PROBE "B"	
		83%	90%
		59%	FORGOT
	MEAN	80%	81%
SELF-RECORDING$_3$ PLUS PRAISE		89%	FORGOT
		93%	FORGOT
		83%	FORGOT
		92%	FORGOT
		81%	66%
		81%	100%
		96%	FORGOT
		88%	100%
	MEAN	88%	89%

study recorded by Liza and the observer during the Self-Recording phases. During the Self-Recording$_1$ phase, Liza recorded study or non-study on the average of 12 times per session. There was very little correlation between Liza's and the observer's estimates of the percent of study on a day-to-day basis. Variations between records ranged up to 29%. However, the means of the overall subject-observer records were similar. For example, the mean of Liza's estimate of her study behavior during Baseline was 76%. The observer's record revealed that Liza actually studied an average of 78% of the time.

During the Self-Recording$_2$ phase, the number of times Liza recorded decreased to 11 marks per class. On four days she did not record at all. Liza's mean estimate of her study was 81%, the observer's was 80%. Again, there was little correlation between Liza's record and the observer's record on a day-to-day basis.

The number of times Liza recorded during the Self-Recording Plus Praise condition declined markedly to 2.3 times per session and Liza recorded on only three of the nine days during this experimental phase. Liza's mean estimate of study was 89%, that of the observer was 88%.

There was, of course, no self-recording during the other phases of the experiment.

EXPERIMENT II

Subject and Setting. The second subject, Stu, was an eighth-grade boy enrolled in a fifth-period math class at the same school. He was referred by his teacher, a man, who expressed a desire to find some means to "shut Stu up." He reportedly talked out in class continually, disturbing both the teacher and his classmates. The class was composed of 28 "low" achieving students. It met for 25 min and then students went to lunch, returning afterward for another 20 min of class.

Observation. Observation records of Stu's behavior were made on sheets identical to those used in the previous experiment. The category of "talking out" was added, however, to the observation code. A talk out was defined as any verbalization that occurred during class which had not been recognized by the teacher and was recorded if it occurred at any time within each 10-sec interval. Since some of Stu's talk outs were not audible to the observer, both audible talk outs and instances when Stu's lips moved while facing another student and while another student was facing him were considered as talk outs. Study behavior and teacher attention to the subject were also recorded. Reliability of observation during each experimental phase was assessed in a manner similar to that used in the first study. Agreement of the records on the number of talk outs ranged from 84 to 100%.

Method. *Baseline₁.* For nine days before experimental procedures were initiated, data were recorded during the first half (Session A) of the period. On Days 1, 4, 5, 6, and 8 data were recorded during the second half of the period (Session B) as well.

Self-Recording, Session A. During the first experimental phase, the teacher handed a slip of paper to Stu at the beginning of class with the instructions to use it and that it would be collected during lunch. A facsimile of the slip is shown in Fig. 3. On it was printed a rectangular box about 2 by 5 in. (5 by 12.5 cm) and the statement "record a mark every time you talk out without permission." at the top of the slip was a place for the subject's name and the date. No further instructions were given.

Self-Recording, Session B. Slips were not issued during Session A but were given to Stu just before Session B. No contingencies were in effect during Session A.

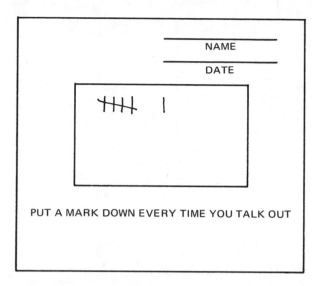

Fig. 3. Sample of self-recording sheet used by Stu.

Self-Recording (Sessions A and B)$_1$. Stu was given the slip at the beginning of class and told to record all period (both Session A and Session B). He was told the slip would be collected at the end of class.

Baseline$_2$. Self-recording slips were not issued for any part of the math period.

Self-Record (Sessions A and B)$_2$. Self-recording slips were issued and Stu was told to record talk outs for the entire period and that the slips would be collected at the end of class.

Results. *Baseline$_1$*. During the Baseline phase, Stu talked out on the average of 1.1 times per minute for the first half of the period and 1.6 times a minute during Session B. (See Fig. 4.)

Self-Recording, Session A. When the teacher began issuing slips to Stu for Session A, the frequency of his talk outs declined during Session A to 0.3 times a minute. The frequency of these talk outs during Session B, however, remained at 1.6 times a minute.

Self-Recording, Session B. After giving Stu the sheet seven days for Session A the teacher commented that "it is the second half of the period which has always been the problem," so contingencies were reversed. Slips were issued only during the second half of the period. The rate of verbalizing without permission during Session B declined to 0.5 times a minute. However, the rate of talking out during Session A, which was not under self-recording contingencies, increased to 1.2 times a minute.

Self-Recording (Sessions A and B)$_1$. When slips were issued for both A and B Sessions, the mean talk-out rate during A was 0.3 times per minute

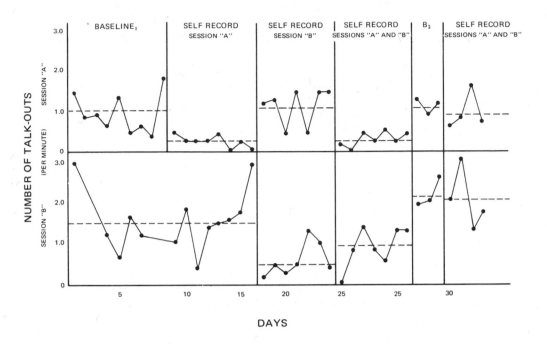

Fig. 4. A record of Stu's talking-out behavior during Sessions A and B of fifth-period math class: *Baseline₁*—Before experimental procedures; *Self-Record, Session A*—Stu recorded his talk outs during Session A only; *Self-Record, Session B*—Stu recorded his talk outs during Session B only; *Self-Record, Sessions (A and B)₁*—Stu recorded his talk outs during both math class sessions; *Baseline₂*—Return to Baseline conditions, self-recording slips withdrawn; *Self-Record (A and B)₂*—Stu recorded his talk outs for both A and B Sessions.

while that for B was 1.0 per minute, both well below baseline rates that were recorded.

Baseline₂. When slips were no longer furnished Stu during a second baseline phase, the rate of talk outs increased to a mean of 1.3 during Session A and 2.3 per minute during Session B.

Self-Recording (Sessions A and B)₂. When self-recording slips were again issued for the entire period, there was a slight but not significant decrease in the number of talk outs to a mean rate of 1.0 per minute in Session A and 2.2 per minute in Session B.

DISCUSSION

These studies indicated that it is possible to use self-recording procedures to modify behaviors of pupils in secondary-level public school classrooms. In Liza's case, self-recording was used to increase an appropriate behavior (study) while in Stu's case self-recording proved effective in decreasing an inappropriate behavior (talking out).

In the experiment with Liza, someone outside the classroom, a counselor, was able to institute procedures that brought about an increase in study to a point that the teacher was able to maintain it with his attention and/or the other reinforcers already available in the classroom. Previous research had shown that systematic teacher attention can be used to increase study rates of elementary pupils (Hall, et al., 1968; Hall, et al., 1968). Broden and Hall (1968) demonstrated that teacher attention was also effective at the junior high school level. There were indications, however, that secondary level teachers were sometimes reluctant to carry out procedures that did not seem to fit their teaching style.

In Liza's case, initially the teacher did not feel that he could systematically increase his attention for study due to the lecture-discussion format he used. On the first day of Baseline$_2$, however, when the self-recording slips had been withdrawn, Liza's study behavior had remained at a high level. An analysis of the data showed that she had received an uncharacteristically high rate of attention from the teacher on that day (five times). This indicated that it might eventually be possible to withdraw the slips and maintain high study rates and that the teacher might willingly increase his attention to Liza for study if her study rate was already at a high level. The drop in study rate on the second day and subsequent days of Baseline$_2$ indicated that Liza was still very much under the control of self-recording.

The effects of issuing self-recording slips was further confirmed in the Self-Recording$_2$ phase. When probes were inserted and she was given no slips on Days 20 and 27 there were accompanying drops in study rates on those days. It is of interest to note that study dropped on Day 27 despite the fact that by this second probe, Liza had begun "forgetting" to record her study and non-study behavior on some days. This would indicate the possibility that the slip itself had become a cue or discriminative stimulus (S^D) for study whether or not it was used for self-recording. Liza's record of her study behavior did not correlate with the observer's record. However, it is important to note that correlation between Liza's estimate and her actual behavior was not necessary to achieve or maintain high study rates.

When the slips were withdrawn in the Praise Only phase, study was maintained at an acceptable level. Even when increased praise was withdrawn in the Baseline$_3$ phase, study remained at acceptable levels. Although it would have been interesting to have continued the Baseline$_3$ phase for a longer period the experiment was terminated due to the close of the school term. Even so, the data indicated that once higher study levels were achieved and maintained for a period of time, slips and high rates of teacher attention could be withdrawn without significant reductions in study. There was some subjective evidence that Liza's increased study may have resulted in increased academic performance because her report card grade in history increased from D– to C.

Although the experiment with Stu was in many ways a replication of the first study there were several important differences. Liza had expressed a desire, in fact had requested help, to improve her study behavior. Her counselor praised her when she reported high study rates on the self-recording slips. Later, her teacher began attending to her and praising her for study once higher rates were achieved.

Stu, on the other hand, had not expressed concern or asked for help in decreasing his talking-out behavior. The teacher rather than a counselor was the agent for dispensing the self-recording slips to Stu. Another difference was that no attempt was made to differentially reinforce Stu with praise or attention for the decreases in talking out that were observed. Previous research (Hall, Fox, Willard, Goldsmith, Emerson, Owen, Davis, and Porcia, 1970) indicates that doing so would have increased the effectiveness of the procedures used. In spite of these factors it seems that initially issuing slips and having Stu record on them did affect his talking-out behavior. As in Liza's case, this was true even though there was very little correlation between the number of talk outs recorded by Stu and the observer's record. This is illustrated by the fact that on Days 10, 11, and 12 the observer's record showed that Stu's talk outs were occurring at 0.4, 0.3, and 0.3 times per minute. On the same days however, Stu recorded 1.5, 0.5, and 0.8 talk outs per minute. That self-recording had little effect during the final phase of the experiment may have been due to the fact that no contingencies were ever applied to differential rates of talking out and the slips thus lost their effectiveness. Further research will be necessary to determine if this is the case. Furthermore, the records kept of his study behavior indicated that initially self-recording of talk outs may have affected his overall study rate. This effect was not conclusive or lasting, however. When self-recording was instituted for Session A, study increased from 30% to 55%. When self-recording was instituted for Session B, study increased from 24% to 42% while it decreased to 32% in Session A. When self-recording was instituted for the entire period, however, study decreased to 24%.

Perhaps the most promising feature of self-recording will be to use it as a procedure for initiating desirable levels of appropriate behavior to a point where the teacher can more easily reinforce the desired behavior with attention, praise, grades, or other reinforcers available in the classroom.

REFERENCES

Barrish, H., Saunders, M., and Wolf, M. M. Good behavior game: effects of individual contingencies for group consequences on disruptive behavior in a regular classroom. *Journal of Applied Behavior Analysis*, 1969, 2, 119–124.

Broden, M. and Hall, R. V. *Effects of teacher attention on the verbal behavior of two junior highschool pupils*. Paper presented at Council for Exceptional Children Convention, New York, 1968.

Broden, M., Hall, R. V., Dunlap, A., and Clark, R. Effects of teacher attention and a token reinforcement system in a junior highschool special education class. *Exceptional Children*, 1970, 36, 341–349.

Evans, G. and Oswalt, G. Acceleration of academic progress through the manipulation of peer influence. *Behaviour Research and Therapy*, 1967, 5, 1–7.

Hall, R. V. and Broden, M. Behavior changes in brain-injured children through social reinforcement. *Journal of Experimental Child Psychology*, 1967, 5, 463–479.

Hall, R. V., Fox, R., Willard, D., Goldsmith, L., Emerson, M., Owen, M., Davis, F., and Porcia, E. The teacher as observer and experimenter in the modification of disputing and talking out behaviors. *Journal of Applied Behavior Analysis*, 1971, 4, 141–149.

Hall, R. V., Lund, D., and Jackson, D. Effects of teacher attention on study behavior. *Journal of Applied Behavior Analysis*, 1968, 1, 1–12.

Hall, R. V., Panyan, M., Rabon, D., and Broden, M. Teacher applied contingencies and appropriate classroom behavior. *Journal of Applied Behavior Analysis*, 1968, 1, 315–322.

Madsen, C., Jr., Becker, W., and Thomas, D. Rules, praise, and ignoring: elements of elementary classroom control. *Journal of Applied Behavior Analysis*, 1968, 1, 139–150.

McKenzie, H., Clark, M., Wolf, M., Kothers, R., and Benson, C. Behavior modification of children with learning disabilities using grades as tokens and allowances as backup reinforcers. *Exceptional Children*, 1968, 34, 745–753.

Thomas, D., Becker, W., and Armstrong, M. Production and elimination of disruptive classroom behavior by systematically varying teacher's behavior. *Journal of Applied Behavior Analysis*, 1968, 1, 35–45.

Zimmerman, E. and Zimmerman, J. The alteration of behavior in a special classroom situation. *Journal of the Experimental Analysis of Behavior*, 1962, 5, 59–60.

The authors wish to express appreciation to observer Betty Smith and to Kenneth Tewell, Robert Clark, Larry Odom, and Leo Richter of the Bonner Springs, Kansas Public Schools for their complete cooperation in making this study possible. This study is part of the research conducted at the Juniper Gardens Children's Project and is partially supported by the National Institute of Child Health and Human Development (HD-03144-03) Bureau of Child Research and Department of Human Development and Family Life, University of Kansas. Reprints may be obtained from R. Vance Hall, Juniper Gardens Children's Project, 2021 North Third Street, Kansas City, Kansas 66101.

TEACHER COMMENTS AND STUDENT PERFORMANCE: A SEVENTY-FOUR CLASSROOM EXPERIMENT IN SCHOOL MOTIVATION*

Ellis Batten Page

Where Often Is Heard An Encouraging Word, There The Students Are Learning All Day. One of the most important skills in using rewards is selecting the right ones. In this article, Page shows that a more personal and encouraging reward works better than a plain, impersonal grade. Many teachers can remember when they were students and were heartened by a personal, encouraging word, perhaps on a paper, perhaps a spoken word. Rewards can include what the student feels about his work too, and in our concentration on external rewards, it's easy to miss the important step of encouraging the student to provide his own rewards. Satisfaction of curiosity, a feeling of pride, a sense of accomplishment, these are rewards too, and it is the student who can provide his own rewards who can begin to take charge of his own learning.

Each year teachers spend millions of hours marking and writing comments upon papers being returned to students, apparently in the belief that their words will produce some result, in student performance, superior to that obtained without such words. Yet on this point solid experimental evidence, obtained under genuine classroom conditions, has been conspicuously absent. Consequently each teacher is free to do as he likes; one will comment copiously, another not at all. And each believes himself to be right.

The present experiment investigated the questions: 1. Do teacher comments cause a significant improvement in student performance? 2. If comments have an effect, which comments have more than others, and what are the conditions, in students and class, conducive to such effect? The questions are obviously important for secondary education, educational psychology, learning theory, and the pressing concern of how a teacher can most effectively spend his time.

PREVIOUS RELATED WORK

Previous investigations of "praise" and "blame," however fruitful for the general psychologist, have for the educator been encumbered by

*From Ellis B. Page, "Teacher Comments and Student Performance," *The Journal of Educational Psychology* 49, no. 4 (August, 1958): 173–181, by permission of the author. Ellis B. Page is Professor of Educational Psychology and Director of the Bureau of Educational Research at the University of Connecticut. This study was conceived as part of a doctoral dissertation and conducted in the San Diego City and County Schools while he was with San Diego Junior College.

certain weaknesses: Treatments have been administered by persons who were extraneous to the normal class situation. Tests have been of a contrived nature in order to keep students (unrealistically) ignorant of the true comparative quality of their work. Comments of praise or blame have been administered on a random basis, unlike the classroom where their administration is not at all random. Subjects have often lacked any independent measures of their performance, unlike students in the classroom. Areas of training have often been those considered so fresh that the students would have little previous history of related success or failure, an assumption impossible to make in the classroom. There have furthermore been certain statistical errors: tests of significance have been conducted as if students were totally independent of one another, when in truth they were interacting members of a small number of groups with, very probably, some group effects upon the experimental outcome.

For the educator such experimental deviations from ordinary classroom conditions have some grave implications, explored elsewhere by the present writer (5). Where the conditions are highly contrived, no matter how tight the *controls*, efforts to apply the findings to the ordinary teacher-pupil relationship are at best rather tenuous. This study was therefore intended to fill both a psychological and methodological lack by *leaving the total classroom procedures exactly what they would have been without the experiment*, except for the written comments themselves.

METHOD

Assigning the subjects. Seventy-four teachers, randomly selected from among the secondary teachers of three districts, followed detailed printed instructions in conducting the experiment. By random procedures each teacher chose one class to be subject from among his available classes.[1] As one might expect, these classes represented about equally all secondary grades from seventh through twelfth, and most of the secondary subject-matter fields. They contained 2,139 individual students.

First the teacher administered whatever objective test would ordinarily come next in his course of study; it might be arithmetic, spelling, civics, or whatever. He collected and marked these tests in his usual way, so that each paper exhibited a numerical score and, on the basis of the score, the appropriate letter grade A, B, C, D, or F, each teacher following his usual policy of grade distribution. Next, the teacher placed the papers in numerical rank order, with the best paper on top. He rolled a specially marked die to assign the top paper to the *No Comment, Free Comment* or *Specified Comment* group. He rolled again, assigning the second-best paper to one of the two remaining groups. He automatically assigned the third-best paper to the one treatment group remaining. He then repeated the process of rolling and assigning with the next three papers in the class, and so on until all students were assigned.

Administering treatments. The Teacher returned *all* test papers with the numerical score and letter grade, as earned. No Comment students received nothing else. Free Comment students received, in addition, whatever comment the teacher might feel it desirable to make. Teachers were instructed: "Write anything that occurs to you in the circumstances. There is not any 'right' or 'wrong' comment for this study. A comment is 'right' for the study if it conforms with your own feelings and practices." Specified Comment students, regardless of teacher or student differences, all received comments designated in advance for each letter grade, as follows:

A: Excellent! Keep it up.
B: Good work. Keep at it.
C: Perhaps try to do still better?
D: Let's bring this up.
F: Let's raise this grade!

Teachers were instructed to administer the comments "rapidly and automatically, trying not even to notice who the students are." This instruction was to prevent any extra attention to the Specified Comment students, in class or out, which might confound the experimental results. After the comments were written on each paper and recorded on the special sheet for the experimenter, the test papers were returned to the students in the teacher's customary way.

It is interesting to note that the student subjects were totally naive. In other psychological experiments, while often not aware of precisely what is being tested, subjects are almost always sure that something unusual is underway. In 69 of the present classes there was no discussion by teacher or student of the comments being returned. In the remaining five the teachers gave ordinary brief instructions to "notice comments" and "profit by them," or similar remarks. In none of the classes were students reported to seem aware or suspicious that they were experimental subjects.

Criterion. Comment effects were judged by the scores achieved on the very next objective test given in the class, regardless of the nature of that test. Since the 74 testing instruments would naturally differ sharply from each other in subject matter, length, difficulty, and every other testing variable, they obviously presented some rather unusual problems. When the tests were regarded primarily as *ranking* instruments, however, some of the difficulties disappeared.

A class with 30 useful students, for example, formed just 10 levels on the basis of scores from the first test. Each level consisted of three students, with each student receiving a different treatment: No Comment, Free Comment, or Specified Comment. Students then achieved new scores on the second (criterion) test, as might be illustrated in Table 1, Part A. On the basis of such scores, they were assigned rankings within levels, as illustrated in Table 1, Part B.

If the comments had no effects, the sums of ranks of Part B would not differ except by chance, and the two-way analysis of variance by ranks

TABLE 1

Illustration of Ranked Data

Level	Part A (Raw scores on second test)			Part B (Ranks-within-levels on second rest)		
	N	F	S	N	F	S
1	33	31	34	2	1	3
2	30	25	32	2	1	3
3	29	33	23	2	3	1
. . .	. . .	. . .	. . .	. . .	. . .	. . .
. . .	. . .	. . .	. . .	. . .	. . .	. . .
. . .	. . .	. . .	. . .	. . .	. . .	. . .
10	14	25	21	1	3	2
Sum:				19	21	20

Note.—N is No Comment; F is Free Comment; S is Specified Comment.

would be used to determine whether such differences exceeded chance. Then the *sums* of ranks themselves could be ranked. (In Part B the rankings would be 1, 3, and 2 for Groups N, F, and S; the highest score is ranked 3 throughout the study.) And a new test, of the same type, could be made of all such rankings from the 74 experimental classrooms. Such a test was for the present design the better alternative, since it allowed for the likelihood of "Type G errors" (3, pp. 9–10) in the experimental outcome. Still a third way remained to use these rankings. The summation of each column could be divided by the number of levels in the class, and the result was *a mean rank within treatment within class*. This score proved very useful, since it fulfilled certain requirements for parametric data.

RESULTS

Comment vs. no comment. The over-all significance of the comment effects, as measured by the analysis of variance by ranks, is indicated in Table 2. The first row shows results obtained when students were considered as matched independently from one common population. The second row shows results when treatment groups within classes were regarded as intact groups. In either case the conclusions were the same. The Specified Comment group, which received automatic impersonal comments according to the letter grade received, achieved higher scores than the No Comment group. The Free Comment group, which received individualized comments from the teachers, achieved the highest scores of all.

Not once in a hundred times would such differences have occurred by chance if scores were drawn from a common population. Therefore it may be held that the comments had a real and beneficial effect upon the students' mastery of subject matter in the various experimental classes.

It was also possible, as indicated earlier, to use the mean ranks within treatments within classes as parametric scores. The resulting distributions, being normally distributed and fulfilling certain other assumptions underlying parametric tests, permitted other important comparisons to be made.[2] Table 3 shows the mean-ranks data necessary for such comparisons.

The various tests are summarized in Tables 4 and 5. The over-all F test in Table 5 duplicated, as one would expect, the result of the Friedman

TABLE 2

The Friedman Test of the Over-all Treatment Effects

Units Considered	N	F	S	df	x	p
Individual Subjects	1363	1488	1427	2	10.9593	< .01
Class-group Subjects	129.5	170.0	144.5	2	11.3310	< .01

TABLE 3

Parametric Data Based Upon Mean Ranks Within Treatments Within Classes

Source	N	F	S	Total
Number of Groups	74	74	74	222
Sum of Mean Ranks	140.99	154.42	148.59	444.00
Sum of Squares of Mean Ranks	273.50	327.50	304.01	905.01
Mean of Mean Ranks	1.905	2.087	2.008	2.000
S.D. of Mean Ranks	.259	.265	.276	
S.E. of Mean Ranks	.030	.031	.032	

TABLE 4

Analysis of Variance of Main Treatment Effects

(Based on Mean Ranks)

Source	Sum of Squares	df	Mean Square	p	Probability
Between Treatments: N, F, S	1.23	2	.615	5.69	< .01
Between Class groups	0.00	73	.000	. . .	
Interaction: T × Class	15.78	148	.108		
Total	17.01	221			

Note.—Modeled after Lindquist (3), p. 157 et passim, except for unusual conditions noted.

test, with differences between treatment groups still significant beyond the .01 level. Comparisons between different pairs of treatments are shown in Table 5. All differences were significant except that between Free Comment and Specified Comment. It was plain that comments, especially the individualized comments, had a marked effect upon student performance.

Comments and schools. One might question whether comment effects would vary from school to school, and even whether the school might not be the more appropriate unit of analysis. Since as it happened the study had 12 junior or senior high schools which had three or more experimental classes, these schools were arranged in a treatments-by--replications design. Results of the analysis are shown in Table 6. Schools apparently had little measurable influence over treatment effect.

TABLE 5

Differences Between Means of the Treatment Groups

Comparison	Differ- ence	S. E. of Diff.	s	Probability
Between N and F	.182	.052	3.500	<.001
Between N and S	.103	.054	1.907	<.05
Between F and S	.079	.056	1.411	<.10(n.s.)

Note.—The t tests presented are those for matched pairs, consisting of the paired mean ranks of the treatment groups within the different classes. Probabilities quoted assume that one-tailed tests were appropriate.

TABLE 6

The Influence of the School Upon the Treatment Effect

Source	Sum of Squares	df	Mean Square	P	Proba- bility
Between Treatments: N, F, S	.172	2	.086	. . .[a]	. . .
Between Schools	.000	11	.000		
Between Classes Within Schools (pooled)	.000	24	.000		
Intersection: T X Schools	1.937	22	.088	. . .	. . .
Interaction: T X Cl. W. Sch. (pooled)	4.731	48	.099		
Total	6.890	107			

Note.—Modified for mean-rank data from Edwards (1, p. 295 *et passim*).

[a]Absence of an important main treatment effect is probably caused by necessary restriction of sample for school year (*N* is 36, as compared with Total *N* of 74), and by some chance biasing.

Comments and school years. It was conceivable that students, with increasing age and grade-placement, might become increasingly independent of comments and other personal attentions from their teachers. To test such a belief, 66 class-groups, drawn from the experimental classes, were stratified into six school years (Grades 7–12) with 11 class-groups in each school year. Still using mean ranks as data, summations of such scores were as shown in Table 7. Rather surprisingly, no uniform trend was apparent. When the data were tested for interaction of school year and comment effect (see Table 8), school year did not exhibit a significant influence upon comment effect.

Though Table 8 represents a comprehensive test of school-year effect, it was not supported by all available evidence. Certain other, more limited tests did show significant differences in school year, with possibly greater responsiveness in higher grades. The relevant data (6, chap. 5) are too cumbersome for the present report, and must be interpreted with caution. Apparently, however, comments do *not* lose effectiveness as students move through school. Rather they appear fairly important, especially when individualized, at all secondary levels.

TABLE 7

Sums of Mean Ranks for Different
School Years

School Year	N	F	S
12	21.08	22.92	22.00
11	19.06	23.91	23.03
10	20.08	23.32	22.60
9	22.34	22.06	21.60
8	21.21	22.39	22.40
7	22.04	22.98	20.93

Note.—Number of groups is 11 in each cell.

TABLE 8

The Influence of School Year Upon Treatment Effect

Source	Sum of Squares	df	Mean Square	F	Probability
Between Treatments: N, F, S	1.06	2	.500	8.25	<.01
Between School Years	0.00	5	.000		
Between Cl. Within Sch. Yr. (pooled)	0.00	60	.000		
Interaction: T × School Year	1.13	10	.113	1.12	(n.s.)
Interaction: T × Class (pooled)	12.11	120	.101		
Total	14.30	197			

Note.—Modified for mean-rank data from Edwards (1, p. 295 *et passim*).

One must remember that, between the present class-groupings, there were many differences other than school year alone. Other teachers, other subject-matter fields, other class conditions could conceivably have been correlated beyond chance with school year. Such correlations would in some cases, possibly, tend to modify the *visible* school-year influence, so that illusions would be created. However possible, such a caution, at present, appears rather empty. In absence of contradictory evidence, it would seem reasonable to extrapolate the importance of comment to other years outside the secondary range. One might predict that comments would appear equally important if tested under comparable conditions in the early college years. Such a suggestion, in view of the large lecture halls and detached professors of higher education, would appear one of the more striking experimental results.

Comments and letter grades. In a questionnaire made out before the experiment, each teacher rated each student in his class with a number from 1 to 5, according to the student's *guessed responsiveness* to comments made by that teacher. Top rating, for example, was paired with the description: "Seems to respond quite unusually well to suggestions or comments made by the teacher of this class. Is quite apt to be influenced by praise, correction, etc." Bottom rating, on the other hand, implied: "Seems rather negativistic about suggestions made by the teacher. May be inclined more than most students to do the opposite from what the teacher urges." In daily practice, many teachers comment on some papers and not on others. Since teachers would presumably be more likely to comment on papers of those students they believed would respond positively, such ratings were an important experimental variable.

Whether teachers *were* able to predict responsiveness is a complicated question, not to be reported here. It was thought, however, that teachers might tend to believe their able students, their high achievers, were also their responsive students. A contingency table was therefore made, testing the relationship between *guessed* responsiveness and letter grade achieved on the first test. The results were as predicted. More "A" students were regarded as highly responsive to comments than were other letter grades; more "F" students were regarded as negativistic and unresponsive to comments than were other letter grades; and grades in between followed the same trend. The over-all C coefficient was .36, significant beyond the .001 level.[3] Plainly teachers believed that their *better* students were also their more *responsive* students.

If teachers were correct in their belief, one would expect in the present experiment greater comment effect for the better students than for the poorer ones. In fact, one might not be surprised if, among the "F" students, the No Comment group were even superior to the two comment groups.

The various letter grades achieved mean scores as shown in Table 9, and the analysis of variance resulted as shown in Table 10. There was consider-

TABLE 9

Mean of Mean Ranks for
Different Letter Grades

Letter Grade	N	F	S
A	1.93	2.04	2.03
B	1.01	2.11	1.93
C	1.90	2.06	2.04
D	2.05	1.99	1.96
F	1.57	2.85	1.88

Note.—Each eligible class was assigned one mean rank for each cell of the table.

TABLE 10

The Relation Between Letter Grade and Treatment Effect

Source	Sums of Squares	df	Mean Square	F	Probability
Between Treatments: N, F, S	2.77	2	1.385	5.41	$<.01$
Between Letter Grades	0.00	4	0.000		
Bet. Blocks Within L. Gr. (pooled)	0.00	65	0.000		
Interaction: T × Letter Grades	4.83	3	.610	2.40	$.05>p>.01$
Residual (error term)	32.99	120	.254		
Total	40.64	209			

Note.—Modified for mean-rank data from Lindquist (3, p. 249). Because sampling was irregular (see text) all eligible classes were randomly assigned to 14 groupings. This was done arbitrarily to prevent vacant cells.

able interaction between letter grade and treatment effect, but it was caused almost entirely by the remarkable effect which comments appeared to have *on the "F" students*. None of the other differences, including the partial reversal of the "D" students, exceeded chance expectation.

These data do not, however, represent the total sample previously used, since the analysis could use only those student levels in which all three students received the same letter grade on Test One.[4] Therefore many class-groups were not represented at all in certain letter grades. For example, although over 10% of all letter grades were "F," only 28 class-groups had even one level consisting entirely of "F" grades, and most of these classes had *only* one such level. Such circumstances might cause a somewhat unstable or biased estimate of effect.

Within such limitations, the experiment provided strong evidence against the teacher-myth about responsiveness and letter grades. The experimental teachers appeared plainly mistaken in their faith that their "A" students respond relatively brightly, and their "F" students only sluggishly or negatively to whatever encouragement they administer.

SUMMARY

Seventy-four randomly selected secondary teachers, using 2,139 unknowing students in their daily classes, performed the following experiment: They administered to all students whatever objective test would occur in the usual course of instruction. After scoring and grading the test papers in their customary way, and matching the students by performance, they randomly assigned the papers to one of three treatment groups. The No Comment group received no marks beyond those for grading. The Free Comment group received whatever comments the teachers felt were appropriate for the particular students and tests concerned. The Specified Comment group received certain uniform comments designated beforehand by the experimenter for all similar letter grades, and thought to be generally "encouraging." Teachers returned tests to students without any unusual attention. Then teachers reported scores achieved on the next objective test given in the class, and these scores became the criterion of comment effect, with the following results:

1. Free Comment students achieved higher scores than Specified Comment students, and Specified Comments did better than No Comments. All differences were significant except that between Free Comments and Specified Comments.

2. When samplings from 12 different schools were compared, no significant differences of comment effect appeared between schools.

3. When the class-groups from six different school years (grades 7–12) were compared, no *conclusive* differences of comment effect appeared between the years, but if anything senior high was more responsive than junior high. It would appear logical to generalize the experimental results, concerning the effectiveness of comment, at least to the early college years.

4. Although teachers believed that their better students were also much more responsive to teacher comments than their poorer students, there was no experimental support for this belief.

When the average secondary teacher takes the time and trouble to write comments (believed to be "encouraging") on student papers, these apparently have a measurable and potent effect upon student effort, or attention, or attitude, or whatever it is which causes learning to improve, and this effect does not appear dependent on school building, school year, or student ability. Such a finding would seem very important for the studies of classroom learning and teaching method.

NOTES

Portions of this paper were read at the National Research Conference of the American Educational Research Association at San Francisco, March 8, 1958. This research depended upon cooperation from many persons. Space limitations prevent the listing of their names. The writer is especially indebted to the teachers who freely donated time and energy after having been randomly selected. Without their participation the study obviously would have been impossible.

[1] Certain classes, like certain teachers, would be ineligible for a priori reasons: giving no objective tests, etc.

[2] It may be noted that the analysis of variance based upon such mean ranks will require no calculation of sums of squares between levels or between classes. This is true because the mean for any class will be $(k + 1)/2$, or in the present study just 2.00.... An alternative to such scores would be the conversion of all scores to T scores based upon each class-group's distribution; but the mean ranks, while very slightly less sensitive, are much simpler to compute and therefore less subject to error.

[3] In a 5×5 table, a perfect correlation expressed as C would be only about .9 (McNemar [4], p. 203).

[4] When levels consisted of both "A" and "B" students, for example, "A" students would tend to receive the higher scores on the second test, regardless of treatment; thus those Free Comment "A" students drawn from mixed levels would tend to appear (falsely) more responsive than the Free Comment "B" students drawn from mixed levels, etc. Therefore the total sample was considerably reduced for the letter-grade analysis.

REFERENCES

1. Edwards, A. *Experimental design in psychological research.* New York: Rinehart, 1950.

2. Friedman, M. The use of ranks to avoid the assumption of normality implicit in the analysis of variance. *J. Amer. Statist. Ass.,* 1937, 32, 675–701.

3. Lindquist, E. F. *Design and analysis of experiments in psychology and education.* Boston: Houghton Mifflin, 1953.

4. McNemar, Q. *Psychological statistics.* (2nd ed.) New York: Wiley, 1955.

5. Page, E. B. Educational research: replicable or generalizable? *Phi Delta Kappan*, 1953, 39, 302–304.

6. Page, E. B. The effects upon student achievement of written comments accompanying letter grades. Unpublished doctoral dissertation, Univer. of California, Los Angeles, 1958.

A NOTE ABOUT RESISTANCE AND OPPOSITION *

Lloyd Homme, Attila Csanyi,
Mary Ann Gonzales, and James R. Rechs

Cherchez la Reinforcement. As the authors of this article imply, it's important to choose an object or activity that *is* rewarding, rather than choosing one that we *wish* were rewarding. It would be nice for us if students found learning to be its own reward, just as it would be nice for the taxpayers if we could all afford to teach for the joy of seeing others learn. Seeing something as a reward, however, is often a result of learning too. For example, if you want students to learn to feel their own pride as a reward, try pairing the hoped-for reward with a current reward, "You can feel proud of your work, Anthony, you got an A on your paper." Sometimes the reward is a feeling or thing that the person likes (positive reinforcement). Sometimes it is escape from the fear or anxiety of an unpleasant situation (negative reinforcement). Most things we do are reinforced in many ways at once, perhaps by a feeling (such as our own pride or sense of accomplishment), sometimes by an object or token (such as a pay check or promotion), sometimes by a social reward (such as an appreciative student or parent), and even at times by escaping an unpleasant situation (such as not paying the bills or escaping bad feelings about ourselves or our work). A little digging will usually turn up a variety of reinforcements.

Contingency management is difficult to teach some people. No one is sure of the reason for this. We will examine a number of possible reasons for this difficulty; the reader is asked to judge for himself whether any of these reasons are relevant to his own reactions to the system.

Contingency Management Concepts Are Too Simple. In a limited sense at least, those who will use this program already know about the effects of reward and punishment. As a matter of fact, those to whom contingency management is difficult to teach will often insist they know all about these classes of events. (It sometimes seems as though the only ones who do not understand these events perfectly are the psychologists who have been studying them for the last fifty years.) As a matter of fact, the concepts involved in contingency management *are* simple. There must be some other source of difficulty.

Is It Inertia? It is often said of educators that they are reluctant to change their ways of doing things. This widespread concept of an educator as one

*From Lloyd Homme, Attila Csanyi, Mary Ann Gonzales, and James R. Rechs, "A Note About Resistance and Opposition," *How to Use Contingency Contracting in the Classroom* (Champaign, Illinois: Research Press, 1971), pp. 61–62, by permission of the authors and publisher. The primary author is manager of research for the Behavior Systems Division of Westinghouse Learning Corporation and also is Clinical Associate, Dept. of Psychiatry, University of New Mexico.

who resists innovation is exemplified by the following quotation from a weekly magazine: "In many American schools, ... the prevailing attitudes are inflexibility, defensiveness and insularity..." (*Time*, January 20, 1967, p. 18).

However, it has been our experience that most teachers are not only willing but eager to try out methods which promise greater control over the behavior of their students.

Is Contingency Management Bribery? The term bribery has strong connotations of immorality. A bribe is used to induce someone to commit an act which is, in some way, illegal or unethical. None of these characteristics is true for the kinds of behavior we are discussing in this program. But there is more to it than that. Many people (particularly parents) somehow resent having to arrange payoffs for the child's behavior. "The child is supposed to behave because I tell him to, not because I am holding out a reward for him," is a common reaction.

This attitude probably arises out of the traditions of our society. There is no instant remedy, but it may help to point out that all of us—children and adults alike—do what we do because of the anticipated (sometimes long-range) consequences of what we do.

The Automatic Nature of Reinforcement. The effects of contingency relationships must be assumed to function at all times, independently of whether they are understood, approved of, hated or loved. People sometimes mistakenly say, for example, "A reinforcement won't work with this subject because he is too young (or mentally retarded or obtuse) to understand why he is being rewarded." This argument does not hold up when one considers that in nature's scheme of things, animals as lowly as insects and worms react to reward and punishment contingencies; and, on the other end of the scale, the extent to which our own adult actions are guided by their real or expected consequences.

In summary, contingencies, whether they are systematically arranged or occur by chance or inadvertence, whether approved or disapproved, understood or not, will have their effect. Always.

CONTINGENCY CONTRACTS *

Harvey F. Clarizio

If You X, Then You Can Y. As Grandma's Law shows, there is nothing new to being clear about what must be done and about what the reward for doing it will be, but unfortunately we aren't always clear to our students. The "reinforcement menu," which Clarizio mentions, is a list of activities, readings, games, etc., which students can select from to choose their own reinforcements. Since rewards vary from person to person and from time to time for one person, a menu saves the teacher from using all her time to plan reinforcements. Some teachers include class suggestions and participation in menu making, and different menu items can "cost" different numbers of points. Contingency contracting often works especially well with students who distrust teachers. Rightly or wrongly, they often feel adults go back on their word. When both the teacher and student have copies of the contract that they both have signed, this gives the student a feeling that he can force the teacher to be "fair," and it gives the teacher a way of showing the student that he hasn't changed requirements for an assignment or made it harder on some students than on others. Also, once contracts are written, they can be revised or reused for later students. While the contract shown here is rather general in its terms, they can be written for specific daily assignments or for whole school years. Helping to write a contract sometimes is a good student exercise in precise writing and clear thinking, too.

The basic rationale of the contingency contract is that "you can do something pleasant, if you perform this task." Homme (1969) states that much of the essence of contingency contracting has been captured in Grandma's Law—"first clean up your plate, then you may have your dessert." In the school setting, the contract specifies that the student can engage in an enjoyable high preference task, for example, art activities, or will receive a very desirable tangible or social reward, if he first engages in a low preference task, for example, a math assignment. To be effective, the contract must offer a reward that is (a) highly attractive, and (b) not obtainable outside the conditions of the contract (Homme, 1969). Educators have utilized this technique for years, but they have not made the terms of the contract explicit, nor have they used contracts systematically. Educational contracts, while useful with elementary school students, are especially effective at the secondary level in that they enhance the adolescent's development of responsibility and yet permit some freedom to choose his goals and rewards.

*From Harvey F. Clarizio, *Toward Positive Classroom Discipline* (New York: John Wiley & Sons, 1971), pp. 41–43, 50–51, by permission of the publisher. The author is Professor of Educational Psychology at Michigan State University and author of *Contemporary Education Psychology*.

Homme (1969), who has done extensive work in this area, lists three basic types of contracts depending on whether the terms are set by a manager, the student himself, or by both. In manager-controlled contracting, the manager determines the amount of the reward, establishes the amount of the task to be accomplished, presents the contract to the student (which he accepts), and delivers the reward. This kind of contracting is quite different from self-contracting in which the student himself determines the amount of the task and the amount of the reward. Self-contracting, however, is usually the last of the three types of contracts entered into, since it demands self-control and initiative on the student's part, In leading the student from manager (teacher)-controlled contracts to self-contracting, it is often necessary to use what is called transitional contracting in which the teacher and student jointly decide on the amount of reinforcement and on the magnitude of the task.

Homme cautions that the contract should be revised when one or more of the following occurs:

1. Incomplete assignments.
2. Complaining.
3. Excessive dawdling.
4. Talking and wasting time.
5. Excessive clock watching.
6. Inattention to instructions or details.
7. Failure to pass more than two progress checks in one subject area.

Sometimes it is necessary to shorten the contract by deleting certain terms or by simplifying the required tasks. If this strategy fails, the teacher might suspect that the rewards are not sufficiently enticing. At times, it may be necessary to lengthen the contract by increasing the number of tasks or their difficulty. On these occasions, it may also be necessary to increase the amount of reward to make the harder assignments more worthwhile. It is important that the student be made to feel that he has achieved a new status, for example, "Jim, you've improved so much that you're now ready for the advanced material." More will be said about the use of educational contracts when we discuss punishment procedures in the next chapter.

The table presents a transitional contract for a 16-year-old student who seldom completed homework assignments in his social studies class. In general, he reacted to his teacher's comments in a negative and sullen manner.

Problem: Underachievement in reading

Reward: Riddles and rhymes
Mike was a bright, eight-year-old boy whose reading skills were deficient with respect to both his grade level and his mental maturity. His lack of

Educational Contract

Between (Student's name) and (Teacher's name)

Student agrees to:

1.	Complete assigned homework—if well done and accurate	5 points 2 extra points
2.	Hand in assignments on date due—if handed in before due date	5 points 2 extra points

Teacher agrees to:
1. Check homework and give appropriate amount of points to the student (as indicated above).
2. Not reprimand or comment when homework is not completed or handed in.
   (a) if two consecutive assignments are not handed in—3 points are subtracted from accumulated total
   (b) if three consecutive assignments are not completed and handed in the contract is considered void.

Student can exchange his points for:
(1) Free period time during class (5 points per 5 minutes)
(2) Access to the driving range (10 points per 15 minutes)
(3) Excuse from the weekly Social Studies quiz (30 points each week)
(4) Being helper to shop teacher (10 points per 15 minutes)
(5) Credits for purchase of pocket book (5 points per credit—10 credits for free book)
(6) Being a student referee for a varsity game (30 points per game)
(7) Access to student lounge during free period (study hall) (30 points per period)

Signed_____
Student

Signed_____
Teacher

confidence in his own reading ability was readily apparent. His resistance was sometimes expressed openly, for example, "How much more of this stuff do I have to do?," "I'll read one more paragraph and that's all." On other occasions his resistance was more passive in nature and took the form of foot dragging.

In an effort to increase Mike's motivation, an educational contract was set up. If Mike concentrated on his reading for 15 minutes, he could select an activity that he enjoyed from a reinforcement menu. Mike had a fascination for riddles and rhymes, as he liked to use them to stump his better reading friends. Accordingly, he selected them as his reward.

Here are some samples:

One for the cut worm,
Two for the crow,
Three for the chickens,
And four to grow.

I had a little dog, his name was Tim:
I put him in a bathtub to see if he could swim;
He drank all the water and ate all the soap,
And almost died with a bubble in his throat.

He wears his hat upon his neck
Because he has no head
And he never takes his hat off
Until you're sick in bed.
(A medicine bottle)

Contingency contracting in conjunction with the use of reinforcement menus over the year resulted in a significant improvement in Mike's reading. These gains kept him from repeating third grade.

Comment. This case depicts the use of an academic activity as a reward. The fact that a poor reader would select this type of activity is, at first glance, somewhat unexpected and highlights the importance of providing a choice in the selection of rewards. Notice that the reward was given after completion of the contingency contract.

PROGRAMMING CREATIVE BEHAVIOR*

Hayne W. Reese and Sidney J. Parnes

Creativity: A Behavioral View. Notice how different this article on creativity is compared with Weisskopf's, Rogers's, or Koestler's. The Freudian, humanistic, and transpersonal authors use anecdote, description and abstract theory. The authors of this article, however, demonstrate a behavioral approach with their step-by-step experimental procedure, the use of tests to actually measure what they are talking about, and the use of statistical comparisons to be as exact as they can—clarity, exactness, and measurability. Here is an example of comparing differing teaching styles by measurement, then being able to base future teaching on the outcome of these measures; this is the "systematic improvement of instruction" that Smith talks of later in this section. The style of writing is also particularly behavioral, with its divisions into clear sections which are demarcated by the statement of the problem, experimental methods, results, and discussion as well as the overall conception of the study into pretest, treatment, and posttest. Comparing this article with the other articles on creativity gives a clear example of the extent that behaviorists value careful methods of investigation and evaluation rather than general feelings, imprecise theory, or broad generalizations.

Creativity, as measured by standard tests, can be increased by training in creative problem solving. To determine whether training with the programmed materials developed by the junior author is effective, high school students were given a 1-semester course with (a) the program alone (2 schools) or (b) the program taught by an instructor (2 schools). (c) Control students in 2 other schools were given no training. (d) Additional control groups within the 4 experimental schools were also included. A battery of creativity tests was given to all Ss at the beginning and end of the semester. In general, the instructor-taught group appeared to improve more on the tests than the program-alone group, and both improved more than the control groups.

Numerous experiments have been conducted to evaluate deliberate methods of developing creative behavior. In a review of the literature reporting such research, Parnes and Brunelle (1967) concluded that the evidence overwhelmingly indicates that creative ability, as measured by existing tests, can be increased.

The purpose of the present study was to evaluate the effects of a *programmed* course in creative problem solving. Research suggests that incremental teaching of subject matter can be more efficient than conventional teaching methods. For example, the findings of Porter (1959)

*From Hayne W. Reese and Sidney J. Parnes, "Programming Creative Behavior," *Child Development* 41 (1970): 413–423, by permission of the authors and publisher. Copyright 1970 by the Society for Research in Child Development, Inc. Hayne W. Reese is Centennial Professor of Psychology at West Virginia University. Sidney J. Parnes is Professor of Creative Studies at Buffalo State University College and co-author of the book *Toward Supersanity: Channeled Freedom.*

showed that students could master a programmed course in spelling four times faster than a conventionally taught course, Schramm's (1964) annotated bibliography cited 36 studies, of which 17 showed significant superiority for students who completed programs as compared with those in conventional classes. In all but one of the remaining 19 studies, no significant differences appeared. In the one exception, the classroom students proved superior to the programmed ones.

Authorities emphasize the value of creative thinking in programming but give much less attention to programming deliberately for creative development. Only a small number of the studies of programming dealt with development of creative thinking (Anderson 1965; Barlow 1960; Day 1961; Olton 1966).

The objective of the present research, at the high school senior level, was to determine whether or not subjects receiving creative problem-solving training with programmed materials alone show increases in creative ability to the same extent as subjects receiving the same error-free programmed materials in an instructor-taught procedure, and whether or not either or both of these groups show a significant gain in creative ability when compared with control subjects receiving no training.

METHOD

Subjects. Six academic high schools from the Buffalo School District were included in the study. In each school, all senior students who indicated that they intended to continue their formal education after graduation were assembled and, after being fully informed about the nature of the experiment, were asked to volunteer to participate. They were told, before being asked to volunteer, that one-quarter unit of high school credit would be given for participation and that attendance at the training sessions would be required of volunteers who were selected to be included. Of some 1,384 apparently eligible students, 957 volunteered.

Subjects included in the study were selected on the basis of IQ and probability of regular attendance at training sessions. The acceptable IQ range was set at 105 to 130. Lorge-Thorndike scores, obtained from school records, were used to evaluate IQ. Volunteers with 10 or more absences per semester in the previous year were excluded as poor risks, except for a few with one or two extra absences who were included in order to fill particular groups. These two criteria, and scheduling problems, reduced the number of students initially included to 193. Five students did not complete the course, leaving 188 subjects.

Materials. The criterion measures were obtained from a battery of eight tests, seven designed to assess five aspects of creative behavior, and one designed to assess a personality characteristic presumably associated with creativity. The tests were the Dominance Scale of the California Psychological Inventory (Gough 1957), the Product Improvement Test (Torrance

1962), and AC (1960) Test of Creative Ability ("Other Uses"), abbreviated forms of four of Guilford's (1966) tests (Apparatus, Planning Elaboration, Alternate Uses, and Consequences), and the unabbreviated form of a fifth Guilford test (Associational Fluency). All tests were administered with the standard instructions and were scored by two independent raters using standard scoring instructions provided by the authors of the tests. The possibility of rater bias and halo effect in the scoring was eliminated by coding the protocols. The raters could not tell what subject, school, or treatment condition any protocol came from, nor whether it was from a pretest or a posttest when the same form was used in both testing sessions. Interrater scoring agreement was computed for random samples of protocols from all of the subjectively scored tests (all except the Dominance Scale of the California Psychological Inventory [CPI], which is objectively scored). The obtained interrater scoring reliabilities are given in Table 1. (Intercorrelations among the scores are given in appendix 1 of Parnes 1966.)

The experimental material was a programmed sequence of 28 booklets designed to teach the principles of creative problem solving described by Parnes (1967). The preparation, preliminary testing, and revision of the programmed booklets required about 2 years (see Parnes 1966, pp. 17–20).

Procedure. Pretests.—The subjects initially selected were given the battery of criterion tests in two 40-minute sessions, 2 days apart. The Associational Fluency, Alternate Uses, Planning Elaboration, Apparatus, and Other Uses tests were given in the first session, and the Consequences, CPI Dominance, and Product Improvement tests were given in the second session. The tests were administered by members of the experimental staff, but no "program-proctor" or "instructor" tested any subjects who were to be in his group.

Treatments.—"Program" and "Instructor" groups were given two 40-minute training sessions per week for 13 weeks, beginning after the pretest sessions. The students in the Program groups were given a new booklet from the sequence at the beginning of each training session (and a second booklet in two sessions), and worked through the booklet during the session without interaction with other students. A program-proctor was present but served only to distribute the materials and to answer administrative kinds of questions.

The Instructor groups were given *exactly* the same material as in the booklets, with no deviations allowed; but the material was presented by instructors in the conventional classroom fashion. During each training session, the subjects in the Instructor groups were encouraged to discuss the material and to interact with one another in developing the kinds of creative responses that the subjects in the Program groups had to develop alone.

TABLE 1

Interrater Agreement for Criterion Measures

Creative Behavior and Measure	Pretest Form	Pretest Scoring Agreement	Posttest Form	Posttest Scoring Agreement
Fluency:				
Associational Fluency	a	0.94	...	...
Other Uses, quantity	b	0.99	...	...
Consequences, total	Items 1–3	0.97	...	...
Product Improvement, Fluency	Toy dog	1.00	Toy monkey	1.00
Flexibility:				
Alternate Uses	Parts I and II	0.96	...	...
Product Improvement, Flexibility	Toy dog	0.82	Toy monkey	0.74
Originality:				
Consequences, Remote	Items 1–3	0.68	...	...
Product Improvement, Originality	Toy dog	0.78	Toy monkey	0.81
Elaboration:				
Planning Elaboration	Part A	0.88	Part B	0.99
Sensitivity:				
Apparatus	Items 1–9	0.80	Items 10–18	0.78

Note.—Dash means that same form was used in posttest as in pretest; reliability computed only on pretest.
[a] Complete unabbreviated form used.
[b] One item, wire coat hanger, from Part V used.

Subjects who were absent from a session were given makeup work to do at home. For the Program groups, the makeup assignment consisted of working through the appropriate booklet. For the Instructor groups, the assignment was to read equivalent material.

Control groups had no contact with the experiment except in the pretest and posttest sessions.

Posttests.—The posttests were given with the same procedures as the pretests, and were given to any one group by the same person who had given the pretests.

Design. The six schools included in the study were divided into two levels on the basis of ratings by three professional members of the experimental staff. The characteristics rated were the extent to which both the school and the neighborhood showed an academic interest and an interest in education as a whole, including cultural and enrichment opportunities. The three schools rated lowest were designated "Level I" schools, and the three rated highest were deisgnated "Level II" schools.

In order to eliminate discussion among subjects given different treatments, and hence to eliminate contamination of the treatment effects, each of the three treatment conditions (Program, Instructor, and Control) was given in separate schools. Two schools, one from each level, were assigned to each condition, using a table of random numbers. The basic design, then, was a 2 X 3 factorial, with two school levels and three treatments.

The Level I schools had ratings that were highly similar to one another, but the Level II schools were less homogeneous. Therefore, additional control groups were included to provide a check on possible sampling errors in the between-school comparisons. These additional control groups were "in-school" controls. Within each of the two Program schools and the two Instructor schools, an in-school control group was selected at random from the eligible volunteers. The in-school control groups were treated exactly like the groups in the two Control schools. Since the results of comparisons with in-school groups were essentially the same as comparisons with the control groups from separate schools, only the latter comparisons are given in the present report. (See Parnes 1966 for the other comparisons.)

For the analyses of the data, the number of subjects was reduced by excluding subjects who had been absent from an excessive number of training sessions and by omitting others at random to balance the group sizes. The group sizes for the final analyses are given in Table 2.

RESULTS

Analyses of variance of the pretest scores indicated that the School Levels by Treatments interaction was significant on every measure except Other Uses and Dominance. The interactions indicated that there were differences among schools within each school level and that the directions

TABLE 2

Sample Sizes for Statistical Analyses

Group	All Tests Except Other Uses		Other Uses	
	Level I Schools	Level II Schools	Level I Schools	Level II Schools
Program	31	31	31	31
Instructor	31[a]	31	17	17[b]
Control	31	31	27[b]	27

[a]Includes one "fictitious subject" (group means) (see Lindquist 1956, p. 148).

[b]Data lost because of expiration of available testing time. (Other Uses was last test in battery.)

of the differences were not the same in both school levels. The differences, besides being statistically significant, were fairly large; and therefore posttest scores were examined with analysis of covariance techniques.

Table 3 presents the means of the adjusted posttest scores, Table 4 summarizes the results of the analyses of covariance of these scores, and Table 5 summarizes the results of t tests of differences between pairs of treatments. There were no significant differences in the adjusted posttest scores of the personality scale (Dominance); but, in general, the analyses of the adjusted posttest measures of creative behavior indicated that the Instructor groups were significantly superior to the Program groups, and both were significantly superior to the Control groups.

Exactly this pattern of results was obtained on three of the four fluency measures, on one of the two flexibility measures, and on the elaboration measure. A similar pattern, with no significant difference between the experimental groups but with both significantly superior to the Control groups, was obtained on the other fluency measure in one school level, on the other flexibility measure, on one of the two originality measures, and on the sensitivity measure. The other originality measure and the Associational Fluency measure in one school level yielded uninterpretable results.

DISCUSSION

The data clearly establish that working alone through a programmed sequence of booklets designed for the purpose can yield significant gains on standard measures of creative behavior, but that working through the same material presented in conventional fashion by an instructor, with class participation and interaction, generally yields larger gains. This finding has important implications not only for the researcher interested in the theoretical problem of creativity but also for the researcher interested in possible classroom applications.

TABLE 3

Adjusted Posttest Means on Criterion Measures

Test	Level I Schools			Level II Schools		
	Program	Instructor	Control School	Program	Instructor	Control School
Assoc. Fluency	15.9	13.4	14.1	16.3	16.1	12.1
Other Uses	12.6	13.3	11.3	13.3	17.2	11.1
Conseq., Total	17.8	19.1	16.1	18.0	21.0	15.3
P.I., Fluency	14.7	17.1	12.4	14.7	17.9	13.7
Alternate Uses	18.9	19.1	15.9	20.3	19.1	15.7
P.I., Flexibility	7.5	8.5	6.9	8.0	8.7	6.1
Conseq., Remote	7.2	8.1	6.3	7.6	8.6	7.1
P.I., Originality	4.8	4.6	3.9	4.9	6.5	3.1
Planning Elab	12.8	14.0	11.7	13.0	14.2	10.6
Apparatus	8.3	8.5	7.2	8.4	8.6	7.3
CPI Dominance	28.4	27.9	27.1	28.2	27.3	26.9

TABLE 4

Summary of Analyses of Covariance of Posttest Scores

Measure	Error Mean Square[a]	F Ratios		
		School Levels $(df = 1)$	Treatments $(df = 2)$	S × T $(df = 2)$
Associational Fluency	14.85	<1.00	9.07***	5.73***
Other Uses	16.56	2.53	10.49***	2.66
Consequences, Total	16.29	<1.00	17.80***	1.75
Product Improvement, Fluency	18.98	1.11	16.23***	<1.00
Alternate Uses	18.83	<1.00	14.01***	<1.00
Product Improvement, Flexibility	2.97	<1.00	22.98***	2.24
Consequences, Remote	11.51	1.32	3.69*	<1.00
Product Improvement, Originality	9.22	<1.00	6.99***	2.95
Planning Elaboration	10.79	<1.00	12.52***	<1.00
Apparatus	7.06	<1.00	4.00**	<1.00
Dominance	19.81	<1.00	1.32	<<1.00

[a]   [a]Error $df = 143$ for Other Uses, 178 for all other tests.

*$p < .05$

**$p < .025$.

***$b < .01$.

TABLE 5

Comparisons of Pairs of Treatments

Creative Behavior and Measure	Instructor vs. Program	Instructor vs. Control	Program vs. Control
Fluency:			
Associational Fluency:			
Level I schools	-2.57*	<1.00	1.79
Level II schools	<1.00	4.05**	4.17**
Other Uses	2.58**	4.70***	2.34*
Consequences, Total	3.04***	5.96***	2.90**
Product Improvement, Fluency	3.04***	5.64***	2.08*
Flexibility:			
Alternate Uses	<1.00	4.24***	4.86**
Product Improvement, Flexibility	2.74**	6.74***	3.99***
Originality:			
Consequences, Remote	1.53	2.71***	1.19
Product Improvement, Originality	1.29	3.67***	2.39*
Elaboration:			
Planning Elaboration	2.05**	4.98***	2.93**
Sensitivity:			
Apparatus	<1.00	2.58*	2.30*

Note.—Body of table gives value of t computed with denominator based on within-cells variance of appropriate analysis of covariance; df of $t = df$ of within-cells variance (Lindquist 1956, p. 327). School levels combined except on Associational Fluency (only measure with significant interaction).

*$p < .05$.
**$p < .01$.

It is important to point out that no discussion at all was allowed between the proctor and the students who took the program on their own. The proctor merely greeted the students on arrival and handed out and collected the booklets. Any questions were related back to the booklets. In classroom usage, the programs could be dealt with much more flexibly.

The junior author observed informally that the students who worked on their own appeared to exert more effort than did the instructor-taught students but appeared to be less interested in the course. This observation, the conclusion of James, Guetzkow, Forehand, and Libby (1962), and pilot work which has already been conducted in other classes, suggest that the best approach may be to combine programmed instruction with classroom participation directed by an instructor.

REFERENCES

AC test of creative ability. Chicago: Education-Industry Service, Industrial Relations Center, University of Chicago, 1960.

Anderson, R. C. Can first graders learn an advanced problem-solving skill? *Journal of Educational Psychology*, 1965, 56, 283–294.

Barlow, J. A. Aspects of programming, learning, and performance. Paper presented at the meeting of the American Psychological Association, Chicago, September 1960.

Day, W. F. Programming a teaching machine course in thinking and problem solving. Unpublished manuscript, University of Nevada, 1961.

Gough, H. C. *Manual for the California Psychological Inventory.* Palo Alto, Calif.: Consulting Psychologists Press, 1957.

Guilford, J. P. Report No. 36 from the Psychological Laboratory. University of Southern California Laboratory, Photoduplication Services Department, Los Angeles, 1966.

James, B. J.; Guetzkow, H.; Forehand, G. A.; and Libby, W. L. Education for innovative behavior in executives. Cooperative Research Project no. 975, Office of Education, U.S. Department of Health, Education, and Welfare, August 1962.

Lindquist, E. F. *Design and analysis of experiments in psychology and education.* Boston: Houghton Mifflin, 1956.

Olton, R. M. A self-instructional program for the development of productive thinking in fifth and sixth grade children. In F. E. Williams (Ed.), *First seminar on productive thinking in education.* St. Paul, Minn.: Creativity and National Schools Project, Macalester College, 1966.

Parnes, S. J. Programming creative behavior. Final Report, Office of Education, U.S. Department of Health, Education, and Welfare, Title VII, Project No. 5-0716, State University of New York at Buffalo, 1966.

Parnes, S. J. *Creative behavior guidebook.* New York: Scribner's, 1967.

Parnes, S. J., & Brunelle, E. A. The literature of creativity. Part 1. *Journal of Creative Behavior,* 1967, 1, 52–109.

Porter, D. Some effects of year long teaching machine instruction. In E. Galanter (Ed.), *Automatic teaching, the state of the art.* New York: Wiley, 1959. Pp. 85–90.

Schramm, W. *The research on programmed instruction.* Washington: U.S. Department of Health, Education, and Welfare, 1964.

Torrance, E. P. *Guiding creative talent.* Englewood Cliffs, N.J.: Prentice-Hall, 1962.

The research reported herein was supported by Title VII, project no. 5-0716, from the Office of Education, U.S. Department of Health, Education, and Welfare. We wish to thank the Consulting Psychologists Press, Inc., Palo Alto, California, for permission to reproduce the Dominance Scale of the California Psychological Inventory. The set of booklets prepared for this research may be secured through the ERIC Document Reproduction Service, 4936 Fairmont Avenue, Bethesda, Maryland 20014. Most of the programmed material has been integrated into the *Creative Behavior Guidebook* (Parnes 1967) and a companion *Creative Behavior Workbook* of the same date by the same author and publisher.

BEHAVIORAL OBJECTIVES? YES! *

Robert M. Gagné

Clearer Thinking for Clearer Teaching. Thinking is one of the greatest human abilities and developable potentials. How can we teachers develop this ability in ourselves and use it to improve our teaching? How can we be clearer to ourselves and to our students about what we are trying to accomplish? When we have helped someone grow, how can we *know* that he has grown? A behavioral-objective approach is one procedure for helping us be clear and exact. As a series of steps to clear thinking, a behavioral-objective approach is useful in education just as formulas are useful in mathematics and the sciences, as grammar helps us organize language, and as rules of the road are good guides to drivers. They all help us to think more clearly and act more efficiently.

Few people who are professionally concerned with education in the United States are unacquainted with "behavioral objectives." Knowledge of this term and its meaning has become widespread. It is therefore timely to pose a question which inquires about the need for behavioral objectives, the possible uses they may have, and the educational functions that may be conceived for them.

NATURE OF INSTRUCTIONAL OBJECTIVES

The statement of a behavioral objective is intended to communicate (to a specified recipient or group of recipients) the outcome of some unit of instruction. One assumes that the general purpose of instruction is learning on the part of the student. It is natural enough, therefore, that one should attempt to identify the outcome of learning as something the student is able to do following instruction which he was unable to do before instruction. When one is able to express the effects of instruction in this way, by describing observable performances of the learner, the clarity of objective statements is at a maximum. As a consequence, the reliability of communication of instructional objectives also reaches its highest level.

To some teachers and educational scholars, it appears at least equally natural to try to identify the outcomes of learning in terms of what capability the learner has gained as a result of instruction, rather than in terms of the performance he is able to do. We therefore frequently encounter such terms as "knowledge," "understanding," "appreciation," and others of this sort which seem to have the purpose of identifying

*From Robert M. Gagné, "Behavior Objectives? Yes!," *Educational Leadership* 29, no. 5 (February, 1972): 394–396, by permission of the author and publisher. Robert M. Gagné is Professor at the College of Education, Florida State University. He is co-author (with J. J. Briggs) of the book *Principles of Instructional Design* (New York: Holt, Rinehart and Winston, 1974).

learned capabilities or dispositions. Mager (1962) and a number of other writers have pointed out the ambiguity of these terms, and the unreliability of communications in which they are used.

Actually, I am inclined to argue that a complete statement of an instructional objective, designed to serve all of its communicative purposes, needs to contain an identification of *both* the type of capability acquired as a result of learning, and also the specific performance by means of which this capability can be confirmed (cf. Gagné, 1971a). Examples can readily be given to show that perfectly good "behavioral" verbs (such as "types," as in "types a letter") are also subject to more than one interpretation. For example, has the individual learned to "copy" a letter, or to "compose" a letter? The fact that no one would disagree that these two activities are somehow different, even though both are describable by the behavior of "typing," clearly indicates the need for descriptions of what has been learned which include more than observable human actions. Complete instructional objectives need to identify the capability learned, as well as the performance which such a capability makes possible.

The implications of this view are not trivial. If in fact such terms as "knowledge" and "understanding" are ambiguous, then we must either redefine them, or propose some new terms to describe learned capabilities which can be more precisely defined. My suggestion has been to take the latter course, and I have proposed that the five major categories representing "what is learned" are motor skills, verbal information, intellectual skills, cognitive strategies, and attitudes (Gagné, 1971b). Completing the example used previously, the statement of the objective would be "Given a set of handwritten notes, *generates* (implies the intellectual skill which is to be learned) a letter *by typing* (identifies the specific action used)."

The alternatives to such "behavioral" statements have many defects, as Mager (1962) and other writers have emphasized. However they may be expanded or embellished, statements describing the *content* of instructional presentations invariably fail to provide the needed communications. The fact that a textbook, or a film, or a talk by a teacher, presents "the concept of the family" is an inadequate communication of the intended learning outcome, and cannot be made adequate simply by adding more detail. The critical missing elements in any such descriptions of instruction are the related ideas of (a) what the student will have learned from instruction, and (b) what class of performances he will then be able to exhibit.

USES OF BEHAVIORAL OBJECTIVES BY SCHOOLS

Statements describing instructional objectives have the primary purpose of *communicating*. Assuming that education has the form of an organized system, communication of its intended and actual outcomes is necessary, among and between the designers of instructional materials, the planners of courses and programs, the teachers, the students, and the parents. In order for the process of education to serve the purpose of learning, communications of these various sorts must take place. When any of them is omitted, education becomes to a diminished degree a systematic enterprise having the purpose of accomplishing certain societal goals pertaining to "the educated adult." There may be those who would argue that education should not serve such goals. Obviously, I disagree, but cannot here devote space to my reasons.

Some of the most important ways in which the various communications about objectives may be used by schools are indicated by the following brief outlines:

1. The instructional designer to the course planner. This set of communications enables the person who is planning a course with predetermined goals to select materials which can accomplish the desired outcomes. For example, if a course in junior high science has the goal of "teaching students to think scientifically," the planner will be seeking a set of materials which emphasize the learning of intellectual skills and cognitive strategies, having objectives such as "generates and tests hypotheses relating plant growth to environmental variables."

In contrast, if the goals of such a course are "to convey a scientific view of the earth's ecology," the curriculum planner will likely seek materials devoted to the learning of organized information, exhibited by such objectives as "describes how the content of carbon dioxide in the air affects the supply of underground water."

2. The designer or planner to the teacher. Communications of objectives to the teacher enable the latter to choose appropriate ways of delivering instruction, and also ways of assessing its effectiveness. As an example, a teacher of foreign language who adopts the objective, "pronounces French words containing the uvular 'r,' " is able (or should be able) to select a form of instruction providing practice in pronunciation of French words containing "r," and to reject as inappropriate for this objective a lecture on "the use of the uvular 'r' in French words."

Additionally, this communication of an objective makes apparent to the teacher how the outcome of instruction must be assessed. In this case, the choice would need to be the observation of oral pronunciation of French words by the student, and could not be, for instance, a multiple-choice test containing questions such as "which of the following French words has a uvular 'r'?"

3. The teacher to the student. There are many instructional situations in which the learning outcome expected is quite apparent to the student, because of his experience with similar instruction. For example, if the course is mathematics, and the topic changes from the addition of fractions to the multiplication of fractions, it is highly likely that the naming of the topic will itself be sufficient to imply the objective.

However, there are also many situations in which the objective may not be at all apparent. A topic on "Ohm's Law," for example, may not make apparent by its title whether the student is expected to recognize Ohm's Law, to state it, to substitute values in it, or to apply it to some electric circuits. It is reasonable to suppose that a student who knows what the objective is will be able to approach the task of learning with an advantage over one who does not.

4. The teacher or principal to the parent. It is indeed somewhat surprising that parents have stood still for "grades" for such a long period of time, considering the deplorably small amount of information they convey. If the trend toward "accountability" continues, grades will have to go. Teachers cannot be held accountable for As, Bs, and Cs—in fact, grades are inimical to any system of accountability. It seems likely, therefore, that the basis for accountability will be the instructional objective. Since this must express a learning outcome, it must presumably be expressed in behavioral terms. Several different forms of accountability systems appear to be feasible; objectives would seem to be necessary for any or all of them.

These appear to be the major communication functions which schools need to carry out if they are engaged in systematically promoting learning. Each of these instances of communication requires accurate and reliable statements of the *outcomes of learning*, if it is to be effective. Such outcomes may be described, accurately and reliably, by means of statements which identify (a) the capability to be learned, and (b) the class of performances by means of which the capability is exhibited. There appears to me to be no alternative to the use of "behavioral objectives," defined as in the previous sentence, to perform these essential functions of communication.

REFERENCES

R. M. Gagné. "Defining Objectives for Six Varieties of Learning." Washington, D.C.: American Educational Research Association, 1971a. (Cassette tape.)

R. M. Gagné. "Instruction Based on Research in Learning." *Engineering Education* 61: 519–23; 1971b.

R. F. Mager. *Preparing Instructional Objectives.* Belmont, California: Fearon Publishers, Inc., 1962.

THE NEW WORLD
OF ACCOUNTABILITY: IN THE CLASSROOM

W. James Popham

Accountability: Show Your Results. Although Popham, like many other behaviorally-oriented educators, claims he is speaking for a silent-majority public, I have found them most often to be speaking for other behaviorists and their influencees. Popham stresses the social-pressure argument for showing that we are teaching; the public demands that we be precise about what we are trying to do and clearly show whether we are doing it. In the next article, Smith stresses the improvement of instruction as a goal. Have you ever wondered what it is that you resent about tests that grade people on a curve or fit your students into national percentiles? What is important to most teachers is not how students compare with each other, but whether they have learned what they are supposed to. Popham's second main point is that we should use tests to see whether our students have met the goals we have set, not where they are on a normal curve. People learn what they are rewarded for learning, and limiting the amount of reinforcement with normal-curve grading limits the amount of learning. Criterion-referenced tests help us increase learning by rewarding it wherever it occurs, not just among those at the top of the curve.

The educational battle lines for the impending accountability showdown are drawn as clearly as in a classic western movie. On one side we have the underdog public school teachers, their portable classrooms drawn into a circle. On the other side is the marauding Accountability Gang who, although they are viewed by teachers as mortal enemies, could hardly be considered *no account* bandits. The Accountability Gang is beginning to fire some pretty potent pistols at the embattled teachers. For instead of Colt six-shooters and Winchester rifles, their guns bear different markings. One is labeled "Teacher Tenure." Another is called "Teacher Evaluation." A third simply says "Taxpayer's Revolt." It is small wonder that bullets from these guns may pick off a teacher or two. And the terrifying part of this script, at least to classroom teachers, is that there may be no cavalry over the next hill coming to the rescue.

AN ERA OF ACCOUNTABILITY

While perhaps a mite less melodramatic, the present real world plight of classroom teachers who are seriously trying to cope with the educational accountability movement is equally serious. Teachers are being quite literally bombarded with requests and/or directives to become more account-

*From W. James Popham, "The New World of Accountability: In the Classroom," *National Association of Secondary School Principals Bulletin* 56, no. 364 (May, 1972) 25–31, by permission of the author. W. James Popham is Professor at the Graduate School of Education, U.C.L.A.

able for their instructional activities. Just what does this mean and how can a willing teacher react sensibly to the current quest for accountability?

Well, in general the concept of educational accountability involves the teacher's producing *evidence* regarding the quality of his or her teaching, usually in terms of what happens to pupils, then standing ready to be judged on the basis of that evidence. An accountable teacher, therefore, takes *responsibility* for the results his or her instruction produces in learners. Characteristically, other individuals, e.g., supervisors, administrators, or school boards, will then take appropriate action based on those results. The "appropriate action" might range from decisions regarding which courses the teacher should teach next year all the way to termination of services or salary increases and decreases. Clearly, the stakes are high.

FROM RHETORIC TO REALITY

Further, the situation has moved well beyond the empty rhetoric stage. California legislators last year enacted a teacher evaluation law requiring each K–12 teacher in the state to be evaluated (probationary teachers annually, all others biennially) by locally devised teacher appraisal systems. These local evaluation systems must include certain *state stipulated* elements. Prominent among these legislatively required elements is the teacher's role in promoting *learner progress* in each area of study toward locally defined standards. Thus, a learner-results criterion has been mandated by California lawmakers for teacher evaluation. A state-wide system of imposed accountability therefore exists in California. Other states will surely be observing the implementation of the California teacher evaluation law with keen interest.[1]

Beyond their individual involvement in the accountability milieu as it affects job security and advancement, teachers are also being asked to play an integral role in the appraisal of larger educational units, e.g., the school or school district. The public is clearly subjecting educational institutions to increased scrutiny. Citizens are not elated with their perceptions of the quality of education. They want dramatic improvements in the schools and, unless they get them, there is real doubt as to whether we can expect much increased financial support for our educational endeavors. And the public is in no mood to be assuaged by promises. "*Deliver the results,*" we are being told. No longer will lofty language suffice, and yesteryear's assurances that "only we professionals know what we're doing" must seem laughable to today's informed layman.

The distressing fact is that we haven't produced very impressive results for the nation's children. There are too many future voters who can't read satisfactorily, can't reason respectably, don't care for learning in general, and are pretty well alienated from the larger adult society.

AN APPROPRIATE RESPONSE

Well, what do educators do about this demand that they produce results? How should they respond to the mounting pressure that they become more accountable? My recommendation is that we do just that— *we produce results and we become accountable!* For that stance, in my estimate, is the only professionally defensible posture available to us, and we should be chagrined that it took external forces to spur us to action.

Putting historical antecedents aside, let's sieze the initiative in this drive to make educators responsible for their actions. The vast majority of American teachers are well intentioned men and women who want only the best for the children under their tutelage. Impeded only by their human limitations (There are only 24 hours available in most days, and most human folk can't psychologically work 18 of those), most teachers would like to do a better job for their pupils if they only knew how. And here's where the school principal comes in—his role should be to increase the teacher's skill in achieving *demonstrable* results with learners, while at the same time making sure those results are the most defensible ones that can be attained.

In brief, I am suggesting that we accept the accountability challenge by increasing classroom teachers' skills in producing evidence that their instruction yields worthwhile results for learners. Not only is this the key ingredient in current accountability strategies, it represents a way of helping teachers do the best job they can for their students.

Space limitations preclude an exhaustive analysis of the numerous ways we can offer succor to the classroom teacher in promoting their increased results-producing competence. Thus, I would like to outline only two such strategies, but two strategies which seem to me to be high payoff schemes for implementing the principal's leadership role in this endeavor.

PROVIDE CRITERION-REFERENCED MEASURES

Since the emphasis is on getting demonstrable results, we should get into the teacher's hands suitable measures of such results. The teacher can then more readily monitor the quality of instruction in relationship to student progress on such measures and, insofar as resources permit, make individual diagnoses and prescriptions for different learners on the basis of their performance on such measures. This is a stance totally compatible with the continuing emphasis on measurable instructional objectives seen so frequently in today's educational circles. But rather than forcing the already too busy teacher to conjure up a host of specific objectives and measures related to them, *we have to provide these measures.*

I believe that criterion-referenced measures related to objectives will prove serviceable merely because experience suggests that explicit objectives will be a more parsimonious way of describing a class of learner behaviors than by using the measuring device itself. And please note that by measuring device I do not mean only paper and pencil tests. Surely the bulk of these measures will, for practicality's sake, be in a paper format. But we can use paper formatted measures for more diverse assessment schemes than the classic multiple choice test. Attitudinal inventories, interest questionnaires, indeed, affective measures of all sorts, can be handled by low cost paper measuring devices.

But why use such criterion-referenced measures rather than the time honored standardized tests? A simple question, with a simple answer. Because *for purposes of measuring results reflecting high quality instruction, standardized tests are usually inappropriate.* They were designed, developed, and refined with a totally different purpose in mind, namely, to permit us to distinguish between different learners. For the purpose for which they were intended, standardized tests are fine. When selections among learners are in order, for instance, in predicting which students will succeed in college, standardized tests are super. Well, at least, until some of their ethnic biases are better eliminated, they're the best available. But for purposes of assessing the quality of instruction and for making specific judgments about what certain pupils have learned, standardized tests will typically yield misleading information.

We need more short duration tests which have better *local curricular validity.* There are several ways school principals can attempt to promote the availability of more of these measures. First, they can bring concentrated pressure on America's major test publishers to encourage them to move more rapidly into the development of criterion-referenced measures. Second, they can inspect the suitability of those criterion-referenced measuring devices currently available. Third, if local resources permit, they can develop at least a few measures to deal with particularly high priority goals (perhaps in concert with neighboring schools or school districts).

Once the measures are available, teachers should be encouraged to use them frequently and to make instructional modifications as dictated by the results. And for purposes of instructional evaluation, not every pupil needs to complete every measure in its entirety. The use of *item sampling,* whereby different pupils complete only a small segment of the measuring device, can yield accurate estimates of group performance while conserving valuable instructional time.

The whole thrust of this particular strategy is to provide measures of pupil outcomes so that teachers will not have to judge intuitively whether their instructional tactics are effective, for such intuitions are often as likely to be wrong as they are to be right. Decisions regarding whether to modify or retain a given instructional sequence can be better made by the classroom teacher on the basis of data yielded from criterion-referenced measures.

INSTRUCTIONAL MINI-LESSONS

One vehicle which appears to offer considerable promise in helping classroom teachers increase their ability to produce desirable results with learners is the *instructional mini-lesson,* or sometimes called the *teaching performance test.* By employing these mini-lessons in a systematic inservice or pre-service program there is evidence that instructors can increase their teaching proficiency. For example, teachers who have attempted to improve their instructional effectiveness through the use of mini-lessons have been able to significantly outperform comparable teachers not participating in a mini-lesson improvement program.[2] Further, teachers well versed in instructional principles and experienced with mini-lessons have been able to dramatically exceed the performance of novice teachers. There is evidence beginning to build up which, although only suggestive at the moment, offers considerable support for the role of mini-lessons in preservice and inservice teacher education programs.

In general, instructional mini-lessons are designed to improve a teacher's skill in accomplishing a prespecified instructional objective while at the same time promoting learner interest in the lesson. Here's how they work:

First, a teacher is given an explicit instructional objective along with a sample measurement item showing how the objective's achievement will be measured.

Second, the teacher is given time to plan a lesson designed to achieve the objective.

Third, the teacher instructs a group of learners for a specified period of time, perhaps as few as a half dozen students or as many as a whole class. Certain mini-lessons are designed to be used with adult learners, others with younger learners.

Fourth, the learners are measured with a post-test based on the objective but unseen previously by the teacher. Learner interest in the instruction is also measured.

On the basis of these two indicators, that is, learners' interest ratings and post-test scores, a judgment of the teacher's instructional skill can be derived. Such a judgment does not reflect all dimensions on which a teacher should be judged, only the teacher's ability to accomplish a pre-specified instructional objective with positive learner affect during a short lesson. Nevertheless, this is an important aspect of a teacher's instructional proficiency.

The use of mini-lessons to bring about increases in a teacher's instructional skill is consistent with a basic assumption regarding teaching, namely, that the chief reason for a teacher's existence in the classroom is to bring about desirable changes in learners. Accordingly, one important competency which a teacher should possess is the ability to promote the learner's attainment of specific instructional objectives. Mini-lessons are designed to assess this ability, that is, the teacher's skill in accomplishing pre-specified instructional objectives. Mini-lessons, therefore, can be used as the central focus of pre-service and inservice programs which set out to improve this key instructional skill.[3] Unlike the increasingly popular micro-teaching procedures, the focus of instructional mini-lessons is on learner outcomes, not the procedures employed by the teacher, that is, mini-lessons are product-focused rather than process-focused.

OTHER ALTERNATIVES

While the two specific procedures described here clearly do not exhaust the range of potential approaches we might employ to aid classroom teachers in improving their ability to produce better results, they are certainly consistent with the general theme of increasing the degree to which a teacher should become accountable. If educators can only capitalize on the correct state of educational affairs, rather than being cast in the role of progress-resistors, we may mark the age of accountability as the beginning of a new era indeed.

NOTES

[1] For a further treatment of the California teacher evaluation law see the following document: W. James Popham, *Designing Teacher Evaluation Systems*, Instructional Objectives Exchange, Box 24095, Los Angeles, Califronia 90024. December, 1971, @ $1.25 per copy.

[2] Martin Levine, "The Effect on Pupil Achievement of a Criterion-Referenced Instructional Model Used by Student Teachers," unpublished doctoral dissertation, University of California, Los Angeles, 1971.

[3] At least one firm is currently distributing mini-lessons such as those described here. For information contact Instructional Appraisal Services, 105 Christopher Circle, Ithaca, N.Y. 14850. Filmstrip-tape programs describing how to construct and use teaching performance tests are also available from Vimcet Associates, P.O. Box 24714, Los Angeles, Calif. 90021.

EDUCATIONAL OBJECTIVES AND THE SYSTEMATIC IMPROVEMENT OF INSTRUCTION *

Richard B. Smith

Reinforce Your Own Good Teaching. Are you teaching better this year than last year? How do you *know* whether you are? In this sequence of frames Smith teaches why it is helpful to know exactly how we are teaching in order to know exactly how well we have done. He shows the behavioral trait of emphasis on clarity by being able to point out the results of what we are doing. By being explicit about what we are trying to teach, we can be precise about how well we are teaching it. This makes it possible to compare styles of teaching, methods of presentation, or materials. When we know what we are trying to teach, then we can compare different ways of teaching it. If one method is better than another, then we have been reinforced by our students' learning more, and we can choose to do it in the future. This results in the gradual and systematic improvement of instruction. Here is an example of how we teachers can use behavioral processes to improve our own teaching behavior, and how we can show the process and its results to ourselves and to others. The programmed style of this article uses the behavioral principle that immediate reward (in this case filling in the blanks correctly) is stronger than delayed reward (taking a test or writing a paper later on).

*From Richard B. Smith, "Educational Objectives in the Classroom and the Systematic Improvement of Instruction," mimeographed (DeKalb, Illinois: Northern Illinois University, 1972), frames 1-1 through 1-72, by permission of the author. Richard B. Smith is Professor of Education at Northern Illinois University.

Keep the answer in the right-hand column covered until you have filled in the blank in in the left-hand column.

1-1. Educational Objectives are statements of the goals that teachers have set for their students. The goals that teachers set for their students are called an/a _____ _____ .	educational objective
1-2. When a teacher says that she wants her students to be able to write an anti-pollution petition, she has stated an/a _____ _____ _____	educational objective

1-3.	A coach states that he wants his players to be able to make seventy-five percent of their free throws, he has formulated an/a _____ _____ .	educational objective
1-4.	If a music teacher states that she wants her students to enjoy all kinds of music, she has stated an/a _____ _____ .	educational objective
1-5.	The primary reason for formulating educational objectives is to facilitate the systematic improvement of instruction. Educational objectives make possible the a. _____ improvement of b. _____ .	a. systematic b. instruction
1-6.	If a teacher has not stated his educational objectives or goals, it is difficult for him to know how effective his _____ has been.	instruction
1-7.	Is it likely that teachers will design effective learning experiences for their students if they have no educational objectives in mind? (Yes or No)	No
1-8.	Is it likely that the evaluation procedures of the teacher will be valid if he has no educational objectives in mind? (Yes or No)	No

Three Classifications of Educational Objectives

1-9. The educational objectives with which teachers are concerned can be divided into three different classes or domains. Objectives concerned with traditional verbal or numerical learning are in the *COGNITIVE DOMAIN*; objectives concerned with the learning of physical skills are in the *PSYCHOMOTOR DOMAIN*, and objectives concerned with emotional learning are in the *AFFECTIVE DOMAIN*. The three classes of educational objectives with which teachers are concerned are a. _____ , b. _____ and c. _____ objectives.	a. cognitive b. psychomotor c. affective In any order
1-10. Educational objectives involving the learning of verbal or numerical material belong in the cognitive domain. An economics teacher has as his objective that his students be able to recall the principle of supply and demand. This objective would be classified in the _____ _____ .	cognitive domain
1-11. If a teacher wants her students to be able to define democracy, this objective is concerned with verbal learning and would be classified in the _____ domain.	cognitive
1-12. An arithmetic teacher wants his students to be able to recite the multiplication tables through ten. This objective is in the _____ _____ .	cognitive domain

1-13. A second type of educational objective with which teachers are concerned involves the learning of motor skills. Objectives involving the learning of _____ _____ are classified as belonging to the *psycho-motor domain*.	motor skills
1-14. A physical education teacher has as an objective that his students be able to touch their toes. This objective requires the learning of an/a a. _____ _____ , and would be classified as belonging in the b. psy _ _ _ m_t _ _ domain.	a. motor skill b. psychomotor
1-15. A home economics teacher wants her students to be able to fold beaten egg whites into cake batter. This objective requires learning an/a a. _____ _____ and would be classified in the b. _____ domain.	a. motor skill b. psychomotor
1-16. The third classification of educational objectives with which teachers are concerned is *Affective Objectives*. Educational objectives involving the learning of interests, attitudes, appreciation and values belong in the *Affective Domain*. The _____ _____ contains educational objectives concerned with student interests, attitudes, appreciations and values.	affective domain

1-17. Objectives in the affective domain are concerned with <u>e m</u> _ _ _ _ _ _ learning.	emotional
1-18. When an English teacher says that he wants his students to enjoy reading, he has specified an educational objective that belongs in the _____ _____ .	affective domain
1-19. When a social studies teacher specifies that he wants his students to appreciate the dignity and worth of the individual, the objective is in the _____ _____ .	affective domain
1-20. A mathematics teacher states that he wants his students to like mathematics. This objective would be classified in the _____ _____ .	affective domain
1-21. *INFORMATION FRAME* It is important that you are able to discriminate between educational objectives in the three domains. The following frames are review frames. You can use these frames to determine if you can discriminate between cognitive, affective and psychomotor objectives.	No response required

1-22. The teachers' objective is that her students: Given corporate earnings for the past ten years, predict future earnings for the company. This objective is in the _____ domain.	cognitive
1-23. When a science teacher says that he wants his students to appreciate nature, he has specified an educational objective which is in the _____ _____ .	affective domain
1-24. A chemistry teacher has as an objective that his students be able to bend glass tubing. This objective would be classified in the _____ _____ .	psychomotor domain
1-25. A science teacher wants his students to be able to "apply" the principle of electromagnetic induction. This educational objective is in the _____ _____ .	cognitive domain
1-26. A teacher wants his students to be able to saw a board along a straight line. This objective is concerned with learning a skill, and would be classified in the _____ domain.	psychomotor

1-27. The teachers' objective is that her students: Enjoy reading. This objective is in the _____ domain.	affective
1-28. The teachers' objective is that his students: Be able to make nine out of ten lay-ups in basketball. This objective is in the _____ domain.	psychomotor
1-29. If a teacher wants her students to appreciate literature this objective is concerned with emotional learning and is in the _____ domain.	affective
1-30. A social studies teacher has as his objective that the student be able to recognize the stated assumptions in the *Declaration of Independence.* This educational objective is in the _____ _____ .	cognitive domain

Educational Objectives and the "Model for Instructional Improvement"

1-31. In order to insure the systematic improvement of instruction the teacher needs to incorporate his educational objectives into a *"Model for Instructional Improvement."* The systematic improvement of instruction requires that the instructor utilize his educational objectives in an/a "_____ _____ _____ _____ ."	Model for Instructional Improvement

1-32. The "Model for Instructional Improvement" consists of at least the following steps:
   1. The specification of broad general objectives.
   2. The reduction of broad general objectives to specific objectives.
   3. The design of the learning experience.
   4. Evaluating to determine the effectiveness of the learning experience.
List the four steps in the "Model for Instructional Improvement."
	1. The specification of broad general objectives.
	2. The reduction of broad general objectives to specific objectives.
	3. The design of the learning experience.
	4. Evaluating to determine the effectiveness of the learning experience.

1-33. The "Model for Instructional Improvement," is important because it makes possible the _____ _____ of instruction.	systematic improvement
1-34. If the teacher does not utilize a model similar to the one suggested above, he (will, will not) be able to determine whether the instructional procedure used this term is better than the one used previously.	will not
1-35. The "Model for Instructional Improvement," makes it possible for the teacher to compare the relative effectiveness of different a. _____ procedures for the attainment of a particular educational b. _____ .	a. instructional b. objective

1-36. The four steps in the "Model for Instructional Improvement," are:
   1. The specification of
      a. _____ _____
         _____ .
   2. The reduction of broad general objectives to
      b. _____ _____ .
   3. The design of the
      c. _____ _____ .
   4. d. _____ to determine the effectiveness of the learning experience.

a. broad general objectives.
b. specific objectives.
c. learning experiences
d. Evaluating

1-37. Once educational objectives are incorporated into the "Model for Instructional Improvement," they perform three important functions for the teacher. These are:
   A. They give direction to the planning of the teacher.
   B. They aid in designing adequate learning experience by:
      1. Making it possible for the teacher to compare the effectiveness of different learning experiences.
      2. Enabling the teacher to apply the results of learning research to facilitate the attainment of the objectives.
   C. They make possible the evaluation of instruction.
List the three major functions of educational objectives.

a. They give direction to the planning of the teacher.
b. They aid in designing adequate learning experiences.
c. They make possible the evaluations of instruction.

1-38. Once the educational objectives of the teacher are incorporated into the "Model for Instructional Improvement," they perform three important functions. First, they give a. _____ to the planning of the teacher; second, they aid in the design of b. _____ _____ ; and third, they make the c. _____ of instruction possible.

a. direction
b. learning experiences
c. evaluation

1-39. Too many classroom teachers approach the problem of educational planning by asking themselves the question:
What shall I do today?
A more appropriate question for the teacher to ask would be:
What do I want my students to learn to do today?
When the teacher asks the first question, it indicates that he lacks a. _____ .
The answers to the second question, however, will help give b. _____ to his learning activities.

a. direction
b. direction

1-40. There is an old saying that one cannot know when he has arrived until he knows where he is going. This saying implies the need for having aims or o b _ _ _ _ _ _ _ _ in life.

objectives

1-41. Does it seem likely that a teacher can adequately plan lessons if she does not know what she wants to achieve? (Yes or No)	No
1-42. Efficient instruction requires that the teacher have a goal or an/a _____ objective that he is trying to achieve.	educational
1-43. Under the pressure of class-room work, some teachers do not clearly identify their objectives. They rely on textbooks or course outlines for lesson planning. Some of these teachers may be just covering c o _ _ _ _ _ without a clear educational direction in mind.	content
1-44. When teachers spend classroom time in covering content, we may suspect that they have no clear educational _____ in mind.	objectives
1-45. Without clearly stated educational objectives, the teachers' activities will lack d i r _ _ _ _ _ _ .	direction
1-46. The first major function of educational objectives is to _____ _____ .	give direction to the planning of the teacher

1-47. Once the educational objectives are specified and incorporated into the "Model for Instructional Improvement," they can perform their second function, which is to aid the teacher in designing an effective _____ _____ .	learning experience
1-48. In addition to providing the teacher with direction for educational planning, educational objectives allow the teacher to a. s y s _ _ m-_ _ _ _ _ _ l l y improve instruction by aiding in the design of b. _____ experiences.	a. systematically b. learning
1-49. Educational objectives facilitate the improvement of instruction by aiding in the design of learning experiences. They do this by: A. Making it possible for the teacher to compare the effectiveness of different a. _____ _____ . B. Enabling the teacher to apply the results of learning b. _____ to facilitate the attainment of educational objectimes.	a. learning experiences b. research
1-50. Once a teacher has formulated the objectives that he wants his students to attain, he is in a position to make judgments about the _____ of the learning experience that has been used.	effectiveness or something that means the same

1-51.   When a teacher selects a learning experience that he believes will lead to the attainment of his objective, he is really hypothesizing that the learning experience will enable the students to reach the objective. If his educational objective has been properly stated, he can determine whether or not his objective was achieved. He can then accept or reject the _____ about the effectiveness of the learning experience.

hypothesis

1-52.   If a teacher is able to determine after a series of lectures on the advantages and disadvantages of the different kinds of interest charged by loan companies, that sixty percent of his students are not able to select the loan that would be most advantageous for them, he is in a position to reject the hypothesis that the lectures led to the attainment of the objective. He can then a. _____ improve instruction by designing and testing other learning experiences which may be more appropriate for the attainment of his b. _____ .

a. systematically
b. educational objectives

1-53.   A golf instructor has as his objective that his students be able to consistently drive a golf ball 175 yards in a straight line. After running his students through a prescribed learning experience, he finds that 70% of his students have severe slices. With this data he is in a position to reject the a. _____ that the prescribed learning experiences were effective. He can then go on to b. _____ modify the learning experiences in an attempt to get a greater portion of the students to attain his objective.

a. hypothesis
b. systematically

1-54.   An English teacher has as an educational objective that his students like poetry. After the first unit, however, he found out that eighty percent of his students think that poetry is irrelevant. This data can be used by the teacher as a justification for modifying the _____ _____ in such a way that a higher percentage of his students will come to like poetry.

learning experiences

1-55.   Educational objectives also enable the teacher to apply the results of *learning research* to facilitate the attainment of specific types of educational objectives.

Educational objectives can be classified according to the kind of learning involved. When this is done, it is possible to utilize the results of a. _____ research to facilitate the attainment of the b. _____ _____ .	a. learning b. educational objective
1-56. When the teacher is able to identify the kind of learning involved in the attainment of an educational objective, he can use the results of the _____ _____ for that particular kind of learning to aid in the attainment of the educational objective.	learning research
1-57. Once a teacher has identified that the educational objective—learning the multiplication tables from one through ten—requires multiple discriminant learning; he can use the findings from research on _____ _____ learning to aid him in designing a learning experience that will lead to the efficient attainment of the objective.	multiple discriminant
1-58. When a teacher recognizes that the educational objective. "the students will be able to identify examples of mammals" involves concept learning, he can utilize the research on concept formation and attainment to help him design an/a a._____ experience that will efficiently lead to the attainment of the b._____ _____ .	a. learning b. educational objective

1-59. List the first and second major functions of educational objectives in the "Model for Instructional Improvement."

a. _____
_____

b. _____
_____

a. give direction to the planning of the teacher
b. aid in the design of learning experiences

1-60. After the educational objectives have been incorporated into the "Instructional Model," they can perform their third function which is to enable the instructor to _____ the outcome of the learning experience.

evaluate

1-61. The third major function of educational objectives in the "Model," is to make it possible for the teacher to a. _____ the attainment of the objective. When teachers formulate specific behavioral objectives, they have specific criteria with which to evaluate the effectiveness of the learning experiences. When educational objectives describe the specific student behaviors, it is possible to judge the effectiveness of the learning experience by determining whether or not the student or students can b. _____ .

a. evaluate
b. perform the behaviors (or something that means the same)

1-62.	Can a teacher actually see learning occur? (Yes or No)	No
1-63.	Because the teacher cannot see learning occur, he must observe changes in the learner's behavior, and from these *infer* that learning has occurred. Learning cannot be directly observed. For this reason the teacher must observe changes in the capabilities of the learner, and from these _____ that learning has occurred.	infer
1-64.	Teachers cannot see learning take place. Teachers can only observe student behavior and make *inferences* about learning based upon changes in the student behavior. If Joe could not do long division problems prior to the learning experience, *but can do* them after the learning experiences, the teacher can _____ that learning has occurred.	infer
1-65.	The evaluation procedures used in the "Model," are *VALID* to the extent that they directly relate to the attainment of the educational objective. Another way of saying this is to say that the evaluation procedure is _____ to the extent that it adequately reflects the desired change in the behavior of the learner.	valid

1-66.	If the educational objective is not specified, is it possible for the teacher to evaluate the attainment of the objective? (Yes or No)	No
1-67.	If the educational objective is not stated, is it possible for the teacher to evaluate the effectiveness of the learning experience? (Yes or No)	No
1-68.	An evaluation procedure is a. _____ to the extent that it indicates the ability of the student to perform the b. _____ stated in the educational objectives.	a. valid b. behaviors
1-69.	Teachers evaluate the learning experiences based upon changes that occur in student behavior. In order to evaluate if Joe has learned his multiplication tables from one to ten, the teacher would ask Joe to _____	recite the multiplication tables from one to ten. (or something that means the same)
1-70.	If a teacher has as his educational objective that his students be able: To pick out the unstated assumptions involved in arguments. He would evaluate the attainment of this objective by giving his students sample arguments and asking them to _____ _____ .	pick out the unstated assumptions

1-71. The educational objective for which a teacher is striving is that his students: Like to grow things. Attainment of this educational objective would be evaluated by observing the extent to which the students are actively and voluntarily involved in _____ _____ .	growing things
1-72. The above seems obvious; however, unless the educational objectives are stated in terms of the specifically desired student behaviors it (is, is not) possible to determine that learning has occurred.	is not

DOING YOUR OWN THING WITH PRECISION: THE ESSENCE OF BEHAVIOR MANAGEMENT IN THE CLASSROOM *

Joseph Zimmerman and Elaine Zimmerman

with Shanron L. Rider, Alice F. Smith and Ruthanna Dinn

The Behavior Modifier as Facilitator. The authors of this article make several behavioral points strongly. First, behavioral education does not specify the goals of education but shows ways of reaching goals. As the authors say, they facilitated the teachers' reaching whatever goals they had in mind. Second, behavioral educational techniques work best when the teacher is explicit about the behavior she wants or doesn't want as in steps A through D in the second and third weekly sessions. The teachers in these projects modified clearly observable, specific actions such as "talking out" instead of a more general vague word such as "not following directions" or "fooling around." Third, behaviorists concern themselves with the specific actions of students, not with underlying reasons or unconscious causes, as Freudians are likely to do.

In January, 1969, the first two authors were asked to design, implement and conduct a behavior modification workshop for elementary school teachers. The purpose of the workshop was to expose volunteer teachers to the rationale and methodology of precision teaching and behavior management. The two specific purposes of this article are to describe the organization and implementation of the workshop and to present some representative results. Our more general purpose is to employ these descriptions as a vehicle with which to present our approach to the problem of teaching teachers to teach.

RECRUITING PARTICIPANTS

We were asked to recruit teachers (K through 4) from seven selected[1] inner-city schools. To stimulate interest in both the workshop and the behavior modification approach, and in an attempt to recruit at least five to ten workshop participants, we employed the following procedures. All the teachers (K through 4) and administrators of the seven schools were invited to attend a two-hour Behavior Modification Institute at a downtown restaurant. The major incentive for attending the Institute was the opportunity to hear about and discuss the application of behavior

*From Joseph Zimmerman et al., "Doing Your Own Thing with Precision: The Essence of Behavioral Management in the Classroom," *Educational Technology* 11, no. 4 (April, 1971): 26–32, by permission of the authors. Joseph Zimmerman is Professor of Psychology at the Indiana University School of Medicine. Elaine Zimmerman is with the Butler University School of Education. Shanron L. Rider, Alice F. Smith and Ruthanna Dinn are with the Indianapolis Public Schools.

modification approaches to problems encountered in the public school classroom. The Institute included a multi-media presentation entitled, "A Fifth Grade Therapist."[2]

At the conclusion of the Institute, the teachers in attendance were given the opportunity to register for a ten-week Precision Teaching and Behavior Management workshop. Registrants could earn either graduate credit (Psychology or Education) with tuition paid, or a $50 honorarium.

We considered these preliminary procedures successful since (a) over 40 of the 70 persons invited attended the Institute and (b) 14 participants were recruited for the workshop, even though the spring semester was six weeks underway and the workshop was scheduled for Saturday mornings.

WORKSHOP GOALS AND BRIEF SUMMARY OF WORKSHOP PROCEDURES

The specific goals of the workshop were to help the teachers acquire the skills of (a) objectively defining academic and conduct behaviors; (b) systematically applying behavior management procedures *of their own choice* to improve academic performance or classroom conduct in individual students or groups of students; and (c) quantitatively assessing the behavioral effects of their management procedures. To meet these goals, we conducted the workshop primarily as a practicum, or laboratory course, in which the teachers used their own students as subjects for classroom management projects. Our functional behavioral target for each participant was that each would conduct at least one management project within his own classroom. To achieve this we made the consequences of participating in the workshop contingent upon the target performance. The participants were informed that in order to earn a grade of "B" or to earn the honorarium, they were required to conduct an acceptable behavior management project in their classroom and turn in a report. A grade of "A" could be earned only if two acceptable behavior projects were conducted. Unfortunately, similar differential reinforcement with respect to the honoraria could not be arranged.

A minimally acceptable behavior management project was defined as one in which (a) a conduct behavior or academic performance is pinpointed (defined in objective and measurable terms); (b) the frequency of the pinpointed behavior is measured daily under specified Baseline (pre-treatment) conditions; and (c) the daily measurement is continued following either a single application of—or under the systematic, daily application of—at least one objectively defined instructional or management treatment.

The workshop started at the level of the teachers' current repertoires and needs. Its primary focus was upon the idiosyncratic problems encountered by the participants in their classrooms and their influence upon and reactions to specified behaviors of their students. Classroom problems encountered and dealt with by other teachers and researchers in other settings were discussed and presented only as they provided a foundation for the participants' own work or as they were relevant to particular problems or solutions proposed by participants. Similarly, behavior management principles were discussed only when directly relevant to the problems stated by and data presented by participants. The only reading materials made available to all participants were those written by Lindsley (1966), Surratt & Wolfe (1969) and Ulrich, Wolfe & Bluhm (1968), each of which emphasizes background and rationale rather than particular "recipes" for behavioral modification.

The participants met weekly on Saturday mornings. These meetings were conducted in an informal manner, and all participants were encouraged to contribute to the discussion.

Since the participants came to the workshop with little knowledge of what others had done in the area of behavior management and with no experience with respect to the formal workshop requirements, during the initial three weeks they were provided with some minimal background and support. This was accomplished, in part, with a formal presentation by Dr. Eric Haughton, who conducted the first session. He initiated the workshop by describing a variety of projects conducted under his consultation with teachers in the Eugene, Oregon Public Schools.

During the second and third weekly sessions, the leaders emphasized general methodology and strategy in the context of having the teachers discuss the specific conduct and academic problems which they faced in their own classes. When a participant presented a problem (i.e., poor classroom conduct or unsatisfactory academic performances in a student or a group of students), he was asked to (a) pinpoint or objectively define the behavior to which he was explicitly referring (i.e., being out of one's seat frequently or spelling few words correctly on spelling tests); (b) suggest how he could objectively measure this pinpointed behavior; (c) state what he generally did (if anything) when the problem behavior was observed; and, finally, (d) suggest a procedure which might successfully alter the problem behavior where it applied systematically. Thus, the strategy of a classroom project was discussed with each participant's own classroom problem(s) as the basic discussion material. Approaches taken by others were sometimes described when appropriate to specific problems raised by participants or when they illustrated alternative measurement or treatment approaches. Such outside material was not usually provided to influence a participant in the direction of a particular treatment or approach. On the contrary, the teachers were strongly encouraged to "do their own thing."

During the initial three weeks of the workshop, the second author visited each classroom during the school day on at least two different occasions. She observed the teachers in their classroom settings and conferred with them on problems and potential methods of implementing the methodology being presented and discussed in the weekly sessions.

At the end of the third session and during the fourth session, participants proposed their first behavior projects. Each project was discussed and refined with the aid of all participants.

In the remaining sessions, second and third proposals were presented by those participants who chose to undertake additional challenges, and participants presented data collected to date. The final weekly session was devoted to summarizing results by having each participant give a 10- to 15-minute summary of his project(s).

OVERVIEW OF THE RESULTS

The participants, as a group, conducted and reported 26 projects. While most initial projects were undertaken for the purpose of decelerating "undesirable" conduct, the majority of the additional projects were devoted to academic acceleration in individual students or groups of students. This was due, at least in part, to promising early returns of several of the initial projects which had been devoted to academic improvement. Of the 26 projects, 10 were conduct deceleration projects, and 16 were academic acceleration projects. The former focused on talk-outs, out-of-seat behavior or coming-up-to-the-teacher behavior. The latter covered many academic areas, but mainly involved arithmetic skills, spelling, and drawing correct symbols and letters.

A large variety of treatments were actually employed. Among these were public measurement, team competition for prizes (inspired by a preprint of the paper of Barrish, Saunders & Wolf, 1969) response-contingent positive reinforcement (with candy, tokens, choice of activity, self-drawn or teacher-drawn smiles, etc.), opportunity to engage in a preferred activity such as serving as class monitor or "teaching" a reading group, and the use of a tutorial system.

Nine of the 14 participants took the workshop for academic credit, while the remaining five took it for the honorarium. A comparison between the performance of these two groups is suggestive, if not instructive. *Each* of the former nine teachers conducted *at least* two projects and as a group they conducted a total of 21 projects. In marked contrast, only four of the latter five teachers conducted a project and a total of only five projects were submitted by this group.

SOME REPRESENTATIVE PROJECTS

In this section we will briefly describe five of the projects in order to give the reader an idea of the kinds of projects which can readily be conducted by a *single* teacher in his or her classroom. The first and fifth projects were conducted by the third author, the second and third were conducted by the fourth author, and the fourth was conducted by the last author.

Project 1. G is a six-year-old kindergarten student. She was generally disruptive and frequently talked out, moved around and bothered other students. Since the teacher felt that talk-outs were the most disruptive of her "undesirable" behaviors, she chose their deceleration as the target of

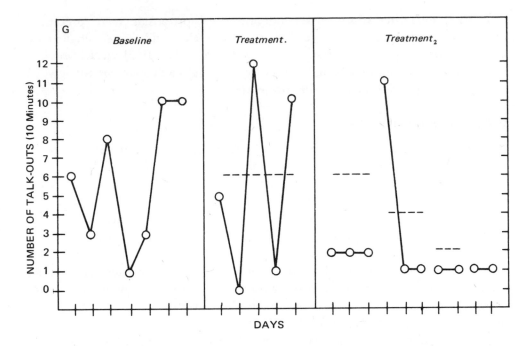

her first behavior project. She measured the number of times that G talked out in a daily ten-minute quiet period. At this time the children were supposed to work quietly and not speak unless they raised their hands and received permission to do so. A talk-out was defined as speaking without receiving such permission. It could comprise a single word or several sentences. The completion of one talk-out was delineated by at least five seconds of quiet. Throughout the 22-day project, the teacher sat quietly at her desk during each ten-minute quiet period and counted G's talk-outs. During the seven Baseline days, no instructions were given to the class and G was ignored when she talked out; G talked out one to ten times in the Baseline sessions. Prior to the eighth session, which occurred on a Monday, the entire class was informed that G's talk-outs would be counted each day during the quiet period. The teacher then promised to take the class to the gym on Friday if G would talk out six or fewer times during each of the five quiet periods of this week.

At the end of each of the five Treatment₁ sessions, the teacher announced the number of talk-outs that G produced. G failed to meet the contingency on the third Treatment₁ day, and, thus, the data taken on the next two days were of no consequence to the class. During the Saturday workshop meeting which followed the 12th session, the data described to this point were presented. One of the participants suggested the use of a *daily* and *immediate* class consequence. Two days later, immediately before the 13th session, the teacher told the class that if G talked out six or fewer times during the quiet period, the class could play a game of their choice for five minutes *immediately following* that period; G talked out only twice in the first Treatment₂ session. As a consequence, the class was reinforced. The instructions were repeated prior to each of the nine subsequent Treatment$_2$ sessions, but the contingency was lowered to four, two and one talk-out, as indicated. G met the given contingency on all but one Treatment$_2$ session. Unfortunately, the semester ended before a contingency involving no talk-outs could be employed. The data suggest, however, that G would have had little trouble meeting such a contingency.

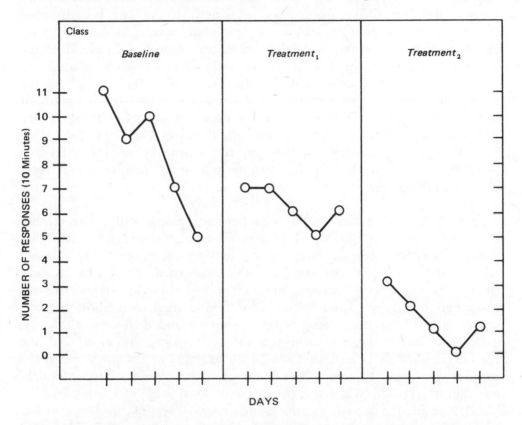

Project 2. This project was conducted with an entire first-grade class. The teacher complained that many of the students left their work and came to her needlessly and without permission throughout the day. She chose the deceleration of this behavior across all students as the target of her first project. She measured the number of times that students came up to her desk without permission in a daily ten-mintute period during which the children were supposed to work quietly at their desks. If a student did so, left, and then came to her again, he contributed two times to the total for the session. When a student came up without permission he was responded to "appropriately and briefly" and then ignored. At no time during the project was the class told that their behavior was being counted.

During the five Baseline days, no special instructions were given to the class. From five to 11 coming-up-to-the-teacher responses were recorded in the Baseline sessions. Unfortunately, the frequency of the behavior was decreasing over these sessions, and the teacher should have continued measuring under Baseline conditions until the data stabilized. Since she did not, it could be argued that the systematic approach which she initially employed could have contributed to the decreasing results. In any case, prior to the sixth session, she applied her first treatment. She discussed the "problem" that she was having with the students coming up to her without permission and suggested that they not do this unless they "thought it to be very important." The results which followed the discussion did not differ from those obtained in the last two Baseline sessions. Prior to the 11th session the "problem" was again discussed with the class, but this time the teacher asked for suggestions. Several of the children "suggested that, because drawn smiles and frowns were used as a class grading system, these could be also used here." During each of the Treatment$_2$ sessions, whenever a child came up to the teacher without permission, a frown was drawn under his name on a chart of names which was already present on one of the blackboards. The data show that Treatment$_2$ was effective in reducing the frequency of the offending behavior. In the final three sessions, only one or two responses were observed per session.

Project 3. C.M. is a first-grader with poor arithmetic skills. Her teacher chose to improve her test performance in this area as the target of her second behavior project. Prior to conducting the project, the teacher constructed ten equivalent tests of ten items each. Each test involved simple first-grade level addition, subtraction and ordinality items. The test construction was done carefully, item by item, so that each whole test was comparable to all the others, both in content and difficulty. C.M. was given a different test daily on ten successive days. On each day, the teacher handed her a test, told her to do as many of the problems as she could in ten minutes, and collected the paper ten minutes later. Throughout the project C.M. was *never* given specific knowledge of her results.

C.M. wrote three to five correct answers on each of the five Baseline tests. Prior to administering the sixth test, the teacher asked C.M. what she would most like to do in the classroom if she had the opportunity to do something that she presently was not permitted to do. She stated that she would like to "teach the low reading group" of which she was a member. The teacher told her that to earn the privilege of doing so she would have to improve her arithmetic skills. She was then briefly shown the five previous tests and her scores, and told that she would indeed teach her reading group on any day that she correctly answered more than five items on a test. Knowledge of results provided to C.M. after each of the subsequent Treatment tests was exclusively confined to her teacher's statement that she earned the privilege of "teaching" her reading group.

The data show that C.M. answered more than five items correctly on *each* of the final five tests. Her Treatment performances, therefore, did not overlap with her Baseline performances. Indeed, she wrote eight or nine correct answers on the final three tests. Her teacher also reported that, as a consequence of her particular choice of reward, C.M.'s reading skills also improved. It was pointed out to the teacher, however, that

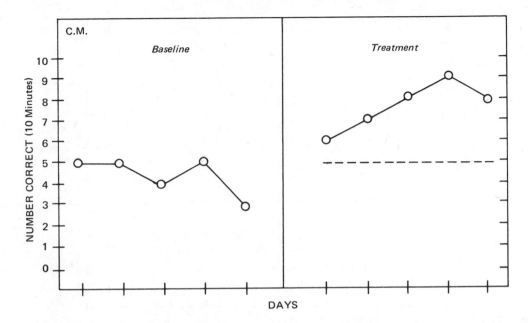

although this made sense (since if you have to "teach," you had better be ahead of your "students"), in the absence of objective data, this observation would have to be considered anecdotal and subjective. It does suggest, however, an obvious and readily assessable method of accelerating academic performance.

Project 4. M is a nine-year-old third-grader who "demands much teacher attention and spends much of his classroom time doing anything but class work." One of his worst academic subjects is spelling, and "he had spelled no more than two or three words correctly all semester." His teacher chose the improvement of his spelling as the target of her first project. Since she considered M's spelling performance to be extremely poor, and since he seemed to completely lack any motivation with respect to spelling, she indicated that she would be satisfied if he would spell 20 words correctly by the end of the semester! When she presented this problem in a workshop session, she also posed the problem of how to give him a daily spelling test without taking teaching time away from the rest of the class. The suggested solution was that she construct a test which called for the spelling of words which corresponded to pictures. She constructed such a test by drawing 20 pictures on a ditto master and running off many copies.

The test called for the spelling of 20 nouns. It included, among others, pictures of a boat, dress, pencil, snake, table, etc. The first item was a picture of a boy's face which she identified to M as a picture of himself. This insured that M could spell at least one of the words correctly, since he had spelled his first name correctly on many previous occasions. Throughout the 24-day project, the teacher gave M a copy of the test at the same time each morning. He was told to look at each picture and spell

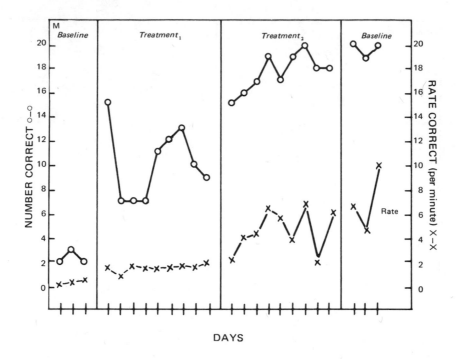

DAYS

the corresponding word on the line which was immediately to the right of the picture. He was asked to spell as many words as he could and then raise his hand as soon as he had done so. When he raised his hand, or when ten minutes had elapsed, the teacher went over to M, marked down the elapsed time on his paper, removed the paper, marked it, and finally told him how many words he had spelled correctly.

Results were obtained over her 24-day project in terms of both the number of words M spelled correctly on each test, and the rate of correct words (number correct divided by elapsed time). The data show that on each of three Baseline tests, M spelled only two or three words correctly. Before administering the fourth test, the teacher told M that he could earn five minutes of free-play time at the end of the school day for each correctly spelled word.[3] She added that if he missed only one word he could also earn the right to visit her home (he had done so once before and enjoyed it), and that if he turned in a perfect paper he could visit her home and bring a classmate of his choice. On the first test under Treatment$_1$, M spelled 15 words correctly. By doing so he earned 75 minutes of free-play time at the end of the day.

On the next eight tests, however, M correctly spelled between seven and 13 words. Although each of these scores markedly exceeded his three Baseline scores, each was lower than his first Treatment$_1$ score. When the results described to this point were presented at a Saturday session of the Workshop, it was suggested that the teacher make the consequences of correct spelling more immediate. The teacher pointed out that, although there had indeed been a three-hour delay between the test and the earned free play, this was necessary in order to provide M with sufficient time to collect his five minutes per correct word under conditions in which he correctly spelled ten or more words. When asked how much time was available between the end of the test and lunch, she indicated that 40 minutes was an absolute maximum. It was then suggested that she decreased the earned time to two minutes of free play per correct word but that this be available *immediately* after the test was marked.

On the first Treatment$_2$ test, M again spelled 15 words correctly. His scores increased thereafter, however; and on each of the final seven Treatment$_2$ tests, M spelled between 17 and 20 words correctly! On the seventh Treatment$_2$ day he earned the right to visit his teacher and bring a classmate along. Prior to administering the test for the 22nd time, the teacher informed M that she wanted to see how well he could do on his own without earning free play for spelling words correctly. On the final three tests, M spelled 20, 19 and 20 words correctly.

Although this project utilized the same 20-word test each day, and one could argue that a motivated student with spelling skills could have learned to write a perfect paper with just two or three test exposures, by conducting the project the teacher learned several things about this student specifically, and about contingency management in general. One notable result was M's performance on the first Treatment$_1$ test. This marked and immediate improvement in spelling performance suggested that M's Baseline performances did not reflect his spelling ability. The second important set of results was that, while under continued application of the Treatment$_1$ contingency M did not maintain his initial performance level, his performances did improve markedly under Treatment$_2$ when the consequences of spelling words correctly were made *immediate*. A third important result is illustrated by a comparison of M's number of correct responses and his *rate of correct responses* over the project. While both his average number of correct problems and his average correct rate (number of problems per minute) increased from condition to condition, the latter measure seemed to be a more sensitive indicator of his improvement. This seems reasonable in light of the fact that the first measure had a ceiling of 20 words, while the rate (or speed) measure had no such ceiling. Both performance measures showed four- to five-fold increases from Baseline to Treatment$_1$. From Treatment$_1$ to Treatment$_2$, however, the average number of correct responses showed less than a two-fold increase, while the average rate showed more than a three-fold increase. The difference in sensitivity of the two measures becomes especially apparent when one compares initial and final test performances. While the final score was ten times as high as the initial score (20 correct compared with two correct), the final correct response rate was *50 times higher* (10.0 per minute compared with 0.2 per minute) than the initial rate.

Project 5. The final project to be described is an outstanding example of those projects which were devoted to tracking and accelerating academic

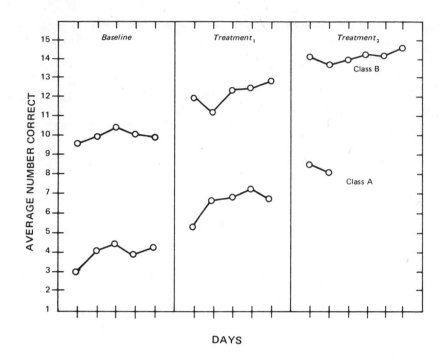

performance in large groups of students or in an entire class. The third author ran such a project with each of her two kindergarten classes. One of these two classes (class A) met in one of the seven selected schools, while the other (class B) did not. She chose as her project target the concurrent tracking and improvement of several skills. These included color discrimination, the recognition and printing of letters, and the recognition of numbers. She constructed one 26-item test in which the correct answer to each item depended upon all of these skills. The test called for printing a given letter in a given color in a particular numbered box. The test form consisted of five rows of numbered boxes. The two items were: "In the box with the number *1*, write a *blue* A; in the box with the number *2*, write a *brown* B." The remaining items similarly called for writing the letters C through Z in boxes 3 through 26, and each letter was to be written in one of eight specified colors.

Throughout the 12-day project[4] conducted with class A and the 16-day project conducted with Class B, the teacher seated the students in pairs, back to back, at the same time each day. She handed each student a set of crayons and the 26-box test form, and then read each of the 26 items, one by one. She waited about 30 seconds after reading each item. An item was marked as correct *only* if the proper letter was written in the proper color *and* in the proper box. In the case of class A the average correct was plotted for the 16 students (out of 22) who were not absent on more than two Baseline days or two Treatment₁ days, and who were present on at least one of the two Treatment₂ days. In the case of class B this average was plotted for the 10 students (out of 11) who were not absent more than two days under any of the three conditions.[5] The nature of the Baseline, Treatment$_1$ and Treatment$_2$ conditions was the same for both classes. During Baseline days, students received no information about their test performances.

The data charted by the teacher show that the class B students averaged about ten items correct while the class A students averaged about four items correct on the fifth Baseline test. In the case of each class, the daily average did not increase from the second through the fifth Baseline test. This latter observation was also representative of the results obtained with most of the individual students. In the case of 11 of the 26 class A and B students, the final Baseline test score actually exceeded the final score in the case of eight of the students. Indeed, only three of the 26 students showed a consistent increase in scores over successive Baseline tests.

After the first five tests were given, the teacher noted *each* student's average Baseline test score in her notebook. Prior to administering the test for the sixth time, the teacher told the children that if they did better than their average on the previous tests or if they scored 23 or more correct, a smiling face would be drawn on their papers. If they did not exceed their average, however, a frowning face would be drawn. The next five tests were marked on the evening of the test day and the students were briefly shown their results at the beginning of the next day's class meeting. The Treatment$_1$ instructions, per se, resulted in a marked increase in the average number of correct items obtained in each class. That is, in comparison with results obtained on the final Baseline test, on the first Treatment$_1$ test, the class B average increased 20 percent while the class A average increased 25 percent. This result was representative of the majority of students in the two classes. Indeed, 17 students obtained a higher score on the first Treatment$_1$ test than on the final Baseline test, while only three students obtained a lower score.

With brief visual exposure to smiles and frowns on their papers, the students' daily scores rose over Treatment$_1$ to averages of more than 12½ correct items and seven correct items in the case of class B and class A, respectively. The improvement in average performance from Baseline to Treatment$_1$ was representative of the vast majority of students. Twenty-three of the 26 students had a higher average on Treatment$_1$ tests than on Baseline tests.

Prior to administering the test for the 11th time, the teacher told the students that from now on any child who received a smile on his paper would earn a choice of a piece of candy or bubble gum, a hero button, or five minutes of an activity of his choice. Among the activities chosen by the children were playing the piano, using the chalkboard, and washing the dishes in the doll corner. In all other ways the Treatment$_2$ conditions were similar to the Treatment$_1$ conditions. The Treatment$_2$ instructions, per se, resulted in a marked increase in the average number of correct items obtained in each class. That is, in comparison with results obtained on the final treatment$_1$ tests, the class B average increased 10 percent while the class A average increased 20 percent. This result was also representative of the majority of students in the two classes. Sixteen students obtained a higher score on the first Treatment$_2$ test than on the final Treatment$_1$ test, while only four students obtained a lower score.

Class B was exposed to Treatment$_2$ for five additional days. With continued brief exposure of these students to smiles and frowns, together with their opportunity to trade in smiles for tangible or activity rewards, class B's daily performance rose over Treatment$_2$ to an average of almost 15 correct items. The improvement in class B average performance from Treatment$_1$ to Treatment$_2$ was representative of the majority of class B students. Seven of these ten students had a higher average on Treatment$_2$ tests than on Treatment$_1$ tests, while only one had a lower average.

The teacher gained much valuable information in the process of conducting this most ambitious group project. First, she observed that the systematic application of management procedures across entire classes could lead to academic acceleration in the majority of students; in fact, only two of the 26 students failed to show at least minimal improvement in skills as a result of being exposed to the conditions applied after the Baseline tests. Second, and perhaps of greater importance, the teacher was able to objectively follow daily progress (or lack of the same) in each of her students within and between each of the project conditions. Thus, by the end of the project she could readily differentiate between those students who accelerated over the project and those who made little or no progress. Furthermore, in the case of the former students, she could readily identify the conditions under which each showed the greatest amount of improvement. Had the teacher completed the project early in the school year, she could have used this information in attempting to accelerate other skills. Finally, in the case of the students who made no progress, she could differentiate between those who performed well on some days but not on others, independent of the conditions, and those who consistently failed to correctly answer more than one or two items per test, throughout the project. Such differential information could certainly have been of great value to her in working with these individuals after the completion of the project, had this occurred earlier in the school year.

One final result of this project may be of considerable importance. While all the daily averages obtained in class B exceeded all those obtained in class A, the treatments applied following the Baseline condition differentially increased the class A averages. In particular, while the class B averages increased about 40 percent from the final Baseline tests to the initial Treatment$_2$ tests, the corresponding class A averages increased 100 percent. It is not possible, given only the teacher's data, to specify the variables which accounted for the greater part of the differential effect. One can argue, however, that this observation does not support the notion that a difficult test[6] would be a poor vehicle with which to attempt to evaluate and accelerate academic performance in groups of students whose Baseline performances suggest a marked lack of academic skills across most members of the group.

DISCUSSION

In designing the teachers' workshop we were guided by two basic considerations. First, we wanted the curriculum to be maximally *relevant* to the pressing needs and dispositions of the participants. Therefore, we placed major emphasis upon the idiosyncratic conduct and academic problems which the participants encountered in their own classrooms, and encouraged them to suggest and apply their own preferred procedures in attempting to deal with those problems. Second, we wanted to conduct a *functional* workshop, or practicum, which would directly provide the participants with behavior management experiences and skills. Therefore, rather than stress the participants' exposure to principles and to information provided by other workers, we placed major emphasis upon the teachers' work in their own classrooms. We did so by making their successful completion of the workshop contingent upon the implementation and completion of one or more classroom behavior management projects.

Since the participants chose both the behavior target and the treatment(s) to be applied in planning their projects, and since the projects required precise definition and daily behavior measurement, the theme of the workshop could have been entitled, "Doing your own thing with precision." We encouraged the participants to "do their own things" for several reasons. First, we saw our role as that of helping the teachers to meet their own classroom goals, rather than specifying what those goals should be. We did not consider it our function to press for or to endorse the choice of any particular behavior target. In addition, we recognized that each teacher would be "the establishment" in his own classroom and would manage it in accordance with his own goals, values and dispositions.

In light of this, we considered it strategically unsound to push for the application of given pet recipes. This tactic often leads to the alienation of teachers who find the use of given procedures to be in conflict with their own values. Finally, we are not invested in specific behavior targets or recipes for modifying behavior. Indeed, as Zimmerman *et al.* (1969) suggested, "The arbitrariness of such investments has too seldom been suggested by advocates of the behavior modification approach, perhaps because, being human ourselves, we also collect pets. It seems obvious to us, however, that until far more objective data of the kind that we advocate are generated, the choice of any specific behavior target and any specific recipe must of necessity remain in the realm of value judgment."

We first expressed these convictions to the participants during the preliminary Institute. When we interacted with the audience at that

Institute, several teachers objected to the use of tangible rewards on the grounds that "students were being *bribed* to do what they were supposed to do anyway." We *did not* respond to these opinions by appealing to the dictionary definition of "bribery" and engaging in logical argument. Instead, we indicated that if a given suggested recipe for improving behavior is objectionable to a given teacher, then the latter should choose a method which he is more disposed to apply. We emphasized this point by indicating that we had no objection to the use of any specific procedure, as long as it did not violate school rules *and* if it could be shown to be effective in improving behavior. As an example we suggested that, if a teacher preferred to yell at a child in order to improve his behavior, yelling would be a fine procedure, if it indeed proved to be effective. If, on the other hand, yelling had little effect, and the teacher failed to discriminate its lack of effect, she could be yelling all semester to no avail.

As we interacted with the workshop participants in the weekly meetings, they confirmed our feelings about the subjective nature of the choice of particular behavior targets and recipes. Our "experts" strongly disagreed with the choices of their fellow participants on many occasions. For example, when some teachers proposed to measure and later decelerate talk-outs or out-of-seat behavior, others expressed disapproval by indicating that they preferred to have movement and chatter in their own classes. Another example of such disagreement was mentioned in the description of Project 4.

We did not sell pet recipes but, on the contrary, strongly encouraged each teacher to "do his own thing." We verbally and functionally indicated that our investment was in the way that "his own thing" was done. What we "pushed" was *objective behavior measurement,* since we consider this to be the *essence* of behavior modification. Such measurement is crucial because it alone can provide the teacher with a clear picture of a student's behavior before a management procedure is applied, and it can subsequently provide unambiguous feedback with respect to the behavioral effects of a management procedure. *By measuring behavior on a daily basis, both before and after the application of the procedures, the teacher can clearly determine whether his procedure improves behavior, has little or no effect, or perhaps even makes things worse.* Finally, we put teeth into our "mouth noise"[7] by requiring that each participant implement and complete at least one classroom management project in order to receive credit for the workshop.

In specifying the requirements for an acceptable project, we made it clear that while improvement in behavior is always a goal to be aimed at, credit for a project DID NOT depend upon the achievement of positive results. Had we insisted upon positive results, we would have probably set the occasion for some "dry-labbing." Our major reason for not including such a requirement was based upon our own previous experiences. While most of our applied research has provided us with valuable information with respect to individual description and treatment effects, *we have never observed that a given treatment "works" for all subjects. Indeed, we have occasionally observed that treatments which are effective for many subjects can actually make things worse in the case of a given subject. Since we find ourselves in a world which is filled with panacea-pushing pitchmen, but which is relatively devoid of direct behavioral assessment of pet recipes, we chose to emphasize process rather than specific outcome in both the design and conduct of this workshop.*

We feel that it is as important to know when a procedure does not work, or when it actually makes things worse, as it is to know when the intended job is being accomplished. Behavior measurement, when carefully applied, will provide this information. A teacher who knows how to *objectively measure behavior* will be able to apply this skill to new problems which will confront him throughout his professional career.

Most teachers want to take responsibility for their practices. With the methodology now available it is no longer tenable to blame the student, pass the buck to other professionals, or wait until achievement test time in order to get feedback about academic progress. The teacher *is* the curriculum and the professional in education. What we have called the essence of the behavior modification approach, objective behavior measurement, is one of the most cogent methods at his disposal for dealing with conduct and academic problems in the classroom.

One year after the workshop was held, we conducted an informal follow-up by telephoning each of the 13 participants who successfully completed the workshop. We asked them whether their classroom practices were influenced by this participation. Ten of the 13 served as classroom teachers during the 1969-1970 academic year. Nine of these ten teachers reported that the workshop significantly influenced their classroom practices. All nine indicated that they employed one or more behavior management techniques during the year. Seven reported and described their use of behavior measurement for the purpose of objectively monitoring classroom behavior and/or assessing the effects of management procedures.

The teachers' workshop described in this article was supported by ESEA Title III Grant No. 68-06757-0 (Behavioral and Learning Disabilities Project) to the Indianapolis Public Schools. We are greatly indebted to Dr. Ogden R. Lindsley and his student, Dr. Eric Haughton, for the inspiration and ideas they provided us through their writings and personal communications.

NOTES

[1] Selected, in part, on the basis of past achievement scores of fourth-graders at these schools.

[2] This narration was prepared and presented by Mr. Paul Surratt. It described the measurement and alteration of behavior in four first-graders with a fifth-grader serving as the major agent of behavior change (see Surratt, Ulrich & Hawkins, 1969). A film version of the presentation should soon be available from Mr. Surratt, who is presently at the Rehabilitation Institute, Southern Illinois University, Carbondale, Illinois.

[3]When this was stated in a weekly workshop session, most of the participants were surprised and expressed disapproval, but the teacher pointed out that M played freely all day anyway, and that she would be merely giving him the opportunity to earn "consented to" free-play time.

[4]The class A project had to be terminated after the 12th day, because of the participation of the class in a special TV instruction program at the end of the school year.

[5]The daily averages plotted for each class are not based upon the marks of only those students present. This is because a daily average could have been markedly influenced by the absence of one or two high-scoring or one or two low-scoring students on the same day. To correct for such possible distortion, in preparing the values we assigned a score for an absentee which was (a) the average of his scores on the day before and the day after his absence if this occurred within a condition or (b) the same as his adjacent score in the same condition if his absence occurred on the first or last day of that condition.

[6]Subjectively, the kindergarten teachers in the workshop considered this to be a difficult test by virtue of the teacher's demand that the correct letter had to be drawn in the correct color and placed in the correct box.

[7]Borrowed from Dr. Ogden R. Lindsley.

REFERENCES

Barrish, H. H., Saunders, M. & Wolf, M. M. Good Behavior Game: Effects of Individual Contingencies for Group Consequences on Disruptive Behavior in a Classroom. *Journal of Applied Behavior Analysis*, 1969, *2*, 119–124.

Lindsley, O. R. An Experiment with Parents Handling Behavior at Home. *Johnstone Bulletin*, 1966, *9*, 27–36.

Surratt, P. R., Ulrich, R. E. & Hawkins, R. P. An Elementary Student as a Behavioral Engineer. *Journal of Applied Behavior Analysis*, 1969, *2*, 85–92.

Surratt, P. R. & Wolfe, M. A Second Look at the King's New Clothes. Unpublished manuscript (available from first author), 1969.

Ulrich, R. E., Wolfe, M. & Bluhm, M. Operant Conditioning in the Public Schools. *Educational Technology Monographs*, 1968, *1*, 1–31.

Zimmerman, J., Overpeck, C., Eisenberg, H. & Garlick, B. Operant Conditioning in a Sheltered Workshop. *Rehabilitation Literature*, 1969, *30*, 326–334.

BEHAVIORAL MANAGEMENT OF SCHOOL PHOBIA*

T. Ayllon, D. Smith and M. Rogers

The Behavioral Moral Question: What Am I Reinforcing? This article nicely exemplifies how several behavioral techniques can be used to complement each other. The authors had a clear idea of the visible behavior they were trying to change, attending school. They didn't bother with other, more cloudy terms. They analyzed the behavior of their subject, an eight-year-old girl, in terms of how she was being rewarded for staying at home, what reinforcements she was getting. They ended the rewards for staying at home and started rewards for attending school. To this positive orientation they added punishment for staying home or leaving school; thus she could escape the punishment by attending school and at the same time get rewarded for her attendance. An interesting side note is that her mother had been teaching Valerie to stay at home, although the mother didn't realize it. We are constantly teaching people things that we aren't aware of by unknowingly reinforcing, extinguishing, and punishing them. This, in fact, is a behavioral approach to social morality. Just as Valerie's mother didn't think of what her actions meant behaviorally, we all could watch our behavior to make sure we reward socially responsible actions.

Summary—In an 8-year-old Negro child diagnosed as suffering from school phobia the problem was re-defined as zero or low probability of school attendance. The implementation of techniques for increasing the probability involved getting the child's mother to withdraw the rewards of staying at home. Then a home-based motivational system was used to reinforce school attendance and refusal to attend school resulted in punishment. School attendance was generated quickly and maintained even after the procedures were withdrawn a month later. No 'symptom substitution' was noticed either by the parents or the school officials within the 9 months of follow-up. An additional important finding was that when the child's school phobia was used to produce aversive consequences on the mother it immediately led the mother to find a 'natural' way to rectify her child's psychiatric condition.

The most widely accepted approach to neurosis is the psychoanalytic one. The phobic object is said to serve as a symbol of some danger that is extremely real to the patient and whose origins are attributed to early childhood. Concern for the underlying dynamics of school phobia has resulted in provocative speculations. For example, sometimes the cause of the child's fear of school is traced to "an unrealistic self-image" (Leventhal and Sells, 1964). More often the mother is blamed for the child's school phobia as she is said to displace her own hostility onto the school (Coolidge, Tessman, Waldfogel and Miller, 1962). It has also been

*From T. Ayllon, D. Smith and M. Rogers, "Behavioral Management of School Phobia," *Journal of Behavior Therapy and Experimental Psychiatry* 1, no. 2 (June, 1970): 125–128, by permission of the authors. The authors are with Georgia State University.

suggested that the hostile impulses of sado-masochistic school personnel toward school phobics leads them to re-enact in the school setting the sado-masochistic relationship alleged to exist between mothers and their children (Jarvis, 1964). Unfortunately, such hypotheses have not led to standardized techniques for its treatment.

An alternative approach to school phobia is that of Wolpe's systematic desensitization technique. The pioneering work of Wolpe constitutes the first effective translation of the conditioning techniques of Pavlov and Hull to therapeutic procedures. Indeed, Wolpe's systematic desensitization technique marks a departure from methods used up to 1958 which was when his book *Psychotherapy by Reciprocal Inhibition* appeared in print.

The effectiveness of this approach, unlike the psychoanalytic one, has received empirical validation (Garvey and Hgrenis, 1966; Lazarus, Davidson and Polezka, 1965; Patterson, Littleman and Hensey, 1964). The impact of Wolpe's work has been such that even when modifications of his work have been explored, such as Patterson's (1965) use of M&M's to reinforce responses to the hierarchy of stimuli presented to the phobic child or Lazarus and Abramovitz's (1962) use of the so-called 'emotive imagery,' the conceptual rationale and procedural details remain those advanced by Wolpe (1958).

A complementary approach to school phobia may now be available through the use of operant techniques. In dealing with 'emotional' or behavioral problems this approach tries to determine through observation and experimentation the particular environmental event likely to be responsible for the behavior. The rationale for an operant approach to school phobia, however, requires that the condition or diagnosis of school phobia be behaviorally redefined. Indeed irrespective of the interpretation to be attached to school phobia the major feature of this condition is immediately accessible to observation: the child's attendance at school. School phobia, therefore, can be redefined behaviorally as an observable event of low frequency or probability of occurrence. Two major methodological advantages are obtained by such a redefinition. First, frequencies and rates of behavior constitute the data of a large body of experimental research. Techniques to increase or decrease rates of behavior initially developed in the laboratory (Skinner, 1938; Ferster and Skinner, 1957) have been successfully extended to the treatment of pathological behaviors in clinical settings (Ayllon and Michael, 1959; Isaacs, Thomas and Goldiamond, 1960; Ayllon and Haughton, 1964; Wolf, Risley and Mees, 1964; Ayllon and Azrin, 1965; Ayllon and Azrin, 1968b).

The second advantage of redefining school phobia as a low probability behavior is that it immediately suggests what the relevant target for treatment is, namely reinstatement of school attendance. Our strategy then was to apply such behavioral procedures to the analysis and modification of school phobia.

It should be recognized that while a legitimate target of treatment may be self-understanding, growth, and insight, these are important only insofar as they are presumed to facilitate the behavioral change from not going to school to normal school attendance. The observable datum, school attendance, then is a legitimate if not the only relevant treatment objective for school phobia. Another objective of the behavioral intervention reported here was to bypass treatment in a clinical situation or in a therapist's office since success in such situations would still have to generalize into the school situation for the success to be relevant to the problem. Therefore, our attempt was to treat the phobia in the environment where it survived. In this manner if our strategy succeeded there would be no school phobia and the problem of generalization would simply not arise.

BACKGROUND

The child. The subject of this study was Valerie, an 8-year-old Negro girl from a low income area. In the second grade she had exhibited episodes of gradually increasing absences from school until she stopped going to school in that grade and this continued on into the third grade.

The family. She had three siblings, a sister who was 9 and two brothers ages 6 and 10. None of her siblings had a history of school phobia. Her father was periodically employed as a construction worker and her mother worked as a cook in a restaurant. Both had high-school level educations.

School phobia. Valerie held an above average school attendance in kindergarten and the first grade. She started skipping school only gradually in the second grade and finished that year with 41 absences. According to school records, Valerie attended no more than the first 4 days of school in the third grade. During her 4 days of attendance, her mother reported that Valerie refused to go to school. Whenever the mother attempted to take her to school, Valerie threw such violent temper-tantrums, screaming and crying, that it was nearly impossible to move her from the house.

Finally, the mother took Valerie to a number of specialists, including a school counselor, a medical specialist and a social worker. All these professionals offered extensive advice. The mother reported that the advice took several forms: 'Ignore the behavior and it will go away'; 'Give her plenty of praise and affection'; and 'Punish her severely if she refuses to go.' Unfortunately, none of this advice worked and Valerie continued to stay away from school.

Val, according to the mother's reports, had much trouble going to sleep and lay awake during much of the night. Val had no friends except for one cousin to whom she felt close. Children did not seek her nor did she seem interested in playing with children at school or in the neighborhood. According to the teacher's reports, when Val did attend school she was as quiet as a mouse in class and simply stood and watched at recess but would not join the games and activities. As the mother became convinced that Valerie had 'something wrong with her nerves' she took her to the local hospital so that she could get some 'pills for her nerves.' Valerie was evaluated by the pediatric staff and her case diagnosed as school phobia.

Diagnostic test results. Several diagnostic psychological tests were administered to Valerie while her case was being presented at the local hospital. The test results were as follows:

> Valerie demonstrated a consistent variability in her overall functioning. Her problem-solving, visual–manual skills (WISC Performance IQ = 78) are considerably below her near average verbal-expressive abilities (WISC Verbal IQ = 90). Within her verbal skills, she ranges from a defective level of functioning in comprehension of social situations and in her fund of information to an above normal level of functioning in her ability to think abstractly. Within her performance skills, she also demonstrated variability (DAP IQ = 87; Peabody IQ = 76). Valerie's variable functioning is due to an extreme inability to concentrate, since on perceptual tasks not requiring concentration she performed at a normal level (Frostig Perceptual Quotient = 98). Emotionally, Valerie's inability to concentrate is related to her extreme fears—especially her fears about men. The only way she can cope with men is to see them as dead. The inconsistency in her functioning seems to be related to the amount of concentration required by various tasks—such as classroom activities. To handle such stressful situations, she is likely to withdraw by not performing.

Social intake evaluation. A social intake evaluation was also done at the pediatric clinic. Excerpts of this evaluation indicate that "when the mother tried to accompany Valerie to school, even as far as getting on the bus with her, as they approached the school, Valerie would become very stiff, begin shaking, screaming and hollering. When Valerie was asked about this, she stated that she was afraid to go to school, that when she went to school she thought about the time she was molested." This was a reference to an incident which took place when the child was 4 years old. According to Valerie's mother, a boy had "played with Valerie's 'private parts.'" Neither the extent of this incident nor any physical evidence could be obtained at the time of its occurrence. After the child had been diagnosed as suffering from school phobia, the mother was advised that the nature of Valerie's difficulties required long-term psychiatric treatment. Since the cost of such treatment was beyond the family means, the mother was left with the understanding that she should resign herself to living with the problem. Quite by accident, one of the authors of this paper was visiting the pediatric facility where Valerie's case was being discussed for the benefit of interns in pediatrics and child psychiatry. It was then that a suggestion was made by the senior author (T.A.) to attempt a behavioral treatment of Valerie's school phobia.

METHODOLOGY

Behavioral strategy. The behavioral approach to school phobia requires to break it down into three major components.

First of all there is the matter of response definition. The relevant dimension, insofar as the school, parent and child are concerned is that of school attendance. Thus, we can define school phobia as a low or near zero level of school attendance. This definition enables us to specify what the target behavior is for a treatment program. If the rate of going to school is low, our aim then is to increase it and maintain it, hopefully under the conditions that obtain in the 'natural' setting of the school environment. The next component involves the matter of consequences or reinforcement for staying away from school. These consequences must be examined as they affect the child and the behavior of those living with her. Finally, there is the issue of redesigning the consequences provided by the environment so as to minimize the probability of skipping school while maximizing the probability of attending school.

To identify the relevant environmental consequences responsible for the child's refusal to attend school, the child's behavior was directly observed and recorded by trained assistant-observers. The initial step was to attempt to quantify the dimensions of the relevant behaviors in the three primary environments of the child: (1) home, (2) a neighbor's home (where she was cared for) and (3) school.

The systematic observational schedule that was conducted each day on a minute-by-minute basis started at 7.00 a.m. and ended at 9.00 a.m. The sampling of observations was conducted for 10 days at home and for 3 days at the neighbor's house. Behavioral observations and procedures designed to reinstate school attendance were implemented by two assistant observers. One observer (M.R.) conducted the prompting-shaping procedures and participated in the observations at the neighbor's apartment. The second observer (D.S.) was responsible for giving instructions to the mother and conducted the observations at Valerie's home. Once the child returned to school as a consequence of the procedures applied, the observations were extended to include the child's behavior at school and on the way to and from school.

Valerie's behavior at home. The observations in the home revealed that Valerie was sleeping an average of 1 hr later than her siblings in the morning, although according to the mother she retired at the same time as they, between 9.00 and 10.00, every night. Her mother had long abandoned any hope of Valerie's going to school and simply allowed her to sleep until she awoke, or until it was time for the mother to leave for work at 9.00 a.m. The mother would usually leave for work approximately 1 hr following the departure of the siblings who left for school at 8.00 a.m.

Except for a few occasions when the mother made breakfast for the children they frequently fixed their own food. Valerie was given no preferential treatment, and was never asked what she would like for breakfast if she slept late. Upon arising, Valerie spoke an average of 14 sentences to the siblings, an average of 10 sentences to her mother and only two sentences to her father. The mother averaged one request each morning asking Valerie to go to school. Physical interaction such as touching, holding or other aggressive or affectionate behavior occurred seldom with her siblings and not at all with her father. On the other hand, Valerie typically followed her mother around the house, from room to room, spending approximately 80 percent of her time within 10 ft of her mother. During these times, there was little or no conversation. When the mother left for work, she would take Valerie to a neighbor's apartment. On every observational occasion, when the mother left the neighbor's apartment to go to work, Valerie would immediately leave and follow the mother. This behavior of quietly following her mother at a 10-ft distance occurred on each of the 10 days of baseline observations. Each time this occurred, the mother would look back and see Valerie, stop and warn her several times to go back, all of which had no effect on Valerie. When the mother began walking once more, Valerie continued to follow at a 10-ft distance, with no verbal response of any type. Also, it was noted that on three occasions that the mother resorted to punishing Valerie with a switching for following, Val would cry quietly but would make no effort to return home until the mother took her back to the neighbor's apartment. Once the mother left again for work, Valerie would continue to follow at about twice the distance, or 20 ft, behind the mother. This daily scene was usually concluded with the mother literally running to get out of sight of Valerie so that Valerie would not follow her into traffic.

Valerie's behavior at the neighbor's apartment. Valerie was observed at the neighbor's apartment for 3 days during which the observer had no interaction with Val but remained nearby recording whatever behavior occurred. During this time Val watched the observer at times but made no effort to interact in any way.

At the neighbor's apartment, Val was free to do whatever she pleased for the remainder of the day. Val showed little interest in television or radio, preferring to be outdoors unless it was raining. If she had to stay inside she pored over a mail order toy catalogue. Very rarely did the neighbor spend time interacting with Val. The few times she did it was after Val's mother had left for work and Val was still crying.

Outdoors, Val found many ways to entertain herself. The observer watched while she played with a jump rope, exploded caps and found a dozen different ways to play with play-dough. If she ran out of things to play with, Val amused herself by hopping on one foot, jumping, running and turning in circles. In addition, Val had some money and at some time during the day made a trip to the corner store where she bought candy, gum or soft drinks.

Val was the only school age child at the neighbor's house and children from toddlers to kindergarten age sought her attention. She was somewhat aloof, but occasionally joined their play. In short, her day was one which would be considered ideal by many grade children—she could be outdoors and play as she chose all day long. No demands of any type were made on Val by anyone and she had the status of being the eldest among the children.

Valerie's behavior in school. Two visits were made to the school to get acquainted with the principal and teachers and to gather information from them about Val's past school performance, work attitude and social adjustment. Copies were obtained of the official records of Val's attendance for kindergarten, 1st grade, 2nd grade, and the current year (3rd grade). The records showed Val's attendance to have been above average during kindergarten and first grade but that absences had increased each quarter during the second grade; 1st quarter, 1; 2nd quarter, 7; 3rd quarter, 13; and fourth quarter, 20, for a total of 41 absences for the year. Excuses had been illness, oversleeping or missing the bus. Scholastic achievement had been normal or average until absences became numerous. Val, it was reported, had never cried or asked to go home. While described as shy, quiet and rather apathetic, Val had never given the impression that she was unhappy or afraid.

The behavioral assessment. The evaluation of Valerie's behavior at home, at the neighbor's apartment and finally at school suggested that Valerie's school phobia was currently maintained by the pleasant and undemanding characteristics of the neighbor's apartment where Val spent her day after everyone had left home in the morning.

Rather than speculating on the 'real' causes or etiology of the phobia itself our initial strategy was to determine the feasibility of having Val return to school by some prompting-shaping procedure (see Ayllon and Azrin, 1968a, for rationale and empirical basis for this procedure). Once this was done it would then be possible to provide for some pleasant experience associated with being in school in order to maintain her school attendance. To design the prompting-shaping procedure it was necessary first to assess Valerie's existing behaviors that had a component relation to the target behavior. Indeed, if attending school were to be meaningful, Valerie had to show sufficient interest to go to school voluntarily and consistently. In addition, she had to be prepared to work with school materials and perform academic work. To determine the presence or absence of these component behaviors, first one assistant (M.R.) took a coloring book, crayons, a set of arithmetic flash cards and other academically related items to the neighbor's apartment. While at the neighbor's apartment, she prompted Val to make the appropriate academically related responses to the stimuli. Val responded appropriately to the academic material and contrary to expectations, she did not panic, 'freeze,' or become at all upset when exposed to academically related material. The next objective was to assess the difficulties associated with leaving the neighbor's apartment. Therefore, the next probe was for the observer to invite Val for a car ride after both had worked on academically related activities. Val offered no resistance and went with the observer for a car ride and later had a hamburger on the way home.

This behavioral assessment assured us (1) that a prompting-shaping procedure could start by taking Val directly to school rather than in gradually increasing steps; (2) that she would do academic work once in the classroom. The next step was to develop the desired response chain eventuating in Valerie's attendance at school. It must be remembered that Val stayed alone with her mother after her siblings left for school at about 8.00 a.m. She remained with her mother until she left for work at 9.00 a.m. If staying with the mother alone was the reinforcing consequence that maintained her refusal to go to school, we reasoned, withdrawal of this consequence might lead Valerie back to school. Before we could try such a procedure, however, it was necessary to determine the probability of Valerie remaining in the classroom once she returned to school. That was in effect the objective of the first procedure. Additional procedures were subsequently implemented to achieve the target behavior.

Specific procedures and results. Table 1 shows all procedural stages as well as their behavioral effects. The target behavior of voluntary and consistent (100 percent) school attendance was achieved in less than 2 months. Four distinct procedures were designed and implemented only after observing and recording their specific effects on Valerie's voluntary school attendance.

Procedure 1. Prompting-shaping of school attendance. Our plan was to manage to have Valerie visit the school at a time when school was almost over for the day. By having the child go to school for a short time only to be dismissed for the day along with the rest of the pupils we attempted to use the 'natural' contingencies of the school to maintain Valerie's presence in school. Permission was obtained from the teacher to bring Val to school for the last hour of the school day and for the assistant to remain in the classroom with her. The plan was to arrive at school progressively earlier until the child's presumed fears were extinguished at which time she would then initiate voluntary school attendance. The first day of this procedure the assistant (M.R.) told Val, about 1.30 p.m., that they would be going to school and that she would stay with Val. Val's eyes widened but she offered no resistance. They drove to school, arriving 1½ hr before closing time and holding hands tightly, went to the third grade classroom. Val was given a desk and the assistant sat nearby until the day was over. The teacher, in a very natural manner, greeted Val and gave her some classroom material. Val immediately started doing some school work. On the way out of school the assistant found Val's siblings. To maximize the probability of Val's getting approval from her siblings, associated with the school, the assistant gave Val some candy to share with the siblings and left her to walk home with them.

The following day, the procedure was repeated except that the assistant left Val in the classroom about 10 min before school was out. Again, the teacher worked with Val just as naturally as if she had been attending all day long. The assistant before leaving the classroom instructed Val to meet her siblings and reassured her that they would wait for her to walk home with them. The next day the time of arrival was moved up so that Val

TABLE 1.
Procedural and Behavioral Progression During
the Treatment of School Phobia

Temporal sequence	Procedure	Valerie's behavior
Baseline observations Day 1–10	Observations taken at home and at the neighbor's apartment where Val spent her day.	Valerie stayed at home when siblings left for school. Mother took Val to neighbor's apartment as she left for work.
Behavioral assessment Day 11–13	Assistant showed school materials to Val and prompted academic work.	Val reacted well to books; she colored pictures and copied numbers and letters.
Behavioral assessment Day 13	Assistant invited Val for a car ride after completing academic work at neighbor's apartment.	Val readily accepted car ride and on way back to neighbor's apartment she also accepted hamburger offered her.
Procedure 1 Day 14–20	Taken by assistant to school. Assistant stayed with her in classroom. Attendance made progressively earlier while assistant's stay in classroom progressively lessens.	Val attended school with assistant. Performed school work. Left school with siblings at closing time.
Day 21	Assistant did not take Val to school.	Val and siblings attended school on their own.
Procedure 1 Day 22	Val taken by assistant to school	Val attended school with assistant. Performed school work. Left with siblings at school closing time.
Return to baseline observations Day 23–27	Observations taken at home.	Val stayed at home when siblings left for school. Mother took Val to neighbor's apartment as she left for work.
Procedure 2 Day 28–29	Mother left for work when children left for school.	Val stayed at home when children left for school. Mother took her to neighbor's apartment as she left for work.
Procedure 3 Day 40–49	Taken by mother to school. Home-based motivational system.	Val stayed at home when siblings left for school. Followed mother quietly when taken to school.

TABLE 1. (Continued)

Temporal sequence	Procedure	Valerie's behavior
Procedure 4 Day 50–59	On Day 50, mother left for school *before* children left home. Home-based motivational system.	Siblings met mother at school door. Val stayed at home.
	15 min of waiting in school, mother returned home and took Val to school.	Val meekly followed her mother.
	On Day 51, mother left for school *before* children left home.	Val and siblings met mother at school door.
	On Day 52, mother left for school before children left home.	Siblings met mother at school door. Valerie stayed at home.
	After 15 min of waiting in school, mother returned home and physically hit and dragged Valerie to school.	Valerie cried and pleaded with her mother not to hit her. Cried all the way to school.
	On Day 53–59, mother left for school before children left home.	Val and siblings met mother at school door.
Fading Procedure Day 60–69	Mother discontinued going to school before children. Mother maintained home-based motivational system.	Val and siblings attended school on their own.
Fading Procedure Day 70	Mother discontinued home-based motivational system.	Val and siblings attended school on their own.

spent 2 hr in school. By now Val had attended the third grade for a total of 4 hr. On the basis of her classroom performance the teacher came to the conclusion that Val was too far behind to catch up with her third grade classmates. Therefore, after careful consideration and discussion with the school principal decided to place her in the second grade class to insure her learning the material she had missed during her prolonged absence from school. Again, the cooperation of the new second grade teacher was obtained to allow Val to keep going to school at rather unusual hours, about 2–3 hr before the end of the school day.

The next day Val was taken to the second grade class for the first time. She gave no evidence of being upset with the shift from classrooms. On succeeding days Val was taken earlier each day. By the time Val was arriving in school at 9.30 a.m. the assistant had gradually decreased her own time in the classroom from the initial 1½ hr to 5 min. Each day the assistant left a sack containing some small prize like a children's magazine, a few pieces of candy, etc., with the teacher to be given to Val when school was over. On the 8th day of this procedure Val left home with her siblings and went to school without the assistant for the first time. The teacher praised her and the assistant went to school and told Val how happy she was that Val had come to school by herself.

On the next day Val stayed home until her mother left for work. As usual she was then taken to the neighbor's apartment. The assistant picked her up and took her to school where she spent the remaining 4½ hr of the school day. The prompting-shaping procedure was discontinued at this time to allow for further behavioral evaluation. For the next 6 days she remained at home when her siblings went to school and, just as before, the mother took Val to the neighbor's apartment as she left for work.

Figure 1 shows the day-to-day behavior of Val under procedure 1. The prompting-shaping procedure demonstrated that Val could go to school and stay all day without running away, causing disturbance in the classroom, or displaying any behavior that might suggest undue fear or panic. Just as significant, Val's behavior in school indicated that the 'natural' reinforcing consequences provided at school were adequate to keep her there once she engaged in the first activity of a complex behavior chain including getting up on time, washing, dressing, leaving the house and going to school. True, this procedure reinstated Valerie's school attendance but failed to maintain it. The problem then was how to provide sufficient motivation to insure her leaving for school. At this point it became necessary to examine and re-design the social consequences provided at home for Valerie's refusal to attend school.

Procedure 2. Withdrawal of social consequences upon failure to attend school. As mentioned before, Val stayed with her mother for 1 hr daily right after her siblings had gone to school. The objective here was to eliminate such a social consequence for staying away from school. Therefore, procedure 2 involved instructing the mother that she was casually to inform all the children the night before that she was going to leave for work *at the same time they left for school.* When additional questions were asked, she was to reply that her working hours had been changed. Valerie gave no verbal or physical reaction to this announcement when it was given. Nothing else was changed. The children were treated the same as on previous occasions. One of the assistant-observers, who had had no interaction with Val, was in the house making standard observations the day the new procedure 2 was initiated and during subsequent intervention. The mother left for work along with the siblings but Val refused to go. Therefore, she was taken to the neighbor's apartment. This procedure was continued for 10 days during which Val did not attend school and was taken to the neighbor's apartment. In addition, Val increased her 'follow-

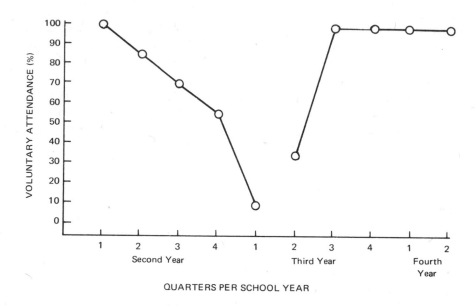

Fig. 1. Valerie's school attendance both when she was escorted to school during the prompting-shaping procedure, and when she went on her own. Each dot represents the actual duration of her stay in the class room per day. The start of Procedure 1 is indicated by the gap between day 13 and 14.

ing behavior' when the mother left for work. Valerie followed at a distance of 3–6 ft behind the mother. When Valerie was punished by her mother she invariably dropped back to about 8–10 ft and continued following her mother. As there were no other observable effects on Valerie's behavior at the end of 10 days, this procedure was terminated. In effect, we had spent over 20 days trying various procedures and we were now back to the original behavior pattern: Val did not go to school and was taken to the neighbor's apartment. As soon as the mother started to leave for work Val followed her despite her mother's efforts to discourage her.

Procedure 3. Prompting school attendance combined with a home-based motivational system. Despite the fact that Val appeared to have remained unchanged as ever through the various procedures, it was clear from results of procedure 1 that she could return to school through a prompting-shaping procedure. The problem was one of maintaining that attendance for any length of time. To find a solution, it was required that we find some source or sources of reinforcement to be used at home contingent on school attendance. Val's mother described some of the things Val liked most. Among these were having her cousin stay overnight with her, soda pop, chewing gum, and ice cream. Therefore, the strategy for designing the new procedure included the prompting-shaping procedure that previously resulted in Val's return to school and a motivational system designed to reinforce Valerie for attending school. This time, the mother rather than an assistant was to use the prompting procedure. In addition and to facilitate implementation of the motivational system, a large chart with each child's name and the days of the week was given to the mother. She announced that a star would signify one day of going to school on a *voluntary* basis and was to be placed on the appropriate spot by each child at the end of each day. Five stars would equal perfect attendance and would result in a special treat or trip on the weekend. In addition to the above, each child who went to school on a voluntary basis would receive, each day, three pieces of a favorite candy. If anyone had to be taken to school (non-voluntary attendance), the reward was only one piece of candy. It was felt to be important to attach some reward value to the school attendance even if, in the beginning, attendance was not voluntary. The occasion of putting up stars, handing out rewards and verbal praise was to be made into a special event each evening when the mother returned home. When Valerie did not leave with the other children to go to school in the morning, the mother was to leave the house 15 min later taking Valerie with her to school. No excuses were to be tolerated with the exception of sickness. Since previously Valerie had used the excuse of being sick to avoid going to school, this time the mother was given a thermometer and taught to use it to decide whether or not Valerie was ill. If the thermometer reading was above 100, the mother would then be justified in allowing Val to stay home. This procedure resulted in Valerie's mother taking her to school daily for 10 consecutive days. Once, Valerie stated that she was sick but since her temperature was within the normal range, her mother took her to school. Procedure 3, just as procedure 1, resulted in Valerie attending school but it failed to initiate Valerie's going to school on her own. In analyzing the procedure carefully, it seemed that what was happening was that the mother taking Valerie personally to school was perhaps adventitiously reinforcing and thus maintaining her refusal to go on her own. After the other children had left for school, the mother in a very matter-of-fact fashion, asked Valerie to get ready to go to school with her. On the way to school, Valerie and the mother appeared quite natural and even after 10 days of this procedure there was no particular irritation or apparent inconvenience experienced by Valerie or by her mother. It should be pointed out here that prior to the present intervention, Valerie would kick and scream and simply refused to go to school even when her mother attempted to take her by force. The results of procedure 3 suggested that the natural consequences for school attendance plus the motivational system employed here increased the probability of Val's going to school escorted, but it failed to prompt her going to school voluntarily. Procedure 4 was designed to introduce a mild aversive consequence for the mother if Val failed to go to school. In addition, the motivational system used in procedure 3 was maintained.

Procedure 4. The effects of aversive consequences on the mother. Procedure 4 involved having the mother get ready for work and leave the house 10 min *before* the children left for school. She was to inform all the children that she had to go to work much earlier but wanted to see that they got to school on time, so she would meet them at school each morning with a reward. This procedure was designed to have a two-fold effect: one, to prompt the behavior on Valerie's part of voluntarily leaving for school with her siblings and to provide reinforcement through the mother upon arrival at school. If Valerie failed to arrive at school with her siblings, the mother had to return home and escort Valerie to school. Since the school was about a mile away from home, Val's failure to go to school required that her mother walk back home a mile and then walk another mile to school—this time with Valerie in tow, for a total of 3 miles walking. By having Valerie's behavior affect her mother's directly, it was hoped that this procedure would in effect have the mother become more actively interested in conveying to Val the importance of going to school. On the first day of this procedure 4, Val behaved just as she had throughout the previous ones: she remained at home after everyone, her mother and later the siblings, had left for school. The mother met the siblings at school, gave them a bit of candy and then waited for Val to come to school. Following the previous instructions she remained at the school door for 15 min before going back home to find Val. Once there she very firmly proceeded to take Val by the hand and with hardly any words between them, they rushed back to school. Val did not protest and quite naturally followed her mother into school. After a few minutes Val's mother left school for work. That evening, the mother rewarded each child with praise and candy for going to school. She gave stars to the siblings and placed them on the board made for that purpose. She also gave Val a piece of candy and noted that she could not get a star since Val had not attended school on her own. The children's reaction to the stars and praise seemed one of excitement. Val, however, appeared some-what unsure of what was happening. The second day of procedure 4, Val got up along with her siblings, dressed, fixed herself some breakfast, and left for school with her siblings. When they arrived at school they met their mother who was waiting for them. The mother was obviously pleased with Val to whom she gave candy along with the siblings. At the end of the school day, the children again were praised at home and given stars by the mother on the special board that hung in the kitchen. Val appeared very interested particularly when the mother explained to her that if she collected 5 stars she would be able to exchange them for the opportunity to have the cousin, of whom Val was very fond, spend the night with her. The next day she went to school along with her siblings. The mother met left for school. Again, the mother waited for 15 min in school. Then she returned home. As it was raining, it was a considerable inconvenience for Val's mother to have to go back home. Once she reached home she scolded Val and pushed her out of the house and literally all the way to school. As Val tried to give some explanation the mother hit her with a switch. By the time they arrived at school, both were soaking wet. That evening, Val received some candy but no stars as she had not gone to school on her own. This was the last time Val stayed away from school. The next day she want to school along with her siblings. The mother met the children at the door and genuinely praised them for their promptness. That evening, Val received a star along with candy and was praised by the mother in front of the siblings. Within 5 days Val had accumulated enough stars to exchange them for the opportunity to have her cousin stay overnight with her. She appeared in very good spirits and seemed to enjoy her cousin's visit. The next school day, Val got up with her siblings, washed, dressed, fixed herself some breakfast cereal, and left for school with them. When they arrived at school they were met by their mother, who again praised them, gave them some candy, and then the children went to their respective classrooms while the mother went off to work. Val and the children continued attending school without any difficulty, even after one aspect of the procedure was withdrawn: namely, the mother waiting for them at school. The home-based motivational system was maintained in force for 1 month and withdrawn at that time. Still, Val and the children continued attending school unaffected by the withdrawal of these formal procedures.

To gain perspective on the dimensions of the school phobia presented here it is necessary to look at Val's overall school attendance per quarter (45 days each quarter). Figure 2 shows that Val went from 95 percent school attendance to 10 percent within 5 quarters. This 10 percent represented the first 4 days of the fifth quarter after which she quit going to school for the remainder of the quarter. The present behavioral intervention was conducted during the latter part of the 6th quarter. The net result was that Val's overall attendance in the 6th quarter increased from 10 to 30 percent. The next quarter, the 7th, her overall attendance increased from 30 to 100 percent. A follow-up for the next 3 quarters indicates that Val had maintained this perfect attendance.

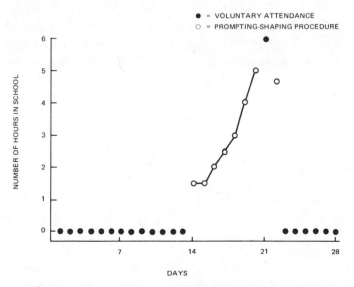

Fig. 2. Valerie's voluntary school attendance. Each dot represents the percentage of voluntary attendance per school quarter (45 days). The behavioral intervention was initiated during the second quarter of the third year of school.

Follow-up. Inquiries were made of Valerie's parents and teachers at 6 and 9 months subsequent to Valerie's return to school. Their comments can be subsumed under school and home evaluation. Finally a psychodiagnostic evaluation was also obtained.

School evaluation. Val's academic progress is shown by her current grades. While previously she was an average C student, she now has A's and B's. Her teacher remarked that Val is well-behaved in class and helpful to the teacher. While she is pleased to volunteer for small errands and clean-up duties to assist the teacher, she has also shown sufficient social skills to be chosen as the school guide for a new girl admitted into her classroom. Val's specific duties as guide consisted of showing and explaining to the new girl the various school facilities such as the school cafeteria, the library, the gym and so on. The teacher was particularly impressed with Val's performance as a guide because the new girl came from Germany and asked more detailed questions than is usually the case for a standard transfer student. Her newly developed social skills appeared to have impressed the Brownie Scouts to extend a cordial invitation for Valerie to join their group. Valerie was thrilled with the prospect and after requesting permission from her mother she joined the Brownies. Every Tuesday afternoon after class she attends the group's meeting which is held in the school. After the meeting she walks home with her girl friends.

A few months after Val resumed normal school attendance an incident took place that suggests the strength of her newly-acquired fondness for school. She was waiting for the school bus when another child snatched her money changer from her, took her bus money and ran away. Instead of crying and returning home, Val ran all the way to school since she did not want to be late.

Home evaluation. Val no longer complains of feeling sick, tired in the morning nor does she suffer from insomnia. She goes to bed about 8.30 p.m. daily with her siblings and gets up at 7.00 a.m. Valerie now fusses and hurries her siblings to finish dressing in the morning in time to go to school. She brings her math and spelling work home to show her mother. The mother very naturally praises her child as she does her other children. Whereas previously Valerie had been rather apathetic in school, she now takes pride in her work there and likes to discuss things she is learning.

Eight months after Val resumed school attendance the mother initiated divorce proceedings against her husband. This situation introduced a definite strain into the home family relations. Still, Val appeared sufficiently motivated to continue attending school without any disruption in her academic or social progress.

Neither the mother nor the school teachers have noticed any other maladaptive behavior or possible 'symptom substitution' since the child resumed normal school attendance. On the contrary, the mother as well as Valerie's teachers were very impressed with the astounding change in her behavior and the promise it now offers for her future both academically and socially.

Psychodiagnostic evaluation. Because Valerie's school phobia was initially presented and diagnosed in the psychiatric unit of a pediatric department at a large urban hospital, the formal procedures for case referral included a psychodiagnostic evaluation prior to and following treatment given to the child.

The conclusion now arrived at by the examiner is interesting!

> Her emotional development is characterized by deviations in the area of maturity and aggression. Her reality testing is marred by an extreme concern over sexuality and men, whom she sees as attacking, ever fighting animal-like creatures. On the basis of the recent results, without considerations to results previous to behavioral management, it would seem that the school phobia may have been treated successfully, but it has not meant anything to this girl.

DISCUSSION

A child diagnosed as suffering from school phobia was cured within 45 days through the combined use of behavioral analysis and techniques. The term *cured* is used here purposely since the functional characteristics of school phobia are straightforward: chronic absence from school. Therefore, reinstating the child's school attendance constitutes the only relevant criterion of successful cure.

The therapeutic intervention reported here is characterized by the following features:

(1) Definition of the psychiatric problem is made in terms of behavioral dimensions. The observable and measurable dimension of school phobia is the child's frequency of school attendance. Hence this is the datum 'par excellence' in the treatment of school phobia.

(2) Evaluation of the treatment objective is made in terms that are amenable to direct observation and measurement. Since the treatment objective was defined as reinstatement of voluntary school attendance, it was easy to evaluate the effectiveness of the behavioral intervention. The psychodiagnostic evaluation illustrates the dangers involved when evaluation of a treatment is on a non-behavioral basis: Speculation on personality factors often are given importance at the cost of minimizing the observable behavioral changes.

(3) The behavioral intervention is conducted in the very environment where the individual's behavior is to be displayed. Hence, rather than working in a clinic or hospital situation, the emphasis is on utilizing behavioral techniques right in the field environment to which any clinic-based therapeutic efforts must generalize for these efforts to be successful.

(4) Description of the procedures used here is also consistent with the stress on directly observable and measurable dimensions. The above provides a self-corrective method for approaching psychiatric problems in general. Each of the several procedures used here gave empirical quantitative information that enabled us to revise each procedure in the light of its effects on the child's behavior. This ongoing, step-by-step self-corrective evaluation is particularly critical for developing effective and inexpensive methods of treatment.

One other finding here was that the use of differential consequences for attending school was more effective than the use of either positive reinforcement or negative reinforcement (punishment) alone. It must be pointed out that during the baseline observations, the mother was observed hitting the child with no change in her refusal to attend school. Also during procedure 2, she was observed hitting the child again without any effect on her refusal to attend school. Similarly, Valerie's refusal to attend school continued when positive reinforcement was made available for going to school escorted by her mother (procedure 3). However, when school attendance was reinforced by the mother immediately at the school door, and at home with an incentive system that made use of the child's own motivation, while refusal to attend school was punished, it took but a few days to reinstate normal school attendance.

Why should punishment have worked this time? A parsimonious explanation of this finding lies in the fact that procedure 4 combined punishment for staying away from school with positive reinforcement for voluntary school attendance. Valerie's mother had used punishment previously but no positive reinforcement for going to school. These findings are consistent with those obtained by Holz, Azrin and Ayllon (1963) under more controlled conditions. In that study, they found that one of the most efficient methods for eliminating an undesirable response of mental patients was to schedule punishment for the undesirable response and concurrently, reinforcement for an alternative competing response.

An important procedural innovation introduced here was arranging the child's refusal to attend school to affect the mother's own behavior. When procedure 3 required that she take Valerie to school she did so without ever appearing inconvenienced by it. It was only when Val's refusal to go to school resulted in her mother having to walk from the school back home and then again back to school that the aversive properties of the procedure led to the mother finding a 'natural' way of putting an end to such inconvenience. Only twice did she have to be inconvenienced. The second time her reaction was such as to convince Valerie that it would be easier to go to school with her siblings. The aversive properties of the procedure set up an escape-avoidance type of behavior in the mother that led Val to prevent such occurrences in the future by attending school.

REFERENCES

Ayllon T. and Azrin N. H. (1965) The measurement and reinforcement of behavior of psychotics. *J. exp. Analysis Behav.* 8, 357–383.

Ayllon T. and Azrin N. H. (1968a) Reinforcer sampling: a technique for increasing the behavior of mental patients. *J. app. Behav. Anal.* 1, 13–20.

Ayllon T. and Azrin N. H. (1968b) *The Token Economy: A Motivational System for Therapy and Rehabilitation.* Appleton-Century-Crofts, New York.

Ayllon T. and Haughton E. (1964) Modification of the symptomatic verbal behavior of mental patients. *J. Behav. Res. & Therapy* 2, 87–97.

Ayllon T. and Michael J. (1959) The psychiatric nurse as a behavioral engineer. *J. exp. Analysis Behav.* 2, 323–334.

Coolidge J., Tessman E., Waldfogel S. and Willer M. (1962) Patterns of aggression in school phobia. *Psychoanal. Study Child* 17, 319–333.

Ferster C. B. and Skinner B. F. (1957) *Schedules of Reinforcement.* Appleton-Century-Crofts, New York.

Garvey W. P. and Hgrenis J. R. (1966) Desensitization techniques in the treatment of school phobia. *Am. J. Orthopsychiat.* 36 (1), 147–152.

Holz W., Azrin N. H. and Ayllon T. (1963) Elimination of behavior of mental patients by response-produced extinction. *J. exp. Analysis Behav.* 6, 407–412.

Isaacs W., Thomas J. and Goldiamond I. (1965) Application of operant conditioning to reinstate verbal behavior in psychotics. *Case Studies in Behavior Modification.* (Eds. L. P. Ullmann and L. Krasner.) pp. 69–72. Holt, Rinehart, & Winston, New York.

Jarvis V. (1964) Countertransference in management of school phobia. *Psychoanalyt. Q.* 33 (3), 411–419.

Lazarus A. and Abramovitz A. (1962) The use of 'emotive imagery' in the treatment of children's phobias. *J. men. Sci.* 180 (453), 191–195.

Lazarus A., Davidson G. and Polefka D. (1965) Classical and operant factors in the treatment of a school phobia. *J. abnorm. Psychol.* 70 (3), 225–229.

Levanthal T. and Sells M. (1964) Self-image in school phobia. *Am. J. Orthopsychiat.* 34 (4), 685–695.

Patterson G. R. (1965) A learning theory approach to the treatment of the school phobic child. *Case Studies in Behavior Modification.* (Eds. L. P. Ullmann and L. Krasner), pp. 279–285. Holt, Rinehart & Winston, New York. .

Skinner B. F. (1938) *The Behavior of Organisms: An Experimental Analysis.* Appleton-Century-Crofts, New York.

Wolf M., Risley T. and Mees H. (1965) Application of operant procedures to the behavior problems of an autistic child. *Case Studies in Behavior Modification* (Eds. L. P. Ullmann and L. Krasner), pp. 138–145. Holt, Rinehart & Winston, New York.

Wolpe J. (1958) *Psychotherapy by Reciprocal Inhibition.* Stanford University Press, Stanford.

*A portion of this paper was read at the Southeastern Psychological Association, New Orleans, 1969. We thank Dr. L. L'Abate for the use of material from psychodiagnostic evaluations. We also acknowledge our deep appreciation to Dr. Joseph Zimmerman and Dr. Zal Newmark for their critical reading of the manuscript.

THE BEHAVIOR THERAPIST IN THE SCHOOLS*

John B. Mordock and Debora R. Phillips

Varieties of Behavioral Experience. These authors describe several behavioral techniques. With Bill, the hyperactive student, they used *shaping* by increasing the interval of paying attention in small steps from one minute to ten minutes. They *selected an appropriate reinforcement*, a horseback ride, and used *social reinforcement* too, allowing the class to share his reward. The teacher used *extinction* by ignoring Bill's wandering. *Behavioral rehearsal* helped Sally to practice what she wanted to do before the actual situations, just as teachers practiced after seeing their behavior modeled. In *contingency management* children are allowed to do something they want *after* they have done what the teacher wants. *Desensitization* is used for learning tolerance; first one accepts small doses of disliked behavior, then larger doses, etc. until he no longer reacts negatively. This article mentions many of the most useful behavior modification techniques. Like anything else, you usually don't do them perfectly at first, but the more you practice, the better you get.

A number of psychotherapists in private or clinic practice are attempting to broaden the scope of therapeutic management by treating the child within the school, in addition to home and clinic. The present paper discusses procedures employed in schools by behaviorally-oriented therapists (Patterson, 1969; Phillips and Mordock, 1970).

Individual Behavioral Counseling. Hyperactivity is one of the most common problems for which children are referred to child guidance clinics (Patterson, 1956). Such children emit low rates of attending behavior and, as a consequence, their behavior is aversive to adults, particularly to teachers. Patterson (1965), and Patterson et al. (1965), demonstrated that conditioning procedures could be employed to increase the frequency of attending behavior in hyperactive children.

These techniques were adapted for use with Bill, age six, a hyperactive child referred by his teacher. Since Bill's base rate of attending behavior was only one minute, the goal was to gradually increase this rate until he could attend to one task for approximately ten minutes. The procedure to be used was explained to Bill as something which would help him to sit longer and he was told he would be rewarded for success. The reinforcement employed should be idiosyncratic to each child, and for Bill, it was acquiring money to enable him to go horseback riding with his father.

*From John B. Mordock, "The Behavioral Therapist in the Schools," *Psychotherapy: Theory, Research, & Practice* 8, no. 3 (Fall, 1971): 231–235, by permission of the authors and publisher. John B. Mordock is Chief Psychologist at the Astor Home for Children, Rhinebeck, New York; he is author of the book *The Other Children: An Introduction to Exceptionality* (New York: Harper and Row, 1975). Debora R. Phillips is with the Princeton Center for Behavior Therapy, Kingston, New York.

A reaction-time apparatus (Lafayette, 6301S) was placed on a desk in front of the child in the therapist's office. Bill was told to draw and that, as he was drawing, he would see a little green light come on from the little box. He was not to pay attention to the light but to keep on drawing. The light coming on simply meant he had earned two points and each time it came on it was simply adding up toward the reward he would get (horseback ride valued at 15 Points).

The light was activated after Bill had been attending to his drawing for the base rate period (one minute), and at a variable interval of ten seconds after that, until he could work for two minutes. This procedure was continued during therapy sessions until Bill had progressed up to four minutes of attending behavior. The time of initial onset of the light was increasingly delayed and the variable interval increased.

At this period in Bill's treatment the therapist extended his training into the classroom. Since the apparatus was operated by remote control, the therapist could seat himself unobtrusively in the back of the room and operate the "work box" from this position.

The procedure was introduced to the class much in the fashion of the old-time school teacher, but carried a bit further: "Johnny has problems in arithmetic so he is getting some supplemental help from his tutor. Jack is having special problems in spelling so he gets help from his Dad. Now Bill has difficulty just sitting quietly in his seat. It's a real problem for him and we're going to work on it in a very special way. This is why you'll see us doing some special things with Bill. Does anyone else present have a special problem that we haven't mentioned and who would like some help?"

Responses to the last question give the teacher insight into the needs of other children under her care. This question is not asked if there are no resources available to help those children who request assistance. Usually, however, their requests are quite simple (help tying shoelaces, counting lunch money, etc.), and assistance presents little difficulty.

When Bill finally was able to attend for ten minutes, the whole class shared in his reward. "Bill has earned 100 pennies. The class gets to share 50 of these pennies while Bill gets the rest." Bill was like a number of hyperactive youngsters, isolated and disliked by other students. The other children had heard teachers tear him down constantly because of his inappropriate behavior. Nearly four out of five comments directed to children like Bill are negative (Madsen and Madsen, 1969; Patterson, 1969). Other children notice this (Kounin, Cump and Ryan, 1961) and eventually only see the outstandingly bad qualities about those children toward whom the teacher constantly responds in a negative manner. Modeling their behavior after that of the teacher, they too administer negative comments, but often more harshly. The child responds inappropriately to their taunts and, eventually, becomes even more isolated; such isolation prevents the development of appropriate social behaviors. (Patterson and Brodsky, 1966, give an excellent description of this spiraling phenomenon.)

The amount of peer reinforcement that is modeled after critical remarks made by parents and teachers is appalling. Children are made to play roles and are continually prevented from recasting themselves differently. When children like Bill are exposed to more than five hours a day of negative reinforcement, it is almost impossible to expect one or even five hours of office therapy per week to have any effect on modifying behavior.

When a child like Bill, however, finally does something correct for a change and the other children are encouraged to notice it and, in addition, to get something out of it, the effect on the child is often substantial. Consequently, it is standard procedure to have the class share concretely a portion of the reward given for appropriate behavior.

In the program described, the classroom teacher was trained to carry out an attention span conditioning program when the therapist was not present. She began to ignore Bill's wandering around the room and gave him praise and points (toward matchbox cars) whenever she noticed him sitting and attending or working. The children in the class were rewarded with extra recess time if they could ignore Bill's negative behavior, in order to remove the powerful reinforcement of peer attention. Follow-up indicates that Bill is still relatively hyperactive, but both teachers and parents report that they are better able to provide beneficial experiences for him.

A second case illustrates the combined use of assertive training (Salter, 1961), behavior rehearsal (Wolpe, 1969), and operant conditioning. Sally, age 13, was referred for extremely immature behavior, characterized by poor impulse control, preoccupation with fantasy, and hyperactivity. She frequently refused to answer questions in class and annoyed others around her because of her restless behavior. Consequently, no one wanted to be seen with her and boys taunted and teased her. Relations with authority figures were extremely poor and teachers described her as an obnoxious brat. Psychological evaluation by the school psychologist highlighted hysterical features in a girl with limited intellect (WICS Verbal I.Q. of 72, Performance I.Q. of 89). A male therapist was selected to treat her since continued exposure to him would serve as an in vivo desensitization to males. The target behavior selected was refusal to answer teacher initiated questions. Her science teacher was asked to cooperate with us since he was young and seemed less negative about her. He was instructed to ask no questions of Sally, but simply to by-pass her when her turn came. Instead, he gave the therapist a list of questions which he would have asked her and which he ranked according to difficulty. These questions were then read to Sally by the therapist, starting with the easier items. At first only a minimal answer was required, followed by elaboration. Sally, at first, would not cooperate in the training enterprise. Completion of the Reinforcement Survey Schedule (Phillips, 1969) revealed several things she wanted but, because of her poor behavior, they had been withheld from her by her parents. With their cooperation, Sally could acquire these privileges by accumulating points earned for answering the questions in therapy. She was not required to study the material, since her study habits were extremely poor, but to answer the questions from cards handed her. Concurrently, she was instructed to make a count of the number of notes she passed in class which asked students whether they were her friends, mad at her, etc. This behavior was reportedly annoying to other students, or gave them reason to ridicule her. She was then told that she could also earn points if she reported having passed less notes of this sort, following an explanation that friends were not gained by such behavior.

Behavior rehearsal was then introduced to help her initiate behaviors which would assist her to develop relationships with peers. A target girl was selected toward whom she would direct compliments. Practice in compliment giving was undertaken until she felt comfortable doing so and then she was encouraged to initiate this behavior toward the girl selected, or toward others if she wished to do so. More detailed information regarding assertive training is given in Phillips and Mordock (1970).

Following this phase, Sally was to answer questions in class and then to volunteer to answer pre-selected questions. During this period, Sally's grade in science improved from 55 to 75, while grades in her other five courses remained the same (50 to 60). Her restless behavior also diminished in science and she was reported to have several friends. Several weeks later other teachers noted improvement and, following her last marking period, she had improved in all courses. She also had a "best friend," which pleased her greatly. Sally was seen for a total of ten sessions.

Our conceptualization regarding many of these cases is similar to the earlier discussion around Bill. Many children, for whatever predisposing reason, suffer isolation from others because of inappropriate behavior. Our bias is not to talk about behavior but to do our best to change it. When friends are found, other inappropriate behaviors diminish since pre-occupation with obtaining attention is absent. Consequently, fantasies diminish, study habits improve, and "stupid answers" are no longer given.

Teacher Workshops. Ideally, the therapist hopes his procedures will be adopted by classroom teachers and, frequently, he is called upon to discuss behavior modification techniques in a formalized workshop. Teacher workshops and other in-service training programs should focus on particular children teachers are having difficulty helping. Simple terms should be employed—what works, what doesn't work. Children are selected for study and programs developed to modify their behavior. Teachers try out the programs and report back to the workshop partici-pants. Usually the therapist goes into selected classes to assist teachers with program implementation. Continual feedback of each teacher's experience is mandatory since their reports broaden the base of experience of workshop participants and serve as a sounding board for discussion.

When situations are presented, and some of the participants feel that the particular program developed will be difficult to carry out, a model of the appropriate behavior is presented (Bandura, 1965). The procedure was adapted from similar work with parents (Rose, 1969). The therapist or teacher who has solved a similar problem, plays the role of the teacher while the other teachers play the roles of children in the class. The teacher whose problem is to be re-enacted functions as the director, instructing the other members in performing their roles and defining the conditions of the problem. The director may initially have to play all the roles to familiarize each workshop participant with the specifics of the situation. The role playing is repeated until the director feels that he can try the modeled behavior himself.

Workshop participants are encouraged to discuss their reactions to the Model's behavior. Alternate behaviors are discussed and also presented by the same or another model. The director, after rehearsing the appropriate behavior himself, is then given the assignment to perform in the classroom some of the behaviors rehearsed in the workshop. All workshop participants should be given the opportunity to present a problem and perform at least once. If this is not possible, then situations selected should have implications for many of the workshop members.

If it can be arranged, teachers observe one another either in pairs or as a group. With younger children, teacher's aides can take over classes enabling one teacher to be observed by the group. Following observation, the group discusses the target child and the value of the modification procedures selected. Having teachers observe one another, however, is an anxiety-arousing situation since frequently teachers are defensive about their behavior. The therapist must be extremely supportive during this process.

Contingency Management. Frequently, the opportunity to engage in a highly desirable activity has been used as a reinforcer of more socially desirable responses; i.e., a child can play checkers for ten minutes if he sits still for ten minutes. The use of these desired activities to control behavior is called contingency management. Such management is based on the Premack Principle that a high probability behavior will reinforce a low probability behavior (Premack, 1959). In application, a child is allowed to engage in an activity he desires, contingent upon his completion of a behavior requested by his teacher or therapist. Frequent use of this technique is employed both in the home and school. Arrangements are also made with ancillary staff; i.e., librarians, gym teachers, so that if a child reads for 15 minutes he can go to gym. Even counseling has been made contingent upon school attendance for chronic non-attenders (MacDonald et al., 1970). With children who look forward to therapy, short extra sessions are made contingent upon certain classroom behaviors. Cooperating teachers are given special "report cards" similar to that described in Bailey, et al. (1970), where the child is evaluated regarding a target behavior and if the behavior diminishes he "earns" extra therapy. Children are encouraged to eventually evaluate their own behavior and to decide if they have earned the right to engage in a desirable behavior. Self-control is always the goal regardless of how machinistic the descriptions of behavioral techniques may appear to practitioners trained in other approaches.

Desensitization. Some teachers, no matter how often they are instructed in positive reinforcement and extinction procedures, are made anxious by certain things children do. If a behavior is ignored (not reinforced by attention and other effects) it will extinguish. Since extinction procedures are so often necessary in treating children, teachers must eventually learn to ignore certain deviant behaviors. If a teacher cannot ignore such negative behavior as a child switching a light on and off, or talking in the classroom, extinction procedures cannot be employed.

One cooperative but very anxious teacher of a class of brain-injured children agreed to try systematic desensitization procedures (Wolpe, 1969) to help alleviate anxiety she experienced in the classroom. The hyperactive behavior of her students was so distressing to her that she was going home each evening with a headache and taking sedatives.

While the details of the procedures will not be given here, they were similar to those described by Wolpe (1969) for treatment of phobias or social anxieties. Systematic desensitization to graded hierarchies of hyperactive and agressive behavior eliminated her headaches, enabled her to employ a token economy system (O'Leary & Becker, 1967) in her classroom and cope more effectively with her students.

Several other teachers were interested in a similar experience. Consequently, a group of teachers met for desensitization in a group (group desensitization procedures as described by Lazarus, 1961). The therapist took a simple, straightforward approach; behaviors which made the teachers anxious were graded. A common hierarchy was constructed and presented for two group sessions.

One teacher in the group had been teaching for 40 years. She was a very authoritarian and rigid person and efforts to have her use contingency management had gotten nowhere, since she couldn't tolerate her children behaving in anything but a well-controlled manner. After the two group desensitization sessions, children in her class were observed painting in the back of her room and they were quite messy about it. When asked about it she said, "When the kids finish a certain amount of work, they are now allowed to go to the back of the room and finger paint."

While there is no extensive backlog of experience in the use of systematic desensitization with teachers, results to date appear promising. In contrast to sensitivity training, this technique may be less threatening to some teachers. The rather rigid teacher referred to previously would never have agreed to participate in a sensitivity group since this would have implied to her that she was "insensitive" to children and their needs. Sensitivity group participation implies personal encounter and change in outlook; many teachers feel no need for such revamping of their personality. These teachers see relaxation and desensitization as a "technique" and, consequently, are more favorably disposed toward trying it.

CONCLUSIONS

In the programs described above, the authors were guided by a basic philosophy which underlies all of their work with children. They consider behavior modification meaningful and usable only in relation to behaviors which are maladaptive for a child—either because they interfere with his learning, isolate him from his peers, and/or cause him anxiety. In other words, procedures are never instituted for the purpose of enabling the teacher to control her class more rigidly, or to effect behavioral conformity within her group. One of the therapeutic goals includes helping the teacher feel comfortable with greater flexibility and freedom within her classroom.

The authors are in agreement with Klein et al. (1969), who report that behavior therapy is not as simple and straightforward as its popular stereotype would imply. Clinical inference and sensitivity to a child's needs are equally important. When used with sensitivity, behavior modification can result in meaningful changes in a child's total functioning.

REFERENCES

Bailey, J. S., Wolf, M. M., & Phillips, E. L. Home-based reinforcement and the modification of pre-delinquents' classroom behavior. *Journal of Applied Behavior Analysis*, 1970, 3, 223–233.

Bandura, A. Behavior modification through modeling procedures. In L. Krasner & L. P. Ullman (Eds.) *Research in Behavior Modification*. New York: Holt, Rinehart and Winston, 1965, pp. 310–340.

Kleim, Marjoris H., Dittman, A. T., Parkloff, M. B. & Gill, M. M. Behavior therapy observations and reflections. *Journal of Consulting and Clinical Psychology*, 1969, 33, 259–266.

Kounin, J. S., Gump, P. V., & Ryan III, J. J. Explorations in classroom management. *The Journal of Teacher Education*, 1961, 12, 235–246.

Lazarus, A. A. Group therapy of phobic disorders by systematic desensitization. *Journal of Abnormal and Social Psychology*, 1961, 63, 504–510.

MacDonald, W. S., Gallimore, R., & MacDonald, Gwen. Contingency counseling by school personnel: an economical model of intervention. *Journal of Applied Behavior Analysis*, 1970, 3, 175–182.

Madsen, C. H., Jr. & Madson, C. K. *Teaching discipline*. Boston: Allyn and Bacon, 1969.

O'Leary, K. D. & Becker, W. C. Behavior modification of an adjustment class: a token reinforcement program. *Exceptional Children*, 1967, 33, 637–642.

Patterson, G. R. An application of conditioning techniques to control a hyperactive child. In L. P. Ullman & L. Krasner (Eds.), *Case Studies in Behavior Modification*. New York: Holt, Rinehart & Winston, 1965, pp. 279–284.

Patterson, G. R. Behavioral intervention procedures in the classroom and in the home. In A. E. Bergin and S. L. Garfield (Eds.), *Handbook of Psychotherapy and Behavior Change*. New York: Wiley, 1969.

Patterson, G. R. & Brodsky, G. D. A behavior modification programme for a child with multiple problem behaviors. *Journal of Child Psychology and Psychiatry*, 1966, 7, 277–295.

Patterson, G. R. & Gullion, M. E. *Living with children: new methods for parents and teachers*. Champaign, Illinois: Research Press, 1968.

Patterson, G. R., Jones, R., Whittier, J., & Wright, M. M. A behavior modification technique for the hyperactive child. *Behavior Research and Therapy*, 1965, 2, 217–226.

Phillips, D. A reinforcement survey schedule for children. Mimeo paper. Princeton Center for Behavior Therapy, Kingston, N.J., 1969.

Phillips, D. & Mordock, J. B. Behavior therapy with children: general guidelines and concrete suggestions. Paper presented at the convention of the American Association of Psychiatric Services for Children, Philadelphia, November, 1970.

Premack, D. Toward empirical behavior laws: I. Positive reinforcement. *Psychological Review,* 1959, 66, 219–233.

Rose, S. D. A behavioral approach to the group treatment of parents. *Social Work*, 1969, 14, 21–29.

Wolfe, J. P. *The Practice of Behavior Therapy.* New York: Pergamon, 1969.

INSTRUCTING BEGINNING TEACHERS IN REINFORCEMENT PROCEDURES WHICH IMPROVE CLASSROOM CONTROL*

R. Vance Hall, Marion Panyan, Deloris Rabon, and Marcia Broden

Good Teacher—Skillful Reinforcer. Here are three more variations on the reinforcement theme: Reward desired behaviors. The teachers were able to select the types of rewards that were effective with their classes and to apply them when the students showed the desired behavior. While none of the reinforcement plans resulted in entirely eliminating the undesired behavior or resulted in establishing the desired actions 100% of the time, the final measurements show dramatic improvements over the previous classroom activity. In a short time these teachers became better teachers. To a large extent teaching is reinforcing, and if we are going to become more skillful teachers, we should become more skillful users of reinforcement. Principals, supervisors, and teacher-educators have a job too: reinforce the use of reinforcement.

Systematic reinforcement procedures were used to increase study behavior in the classrooms of three beginning teachers experiencing problems of classroom control. Classroom study rates were recorded during a baseline period. During subsequent experimental periods, the teachers changed one or more reinforcement contingencies (teacher attention, length of between-period break, a classroom game) to bring about increased study rates and concomitant reductions in disruptive behaviors. A brief reversal period, in which these contingencies were discontinued, again produced low rates of study. Reinstatement of the contingencies resulted once again in marked increases in study behaviors.

Previous studies (Hall, Lund, and Jackson, 1968; Evans and Ozwalt, 1968; Thomas, Becker, and Armstrong, 1968) have shown that teacher-applied contingencies could be used to increase or decrease study rates and academic performance of dawdling or disruptive pupils in regular school classrooms. These studies, like almost all of those which have demonstrated that teacher-applied contingencies can be effective in special education classrooms (Wolf, Giles, and Hall, 1968; Clark, Lachowicz, and Wolf, 1968; O'Leary and Becker, 1967; Hall and Broden, 1967; McKenzie, Clark, Wolf, Kothera, and Benson, 1968), were carried out by experienced teachers. Often, the teachers had been selected because of their excellent classroom management skills and the high probability that they could carry out the experimental procedures successfully.

*From R. Vance Hall et al., "Introducing Beginning Teachers in Reinforcement Procedures Which Improve Classroom Control," *Journal of Applied Behavioral Analysis* 1, no. 4 (Winter, 1968): 315–322, by permission of the authors. The authors are with the University of Kansas, with the exception of Marion Panyan, who participated as a graduate student intern of the Southern Illinois University Behavior Modification Program. Dr. Hall is Director of Juniper Gardens Children's Project, Kansas City, Kansas.

These demonstrations have been important, but they have not addressed themselves to one of the most significant aspects of classroom management in education: the training of beginning teachers in the principles and procedures which will bring about classroom control.

The present studies were carried out in the classrooms of three first-year teachers. Not only were they initially unfamiliar with learning theory principles and the systematic application of contingencies, but each was experiencing significant problems of general classroom control.

Teacher One. The first teacher had received his B.A. in education the previous year. His first teaching assignment was a class of 30 sixth-graders in a public school located in a low socio-economic area of Kansas City, Kansas. His class was selected for study on the principal's recommendation because of continued high rates of disruptive and other student non-study behaviors. In the principal's words, the class was "completely out of control."

Data were recorded every day during the first hour of the school day during the reading period. The recording system was essentially that used in previous studies with individual pupils in which an observer recorded pupil behavior every 10 sec during a 30-min observation session, except that instead of observing the same pupil throughout the session, each was observed for 10 sec on a consecutive rotating basis. If the pupil being observed was out of his seat, or if he talked without being recognized by the teacher any time during the 10-sec interval, an "N" for non-study was scored for the interval. Otherwise, the student's behavior at the end of the 10 sec determined the rating. If he was looking out the window, playing with cards, fighting or poking a classmate, tapping pencils on books, cleaning out his desk or engaging in any of a variety of other such behaviors, an "N" was recorded. If there was no "N" behavior an "S," indicating study, was scored for the interval. Study behaviors included writing the assignment, looking in the book and answering the teacher's questions.

When every class member had been observed in turn, recording began again with the first child, until all were observed again in the same order. From this time-sampling procedure the percent of study for the entire class was computed by dividing the number of study intervals by the total number of observation intervals and multiplying by 100.

The teacher's verbal attention, defined as a verbalization directed to a pupil or pupils, was also analyzed. The teacher's comment was recorded as a "+" if it followed appropriate study behavior, and a "-" if it followed an instance of non-study behavior. These comments were recorded when they occurred. Almost without exception those that followed study behavior were approving and those that followed non-study behavior were in the form of a verbal reprimand. See Broden (1968) for a more detailed description of these interval recording procedures.

Periodically, and at least once during every experimental condition, a second observer made a simultaneous observational record. Correspondence of the two records interval-for-interval yielded the percentage of interobserver agreement. For this study, the percentage of agreement for class study behavior and for teacher attention ranged from 87 to 93%.

Figure 1 presents the class study rates for the various phases of the experiment and the frequency of teacher comments following study and non-study behaviors. The broken horizontal lines indicate the mean study rates for each experimental condition.

During Baseline, the mean class study rate was 44%. The mean number of intervals in which the teacher made comments following study behavior was 1.4 per session. The class study rate rose to 90% when the helping teacher presented a demonstration lesson. The points at which the teacher met with the principal to discuss organizational procedures are indicated. After the first meeting, the teacher began writing all assignments on the board. After the third, he changed the class seating arrangements. As can be seen, these counseling procedures seemed to have some beneficial effects, but the improvement was not enough to eliminate concern.

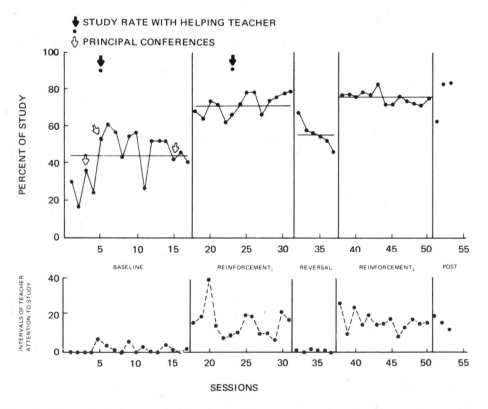

Fig. 1. A record of class study behavior and teacher attention for study behavior during reading period in a sixth-grade classroom: Baseline—before experimental procedures; Reinforcement₁—increased teacher attention for study; Reversal-removal of teacher attention for study; Reinforcement₂—return to increased teacher attention for study; Post-follow-up checks up to 20 weeks after termination of experimental procedures.

Before the first day of the second phase, reinforcement principles and procedures used in other studies which had been effective in increasing study behavior of individual pupils were discussed with the teacher. He was shown the class baseline study record and the record of the frequency of teacher comments following study behavior. He was instructed to increase the frequency of positive comments for appropriate study. Each day he was shown the records of the class study rates and the frequency of his comments following appropriate study. Under these conditions the mean frequency of teacher comments following study behavior increased to 14.6 per session. There was a dramatic and sustained concomitant increase in study behavior to a mean rate of 72%. According to the subjective observations of the teacher, principal, and the observers, the class was under better control and classroom noise had decreased significantly.

During a brief Reversal phase, the teacher provided almost no reinforcement for study behavior. This resulted in a sharp decrease in study, which by the sixth session was well within the Baseline range. According to the subjective judgments of the teacher, principal, and observers, disruptive behaviors and high noise levels also returned.

During the Reinforcement$_2$ phase, an immediate sustained increase in study to a mean rate of 76% accompanied an increase of "+" teacher comments to a mean frequency of 14 per session. In the final nine sessions (43 to 52) of the Reinforcement$_2$ phase, the teacher was instructed to continue reinforcing study behavior but to discontinue making comments following non-study behaviors. Up to that point, the level of these "−" comments had remained fairly constant, occurring in about 12 intervals per session. When the teacher decreased "−" comments so that they occurred in only 4.5 intervals per session there was no significant change in the class study rate. Therefore, study behavior seemed to be unaffected by comments (usually reprimands) following non-study.

Continuous observation was terminated at the end of the Reinforcement$_3$ phase when the primary observer, who was a student intern, returned to her university classes. Post checks taken at one-, three-, and five-month intervals, however, indicated that the relatively high rates of study and teacher attention for study were being maintained.

Teacher Two. The second teacher was also a recent college graduate and in her first year of teaching. She had been assigned to teach a first-grade class of 24 pupils in the same Kansas City, Kansas school. Again the principal and helping teacher had recommended and demonstrated procedures to the teacher for improving classroom management. The results were deemed unsatisfactory because both principal and teacher felt non-study behaviors were still too high.

Data were recorded every day the first 30 min of the morning reading period. This time was selected at the request of the teacher because of her concern about the low study rate of pupils at their desks doing "seat-work" while she was working with one or another of the three classroom reading groups in a circle at the front of the room.

The recording procedures were essentially those used with Teacher One. The percentage of agreement between observers for class study behavior and teacher attention ranged from 85 to 88%.

Figure 2 presents the class study rates for the various phases of the experiment. Mean rates for each condition are shown by a broken horizontal line. During the Baseline phase, the mean study rate of pupils at their desks not participating in reading circle was 51%. The mean frequency of intervals of teacher attention following study behavior was 1.6.

Before the first experimental phase (Reinforcement$_1$) reinforcement principles and procedures were explained to the teacher and she was shown the Baseline study record and the record of her verbal attention following study behavior. She was asked to increase the frequency of her attention for appropriate study of pupils working at their desks. As a

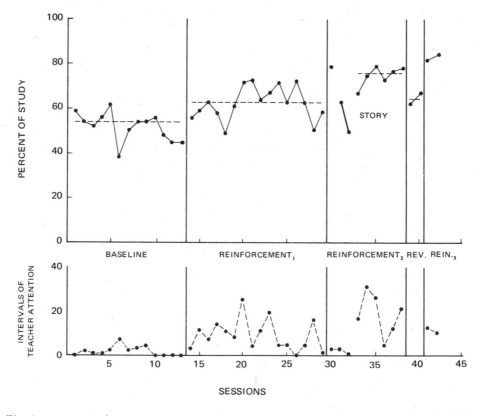

Fig. 2. A record of study rates and teacher attention for study of pupils at desks during a first-grade reading period; Baseline-before experimental procedures; Reinforcement$_1$ — increased teacher attention for study; Reinforcement$_2$ —study game following reading period; Reversal—removal of study game and attention for study; Reinforcement$_3$ — reinstatement of study game and attention for study.

result of these instructions, the frequency of teacher attention following appropriate study was increased to nine per session. The mean rate of appropriate study increased to 62%. The teacher, however, was still not satisfied with this study rate. So a second condition, the study game, was introduced as a contingency.

The study game was the simple classroom game, familiar to many teachers, commonly called "7 Up." In it the teacher selects seven pupils, in this case the seven best studiers, to go to the front of the room. Then the rest of the class members put their heads down on their desks and close their eyes. The seven tiptoe around the room, touch one of the seated pupils lightly on the head and return to the front of the room. The seated pupils then open their eyes. The seven who were touched stand and in turn attempt to guess which of those who are up in front touched them. If they succeed they get to go to the front of the room and be "it" on the next round. "7 Up" was renamed the "study" game. It was used because it is a favorite of elementary pupils up through the sixth grade, it is quiet, and it requires little or no teacher supervision.

The "study" game was introduced to the children before reading period on the first day of the Reinforcement$_2$ phase. This was a priming procedure similar to that described by Allyon and Azrin (1968). Teacher judgment was the sole criterion as to whether or not pupils studied enough to play the "study" game.

When the "study" game followed the reading period in the Reinforcement$_2$ phase, study rose to 79%. An unplanned reversal effect was observed in the next two sessions of Reinforcement$_2$ when the teacher read a story to her students after the reading period in lieu of the "study" game. By the second session, study had dropped to 50%. When the "study" game was reinstituted as a contingency for study, the class study rate rose to higher levels.

The next phase was a planned reversal in which the teacher was instructed not to reinforce study and told the pupils they could not play the "study" game. The mean study rate for Reversal was 63%.

The mean rate of study during the two days of the Reinforcement$_3$ phase, when the "study" game was again used as reinforcement for appropriate study, was 82%. Since these last two sessions were during the last week of the school year, the teacher was particularly pleased at the high study rate achieved and the almost complete lack of disruptive behavior in the class.

TEACHER THREE

In the third study, the teacher taught a class of 30 seventh graders enrolled in an afternoon unified studies (English and social studies) class in the small town of Bonner Springs, Kansas which is just outside Kansas City. The class met daily for 40 min with a 5-min break and then met for another session of 45 min.

The class was selected on the principal's recommendation because the teacher was in his first year and there was concern because of the high rate of disruptive behaviors. These included talking without permission, being out of their seats, fighting, and throwing paper. The noise level was so high and so constant that the teacher kept the classroom door closed and the shade over the door window pulled at all times.

Observations were made daily during the first 30 min of the period before the 5-min break.

The recording system was essentially that used in the first two experiments, except that the recording interval was 5 sec rather than 10. Thus, the recorded behavior for the first pupil was that which was occurring after the next 5 sec of observation, the behavior of the second pupil was recorded after the next 5 sec of observation, and so on, so that the behavior of a different pupil was recorded each 5 sec interval until the entire class had been observed. Then the observation sequence was repeated. Teacher attention for both study and non-study was also recorded as it occurred. Reliability checks made during each phase of the study showed an inter-observer agreement which ranged from 80 to 90%.

Figure 3 shows that the mean class study rate for the baseline period of 25 days was 47%. The mean frequency of teacher attention following study behavior was six times per session. The frequency of attention for non-study was over 20 per session; most often this attention was in the form of the command, "Let's have it quiet in here."

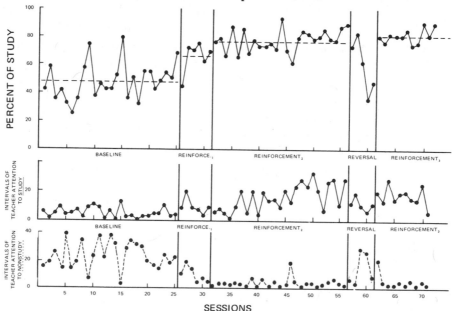

Fig. 3. A record of class study rates and teacher attention for study and non-study during a seventh-grade unified studies period: Baseline-before experimental procedures; Reinforcement$_1$—increased attention for study; Reinforcement$_2$—increased attention for study and shortened between-period break for disruptive behavior; Reversal—removal of punishment for disruptive behavior; Reinforcement$_3$—reinstatement of punishment for disruptive behavior.

During the first Reinforcement phase, the teacher was asked to try to increase the amount of attention to study and decrease the amount of attention for non-study. As a result, teacher attention for study increased to nine times per session while attention for non-study decreased to about nine per session. The study rate under these conditions increased to 65%. According to the subjective judgment of the teacher, principal, and the experimenters, however, the classroom noise still remained at a disruptive level.

In the next phase (Reinforcement$_2$), the teacher added an additional condition. He placed a chalk mark on the chalk board if any student got out of his seat without permission or disturbed the class. For each mark placed on the board 10 sec were deducted from the five-min between-period break. If as many as 24 marks were accumulated there was to be no break. The teacher paused about 5 sec before placing a mark on the board. If the class became quiet and the disruptions stopped within the 5-sec period, no mark was put on the board.

Under these conditions study increased to 76%. A marked decrease in classroom noise was noticed by the observers and the teacher began to leave the door to the room open. He also, for the first time, left the room for brief periods without losing control.

After the first two days of Reversal, when punishment of noisy behavior was discontinued, the rate of study behavior dropped sharply. At the same time, teacher attention for non-study behaviors increased, as did the high level of classroom noise, according to the judgment of the observers.

During the final reinforcement phase, the study behavior rose immediately to 81% and was maintained at that level to the end of the study.

DISCUSSION

The beginning teacher faces a formidable challenge. Except for a brief exposure to student teaching, where the classroom is organized and supervised by an experienced teacher, he or she has had no pedagogical experience. Often the practice teaching is at a different grade level than the one assigned the new teacher when he gets his own classroom. Thus, on the first day of school the teacher suddenly finds himself alone, facing a classroom of 30 or so pupils with responsibility for providing them an effective learning environment. All too often he finds that he is ill-prepared to cope with the management and control problems which face him, for his professors have not specified precisely enough what procedures should be followed to bring about classroom control.

Most teachers do learn over time the techniques which are effective in getting pupils to study, rather than to engage in non-study behaviors. Often another teacher, the principal, or in some districts a helping teacher, suggest or demonstrate ways for achieving classroom control. Even this help, however, is often ineffective. Sometimes it is well into the year before a semblance of good classroom control has been achieved. Some new teachers never make it and drop out during or after that first year. Those that do succeed, often look back and realize that both they and their pupils wasted a great deal of time and energy that first year until they "caught on" on how to manage a class.

The results of the present experiments showed that beginning teachers of three different grade levels experiencing problems of classroom control could be taught to use systematic reinforcement procedures to increase classroom study behavior even when previous attempts at assistance by principals and helping teachers had been relatively ineffective.

In the first experiment, before the changes brought about, the principal had termed the sixth-grade teacher's status as "precarious." He had contemplated replacing him during the year and certainly could not have offered him a contract for a second year if considerable improvement in control had not occurred. The teacher's awareness of his situation was reflected in a remark made to the observer after the third day of the first reinforcement phase, when an improved classroom atmosphere was already evident. He said: "You know, I think I'm going to make it." He did make it, and was offered and accepted a contract to continue teaching.

In the cases of the first- and seventh-grade teachers there was less immediate concern about imminent failure. Even so, both the teachers and the principals reported that the improvements seen in class control were dramatic.

One notable aspect of all three studies is that the teachers were able to carry out the procedures after an initial explanatory session of between 15 and 30 min at the beginning of each experimental period and daily feedback of the results. The feedback sessions were also used to provide social reinforcement to the teacher for carrying out the procedures. It seems likely that for all three teachers, the fact that their classes became more manageable served to reinforce and thus maintain the changes in the teacher's reinforcement behavior. They reported it was actually less work to teach using the procedures than when they had not used them. In the case of the seventh-grade teacher, this was borne out by the fact that, whereas he provided attention (mostly verbal reprimands) almost once a minute during Baseline, he was able to maintain a much higher study rate during the reinforcement phases with about half as much total teacher attention.

We are well aware that good teachers (who had "caught on") had been using these same techniques effectively long before B. F. Skinner formulated the principles of operant conditioning. Even these teachers, however, had not looked at behavior closely enough and with enough understanding to be able to specify precisely what they had done and what the ineffective teacher needed to do to bring about the desired pupil behavior. These studies indicate that a behavior analysis approach will allow educators, including principals and helping teachers, to help the beginning teacher who otherwise may have been doomed to failure or at least to a fumbling and frustrating trial and error period, quickly to learn to manage his classroom through systematic use of the reinforcing contingencies available to him.

Furthermore, college instructors should now be able to give prospective teachers functional information regarding the relationship of their behavior to that of their pupils. This information can be specific and precise enough so that the new teacher can apply it in the classroom.

Finally, it should be noted that the procedures were carried out with telling effect within the existing school structure. Teacher attention, a classroom game, and access to a between-period break were used rather than reinforcers extrinsic to the situation. The procedures described (or others that are similar) which use the reinforcers already available in the schools can be employed by teachers in any classroom without added expense and without major administrative revision.

REFERENCES

Allyon, T. and Azrin, N. H. Reinforcer sampling: a technique for increasing the behavior of mental patients, *Journal of Applied Behavior Analysis*, 1968, 1, 13–20.

Broden, Marcia. Notes on recording. *Observer's Manual for Juniper Gardens Children's Project*, Bureau of Child Research, 1968.

Bushell, D., Wrobel, P. A., and Michaelis, M. L. Applying "group" contingencies to the classroom study behavior of preschool children. *Journal of Applied Behavior Analysis*, 1968, 1, 55–61.

Clark, M., Lachowicz, J., and Wolf, M. M. A pilot basic education program for school dropouts incorporating a token reinforcement system. *Behavior Research and Therapy*, 1968, 6, 183–188.

Evans, G. and Ozwalt, G. Acceleration of academic progress through the manipulation of peer influence. *Behaviour Research and Therapy*, 1967 Vol. 5, pp 1–7.

Hall, R. Vance and Broden, Marcia. Behavior changes in brain-injured children through social reinforcement. *Journal of Experimental Child Psychology*, 1967, 5, 463–479.

Hall, R. Vance; Lund, Diane and Jackson, Deloris. Effects of teacher attention on study behavior. *Journal of Applied Behavior Analysis*, 1968, 1, 1–12.

McKenzie, Hugh; Clark, Marilyn; Wolf, Montrose; Kothera, Richard, and Benson, Cedric. Behavior modification of children with learning disabilities using grades as token reinforcers. *Exceptional Children*, 1968, 34, 745–752.

O'Leary, K. D. and Becker, W. C. Behavior modification of an adjustment class: a token reinforcement system. *Exceptional Children*, 1967, 33, 637–642.

Thomas, Dan R., Becker, Wesley C., and Armstrong, Marianne. Production and elimination of disruptive classroom behavior by systematically varying teachers' behavior. *Journal of Applied Behavior Analysis*, 1968, 1, 35–45.

Wolf, Montrose M., Giles, David K., and Hall, R. Vance. Experiments with token reinforcement in a remedial classroom. *Behavior Research and Therapy*, 1968, 6, 51–54.

*The authors wish to express appreciation to Dr. O. L. Plucker, Dr. Bertram Caruthers, Alonzo Plough, Curtis Reddic, and Barbara Gaines of the Kansas City, Kansas Public Schools and Kenneth Tewell, Robert Clark, and John Beougher of the Bonner Springs, Kansas Public Schools without whose cooperation and active participation these studies would not have been possible. We are also indebted to Dr. R. L. Schiefelbusch, Director, and R. H. Copeland, Associate Director of the Bureau of Child Research, who provided essential administrative support and counsel. Reprints may be obtained from R. Vance Hall, Juniper Gardens Children's Project, 2021 North Third Street, Kansas City, Kansas 66101.

The research was carried out as a part of the Juniper Gardens Children's Project, a program of research on the development of culturally deprived children and was partially supported by the National Institute of Child Health and Human Development: (HD 03144-01) and the Office of Economic Opportunity: (GG 8180) Bureau of Child Research, University of Kansas.

PART THREE

Humanistic Psychology

INTRODUCTION
THE EDITOR

One of the most ambiguous words in educational terminology is "humanistic." Because of the many meanings of the word, it is helpful to say what it doesn't mean before saying what it does mean. The first series of inappropriate meanings has to do with religion. These religion-centered uses of "humanistic" and "humanism" mean such things as *a*) a disbelief in the super-natural and a belief in man's improvement through reason and science, *b*) an interest in human concerns rather than divine concerns, *c*) a belief that Jesus was an extraordinary human, not a supernatural being, or *d*) a belief that man's highest nature can be developed through a specific religion, e.g., Christian humanism. Another use of "humanistic" has to do with values. In this field "humanistic" means a devotion to human welfare. "Humanitarian" and "humane" catch this consideration and compassion. In the academic world "humanistic" implies having to do with the humanities or refers to studies which promote human culture. A specialized sub-meaning of this refers to the classical studies of the fourteenth through sixteenth centuries, especially studies of ancient Greece and Rome.

If "humanistic" as it is used in educational psychology doesn't have the meanings above, what does it mean? Kirschenbaum's article "What Is Humanistic Education?" answers this question. In fact, he answers it eight ways, and here is one of the problems of trying to talk about the applications of humanistic psychology to education. Even in this restricted field, "humanistic" has a variety of meanings, so that the first task when humanistically-oriented educators get together is to agree on what they mean by "humanistic." Otherwise they end up talking at cross purposes and misunderstanding each other. As Kirschenbaum's article points out, a school, class, or a teacher can be judged more or less humanistic by several criteria simultaneously. The articles in this section show differing types of humanistic approaches to education. Through them, however, a collection of ideas emerge, disappear, and re-emerge. These thematic ideas form the warp and woof of humanistic psychology.

In "Some Educational Implications of the Humanistic Psychologies" Abraham Maslow summarizes some of the disadvantages that humanistic psychologists see in behavioral and Freudian psychologies. The idea of *human potential* points to one of these, and this theme reappears consistently in humanistic education. As pointed out in the introduction to the Freudian section, those psychologists tend to look for sickness, and they interpret their task as curing, or perhaps as preventing sickness. Because they use the medical, curative model of psychology, they are interested primarily in therapy. Humanistic educators, on the other hand, are more interested in developing our abilities once sickness has been cured or in people who have had no particular sicknesses. It is not fully human, they say, merely to be free of problems. Once a person is normally healthy, what then? They try to go beyond the mere absence of problems into the positive ability to do things. These positive abilities are called human potentials, and humanistic educators usually focus their teaching on these abilities. Terry Borton and Arthur Combs stress this idea in the first two articles in this section. As they point out, we are constantly revising our concept of human potentials upward as individuals and groups discover new abilities. The human potential theme in humanistic education says that there is more to education than the 3 R's and our current subjects. The articles in this section show us some additional skills that humanistic educators would like to see included in our curricula.

Perhaps the largest group of human abilities that are the concern of humanistic educators are the *human relations* skills. This theme shows up in the desire to help people get along with others more skillfully and happily while getting along with themselves, too. Himber's article on sensitivity training with teenagers exemplifies this typically humanistic concern. She shows that there are ways to teach people to build warm relationships with each other and ways to teach trust, acceptance, awareness of others' feelings, interpersonal honesty, and other kinds of social knowledge. With a typical human potentials thrust, the emphasis in her article isn't on curing interpersonal problems so much as on improving day-to-day living and adding enjoyment and enrichment to our social lives. One kind of typical humanistic content concerns itself with getting to know others and learning how to increase man's social potentials. Often this includes getting to know oneself, and through better knowledge of oneself as one human, getting to know others as humans.

Besides stressing human relations, or group dynamics, humanistic educators see other human abilities that we under-teach in schools. In addition to the cognitive skills and social relations, humanistic educators try to plan classes that help us improve our abilities to perceive, feel, move, wonder, intuit, sense, create, fantasize, imagine, and experience. Although the current resurgence of interest in humanistic education is new, in one sense it is a return to one of the oldest traditions in educational philosophy, education of the whole man. Humanistic educators try to look at a broad spectrum of human behavior and ask, "How many things can people do? How can I help them do all these things better?"

Probably the major thrust of humanistic education is the recognition of the importance of the emotions in education. While we traditionally see emotions from a Freudian perspective as interfering with cognition, humanistic psychologists are more likely to stress the benefits of education of the emotions. The importance of the emotional or *affective domain* is one of the strongest characteristics of humanistic educators. Since thinking and feeling almost always accompany each other, neglecting the proper education of our feelings is stunting one of our greatest potentials. We can learn to use our emotions and benefit from this type of learning just as we do from our cognitive educations. The rationale behind the education of the emotions is elaborated on by several authors in this section, e.g., Roberts, Mills and Scher, and Himber.

Strzepek picks up the idea of *learning to enjoy life* from humanistic psychology too. In "Fiction and the Human Potentiality" he notes that most high school literature neglects the positive side of being human. The way to redress this balance is to present literature that shows both desirable and undesirable human traits. Rather than trying to explain away desirable human behavior by reducing it to basic physiological drives as the behaviorists do or to a variety of sexual pleasure as the Freudians do, humanistic psychologists tend to see human behavior as a mixture of higher and lower motivations.

This brings up another trait of humanistic psychology: instead of seeing human behavior only in terms of sickness or in terms of motivation that applies also to lower animals, humanistic psychologists emphasize the human view based on ". . . the prime reality—human experience itself—and starting from there to derive the concepts, the necessary abstractions and the definitions of real human experience and human needs, goals and values . . ." (Maslow, 1967). Thus, humanistic psychology *starts with human behavior*, not with the behavior of other species. Beginning with human behavior, not rat behavior, it is "humanistic," not "rodentistic."

One of the results of starting with human behavior in psychology is a humanistic view of motivation. While we share some motivation with other animals, we also have some especially human motivation; these are the *higher needs* which humanistic psychologists discuss. Maslow's needs-hierarchy theory of human motivation posits the desires for being with others, for competence and recognition, and for self-actualization as parts of human motivation, as well as the lower desires for physiological needs and security. As educators, we too should consider these higher needs and plan our individual courses and overall curricula to meet these higher needs. Some humanistic psychologists see us as having a natural desire for growth, improvement, and learning. Schools should be careful not to kill this instinct by forcing children to learn about topics before they are ready. Since one of the natural human traits is the desire for knowledge, forcing a child to learn a set curriculum or at a specific time is pushing him before he is psychologically ready and willing. He will show this readiness by learning when he wants to learn. As Kirschenbaum points out, one of the humanistic roles of the teacher is to assist students to learn what they want to when they want to. This is the *teacher as humanistic facilitator* to help people meet their higher, human needs, rather than the teacher as a Freudian counselor or behavioral engineer. The assumption of higher needs shows up in the goals of education too. Humanistic psychologists see one of the purposes of life as living as full and rewarding a life as one can. Instead of using "need" in a minimal sense to refer to those things which are necessary only to sustain life, a humanistic use of the word refers to those things which are necessary to live as full a life as one can. They are *needs for maximum living*, not needs for the maintenance of life and nothing more.

In summary, a humanistic approach to educational psychology emphasizes possibilities for positive growth. The human potentials approach looks for abilities people can develop and focuses on helping to develop them. These include a wide range, and especially concern the social, interpersonal abilities and methods for self-development. The emphasis is on enriching and enjoying oneself, one's life, and society.

The characteristics of humanistic psychology that I've mentioned in this introduction are generally true and accurate for *most* humanistic psychologists, but not for all. Because of the variety of people and interests among this group, the list of characteristics mentioned here is incomplete; it includes, however, those that are most relevant to educators and most helpful to reading and understanding the articles which follow. Other writings by the authors of these articles will provide further information on how humanistic psychology can help teachers and administrators. In addition to these sources, the references in the bibliography by Canfield and Phillips (Appendix A) will open further the door of humanistic psychology.

TEACHING FOR PERSONAL GROWTH *

Terry Borton

Education for Life Enrichment, The Humanistic Goal. In this article Borton sets the theme for most educators who base their practices on humanistic psychology. Education is not just for personal survival or to increase one's income or power over others, but it is also for enriching one's life, for personal growth beyond survival and income. Thus, humanistic psychologists look at human motivation in a broader sense to include developing beyond the more basic levels. They tend to see human goals as more than the absence of fear, pain, anxiety, or other unwanted feelings. As well as education to help in the removal of these, they see the creation of positive aspects of humanity. The other articles in this section will develop this idea more fully.

When you get to the end of this paragraph, stop, and think back to when you were in sixth grade. Remember a particular moment in that year, close your eyes, and let your mind rest there for a while. Don't cheat. Stop and go back to sixth grade.

Do you remember much about your old class? Do you remember whether other people were close, or far away? Were you warm or cold? Do you remember where the class bully was sitting? The boy with the mossy teeth? The one with the snotty nose? The kid who sucked his thumb? Who supplied the dirty pictures? How did you feel about him? Who were the special people? How were you going to get near them? Who was the teacher? Do you remember the lesson? . . . At the end of this paragraph, close your eyes again. Let yourself drop down those years, until you find your sixth-grade you. What was school like, really? Stop, and give yourself time to remember it as you experienced it. Stop and allow yourself to remember school as you experienced school.

If you tried this opening exercise, you might generate a more personal understanding of the importance of feelings and attitudes in the classroom. Unless you had an exceptional teacher, you probably don't remember the lesson that was being taught back there in sixth grade. Instead, you probably remember your feelings—your own concerns about yourself, your relationships with your friends, and the power struggles swirling through the room. And, if you think back to the last time you were in a college class, you will probably discover that you had not changed very much, that the things that

---

*From Terry Borton, "Teaching for Personal Growth: An Introduction to New Materials," *Mental Hygiene* 53, no. 4 (October, 1969): 594–599, by permission of the author. Terry Borton is Director of the Dual Audio-Television Project of the Philadelphia Board of Education and author of the book *Reach, Touch, and Teach* (New York: McGraw-Hill, 1970).

were important to you, that you remember, and that had an effect on how you grew as a person, had relatively little to do with the content of the subject being taught and a great deal to do with your feelings, fantasies, and subjective thoughts.

These "affective" components of student life—feelings, motives, fantasies, interpersonal relations, and attitudes—have received new attention from educators within the last several years, because it has become increasingly clear that such factors are of tremendous importance for students' academic achievement as well as for their personal growth and mental health. For instance, James Coleman, describing the results of his mammoth survey *Equality of Educational Opportunity*, concluded that, of all factors studied (family background, teacher salary, school facilities, curriculum materials, etc.), *attitudes*, such as interest in school, self-concept, and sense of control, showed the strongest relation to achievement. At a more intuitive level, John Holt, in his *How Children Fail*, has documented the power of anxiety to cripple learning in even the best "progressive" schools. And Jonathan Kozol's *Death at an Early Age* has given an appalling picture of the way the same factor is intensified in the urban schools of our big cities.

These criticisms of school—reinforced by such indices of the general society's mental condition as a soaring crime rate, widespread divorce, the generation gap, and increasing mental illness—have encouraged educators and psychologists to begin developing new approaches to the emotional and personal lives of students within the school. These new approaches supplement the work of the traditional psychologist in the school. They do not involve delving back into a child's past, exploring personal relations with parents, or giving psychological tests and classifying students' problems. Instead, they direct attention to normal children within a classroom setting and rely on materials that are within a teacher's competence to handle. They provide ways for the students to recognize, analyze, and express the feelings that are always present in the classroom. In some of the materials, the goal is simply to make these feelings legitimate and help the student understand them more fully; other programs attempt to use this understanding to increase the relevance of regular school work or to stimulate creativity.

Besides the "here and now" attention to the child's feelings, the new approaches have a number of other characteristics in common:

1. They make the student himself the content—that is, he learns about his *own* feelings and actions, not about psychology in general.

2. They recognize that a student's imagination, as reflected in art, dreams, stories, and fantasies, is an important part of his life that he can share with classmates and use to think creatively.

3. They pay particular attention to nonverbal expression (such as gesture and tone), since it is through such means that many feeling states and attitudes are communicated.

4. They use games, improvisations, and role-playing as a way of simulating behavior so that it can be studied and changed.

5. They teach in an explicit fashion some of the basic principles of group dynamics so that students can have more responsibility for the conduct of their own affairs.

There are problems in the new materials—problems of ethics, professionalism, and politics inherent in the fact that they represent the exploration of a new area. Perhaps the most basic problem is that they raise the expectation that student feelings will be handled in a considerate and sensitive fashion—both by other students and by the teacher. If this expectation is violated, then materials that open up the realm of the emotions may do more harm than good.

There are a few rules-of-thumb that can help ensure that the materials are used with a sensitivity that gives students their full benefits:

1. The teacher should never take students into areas of experience in which he himself is uncomfortable. The teacher should teach for the students' needs, not his own.

2. The teacher should never push a student to reveal something he is reluctant to reveal, participate when he doesn't want to participate, or explore territory he does not want to explore. The student is his own best guide to what he is comfortable doing.

3. The teacher should never manipulate students by pretending that he is doing one thing when he is doing another. A good test is to see if an exercise can be used twice with students; if so, then they are not being tricked.

It is helpful for teachers to have had some experience in exploring their own feelings before working with students on a feeling level. There are many groups set up for this purpose, but teachers should take care in choosing one to join. Groups not affiliated with some organization should be avoided; and the personal, professional, or experiential qualifications of the leader should be carefully examined. More and more schools of education are offering courses in "group process," "sensitivity groups," "human psychology," or "affective education" in which good training can be had under careful supervision. The National Training Laboratory, an associate of the National Education Association, 1201 Sixteenth St., N.W., Washington, D.C., conducts training sessions for all levels of school personnel. In addition, there are a number of "growth centers" or informal institutes where experienced leaders conduct short-term training sessions. A list of these centers can be obtained from the Association of Humanistic Psychology, 325 Ninth Street, San Francisco, California.

NEW CONCEPTS OF HUMAN POTENTIALS:
NEW CHALLENGE FOR TEACHERS*

Arthur W. Combs

Some Humanistic Assumptions. Each of Combs' points in this article illustrates a position typical of humanistic educators; while he makes them explicit here, many of the other authors are less exact in their assumptions. Combs's five points also demonstrate other humanistic attitudes: We must consider the complex interactions of physiological, social, and psychological elements. We are just beginning to tap our vast personal and interpersonal abilities. Human relations, including intergroup relations, should be improved in order to create the conditions necessary to allow each person to develop his potentials. The way a person feels about himself and his development are important. The removal of adverse social and psychological conditions is a necessary first step to allow further growth. Finally, Combs uses "needs" in three ways that are particularly humanistic: first, as a hierarchy of human motivation, such that when one need becomes satisfied, the next becomes predominant (see Roberts's article); second, as what each person wants, as in "felt needs"; third, as those conditions necessary for full growth, or self-actualization. In this last sense it is especially humanistic to see "needs" in terms of what is necessary for complete development, not, as many other psychologies do, what is necessary only to maintain life.

We are living in a world today with new ideas about the nature of human capacity, about what is possible for human beings. These revolutionary ideas pose vast new challenges to people who work with children.

Each of us behaves in terms of his beliefs about other people. If you believe a man is honest, you will trust him; if you don't believe he is honest, you will not. And any kind of change in our beliefs about what is possible for people must have far-reaching implications for every aspect of life. It makes a lot of difference, for example, whether you believe that children are able or unable. If you believe they are able, you *let* them. But if you don't believe they are able, you don't dare let them.

We now understand that a human organism is like an engineer's bridge. When an engineer constructs a bridge he builds in a safety factor some ten or fifteen times over what the bridge will ever be expected to withstand. He overbuilds it; in the same way the human organism is also overbuilt.

*From Arthur W. Combs, "New Concepts of Human Potentials: New Challenge for Teachers," *Childhood Education* 47, no. 7 (April, 1971): 349–355, by permission of the author and the Association for Childhood Education International, 3615 Wisconsin Avenue, N.W., Washington, D.C. Copyright 1971 by the Association. Adapted by Arthur W. Combs from the keynote address he presented to the Annual Study Conference of the Association for Childhood Education International at Atlanta, Georgia, on March 30, 1970. Arthur W. Combs is Professor of Education at the University of Florida, Gainesville. He is the author, with D. Avila and W. Purkey, of *Helping Relationships: Basic Concepts for the Helping Professions* (Boston: Allyn and Bacon, 1971).

Each of us has vastly more capacity than we ever dreamed of. Most of us use only a very small portion of our possibilities.

Today we know that intelligence itself can be created. If you doubt this, let me recommend J. McVicker Hunt's book, *Intelligence and Experience*, which reviews the evidence of why we now understand this is true. We know, for example, that the longer a child has been in an institution, the lower his IQ; when you put him in a rich environment, his IQ rises. We know that when we provide opportunities for people in the ghettos their intelligence levels rise. We know that between World War I and World War II the intelligence levels of men taken into the armed forces rose significantly. How do you suppose that happened? (It certainly *didn't* happen by selective breeding, because we still pick our mates in the same old sloppy way we always did, by falling in love.) This change came about as a consequence of changes in our society and in the way we have learned to deal with human beings.

The idea that intelligence is not fixed and immutable is tremendously exciting for all of us working with young people. It means that you and I are not the victims of the child's intelligence; we are in the business of creating it! It means also that the Great Society LBJ talked about, and the rest of us hoped for, is possible. It changes our thinking in many directions. Take our conception of the gifted. If intelligence is something that can be created, the gifted child is our outstanding accomplishment, the child with whom we have been enormously successful. Our job is not to find such children and give them special nourishment, but to find out how we did it and get about the business of producing more of them as quickly as we can.

With all this change in our conception of what is possible, however, we still have children who are deeply limited, who are not achieving, who are not finding the kinds of life we know is possible. We know that a child can live in an expanded world and be unable to profit by it. Limits exist.

PHYSIOLOGICAL LIMITS

Let's take a look at some of those limits. *First*, we know that children are limited by their physiology. In order to be able to use the world, one needs a body in good condition. People in medicine today are talking not just about being sick or being well but about the concept of high-level wellness. We know what could be done for children physically, and yet we go on talking about cutting budgets for school lunches. We have starving children in our land; we have children living on Indian reservations without enough to eat. And yet the cost of one single helicopter shot down over Vietnam would feed thousands and thousands of children a free lunch every day for months and months. Not long ago I was at Cape Kennedy and as our beautiful rocket lifted off the pad the man from NASA said, "There goes 329 million dollars!" I thought of what we could do with that kind of money for education.

We have enough know-how and wealth to provide every child in this country with the ultimate in physical health. What kind of world could we produce if we provided for every child adequate care and nutrition? What kind of new generation would we have before us?

OPPORTUNITY

Second, we know that realization of human capacities is limited by lack of opportunity. The child's world is determined by the opportunities he has had and his knowledge acquired as a consequence of experience. But the experience of the child is dependent upon us. Earl Kelley once said, "Whenever we start to worry about the next generation, we need to remind ourselves they were all right when we got them." You and I provide opportunity for children. The information explosion has given us magnificent techniques for providing young people with opportunities; but still some—many—live with no opportunity in the midst of such riches. In the ghettos children are living who do not develop language because nobody is there for them to speak to. Some children are left alone all day every day in a one-room apartment while Mother and Father (if there is one) go to work. Nobody speaks to these children, and they grow up without the language development so significant and important for full intellectual growth.

At the University of Florida Ira Gordon is doing some fascinating experiments on early childhood stimulation. Beginning with babies at the age of six weeks, he shows their mothers how to provide them with opportunities for a more stimulating environment, using things found in the home. He is finding that when he provides these children with increased stimulation, even those from the most deprived kinds of home situations show increased intelligence levels.

We now know that human capacities increase with use and atrophy with disuse; that if we do not provide the opportunities for a person to utilize what he has, it dies aborning. Too many of our schools, which are supposed to provide stimulation for children, are deadly dull, monotonous and stupifying. Simply providing schools is no guarantee that children will be able to use them.

Here we are, a nation on wheels, and yet we cannot find ways to expand the world of the ghetto child. Some even fight tooth and nail to prevent the movement of children to enriching experience. The principle is clear—from the psychologist's point of view, human behavior is a function of opportunity. What kind of world could we create if we were really to provide every child with opportunities to experience the kinds of things that would make it possible for him to develop his ultimate capacities?

HUMAN NEEDS

A *third* thing psychologists know about limitations upon human beings has to do with human needs. Each of us is continuously searching for the satisfaction of his needs, which in turn provides us with drive and direction, motivations for obtaining further experience. We know that human needs exist in a hierarchy from those very basic ones like staying alive and getting enough to eat on up to those beautiful ones like love and self-fulfillment. But we also know that you can't do much with higher needs until lower ones are taken care of. You can't think much about nice ideas of democracy on an empty belly. The child who comes to school worried because Mama went to the hospital last night is in no condition to learn the principal exports of Venezuela.

We know today that human failure, maladjustment, stupidity, criminality are often consequences of deprivation. As Abe Maslow once put it, the deviant behavior of the maladjusted represents "the screams of the tortured at the crushing of their psychological bones." What a statement! Illness, physiologically, is a failure of the body to be able to satisfy its need for growth and health. In the same fashion, psychological illness is a failure of the organism to achieve its human needs for self-fulfillment.

Now, we don't say about a child when he is physically ill, "Let's give this child all the diseases we can as early as possible." We say, "Let's keep this child from getting the disease as long as we possibly can." Or, as with a vaccination or an immunization, we give him the disease in such an attentuated form that he will be successful with it and better able to deal with the real thing when it comes along.

But look what we do psychologically. Some children fail every day of their lives—are *forced* to fail, by the conditions they are placed in. We know today that illness is a lack of fulfillment physiologically or psychologically.

We have known for a long time that people behave in terms of their needs and yet we have not really implemented that fact in our dealings with youngsters. We have created schools that are largely irrelevant, out of touch with the needs of the kids. In our schools we have said, "I'm not interested in what you think about that, Jimmy; what does the book say?" Which is a way of saying to him that his needs are unimportant and without value.

Donald Snygg once described the illness of American education in these terms: "We are madly providing children with answers to problems they ain't got yet." We are often unwilling to fulfill people's needs. Instead we insist that they be right *now* what we hope to make them one day. Take for example what we do to the delinquent, who for fifteen years has been learning "Nobody likes me, nobody wants me, nobody cares about me" and who comes to the conclusion, "Well, I don't care about nobody neither!" He comes lunging into the office acting surly and ill-mannered. We say to him, "Now, look here, young man, you behave yourself! Sit up there! Be polite!" In his society being polite would ruin him.

We are asking him to be today what the school ought someday to help him become. This is like going to the doctor's and being told, "Go away and get better, and come back and I'll help you!" No wonder we have children who feel their needs are not being satisfied in schools! To drop out is intelligent in that kind of circumstance (it's ridiculous to subject yourself to conditions that have nothing to offer you).

One of the things we have been discovering in our studies of self-actualizing people who are able to be all kinds of things, who are successful and happy and satisfied, effective in the community, is that they are people who grew up with needs fulfilled. As a consequence they are better adjusted, more stable, more successful. We also know that when we help other people to fulfill their needs, they fulfill ours too. I ask again, what kind of world could we create if we were really to put our minds to the problem of helping every child fulfill his basic needs for love, affection, physiological health, opportunity?

SELF-CONCEPT

The *fourth* limitation that we know hampers people in expanding their world has to do with the self-concept, which we now recognize as perhaps the most important single factor in determining what a person is able to do under any given circumstance. People behave in terms of their self-concept. What a person believes about himself affects everything he does, even what he sees and hears—and, hence, is of tremendous significance in determining how effectively he will be able to deal with the world in which he lives.

Intelligence itself is a function of a person's self-concept. Those who have positive self-concepts because they feel good about themselves are *able* to try, to be creative, to go out into the blue and make use of their world. They have a better approach to life, are more open to their experiences and being more open are more likely to have better answers—which is what we mean by intelligence.

We know also that what a person believes about himself will determine whether he is likely to be well adjusted or badly adjusted. Well-adjusted people see themselves as liked, wanted, acceptable and able, dignified and worthy, whereas the maladjusted are those who see themselves as unwanted, unliked, unacceptable, unable and undignified. A positive view of self provides a tremendous resource for a person to be able to make the fullest possible use of his world.

But, of course, the self is something we learn. You learn who you are, what you are, from the significant others in your life—the ways people have treated you. We can ask, therefore: How can a child feel liked unless someone likes him? How can a child feel wanted unless somebody wants him? How can a child feel acceptable unless someone accepts him? And how can a child feel able unless somewhere he has some success? Thousands of people in our society are trapped, prisoners of their own perception, believing they can only do x-much. Then the rest of us see them only doing x-much, so we say "That is an x-much person"—which only proves what he already thought in the first place! Millions of people in this world are walking around with beliefs about themselves that are self-limiting, self-destructive. It is so also with children in all school subjects.

Let's take reading, for example. Most children who come to the reading clinic do not have anything wrong with their eyes. They are children who *believe* they can't read. Because they believe they can't read, they don't try; because they don't get any practice, they don't do it very well. Then, when the teacher asks them to read, they don't read very well and the teacher says, "My goodness, Jimmy, you don't read very well." And to add to that, we bring the parents in on the act by sending home a failing grade so they can tell him also.

Somehow, we have to find ways of breaking out of this vicious circle in which people are trapped, as James Agee said, "like mirrors locked face to face in an infinite corridor of despair."

A child brings his self-concept with him—he doesn't park it at the door; whatever we do affects his self-concept, even when we are teaching him mathematics, languages, or how to roller-skate. If the self-concept is as important as psychologists are telling us today, then you and I must pay attention to it. The laws of learning cannot be suspended because they are inconvenient—they go right on in spite of us. We need to ask ourselves, "What are we teaching?"

Take the child who is reading at the third-grade level in the sixth grade. Day after day, hour after hour, week after week he is condemned to one failure experience after another—because you and I cannot adjust to a third-grade reader who happens to be twelve years old.

If the self-concept is learned, then in order to help children grow effectively we've got to find ways of helping them see themselves in positive fashion. In the answers to the questions I've stated before (how can a child feel liked unless someone likes him, and how can he feel successful unless somewhere he has success), we'll discover what we need to do to help the child expand his world.

CHALLENGE AND THREAT

A *fifth* factor that influences how well a person can make use of the world in which he lives has to do with challenge and threat. I remember asking a little girl, "What did you learn today?" "Nothing," she replied, "but was my teacher mad! Wow!" She illustrated a very important psychological point, that a person being threatened can pay attention to nothing but that which threatens him. His capacity to perceive is narrowed down to the object of threat. Obviously, this condition is precisely the opposite of what we seek in expanding a child's world. We don't want him to narrow his perceptions; we want him to open them up.

When people are threatened, they are also forced to defend their existing position. The hotter the argument gets, the more a person sticks to the position he had in the first place. Again, this is directly antithetical to everything we are seeking to accomplish in helping a person use his world effectively.

What do we mean by threat? People feel challenged when confronted with a problem that interests them and with which they believe they have a chance to succeed. People feel threatened when confronted with a problem they do not feel able to handle. Whether a child feels challenged or threatened is not a question of how it looks to his teacher—it's a question of how it looks to him.

Whether a person feels challenged or threatened determines how effectively he will be able to make use of the world in which he lives. Our problem then becomes one of finding ways to challenge people without threatening them. Again I ask, what kind of world could we create if we were really to put our minds to the problem of finding ways of challenging children without threatening them?

RECAPITULATION

After all, what children make of the world is dependent on us, on you and me. Science has provided us with answers and directions. These exciting new concepts of what is possible for human beings are world-shaking. No human interaction is in vain unless we make it so. Every good experience a person is given is given him forever.

To help a deeply deprived child is like helping a child to fill up a deep pit. It takes a lot of giving and sometimes it is necessary to go on in sheer faith that eventually it will make a difference. So it is with deeply deprived people. A single thing you do on a nice Tuesday afternoon may not be enough; but neither is that good thing ever in vain, unless you make it so. Unfortunately we sometimes get into too much of a hurry.

For instance, take the "delinquent" I was talking about earlier who feels, "Nobody likes me, nobody wants me, nobody cares about me; well, I don't care about nobody neither." A well-meaning teacher comes along and says, "Eddie, I like you," and Eddie swears at her. Why? Because all his life all his experiences have taught him that he can't trust people who talk like that. He thinks, "Either she's lying and in that case she deserves to get punished, or she is making fun of me, and in that case she deserves it all the more." So he swears at the teacher and she clouts him across the mouth—which, of course, just proves what he thought in the first place: she didn't mean it either!

Somehow we have to recognize that every good experience is given forever—but somebody has to start. We talk much about rejected children at home; there are also rejected children at school. And teachers who say, "What can I do with a child from a home like that?"

In my own clinical experience I have seen children change their homes because of their experience in school. Let me give you an illustration. Eddie Smith is unhappy, bugging his mother, driving her nuts. He comes to school, where he has a teacher who makes him feel just a little bit better. As a result, when Eddie goes home he doesn't bug Mama quite so much. In turn Mama, because she finds Eddie is a little bit better that day, doesn't take it out on Papa when he comes home. Papa finds that

Mama is a little bit nicer tonight than she has been lately, so when he sits down to read the paper and his daughter wants to climb onto his lap, instead of pushing her away he says, "OK, honey, come on." She climbs up in his lap and has a good experience too. Because she feels better about her daddy, she doesn't tease Eddie so much (he was our problem in the first place!). I have seen it happen.

Many teachers believe that what they do is unimportant. This is never so! It is never unimportant because you cannot "unexperience" a good experience. Even a holding operation can be a positive thing. When everything in a child's life is pushing him downhill and all you do is keep him as bad as he is, that's progress. Fritz Redl, talking about juvenile delinquents, once put it very nicely when he said, "There's not much difference between a good child and a naughty child, but there is a world of difference between a naughty child and a real tough delinquent." And then he said, "Gee, if we could just keep them naughty!" I find that very reassuring.

With our new understanding of human potential, we now understand that stupidity and maladjustment are not "the will of God" but the *lack* of will of man. A theological concept holds that a man has not sinned if he doesn't know any better. In previous times our production of stupid and depraved people was excusable because we didn't know. That excuse no longer exists! We now know that constant deprivation leads to depravity, while *being given* leads to growth. In the light of that knowledge, we live in grievous sin if we do not act upon it. If we do not help the next generation to expand its world, we have failed everyone—the child, the parents, our institutions, the nation itself. It is in our own best interest to help expand the world of children. But, even if we do not act upon our new understandings for such selfish reasons, we ought to do it anyhow—just because we love them.

SOME EDUCATIONAL IMPLICATIONS OF THE HUMANISTIC PSYCHOLOGIES[1]*

Abraham H. Maslow

New Ideas And A New View of Man For A New Education. Maslow probably invented and developed more ideas in humanistic psychology than any other psychologist. In this section his hierarchy of needs is the basis for "Developing Thoughts on Developmental Psychology." Strzepeck's article looks for "self-actualization" and "peak experiences" in fiction. Most of the articles concern themselves with human emotions, and the blending of emotion and cognition is a recurrent theme in humanistic education. More than these, Maslow points toward the goal of learning to be a fully-functioning person as a rediscovered goal of education; these open a whole new realm of educational goals and methods. In this article he draws together many of his own and others' thoughts on humanistic educational psychology.

The upshot of the past decade or two of turmoil and change within the field of psychology can be viewed as a local manifestation of a great change taking place in all fields of knowledge. We are witnessing a great revolution in thought, in the Zeitgeist itself: the creation of a new image of man and society and of religion and science (1, 16). It is the kind of change that happens, as Whitehead said, once or twice in a century. This is not an *improvement* of something; it is a real change in direction altogether. It is as if we had been going north and are now going south instead.

Recent developments in psychological theory and research are closely related to the changes in the new image of man which lie at the center of the larger revolution. There are, to oversimplify the situation, two comprehensive theories of human nature which dominate psychology today. The first is the behavioristic, associationistic, experimental, mechanomorphic psychology; the psychology which can be called "classical" because it is in a direct line with the classical conception of science which comes out of astronomy, mechanics, physics, chemistry, and geology; the psychology which can be called "academic" because it has tended to emanate from and flourish in the undergraduate and graduate departments of psychology in our universities. Since its first detailed and testable formulation by Watson (24), Hull (5), and Skinner (21), "classical," "academic" psycholo-

From Abraham H. Maslow, "Some Educational Implications of Humanistic Psychologies," *Harvard Educational Review* 38, no. 4 (Fall, 1968): 685–696, by permission of Bertha G. Maslow. Based on a talk given to Superintendents of member schools in the New England School Development Council, July 12, 1967. Abraham Maslow's posthumous work *Dominance, Self-Esteem, Self-Actualization: Germinal Papers of A. H. Maslow* is edited by Richard Lowry (Monterey, Cla.: Brooks/Cole Publishing Co., 1973). Forthcoming is another posthumous work *The Journals of A. H. Maslow, 1958–1970* (Monterey, Cal.: Brooks/Cole Publishing Co., 1974).

gical theory has been widely applied beyond its original limited focus in such diverse areas as acquisition of motor skills, behavior disorders and therapy, and social psychology. It has answers of a kind to any questions that you may have about human nature. In that sense, it is a philosophy, a philosophy of psychology.

The second philosophy of psychology, the one which dominates the whole field of clinical psychology and social work, emerged essentially from the work of Freud and his disciples and antagonists. In light of its emphasis upon the interplay between unconscious emotional forces and the conscious organization of behavior, I refer to this school of thought as a "psychodynamic" or "depth" psychology. It, too, tries to be a comprehensive philosophy of man. It has generated a theory of art, of religion, of society, of education, of almost every major human endeavor.

What is developing today is a third, more inclusive, image of man, which is now already in the process of generating great changes in all intellectual fields and in all social and human institutions (2, 6, 8, 20, 25). Let me try to summarize this development very briefly and succinctly because I want to turn as soon as I can to its meaning for learning and education.

"Third Force" psychology, as some are calling it, is in large part a reaction to the gross inadequacies of behavioristic and Freudian psychologies in their treatment of the higher nature of man. Classical academic psychology has no systematic place for higher-order elements of the personality such as altruism and dignity, or the search for truth and beauty. You simply do not ask questions about ultimate human values if you are working in an animal lab.

Of course, it is true that Freudian psychology has confronted these problems of the higher nature of man. But until very recently these have been handled by being very cynical about them, that is to say, by analyzing them away in a pessimistic, reductive manner. Generosity is interpreted as a reaction formation against a stinginess, which is deep down and unconscious, and therefore somehow more real. Kindliness tends to be seen as a defense mechanism against violence, rage, and the tendency to murder. It is as if we cannot take at face value any of the decencies that we value in ourselves, certainly what I value in myself, what I try to be. It is perfectly true that we do have anger and hate, and yet there are other impulses that we are beginning to learn about which might be called the higher needs of man: "needs" for the intrinsic and ultimate values of goodness and truth and beauty and perfection and justice and order. They are there, they exist, and any attempt to explain them *away* seems to me to be very foolish. I once searched through the Freudian literature on the feeling of love, of wanting love, but especially of giving love. Freud has been called the philosopher of love, yet the Freudian literature contains nothing but the pathology of love, and also a kind of derogatory explaining-away of the finding that people do love each other, as if it could be only an illusion. Something similar is true of mystical or oceanic experiences: Freud analyzes them *away*.

This belief in the reality of higher human needs, motives and capacities, that is, the belief that human nature has been sold short by the dominant psychological theories, is the primary force binding together a dozen or so "splinter groups" into the comprehensive Third Force psychology.[2] All of these groups reject entirely the whole conception of science as being value-free. Sometimes they do this consciously and explicitly, sometimes by implication only. This is a real revolution because traditionally science has been defined in terms of objectivity, detachment, and procedures which never tell you how to find human ends. The discovery of ends and values are turned over to non-scientific, non-empirical sources. The Third Force psychology totally rejects this view of science as merely instrumental and unable to help mankind to discover its ultimate ends and values (11, 18).

Among the many educational consequences generated by this philosophy, to come closer to our topic now, is a different conception of the self. This is a very complex conception, difficult to describe briefly, because it talks for the first time in centuries of an *essence*, of an *intrinsic* nature, of specieshood, of a kind of animal nature (9, 14). This is in sharp contrast with the European existentialists, most especially with Sartre, for whom man is *entirely* his own project, *entirely* and merely a product of his own arbitrary, unaided will. For Sartre and all those whom he has influenced, one's self becomes an arbitrary choice, a willing by fiat to be something or do something without any guidelines about which is better, which is worse, what's good and what's bad. In essentially denying the existence of biology, Sartre has given up altogether any absolute or at least any species-wide conception of values. This comes very close to making a life-philosophy of the obsessive-compulsive neurosis in which one finds what I have called "experiential emptiness," the absence of impulse-voices from within (12, 14).

The American humanistic psychologists and existential psychiatrists are mostly closer to the psychodynamicists than they are to Sartre. Their clinical experiences have led them to conceive of the human being as having an essence, a biological nature, membership in a species. It is very easy to interpret the "uncovering" therapies as helping the person to *discover* his "identity," his "real self," in a word, his own subjective biology, which he can *then* proceed to actualize, to "make himself," to "choose." The Freudian conception of instincts has been generally discarded by the humanistic psychologists in favor of the conception of "basic needs," or in some cases, in favor of the conception of a single overarching need for actualization or growth (19). In any case, it is implied, if not made explicit, by most of these writers that the organism, in the strictest sense, has *needs* which must be gratified in order to become fully human, to grow well, and to avoid sicknesses (9, 14). This doctrine of a "real self" to be uncovered and actualized is also a total rejection of the *tabula rasa* notions of the behaviorists and associationists who often talk as if *anything* can be learned, *anything* can be taught, as if the human being is a sort of passive clay to be shaped, controlled, reinforced, modified in any way that somebody arbitrarily decides.

We speak then of a self, a kind of intrinsic nature which is very subtle, which is not necessarily conscious, which has to be sought for, and which has to be uncovered and then built upon, actualized, taught, educated (13). The notion is that something is there but it's hidden, swamped, distorted, twisted, overlayed. The job of the psychotherapist (or the teacher) is to help a person find out what's already in him rather than to reinforce him or shape or teach him into a prearranged form, which someone else has decided upon in advance, *a priori*.

Let me explore what I call "introspective biology" and its relation to new ideas for education. If we accept the notion of the human essence or the core-self, i.e., the constitutional, temperamental, biological, chemical, endocrinological, given raw material, if we do accept the fact that babies come into the world very different from each other (anyone of you who has more than one child knows that), then the job of any helper, and furthermore the first job of each of us for ourselves, is to uncover and discover what we ourselves are. A good example for pedagogical purposes is our maleness and femaleness, which is the most obvious biological, constitutional given, and one which involves all the problems of conflicts, of self-discovery, and of actualization. Practically every youngster, not to mention a good proportion of the older population also, is mixed up about what it means to be a female and what it means to be a male. A lot of time has to be spent on the questions: How do I get to be a good female, or how do I get to be a good male? This involves self-discovery, self-acceptance, and self-making; discoveries about both one's commonness and one's uniqueness, rather than a Sartre-type decision on whether to be a male or a female.

One constitutional difference that I have discovered is that there are differences in triggers to peak-experiences between the sexes. The mystical and peak-experiences, the ultimate, esthetic, poetic experiences of the male, can come from a football game, for example. One subject reported that once when he broke free of the line and got into the open and then ran—that this was a true moment of ecstasy. But Dr. Deborah Tanzer has found women who use the same kinds of words, the same kind of poetry, to describe their feelings during natural childbirth. Under the right circumstances these women have ecstasies which sound just the same as the St. Theresa or Meister Eckhardt kind of ecstasy. I call them peak-experiences to secularize them and to naturalize them, to make them more empirical and researchable.

Individual constitutional differences, then, are an important variable. It continually impresses me that the same peak-experiences come from different kinds of activities for different kinds of people.[3] Mothers will report peak-experiences not only from natural childbirth but also from putting the baby to the breast. (Of course this doesn't happen all the time. These peak-experiences are rare rather than common.) But I've never heard of any man getting a peak-experience from putting his baby to *his* breast. It just doesn't happen. He wasn't constructed right for this purpose. We are confronting the fact that people are biologically different, but have species-wide emotional experiences. Thus I think we should examine individual differences in all of our given biochemical, endocrine, neurological, anatomical systems to see to just what extent they carry along with them psychological and spiritual differences and to what extent there remains a common substratum (14).

The trouble is that the human species is the only species which finds it hard to be a species. For a cat there seems to be no problem about being a cat. It's easy; cats seem to have no complexes or ambivalences or conflicts, and show no signs of yearning to be dogs instead. Their instincts are very clear. But we have no such unequivocal animal instincts. Our biological essence, our instinct-remnants, are weak and subtle, and they are hard to get at. Learnings of the extrinsic sort *are more powerful than our deepest impulses*. These deepest impulses in the human species, at the points where the instincts have been lost almost entirely, where they are extremely weak, extremely subtle and delicate, where you have to dig to find them, *this* is where I speak of introspective biology, of biological phenomenology, implying that one of the necessary methods in the search for identity, the search for self, the search for spontaneity and for naturalness is a matter of closing your eyes, cutting down the noise, turning off the thoughts, putting away all busyness, just relaxing in a kind of Taoistic and receptive fashion (in much the same way that you do on the psychoanalyst's couch). The technique here is to just wait to see what happens, what comes to mind. This is what Freud called free association, free-floating attention rather than task-orientation, and if you are successful in this effort and learn how to do it, you can forget about the outside world and its noises and begin to hear these small, delicate impulse-voices from within, the hints from your animal nature, not only from your common species-nature, but also from your own uniqueness.

There's a very interesting paradox here, however. On the one hand I've talked about uncovering or discovering your idiosyncrasy, the way in which you are different from everybody else in the whole world. Then on the other hand I've spoken about discovering your specieshood, your humanness. As Carl Rogers has phrased it: "How does it happen that the deeper we go into ourselves as particular and unique, seeking for our own individual identity, the more we find the whole human species?" Doesn't that remind you of Ralph Waldo Emerson and the New England Transcendentalists? Discovering your specieshood, at a deep enough level, merges with discovering your selfhood (13, 14). Becoming (learning how to be) fully human means *both* enterprises carried on simultaneously. You are learning (subjectively experiencing) what you peculiarly are, how you are you, what your potentialities are, what your style is, what your pace is, what your tastes are, what your values are, what direction your body is going, where your personal biology is taking you, i.e., how you are *different* from others. And at the same time it means learning what it means to be a human animal like other human animals, i.e., how you are *similar* to others.

It is such considerations as these that convince me that we are now being confronted with a choice between two extremely different, almost mutually exclusive conceptions of learning. What we have in practically all the elementary and advanced textbooks of psychology, and in most of the brands of "learning theory" which all graduate students are required to learn, is what I want to call for the sake of contrast and confrontation, *extrinsic learning*, i.e., learning of the outside, learning of the impersonal, of arbitrary associations, of arbitrary conditioning, that is, of arbitrary (or at best, culturally-determined) meanings and responses. In this kind of learning, most often it is not the person himself who decides, but rather a teacher or an experimenter who says, "I will use a buzzer," "I will use a bell," "I will use a red light," and most important, "I will reinforce this but not that." In this sense the learning is extrinsic to the learner, extrinsic to the personality, and is extrinsic also in the sense of *collecting* associations, conditionings, habits, or modes of action. It is as if these were *possessions* which the learner accumulates in the same way that he accumulates keys or coins and puts them in his pocket. They have little or nothing to do with the actualization or growth of the peculiar, idiosyncratic kind of person he is.

I believe this is the model of education which we all have tucked away in the back of our heads and which we don't often make explicit. In this model the teacher is the active one who teaches a passive person who gets shaped and taught and who is *given* something which he then accumulates and which he may then lose or retain, depending upon the efficiency of the initial indoctrination process, and of his own accumulation-of-fact process. I would maintain that a good 90 percent of "learning theory" deals with learnings that have nothing to do with the intrinsic self that I've been talking about, nothing to do with its specieshood and biological idiosyncracy. This kind of learning too easily reflects the goals of the teacher and ignores the values and ends of the learner himself (22). It is also fair, therefore, to call such learning amoral.

Now I'd like to contrast this with another kind of learning, which is actually going on, but is usually unconscious and unfortunately happens more outside the classroom than inside. It often comes in the great personal learning experiences of our lives.

For instance, if I were to list the most important learning experiences in my life, there come to mind getting married, discovering my life work, having children, getting psychoanalyzed, the death of my best friend, confronting death myself, and the like. I think I would say that these were more important learning experiences for me than my Ph.D. or any 15 or 150 credits or courses that I've ever had. I certainly learned more about *myself* from such experiences. I learned, if I may put it so, to throw aside many of my "learnings," that is, to push aside the habits and traditions and reinforced associations which had been imposed upon me. Sometimes this was at a very trivial, and yet meaningful, level. I particularly remember when I learned that I really hated lettuce. My father was a "nature boy," and I had lettuce two meals a day for the whole of my early life. But one day in analysis after I had learned that I carried my father inside me, it dawned on me that it was my father, through *my* larynx, who was ordering salad with every meal. I can remember sitting there, realizing that *I* hated lettuce and then saying, "My God, take the damn stuff away!" I was emancipated, becoming in this small way me, rather than my father. I didn't eat any more lettuce for months, until it finally settled back to what my body calls for. I have lettuce two or three times each week, which I now enjoy. But *not* twice a day.

Now observe, this experience which I mentioned occurred just once and I could give many other similar examples. It seems to me that we must call into question the generality of repetition, of learning by drilling (4). The experiences in which we uncover our intrinsic selves are apt to be unique moments, not slow accumulations of reinforced bits. (How do you repeat the death of your father?) These are the experiences in which we discover identity (16). These are the experiences in which we learn who we are, what we love, what we hate, what we value, and what we are committed to, what makes us feel anxious, what makes us feel depressed, what makes us feel happy, what makes us feel great joy.

It must be obvious by now that you can generate consequences of this second picture of learning by the hundred. (And again I would stress that these hypotheses can be stated in testable, disconfirmable, confirmable form.) One such implication of the point of view is a change in the whole picture of the teacher. If you are willing to accept this conception of two kinds of learning, with the learning-to-be-a-person being more central and more basic than the impersonal learning of skills or the acquisition of habits; and if you are willing to concede that even the most extrinsic learnings are far more useful, and far more effective if based upon a sound identity, that is, if done by a person who knows what he wants, knows what he is, and where he's going and what his ends are; then you *must* have a different picture of the good teacher and of his functions.

In the first place, unlike the current model of teacher as lecturer, conditioner, reinforcer, and boss, the Taoist helper or teacher is receptive rather than intrusive. I was told once that in the world of boxers, a youngster who feels himself to be good and who wants to be a boxer will go to a gym, look up one of the managers and say, "I'd like to be a pro, and I'd like to be in your stable. I'd like you to manage me." In this world, what is then done characteristically is to try him out. The good manager will select one of his professionals and say, "Take him on in the ring. Stretch him. Strain him. Let's see what he can do. Just let him show his very best. Draw him out." If it turns out that the boxer has promise, if he's a "natural," then what the good manager does is to take that boy and train him to be, if this is Joe Dokes, a *better Joe Dokes*. That is, he takes his style as given and builds upon that. He does not start all over again, and say, "Forget all you've learned, and do it this new way," which is like saying, "Forget what kind of body you have," or "Forget what you are good for." He takes him and builds upon his *own* talents and builds him up into the very best Joe Dokes-type boxer that he possibly can.

It is my strong impression that this is the way in which much of the world of education could function. If we want to be helpers, counselors, teachers, guiders, or psychotherapists, what we must do is to accept the person and help him learn what kind of person he is already. What is his style, what are his aptitudes, what is he good for, not good for, what can we build upon, what are his good raw materials, his good potentialities? We would be non-threatening and would supply an atmosphere of acceptance of the child's nature which reduces fear, anxiety and defense to the minimum possible. Above all, we would care for the child, that is enjoy him and his growth and self-actualization (17). So far this sounds much like the Rogerian therapist, his "unconditional positive regard," his congruence, his openness and his caring. And indeed there is evidence by now that this "brings the child out," permits him to express and to act, to experiment, and even to make mistakes; to let himself be seen. Suitable feedback at this point, as in T-groups or basic encounter groups, or non-directive counseling, then helps the child to discover what and who he is.

In closing, I would like to discuss briefly the role that peak-experiences can play in the education of the child. We have no systematic data on peak-experiences in children but we certainly have enough anecdotes and introspections and memories to be quite confident that young children have them, perhaps more frequently than adults do. However, they seem at least in the beginning to come more from sensory experiences, color, rhythm, or sounds, and perhaps are better characterized by the words wonder, awe, fascination, absorption, and the like.

In any case, I have discussed the role of these experiences in education in (15), and would refer the reader to that paper for more detail. Using peak-experiences or fascination or wonder experiences as an intrinsic reward or goal at *many* points in education is a very real possibility, and is congruent with the whole philosophy of the humanistic educator. At the very least, this new knowledge can help wean teachers away from their frequent uneasiness with and even disapproval and persecution of these experiences. If they learn to value them as great moments in the learning process, moments in which both cognitive and personal growth take place simultaneously, then this valuing can be transmitted to the child. He in turn is then taught to value rather than to suppress his greatest moments of illumination, moments which can validate and make worthwhile the more usual trudging and slogging and "working through" of education.

There is a very useful parallel here with the newer humanistic paradigm for science (11, 18) in which the more everyday cautious and patient work of checking, validating and replicating is seen, not as *all* there is to science but rather as follow-up work, *subsequent* to the great intuitions, intimations, and illuminations of the creative and daring, innovative, break-through scientist. Caution is then seen to *follow* upon boldness and proving comes *after* intuition. The creative scientist then looks more like a gambler than a banker, one who is willing to work hard for seven years because of a dazzling hunch, one who feels certain in the *absence* of evidence, *before* the evidence, and only *then* proceeds to the hard work of proving or disproving his precious revelation. First comes the emotion, the fascination, the falling in love with a possibility, and *then* comes the hard work, the chores, the stubborn persistence in the face of disappoint-ment and failure.

As a supplement to this conception in which a noetic illumination plays such an important role, we can add the harsh patience of the psychothera-pist who has learned from many bitter disappointments that the break-through insight doesn't do the therapeutic job all by itself, as Freud originally thought. It needs consolidation, repetition, rediscovery, applica-tion to one situation after another. It needs patience, time and hard work—what the psychoanalysts call "working through." Not only for science but also for psychotherapy may we say that the process *begins* with an emotional-cognitive flash but *does not end there!* It is this model of science and therapy that I believe we may now fairly consider for the process of education, if not as an exclusive model, at least as an additional one.

We must learn to treasure the "jags" of the child in school, his fascination, absorptions, his persistent wide-eyed wonderings, his Dionysian enthusiasms. At the very least, we can value his more diluted raptures, his "interests" and hobbies, etc. They can lead to much. Especially can they lead to hard work, persistent, absorbed, fruitful, educative.

And conversely I think it is possible to think of the peak-experience, the experience of awe, mystery, wonder, or of perfect completion, as the goal and reward of learning as well, its end as well as its beginning (7). If this is true for the *great* historians, mathematicians, scientists, musicians, philosophers and all the rest, why should we not try to maximize these studies as sources of peak-experiences for the child as well?

I must say that whatever little knowledge and experience I have to support these suggestions comes from intelligent and creative children rather than from retarded or underprivileged or sick ones. However, I must also say that my experience with such unpromising adults in Synanon, in T-groups (23), in Theory Y industry (10), in Esalen-type educative centers (3), in Grof-type work with psychedelic chemicals, not to mention Laing-type work with psychotics and other such experiences, has taught me never to write *anybody* off in advance.

NOTES

[1] I would like to acknowledge the assistance of David Napior, Barbara Powell, and Gail Zivin of the *Harvard Educational Review* in preparing this article.

[2] See (16), Appendix, for list.

[3] For some ways in which educators can use peak-experiences, see (15).

REFERENCES

1. Braden, W. *The private sea: LSD and the search for God.* Chicago: Quadrangle, 1967.

2. Bugental, J. (ed.) *Challenges of humanistic psychology.* New York: McGraw-Hill, 1967.

3. Esalen Institute. *Residential program brochure.* Big Sur, California, 1966 and subsequent years.

4. Holt, J. *How children fail.* New York: Pitman, 1964.

5. Hull, C. L. *Principles of behavior.* New York: Appleton Century-Crofts, 1943.

6. *Journal of Humanistic Psychology.* (Periodical.) American Association of Humanistic Psychology, Palo Alto, California.

7. Leonard, G. *Education and ecstasy.* New York: Delacorte Press, 1968.

8. *Manas.* (Periodical.) Cunningham Press, South Pasadena, California.

9. Maslow, A. Criteria for judging needs to be instinctoid. In M. J. Jones (ed.), *Human motivation: A symposium.* Lincoln, Neb.: University of Nebraska Press, 1965.

10. Maslow, A. *Eupsychian management: A journal.* New York: Irwin-Dorsey, 1965.

11. Maslow, A. *The psychology of science: A reconaissance.* New York: Harper and Row, 1966.

12. Maslow, A. Neurosis as a failure of personal growth. *Humanitas,* III (1967), 153–169.

13. Maslow, A. Self-actualization and beyond. In J. Bugental (ed.), *Challenges of humanistic psychology.* New York: McGraw-Hill, 1967.

14. Maslow, A. A theory of metamotivation: The biological rooting of the value-life. *Journal of Humanistic Psychology,* I (1967), 93–127.

15. Maslow, A. Music education and peak-experiences. *Music Educators Journal,* LIV (1968), 72–75, 163–171.

16. Maslow, A. *Toward a psychology of being.* (Revised edition) Princeton, N.J.: D. Van Nostrand, 1968.

17. Moustakas, C. *The authentic teacher.* Cambridge, Mass.: Howard A. Doyle Publishing Co., 1966.

18. Polanyi, M. *Personal knowledge.* Chicago: University of Chicago Press, 1958.

19. Rogers, C. *On becoming a person.* Boston: Houghton Mifflin, 1961.

20. Severin, F. (ed.) *Humanistic viewpoints in psychology.* New York: McGraw-Hill, 1965.

21. Skinner, B. F. *Science and human behavior.* New York: Macmillan, 1938.

22. Skinner, B. F. *Walden two.* New York: Macmillan, 1948.

23. Sohl, J. *The lemon eaters.* New York: Simon and Schuster, 1967.

24. Watson, J. B. *Behaviorism.* New York: Norton, 1924 (rev. ed., 1930). Also *Psychology from the standpoint of a behaviorist.* Philadelphia: Lippincott, 1924.

25. Wilson, C. *Introduction to the new existentialism.* Boston: Houghton Mifflin, 1967.

EDUCATION ON THE NONVERBAL LEVEL *

Aldous Huxley

Multiple Education for Multiple Man. We are animals and thinkers, says Huxley, but much more than only these, and it is up to us to build an education for these other abilities. Huxley's emphasis is on many of the human potentials we neglect, many of them blending into the transpersonal realm. He tells us to include more human potentials in our view of man and to enlarge our view of education too. Curriculum makers at many educational levels will find the sources he cites valuable guides to broadening the curriculum to include the education of more ways to be human; teachers will find innovative techniques to be adapted to their students and to their subjects; and educational researchers will find a rich store of mind-opening ideas for further investigation.

Early in the mid-Victorian period the Reverend Thomas Binney, a Congregationalist divine, published a book with the alluring title, *Is It Possible to Make the Best of Both Worlds?* His conclusion was that perhaps it might be possible. In spite of its unorthodox message, or perhaps because of it, the book was a best seller, which only showed, said the more evangelical of Mr. Binney's Nonconformist colleagues and Anglican opponents, how inexpressibly wicked Victorian England really was.

What Mr. Binney's critics had done (and their mistake is repeated by all those who use the old phrase disapprovingly) was to equate "making the best of both worlds" with "serving two masters." It is most certainly difficult, perhaps quite impossible, to serve Mammon and God simultaneously—to pursue the most sordid interests while aspiring to realize the highest ideals. This is obvious. Only a little less obvious, however, is the fact that it is very hard, perhaps quite impossible, to serve God while failing to make the best of both worlds—of *all* the worlds of which, as human beings, we are the inhabitants.

Man is a multiple amphibian and exists at one and the same time in a number of universes, dissimilar to the point, very nearly, of complete incompatibility. He is at once an animal and a rational intellect; a product of evolution closely related to the apes and a spirit capable of self-transcendence; a sentient being in contact with the brute data of his own nervous system and the physical environment and at the same time the creator of a homemade universe of words and other symbols, in which he lives and moves and has anything from 30 to 80 percent of his being.

*From Aldous Huxley, "Education on the Nonverbal Level," *Science and Technology in Contemporary Society, Daedalus* 91, no. 2 (Spring, 1962): 279–293, by permission of Laura Huxley and *Daedalus,* Journal of the American Academy of Arts and Sciences, Boston, Massachusetts. *This Timeless Moment—A Personal View of Aldous Huxley,* by Laura Huxley, will be published by Farrar and Straus.

He is a self-conscious and self-centered ego who is also a member of a moderately gregarious species, an individual compelled by the population explosion to live at ever closer quarters, and in ever tighter organizations, with millions of other egos as self-centered and as poorly socialized as himself. Neurologically, he is a lately evolved Jekyll-cortex associated with an immensely ancient brain-stem-Hyde. Physiologically, he is a creature whose endocrine system is perfectly adapted to the conditions prevailing in the lower Paleolithic, but living in a metropolis and spending eight hours a day sitting at a desk in an air-conditioned office. Psychologically, he is a highly educated product of twentieth-century civilization, chained, in a state of uneasy and hostile symbiosis, to a disturbingly dynamic unconscious, a wild phantasy and an unpredictable id—and yet capable of falling in love, writing string quartets, and having mystical experiences.

Living amphibiously in all these incommensurable worlds at once, human beings (it is hardly surprising) find themselves painfully confused, uncertain where they stand or who they really are. To provide themselves with a recognizable identity, a niche in the scheme of things that they can call "home," they will give assent to the unlikeliest dogmas, conform to the most absurd and even harmful rules of thought, feeling, and conduct, put on the most extravagant fancy dress and identify themselves with masks that bear almost no resemblance to the faces they cover. "Bovarism" (as Jules de Gaultier calls it) is the urge to pretend that one is something that in fact one is not. It is an urge that manifests itself, sometimes weakly, sometimes with overpowering strength, in all human beings, and one of the conditions of its manifestation is precisely our uncertainty about where we stand or who we are. To explore our multiple amphibiousness with a view to doing something constructive about it is a most laborious process. Our minds are congenitally lazy, and the original sin of the intellect is oversimplification. Dogmatism and bovaristic identification with a stereotype are closely related manifestations of the same kind of intellectual delinquency. "Know thyself." From time immemorial this has been the advice of all the seers and philosophers. The self that they urge us to know is not, of course, the stylized persona with which, bovaristically, we try to become identified; it is the multiple amphibian, the inhabitant of all those incompatible worlds that we must somehow learn to make the best of.

A good education may be defined as one which helps the boys and girls subjected to it to make the best of all the worlds in which, as human beings, they are compelled, willy-nilly, to live. An education that prepares them to make the best of only one of their worlds, or of only a few of them, is inadequate. This is a point on which, in principle, all educators have always agreed. *Mens sana in corpore sano* is an ancient educational ideal and a very good one. Unfortunately, good ideals are never enough. Unless they are accompanied by full instructions regarding the methods by which they may be realized, they are almost useless. Hell is paved with good intentions, and whole periods of history have been made hideous or grotesque by enthusiastic idealists who failed to elaborate the means whereby their lofty aspirations might be effectively, and above all harmlessly, implemented.

Just how good is modern education? How successful is it in helping young people to make the best of all the worlds which, as multiple amphibians, they have to live in? In a center of advanced scientific and technical study this question gets asked inevitably in terms of what may be called the paradox of specialization. In science and technology specialization is unavoidable and indeed absolutely necessary. But training for this unavoidable and necessary specialization does nothing to help young amphibians to make the best of their many worlds. Indeed, it pretty obviously prevents them from doing anything of the kind. What then is to be done? At the Massachusetts Institute of Technology and in other schools where similar problems have arisen, the answer to this question has found expression in a renewed interest in the humanities. Excessive scientific specialization is tempered by courses in philosophy, history, literature, and social studies. All this is excellent so far as it goes. But does it go far enough? Do courses in the humanities provide a sufficient antidote for excessive scientific and technical specialization? Do they, in the terminology we have been using, help young multiple amphibians to make the best of a substantially greater number of their worlds?

Science is the reduction of the bewildering diversity of unique events to manageable uniformity within one of a number of symbol systems, and technology is the art of using these symbol systems so as to control and organize unique events. Scientific observation is always a viewing of things through the refracting medium of a symbol system, and technological praxis is always the handling of things in ways that some symbol system has dictated. Education in science and technology is essentially education on the symbolic level.

Turning to the humanities, what do we find? Courses in philosophy, literature, history, and social studies are exclusively verbal. Observation of and experimentation with nonverbal events have no place in these fields. Training in the sciences is largely on the symbolic level; training in the liberal arts is wholly and all the time on that level. When courses in the humanities are used as the only antidote to too much science and technology, excessive specialization in one kind of symbolic education is being tempered by excessive specialization in another kind of symbolic education. The young amphibians are taught to make the best, not of all their worlds, but only of two varieties of the same world—the world of symbols. But this world of symbols is only one of the worlds in which human beings do their living and their learning. They also inhabit the nonsymbolic world of unconceptualized or only slightly conceptualized experience. However effective it may be on the conceptual level, an education that fails to help young amphibians to make the best of the inner and outer universes on the hither side of symbols is an inadequate education. And however much we may delight in Homer or Gibbon, however illuminating in their different ways Pareto and William Law, Hui-neng and Bertrand Russell may strike us as being, the fact remains that the reading of their works will not be of much help to us in our efforts to make the best of our worlds of unconceptualized, nonverbal experience.

And here, before I embark on a discussion of these nonverbal worlds, let me add parenthetically that even on the verbal level, where they are most at home, educators have done a good deal less than they might reasonably have been expected to do in explaining to young people the nature, the limitations, the huge potentialities for evil as well as for good, of that greatest of all human inventions, language. Children should be taught that words are indispensable but also can be fatal—the only be-getters of all civilization, all science, all consistency of high purpose, all angelic goodness, and the only begetters at the same time of all supersti-tion, all collective madness and stupidity, all worse-than-bestial diabolism, all the dismal historical succession of crimes in the name of God, King, Nation, Party, Dogma. Never before, thanks to the techniques of mass communication, have so many listeners been so completely at the mercy of so few speakers. Never have misused words—those hideously efficient tools of all the tyrants, war-mongers, persecutors, and heresy-hunters—been so widely and so disastrously influential as they are today. Generals, clergymen, advertisers, and the rulers of totalitarian states—all have good reasons for disliking the idea of universal education in the rational use of language. To the military, clerical, propagandist, and authoritarian mind such training seems (and rightly seems) profoundly subversive. To those who think that liberty is a good thing, and who hope that it may some day become possible for more people to realize more of their desirable potentialities in a society fit for free, fully human individuals to live in, a thorough education in the nature of language, in its uses and abuses, seems indispensable. Whether in fact the mounting pressures of overpopulation and overorganization in a world still enthusiastically dedicated to national-istic idolatry will permit this kind of subversive linguistic education to be adopted by even the more democratic nations remains to be seen.

And now, after this brief digression, let us return to our main theme, the education of multiple amphibians on levels other than the verbal and the symbolic. "Make the body capable of doing many things," wrote Spinoza. "This will help you to perfect the mind and come to the intellectual love of God." Substitute "Psychophysical organism" for "body," and you have here the summary of a program for universal education on the nonsymbolic level, supplemented by a statement of the reasons why such an education is desirable and indeed, if the child is to grow into a fully-human being, absolutely necessary. The detailed curricu-lum for an education in what may be called the nonverbal humanities has still to be worked out. All I can do at this time is to drop a few fragmentary hints.

Two points, to begin with, must be emphatically stressed. First, educa-tion in the nonverbal humanities is not just a matter of gymnastics and football, of lessons in singing and folk dancing. All these, of course, are good, but by themselves not good enough. Such traditional methods of training young people in nonverbal skills need to be supplemented, if they are to yield their best results, by other kinds of training, beginning with a thorough training in elementary awareness. And the second point to be remembered is that education in the nonverbal humanities is a process that should be started in the kindergarten and continued through all the years of school and college—and thereafter, as self-education, throughout the rest of life.

At the end of a delightful anthology entitled *Zen Flesh, Zen Bones*, its editor, Mr. Paul Reps, has printed an English version of an ancient Tantrik text in which Shiva, in response to Parvati's questions about the nature of enlightened consciousness, gives a list of 112 exercises in the art of being aware of inner and outer reality on its nonsymbolic levels. *Gnosce Teipsum*. But how? From the vast majority of our pastors and masters no answer is forthcoming. Here, for a blessed change, is a philosophical treatise that speaks of means as well as of ends, of concrete experience as well as of high abstractions. The intelligent and systematic practice of any half-dozen of these 112 exercises will take one further towards the realization of the ancient ideal of self-knowledge than all the roaring or pathetic eloquence of generations of philosophers, theologians, and moralists. (Let me add, in passing, that whereas Western philosophy tends to be concerned with the manipulation of abstract symbols for the benefit of the speculative and moralizing intellect, oriental philosophy is almost always essentially operational. "Perform such and such psychophysical operations," the exponents of this philosophy say, "and you will probably find yourself in a state of mind which, like all those who have achieved it in the past, you will regard as self-evidently and supremely valuable. In the context of this state of mind, speculation about man and the universe leads us, as it led earlier thinkers, to the metaphysical doctrine of *Tat tvam asi* [thou art That], and to its ethical corollary—universal compassion. In this philosophy it is the experiential element that is important. Its speculative superstructure is a thing of words, and words, though useful and necessary, should never be taken too seriously.")

Education in elementary awareness will have to include techniques for improving awareness of internal events and techniques for improving awareness of external events as these are revealed by our organs of sense. In his introductions to several of F. M. Alexander's books, John Dewey insisted upon the importance of a properly directed training in the awareness of internal events. It was Dewey's opinion that the training methods developed by Alexander were to education what education is to life in general—an indispensable condition for any kind of improvement. Dewey had himself undergone this training and so knew what he was talking about. And yet in spite of this high praise bestowed by one of the most influential of modern philosophers and educational reformers, Alexander's methods have been ignored, and schoolchildren still receive no training in the kind of internal awareness that can lead to what Alexander described as "creative conscious control."

The educational and therapeutic values of training aimed at heightening awareness of internal events was empirically demonstrated during the first quarter of the present century by the eminently successful Swiss psychiatrist, Dr. Roger Vittoz. And in recent years methods similar to those of Vittoz and to the Tantrik exercises attributed many centuries ago to Shiva have been developed and successfully used both in the treatment of neurotics and for the enrichment of the lives of the normal by the authors of *Gestalt Therapy*, Drs. Frederick F. Perls, Ralph F. Hefferline, and Paul Goodman.

All our mental processes depend upon perception. Inadequate perceiving results in poor thinking, inappropriate feeling, diminished interest in and enjoyment of life. Systematic training of perception should be an essential element in all education.

Our amphibiousness is clearly illustrated in the two modes of our awareness of external events. There is a receptive, more or less unconceptualized, aesthetic and "spiritual" mode of perceiving; and there is also a highly conceptualized, stereotyped, utilitarian, and even scientific mode. In his "Expostulation and Reply" and "The Tables Turned," Wordsworth has perfectly described these two modes of awareness and has assigned to each its special significance and value for the human being who aspires to make the best of both worlds and so, by teaching his psychophysical organism to "do many things," to "perfect the mind and come to the intellectual love of God."

"Why, William, on that old grey stone,
Thus for the length of half a day,
Why William, sit you thus alone,
And dream your time away?

Where are your books?—that light bequeathed
To beings else forlorn and blind?
Up! Up! and drink the spirit breathed
From dead men to their kind.

You look round on your Mother Earth,
As if she for no purpose bore you;
As if you were her first-born birth,
And none had lived before you."

One morning thus, by Esthwaite lake,
When life was sweet, I knew not why,
To me my good friend Matthew spake,
And thus I made reply.

"The eye it cannot choose but see;
We cannot bid the ear be still;

Our bodies feel, where'er they be,
Against or with our will.

Nor less I deem that there are Powers
Which of themselves our minds impress;
That we can feed this mind of ours
In a wise passiveness.

Think you, 'mid all this mighty sum
Of things for ever speaking,
That nothing of itself will come,
But we must still be seeking?

Then ask no wherefore, here, alone,
Conversing as I may,
I sit upon this old grey stone
And dream my time away."

In "The Tables Turned" it is the poet who takes the offensive against his studious friend. "Up! Up! my Friend," he calls, "and quit your books." And then, "Books!" he continues impatiently,

Books! 'tis a dull and endless strife;
Come, hear the woodland linnet;
How sweet his music! on my life,
There's more of wisdom in it.

And hark how blithe the throstle sings!
He too is no mean preacher.
Come forth into the light of things,
Let Nature be your teacher.

One impulse from a vernal wood
May teach you more of man,
Of moral evil and of good
Than all the sages can.

Sweet is the lore which Nature brings;
Our meddling intellect
Mis-shapes the beauteous forms of things—
We murder to dissect.

Enough of Science and of Art;
Close up those barren leaves;
Come forth and bring with you a heart
That watches and receives.

Matthew and William—two aspects of the multiple amphibian that was Wordsworth, that is each of us. To be fully human, we must learn to make the best of William's world as well as Matthew's. Matthew's is the world of books, of the social heredity of steadily accumulating knowledge, of science and technics and business, of words and the stock of second-hand notions which we project upon external reality as a frame of reference, in terms of which we may explain, to our own satisfaction, the enigma, moment by moment, of ongoing existence. Over against it stands William's world—the world of sheer mystery, the world as an endless succession of unique events, the world as we perceive it in a state of alert receptiveness with no thought of explaining it, using it, exploiting it for our biological or cultural purposes. As things now stand, we teach young people to make the best only of Matthew's world of familiar words, accepted notions, and useful techniques. We temper a too exclusive concentration on scientific symbols, not with a training in the art of what William calls "wise passiveness," not with lessons in watching and receiving, but with the injunction to concentrate on philosophical and sociological symbols, to read the books that are reputed to contain a high concentration of "the spirit breathed from dead men to their kind." (Alas, dead men do not always breathe a spirit; quite often they merely emit a bad smell.)

It is related in one of the Sutras that on a certain occasion the Buddha preached a wordless sermon to his disciples. Instead of saying anything, he picked a flower and held it up for them to look at. The disciples gaped uncomprehendingly. Only Mahakasyapa understood what the Tathagata was driving at, and all that he did was to smile. Gautama smiled back at him, and when the wordless sermon was over, he made a little speech for the benefit of those who had failed to comprehend his silence. "This treasure of the unquestionable teaching, this Mind of Nirvana, this true form that is without forms, this most subtle Dharma beyond words, this instruction that is to be given and received outside the pale of all doctrines—this I have now handed on to Mahakasyapa." Perceived not as a botanical specimen, not as the analyzed and labeled illustration of a pre-existent symbol system, but as a nameless, unique event, in which all the beauty and the mystery of existence are manifest, a flower can become the means to enlightenment. And what is true of a flower is true, needless to say, of any other event in the inner or outer world—from a toothache to Mount Everest, from a tapeworm to *The Well-Tempered Clavichord*—to which we choose to pay attention in a state of wise passiveness. And wise passiveness is the condition not only of spiritual insight. ("In prayer," wrote St. Jeanne Chantal, "I always want to *do* something, wherein I do very wrong. ... By wishing to accomplish something myself, I spoil it all.") In another context, wise passiveness, followed in due course by wise hard work, is the condition of creativity. We do not fabricate our best ideas: they "occur to us," they "come into our heads." Colloquial speech reminds us that, unless we give our subliminal mind a chance, we shall get nowhere. And it is by allowing ourselves at frequent intervals to be wisely passive that we can most effectively help the subliminal mind to do its work. The *cogito* of Descartes should be emended, said von Baader, to *cogitor*. In order to actualize our potentialities, in order to become fully human and completely ourselves, we must not merely think; we must also permit ourselves to be thought. In Gardner Murphy's words, "Both the historical record of creative thought and the laboratory report of its appearance today, indicate clearly that creative intelligence can spring from the mind that is not strained to its highest pitch, but is utterly at ease." Watching and receiving in a state of perfect ease or wise passiveness is an art which can be cultivated and should be taught on every educational level from the most elementary to the most advanced.

Creativity and spiritual insight—these are the highest rewards of wise passiveness. But those who know how to watch and receive are rewarded in other and hardly less important ways. Receptivity can be a source of innocent and completely harmless happiness. A man or woman who knows how to make the best of both worlds—the world revealed by wise passiveness and the world created by wise activity—tends to find life enjoyable and interesting. Ours is a civilization in which vast numbers of children and adults are so chronically bored that they have to resort during their leisure hours to a regimen of nonstop distractions. Any method which promises to make life seem enjoyable and the commonplaces of everyday experience more interesting should be welcomed as a major contribution to culture and morality.

In *Modern Painters* there is a remarkable chapter on "the Open Sky"—a chapter which even by those who find Ruskin's theology absurd and his aesthetics frequently perverse may still be read with profit and admiring pleasure. "It is a strange thing," Ruskin writes, "how little in general people know about the sky. It is the part of creation in which nature has done more for the sake of pleasing man, more for the sake and evident purpose of talking to him and teaching him, than in any of her works; and it is just the part in which we least attend to her. . . . There is not a moment in any day of our lives in which nature is not producing (in the sky) scene after scene, picture after picture, glory after glory, and working always upon such exquisite and constant principles of the most perfect beauty, that it is quite certain it is all done for us and intended for our perpetual pleasure." But, in point of fact, does the sky produce in most people the perpetual pleasure which its beauty is so eminently capable of giving? The answer, of course, is No. "We never attend to it, we never make it a subject of thought. . . . We look upon it . . . only as a succession of monotonous and meaningless accidents, too common or too vain to be worthy of a moment of watchfulness or a glance of admiration. . . . Who, among the chattering crowd, can tell me of the forms and the precipices of the chain of tall white mountains that girded the horizon at noon yesterday? Who saw the narrow sunbeam that came out of the south and smote their summits until they melted and mouldered away in a dust of blue rain? . . . All has passed unregretted as unseen; or if the apathy be ever shaken off, if even for an instant, it is only by what is gross or what is extraordinary." A habit of wise passiveness in relation to the everyday drama of the clouds and mist and sunshine can become a source, as Ruskin insists, of endless pleasure. But most of the products of our educational system prefer Westerns and alcohol.

In the art of watching and receiving Ruskin was self-educated. But there seems to be no reason why children should not be taught that wise passiveness which gave this victim of a traumatic childhood so much pleasure and kept him, in spite of everything, reasonably sane for the greater part of a long and productive life. A training in watching and receiving will not turn every child into a great stylist but, within the limits imposed by constitution, temperament, and the circumambient culture, it will make him more sensitive, more intelligent, more capable of innocent enjoyment and, in consequence, more virtuous and more useful to society.

In the United States life, liberty, and the pursuit of happiness are constitutionally guaranteed. But if life hardly seems worth living, if liberty is used for subhuman purposes, if the pursuers of happiness know nothing about the nature of their quarry or the elementary techniques of hunting, these constitutional rights will not be very meaningful. An education in that wise passiveness recommended by the saints and the poets, by all who have lived fully and worked creatively, might help us to transform the paper premises of a democratic constitution into concrete contemporary fact.

Let us now consider very briefly two other areas in which an education in the art of making the best of all our seemingly incommensurable worlds would certainly be helpful and might also turn out to be practicable within the system now prevailing in our schools and colleges. It is a matter of observable fact that all of us inhabit a world of phantasy as well as a world of first-order experience and a world of words and concepts. In most children and in some adults this world of phantasy is astonishingly vivid. These people are the visualizers of Galton's classical dichotomy. For them the world presented to their consciousness by their story-telling, image-making phantasy is as real as, sometimes more real than, the given world of sense impressions and the projected world of words and explanatory concepts. Even in nonvisualizers the world of phantasy, though somewhat shadowy, is still real enough to be retreated into or shrunk from, tormented by or voluptuously enjoyed. The mentally ill are the victims of their phantasy, and even more or less normal people find themselves tempted into folly, or inhibited from behaving as they know they ought to behave, by what goes on in the supernal but unrealistic world of their imagination. How can we make the best of this odd, alien, almost autonomous universe that we carry about with us inside our skulls?

The question has been partially answered by the apostles of those numerous religious movements stemming from "New Thought." Using a vaguely theological language and interpreting the Bible to suit themselves, they have given a religious form to a number of useful and practical methods for harnessing imagination and its suggestive power in the service of individual well-being and social stability. For about a quarter or perhaps a third of the population their methods work remarkably well. This is an important fact, of which professional educators should take notice and from whose implications they should not be ashamed to learn. Unfortunately, men and women in high academic positions tend to be intellectually snobbish. They turn up their noses at the nonscientific, distressingly "inspirational" but still astute and experienced psychologists of the modern heretical churches. This is deplorable. Truth lives, proverbially, at the bottom of a well, and wells are often muddy. No genuinely scientific investigator has any right to be squeamish about anything.

And here is another truth-containing well abhorred by academic scientists of the stricter sort. Excellent techniques for teaching children and adults to make the best of the chaotic world of their phantasy have been worked out by the Dianeticists and their successors, the Scientologists. Their Imagination Games deserve to be incorporated into every curriculum. Boys and girls, and even grown men and women, find these games amusing and, what is more important, helpful. Made the worst of, our imagination will destroy us; made the best of, it can be used to break up long-established habits of undesirable feeling, to dissipate obsessive fears, to provide symbolic outlets for anger and fictional amends for real frustrations.

In the course of the last three thousand years how many sermons have been preached, how many homilies delivered and commands roared out, how many promises of heaven and threats of hell-fire solemnly pronounced, how many good-conduct prizes awarded and how many childish buttocks lacerated with whips and canes? And what has been the result of all this incalculable sum of moralistic words, and of the rewards and savage punishments by which the verbiage has been accompanied? The result has been history—the successive generations of human beings comporting themselves virtuously and rationally enough for the race to survive, but badly enough and madly enough for it to be unceasingly in trouble. Can we do better in the future than we are doing today, or than our fathers did in the past? Can we develop methods more effective than pious talk and Pavlovian conditioning?

For an answer to these questions—or at least for some hints as to the nature of a possible answer—we must turn to history and anthropology. Like many primitive societies today, many highly civilized socieites of the past provided their members with realistically amphibious methods for dealing with negative emotions and the instinctive drives that are incompatible with communal living. In these societies morality and rational behavior were not merely preached and rewarded; they were made easier by the provision of religiously sanctioned safety valves, through which the angry, the frustrated, and the anxiously neurotic could release their aggressive or self-destructive tendencies in a satisfyingly violent and yet harmless and socially acceptable way. In Ancient Greece, for example, the orgies of Dionysus and, at a somewhat later date, the Corybantic dances, sacred to the Great Mother, were safety valves through which rage and resentment found an innocuous outlet, while the paralyzing inhibitions of anxiety were swept away in a wild rush of nervous, muscular, and hormonal activity. In this ethical and therapeutic context Dionysus was known as Lusios, the Liberator. His orgies delivered the participants from the dismal necessity of running amok, or retreating into catatonia, or stoically bottling up their feelings and so giving themselves a psychosomatic illness. Corybantic dancing was regarded as a form of medical treatment and at the same time as a religious rite, cathartic to the soul no less than to the adrenalin-charged body. Which did most for morality and rational behavior—the dialogues of Plato or the orgies of Dionysus, Aristotle's *Ethics* or the Corybantic dances; My guess is that, in this competition, Lusios and the Great Mother would be found to have won hands down.

In a society like ours it would doubtless be impracticable to revive Maenadism or the congregational antics of the Dionysian orgies. But the problem of what multiple amphibians should do about their frustrations and their tendencies to aggression remains acute and still unsolved. Sixty years ago William James wrote an essay entitled *The Moral Equivalent of War*. It is an excellent essay as far as it goes; but it does not, unfortunately, go far enough. Moral equivalents must be found not only for war but also for delinquency, family squabbles, bullying, puritanical censoriousness, and all the assorted beastliness of daily life. Preaching and conditioning will never of themselves solve these problems. It is obvious that we must take a hint from the Greeks and provide ourselves with physical safety valves for reducing the pressure of our negative emotions. No ethical system which fails to provide such physical safety valves, and which fails to teach children and their elders how to use them, is likely to be effective. It will be the business of psychologists, physiologists, and sociologists to devise acceptable safety valves, of moralists and clergymen to provide rationalizations in terms of the local value systems and theologies, and for educators to find a place in the curriculum for courses in the indispensable art of letting off steam.

And there is another art that merits the educator's closest attention—the art of controlling physical pain. Pain, as recent studies have made abundantly clear, is not simply a mechanical affair of peripheral receptors and special centers in the brain, and its intensity is not directly proportional to the extent of the injury which is its cause. Pain may be aggravated or inhibited by numerous psychological and even cultural factors. Which means, of course, that to some extent at least pain is controllable. This fact, needless to say, has been known from time immemorial, and for the last century and a half (from the days of Elliotson and Esdaile) has been systematically exploited in hypnotic anesthesia. Neurological research is now discovering the organic and functional reasons for these old observations and empirical practices; a somewhat disreputable "wild" phenomenon is in process of being turned into a domesticated scientific fact, consonant with other well-known facts and safely caged within a familiar symbol-system. Taking advantage of the newfound respectability of hypnosis and suggestion, educators should now include elementary pain control in the curriculum of physical training. Control of pain through suggestion and autosuggestion is an art which, as every good dentist knows, can be learned by most children with the greatest of ease. Along with singing and calisthenics, it should be taught to every little boy and girl who can learn it.

Training in a closely similar art may prove to be very useful as a part of ethical education. In his book *Auto-Conditioning* Professor Hornell Hart has outlined simple and thoroughly practical methods for changing moods, intensifying motivations, and implementing good intentions. There are no educational panaceas, no techniques that work perfectly in every case. But if auto-conditioning produces good results in only 20 or 30 percent of those who have been instructed in the art, it deserves to take its place in every educator's armamentarium.

That we are multiple amphibians is self-evident, and the corollary of this self-evident truth is that we must attack our problems on every front where they arise—on the mental front and on the physiological front, on the front of concepts and symbols and on the front of wordless experience, on the rational front and on the irrational front, the individual front and the social front. But what should be our strategy? How are we to learn and successfully practice the art of attacking on all the fronts simultaneously? Many valuable discoveries were made by the amphibians of earlier times and alien cultures, and many discoveries are being made within our own culture today. These empirical findings of the past and the present should be studied, tested, related to the best scientific knowledge now available, and finally adapted for practical use within our educational systems. Ten million dollars from the coffers of one of the great foundations would pay for the necessary research and large-scale experimentation. Out of such research and experimentation might come, within a few years, a radical improvement in the methods currently used to prepare young people to meet the challenges of their manifold amphibiousness and to make the best of all the strangely assorted worlds in which, as human beings, they are predestined to live.

WHAT IS HUMANISTIC EDUCATION?*

Howard Kirschenbaum

The Many Meanings of "Humanistic." In many schools and in many colleges of education the word "humanistic" gets applied in practically any way that people want. Depending on their point of view, it is either a praising or a damning word, but regardless of the value attached, in most cases its meaning is ambiguous. In addition, various humanistically-oriented educators add to the confusion by doing all sorts of different things and calling them "humanistic." In this short and important catalog of meanings, Kirschenbaum presents the various meanings and differentiates among them. It is important to notice that a teacher, program, or school can be humanistic in several ways at once. Sometimes in their over-emphasis on the more neglected, non-cognitive human potentials, educators forget that thinking and language are two of the most important human abilities. Kirschenbaum gives us an example of developing the potentials of clarity and precision in the cognitive domain. When you read the other articles in this section, and when you hear someone use the word "humanistic," it will help you to be clear about his meaning by figuring out which meaning(s) he has in mind. Clear thinking is humanistic too.

For one thing, the term is an umbrella that encompasses several similar approaches—affective education, psychological education, confluent education, and others. It's also a vague term. Many people are for it, but few can coherently define or describe it. And it certainly is a loaded term. Depending on whether or not one is a proponent of humanistic education, the term becomes associated with "us" and "them," with all the forces of good and evil in the community.

Without defending or critiquing this approach, I would like to present two ways of describing humanistic education which try to be helpful by being specific.

The first approach takes a look at what different people, projects and districts are actually doing under the label of humanistic education, when it comes to building curriculum and structuring the school or classroom. I see three types of approaches which people are taking. *They often overlap.* Some curricula or programs use all three approaches.

HUMANISTIC CONTENT CURRICULA

This approach takes some areas of human concern and focuses on those areas. The Unitarian Church has a course for secondary school students on

---

*From Howard Kirschenbaum, "What is Humanistic Education?," mimeographed, 2 pp., by permission of the author. Copyright by Howard Kirschenbaum. Howard Kirschenbaum is Director of the Adirondack Mountain Humanistic Education Center, Upper Jay, New York. He is co-author of the recent book *Values Clarification: A Handbook of Practical Strategies.*

"Human Sexuality." The Lakewood, Ohio Public Schools have developed a curriculum concerning "Aggressive Behavior." Drug abuse education courses and curricula abound. Conceivably, these courses or units could be taught in a traditional fashion; although curriculum builders in these areas tend to favor experiential learning. What is humanistic about these curricula is that, theoretically, they are "relevant." That is, they explore areas that will help students deal more effectively with particular issues in their lives.

HUMANISTIC PROCESS CURRICULA

This approach attempts to teach students processes or skills they need or will need to guide their lives and successfully deal with issues of "identity, power and connectedness." Values clarification is one such approach, emphasizing the processes of prizing, choosing and acting. Human relations training (in many forms, including communications exercises, Parent Effectiveness Training, encounter groups, etc.) is another example, teaching the processes of listening, giving and receiving feedback, handling conflict, etc. Achievement Motivation is another process approach, emphasizing goal setting, moderate risk taking and achievement planning.

HUMANISTIC SCHOOL (AND GROUP) STRUCTURES

Here, the approach is to structure the learning environment in such a way as to allow students to pursue humanistic and other content areas of their own choosing and to encourage them to learn and practice humanistic processes as a part of their education. Some examples of this approach are: the open classroom, with teacher as facilitator; the open school; class meeting; finding alternatives to traditional grading; etc.

A second way of describing humanistic education looks more closely than the first at what actually happens in the classroom. I see five dimensions, or continua, along which classes seem to move, when teachers attempt to facilitate a more humanistic education. (Many of these approaches overlap also.)

Choice or Control. All their lives, the students will be setting goals and making decisions. In a humanistic education, the students learn to do this more effectively by exercising more and more control and choices concerning the course of their education—both their educational goals and their day-to-day activities.

Felt Concerns. As a classroom becomes more humanistic, the curriculum tends to focus more and more on the felt concerns and interests of the students. One student may be more concerned about black literature than Shakespeare; but another may be more concerned about improving his writing than in sex education. Relevant vs. irrelevant is not **the** same as modern vs. traditional.

Life Skills (The Whole Person). School education has traditionally been cognitive. Humanistic education tends to involve the whole person, not just the mind. It moves toward integrating thinking skills with the other life skills necessary to be an effective person—feeling, choosing, communicating and acting.

Self-Evaluation. Adult learners evaluate their own learning progress, occasionally choosing to take tests, occasionally asking for others' feedback, occasionally gathering data about themselves. Humanistic education tends to move away from teacher controlled evaluation and shift the locus of evaluation back to the student, as he learns to evaluate his own progress toward his goals.

Teacher as Facilitator. The teacher moves from a director of learning to a facilitator or helper. He tends to be more supportive than critical, more understanding than aloof and judgmental, more real and genuine than playing a role. Roles tend to be more reciprocal, with the "teacher" often being a learner and the "students" often helping and teaching each other.

This conception suggests that whether a classroom is "humanistic" or not is not an either-or proposition. Rather, each classroom can be assessed by the degree to which students make choices, the degree to which they feel their education relates to their concerns, the balance of emphasis placed on the cognitive and other life skills, the degree of self-evaluated learning, and the extent to which the teacher facilitates or dictates. By specifying five goals for the classroom or school, perhaps these categories will be helpful to educators who want to humanize education and to researchers who want to measure it.

For information on materials available and workshops offered in humanistic education, please write to: the Adirondack Mountain Humanistic Education Center, Upper Jay, New York 12987.

SEVEN MAJOR FOCI OF AFFECTIVE EXPERIENCES: A TYPOLOGY FOR EDUCATIONAL DESIGN, PLANNING, ANALYSIS, AND RESEARCH

Thomas B. Roberts

To Delight AND Instruct. Although affective techniques may be fun, they are primarily ways of teaching people things, not entertainment. This article shows seven educational goals that can be served by affective teaching methods. And, like the meanings of the word "humanistic" in Kirschenbaum's article, several of these may be present at once. Involving students' feelings as well as their thoughts in education, humanistic techniques try to increase learning two ways: 1) by including education of the emotions as well as the intellect and 2) by recombining the affective side of learning with the cognitive side for their mutual improvement.

If this is supposed to be an affective learning technique, WHO is supposed to learn WHAT?

As a fast-growing educational activity, affective education tries to educate people's emotions just as cognitive education tries to educate their intellects. Or, these may be combined into humanistic, or "confluent," education. An expanding number of works present examples of humanistic and affective education. They describe affective techniques, explain the theoretical backing for them, and try to anticipate and answer skeptics. (A list of selected references is in the Appendix.) Although they describe many affective methods, they offer little guidance to a teacher who wants to design her own experiences, to an administrator or to a member of the public who wants to understand what's going on, or to a planner or researcher who wants to think about or analyze what's going on. At the present these people must rely on their own intuition and imagination practically unaided by their cognitive capacities. Just as humanistic educators judge cognitive-only education as one-sided, so too is educational planning if it is left entirely to affective capacities unaided by thought.

The following classification of kinds of affective education gives teachers, curriculum designers, administrators, and others a way of adding reason in their selection of affective experiences instead of just, "I guess this ought to work," or, "This feels like a good experience." While the following types are conceptually different, any particular instance may be in more than one catagory. A perfect technique would meet the criteria of all seven.

*From Thomas B. Roberts, "Seven Major Foci of Affective Experiences: A typology for Educational Design, Planning, Analysis, and Research," *Research in Education*, ED-063-215, ERIC (1973), by permission of the author.

Personal development. *The goal of this type is the individual, personal growth of students. Such phrases as self-awareness and self-insight apply here. The student becomes more in touch with himself and knows more about himself.*

Two subtypes are *individual* personal awareness and *general* awareness. The former concerns the person's uniqueness, how he differs from other people, how he is an individual with his own history, desires, capacities, and potentials. After a blindfolded walk, for example, he may find that he was aware of how his clothes felt on him. This is an unusual awareness. Likewise he may be especially creative in some ways, or he may become aware of how his own, unique life has contributed to the kind of person he is now. One of the suppositions of humanistic psychology, which is a major theoretical base for humanistic education, is that we use only a small fraction of our capacities. Becoming aware of these abilities and practicing them are two of the goals of individual personal development.

Another teaching of humanistic education is that we share much with our fellow humans, and when we see something new in ourselves, we are on the way to seeing and appreciating it in others. A blind walk may also lead to knowledge of others through knowledge of oneself. A blindfolded person may enjoy freedom from responsibility when someone else leads him and makes decisions. He can better understand social-political situations such as the rise of totalitarianism which Erich Fromm writes of in *Escape from Freedom* or Eric Hoffer describes in *The True Believer*. By experiencing dependency in himself and by learning to learn through his feelings, a person learns to understand more in other people too.

Creative behavior. *This goal values originality, creativity, imagination, new interpretations, novel meanings, and so forth.*

Closely related to the goals of personal development, these goals are approached affectively through fantasy, free associations, mining one's unconscious, intuition, and so on. Unfortunately, some people have learned to ignore these affective capacities, "Oh, it's only your imagination." They haven't found that the imagination is also a storehouse of good ideas, "How imaginative she is!" Affective skills can tap this source; afterwards cognitive skills can judge, analyze, and refine them.

Imagination games such as "Once Upon a Time" help strengthen these affective abilities. In this exercise a small group of students uses the last word of one phrase as the first word of the next, for example: "Once upon a time waits for no man is an island of the damned if you do damned if you don't" ... and so forth. What is important here is that a person learns to "read" his unconscious as one possible, and often neglected, source of information. Problem reformulation, problem insight, novel solutions, seeing similarities in different things or regularities in chaos are some instances of intellectual creative behavior. Learning to follow the wanderings of one's mind is a key to intellectual concept formation as well as to non-verbal creation.

Interpersonal awareness. *The emphasis here is on how people influence each other. Social interaction, group processes, leadership, and communication are classic topics of this field.*

Interpersonal feedback protocols such as, "You impress me as —————," and, "I like your —————, but I resent —————" help someone become aware of *how others react to him.* Conversely, the same techniques require him to focus on his *reactions to others* and to verbalize his feelings. These are different subtypes of affective experience, however. This illustrates how one affective experience may serve more than one purpose; learning about how one interacts with others can result in both interpersonal and personal awareness. Many feelings such as anger, frustration, dependency, love, and others have interpersonal as well as personal origins. How someone reacts to others and how they react to him both stress individual person-to-person interactions.

Two other subtypes of interpersonal awareness emphasize group relations, *person-group*, and *group-group*. What does it feel like to have a group decide to exclude you from membership? How does it feel to go through an initiation and be declared a full group member? Some affective techniques require the group to choose one member to exclude. Others have the group develop a ritual and initiate a new member of the one they had previously excluded. How do the outsiders or excluded people feel? How do the remaining insiders feel? The results are sometimes surprising, and when the participants get in touch with their feelings, they sometimes become more aware of analogous situations in schools and society.

This technique can develop into a group-group exercise if the excluded members are all brought together to form their own group of outsiders. How will they rationalize their exclusion? Will they compensate or over-compensate for their apparently low status? Some may want to withdraw, "Let's forget them." Some may insist that their own characteristics are superior, "Superior people make inferiors nervous, and are excluded." Some take out their rejection on other group members, "There must be something the matter with you. I don't want to be in a group with you." Discussions of rivalry between groups, prejudice, and class conflict can be enriched as can the personal feelings of rejection, popularity, and inclusion by members of in-groups and out-groups.

Subject or discipline orientation. *The focus here is on a student's feelings about a whole subject or broad field of study.*

Many students report they "hate math" or "love English," or have some other feelings about general fields of study. Charges of irrelevance and boredom can be signs of affective hollowness in curricula. "Why study the Revolutionary War?" An intellectual answer about something to do with our history and how our lives and the world would be different today may satisfy questions of intellectual hunger, but how many courses underfeed students intellectually and overfeed them affectively? A cry for relevance is often a cry for affective content. The American colonists felt angry and frustrated, betrayed and neglected in their dealings with their English government. Wars come from emotional problems of anger, self-righteousness, fear, and pride just as they do from economic and political forces. Feeling one's own frustration, anger, anxiety, and aggression can add relevant affective content and can aid in the understanding of war as mass passion. Learning to recognize, accept, arouse, determine, and control one's emotions can be steps to intellectual understanding of emotions in others as well as steps to personal, group, and international peace.

In addition to *affective content*, a second field-of-study subgoal has to do with the *students' own feelings about the subject*. When he says, "I hate math," he may mean, "I feel stupid when I don't get a problem right, and I don't like to feel stupid." If he has been in a school system that marks off for wrong answers and which punishes mistakes, he has probably been sensitized to pay more attention to errors, his faults, and avoiding new things than he has to correct answers and to trying new things. His idea of learning may be never making a mistake rather than trying new things, which, of course, leads to a number of mistakes.

Sometimes the dislike has little to do with the cognitive aspects of the subject. A younger brother, for example, may "hate" math because his older brother was very good at it. If his dislike is due to his desire to establish his own identity separate from being his brother's younger brother, affective experiences which help him increase his awareness of uniqueness may, as a side effect, help him in math. As many teachers know, parents, fellow students, and other "significant others" play important roles in developing student attitudes toward learning in general and toward particular subjects. Much work remains to develop affective methods for generalized attitudes.

If the student is in a field with low status, he may resent the status because he adapts it as part of his own self image. This, in turn, leads to lower self-expectations and lower other-expectations, and these too frequently are self-fulfilling and self-perpetuating. In most educational institutions applied fields such as home economics, business, and job-oriented courses suffer from low status compared with the academic fields. Little has been done in designing affective techniques to cope with this set of problems. A getting acquainted protocol which George Brown used at the Association for Humanistic Psychology Convention in 1971 may be a step in that direction. He divided the participants into small groups and had each person tell the others about something he was proud of accomplishing. This raised both self images and group expectations.

Specific content. *The goal of this type of technique is humanistic learning (both affective and cognitive) of a specific bit of course content such as a reading or historical event.*

An example of this in *Human Teaching for Human Learning* shows students feeling and discussing their own courage, bravery, and fears. Awareness of these makes *The Red Badge of Courage* and its hero's feelings more understandable. *The Red Badge of Courage* is, among other things, about dealing with one's fears. Henry Fleming, the hero, also left and joined various groups during the book: student experiences of social acceptance/rejection make this part of the novel more alive, and when the students become aware of their own feelings in such situations, this piece of literature takes on personal affective relevance.

Method of teaching. *What are the affective possibilities for different ways of conducting a class and for in-classroom and out-of-classroom experiences?*

Different sorts of students like and dislike different approaches. Those who are insecure usually prefer unambiguous questions with clearly right/ wrong answers. Does a structured atmosphere make them feel more secure? Are there affective techniques which can add to their security? Can these lessen their fear of change and uncertainty or open them to new experiences and teaching methods? Other students prefer the social inter-action of discussions and group work. Another type prefers individual work on their own projects.

Much research and development is needed in this field. What are the affective and cognitive results and possibilities of various classroom methods? If a student learns cognitive materials best in a structured class, is this the preferable way to teach him, or should educators try to make him comfortable with a wider repertoire of methods? The interactions of students' and teachers' affective styles need analysis. If teaching methods are developed in schools with one affective climate, how applicable are they to schools with different climates?

Teachers and administrators. *The focus here is on the educator as a growing person and a model for students.*

A teacher who is an enthusiastic learner sets a good example for his students. He realizes that he doesn't know everything; but he is always willing to improve and learn. When students can see these attitudes of personal growth, they receive help in accepting the facts of their own, personal limits. They can see a teacher-model who recognizes and tries to expand beyond his limitations. Many teachers and administrators can accept the idea of themselves as learning models in the cognitive domain; they don't mind admitting cognitive imperfection. But they don't like to see themselves in the analogous affective role, as people who are affectively imperfect, but who are trying to grow affectively too. George Brown's book describes a weekend in-service training program for educators. The affective methods that he and his colleagues developed in the Ford Foundation—Esalen Institute project can help administrators, teachers, and other educators grow toward a healthier, fuller humanity, a good model for anyone to emulate.

Summary. What makes an activity an affective learning experience rather than just a good time? This taxonomy described some objectives, or foci, of learning experiences. This typology presented seven major types of affective work and eight subtypes:

1. Personal awareness
   a. individual uniqueness
   b. shared humanness
2. Creative behavior
3. Interpersonal awareness
   a. how others react to the person
   b. how the person reacts to others
   c. person-group
   d. group-group
4. Subject or discipline orientation
   a. affective content
   b. feelings about subject or discipline
5. Specific content, joining affective and cognitive
6. Affective styles of teaching/learning
7. Teacher, administrator, and other educators

The purpose of analyzing affective methods into these categories is to help educators use their cognitive capacities when planning or considering affective experiences. Does the technique enrich or contribute to one or more of the foci listed? How is it expected to do so? What sorts of techniques are most appropriate for the various goals?

While this typology applies to educational situations, it may be adapted to other fields too. Here we considered the learner, what he learns, and his social environment. When considering business situations, appropriate transpositions may be the employee, his work, and the company he works for. If affective techniques can enrich education, perhaps they can enrich other institutions and other parts of life too. Just as we expect the cognitive content of education to contribute to an individual's life and to society at large, perhaps we can expect affective content to enrich ourselves and our society too.

For references on humanistic education, see the appendix.

A CONFLUENT APPROACH
TO EDUCATION IN THE SCIENCES*

David Mills and Stanley Scher

Feelings In All We Do. To many teachers, affective methods are naturals for younger students or for the social sciences, languages, and the arts, but not for other subjects. By using George Brown's model of combining affective and cognitive teaching, Mills and Scher give examples of how to use a confluent approach in the sciences. I have seen examples in high school algebra, business education, and even automotive shop. Helpful questions to ask when trying to develop affective teaching styles are: How are my students' emotions involved in learning (doing) this? And how are (were) the emotions of people who do (did) this affected?

INTRODUCTION & RATIONALE

During the past two decades, the primary activity in science education has been the development of materials for teaching science, with much less emphasis on programs concerned with methodology. The fullest use of such materials, however, depends on a corresponding development of methodological approaches.

The necessity for a confluent approach to education in general has been outlined by George Brown (1), Weinstein & Fantini (2), and others. The confluent approach, a synthesis of Humanistic Psychology—especially Gestalt Therapy—and education, involves the integration of cognitive and affective elements in teaching. In the context of these two basic modes of consciousness (3), *cognitive* refers to thinking; to verbal, logical, analytic, rational and intellectual ways of knowing; and *affective* to feeling; to ways of knowing involving visual—spatial imagery, fantasy, gestalt perception, metaphor and intuition; and to consideration of values.

The natural sciences have long been taught almost exclusively in the cognitive mode—as a mere accumulation of facts and theories. In contrast to this, however, the *practice* of science always involves affective elements. These include the desire for knowledge, the use of intuition and imagination in creative efforts, the experience of excitement, frustration, and so on. As Polanyi (4) notes, "It is the passion of the scholar that makes for a truly great scholarship." The *process* of science, how science is done, is fully as important to teach as its content.

*From David Mills and Stanley Scher, *A Confluent Approach to Education in the Sciences* (Santa Cruz: Santa Cruz Workshop, 1973), 6 pp., by permission of the authors. David M. Mills, a physicist and astronomer, teaches at the University of California Extension and is a Gestalt practitioner at the Santa Cruz Workshop. Stanley Scher, a microbiologist, is Professor of Natural Sciences at the New College of California, Sausalito.

336

Further, all *applications* of science can invoke affective components, including consideration of values. Even learning the content of scientific knowledge is enhanced by the (usually implicit) use of affective processes such as fantasy and imagery. Rarely are these kinds of issues examined in the classroom. If the teaching of science is not to remain one-sided, if science is to be taught in a spirit consonant with what actually happens in science, science teaching must also involve the explicit consideration and integration of these affective and cognitive elements.

MEANS & GOALS OF A CONFLUENT SCIENCE EDUCATION PROGRAM

In addition to the integration of affective and cognitive elements, the confluent approach provides a guide to desired means and goals. Regarding means, we agree with Montz (5) that "It is the teacher's responsibility to make it clear to students at all times that they have more than one option in the class (even if it is only) not participating with no penalty or stigma whatever." Further, "The confluent teacher's function is to become increasingly dispensable—to enable the student to rely upon the teacher less and less and upon himself more and more." The end-goal is developing the student's responsibility for his own learning; the teacher helps the student not only by providing reasonable choices for his learning, but by, when necessary, increasingly *refusing* to take the responsibility for doing for the student what he *can* do for himself.

The overall goals of the confluent approach have been summarized (5) as the development of student *awareness, response,* and *responsibility: awareness* of himself and the world around him; the ability to use this awareness to *respond* to his environment in a variety of ways, taking his internal clues into account; and the ability to take *responsibility* for his choice of response. Within this context, a confluent science education program would have as particular goals: 1) to help students experience the practice (process) of science, including the discovery of new ideas, as both an intellectual and an affective process; 2) to help them achieve a sense of confidence in their ability to explore and understand themselves and the world in a scientific way; 3) to increase their understanding and retention of concepts and ideas in science; 4) to explore with them the implications of possible applications of scientific knowledge; and 5) to enable students to apply both scientific process and knowledge to their personal and everyday concerns—in short, to increase the students' awareness of their world and their choices for responsible action.

INTEGRATING AFFECTIVE & COGNITIVE ELEMENTS IN TEACHING SCIENCE

Brown (1) has shown how affective and cognitive elements can be integrated in teaching social science. Two examples of how this model can be adapted to the natural sciences are shown in the accompanying diagram. One characteristic of this model is its flexibility. Starting with a given cognitive lesson, it is possible to move to a number of affective

Physics

Cognitive		Affective	
Straight Cognitive	Abstract Cognitive	Abstract Affective	Straight Affective
Newton proposes a theory which relates the fall of an apple on Earth to the Moon's orbit.	Matter in space is like matter on earth; binary star motions are related to Earth-Moon rotation. / All future motions can be calculated in principle; beginning of determinism.	What motivates a scientist to seek to understand? What are the rewards to him?	Why do I want to learn? How do I feel when I find out something new by myself?

It is possible to understand the universe
in a certain way.

The scientist and I both seek to understand for the same human rewards.

I want to understand the universe for the same reasons (other) scientists do,
and I am able to do so in the same way that they do.

Biology

Cognitive		Affective	
Straight Cognitive	Abstract Cognitive	Abstract Affective	Straight Affective
Watson and Crick propose a model of DNA consistent with observed properties: the Double Helix.	Model provides explanation at molecular level for heredity & development of all organisms. / Suggests the possibility of creating life; beginning of genetic engineering.	How will people feel if scientists do create life to specifications? Is it a good idea?	How would you feel if you were an engineered child? Parallel to adopted child.

A new theoretical model can lead to
incredible possibilities for all mankind.

What scientists do may have very
important implications for my life.

I understand some advances in biology and the possible consequences,
and I have some feelings about the uses to which these *should* be put.

Two Examples

issues. Conversely, one might start with a given affective issue, and move to a number of cognitive elements. Thus, the order in which the issue or element is raised is somewhat arbitrary, and depends upon the goals for teaching at a given level, some of which have been discussed above.

The application of this approach to the actual classroom situation can best be illustrated by the following examples:

(A) An instructor brings copies of an original research paper to class. After everyone has read the paper, the instructor explains unfamiliar terms and concepts. All of the content is supplied through such digressions, and only as the students request it. The major thrust is on what the scholar does, on re-experiencing the events that lead to the discovery of important ideas, rather than the accumulation of facts. The students are encouraged to propose criteria by which the paper can be judged. After several hours of discussion, the once formidable paper seems to be riddled with imperfections and ambiguities. Promising avenues for further research emerge from the discussion. The instructor asks the students to select the directions that the research might next move, and makes a note to bring copies of the follow-up papers to the next class meeting.

(B) Another teacher asks her students to pretend that they are Isaac Newton, sitting under an apple tree. After introducing through this fantasy the idea that the moon falls around the earth much as an apple falls on it, she brings the class back to the present with a discussion of how artificial satellites stay in orbit. She then proposes a game in which the students divide into teams to role-play being astronauts in a space station. The astronauts are in an emergency situation and have exactly ten minutes to decide what to do. Afterwards, each team presents its solution. (The students are relieved to find that there is no one, "correct" answer.) The teacher encourages them to discuss also *how* they arrived at their solution.

(C) Another instructor begins her class by asking the students to concentrate on the light reflected by the pigments in a flower. She then leads a guided fantasy asking the students to imagine that they are a photon of light generated at the center of the sun. They follow the path taken by the photon through space, into the Earth's atmosphere, until the photon strikes the flower and is re-emitted to strike the pigment of the eye. Down the hall, a biology class role-plays being groups of atoms in a DNA chain. They perform a dance, illustrating the replication and transcription of the genetic code. In another school, a teacher holds up a Tulip bulb, and asks her students to close their eyes and imagine that they are that bulb, being planted, watered, and then growing into a flower. Afterwards, some of the students write stories about their experience as a flower, others read texts on flowers, and some decide to plant flowers themselves to observe their growth.

While all of the above examples are similar, and might be used in a single day by a single teacher, the first example (A) has a more cognitive, scholarly emphasis with generally implicit affective dimensions (this approach has also been developed extensively by Epstein (6)); the second example (B) emphasizes more affective elements; and the last (C) uses affective processes to emphasize cognitive elements.

DISCUSSION

The concepts presented here have been used by the authors over the past few years as a basis for teacher education courses at the University of

Califonia Extension, and in science courses at the University of California at Santa Cruz and at New College of California. What follows is our impressions based on this experience.

In teaching science at the elementary and secondary levels, teachers and students have responded very readily to the explicit use of fantasy, role-playing and games (as exemplified by (B) and (C) above). In fact, because of the excitement generated by these activities, teachers sometimes report that students are reluctant to return to the more usual cognitive emphasis. At the college and university level, the scholarly approach (A) has been widely, and successfully, used. While the more affective approaches have been applied less, these can be quite useful in appropriate situations. Hewitt's approach (7) is a good example of this, and his text contains some excellent illustrations of the use of fantasy and imagination in teaching descriptive physics at the college level.

It is a common misconception that innovative methods take more time than traditional approaches. It is our experience that, with adequate training in the presentation of affective elements, teaching confluently can take even less time. The scholarly approach particularly has been recommended (6) for research-oriented instructors, postdoctoral fellows and graduate students who would like to teach without serious disruption of their research activities.

ACKNOWLEDGMENTS

The authors would like to thank Stewart Shapiro and George Brown for valuable discussions in beginning this work. This work originated as part of the *Project for Innovative Education* (1971–1972) at the University of California at Santa Cruz, a Kresge College program supported by funds from the Danforth Foundation: a report on this phase of the work is available elsewhere (8).

REFERENCES

1. Brown, G. I., *Human Teaching for Human Learning*, Viking Press, N.Y., 1971.

2. Weinstein, G., and Fantani, M., *Toward a Humanistic Education: A Curriculum of Affect*, Praeger, N.Y., 1971.

3. Ornstein, R. E., *The Psychology of Consciousness*, Freeman, San Francisco, 1972.

4. Polanyi, M., *The Tacit Dimension*, Doubleday, N.Y., 1966.

5. Montz, R. D., "Awareness, Response and Responsibility—A Model of the Confluently Educated Person," DRICE Occasional Paper No. 13, Grad. School of Educ., U. of Cal. Santa Barbara, 1972.

6. Epstein, H. T., *A Strategy for Education*, Oxford University Press, N.Y., 1970.

7. Hewitt, P., *Conceptual Physics—A New Introduction to Your Environment*, Little, Brown & Co., 1971.

8. Mills, D., Scher, S. and Kramarz, R., "To Crash an Airplane: The Project for Innovative Education at UCSC," a report submitted to the Danforth Foundation, 1972.

TOWARD A THEORY OF CREATIVITY[1]*

Carl. R. Rogers

Creativity, A Natural Growth Activity. In Freudian psychology we saw creativity as an act of the unconscious becoming conscious at the moment of insight, or illumination; thus displaying the Freudian preoccupation with the unconscious. Rogers attributes creativity, in a typically humanistic move, to "man's tendency to actualize himself, to become his potentialities." The assumption of this trend toward growth is frequently strong in humanistic educators who see a person as naturally growing and the teacher's role as a helper or facilitator of that natural urge. Like Combs, Rogers sees society's role as removal of threat and as providing a psychologically safe greenhouse in which creativity can blossom. As with Lesh and the other transpersonal psychologists, Rogers values openness to both external and internal reality.

I maintain that there is a desperate social need for the creative behavior of creative individuals. It is this which justifies the setting forth of a tentative theory of creativity—the nature of the creative act, the conditions under which it occurs, and the manner in which it may constructively be fostered. Such a theory may serve as a stimulus and guide to research studies in this field.[1]

THE SOCIAL NEED

Many of the serious criticisms of our culture and its trends may best be formulated in terms of a dearth of creativity. Let us state some of these very briefly:

In education we tend to turn out conformists, stereotypes, individuals whose education is "completed," rather than freely creative and original thinkers.

In our leisure time activities, passive entertainment and regimented group action are overwhelmingly predominant while creative activities are much less in evidence.

In the sciences, there is an ample supply of technicians, but the number who can creatively formulate fruitful hypotheses and theories is small indeed.

In industry, creation is reserved for the few—the manager, the designer, the head of the research department—while for the many life is devoid of original or creative endeavor.

In individual and family life the same picture holds true. In the clothes

From Carl R. Rogers, "Toward a Theory of Creativity," *ETC: A Review of General Semantics,* 11, no. 4 (Summer, 1954): 249–260, by permission of the author. Carl Rogers is Resident Fellow at the Center for Studies of the Person, La Jolla, California. His book, *Freedom to Learn* will especially interest educators.

we wear, the food we eat, the books we read, and the ideas we hold, there is a strong tendency toward conformity, toward stereotype. To be original, or different, is felt to be "dangerous."

Why be concerned over this? If, as a people, we enjoy conformity rather than creativity, shall we not be permitted this choice? In my estimation such a choice would be entirely reasonable were it not for one great shadow which hangs over all of us. In a time when knowledge, constructive and destructive, is advancing by the most incredible leaps and bounds into a fantastic atomic age, genuinely creative adaptation seems to represent the only possibility that man can keep abreast of the kaleido-scopic change in his world. With scientific discovery and invention pro-ceeding, we are told, at the rate of geometric progression, a generally passive and culture-bound people cannot cope with the multiplying issues and problems. Unless individuals, groups, and nations can imagine, con-struct, and creatively revise new ways of relating to these complex changes, the lights will go out. Unless man can make new and original adaptations to his environment as rapidly as his science can change the environment, our culture will perish. Not only individual maladjustment and group tensions, but international annihilation will be the price we pay for a lack of creativity.

Consequently it would seem to me that investigations of the process of creativity, the conditions under which this process occurs, and the ways in which it may be facilitated, are of the utmost importance.

It is in the hope of suggesting a conceptual structure under which such investigations might go forward, that the following sections are offered.

THE CREATIVE PROCESS

There are various ways of defining creativity. In order to make more clear the meaning of what is to follow, let me present the elements which, for me, are a part of the creative process, and then attempt a definition.

In the first place, for me as scientist, there must be something observ-able, some product of creation. Though my fantasies may be extremely novel, they cannot usefully be defined as creative unless they eventuate in some observable product—unless they are symbolized in words, or written in a poem, or translated into a work of art, or fashioned into an invention.

These products must be novel constructions. This novelty grows out of the unique qualities of the individual in his interaction with the materials of experience. Creativity always has the stamp of the individual upon its product, but the product is not the individual, nor his materials, but partakes of the relationship between the two.

Creativity is not, in my judgment, restricted to some particular content. I am assuming that there is no fundamental difference in the creative process as it is evidenced in painting a picture, composing a symphony, devising new instruments of killing, developing a scientific theory, dis-covering new procedures in human relationships, or creating new formings of one's own personality as in psychotherapy. (Indeed it is my experience in this last field, rather than in one of the arts, which has given me special interest in creativity and its facilitation. Intimate knowledge of the way in which the individual remolds himself in the therapeutic relationship, with originality and effective skill, gives one confidence in the creative potential of all individuals.)

My definition, then, of the creative process is that it is the emergence in action of a novel relational product, growing out of the uniqueness of the individual on the one hand, and the materials, events, people, or circumstances of his life on the other.

Let me append some negative footnotes of this definition. It makes no distinction between "good" and "bad" creativity. One man may be discovering a way of relieving pain, while another is devising a new and more subtle form of torture for political prisoners. Both these actions seem to me creative, even though their social value is very different. Though I shall comment on these social valuations later, I have avoided putting them in my definition because they are so fluctuating. Galileo and Copernicus made creative discoveries which in their own day were evaluated as blasphemous and wicked, and in our day as basic and constructive. We do not want to cloud our definition with terms which rest in subjectivity.

Another way of looking at this same issue is to note that to be regarded historically as representing creativity, the product must be acceptable to some group at some point of time. This fact is not helpful to our definition, however, both because of the fluctuating valuations already mentioned, and also because many creative products have undoubtedly never been socially noticed, but have disappeared without ever having been evaluated. So this concept of group acceptance is also omitted from our definition.

In addition, it should be pointed out that our definition makes no distinction regarding the degree of creativity, since this too is a value judgment extremely variable in nature. The action of the child inventing a new game with his playmates; Einstein formulating a theory of relativity; the housewife devising a new sauce for the meat; a young author writing his first novel; all of these are, in terms of our definition, creative, and there is no attempt to set them in some order of more or less creative.

THE MOTIVATION FOR CREATIVITY

The mainspring of creativity appears to be the same tendency which we discover so deeply as the curative force in psychotherapy—*man's tendency to actualize himself, to become his potentialities.* By this I mean the directional trend which is evident in all organic and human life—the urge to expand, extend, develop, mature—the tendency to express and activate all the capacities of the organism, to the extent that such activation enhances the organism or the self. This tendency may become deeply buried under layer after layer of encrusted psychological defenses; it may be hidden behind elaborate facades which deny its existence; it is my belief however, based on my experience, that it exists in every individual, and awaits only the proper conditions to be released and expressed. It is this tendency which is the primary motivation for creativity as the organism forms new relationships to the environment in its endeavor most fully to be itself.

Let us now attempt to deal directly with this puzzling issue of the social value of a creative act. Presumably few of us are interested in facilitating creativity which is socially destructive. We do not wish, knowingly, to lend our efforts to developing individuals whose creative genius works itself out in new and better ways of robbing, exploiting, torturing, killing other individuals; or, developing forms of political organization or art forms which lead humanity into paths of physical or psychological self-destruction. Yet how is it possible to make the necessary discriminations such that we may encourage a constructive creativity and not a destructive?

The distinction cannot be made by examining the product. The very essence of the creative is its novelty, and hence we have no standard by which to judge it. Indeed history points up the fact that the more original the product, and the more far-reaching its implications, the more likely it is to be judged by contemporaries as evil. The genuinely significant creation, whether an idea, or a work of art, or a scientific discovery, is most likely to be seen at first as erroneous, bad, or foolish. Later it may be seen as obvious, something self-evident to all. Only still later does it receive its final evaluation as a creative contribution. It seems clear that no contemporary mortal can satisfactorily evaluate a creative product at the time that it is formed, and this statement is increasingly true the greater the novelty of the creation.

Nor is it of any help to examine the purposes of the individual participating in the creative process. Many, perhaps most, of the creations and discoveries which have proved to have great social value, have been motivated by purposes having more to do with personal interest than with social value, while on the other hand history records a somewhat sorry outcome for many of those creations (various Utopias, Prohibition, etc.) which had as their avowed purpose the achievement of the social good. No, we must face the fact that the individual creates primarily because it is satisfying to him, because this behavior is felt to be self-actualizing, and we get nowhere by trying to differentiate "good" and "bad" purposes in the creative process.

Must we then give over any attempt to discriminate between creativity which is potentially constructive, and that which is potentially destructive? I do not believe this pessimistic conclusion is justified. It is here that recent clinical findings from the field of psychotherapy give us hope. It has been found that when the individual is "open" to all of his experience (a phrase which will be defined more fully), then his behavior will be creative, and his creativity may be trusted to be essentially constructive.

The differentiation may be put very briefly as follows. To the extent that the individual is denying to awareness (or repressing, if you prefer that term) large areas of his experience, then his creative formings may be pathological, or socially evil, or both. To the degree that the individual is open to all aspects of his experience, and has available to his awareness all the varied sensings and perceivings which are going on within his organism, then the novel products of his interaction with his environment will tend to be constructive both for himself and others. To illustrate, an individual with paranoid tendencies may creatively develop a most novel theory of the relationship between himself and his environment, seeing evidence for his theory in all sorts of minute clues. His theory has little social value, perhaps because there is an enormous range of experience which this individual cannot permit in his awareness. Socrates, on the other hand, while also regarded as "crazy" by his contemporaries, developed novel ideas which have proven to be socially constructive. Very possibly this was because he was notably nondefensive and open to his experience.

The reasoning behind this will perhaps become more clear in the remaining sections of this paper. Primarily however it is based upon the discovery in psychotherapy

> ... that if we can add to the sensory and visceral experiencing which is characteristic of the whole animal kingdom the gift of a free and undistorted awareness of which only the human animal seems fully capable, we have an organism which is as aware of the demands of the culture as it is of its own physiological demands for food or sex; which is just as aware of its desire for friendly relationships as it is of its desire to aggrandize itself; which is just as aware of its delicate and sensitive tenderness toward others as it is of its hostilities toward others. When man's unique capacity of awareness is thus functioning freely and fully, we find that we have, not an animal whom we must fear, not a beast who must be controlled, but an organism able to achieve, through the remarkable integrative capacity of its central nervous system, a balanced, realistic, self-enhancing, other-enhancing behavior as a resultant of all these elements of awareness. To put it another way, when man is less than fully man—when he denies to awareness various aspects of his experience—then indeed we have all too often reason to fear him and his behavior, as the present world situation testifies. But when he is most fully man, when he is his complete organism, when awareness of experience, that peculiarly human attribute, is most fully operating, then he is to be trusted, then his behavior is constructive. It is not always conventional. It will not always be conforming. It will be individualized. But it will also be socialized.[2]

THE INNER CONDITIONS OF CONSTRUCTIVE CREATIVITY

What are the conditions within the individual which are most closely associated with a potentially constructive creative act? I see these as possibilities.

A. Openness to experience: Extensionality. This is the opposite of psychological defensiveness, when to protect the organization of the self, certain experiences are prevented from coming into awareness except in distorted fashion. In a person who is open to experience each stimulus is freely relayed through the nervous system, without being distorted by any process of defensiveness. Whether the stimulus originates in the environment, in the impact of form, color, or sound, on the sensory nerves, or whether it originates in the viscera, or as a memory trace in the central nervous system, it is available to awareness. This means that instead of perceiving in predetermined categories ("trees are green," "college education is good," "modern art is silly") the individual is aware of this existential moment as *it* is, thus being alive to many experiences which fall outside the usual categories (*this* tree is lavender; *this* college education is damaging; *this* modern sculpture has a powerful effect on me).

This last suggests another way of describing openness to experience. It means lack of rigidity and permeability of boundaries in concepts, beliefs, perceptions, and hypotheses. It means a tolerance for ambiguity where ambiguity exists. It means the ability to receive much conflicting information without forcing closure upon the situation. It means what the general semanticist calls the "extensional orientation."

This complete openness of awareness to what exists at this moment is, I believe, an important condition of constructive creativity. In an equally intense but more narrowly limited fashion it is no doubt present in all creativity. The deeply maladjusted artist who cannot recognize or be aware of the sources of unhappiness in himself, may nevertheless be sharply and sensitively aware of form and color in his experience. The tyrant (whether on a petty or grand scale) who cannot face the weaknesses in himself may nevertheless be completely alive to and aware of the chinks in the psychological armor of those with whom he deals. Because there is the openness to one phase of experience, creativity is possible; because the openness is *only* to one phase of experience, the product of this creativity may be potentially destructive of social values. The more the individual has available to himself a sensitive awareness of all phases of his experience, the more sure we can be that his creativity will be personally and socially constructive.

B. An internal locus of evaluation. Perhaps the most fundamental condition of creativity is that the source or locus of evaluative judgment is internal. The value of his product is, for the creative person, established not by the praise or criticism of others, but by himself. Have I created something satisfying to *me*? Does it express a part of me—my feeling or my thought, my pain or my ecstasy? These are the only questions which really matter to the creative person, or to any person when he is being creative.

This does not mean that he is oblivious to, or unwilling to be aware of, the judgments of others. It is simply that the basis of evaluation lies within himself, in his own organismic reaction to and appraisal of his product. If to the person it has the "feel" of being "me in action," of being an actualization of potentialities in himself which heretofore have not existed and are now emerging into existence, then it is satisfying and creative, and no outside evaluation can change that fundamental fact.

C. The ability to toy with elements and concepts. Though this is probably less important than A or B, it seems to be a condition of creativity. Associated with the openness and lack of rigidity described under A is the ability to play spontaneously with ideas, colors, shapes, relationships—to juggle elements into impossible juxtapositions, to shape wild hypotheses, to make the given problematic, to express the ridiculous, to translate from one form to another, to transform into improbable equivalents. It is from this spontaneous toying and exploration that there arises the hunch, the creative seeing of life in a new and significant way. It is as though out of the wasteful spawning of thousands of possibilities there emerges one or two evolutionary forms with the qualities which give them a more permanent value.

THE CREATIVE ACT AND ITS CONCOMITANTS

When these three conditions obtain, constructive creativity will occur. But we cannot expect an accurate description of the creative act, for by its very nature it is indescribable. This is the unknown which we must recognize as unknowable until it occurs. This is the improbable that becomes probable. Only in a very general way can we say that a creative act is the natural behavior of an organism which has a tendency to arise when that organism is open to all of its inner and outer experiencing, and when it is free to try out in flexible fashion all manner of relationships. Out of this multitude of half-formed possibilities the organism, like a great computing machine, selects this one which most effectively meets an inner need, or that one which forms a more effective relationship with the environment, or this other one which discovers a more simple and satisfying order in which life may be perceived.

There is one quality of the creative act which may, however, be described. In almost all the products of creation we note a selectivity, or emphasis, an evidence of discipline, an attempt to bring out the essence. The artist paints surfaces or textures in simplified form, ignoring the minute variations which exist in reality. The scientist formulates a basic law of relationships, brushing aside all the particular events or circumstances which might conceal its naked beauty. The writer selects those words and phrases which give unity to his expression. We may say that this is the influence of the specific person, of the "I." Reality exists in a multiplicity of confusing facts, but "I" bring a structure in my relationship to reality; I have "my" way of perceiving reality, and it is this (unconsciously?) disciplined personal selectivity or abstraction which gives to creative products their esthetic quality.

Though this is as far as we can go in describing any aspect of the creative act, there are certain of its concomitants in the individual which may be mentioned. The first is what we may call the Eureka feeling—

"This is *it*!" "I have discovered!" "This is what I wanted to express!"

Another concomitant is the anxiety of separateness.[3] I do not believe that many significantly creative products are formed without the feeling, "I am alone. No one has ever done just this before. I have ventured into territory where no one has been. Perhaps I am foolish, or wrong, or lost, or abnormal."

Still another experience which usually accompanies creativity is the desire to communicate. It is doubtful whether a human being can create, without wishing to share his creation. It is the only way he can assuage the anxiety of separateness and assure himself that he belongs to the group. He may confide his theories only to his private diary. He may put his discoveries in some cryptic code. He may conceal his poems in a locked drawer. He may put away his paintings in a closet. Yet he desires to communicate with a group which will understand him, even if he must imagine such a group. He does not create in order to communicate, but once having created he desires to share this new aspect of himself-in-relation-to-his-environment with others.

CONDITIONS FOSTERING CONSTRUCTIVE CREATIVITY

Thus far I have tried to describe the nature of creativity, to indicate that quality of individual experience which increases the likelihood that creativity will be constructive, to set forth the necessary conditions for the creative act and to state some of its concomitants. But if we are to make progress in meeting the social need which was presented initially, we must know whether constructive creativity can be fostered, and if so, how.

From the very nature of the inner conditions of creativity it is clear that they cannot be forced, but must be permitted to emerge. The farmer cannot make the germ develop and sprout from the seed; he can only supply the nurturing conditions which will permit the seed to develop its own potentialities. So it is with creativity. How can we establish the external condition which will foster and nourish the internal conditions described above? My experience in psychotherapy leads me to believe that by setting up conditions of psychological safety and freedom, we maximize the likelihood of an emergence of constructive creativity. Let me spell out these conditions in some detail, labelling them as X and Y.

X. Psychological safety. This may be established by three associated processes.
1. Accepting the individual as of unconditional worth. Whenever a teacher, parent, therapist, or other person with a facilitating function feels basically that this individual is of worth in his own right and in his own unfolding, no matter what his present condition or behavior, he is fostering creativity. This attitude can probably be genuine only when the teacher, parent, etc., senses the potentialities of the individual and thus is able to have an unconditional faith in him, no matter what his present state.

The effect on the individual as he apprehends this attitude, is to sense a climate of safety. He gradually learns that he can be whatever he is, without sham or facade, since he seems to be regarded as of worth no matter what he does. Hence he has less need of rigidity, can discover what it means to be himself, can try to actualize himself in new and spontaneous ways. He is, in other words, moving toward creativity.

2. Providing a climate in which external evaluation is absent. When we cease to form judgments of the other individual from our own locus of evaluation, we are fostering creativity. For the individual to find himself in an atmosphere where he is not being evaluated, not being measured by some external standard, is enormously freeing. Evaluation is always a threat, always creates a need for defensiveness, always means that some portion of experience must be denied to awareness. If this product is evaluated as good by external standards, then I must not admit my own dislike of it. If what I am doing is bad by external standards, then I must not be aware of the fact that it seems to be me, to be part of myself. But if judgments based on external standards are not being made then I can be more open to my experience, can recognize my own likings and dislikings, the nature of the materials and of my reaction to them, more sharply and more sensitively. I can begin to recognize the locus of evaluation within myself. Hence I am moving toward creativity.

To allay some possible doubts and fears in the reader, it should be pointed out that to cease evaluating another is not to cease having reactions. It may, as a matter of fact, free one to react. "I don't like your idea" (or painting, or invention, or writing), is not an evaluation, but a reaction. It is subtly but sharply different from a judgment which says, "What you are doing is bad (or good), and this quality is assigned to you from some external source." The first statement permits the individual to maintain his own locus of evaluation. It holds the possibility that I am unable to appreciate something which is actually very good. The second statement, whether it praises or condemns, tends to put the person at the mercy of outside forces. He is being told that he cannot simply ask himself whether this product is a valid expression of himself; he must be concerned with what others think. He is being led away from creativity.

3. Understanding empathically. It is this which provides the ultimate in psychological safety, when added to the other two. If I say that I "accept" you, but know nothing of you, this is a shallow acceptance indeed, and you realize that it may change if I actually come to know you. But if I understand you empathically, see you and what you are feeling and doing from your point of view, enter your private world and see it as it appears to you—and still accept you—then this is safety indeed. In this climate you can permit your real self to emerge, and to express itself in varied and novel formings as it relates itself to the world. This is a basic fostering of creativity.

Y. Psychological freedom. When a teacher, parent, therapist, or other facilitating person permits the individual a complete freedom of symbolic expression, creativity is fostered. This permissiveness gives the individual complete freedom to think, to feel, to be, whatever is most inward within himself. It fosters the openness, and the playful and spontaneous juggling of percepts, concepts, and meanings, which is a part of creativity.

Note that it is complete freedom of *symbolic* expression which is described. To express in behavior all feelings, impulses, and formings may not in all instances be freeing. Behavior may in some instances be limited by society, and this is as it should be. But symbolic expression need not be limited. Thus to destroy a hated object (whether one's mother or a rococo building) by destroying a symbol of it, is freeing. To attack it in reality may create guilt and narrow the psychological freedom which is experienced. (I feel unsure of this paragraph, but it is the best formulation I can give at the moment which seems to square with my experience.)

The permissiveness which is being described is not softness or indulgence or encouragement. It is permission to be *free*, which also means that one is responsible. The individual is as free to be afraid of a new venture as to be eager for it; free to bear the consequences of his mistakes as well as of his achievements. It is this type of freedom, responsibly to be oneself, which fosters the development of a secure locus of evaluation within oneself, and hence tends to bring about the inner conditions of constructive creativity.

PUTTING THE THEORY TO WORK

There is but one excuse for attempting to discover conceptual order and stating it in a theory; that is to develop hypotheses from the theory which may be tested. By such testing profitable directions for action may be found, and the theory itself may be corrected, modified, and extended. Thus if this theory which I have tentatively formulated is worthwhile, it should be possible to develop from it hypotheses which might be objectively tested in classes in the arts; in education outside of the arts; in leadership training groups whether in industry or the military services; in problem-solving groups of any sort. Let me suggest a few of the general hypotheses which might be given more specific and operational form for any of the above groups. They would apply whether one was concerned with the development of creative artists or creative leaders; with originality of design or creative methods of problem-solving.

Hypotheses regarding inner conditions. 1. Individuals who exhibit a measurably greater degree of conditions A, B and C (openness, internal locus of evaluation, ability to toy with materials) will, over any given period of time spontaneously form more products judged to be novel and creative, than a matched group who exhibit a lesser degree of A, B and C.

2. The products of the first group will not only be more numerous, but

will be judged to be more significant in their novelty. (Such a hypothesis could be given operational definition in art classes, problem-solving groups, or leadership training groups, for example.)

3. Condition A (openness to experience) can be predicted from conditions B or C, which are more easily measurable. (It is not at all certain that this hypothesis would be upheld, but it would be worth careful investigation. If conditions A, B and C are highly intercorrelated, then they could jointly be predicted from the one which proved most easily measurable. Thus we might gain clues as to how we might less laboriously select graduate students, for example, with a high creative potential.)

Hypotheses re: fostering constructive creativity. 4. Given two matched groups, the one in which the leader establishes a measurably greater degree of conditions X1, X2, X3 and Y (psychological safety and freedom) will spontaneously form a greater number of creative products, and these products will be judged to be more significantly novel.

5. Conditions X1, X2, X3 and Y are not of equal importance in fostering creativity. By comparing different groups in which one or another of these conditions is emphasized or minimized it may be possible to determine which of these conditions is most effective in facilitating creativity.

6. A group in which conditions X1, X2, X3 and Y are established should, according to our theory, have more effective and harmonious interpersonal relationships than a matched group in which these conditions are present to a lesser degree. (The reasoning is that if creativity is all of a piece, then a group in which the fostering conditions are established should be more constructively creative in social relationships.)

7. The extent to which different groups in our culture provide the fostering conditions (X and Y) could be measured. In this way one could determine whether creativity is now being fostered to a greater degree by the family group, classes in schools and colleges, bull sessions, social clubs and groups, interest groups, military groups, industrial groups. (One wonders how college classes would show up in such a comparison.)

CONCLUSION

I have endeavored to present an orderly way of thinking about the creative process, in order that some of these ideas might be put to a rigorous and objective test. My justification for formulating this theory, and my reason for hoping that such research may be carried out is that the present development of the physical sciences is making an imperative demand upon us as individuals and as a culture, for creative behavior in adapting ourselves to our new world if we are to survive.

NOTES

[1]That I am much indebted to the thinking of others will frequently be evident, but especially I am indebted to the Conference on Creativity called together by a sponsoring group from Ohio State University, which nourished and vitalized my thinking and led me to produce the rough notes upon which this paper is based. The Conference was held at Granville, Ohio, December 5–8, 1952.

[2]From "Some of the Directions and End Points of Therapy," by Carl R. Rogers, in *Psychotherapy—Theory and Research Methods*, ed. by O. H. Mowrer (New York: Ronald Press, 1953).

[3]For this and the idea in the following paragraph I am specifically indebted to my student and colleague, Mr. Robert Lipgar.

EVALUATING SENSITIVITY TRAINING FOR TEEN-AGERS *

Charlotte Himber

Feelings: Learning a Humanistic Potential. Several humanistic ideas show through Himber's article and relate her ideas and observations to other authors in this book. The emphasis on the importance of self-knowledge and exploring one's inner world of feelings echoes many of the Freudian authors, especially Kubie. The connection between self-acceptance and learning to get along with others is picked up by Jersild and Bower in the Freudian tradition and Lesh, who writes from a transpersonal orientation. The emphasis on belonging to a group and developing one's potentials through group membership show in Tenenbaum's article on group therapy as well as here. Both Erikson and Roberts say that adolescence is a period of peer-orientation too, and this article describes a kind of education that is especially appropriate to learning healthy interpersonal relations. While the studies of sensitivity training, like anything else, show mixed results, the preponderance of them support Himber's conclusions and show that scores of self-actualization usually increase too.

At a meeting of some 43 trained staff leaders of the teen-agers' sensitivity training program for the YMCA, psychologist Jack Gibb, who was consultant for the program, commented: "There's no book that says all the things that kids feel have happened, or describes how tremendously life has changed."

Throughout the Young Men's Christian Associations in the United States, more than 7,000 teen-agers have participated in sensitivity training experiences, ranging from three-day weekends to 10-day laboratories. Some form of evaluation is usually built in as part of the program design. One formal study evaluating the "Self-Perceived Gains" of teen-agers was made in 1968 (643 were sent questionnaires, of whom 420 responded). A follow-up to the same subjects six months later largely corroborated the first overwhelmingly positive findings. Many other interactional programs using sensitivity training with teen-agers have been introduced, and the results are sufficiently positive in the YMCA to warrant wider exploration with this type of program for young people.

A boy in his teens experiencing sensitivity training remarks:

I realize what a phony I am. Everybody thinks I'm a happy-go-lucky. Inside I'm always worrying.

*From Charlotte Himber, "Evaluating Sensitivity Training for Teenagers," *Journal of Applied Behavioral Science* 6 (July, 1970): 307–322, by permission of the author. Charlotte Himber is Editor of the *Y-Circulator*, a professional YMCA directors' publication.

But now I'm not so happy-go-lucky outside. You guys here keep sayin' how serious I am. And it seems to me, the more I can let you in on how serious I am, the more happy-go-lucky it makes me feel *inside*. [Shaking his head and clicking his tongue] It's a funny thing.

Two behavioral scientists reporting on a review and analysis of 44 research efforts to determine the effectiveness of T-Group experiences in managerial training and development conclude: "The evidence, *though limited*, is reasonably convincing that T-Group training does induce behavioral changes in the 'back-home' setting, but the utility of these changes for the performance of individuals in their organizational roles remains to be demonstrated."[1]

My attention in this investigation was focused on the first part of the behavioral scientists' conclusion. I compared their interpretation of the personal growth aspect of a laboratory training experience with the YMCA's assessment of its sensitivity training programs for teen-agers. They describe as "limited" even the positive findings claimed by the research. I labored through their impersonal professional discourse and was depressed by the tenuousness of the supporting research evidence. Anyone who has experienced, over and over, living with teen-agers during and after sensitivity training must be discouraged by such weak affirmations of a process that thousands of participants have declared to be electrifying in its influence on their lives. The researchers of the researches conclude that it is not so much the T-Group experience itself which is in trouble as the research designs which have been used. They mention "lack of control, zero degrees of freedom, susceptibility to contaminating influences." Their suggestions for the type of research that is needed warrant fuller treatment, not to be attempted in this article. But Campbell and Dunnette's look at the stubborn, puzzling question—*"How do you prove it works?"* —is important as a preface to what I am about to describe, because it puts into proper focus the YMCA story.

Statistics confirm that most teen-agers who are offered sensitivity training as one of the YMCA approaches with this constituency respond dramatically to the experience. But also, I have my own personal experiences as a group leader.

Let us take the story of Steve who had been hating his mother for four years out of loyalty to his estranged father. In a psychodrama session (which teen-agers do so effectively) he plays the parts of his father, his mother, and his 12-year-old brother who is "spoiled rotten" by the mother. Ellen declares he has done a "stupid" performance as the mother and plays out her version. He sees his mother for the first time as bereft, pleading for some affectionate support from the 12-year-old, in the face of Steve's hostility. Ellen as mother suddenly stirs a denied emotion in Steve, and tears of release spring to his eyes when he allows himself to acknowledge love for his mother. Dick, who two days earlier had vociferated that men who are masculine rarely show emotion, now rushes up to put an arm around Steve; they lock in an embrace. Back at home, Steve may not mention a word of what went on, but the family benefits enormously. The YMCA learns of this from a parent's letter to Steve's club adviser: "He has been a changed person—a joy to have around—ever since. . . ."

Over the years we at the YMCA continue to struggle with our vulnerability, like other agencies and researchers who attempt to study the effects of sensitivity training, to the skepticism of critics about the conclusions we are willing to draw based on these—possibly "contaminated"—researches. It is my hope that the following summaries describing our evaluations will be as convincing and as supportive of our program to others as they are to us.

Beginning in 1948, when Tilden Harrison[2] attended a human relations laboratory at Bethel, Maine, the YMCA introduced sensitivity training for staff or leaders as a way of working with groups.[3] The use of sensitivity training with teen-age youth was pioneered in the San Francisco YMCA by V. M. Robertson, who is continually developing and testing methods for working with young people. The YMCA program in the United States has enabled more than 7,000 teen-agers to participate in sensitivity training experiences, ranging from three-day weekends to 10-day laboratories. Some form of evaluation is usually built in as part of the program design. In a few instances a more sophisticated type of research has been utilized, as evidenced in the latest study of "Self-Perceived Gains by Adolescents," 643 of whom participated in a sensitivity training session totaling approximately 28 hours during a six-day period.

The YMCA has been experimenting with a variety of other sensitivity training programs and examining the results. Because the report on "Self-Perceived Gains by Adolescents" is the most comprehensive evaluation and the most recent, I shall deal with it first and in greater detail.

SELF-PERCEIVED GAINS BY ADOLESCENTS

Immediate Postlaboratory Questionnaire One. All the information and data on a sensitivity laboratory offered to participants in the Twelfth National Hi-Y Assembly held at St. Olaf College in Northfield, Minnesota, July 2 to 8, 1968, were studied and reported in a carefully prepared document by YMCA executives V. M. Robertson and Stan Wallace. Several verbatim sections and tables from their 45-page report have been included here in an effort to represent the nature of the self-perceived gains by adolescents from this experience.

This event was an authorized program of the National Council of YMCAs. From an attendance of approximately 825, about 650 were participants of high school age. The remainder were college-age dormitory counselors, adults who came as supervisors of local delegations, and the training staff.

There were two main components of the program. Each youth delegate was assigned to a "Development" Group of 12 to 14 members and an adult trainer. These groups were scheduled for 12 sessions, totaling approximately 28 hours of meeting time. Another nine hours were devoted to the second component—six general assemblies. These were largely nonverbal experiences designed to help individuals focus on self and to have the experience of relating to others.

Jack Gibb, formerly with the Western Behavioral Sciences Institute, who works with industrial, educational, and government organizations, was the consultant for the total conference. He conducted the nonverbal experience for the entire attendance of 825 during these general assemblies.

Following the Assembly, a questionnaire was mailed to each participant. Respondents were asked (1) to indicate the extent to which they had changed either positively or negatively as a result of the experience, (2) to answer an open-ended question "What did you get out of the experience?" and (3) to check the degree in which six statements of potential learning were true for them. A similar questionnaire was sent to the trainers. The researchers were able to match the responses of 28 trainers who returned the questionnaire with the responses of 244 youths who had been in their groups.

A question arose as to whether those who did not respond (31 percent) might have refrained because they were less enthusiastic than the respondents about the experience. Inspection of the returns, however, seemed to indicate that strong negative feelings might have been as motivating as strong positive ones in filling out the questionnaire.

The first question asked was for a general overall reaction: "How much do you think you have changed because of things which happened to you at the Assembly?" Like all the other questions in this study, this question deals strictly with a youth's self-perception. We are aware that eyebrows are sometimes raised at the subjectivity of such a procedure, but no one can seriously quarrel with a youth who is honestly telling you how he feels. It is important to recognize that one who sees himself as having moved from one point to another on a behavior scale is highly motivated to act according to such a perception. For example, a youth who says, "I find myself searching for the true feelings of others now more so than before," is probably really trying to do so. The one who says, "I learned to express my feelings without being so embarrassed," is more likely to take the risk of self-disclosure. The youths who said, "I learned I'm not so open as I thought I was," and, "I realized that I was a fake—and didn't have to be," may have made themselves more available for change as a result of such insight.

Over two-thirds of the participants indicated that they had changed either "much" or "a great deal" because of the experience. The responses they made to the question "What are the most important things you got out of the experience?" follow in Table 1.

The questionnaire also elicited responses in six areas of potential learning for respondents: understanding of *self*; learning about *groups*; the extent of feeling "I am a *lovable* person"; experiencing *closeness*; accept-

TABLE 1.

Teen-Agers' Answers to Question, "What Are the Most Important Things You Got Out of the Experience?"

	RANK AND NUMBER (by frequency of mention)		
	Total	Boys	Girls
Better understanding of others	1 (218)	2 (90)	1 (128)
Increased self-identity	2 (200)	1 (91)	2 (109)
Making new friends	3 (94)	3 (40)	3 (54)
Better able to express self	4 (69)	9 (18)	4 (51)
Increased trust	5 (68)	5 (11)	5-6 (47)
Reaching out to others	6-7 (64)	6-7 (20)	7 (44)
Experiencing love	6-7 (64)	10 (27)	5-6 (47)
Less prejudice	8 (61)	4 (22)	9 (39)
More accepting of others	9 (57)	6-7 (20)	10 (37)
More open, less facade	10-11 (54)	12 (14)	8 (40)
Experiencing closeness	10-11 (54)	8 (19)	11 (35)
Back-home dividends	22 (49)	11 (16)	12 (33)
More confidence	13 (40)	11 (14)	14 (25)
Acceptance of others	14 (38)	14-15 (12)	13 (25)
Nonverbal relating	15 (31)	14-15 (12)	15 (19)
More autonomy	16 (27)	16 (11)	16 (16)
Willingness to risk	19-20 (17)	20-22 (3)	17-19 (14)
Feeling needed	19-20 (17)	20-22 (3)	17-19 (14)
Feeling I am lovable	17-18 (18)	19 (4)	17-19 (14)
Knowing how I affect others	17-18 (18)	18 (6)	20 (11)
Acceptance of feedback	21 (16)	17 (10)	21 (6)
Being understood	22 (5)	20-22 (3)	21 (2)

N = 430

ing the *uniqueness* of others; and the feeling of being *wanted*. Respondents were to indicate whether in each area learning was (1) *not true for me*, (2) *a little true*, (3) *somewhat true*, (4) *true for me*, or (5) *very true*.

Reproduced herewith is one of the final tables designed to summarize the preceding tables in the report. It is derived by adding the top two responses *true for me* and *very true* to form a *high* (H) score and adding the two bottom responses *not true for me* and *a little true* to make a *low* (L) score. The middle response, *somewhat true*, is omitted. The third column is a ratio of *high* to *low* (H/L) and gives an indication of the "positiveness" of the responses in each category. (See Table 2 and subsequent explanation.)

Girls tend to rate all experiences more positively than do boys. This tendency is most evident when "high" scores of boys and girls are compared. Such a comparison shows that there is a significant difference (at the .05 level) for the categories, *Self, Lovable, Uniqueness, Wanted,* and possibly for *Groups*. However, comparison of "low" scores for

TABLE 2.

Comparison of High and Low Responses of Teen-Agers to Six Questions About Potential Learning Areas

	Boys			Girls			Totals		
	H	L	H/L	H	L	H/L	H	L	H/L
Self	65	12	5-4	79	9	8.8	72	11	6.3
Groups	68	9	7-5	77	7	11.0	73	9	8.1
Lovable	47	27	1.7	62	10	6.2	56	19	2.9
Closeness	83	6	13.8	93	3	31.2	89	4	22.2
Uniqueness	77	7	11.0	84	3	28.0	81	5	16.2
Wanted	67	25	4.3	84	6	14.0	77	9	3.6

N = 439

Lovable and *Wanted* also indicates a significant difference (at the .05 level) between the two sexes. Nearly all variations can be accounted for in the boys' greater reluctance to say "Very true." The similarity of the distributions suggests that the boy-girl difference is mainly a difference in language usage between the two sexes.

Comparison with Trainers' Responses. Enough responses came in from 28 trainers so that the researchers could match those alongside the statements of 284 youths who had been in their particular groups. The trainers rated the participant's experience lower than did the participant himself, but their scores provide some validation for the teen-agers' responses. The average overall response of youths to all six questions was 4--*true for me.* The average rating of the 28 trainers was 3.5, which is between *somewhat true* and *true for me.* There was greatest agreement on *feeling lovable* and *experiencing closeness.* Researchers Robertson and Wallace suggest that the trainer was using a different norm or base from that used by the youths. The sensitivity group experiences at the Hi-Y Assembly were new for most participants. The trainers, on the other hand, were experienced in the various processes (both verbal and nonverbal) and therefore might have been less dramatically affected.

One cannot help being impressed that there was in fact considerable agreement in the evaluation of two significant aspects of awareness and self-perception—"feeling lovable" and "experiencing closeness"—since such corroboration does seem to support the validity of self-perceived evaluations of sensitivity training.

Teen-Agers' Comments. There seemed overwhelming confirmation that the youths had achieved more insight into themselves. Self-identity and self-acceptance—so essential for this age group to achieve—were constantly mentioned. Teen-age participants felt that they had become more open, more affectionate, more wanted, and more willing to try to express themselves. They said that they understood others, trusted others more, and accepted others' differences.

Here are a few quotations out of the long, detailed, and effusive paragraphs these teen-agers included gratuitously in their reports.

> I learned that "every day is the first day of the beginning of the rest of [my] life."

> Another change in me started my seeing life through other people's eyes. Now I really believe I can put myself in another's shoes, and feel how life is to them. I guess this is the result of becoming so close to some of the black people there.

> The conference made me feel more alive and vibrant than I have felt for many months.

> For the first time in my life I got the feeling of being wanted and accepted by a group. I also learned to be at ease around other people and react to their feelings.

> I learned that I'm not so open as I thought I was.

> I learned that I'm afraid.

> I have been part of a group where I was not looked on as an outsider because I'm a *black* man.

> My problem was that I could never talk around people. I didn't know, so of course at the Assembly I didn't say too much. But they encouraged me to participate more and feel wanted. I guess that was the most important thing that happened. Instead of always taking myself down, I'm going to try to feel just as good as everyone else.

> I learned how to express my feelings and emotions a lot better. My group gave me assurance that I wouldn't be rejected and I wasn't.

> The first thing I got out of this experience was that I didn't realize what kind of impression I had made on people until the conference.

TEEN-AGERS' RESPONSES SIX MONTHS LATER

Questionnaire Two. In time for inclusion with this article I have received a report of a follow-up procedure by the same research team. Robertson and Wallace mailed out a follow-up questionnaire to the respondents six months after the Hi-Y Assembly at St. Olaf. They studied the replies of the teen-agers in which the respondents identified behavioral changes in themselves *six months later*, as a result of sensitivity training. Results were measured from 384 respondents who had filled out both Questionnaire 1 in 1968 and Questionnaire 2 in 1969.

Eighty-five percent of the responses to the second questionnaire (Q_2) were within a ±1 range of the original score. Five percent showed a gain, and 10 percent of the scores showed regression. *The high positive response to the first questionnaire was in a substantial degree present six months later.*

The least amount of change between the first and second measures was in *closeness to others. The feeling of being wanted* showed the greatest regression. *Learning about groups* reflected the most gain. It should be noted that there was a range of only 5 percentage points between the highest and lowest indicator.

The most common pattern (44 percent) in the Q_2 returns showed all six scores of participants to be within ±1 of the original score. In 29 percent there was a regression of 2 or more points in one or more scores. Sixteen percent of the individuals showed gains in one or more scores of at least 2 points. Ten percent showed both regression and gain.

The boy–girl differential which was apparent in the Q_1 returns was duplicated in the returns to the second questionnaire.

In the answers to the question "Are you now behaving differently because of the Assembly experience?" the most frequent responses specified *better understanding of others, increased self-identity, more acceptance of others, increased trust, openness and availability, increased ability to express self*, and *greater autonomy.*

Ninety percent of all youth participants responded to either Q_1 or Q_2 or both. There is no indication that the remaining 10 percent differ in any significant way.

Table 3, which compares the overall returns of Q_1 and Q_2 responses, shows variations in the upper three categories: "somewhat true," "true," and "very true." There is apparently a slippage from the top category, "very true," to the next category, "true," and from "true" to "somewhat true." Thus the overall response, while somewhat less positive, remains unquestionably positive.

It is noteworthy that the original group, from whose reactions the teen-agers derived their initial impression of "closeness," "being wanted," and "lovable" has never again met as a group. Their second response is derived largely from how they see themselves generally in a normal environment consisting of people who had not participated with them in the St. Olaf experience. This seems to me, therefore, a remarkable affirmation of the value of the sensitivity training experience as these teen-agers perceive it.

Researchers Robertson and Wallace conclude their second inquiry with the following statement:

> For nearly a year the authors have been immersed in the event of sensitivity training at this teen-agers' Assembly: being there, experiencing some of the things the kids write about, serving as trainers in the small groups, conducting the two inquiries. We now feel that we know something of the nature of what the gains were.
>
> First of all, the Assembly provided an experience in closeness to others. Kids were members of small groups in which the focus was upon themselves and their

TABLE 3.

Comparison of Q_1 (N=445) and Q_2 (N=491) Frequency Scores for Six Measures of Learning from Sensitivity Training

	Understanding of Self				Learning About Groups				Feeling I Am Lovable				Being Close to Others				Accepting Uniqueness of Others				Feeling Wanted			
	Q_1	N	Q_2	N	Q_1	N	Q_2	N	Q_1	N	Q_2	N	Q_1	N	Q_2	N	Q_1	N	Q_2	N	Q_1	N	Q_2	N
Not true	3%	(13)	3%	(14)	2%	(7)	1%	(5)	3%	(13)	8%	(37)	2%	(6)	3%	(13)	1%	(6)	2%	(12)	3%	(15)	4%	(11)
A little true	8	(13)	7	(32)	7	(29)	4	(10)	14	(61)	12	(59)	3	(15)	4	(20)	4	(17)	2	(11)	5	(18)	8	(38)
Somewhat true	17	(74)	25	(119)	19	(24)	23	(111)	25	(111)	34	(163)	7	(19)	10	(51)	14	(42)	12	(60)	13	(59)	22	(104)
True	38	(169)	39	(188)	37	(165)	40	(197)	28	(124)	28	(136)	17	(74)	27	(133)	34	(148)	35	(172)	24	(104)	32	(149)
Very true	34	(154)	37	(133)	36	(158)	32	(156)	28	(223)	19	(91)	72	(315)	56	(270)	47	(210)	47	(230)	53	(233)	59	(168)
T	100	(442)	101	(436)	101	(443)	100	(489)	100	(442)	101	(486)	100	(439)	100	(437)	100	(443)	94	(486)	98	(439)	100	(480)

relations to others in the group. The result was essentially humanizing, an experience of learning to care for others and of being cared for. In these groups participants learned to experience others as unique human beings. They felt wanted. Many members took home with them a new view of what relating to others in more than superficial ways could really mean.

The second gain has to do with the growth of self; more awareness, more understanding, perhaps more acceptance of their own worth and individuality. The increase in self-appreciation was in our judgment one of the signal achievements of the Assembly.

OTHER SENSITIVITY TRAINING EVALUATION STUDIES

Experiment with Styles of Leadership. The teen-agers' program of the previous Hi-Y Assembly in 1965 was also designed to give each participant a sensitivity training experience. However, groups were organized under four different types of leadership: (a) adult leader, (b) teen-age leader, (c) one adult and one teen-age leader in the same group, and (d) leaderless. The purpose of this design was to determine whether various types of leadership in adolescent sensitivity training groups made any significant differences in the development of either the groups or the individual participants.

Measuring growth from the third to the eleventh session, the factor that yielded significant findings was growth of the individual toward greater awareness and skills in interpersonal relationships. Those in the leaderless groups had highest scores on this factor, those in the adult-led groups had moderate scores, and those in the youth-led groups had negative scores. (No significant finding emerged where one adult plus one youth led groups.)

Within the adult-led groups, the more effective adults were seen to be those who had had more experience with sensitivity training (irrespective of the amount of experience they had had working with teen-agers). The male adult leaders, in general, were seen to be more effective than the few female adult leaders present; but this may also be due to the fact that the female leaders in general had had far less experience with sensitivity training.

In spite of the implications about the effectiveness of leaderless groups, YMCA executives did not reintroduce this procedure at the following national Hi-Y Assembly. It is an area in which they plan to explore further but only after the Research and Development Division and the executives responsible for work with high school age youth can develop a sound, comprehensive, and appropriate program design and a contiguous research design that will deal reliably with the reported evaluations.

Evaluation of Parents' Reactions. Several studies have been made to gather together the observations and evaluations of parents after their youngsters had had an experience in sensitivity training. Typical and most revealing are the findings from a questionnaire mailed out to 47 parents in Dallas in

1963, five months after their youngsters had had such an experience. In answer to the question, "When your son [daughter] came home did you notice any change in his [her] attitudes or behavior?" 72 percent said "yes," and 11 percent said "not sure." The greatest changes that parents described were "more tolerant of others" or "seemed more mature." In 40 percent the change was said to have persisted; in 17 percent parents were "not sure." Parents reported improved relationships in the family and with peers. This was true for both boys and girls, but somewhat more for girls.

The following comments by various parents reflect the general reaction of a majority of them:

> I still know very little about the workshop as my son found it difficult to describe exactly what went on. I do know he came back more mature in his thinking, more tolerant of his sister, and an adolescent who has been a pleasure to have around.

> My daughter came home on a "cloud," so to speak. She saw the world through different eyes. She has made a tremendous change in her behavior. To me it was a miracle.

> We feel this was the most wonderful experience our daughter has had in helping her to appraise herself and see her worth.

SENSITIVITY TRAINING AND COMMUNITY ACTION GOALS

Many explorations are now taking place around the country, sponsored by the YMCA, in utilizing the arena of a sensitivity training group to deal with critical problems in our times among youths, and between youths and adult. The objectives of these no longer focus exclusively on personal growth although considerable personal growth seems to take place. A discussion of results of such groups follows.

Black-White Confrontation. In a four-day camp session in Oregon in 1968, five black youths, members of a black militant group, met with eight other black and white youths for a confrontation on inter-racial problems that had become critical in the local high school. It was a difficult group to lead. Meetings were infrequent at first until real group feeling was established. To bridge the adult-youth age gap and establish group strength, the entire group slept together on the floor of the dining room lodge, ate together, and shared recreation. A midnight hike without flashlights and a 3-mile rowboat cruise in high winds and threatening swells provided experiences that strengthened the group. As this developed, a high level of trust was invested by each individual. The group's perceptiveness and changed attitude back in the high school have caused an outcry by the rest of the student body for sensitivity training experiences. The principal has now found them to be a supportive group in the school.

Youth–Adult Groups. Results of sensitivity training in groups where youth and adults are both participants have not been documented sufficiently to satisfy research standards, although an attempt was made in 1968 to combine inner-city black youth and local police. There is enough evidence, from programs begun as early as 1965, that this is one valid approach to deal with the mounting generation gap, and more programs of this nature will be introduced in the coming months. Young people seem to feel that in this kind of setting adults (as a captive audience) are more likely to listen, which—it is repeatedly charged—they do not ordinarily do!

Youth-Young Adult Groups. The results of combining teen-agers and young adults in a group in 1968 were reported as highly satisfying to both the teen-agers and the 21–22-year-olds. Nevertheless, when in the following year the same YMCA offered to set up a similar sensitivity training program, the planning commission of three teen-agers and two young adults opted strongly for separate training laboratories for each age range. Both claimed that they had been somewhat inhibited in the mixed-age group and would expect to go deeper and open up more fully and honestly with their peers. They also observed that the laboratory dealt overwhelmingly with the single problem of the age gap.

Some have made the observation that a wider gap is developing today between these age groups than that between teen-agers and adults. It would be tempting to speculate on the reasons for this. For example, President Nathan Pusey has said that the senior class at Harvard appears somewhat embarrassed by the sophistication of the incoming freshmen. (We had better get off this tack here!)

THE MEASURABLE AND THE IMMEASURABLE

Perhaps no other program that the YMCA has undertaken has elicited from so many participants the following two statements, so deeply felt that the words break through the most dauntless reserve: "The sensitivity training experience has changed my whole life" and "This has been the most valuable experience of my life." How does an outside observer, armed with data-processing machinery and a soundly "objective" statistical research design, document the depth of spiritual release and enlightenment that assails the awakening psyche? We can, perhaps, measure changed behavior, reaction of peers, effectiveness of functioning. We cannot be sure to what extent such measurable factors do indeed reflect the inner joy or peace that so many of these participants have expressed—not only immediately after the experience but in letters often spontaneously written and mailed out to "Y" leaders and friends months and years later.

A blast of derogatory journalism has been flooding the news media about sensitivity training. The attacks may be justified in cases where incompetent leadership and sponsorship have invaded the field. But for every individual who has been disappointed in the results, there are hundreds who are convinced that this method of self-discovery through exposure in groups has been a mountain-top experience in self-transcendence.

Fully committed to a process that has shown such incontrovertible gains, those in the YMCA who have vigilantly protected this program of personal growth from incompetence and charlatanism are continuing to develop new and better program designs.

The results to date are encouraging greater and greater commitment on the part of the "Y" staff to utilize sensitivity training as a program support, in all its variations, including verbal and nonverbal techniques, to develop interpersonal understanding, self-fulfillment, and responsible social involvement in our times.

NOTES

[1]Campbell, J. P., & Dunnette, M. D. Effectiveness of t-group experiences in managerial training and development. *Psychol. Bull.*, August 1968, 70, 73–104.

[2]Tilden Harrison is associate executive director, Personnel and Management Services Division, National Council of the Young Men's Christian Associations of the United States of America, New York, New York.

[3]Many of the historical and review data in this article have been drawn from the pages of an excellent survey entitled *Using sensitivity training and the laboratory method* by Richard L. Batchelder and James M. Hardy, Association Press, New York, 1968.

FICTION AND THE HUMAN POTENTIALITY *

Joseph E. Strzepek

Literary Criticism: A Humanistic Beginning. In Freudian and behavioral psychologies the prosocial, or positive characteristics of human behavior are reduced to biological drives and "explained away" as being physiologically-based, self-serving, antisocial, or egotistical. This view of man is particularly threatening when one combines it with the idea that people's expectancies determine outcomes, as in the Jacobson and Rosenthal article later in this section. The problem of a one-sided interpretation of human nature that Strzepek points to is a result of this Freudian-behavioral bias as it shows in a literature which picks up the motivational assumption that the "real reasons" people act are for personal benefit. In Maslow's needs-hierarchy theory of motivation, however, the early stages are similar to the Freudian and behavioral assumption, but as love-belongingness, esteem, and self-actualization become predominant, the "higher" or more humane motivations appear in human behavior. Interestingly, in over 200 studies of Maslow's needs-hiearchy, only two works, both unpublished, are in literature. This may indicate the extent to which Freudian psychology controls literary thought. In this article Strzepek starts a more motivationally balanced and psychologically updated literary criticism by bringing in the idea of self-actualization from humanistic psychology. It appears that the new humanistic zeitgeist that Maslow mentioned in "Some Educational Implications of the Humanistic Psychologies" is beginning to show in the teaching of literature too.

Some eight or nine years ago, I began to notice some disturbing, or at least disappointing, characteristics of dramatic and literary fiction. My high school students often remarked (usually after reading and discussing something tragic or depressing such as Liam O'Flaherty's *The Informer*, an Irish civil war story, Alan Paton's *Cry, The Beloved Country*, about South Africa and apartheid, or *Romeo and Juliet*) that they wished we would read something happy for a change, that almost everything we read seemed to emphasize the worst side of human nature, the agonies of the human condition. They were right. The high school curriculum in English and American literature, even in the ninth and tenth grades, is overwhelmingly populated by literary characters who fail themselves and their friends. Even the heroes and heroines are losers. Consider Macbeth, Heathcliffe, Willy Loman, Holden Caulfield, Thomas Sutpen, and Jay Gatsby.

Spurred by my feeling that my students were right, I started asking myself a series of questions which have stayed with me throughout my career as an English educator:

*From Joseph E. Strzepek, "Fiction and the Human Potentiality," paper presented at the American Educational Studies Convention, Denver, Colorado, November 2, 1973; mimeographed, 17 pp.; by permission of the author. Joseph Strzepek is Assistant Professor of English Education at the University of Virginia and author of the forthcoming book *Situations from Teaching English*.

1. Why are the literature curricula in schools (and colleges also) dominated by tragic and depressing books? Just last week I reviewed a curriculum guide used in one of the largest school systems in Virginia which contained as the major literature unit an extensive course entitled "Disillusioned Man in the Twentieth Century." The major objectives of the course are to show how man came to disillusionment. Unfortunately, this unit is symptomatic rather than atypical of the messages students are being sent by their books and their teachers.

2. A good researcher would question to what extent my impression/ assertion that literature read in schools deals mainly with human failures could be verified by an actual empirical count. I will suggest this question to my doctoral students or perhaps pursue it myself later, but for the purpose of this paper, let me assume that my impression is correct.

3. What are some examples of literature whose characters succeed rather than fail in life? I will attempt an answer to this central question later in this paper.

4. How can scholars, teachers, and students distinguish between characters who "succeed" and those who "fail"? That is, are there some better or more accurate terms for making these distinctions than the few I have used or implied so far: success—failure; happy—depressing; winner— loser; best—worst; ecstasy—agony; comic—tragic? I have found (and had a number of teachers agree) that it is difficult to find much comic fiction or drama which holds up under classroom study or performance, either because the comedy is peculiar to a historical period, because it is too highly intellectual or satirical for high school students, (and satire makes negative statements about mankind), or because it is so light and diverting that it is trivial. This difficulty suggests two more questions:

5. Are there qualitative differences between literature about successes and literature about failures which account for the apparent dominance of the latter in schools and colleges? And 6. Can it be that writers are more interested in, (or teachers obsessed by), human faults than human virtues?

I had not made much conscious progress in answering these questions until the last few months when I began to relate what I had learned from my wife about humanistic psychology, my questions about the view of man revealed in literature, and my opportunity to do a paper for this conference. Recalling my wife's statement that humanistic psychologists, specifically Abraham Maslow, studied human strengths rather than weaknesses, I wondered how Maslow's research on healthy human beings related to my interest in finding healthy fictional characters. So I have begun reading Maslow, and what I found so far excites me. Because I think I have found in Maslow's concept of the "self-actualizing" human being, a fertile, dynamic standard, category, or continuum for analyzing and evaluating fictional characters and fiction.

In *The Farther Reaches of Human Nature*, a collection of Maslow's essays, speeches, and notes published in 1972 by Viking Press, Maslow discusses his efforts to discover the answers to the question, "of what are human beings capable?" and explains why he decided to select a deliberately biased sample, a small and superior group rather than the usual random sample.

> If we want to answer the question how tall can the human species grow, then obviously it is well to pick out the ones who are already tallest and study them. If we want to know how fast a human being can run, then it is no use to average out the speed of a "good sample" of the population; it is far better to collect Olympic gold medal winners and see how well they can do. If we want to know the possibilities for spiritual growth, value growth, or moral development in human beings, then I maintain that we can learn most by studying our most moral, ethical, or saintly people.
>
> On the whole, I think it fair to say that human history is a record of the ways in which human nature has been sold short. The highest possibilities of human nature have practically always been underrated. Even when "good specimens," the saints, sages, and great leaders of history, have been available for study, the temptation too often has been to consider them not human but supernaturally endowed. (p. 7)

And the same is true for literature and its study, Professor Maslow.

Maslow says that self-actualizing people can be "biological assays" to tell the rest of us what we might become, what we ought to value. I will try to summarize the attributes Maslow cites as being characteristic of "good human specimens."

Good humans are self-actualizing, they fulfill their humanness by knowing who they are and who they are not, what they like and what they do not like. They are psychologically healthy, biologically sound, cognitively and perceptually superior. They are good choosers, valuers: they don't get confused when the majority disagrees with them. They have a Taoistic attitude of accepting themselves and others. They take responsibility for evolving themselves. They can transcend problems of mind and body, selfishness and unselfishness. They seek growth and challenges rather than evade, like the Biblical Jonah, their highest possibilities. They dare to be great, but they can integrate pride and humility because they can laugh at themselves and human pretension. They are aware of godlike possibilities, but also of existential human limitations.

They have "peak experiences," transient moments of intense self-actualization which give way to noecstatic serenity. They are capable of wonder at and absorbtion in the here and now of everyday events, capable of creating conditions which make peak experiences more likely. They learn to recognize peak experiences and to communicate about them. They learn to be "surprised by joy" (C. S. Lewis). They are committed to a career or a cause outside themselves, to what Maslow calls the Being values.

They are good workers *and* they are very creative. They listen to and trust their impulse voices. They can improvise, brainstorm first—be critical and follow through later. They can voluntarily regress into childlike play and fantasy in the service of their egos and intellects. They can savor, enjoy, appreciate life and care about people in a Taoistic, non-interfering way. They are spontaneous, courageous, authentic, positive, aesthetic, together. (This sounds like the Scout Law!)

Maslow calls this list of descriptors a syndrome of the self-actualizing person which he discovered while studying intensively some two dozen people from western cultures. He is unsure of what self-actualization means in other cultures. He makes the important point that the degree to which a person can be self-actualizing is largely dependent on his environment. There are societies and institutions which are low in synergism, that is, the values of the individual are not harmonious with or reinforced by those of the society. Finally, Maslow says self-actualization is an ongoing process, not a state one achieves and holds.

Armed with my understanding of Maslow's concept of self-actualizing human beings as summarized above, I have begun a primitive inquiry, a "research" Maslow would say, to find self-actualizing literary characters. I reviewed my own knowledge of literature, surveyed bibliographies, plot and character summaries, and pestered my students and colleagues in English and education. I was Taoistically open to all suggestions at first, because I thought that when I began applying the full grid of self-actualizing characteristics, the list might shrink rapidly. Here is the list, including the suggestions which surprised me.

Zorba of Nikos Kazantzaki's *Zorba the Greek*
Huw Morgan of Richard Llewellyn's *How Green Was My Valley*
Jane of Charlotte Bronte's *Jane Eyre*
Joan of Bernard Shaw's *Saint Joan*
Cervantes' *Don Quixote*
Phineas Fogg of Jules Verne's *Around the World in Eighty Days*
Jim of Joseph Conrad's *Lord Jim*
Phineas of John Knowles's *A Separate Peace*
Hester Pryne of Hawthorne's *Scarlet Letter*
Martin Arrowsmith of Sinclair Lewis's *Arrowsmith*
the Doctor in Camus's *The Plague*
Henderson of Bellows' *Henderson the Rain King*
Augie of Bellow's *Adventures of Augie March*
Norman Moonbloom of Edward Lewis Wallant's *The Tenants of Moonbloom*
the Spenser family of Earl Hamner's *Spenser's Mountain*
Santiago of Hemingway's *Old Man and the Sea*
Richard Bach's *Jonathan Livingston Seagull*
Randle McMurphy of Kesey's *One Flew Over the Cuckoo's Nest*
Jack Jefferson of *The Great White Hope*
Jane Pittman of Ernest J. Gaines's *Autobiography of Miss Jane Pittman*
Newt of Gordon Parks's *The Learning Tree*
Shakespeare's Hamlet
Ulysses of Tennyson's poem "Ulysses"
Howard Roarke of Ayn Rand's *The Fountainhead*
the heroes of Kerouac's *Dharma Bums*
Natty Bumpo of Cooper's *Leatherstocking Tales*

Dorthea Brooke of George Elliot's *Middlemarch*
Moll of Daniel Defoe's *Moll Flanders*
the unnamed narrator of Richard Brautigan's *In Watermelon Sugar*
Douglas Spaulding of Ray Bradbury's *Dandelion Wine*

This is as far as I am so far, a grossly inadequate sample to be sure, but large enough to be suggestive and too large for me to have closely analyzed yet. I do have some initial reactions. I wondered whether it would be difficult to find black or female self-actualizing characters. It was not. I arbitrarily excluded actual biographies and autobiographies, though they certainly should be examined later. Publishers and library records indicate that when left to their own out-of-school impulses, people prefer nonfiction, particularly biography and autobiography, to fiction.

Just from a cursory review of this list a number of questions appear pertinent: How do the genre, historical period of the work, historical period of the author, national origin of the author, the race and sex of the author affect the likelihood that a book's characters will be self-actualizing? How does self-actualization relate to the traditional literary concepts used by critics and teachers such as character growth or development, archetypes, themes such as initiation, loss of innocence, maturation? How does it relate to different conceptions of the hero, to systems of philosophical, social, and psychological analyses of literature?

In a hasty search through literary criticism, I came across one article which I thought from its title should relate to my questions. But the characters David D. Galloway discusses in "Clown and Saint: The Hero in Current American Fiction," which appeared in *Critique: Studies in Modern Fiction*, Spring–Summer 1965 edition, are not really self-actualizing. The clowns, Stanley Elkin's Bosell, Terry Southern's Guy Grand and Candy, Heller's Yossarian, John Hawks's Papa Cue Ball, and Bellows's Henderson, and the saints, Wallant's Moonbloom, Updike's George Caldwell (*The Centaur*), and Salinger's Seymour struggle to cope with and survive in a sick urban society, but they rarely transcend their problems. Galloway's own words give the flavor of their lives.

> There are saintly clowns and clownish saints, and indeed the distinctions begin to blur meaningfully when we realize that both figures wage the battle of the spirit in a world of curtailed expectations, threading the increasingly narrow path round suicide and despair and toward a refurbished vision of man. (p. 64)

Just as literary concepts are useful in describing, interpreting, and evaluating literature, the concept of self-actualization could be a fertile device for teachers and critics. I can imagine some very exciting arguments and class discussions about the extent to which Ayn Rand's individualistic architect Howard Roarke and Shakespeare's Hamlet are self-actualizing. The latter could be viewed as a tragic figure whose great potential for self-actualization is wasted in a sick society. I would expect such discussions to reveal how students perceive and respond to characters, and what their naive impressions of self-actualization are.

I see two more possible results of a systematic application of Maslow's concept to literature. First, bibliographies of works with self-actualizing characters could be generated for teachers to counter-balance the dark fare they usually offer students. Second, the study of fictional self-actualizers could add to or refine Maslow's definition of self-actualization. Maslow himself suggests that the writing and reading of Utopias such as Aldous Huxley's *Island* are good ways to attempt to answer the question, "What are the best social conditions for bringing human nature to full humanness?"

Of the titles I offered earlier, I believe Ray Bradbury's *Dandelion Wine* has the largest number of self-actualizing characters, and they have the highest degree of self-actualization. Significantly, the major characters, Doug and Tom Spaulding, are ten and twelve years old. As Maslow says, children seem especially capable of peak experiences and self-actualization. Somehow most people are much less capable when they reach adulthood. Many of the adults in *Dandelion Wine* are still self-actualizing, however. The story takes place in the village of Green Town, Ohio. In many ways the Spaulding family and their neighbors are like the characters on the television series, "The Waltons," which is based on Earl Hamner's *Spenser's Mountain*.

The locale and historical period are very similar to those in Sherwood Anderson's *Winesburg, Ohio*. Anderson's characters are, to use his word, "grotesques," pathetic, lonely creatures who fail to communicate with themselves or each other, but Bradbury's characters have rich, creative imaginations which enable them to comprehend fully life's joys and sorrows, emotionally and intellectually.

For Doug, waking up on an early June morning is the first of many peak experiences that summer.

Each day brings a new adventure or discovery. Doug and Tom gather dandelions with Grandfather to make dandelion wine which holds the flavor and memories of summer's experiences throughout the year. In the middle of a berry picking expedition with Tom and his father, Doug realizes with great wonder that he "is alive."

Tom and Doug keep a diary of the summer and divide it into two parts. The first they called Rites and Ceremonies, the descriptions of first-time and repeated events. The second they called Discoveries, Revelations, Illuminations, and Intuitions, where they wrote whatever they thought about the Rites, "crazy or not." Notice how, like Maslow's good specimens, they try to be aware of life.

The boys and their friends visit old Colonel Freeleigh, their "Time Machine" who entrances them with his memories of Ching Ling Soo's death during his bullet trick at the Boston Variety Theatre in 1910, of Pawnee Bill and the buffalo, and of the Civil War. They watched the matter of fact and satisfied way their great grandmother accepted death, and they see the village strangler called the Lonely One meet a horrible death, stabbed with the scissors of a terrified young woman.

They see Leo Auffman's Happiness Machine almost break up his happy family. Doug sees old Miss Fern and Roberta run over drunk Mr. Quartermain in their electric Green Machine. Tom sees the hilariously spastic Elmira Brown challenge Clara Goodwater for the women's club's presidency, and accuse Clara of being a witch. They witness the bittersweet love affair between 95-year-old Helen Loomis and 30-year-old Bill Forrester, a couple whose imaginations permit them to transcend their mistimed births.

When the weight of the summer's experiences gets to be too much for Doug, as he realizes that someday he too must die, he almost succumbs to a mysterious fever. He regains his will to live after a visit from Mr. Jonas, a businessman turned Junkman. Mr. Jonas travels the streets befriending anyone in need. Doug "passes it on," repaying Mr. Jonas and everyone in the Spaulding house, family and boarders, by helping Grandmother regain her magically creative touch as a cook. She had been ruined temporarily by visiting Aunt Rose, who had cleaned up and reoganized Grandmother's kitchen, and worst of all, bought her a cookbook.

There are many more correspondences between the behavior of the characters in *Dandelion Wine* and Maslow's definition of self-actualizing people. The Spaulding adults can voluntarily regress to childlike behavior; they Taoistically accept their children and allow them freedom. Mr. Spaulding even helps his sons salvage the mechanical Tarot witch from the deranged owner of the penny arcade. The emotional enjoyment and intellectual contemplation of peak experiences abound, without the unreasonable desire to live every moment in a state of ecstasy, as Leo Auffmann learned through the destruction of his Happiness Machine. All of the people in Doug's family and many of the other characters either have, or learn to have, the ability to savor experience, to appreciate the present.

Dandelion Wine sounds sentimental and fantastical. It is. But to the extent that English teachers agree with Maslow that the purpose of education is to create the best kinds of human beings by studying models of the best, perhaps they should be exposing their students to *Dandelion Wine* and other literature with self-actualizing characters. I would like to encourage teachers and their students to participate in the inquiry I have barely begun in this paper.

REFERENCES

Bradbury, Ray, *Dandelion Wine* (New York: Bantam Pathfinder Editions, 1969)

Calloway, David D., "Clown and Saint: The Hero in Current American Fiction" Critique: Studies in Modern Fiction, Spring–Summer 1965

Maslow, Abraham H. *The Farther Reaches of Human Nature* (New York: The Viking Press Compass Edition, 1972)

DEVELOPING THOUGHTS ON DEVELOPMENTAL PSYCHOLOGY AND MORAL DEVELOPMENT: BEGINNING A HUMANISTIC NORMAL SCIENCE*

Thomas B. Roberts

Values and Morals: Two Humanistic Views. In many ways humanistic psychology is closer to Freudian psychology than to behavioral psychology. Here, for example, child development is viewed as a progression of stages similar to Erikson's naturally developing sequence rather than as the result of external reinforcement contingencies, as Baer sees it. This article illustrates the humanistic trait of emphasis on interpersonal relations, exemplified here by the topic, values and moral development. Since many moral decisions influence other people, this topic is a natural one for human-relations-oriented educators. This author, under the influence of Kohlberg, shows the humanistic trait of looking for agreement or commonness among apparently diverse people. In this case the sequence of moral development is interpreted as a cross-cultural human trait; thus, recognizing one's own moral feelings and development would lead to understanding the similarity in others. A different, although complimentary, emphasis comes from humanistic educators who primarily want to help students be clear about their own values, the value clarification group. The topics of self-knowledge, valuing, and decision-making are usually grouped together in this approach, which frequently assumes individual diversity and socio-cultural relativity; in contrast, this article uses the universal-values approach.

As I look through our program for these Wurzburg meetings, I remember the story of the blind men and the elephant. Each man felt a different part of the beast—a leg, the trunk, a tusk, and so forth—and, consequently each described an elephant as a very different sort of animal. But when the partial descriptions were put together, the image of a magnificent pachyderm emerged.

THIS MOMENT IN HUMANISTIC CONCEPTUAL HISTORY

Something very exciting is going on in the world, something similar to what the blind men did. This conference is part of it. Here, too, we are collecting, combining, and refining partial images. From our papers another image of a magnificent being is emerging. We are creating the image of healthy, self-actualizing, multi-potentialed man. And when the

*Adapted from Thomas B. Roberts, "Developing Thoughts on Developmental Psychology and Moral Development: Beginning a Humanistic Normal Science," paper presented at the Second International Invitational Conference on Humanistic Psychology, Wurzburg, Germany, July 21–24, 1971. Published in *Research in Education*, Document ED-056-934, ERIC (1972); reprinted by permission of the author. The research for this paper was largely supported by an Organized Research Grant (Dean's Fund), Northern Illinois University, DeKalb, Ill., U.S.A.

image changes, all else changes. This theme runs throughout the new psychological humanism. From his psychological orientation, Abraham Maslow called this emerging image "a new zeitgeist" (1). From within the human potential movement Willis W. Harman compares our new image of mankind to the reconceptualization of man that occurred with the Darwinian and Copernican revolutions by calling this "The New Copernican Revolution" (2). From a theological bent Michael Novak calls for a new theology (3,4).

These three, and others, all point to a switch in image, theory, and conceptualization that marks a scientific revolution, what Thomas Kuhn calls a new "paradigm" (5). Each of us here at Wurzburg, and others who aren't here, are fellow collaborators on this paradigm of man. In our own ways, we are all helping to enlarge, build, create, and revise this new and still growing paradigm of humanity.

When a new paradigm bursts against the scientific sky, it signals a trend of scientific activity to follow. This new "normal science" consists of reinterpreting existing studies, reformulating old questions, asking new ones, and embarking on new studies, and research. At this moment in the humanistic social sciences, we have done a fair amount of work on our paradigm (although more is to be done), and we are ready to embark on a new normal science.

In this paper I want to give an example of how we can reformulate current intellectual interests in terms of an emerging humanistic paradigm; this paper selects developmental psychology in general and moral development, specifically.

I feel that developmental psychology is itself especially relevant to humanistic concerns. As people who want to increase our human potentials for brotherhood, cooperation, peace, and social and self-fulfillment, we naturally ask, "How do we encourage these qualities in ourselves and in our society? How do children become fully human, in the best senses of the word *human*? How can we help them and ourselves?" A new image of man reformulates these questions and suggests new answers. There are many partial answers to these questions. One set of them concerns the education of the young.

A THEORY OF HUMAN DEVELOPMENT

The theory I've found useful is an adaptation of Abraham H. Maslow's theory of motivation (14). It is my opinion that as a child grows older he tends to pass through a chain of stages. At each period of transition the child and his world become transformed. How a child's personal history, his family, and social interactions may help or retard this passage from one stage to the next provide a series of new questions for humanistic developmental psychologists. Maslow's types of motivation and my adaptations of them are:

MASLOW	DEVELOPMENTAL STAGES
physiological	survival
safety	stability
love	sociability
esteem	expertise
self-actualization	self

I have used broader categories in order to include human political, economic, and social action within this theoretical framework. (For details see 6, 7, and 8.)

Adapting Erikson's epigenetic chart (9), we come to a matrix of usual, healthy human development.

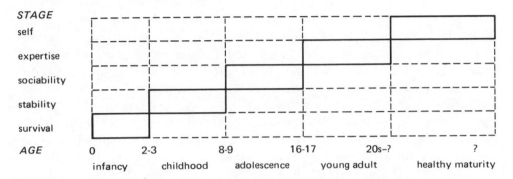

Survival stage—infancy. From birth through infancy a child's main "work" is learning to control his own body. Of course one continues to learn to use one's sensory-motor apparatus throughout life, but it is the main concern of infancy. Maslow's "physiological" fits this stage well.

Stability stage—childhood. The stability stage is marked by learning the rules and mores of one's family and society. A child learns what his roles are and what others' are. He learns what he is allowed to do and not allowed to do. Characteristics of stability are seeing society as given, a set structure which does not change. Childhood manifestations of stability are the childhood rituals, for example bedtime rituals, a security blanket, the desire for an orderly and predictable world, fixity in game rules, and so forth.

One of the most important tasks of the stability world is learning one's language. Language is, for one thing, a set of rules for conceptualizing, categorizing experience, naming things, and forming certain sorts of relationships among them. This structures a person's world, and the desire for form, structure, rules and regulations is primarily a stability trait.

Sociability stage—adolescence. As late childhood ripens into adolescence, a person's conceptual, emotional, and social development become rearranged away from a given set of rules and forms and towards an other-directed world. Instead of a world that is set, formalized, and predetermined, the adolescent discovers a world of social convention, social contract, and mutual agreement. People outside the family take on a new and stronger significance. This is clearest in the well-known peer orientation of adolescence. Parents, teachers, and siblings become less significant. An adolescent typically desires popularity.

James Coleman in his study *The Adolescent Society* (10) reports that typical American high school students want to be popular, leaders in activities, and/or athletes. Within a teen-age subculture, he says, these are all forms of social recognition. Coleman, however, laments this preference for sociability values and wishes that adolescents wanted to be more intellectual, or brilliant students academically. Coleman's preference for intellectuality is understandable when we remember that he is speaking from an expertise value system that emphasizes knowledge and specialization in one's field. Although his position is understandable, my evaluation is opposite. Just as the "work" of infancy is learning to use and control one's body, the tasks of adolescence are to develop one's relationships with others. Otherwise this need may remain unfilled and interfere with one's further development. One origin of the other-directed society in the U.S. (11) may be a school system that tries to take adolescents on to the fourth stage before they have completed the third. Instead of teaching Johnny to think like a teen-age mathematician or like a teen-age historian, we should teach him to think like a teen-age teen-ager. Then when he gets to be an adult, he won't continue to be an adolescent adult.

Expertise stage—young adulthood. Late in secondary school, in higher education, or on-the-job we expect youths to select and start to become proficient in their future occupations. Young adulthood in our society (I mean in the advanced industrialized nations for the most part) is predominantly within an expertise society, the "technological society" as Jacques Ellul calls it (12). Most people (mistakenly) think of adulthood only, or predominantly, in terms of taking one's place in the vocational structure and becoming proficient in one's occupation. This is the way things are now; however, I think they are changing. Part of the new image that humanistic social scientists are building is a new idea of healthy maturity. Freud's definition of health as love and work may be all right for societies in a sociability and/or expertise cultural stage, but for us it is incomplete. Shall we add something to working and loving? These two are helpful, but not enough.

Self-stage—maturity re-envisioned. I'd like to add "self-fulfillment" or "self-actualization" to work and love. And I am including the goals and activities of transpersonal health, too (13); although there may be reason to believe that transpersonalism is actually a sixth stage or state of consciousness. Maslow says that self-actualizing people tend to be middle-aged or older adults (14). The few who make it beyond expertise in our technological society are exceptions. Suppose we were to recognize the goals of self-actualization as the ultimate priority for our culture. How could we build a culture which would make it possible for more people to become self-actualizing?

When we switch this image of man and society, our view of social institutions, such as education, changes too. Many people now see a good education as one that prepares students for success in our *technological* (expertise) society. As our culture evolves, however, these institutions may lag behind society and seem to be dehumanizing our youth (15). Our current schools aid children as far as expertise development, but interfere with their self-fulfillment as human beings (6).

In this section I outlined some characteristics of what I estimate will be the developmental aspect of our broader, humanistic paradigm of man, and I've tried to show that developmental psychology is one site on which to build a new normal science based on that paradigm. I hope I've pointed out some possibilities to you so that we can get a full-fledged humanistic developmental psychology started. If so, perhaps we can influence child-rearing and education.

So far, I've found that when we view human development by this overall scheme, many previously unconnected bits of information assume new and meaningful relationships with each other under the organization of an encompassing theory. For example, in this paper I've connected the learning of language with stability-childhood and have connected peer orientation with sociability-adolescence. Thus language and the adolescent peer orientation become related to each other through this theory. Here, at least, is one step toward a holistic social science. (For more examples of how various specialties in the social sciences can become related, see 6, 7, and 8.)

MORAL DEVELOPMENT

Can we use this approach to reinterpret some topics within developmental psychology? I think this approach is equally applicable to socialization, language development, types of parental discipline, some aspects of applied reinforcement theory, ethnic and social class differences in socialization, and other topics. In this section I concentrate on moral development. This topic is especially interesting because the metamorphosis our society is going through seems to be in large part a value-shift. Moral development, especially among youth, shows this overlay of an additional set of values—the self values (15).

Stability to sociability—Piaget. Piaget believes that moral development in children is predominantly a switch from unquestioned acceptance of adult authority to concern with equality and a sense of autonomous justice (16, 17, 18). In the early stage of moral development children show what is, in humanistic interpretation, a stability orientation to the sense of justice. Piaget calls this a "heteronomous" attitude, and this consists of stability as opposed to the "autonomous" attitudes. In Piaget's ten comparisons below, we see that the younger stage is characterized by an authoritarian orientation (stability), while the older stage is characterized by an awareness of other people (sociability).

To point out one possible relationship with studies of social class, it is interesting to note that Cohen and Hodges note this same difference between the lower blue-collar class and the lower middle-class. Middle-class people are required by their socialization and their occupations to consider themselves in the position of other people. This may be one of the origins of middle-class sociability (19, 20).

Kohlberg reports, "Piaget is correct in assuming a culturally universal age development of a sense of justice, involving progressive concern for the needs and feelings of others." (18, p. 489.) Piaget notes the following ten differences. Younger children show:

1. conformity to rules rather than to intent
2. unchangeability to rules rather than flexibility
3. absolution of value rather than relativism
4. moral wrongness defined by sanctions rather than made independently of sanctions
5. duty as obedience to authority rather than conformity to peers
6. ignorance of reciprocal obligations rather than contract and exchange
7. severe, painful punishment rather than restoration to victim
8. culprit injured by natural consequences of misdeed rather than nature and physical laws being morally neutral
9. punishment by authority rather than retaliation by victim
10. favoritism of authority in distributing goods rather than impartiality, equality, and distributive justice.

With increased interaction with other children (sociability) as a child grows older, the stability orientation is replaced by one of interpersonal reciprocity, equality, and justice. This transition, Piaget reports, usually occurs from ages 8 to 10.

An example he gives is children's reactions to a story in which a scoutmaster tells a boy who has already done his chore for the day to do an additional one. Do children think that the request was just and that it should be obeyed? These are the results Piaget reports (16, p. 278):

Age	Obedience (Stability)	Equality (Sociability)
6	95%	5%
7	55%	45%
8	33.3%	66.6%
9	16.6%	83.4%
10	10%	90%
11	5%	95%
12	0%	100%

In terms of the humanistic theory we see Piaget documenting the transition from a stability stage to a sociability stage.

From sociability to expertise and self. Piaget reports that one of his investigators discovered a third step. In this story a mother gives her children a roll to eat. The youngest drops his into a river. What do the children who hear the story think should be done? The investigators interpreted not giving him a roll as "punishment." Giving him a roll because everyone should have a roll was interpreted as "equality." And giving him a roll because he was small was called "equity"; it allowed for his special circumstance (youth) as different from the older children. This is what the investigator, Mlle Rambert, found (16, pp. 268–269):

Age	Punishment (Stability)	Equality (Sociability)	Equity (Self)
6–9	48%	35%	17%
10–12	3%	55%	42%
13–14	0%	5%	95%

Equity is interpreted as associated with self, because it suggests that individual circumstances and differences are important in deciding what should be done rather than strict rule enforcement or equality, which are based on blindness to individual differences.

Kohlberg presents three major stages of moral development with two substages in each (18, 21). In the premoral or preconventional stage (survival), a person is out to get whatever he can for himself regardless of others. In the conventional stage (stability and sociability), he is very rule conscious and internalizes the rules of his society. In the principled stage (possibly expertise and probably self), he is more interested in the values that the rules are made to promulgate. If existing rules do not lead to the achievement of the values, they should be changed and/or not followed.

The first of the premoral substages is an obedience-punishment orientation. "Whatever I can get away with is right." Kohlberg's second preconventional stage is naive instrumental hedonism (18) or instrumental relativism (21). In this substage a right action still satisfies one's own needs and occasionally others'. Here one conforms to obtain rewards and to have favors done in return. There still is no idea of rules being absolutely right, as expressing a social contract, or derived from a set of abstract values.

Kohlberg's first stage under conventional morality is "personal concordance." In this stage a person wants to maintain the approval of others by fitting a "good-boy" or "good-girl" image. Conformity to a stereotyped two-value orientation (good/bad) suggests a stability approach. The assumption that these stereotypes are held by a majority, or many other people, assists a tendency to move toward sociability.

The second conventional stage is the authority-maintaining stage, or the "law and order" stage. Here one follows the rules to avoid censure by legitimate (i.e., socially accepted) authorities. Interest in the earned regard for others' expectations suggests sociability, for example, "authority and social order maintaining . . . doing duty and showing respect for authority" (read "others") suggest sociability. In terms of the humanistic differences between stability-authority, which is based on rules, eternal truth, power, compliance, and orderliness, and sociability-authority, which is based on group-derived laws, social consensus, and conformity to the majority, Kohlberg's third and fourth stages are transitions from stability to sociability.

The first substage of the post-conventional orientation also shows sociability characteristics, with some expertise mixed in. This stage is the social contract stage. Here socially-derived and democratically-accepted law is the basis for moral judgments, not personal gain or moral absolutism. People recognize that many laws are social conventions and can be changed by group agreement. This democratic basis of laws certainly indicates sociability. Moral judgments may be made from the point of view of an impartial judge who has the welfare of the community in mind, and this introduces an expertise element. The impartial judge may be considered an expert in community welfare and majority rule.

The avoidance of interfering with the will or rights of others may mark the beginning of the self stage by seeing importance in individuals and in individuation. This may be a forerunner of the self point of view. The last stage is one of individual principles. This is a self orientation. It is the "morality of individual principles of conscience." Universal values, principles of justice beyond the written law and beyond majority will, and transcendence of social convention indicate one of Maslow's "being values" (14).

Radical morality. Beyond merely trying to organize concepts and observations that have to do with moral punishment, the humanistic approach sheds some light on one kind of student activism. The Haan, Smith, and Block study (21) investigated the backgrounds of students arrested in the Free Speech Movement in Berkeley, California in 1964 at San Francisco State College. They found that 88% of the nonprotestors were preconventional or conventional; while among protestors 56% were postconventional. (See chart on next page.)

Part of our cultural metamorphosis might be best understood as a value-shift. The fact that only 12% of the nonprotestors were in the post-conventional stage and 56% of the protestors were in the post-conventional stage suggests that part of the generation gap is also a gap in the sense of the basis for morality. Within this humanistic theory we can think of it as the emergence of a new societal stage.

In Milgrim's experiments he requested his subjects to shock a confederate for mistakes in learning even when the confederate reported the shocks were painful, that he wanted to leave, that he had a bad heart, and even after he stopped responding (feigning death?) (23). Kohlberg found that only 13% of the combined conventional and preconventional (survival through expertise?) subjects stopped the administration of shocks. But among the people in the personal principled stage (self), 75% refused to administer the shocks (24).

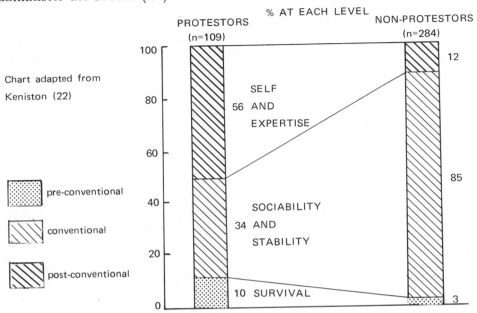

% AT EACH LEVEL

PROTESTORS (n=109)   NON-PROTESTORS (n=284)

Chart adapted from Keniston (22)

SELF 56 AND EXPERTISE

SOCIABILITY 34 AND STABILITY

10 SURVIVAL

pre-conventional

conventional

post-conventional

12

85

3

While some people interpret the "new morality" as an attack on middle-class, conventional morals (25), they might more accurately see the "new morality" as post-conventional, or self morality (26). Weirsma reports that self values form an important part of the value orientations in American communes (27). If our society is moving toward the self end of the humanistic continuum, then social planners, parents, educators, and lawmakers should take the values and behaviors of the self system into account in their decision-making.

SUMMARY

This Maslow-based humanistic conceptual framework helps us to understand some of Piaget's and Kohlberg's observations about moral development by putting them into a wider theoretical framework.

I believe a whole, integrated theory of child development may be derived from this approach (8). Differences in humanistic stages show not only in moral development, but also in socialization practices, the use of language, parental discipline, and dependency. The means of categorizing we have used until now may have to be reformulated. "Authority," "dependency," and other concepts have one meaning when talking about survival, a second for stability, another for sociability, a fourth for expertise, and a fifth for self. When we wish to use the humanistic paradigm I've suggested here, we should ask ourselves, "How does the topic or behavior we are investigating differ from stage to stage or group to group?"

There are many steps to take on the road toward a holistic view of man—the reinterpretation of present studies, re-asking old questions, asking new questions, and reformulating and reinvestigating the topics that interest us. By using this holistic approach in the future, however, we may be able to construct a view of man that synthesizes our many current, separate approaches and specialties. Drews lists 14 stage-sequence typologies which parallel the Maslow-Piaget-Kohlberg synthesis presented here (28, 29). There are over 250 investigations of the Maslow needs-hierarchy (30), and work continues on it. Piaget's theories are generating hundreds of more studies. Using Kohlberg's six stages, Hampden-Turner categorizes a broad spectrum of social science theories, assumptions, and approaches (31). Jones aligns nine stage theories of child development and finds much agreement among them (32). In many ways they parallel the stages presented here. Taken as a whole, these are a formidable convergence of information from disparate fields. A critical mass of new information is being built-up, and the intellectual energy from it can drive a humanistic social science, including new images of man and new possibilities for society.

CITED REFERENCES

1. Abraham Maslow, "Further Reaches of Human Nature," pp. 1–9, *The Journal of Transpersonal Psychology*, Spring 1969.

2. Willis W. Harman, "The New Copernican Revolution," pp. 127–134, *Journal of Humanistic Psychology*, Vol. 9, No. 2, 1969.

3. Michael Novak, *A Theology for Radical Politics*, Herder and Herder, New York, USA, 1969.

4. Michael Novak, "The Enlightenment is Dead," pp. 13–20, *The Center Magazine*, Vol. 4, No. 2, March–April, 1971.

5. Thomas S. Kuhn, *The Structure of Scientific Revolutions*, The University of Chicago Press, Chicago, Ill., USA, 1968.

6. Thomas B. Roberts, *A Humanistic Social Theory: A Human Systems Theory Applied to Youth, Higher Education, and Our Cultural Metamorphosis, Research in Education*, ED-963-179, ERIC, 1972.

7. Thomas B. Roberts, "Toward a Humanistic Social Science: A Consciousness Theory Outlined and Applied," pp. 1204–1227, *The Journal of Human Relations*, Fourth Quarter, 1970.

8. Thomas B. Roberts, *A Humanistic Social Typology: Applications to a Study of Higher Education and Suggestions for a Social Theory*, unpublished doctoral dissertation, Stanford University, 1973.

9. Erik H. Erikson, *Childhood and Society* p. 273, W. W. Norton & Co., New York, USA, 1963.

10. James S. Coleman, *The Adolescent Society: The Social Life of the Teenager and Its Impact on Education*, The Free Press, Glencoe, Ill., USA, 1961.

11. David Riesman with Nathan Glazer and Reuel Denney, *The Lonely Crowd: A Study of the Changing American Character*, Yale University Press, New Haven, Conn., USA, 1961.

12. Jacques Ellul, *The Technological Society*, translated by John Wilkinson, Vintage Books, Random House, New York, USA, 1964.

13. Anthony J. Sutich, "Transpersonal Psychology: An Emerging Force," pp. 77–78, *Journal of Humanistic Psychology*, Spring 1968.

14. a.) Abraham H. Maslow, *Toward a Psychology of Being*, D. Van Nostrand Co., Princeton, N.J., USA, 1962.

    b.) Abraham H. Maslow, *Motivation and Personality*, Harper and Row, New York, USA, 1970.

15. Thomas B. Roberts, "Freedom of the Mind: Humanistic Consciousness and Student Activism," pp. 188–211, *The Journal of Human Relations*, due in Vol. 19, No. 1, 1971.

16. Jean Piaget, and others, *The Moral Judgment of the Child*, The Free Press, New York, USA, 1965.

17. Lawrence Kohlberg, "Moral Development and Identification," pp. 277–332, in *Child Development*, Sixty-Second Yearbook of the National Society for the Study of Education, Harold W. Stevenson (ed), Univ. of Chicago Press, Chicago, Ill., USA, 1963.

18. Lawrence Kohlberg, "Moral Development," pp. 483–494, *International Encyclopedia of the Social Sciences*, Vol. 10, The Free Press and Macmillan Co., New York, NY, USA, 1968.

19. Albert H. Cohen and Harold M. Hodges, "Characteristics of the Lower-Blue-Collar-Class," pp. 303–334, *Social Problems*, Vol. 10, 1963.

20. Melvin Kohn, "Social Class and Parent-Child Relationships: An Interpretation," pp. 471–480, *American Journal of Sociology*, Vol. 68, 1963.

21. Norma M. Haan, Brewster Smith, Jeanne Block, "Moral Reasoning of Young Adults: Political-Social Behavior, Family Background, and Personality Correlates," pp. 183–201, *Journal of Personality and Social Psychology*, Vol. 10, No. 3, 1968.

22. Kenneth Keniston, "Moral Development, Youthful Activism, and Modern Society," pp. 110–127, *Youth and Society*, Vol. 1, No. 1, Sept., 1969.

23. Stanley Milgrim, "Some Conditions of Obedience and Disobedience to Authority," pp. 57–76, *Human Relations*, Vol. 18, 1965.

24. Lawrence Kohlberg, "Education for Justice: A Modern Statement of the Platonic View," Harvard University Burton Lecture on Moral Education, Cambridge, Mass., USA, 1968. Cited in 18.

25. Edwin A. Roberts, Jr., "The Middle Class Does the Work, Pays the Bills, and Gets Blamed for Everything," pp. 20–22, *Today's Education: NEA Journal*, Jan. 1970.

26. Thomas B. Roberts, "Many Student Activists Feel that Middle-Class Society Needlessly Blocks Personal Growth," pp. 22–23, *Today's Education: NEA Journal*, Jan. 1970.

27. Jacquelyn Weirsma, "An Analysis of the Task Productions of Communes and Social Change Communities as Societal Alternatives: Functions of Changes in Personal and Interpersonal Dynamics," Unpublished manuscript and Personnel Communications, Pipestone, Minn., USA, 1970.

28. Elizabeth M. Drews, *Policy Implications of a Hierarchy of Values*, Educational Policy Research Center, Stanford Research Institute, Menlo Park, Calif., 1970.

29. Elizabeth Monroe Drews, and Leslie Lipson; *Values and Humanity*, St. Martin's Press, New York, 1971.

30. Thomas B. Roberts, "Maslow's Human Motivation Needs Hierarchy: A Bibliography," *Research in Education*, Document ED-069-591, ERIC, 1973.

31. Charles Hampden-Turner, "On the Future of American Political Science Education," Paper presented at the Second International Conference on Humanistic Psychology, Wurzburg, Germany, July 21–24, 1971. Printed as "Radical Man and the Hidden Moralities of Social Science," *Interpersonal Development*, pp. 222–237, Vol. 2, No. 4, 1971–72.

32. Richard M. Jones, *Fantasy and Feeling in Education*, Harper and Row, New York, 1968.

TEACHERS' EXPECTANCIES:
DETERMINANTS OF PUPILS' IQ GAINS[1] *

Robert Rosenthal and Lenore Jacobson

The Power of Positive Thinking. Humanistic psychologists are fond of asking, "What effect does our self-concept have on us?" In this article, Rosenthal and Jacobson go a step further, "What effect does our concept of our students have on them?" Quite a bit, it appears. As the table of IQ gains shows, telling the teacher to expect IQ growth actually produced it, especially among the younger elementary pupils. How did this work? Do the teachers behave differently toward the predicted "bloomers"? The teachers said they had forgotten which students were predicted to "bloom" that year. What would happen if teachers expected more out of all their students? Is this part of the secret of successful teachers? Because they judge themselves as competent, they expect their students to learn more, and thinking makes it so. What would happen to teachers and students if a class weren't called "remedial," "average," "college prep," or some other expectation-setting label? Rosenthal and Jacobson's book *Pygmalion in the Classroom* has touched off a string of studies and controversies.

Summary.—Within each of 18 classrooms, an average of 20% of the children were reported to classroom teachers as showing unusual potential for intellectual gains. Eight months later these "unusual" children (who had actually been selected at random) showed significantly greater gains in IQ than did the remaining children in the control group. These effects of teachers' expectancies operated primarily among the younger children.

Experiments have shown that in behavioral research employing human or animal Ss, E's expectancy can be a significant determinant of S's response (Rosenthal, 1964, in press). [E = experimenter; S = subject.] In studies employing animals for example, Es led to believe that their rat Ss had been bred for superior learning ability obtained performance superior to that obtained by Es led to believe their rats had been bred for inferior learning ability (Rosenthal & Fode, 1963; Rosenthal & Lawson, 1964). The present study was designed to extend the generality of this finding from Es to teachers and from animal Ss to school children.

Flanagan (1960) has developed a nonverbal intelligence test (*Tests of General Ability* or *TOGA*) which is not explicitly dependent on such school-learned skills as reading, writing, and arithmetic. The test is composed of two types of items, "verbal" and "reasoning." The "verbal"

*From Robert Rosenthal and Lenore Jacobson, "Teacher Expectancies: Determinants of Pupils' IQ Gains," *Psychological Reports* 19 (1966): 115–118, by permission of the authors. Copyright 1966 by Southern Universities Press. Robert Rosenthal is Professor of Social Psychology at Harvard University. Lenore Jacobson is Principal of the Ponderosa School in San Francisco.

items measure the child's level of information, vocabulary, and concepts. The "reasoning" items measure the child's concept formation ability by employing abstract line drawings. Flanagan's purpose in developing the TOGA was "to provide a relatively fair measure of intelligence for all individuals, even those who have had atypical opportunities to learn" (1960, p. 6).

Flanagan's test was administered to all children in an elementary school, disguised as a test designed to predict academic "blooming" or intellectual gain. Within each of the six grades in the school were three classrooms, one each of children performing at above average, average, and below average levels of scholastic achievement. In each of the 18 classes an average of 20% of the children were assigned to the experimental condition. The names of these children were given to each teacher who was told that their scores on the "test for intellectual blooming" indicated that they would show unusual intellectual gains during the academic year. Actually, the children had been assigned to the experimental condition by means of a table of random numbers. The experimental treatment for these children, then, consisted of nothing more than being identified to their teachers as children who would show unusual intellectual gains.

Eight months after the experimental conditions were instituted all children were retested with the same IQ rest, and a change score was computed for each child. Table 1 shows a mean gain in IQ points among experimental and control Ss in each of the six grades.[2] For the school as a whole those children from whom the teachers had been led to expect greater intellectual gain showed a significantly greater gain in IQ score than did the control children ($p = .02$, one-tail). Inspection of Table 1 shows that the effects of teachers' expectancies were not uniform across the six grade levels. The lower the grade level, the greater was the effect ($rho = -.94$, $p = .02$, two-tail). It was in the first and second grades that

TABLE 1

Mean Gains in IQ

Grade	Controls		Experimentals		Diff.	t	p†
	M	σ	M	σ			
1	12.0	16.6	27.4	12.5	15.4	2.97	.002
2	7.0	10.0	16.5	18.6	9.5	2.28	.02
3	5.0	11.9	5.0	9.3	0.0		
4	2.2	13.4	5.6	11.0	3.4		
5	17.5	13.1	17.4	17.8	−0.1		
6	10.7	10.0	10.0	6.5	−0.7		
Weighted M	8.4*	13.5	12.2**	15.0	3.8	2.15	.02

*Mean number of children per grade = 42.5.
**Mean number of children per grade = 10.8.
†p one-tailed.

the effects were most dramatic. The largest gain among the three first-grade classrooms occurred for experimental *S*s who gained 24.8 IQ points *in excess* of the gain (+16.2) shown by the controls. The largest gain among the three second grade classrooms was obtained by experimental *S*s who gained 18.2 IQ points in excess of the gain (+4.3) shown by the controls.

An additionally useful way of showing the effects of teachers' expectancies on their pupils' gains in IQ is to show the percentage of experimental and control *S*s achieving various magnitudes of gains. Table 2 shows such percentages for the first and second grades only. Half again as many experimental as control *S*s gained at least 10 IQ points; more than twice as many gained at least 20 IQ points; and more than four times as many gained at least 30 points.

TABLE 2

Percentages of Experimental and Control *S*s
Gaining 10, 20, or 30 IQ Points
(First and Second Grade Children)

IQ Gain	Control *S*s*	Experimental *S*s**	χ^2	*p*†
10 points	49	79	4.75	.02
20 points	19	47	5.59	.01
30 points	5	21	3.47	.04

*Total number of children = 95.
**Total number of children - 19.
†*p* one-tailed.

An important question was whether the gains of the experimental *S*s were made at the expense of the control *S*s. Tables 1 and 2 show that control *S*s made substantial gains in IQ though they were smaller than the gains made by experimental *S*s. Better evidence for the proposition that gains by experimental *S*s were not made at the expense of control *S*s comes from the positive correlation between gains made by experimental and control *S*s. Over the 17 classrooms in which the comparison was possible, those in which experimental *S*s made greater gains tended also to be the ones where control *S*s made greater gains (*rho* = .57, *p* = .02, two-tail).

Retesting of the children's IQ had been done in classroom groups by the children's own teacher.[3] The question arose, therefore, whether the greater gain in IQ of the experimental children might have been due to the teacher's differential behavior toward them during the retesting. To help answer this question three of the classes were retested by a school administrator not attached to the particular school. She did not know which children were in the experimental condition. Results based on her retesting of the children were not significantly different from the results based on the children's own teachers' retesting. In fact, there was a tendency for the results of her retesting to yield even larger effects of teachers' expectancies. It appears unlikely, then, that the greater IQ gains made by children from whom greater gains were expected could be attributed to the effect of the behavior of the teacher while she served as an examiner.

There are a number of possible explanations of the finding that teachers' expectancy effects operated primarily at the lower grade levels, including: (a) Younger children have less well-established reputations so that the creation of expectations about their performance would be more credible. (b) Younger children may be more susceptible to the unintended social influence exerted by the expectation of their teacher. (c) Younger children may be more recent arrivals in the school's neighborhood and may differ from the older children in characteristics other than age. (d) Teachers of lower grades may differ from teachers of higher grades on a variety of dimensions which are correlated with the effectiveness of the unintentional communication of expectancies.

The most important question which remains is that which asks how a teacher's expectation becomes translated into behavior in such a way as to elicit the expected pupil behavior. Prior research on the unintentional communication of expectancies in experimentally more carefully controlled interactions suggests that this question will not be easily answered (Rosenthal, in press).

But, regardless of the mechanism involved, there are important substantive and methodological implications of these findings which will be discussed in detail elsewhere. For now, one example, in question form, will do: How much of the improvement in intellectual performance attributed to the contemporary educational programs is due to the content and methods of the programs and how much is due to the favorable expectancies of the teachers and administrators involved? Experimental designs to answer such questions are available (Rosenthal, in press) and in view of the psychological, social and economic importance of these programs the use of such designs seems strongly indicated.

NOTES

[1] This research was supported by Research Grants GS-177 and GS-714 from Division of Social Sciences of the National Science Foundation. We thank Dr. Paul Nielsen, Superintendent, South San Francisco Unified School District, for making this study possible; Dr. David Marlowe for his valuable advice; and Mae Evans, Nancy Johnson, John Laszlo, Susan Novick, and George Smiltens for their assistance. A more extended treatment of this material will be published by Holt, Rinehart and Winston as a chapter in a book tentatively entitled *Social Class, Race, and Psychological Development*.

[2] There were no differences in the effects of teachers' expectancies as a function of Ss' initial level of educational achievement; therefore, the three classrooms at each grade level were combined for Table 1. In one of the three classrooms at the fifth grade level, a portion of the IQ test was inadvertently not re-administered so that data of Table 1 are based on 17 instead of 18 classrooms.

[3] Scoring of the tests was done by the investigators, not by the teachers.

REFERENCES

Flanagan, J. C. *Tests of general ability: technical report.* Chicago, Ill.: Science Research Associates, 1960.

Rosenthal, R. The effect of the experimenter on the results of psychological research. In B. A. Maher (Ed.), *Progress in experimental personality research.* Vol. I. New York: Academic Press, 1964. Pp. 79–114.

Rosenthal, R. *Experimenter effects in behavioral research.* New York: Appleton-Century-Crofts, in press.

Rosenthal, R., & Fode, K. L. The effect of experimenter bias on the performance of the albino rat. *Behavioral Science,* 1963, 8, 183–189.

Rosenthal, R., & Lawson, R. A longitudinal study of the effects of experimenter bias on the operant learning of laboratory rats. *Journal of Psychiatric Research,* 1964, 2, 61–72.

*E = experimenter; S = subject

Editor's Note: The extent of experimenter bias, subject expectations, and the "pygmalion effect" are not clearly established. For a critique of the study above, see:

Barber, Theodore X. and others, "Five Attempts to Replicate the Experimenter Bias Effect," *Journal of Consulting and Clinical Psychology*, 33 (1): 1–14, 1969.

TEACHER SENSITIVITY:
AFFECTIVE IMPACT ON STUDENTS

Dwight Webb

It's Not What You Do, It's How You Do It. Webb's first paragraph summarizes a feeling that most humanistically-oriented teachers have, but is there any
evidence to support this feeling? Webb describes a short survey which does
provide such evidence. In keeping with the assumption that cognition and
affect are compatible with each other, Webb finds not only that student
morale and interest improved, but also that they reported they learned more
content in English and scored higher in math achievement. This article should
challenge teacher-educators to include sensitivity training in their programs
and encourage superintendents and principals to seek and foster sensitive
qualities in teachers, especially those who work with students who are not at
the top in academic ability. Here, too, is another element to consider in merit
pay increases.

The way a teacher behaves, not what he knows, may be the most
important issue in the transmission of the teaching-learning exchange. The
psychological behavior, the quality of how the teacher relates to the child,
is perhaps the most important basis for the learning attitude held by the
child.

It has been demonstrated that children behave differently while under
the training or supervision of different types of adults. Anderson and
Brewer (3) point out that second-grade children with a teacher who
promoted social interchange and cooperation in interaction had significantly lower frequencies in distractibility, whispering, playing with foreign
objects, conforming to teacher domination, and significantly higher frequencies of spontaneity, initiative, and social contributions to others than
did a similar group of students with a teacher who was more directive,
authoritarian, and controlling. Amidon and Flanders (1) found that
dependent-prone students learned more in classrooms where the teacher
gave fewer directions, less criticism, more praise, used less lecturing, and
encouraged student participation. Students with more directive, businesslike teachers became more compliant, less free to express doubts and ask
questions, and their achievement in geometry was not so high.

White and Lippitt (8) studied the effects of authoritarian, democratic
and laissez-faire leadership on eleven-year-olds in club activities. They
found that these boys had a greater feeling of discontent with the adult

*From Dwight Webb, "Teacher Sensitivity: Affective Impact on Students," *Journal of Teacher
Education* 22, no. 4 (Winter, 1971): 455–459, by permission of the author. Dwight Webb is Associate Professor of Education at the University of New Hampshire and author of the forthcoming
book *A New Model for Elementary School Counseling: Paraprofessional Community Counselors.*

leaders in authoritarian and laissez-faire groups than they did in the democratic groups. They further reported that authoritarian leadership was met with considerable frustration and aggression by eleven-year-olds, who were more dependent on the authoritarian leader and initiated less self-directed efforts in learning.

Educators have known for some time the importance of the human dimension in teaching. Anderson and Kennedy (4) emphasized that the mental attitude of the teacher is probably the most important element in the atmosphere of the classroom:

> ... the disgruntled, sour, sarcastic, sharp and bitter teacher has a general attitude of mind that is most dangerous to the shy, timid, over-sensitive child. The suspicious, doubting, supercilious teacher does untold damage to the pupil whose daily life is filled with one long series of threats against his own security (p. 300).

Getzels and Jackson (5) argued that the personality of the teacher is perhaps the most significant variable in the classroom:

> Despite the critical importance of the problem and a half-century of prodigious research effort, very little is known for certain about the nature and measurement of teacher personality, or about the relation between teacher personality and teaching effectiveness (p. 574).

The notion of meeting individual differences of students is a concept widely accepted as a desirable function of education, and yet we have not attended to the impact of the individual differences among teachers as they address themselves to this task. It seems reasonable to conclude that student individualization will be realized more fully if teacher characteristics are considered in attempting to create the most compatible teaching-learning relationship.

PURPOSE

It was the purpose of this study to compare the effect of teachers rated as sensitive or less sensitive on students in two ability groups who had been identified as (1) insecure, (2) school problems, and (3) problem-free.

PROCEDURE

All of the students involved in this study were in the eighth grade in a suburban community near San Francisco, California. The experiment took place during the first semester of the school year as part of the regular instructional program, with the permission and cooperation of the administration. Teachers and students were not aware of the experimental proceedings.

Teachers were selected from the courses common to all eighth-grade students—history, English, and math. The five full-time counselors, one administrator, and one teacher entering the counseling staff served as raters. A sensitive teacher was defined in the rating as one who is understanding, helpful, and concerned with individual differences among students, one who would not likely embarrass or humiliate a student in order to shape his behavior. The two teachers in each course area rated as most sensitive and the two rated as least sensitive served as the basis for the contrasting treatment groups. Agreement among raters was high, averaging 82 percent.

From the total eighth-grade class (n = 148), 91 students were identified for the study: 44 in the insecure, 24 in the school problem, and 23 in the problem-free subgroups. The ability variable was controlled to determine if students of higher ability ("B" lane) were different from students of somewhat less academic aptitude ("C" lane) in their responses to the sensitivity factor in teachers. Of the 91 students, 48 were in the "B" lane, with SCAT (School and College Abilities Test) scores ranging between the 70th and 85th percentiles; and 43 in the "C" lane, with scores ranging from the 50th to the 70th percentile.

HYPOTHESIS

It was hypothesized that the insecure, the school-problem, and the problem-free students would demonstrate fewer educationally negative responses on the evaluative criteria when placed with teachers rated as highly sensitive than would similar students placed with teachers of less sensitivity.

CRITERIA

The dependent variables were:

(a) the pretest, post-test comparisons on the MPCL[1] subscales on insecurity and school problems
(b) the index of student attitude toward teachers (constructed specially for this study)
(c) the index of course satisfaction (also constructed for this study)
(d) raw score achievement data on math quarter and semester examinations
(e) student and/or parent requests for transfer based on teacher-student conflict
(f) tardies
(g) referrals for disciplinary action

The statistical analysis for mean differences between type of teacher placement groups included a 2 x 2 analysis of covariance (for the two MPCL subscales, using the pretest as the covariate); a 2 x 2 analysis of variance; and a t-test. Proportional differences among students responding in an educationally positive or negative way were analyzed by the chi-square method.

RESULTS

The main effects of teacher differences may be summarized with the following generalizations:

(1) The greatest educationally negative impact of the less sensitive teachers was felt among the students of lower ability or "C" lane.

(2) The response of insecure and school-problem students was significantly more educationally negative to teachers rated low in sensitivity than to teachers rated high in sensitivity.

(3) The insecure students were more affected in educationally negative ways by less sensitive teachers than were the school-problem students.

(4) Problem-free students did not appear to respond in significantly different ways when placed with teachers rated high in sensitivity from what they did when placed with teachers rated low in sensitivity.

Specific findings are summarized in Table 1.[2]

DISCUSSION

Seventeen areas of significant differences were found supporting the hypothesis, indicating a prevailing trend of more positive student attitudes associated with the more sensitive teacher placement. The greatest educationally negative impact of the less sensitive teachers was felt among the

TABLE 1

Summary of the Significant Findings Supporting the Hypothesis

When placed with more sensitive teachers

Insecure students
1. At the "C" lane reported they had fewer school problems $(p < .01)$
2. At the "C" lane reported they had more positive attitudes about their teachers $(p < .05)$
3. At the "B" lane expressed more interest in math $(p < .01)$

School problem students
1. At the "C" lane reported they felt more secure $(p < .025)$
2. At the "C" lane reported they had fewer school problems $(p < .05)$
3. At the "C" lane expressed more interest in English $(p < .001)$
4. At the "C" lane reported they learned more in English $(p < .05)$

Total class of students (combined subgroups) at "C" Lane
1. Reported they felt that they learned more in English $(p < .03)$
2. Had greater achievement in math on the quarter examination $(p < .025)$
3. Did not seek to transfer from class as frequently $(p < .001)$
4. Reported having more positive attitudes about their teachers. Specifically: $(p < .025)$
   (a) they got along better with their teachers $(p < .02)$
   (b) they did not feel so overly criticized by their teachers $(p < .02)$
   (c) they felt their teachers were more fair $(p < .05)$
   (d) they did not feel so "cut down" by their teachers $(p < .01)$

Total class of students (combined subgroups) at "B" lane
1. Reported they had more positive attitudes toward their teachers $(p < .025)$
2. Indicated they were not upset by teachers for long periods of time $(p < .05)$

students of lower academic aptitude and among those identified either as insecure or as having school problems. Although the meaning of this is not immediately certain, the following speculations seem warranted: (a) that lower-ability, problem-oriented students are more dependent upon a patient, nurturing, and understanding teacher for a successful school experience than are the more able and problem-free students who, by comparison, seem somewhat immune to the negative impact of the less sensitive teacher; (b) that the less sensitive teacher may treat lower-ability and problem-oriented students with less patience, interacting with them in harsher, more sarcastic, and cutting ways than they do with the abler and better adjusted students.

CONCLUSION

This is not to condemn the task-oriented or rigorously academic teacher; in fact, it could be argued that for some students the more objective teachers are more interesting and stimulating. Ryans (6) points this out:

> Pupil F . . . may differ widely from pupil G in his assessment of the essential attributes of an effective teacher. If pupil F is relatively bright, academically minded, well-adjusted, and independent, he may value most the teacher who is serious, rigorously academic, and perhaps even relatively impersonal. If pupil G, on the other hand, is more sensitive, and requires considerable succor, he may find the teacher just described not at all to his liking, and literally "impossible." In the mind of pupil G, the better teacher may very well be one who is characteristically sympathetic, understanding, and the like (p. 3).

Although the bias of the hypothesis is in the direction of making a case for the humanistic, person-oriented teacher, it could also be maintained that the ideal to be approximated would include strong cognitive as well as affective components. The primary aim of this study, however, is to call attention to the effects that lack of sensitivity in teachers may have on certain kinds of students. The data obtained clearly indicate that teacher personality is a critical variable in the classroom. Lack of teacher sensitivity to students who are shy and insecure or to those who have poor opinions about school and themselves has a marked negative effect on their self-esteem and consequent learning attitudes. This is particularly true for pupils of average ability. The findings of this study could serve as guidelines for all educators who are truly concerned with the ultimate product of education—the student.

NOTES

[1] Mooney Problems Checklist (junior high school form).

[2] Only significant findings are presented here. Readers desiring more details are referred to Webb (7).

REFERENCES

1. Amidon, E., and Flanders, N. A. "The Effects of Direct and Indirect Teacher Influence on Dependent-Prone Students Learning Geometry." *Journal of Educational Psychology* 52:286–91; December 1961.

2. Anastasiow, N. "The Relationship of Sex Role Patterns of First-Grade Boys to Success in School." Doctor's thesis. Palo Alto, Calif.: Stanford University, 1963. (Unpublished)

3. Anderson, H. H., and Brewer, J. E. *Effects of Teachers' Dominative and Integrative Contacts on Children's Classroom Behavior.* Studies for Teachers' Classroom Personalities, II. Palo Alto, Calif.: Stanford University Press, 1946. pp. 83–96.

4. Anderson, V. V., and Kennedy, W. M. *Psychiatry in Education.* New York: Harper, 1932. pp. 300–301.

5. Getzels, J. W., and Jackson, P. W. "The Teacher's Personality and Characteristics." *Handbook of Research on Teaching.* (Edited by N. L. Gage.) Chicago: Rand McNally, 1963. pp. 506–82.

6. Ryans, D. G. *Characteristics of Teachers: Their Description, Comparison, and Appraisal.* Washington, D. C.: American Council on Education, 1960.

7. Webb, W. D. "The Effects of Teacher Sensitivity on Insecure, School-Problem and Problem-Free Students." Doctor's thesis. Palo Alto, Calif.: Stanford University, 1967.

8. White, R., and Lippitt, R. "Leader Behavior and Member Reaction in Three 'Social Climates'." *Group Dynamics: Research and Theory.* Second edition. (Edited by D. Cartwright and A. Zander.) Evanston, Ill.: Row, Peterson, 1960. pp. 527–53.

PART FOUR

Transpersonal Psychology

INTRODUCTION
THE EDITOR

To what extent are we using our full capacities? Psychologists differ on their estimations. Some say we are letting three-quarters of our possibilities lie fallow. Others say we are using only ten percent. Whatever the figure, they judge that we are using only a small portion of our potential. This, of course, raises the question: How can we learn to use underdeveloped psychological capabilities? This is the central question which runs through transpersonal psychology as it applies to education. To put it another way: What *are* we able to learn, and how can we learn it?

Some transpersonal psychologists are interested in these broad questions and their implications for schools. Others are advocates of one or another specialized ability and want to explore it and its ramifications. Authors who are interested in the broader question frequently see a new image of human nature and human capacities emerging (Harman, 1969). They tend to try to pull together information from many sources and synthesize a variety of specializations. In this section the articles "The Affective Domain and Beyond," "Education for Transcendence," and "An Outline of Transpersonal Psychology: Its Meaning and Relevance for Education" show this synthetic trend.

Transpersonal Psychology and Psychologists

Unlike Freudian or behavioral psychology, transpersonal psychology does not have an organized theory or an agreed-upon, clearly defined set of concepts and relationships. This lack of organization is typical in the early stages of the formation of a new science (Kuhn, 1964). Because of this early stage of development of transpersonal psychology, a description of the field is less systematically organized than behavioral or Freudian psychology. An overall view of this psychology describes the psychologists in the field and their characteristic interests and approaches rather than a body of well-formulated ideas and concepts. The interests which are described below list some topics which are especially relevant to education. For a more complete catalogue of the whole field, scan the current issues of *The Journal of Transpersonal Psychology*.

Much of the work of transpersonal psychologists consists of finding compatible or corroborative information and trying to accumulate various pieces of what may someday be a more concise and efficient way of looking at things. Sometimes this information comes from what seems far afield to our usual ways of looking at things. For example, in "The Ins and Outs of Mind-Body Energy" the authors cite Hindu philosophy and parapsychological studies, and in "Zen Meditation and the Development of Empathy in Counselors," Lesh draws on Freudian and humanistic ideas in his background discussion. As a new science is developed, or as a new paradigm within a science starts to grow, one of the activities that the new type of scientists engage in is thinking about existing data in a new way. Lesh and the Greens portray this aspect of transpersonal psychology, too.

Like the humanistic psychologists, the transpersonal psychologists assume that we have large, untapped abilities. While the humanistic psychologists tend to explore interpersonal, human relations in their search for these new potentialities, transpersonal psychologists trend toward the subjective, transcendent, and more unusual human experiences. In an effort to leave no stone unturned, this exploratory research often takes them far afield from the usual realms of academic psychology. Like any exploration, some leads turn out to be dead ends. Other leads show promise and need further exploration. Thus, another usual trait of transpersonal psychologists is an openness to new experiences and a willingness not to close the door on any possible avenue of investigation even if the topic is scientifically heretical.

Most of the articles in this section deal with at least one topic that is new to recent serious scientific consideration in Western psychology. The topic of altered states of consciousness is evident in "The Word and the Vision" and "Do You Have Your Dream for English?" In "Excerpts from *The Natural Mind*" Weil says that the desire for these states is part of human psychology. Thus, he and these other authors try to bring this taboo topic up for systematic, scientific investigation.

Parapsychology, including extrasensory preception, is still an outlawed topic for many psychologists. But if we are to learn about the neglected human abilities and possibly learn to use them and to teach them, then parapsychology and other unusual abilities should not be neglected as possible leads. Krippner and Murphy, and Targ and Hurt raise the possibilities that we can learn to control these occasional spontaneously occurring phenomena.

Beside altered states of consciousness and parapsychology, other areas of search are in cultures other than our own which may have developed abilities we have left dormant. The articles on meditation exemplify practical educational uses of Eastern psychology. In "Artifical Reincarnation" Ostrander and Schroeder discuss Russian uses of hypnosis as an aid to learning. Their book, with its descriptions of Soviet research into a variety of fields taboo to our psychologists, is a bigger challenge to Western science than Sputnik was. Weil, author of *The Natural Mind*, has made trips to the Amazon in hopes of learning some of the native Brazilians' pharmacopia for altered consciousness.

Some transpersonal psychologists center their research on the speculation that there is a form of energy that we are just beginning to explore systematically. In Ogletree's approach to developmental psychology, he says that these bioplasmic forces corroborate some of Piaget's work on developmental psychology, and he implies that they are a key to a readiness-stage learning theory. Just as mankind has discovered how to use and control such forms of energy as electricity, magnetism, and radioactivity, we may be on the verge of discovering and controlling another kind of biological energy that has to do with parapsychology, the occult, psychic phenomena, and other unusual occurrences whose mechanism and variables are still unknown. Since new forms of energy and new sources of already recognized forms have been discovered periodically in human history, the energy-group of transpersonal psychologists speculate that we too may not know of some of these kinds of energy or of their sources. Perhaps meditation, yoga, and biofeedback are some of the techniques for controlling this energy in ourselves. There is even the possibility that this form of energy does not obey the usual parameters of time and space (see *Psychic Discoveries Behind the Iron Curtain*).

Other transpersonal psychologists' main field of exploration has to do with how we can use our subjectively experienced inner states. These include imagination, dreams, and fantasy (Clark, Westheiner, and Hayes); reverie (Koestler); and concentration (Richard). A useful image for understanding this approach is to consider all the inputs into our nervous system, including both external and internal. Usually the external signals are stronger and block out the weaker internal ones, but through relaxation and concentration we can learn to shut out the external signals temporarily and listen to the internal ones. This assumption shows up not only in works of the authors mentioned immediately above, but also in the biofeedback work at the Menninger Foundation and in the meditation articles. The biofeedback researchers amplify these weak internal signals so they can be picked up by the externally oriented senses, while the meditation researchers try to increase the sensitivity of the person to what is going on inside him.

Another series of inputs into transpersonal psychology comes from physiological research. In this collection of articles the biofeedback work of Green, Green, and Walters also represents these inputs. When we are reasoning, calculating, and doing other rigorously logical types of thinking, our brains are likely to be emitting a brain wave pattern called *beta*. (See the biofeedback article for a fuller explanation.) These are predominantly the types of thinking we encourage in schools. We have developed our curricula to teach this in schools, and our society has benefited from this "beta-curriculum" in such things as science and technology. But what about the other brain rhythms? Perhaps we could develop curricular use of the slower alpha, theta, and delta patterns too. Could these provide leads for some of our untapped human potentials? Another way of conceiving this challenge is through the work of Robert Ornstein. It used to be thought that the left and right hemispheres of the brain were almost duplicates. Now some scientists speculate that the left half is the reasoning, analytical, logical half and uses language for its sequential thinking, while the right half is spatial, artistic, intuitive and integrates material simultaneously in its thinking. Whether or not this speculation is accurate, we can ask, "Have we developed a school curriculum that ignores the 'right half's' potentials?"

In summary, then, transpersonal psychologists are exploring a variety of human behavior and trying to bring these topics within the realm of systematic psychological study. The topics are widely diverse but intersect in several ways. These include the following, but are not limited to them: 1) a new image of man, 2) a synthesis of widely separated fields, 3) our impulse toward self-transcendence and spiritual growth, 4) altered states of consciousness, 5) parapsychology and psychic phenomena, 6) other cultures and their psychologies, 7) a new form of energy, 8) subjective, inner states, and 9) recent physiological discoveries. While a transpersonal psychologist who is interested in one or more of these fields may judge any of the others as full of promise or as a dead end, he generally recognizes that he may be wrong and is willing to consider the other fields with an open mind.

Educational Applications

Since transpersonal psychology is in the formative stages, so are its applications to education. The tone of most of the articles in this section is one of the excitement of discovery and excited anticipation about the possible use of the ideas contained in the writings. For the classroom teacher who likes to be told what to do, these articles contain some specific ideas, but at this stage of development, transpersonal education is more of a challenge to creative and innovative teachers than it is a recipe book of lesson plans. A helpful way to think about educational applications is in terms of a) general transpersonal abilities which contribute to all or many current courses, b) the use of transpersonal elements and content in specific courses, and c) a whole, new image of man, what we are capable of learning, and the values and experiences of transcendence.

Examples of two general abilities that can be developed are shown in meditation and creativity. Driscoll reports that meditation improved grades generally, helped in the social relationships of his students, and lowered drug abuse. The last is especially interesting in light of Weil's contention that people have a natural desire to experience altered states of consciousness. If we assume that Weil is correct, then meditation and other forms of altered consciousness might be useful substitutes for drugs. A transpersonal drug education program would teach people how to control and explore their consciousness in non-drug ways.

At least one kind of creativity seems to be linked with altered states, too, as Koestler shows. It is interesting to note that his work and that of the biofeedback researchers, Clark's "Imagination and Fantasy," Hayes's "Do You Have Your Dream for English?" and other articles show how to tune in to our internal signals a source of creativity, in the sciences as well as in the arts. The abilities to block out external signals temporarily and to relax and focus on the processes going on inside us seem to be skills that are useful in many studies and in various situations. Here too are some general skills that might be part of the curriculum in many classes. Westheimer reports that a fantasy journey may take up class time that seems to be unproductive on the face of it, but that the journey results in a more orderly classroom and increased learning because the students are in a receptive learning mode. Perhaps students don't need more stimulation as much as they need to focus on the stimulation that is already there. By controlling their mental states, people may learn to be passive receivers and accumulators of information at some times and be analytical, intellectually active, and critical at others. These may be prior psychological readiness abilities for optimum learning, just as one's psychological capacities will be a facilitating skill like learning to read or doing arithmetic.

Transpersonal content can be used to enrich and round out several subjects. When the so-called scientific method is taught, for instance, a complete treatment of that topic should include the sort of information that Koestler presents about how scientists actually do science, as differentiated from the step-by-step logical approach that is frequently taught. This approach should help overcome the stereotyped objection that scientists are only cold, logical, reasoning, and unimaginative people. The content of the sciences can be made more lively, too. Biofeedback is a way to experience human biology. Meditation can be a door to understanding other cultures as well as understanding oneself; it can also be a topic in biology. If Weil's assumption that the desire for altered states is a part of human nature is correct, then learning about other peoples can include information on how they interpret and achieve these states. This is likely to be part of their religions and/or world views. Poetry, music, and the other arts are often attempts to capture and create the peak-experience altered state. The introduction to "The Ins and Outs of Mind-Body Energy" suggests that this may be the physical education of the future. It could also be a part of biology, an introduction to the study of India, health education, and training in creativity; constructing the biofeedback machines would be an exciting industrial technology project. Since transpersonal psychology tends to cut across current subject lines, it provides a natural route for integrative and interdisciplinary courses.

How can we teach students that not all questions have a right or wrong answer? How can they learn that there are fields in which people don't know the answers, but are trying to find out? How can we teach them that experts and specialists disagree? How can we teach them to accept ambiguity, to be open-minded, to make a decision on incomplete evidence, to revise their tentative conclusions as more information comes in? Since transpersonal psychology leads into some frontiers of human knowledge and experience and includes many controversial topics, it is a natural path for these higher intellectual skills. The articles in this section present topics which can be worked into most current high school curricula. Because these topics are exploratory and speculative, at least in our culture, they are natural topics for teaching students that education is more than knowing facts and solving problems correctly. Explorers of the mind, like explorers of geography, are constantly opening up and mapping new territories. Whether the new territory is ESP, meditation, our inner awareness, or other aspects of transpersonal consciousness the psychological maps and new discoveries are not clearly drawn or completely filled in. These fields which are in the process of being formulated provide current examples of how science is growing and of how people handle problems with unknown answers. Biofeedback, yoga, parapsychology, altered consciousness, and other transpersonal topics exemplify how new interests can be handled; and the people working and writing in these fields show open-mindedness and the ability to change paradigms and to explore new realities as new evidence comes in.

Finally, what could education be if the possibilities in these articles turn out to be capabilities that we all can develop? What if our view of man expands again as it has done before when we've found that we can do more than we previously thought was possible? (Harman, 1969.) Each of these articles points to skills that we may be able to develop in ourselves and our students. Some of these skills seem far-fetched, almost as unbelievable as the products of our science and technology would have seemed to someone living three hundred years ago. Can we learn to tune in the creative signals of our brains? Can we learn to control the autonomic nervous system? Can we increase our ability to concentrate so that we can learn more and faster? Can we develop education for the right half of our brains as well as for the left half and for the delta, theta, and alpha rhythms as well as for beta? What else may be possible? Suppose only one or two of these potentials become actualized. What would happen if we started to use fifteen percent of our capacities instead of only ten percent? These are the questions which fascinate transpersonal educators and transpersonal psychologists. What we thought was the horizon of our potentials is turning out to be only the foreground. The articles in this section show a few first steps beyond yesterday's horizon. The next steps into our future may be the most exciting and educational trip mankind has taken.

REFERENCES

Association for Transpersonal Psychology, P.O. Box 3049, Stanford, California, 94305.

Green, Elmer and Alyce Green, "The Ins and Outs of Mind-Body Energy," In *Science Year, 1974: World Book Science Annual*, pp. 137–147, Field Enterprises Educational Corporation, Chicago, 1973.

Harman, Willis, "The New Copernican Revolution," *Journal of Transpersonal Psychology*, Vol. 1, No. 2, Fall 1969.

Hartley Productions, movies "Potentially Yours," "Psychics, Saints, and Scientists," "Inner Spaces," "The Ultimate Mystery," Cos Cob, Conn.

The Journal for the Study of Consciousness.

The Journal of Transpersonal Psychology.

Kuhn, Thomas C., *The Structure of Scientific Revolutions*, University of Chicago Press, 1970.

Masters, R. E. L. and Jean Houston, *Mind Games: The Guide to Inner Spaces*, Dell, 1972.

Ornstein, Robert, *The Psychology of Consciousness*, Viking, 1973.

——————, "Right and Left Thinking," *Psychology Today*, May, 1973.

Ostrander, Sheila and Lynn Schroeder, *Psychic Discoveries Behind the Iron Curtain*, Bantam Books, 1971.

Savary, Louis and Marianne S. Anderson, *Passages: A Guide for Pilgrims of the Mind*, Harper and Row, 1973.

Tart, Charles, *Altered States of Consciousness*, Anchor-Doubleday, 1972.

THE WORD AND THE VISION *

Arthur Koestler

The Art of Science. Does Koestler present another way to use our minds, a way which some people have developed powerfully? Can the rest of us learn to use this ability too? How can we teach our students that there are other useful ways of thinking, which are not like the usual verbal-sequential way we specialize in during most of our schooling? Koestler's collection of anecdotes fills in the third part of the four-stage model of creativity that Weisskopf mentioned in the Freudian section: preparation, incubation, illumination, and verification. If this is an important part of the way creative science is done, let's teach our future scientists to use their incubative and illumination capacities as well as the usual factual preparation and logical verification.

Let us return from poets to scientists, and to the question what guidance the latter could possibly derive from the intervention of unconscious processes. The answer which, by analogy, now suggests itself is that *the temporary relinquishing of conscious controls liberates the mind from certain constraints which are necessary to maintain the disciplined routines of thoughts but may become an impediment to the creative leap; at the same time other types of ideation on more primitive levels of mental organization are brought into activity*. The first part of this sentence indicates an act of abdication, the second an act of promotion. It will be useful to remember this dual aspect of the Eureka act; it will be seen, later on, to correspond to the destructive-constructive character of all great revolution in the history of thought.

The scientific counterpart of the Coleridge episode is the Kekulé episode. But the vision of the serpent biting its tail was only the last one in a series, which extended over a period of seven or eight years. This is how Kekulé described one of the early but decisive quasi-hallucinations, which led to his theory of molecular constitution—he was then living in London:

'One fine summer evening,' he relates, 'I was returning by the last omnibus, "outside" as usual, through the deserted streets of the metropolis, which are at other times so full of life. I fell into a reverie, and lo! the atoms were gambolling before my eyes. Whenever, hitherto, these diminutive beings had appeared to me, they had always been in motion; but up to that time, I had never been able to discern the nature of their motion. Now, however, I saw how, frequently, two smaller atoms united to form a pair; how a larger one embraced two smaller ones; how still larger ones kept hold of three or even four of the smaller; whilst

*From Arthur Koestler, *The Act of Creation* (London: The Hutchinson Publishing Group), pp. 169–173, by permission of the author and of A. D. Peters & Company, Literary Agents. He is author of many books, including *Roots of Coincidence*, a treatment of physics and parapsychology.

the whole kept whirling in a giddy dance. I saw how the larger ones formed a chain ... I spent part of the night putting on paper at least sketches of these dream forms.'

The whirling, giddy vision reminds one of the hallucinations of schizophrenics, as painted or described by them. Kekulé's case is rather exceptional, but nevertheless characteristic in one respect: the sudden abdication of conceptual thought in favour of semi-conscious visual conceits.

Another example is Michael Faraday, one of the greatest physicists of all time, who also was a 'visionary' not only in the metaphorical but in the literal sense. He saw the stresses surrounding magnets and electric currents as curves in space, for which he coined the name 'lines of forces,' and which, in his imagination, were as real as if they consisted of solid matter. He visualized the universe patterned by these lines—or rather by narrow tubes through which all forms of 'ray-vibrations' or energy-radiations are propagated. This vision of curved tubes which 'rose up before him like things' proved of almost incredible fertility: it gave birth to the dynamo and the electric motor; it led Faraday to discard the ether, and to postulate that light was electro-magnetic radiation. Perhaps the most remarkable fact about Faraday is that he lacked any mathematical education or gift, and was 'ignorant of all but the merest elements of arithmetic'; and mathematics is of course regarded as an indispensable tool of the physicist. In his Faraday memorial lecture in 1881, von Helmholtz—himself one of the greatest mathematical physicists of the century—remarked:

> It is in the highest degree astonishing to see what a large number of general theorems, the methodical deduction of which requires the highest powers of mathematical analysis, he found by a kind of intuition, with the security of instinct, without the help of a single mathematical formula.

Kekulé's visions resemble hallucinatory flights; Faraday's, the stable delusional systems of paranoia. Kekulé's serpent reminds one of paintings by Blake; the curves of force which crowd Faraday's universe recall the vortices in Van Gogh's skies.

Around fifty—like Newton, and at the same age—Faraday had a nervous breakdown. He had always hated writing letters and had stopped lecturing; now he seemed to have developed an abhorrence of language itself:

> This is to declare in the present instance, when I say I am not able to bear much talking, it means really, and without any mistake, or equivocation or oblique meaning, or implication, or subterfuge, or omission, that I am not able, being at present rather weak in the head and able to work no more.

Distrust of words is a trait often found among those who create with their eyes.

Let us leave the borderlands of pathology. Nobody could have been further removed from it than the mild, sober, and saintly Einstein. Yet we find in him the same distrust of conscious conceptual thought, and the same reliance on visual imagery. In 1945 an inquiry was organized among eminent mathematicians in America to find out their working methods. In reply to the questionnaire which was sent to him, Einstein wrote:

> The words or the language, as they are written or spoken, do not seem to play any role in my mechanism of thought. The physical entities which seem to serve as elements in thought are certain signs and more or less clear images which can be 'voluntarily' reproduced and combined. . . .
>
> . . . Taken from a psychological viewpoint, this combinatory play seems to be the essential feature in productive thought—before there is any connection with logical construction in words or other kinds of signs which can be communicated to others.
>
> The above-mentioned elements are, in any case, of visual and some of muscular type. Conventional words or other signs have to be sought for laboriously only in a secondary stage, when the mentioned associative play is sufficiently established and can be reproduced at will.
>
> According to what has been said, the play with the mentioned elements is aimed to be analogous to certain logical connections one is searching for.
>
> In a stage when words intervene at all, they are, in my case, purely auditive, but they interfere only in a secondary stage, as already mentioned.

The inquiry was organized by Jacques Hadamard, whom I have repeatedly quoted, since he is to my knowledge the only mathematician who has made a systematic research into the psychology of mathematical creation. Of himself he said:

> I distinctly belong to the auditory type; and precisely on that account my mental pictures are exclusively visual. The reason for that is quite clear to me: such visual pictures are more naturally vague, as we have seen it to be necessary in order to lead me without misleading me.

He summed up the results of the inquiry as follows:

> Among the mathematicians born or resident in America . . . phenomena are mostly analogous to those which I have noticed in my own case. Practically all of them . . . avoid not only the use of mental words but also, just as I do, the mental use of algebraic or any other precise signs; also as in my case, they use vague images. . . . The mental pictures . . . are most frequently visual, but they may also be of another kind, for instance, kinetic. There can also be auditive ones, but even these . . . quite generally keep their vague character.

It rather sounds as if mathematical discoveries were born out of the airy nothings of *A Midsummer Night's Dream*:

> . . . as imagination bodies forth
> The forms of things unknown, the poet's pen
> Turns them to shapes, and gives to airy nothing
> A local habitation and a name.

The inquiry brought conclusive proof that among mathematicians, verbal thinking plays only a subordinate part in the decisive phase of the creative act; and there is a mass of evidence to show that this is also the rule among original thinkers in other branches of science.

This is a rather startling discovery in view of the fact that language is the proudest possession of *homo sapiens*, and the very foundation on which mental evolution could build. 'Logic' derives from *logos*, which originally means 'language,' 'thought,' and 'reason,' all in one. Thinking in concepts emerged out of thinking in images through the slow development of the powers of abstraction and symbolization, as the phonetic script emerged by similar processes out of pictorial symbols and hieroglyphs. Most of us were brought up in the belief that 'thinking' is synonymous with verbal thinking, and philosophers from Athens to Oxford have kept reasserting this belief. The early Behaviourists went even further, asserting not only that words were indispensable to thought, but also that thinking is nothing more than the subliminal movements of the vocal chords, an inaudible whispering to oneself. Yet if all thinking were verbal thinking Einstein would not qualify as a thinker. In fact, the whole evidence points in the opposite direction, summed up in a single sentence in Woodworth's classic textbook of experimental psychology: 'Often we have to get away from speech in order to think clearly.' And we heard one testimony after another from great scientists, which show that in order to create they had to regress at times from the word to the picture-strip, from verbal symbolism to visual symbolism—some, like Einstein, even to the kinesthetic sensation of muscle-motions. The word 'regression' is appropriate, because the high *aesthetic* value which we put on visual imagery should not obscure the fact that *as vehicles of thought*, pictorial and other non-verbal representations are indeed earlier, both phylogenetically and ontogenetically older forms of ideation, than verbal thinking. Kekulé's 'Let us dream, gentlemen,' is an invitation to regression and retreat—but a regression which prepares the forward leap, a *reculer pour mieux sauter*.

THE AFFECTIVE DOMAIN AND BEYOND*

Robert E. Kantor

A Transpersonal Education for a Transpersonal Man. Kantor says that the nature of psychology is changing; as a result, education is changing too. By bringing in evidence from studies of creativity and dreams, and from other psychologies, he says education is now beginning to focus on the subjective self. This is similar to the "self" that Crampton writes of in her article on psychosynthesis applied to education. Kantor also mentions other themes of transpersonal educational psychology which appear in this section. The interest in dreams is picked up in the article that immediately follows this one. Grof's work with the medical and psychotherapeutic uses of psychedelic drugs is put in a different perspective by Weil's claim that humans naturally desire altered consciousness. Barron's research on creativity echoes the previous article by Koestler. Clark's exercises for imagination and fantasy have overtones of Jungian intuition. While these topics have yet to be systematically related to each other, Kantor begins collecting them together.

INTRODUCTION

I speak to you today from a platform provided by a basic training in social science, and I am going to discuss how the future of affective education looks to one somewhat aberrant psychologist. There will be no pretense of a thorough review of the data or a careful weighing of evidence. If any of you are looking for some sort of utility or relevance in these remarks, I hope you will find it as the kind of help one occasionally gets from a frank brother, prompted by a mixture of love, sympathy, and sibling rivalry to give improving advice to other members of his family.

Since psychology is basic to education in the same way that biology is to medicine, a revolution in psychology usually foreshadows a revolution in education. And to my mind, there is a revolution in psychology underway. The signs are plainest in psychopathology, as usual, since the psychopathological is the caricature by which we identify the normal. Therefore, the signs exist most clearly in psychotherapy (T-groups, sensitivity training, encounter groups, Gestalt therapy and so forth), and in the rebirth of certain topics for psychologists, such as hypnosis, death, creativity, and expanded awareness.

In other words, most of our knowledge of personality structure comes from contemplation of abnormality rather than from a search for regular-

*From Robert Kantor, "The Affective Domain and Beyond," *Journal for the Study of Consciousness* 3, no. 1 (Jan.–June, 1970): 20–42. Reprinted by permission of the author and publisher. Abridged by the editor.

Robert E. Kantor is President of Multi-Media Productions, Inc., Stanford, California, and co-author of the recent book *Contemporary School Psychology*.

ity. But there is yet no good explanation of why most people function as well as they do. All of us have had less than perfect mothers and fathers, and all of us are subjected from time to time to severe psychological stress. Feelings of hostility, inferiority, and dependency are the lot of every one of us. Why do most people bear them so well and others succumb so easily? Nobody knows. Worse than that, nobody, except a few middle-aged psychologists, disillusioned with the neat formulas of their training days, seems to care.

We shall adopt, for better understanding, a conceptual model of personality based on the self-image, because the self-image offers a useful way of summarizing the diversity of techniques that have been used to implement personality development. The self-image (Self-concept of Bugental [1965], personal construct system of Kelly [1955]) is, of course, a much more complex thing than the name suggests. It is by no means free of inconsistencies and fragmentation, but for our purposes we may oversimplify and speak as though it were a unified pattern of feelings and behavior. It has been likened to the input signal of a feedback control system; the personality and behavior-pattern structure tend to "follow" the self-image. We become as we imagine ourselves to be: "As a man thinketh in his heart, so is he." In a more elaborate metaphor, Lilly (1966) views conscious and unconscious mental processes as a hierarchy of programs available to the brain-computer, with the self-image as a "meta-program" that modifies controls, and creates the programs giving rise to behavior.

Research in psychology and psychiatry has emphasized the extent to which mental health is defined as a man's view of himself, as the accessibility of the self to consciousness, and as acceptance of the self. Erikson has helped us to understand how crucial and how perilous is the young person's search for identity. Josh Billings said: "It is not only the most difficult thing to know oneself, but the most inconvenient one, too." Human beings have always had an enormous variety of clever devices for running away from themselves, and modern society is particularly rich in such stratagems. A rational society requires a narrow, specialized focus. Its citizens can acquire this focus most effectively by stuffing their heads with so much knowledge that they never have time to probe the fearful and wonderful world within.

The cure for our fears is not resistance to the new teaching techniques, but insistence on trying them carefully, observing them, and then discussing and deciding how they can be fitted in to give children a faster and easier education in things that are best taught this way. At the same time, teachers and parents should be allowed not less but more time for the education in affect that we call variety and humanity and warmth and love.

We have had to spend so much time on the facts and skills segment in the past that we have not done what we would have liked with the rest of the curriculum. Now the prospect of success in teaching the facts and skills means that we will have the time and space to do more with the rest. What we are faced with at the prospect of success in cognitive instruction is the necessity of redeveloping the curriculum to do more with the affective learnings.

What is entailed in this task? The first step is to clarify the differences between cognitive and affective learnings in terms of the elements already defined. Let us run through these quickly, to establish the fact that there are genuine differences.

Goals. For affective learnings, the goal is not mastery. There is no reachable end-point on the way to which highly specific steps or objectives can be spelled out. Continuous growth is the goal.

Nature of the Learner. The question of equality of capacity is not central, since mastery is not the goal. What is of concern is "an ability, a power . . . the possibility of growth."

Content Analysis. With the emphasis on the development of powers or their growth, analysis of what needs to be learned is very different here. It is concerned with the nature of the process through which powers develop.

Materials. The total environment is of greater concern than any piece of material. The concern is for richness and diversity rather than precision.

Methodology. Powers are personal. Their growth comes necessarily from individual use. The concern is to provide many opportunities for their responsible exercise.

Evaluation. Since growth of "carrying power forward" is the goal, evaluation is concerned with the individual rather than with the group, and is likely to be seen in global rather than concrete terms.

Organization. While room needs to be made to ensure independent functioning, many personal powers require the presence of others in the picture for their proper development. The isolation booth is an inappropriate site for the larger learnings.

By now, a conversation is appropriate between the educator and the scientist, during which the former asks of the latter: "Are you doing pure research, or do you have something in mind?"

Let us briefly reconsider the relationship between individuals and the culture in which they live. One definition of culture would be, I think, a machine for making it possible for human beings to develop their potentials. Obviously, outside an organized culture it is virtually impossible for even the most gifted human being to develop and actualize what lies latent within him. However, this condition is paradoxical, because culture is not only a machine helping us to actualize potentialities; it is also a machine for preventing us from actualizing them. And it may, moreover, be a machine for helping us to actualize the most undesirable potentialities. We must never forget, after all, that while human beings are perfectly capable of being human, they are also perfectly capable of being like beasts, and much worse than beasts. There have been cultures that have not only prevented human beings from actualizing their desirable factors, but have positively encouraged them to actualize the most undesirable ones.

Somehow, we have to work out a society that is sufficiently stable and rigid to support the human being and allow him to function out of its rigidity, but at the same time sufficiently elastic to permit him to go beyond its bounds. For it is only by transcending the limits of the culture that an advance can be made. Needless to say, it is only in a perfect culture that we should be able to get the highest possible development of the individual, but we are certainly not going to get a perfect culture within any measurable time. I propose not to be utopian and talk about no place, but to be realistic and talk about something that can happen in the kind of place in which we find ourselves at this time. What could be done within the limitations of the culture in which we exist today?

We see at once that what needs to be done is a part of something much larger—a thorough investigation of man's inner world, a great project of mind exploration that could and should rival and surpass space exploration in interest and importance. This would open a new realm of being for man, a realm of mental realities, built on but transcending the realm of material realities, a world of satisfactions transcending physical satisfactions, in some way more absolute and more perfect. Ordinary men and women obtain occasional glimpses of it through falling in love, or through other overwhelming experiences of ecstasy, beauty, or awe. And we have the reports of the occasional mental explorers, poets, thinkers, scientists and mystics who have penetrated into its interior. Think of Wordsworth anticipating Freud by revealing in us the "high instincts before which our moral nature doth tremble."

SUBJECTIVE SELF

To the question of "who am I?" many will probably answer with "a school superintendent," "a middle class American," and so on, and as such they will experience themselves in their everyday lives, rather than out of the unlabelled totality of their being. The "subjective self" is not another aspect or fragment of the personality, but a "center of gravity;" a person identifying with the persona is believing a part of him to be his whole psychological reality. Much the same idea is expressed by the metaphor that we are usually living in only a room of our house. This house is actually a palace, with towers, salons, and gardens, but we are locked up in the kitchen or perhaps in the cellar, believing that this is the whole house.

In Gestalt therapy, the main approach to "reassimilating the disowned" is perhaps that of enacting one's involuntary processes. By voluntarily doing that which is commonly automatic in us, we establish—or re-discover—a link between ourselves. By acting out a character in a dream, for instance, we may discover that this was a projection—i.e., only an illusory "other," and contact that core of experience that was expressing itself indirectly through such otherness. Likewise, in impersonating our voice, or any other spontaneous movement—a rocking in the chair, a nod, a smile—by "becoming" them and giving them a voice, we may find that we are only becoming what we already are: somebody wanting to do all that, choosing to do so and finding some satisfaction in it, rather than a passive victim of such occurrences.

In the above discussion, I have been viewing the therapeutic process as one in which the alternative to identification with a self-image is the experiencing of the self, direct contact with one's reality rather than a substitution of a "better" self-image in place of the old one.

I would reemphasize that both religious and psychiatric ideas are not so much the outcome of speculation as the formulation of experiences. The notion of a subjective self in psychological writing reflects the experience of such in persons who have undergone therapy, just as the religious conception of the subjective self is the reflection of the mystical experience.

The point of contact between the religious and the secular forms may be provided by the notion of openness to experience, a concept linking our discussion of identity with that of grasp on reality. Studies on openness to experience (such as Barron's on "complexity" and Taft's on egopermissiveness) suggests that in our "normal state" our range of experience is limited by contact with the world, just as our subjective self-identity is substituted for by our conceptual, mnemonic, social self-image.

Aldous Huxley reflects on the idea of repressive civilization this way:

Each one of us is potentially Mind at Large. But insofar as we are animals, our business is at all costs to survive. To make biological survival possible, Mind at Large has to be funnelled through the reducing valve of the brain and nervous system. What comes out at the other end is a measly trickle of the kind of consciousness which will help us to stay alive on the surface of this particular planet. To formulate and express the contents of this reduced awareness, man has invented and endlessly elaborated those symbol-systems and implicit philo-sophies which we call languages. Every individual is at once the beneficiary and the victim of the linguistic tradition into which he has been born—the beneficiary inasmuch as language gives access to the accumulated records of other people's experience, the victim insofar as it confirms him in the belief that reduced awareness is the only awareness and as it bedevils his sense of reality, so that he is all too apt to take his concepts for data, his words for actual things. That which, in the language of religion, is called 'this world' is the universe of reduced awareness, expressed, and as it were, petrified by language. The various 'other worlds' with which human beings erratically make contact are so many elements in the totality of the awareness belonging to Mind at Large. Most people, most of the time, know only what comes through the reducing valve and is conse-crated as genuinely real by the local language. Certain persons, however, seem to be born with a kind of by-pass that circumvents the reducing valve. In others temporary by-passes may be acquired either spontaneously, or as the result of deliberate 'spiritual exercises,' or through hypnosis, or by means of drugs. Through these permanent or temporary by-passes there flows, not indeed the perception 'of everything that is happening everywhere in the universe' (for the by-pass does not abolish the reducing valve which still excludes the total content of Mind at Large), but something more than, and above all something different from, the carefully selected utilitarian material which our narrowed, individual minds regard as a complete, or at least sufficient, picture of reality.

However, there exists an important area of living in which the world's sway fades, and in which the subjective self rules supreme. This area is that of dreams, a form of symbolic expression that we all share and that constitutes, perhaps, our most spontaneous activity. Dream symbolism expresses us better than concepts can, but it stands as an entity separated from us, a subjective self. It is a message from our depths, but only when we understand its language and recognize it as our own expression. Psychotherapy has paid a great deal of attention to dreams, whether in terms of interpretation (psychoanalysis), underlying the archetype qualities (Jungian analysis), or unfolding their contents through enacting (psycho-drama, Gestalt therapy). Yet aside from the therapy context, there is a sharp split between our dream life and our conscious concern for it (which seems characteristic of our culture). This is not the case in the so-called primitive cultures, and especially in those where shamanism is more alive. Among these, a pervasive interest in dreams goes hand-in-hand with a collaborative relationship between subjective self and social self.

A particular approach to dream life that deserves mention among the ways of growth presented in this paper is the very systematic handling of these productions among the Senoi, a remarkable culture in Malaya. They were studied by Kilton Stewart of the Royal Anthropological Society (London), and he expressed his astonishment at their high state of psychological success. The Senoi, led by Tohats (a combination of educators and doctors) had not had a violent crime or an intercommunal conflict for nearly 300 years. The foothill tribes that surround the land of the Senoi have such a firm belief in the powers of this highland group that they avoid any pugnacious entry into Senoi territory. From all Stewart could learn, this respect of the lowlanders for the Senoi is a very old one. Because of their psychological knowledge of strangers in their territory, the Senoi said it was simple to devise ways of keeping them off.

Stewart's investigation of the Senoi convinced him that they have arrived at their intriguing state of social serenity through the system of psychology that they have invented and developed. Dream interpretation is the center of their system. It is an established custom among this people that at the beginning of every day the family discusses their night's dreams. Each head of the family is to some extent a dream expert. Not only are the dreams told and listened to, they are evaluated, and the father gives advice to the children. A child may have dreamed that he was falling, for instance, and the father may comment: "There must have been a purpose in your fall. The spirit of the depth must have been pulling you down. What did you see under you?" And if the child did not see anything in his nightmarish panic, he may be given the advice to look next time to see where he is going and discover the purpose of the fall. The child may have a dream in the following nights where he starts to fall, but remembering the advice, he stops resisting it, and the fall becomes flight. When his father hears this report, he may still feel that this dream is unfinished, for he has not found anything or met anybody, and his further directions will modify subsequent dreaming until the child learns something from the dream. Only then is a dream considered complete among the Senoi: when the dreamer has found in it something that he may bring back to the community, a new song, a dance, an invention, or an idea.

I have touched on a single aspect of the Senoi's handling of dream material, but this may suffice to point out the possibility of what amounts to a cultivation of dream life and at the same time the establishment of a link between the activities of the dreaming and wakeful mind. The subject is led into an attitude of taking responsibility and feeling himself to be a doer of his dreams, as he is of his conscious actions, and thus he learns how to master his dreams without detracting from their spontaneity and their potential for revelation. On the contrary, he learns how to live them out to the fullest, just as an artist learns to develop a theme to its complete expression. Since dreaming is a symbolic display of a person's feeling-life, the practice of the Senoi seems a salutary cultural means of developing unity between feeling, thinking, and doing.

Stewart's data on the dream life of the various Senoi people indicate to him how dreaming can and does become the deepest avenue of creative thought. He speculates on the waste that occurs in modern civilization because people have shed, or failed to encourage, one-third their power to think—perhaps the most important third. In the West, Stewart goes on to say, the thinking we do while asleep is chaotic, childish, unfocused, because we do not respond to dreams as socially important, nor do we include dreaming in the educative process. This social neglect of a significant aspect of man's reflective side, when his creative channels are most open, seems poor education to Stewart.

Summing up the essentials of this section, we may reassert that the end-state that is implicitly sought by man and that is the object of the various traditions, schools, or systems under discussion is one that is characterized by the experience of openness to the reality of every moment. It is also an experience of self-acceptance, where "self" does not stand for a preconceived notion or image but for the experiential, subjective self-reality, moment after moment.

SUBJECTIVE SELF AND CREATIVITY

What, then, are the characteristics of people who are near to their subjective selves? Here is Joseph Conrad's version (preface to *The Nigger of the Narcissus*):

The artist descends within himself, and in that lonely region of stress and strife, if he be deserving and fortunate, he finds the terms of his appeal. His appeal is made to our less obvious capacities: to that part of our nature which, because of the warlike conditions of existence, is necessarily kept out of sight within the more resisting and hard qualities—like the vulnerable body within a steel armour. His appeal is less loud, more profound, less distinct, more stirring—and sooner forgotten. Yet its effect endures forever.

How does scientific psychology characterize these people? The data accruing in the researches of Walter Pahnke and Charles Savage at the Spring Grove Hospital, of Abraham Maslow at Brandeis, of Robert Mogar, and others now in the field, seem to indicate that those persons who have been demonstrably closer to their subjective selves have some personality attributes in common:

They are more open to hidden levels of meaning in art and science, and see the beauty in complex forms, even when these forms are not conventionally or officially regarded as beautiful. They have a clearer view of the ideal, of the perfect, and therefore of what might be possible to accomplish. They are very apt to be innovators.

Such persons use easily, naturally, and normally the language of the poets, seers, mystics, and artistic men. They employ paradoxes, parables, art, and nonverbal modes with clarity and fruitfulness. They dwell in the sensory world with delight; they have little recourse to final judgments. An anecdote is told of Einstein riding along the countryside in a car with a friend, who commented that some sheep were newly shorn. Einstein looked at them with interest and observed that the sheep were shorn on this side, at any rate.

Those close to their subjective selves very frequently report feelings of illumination and insight that, with the force of absolute certainty, they have entered another world. William James, having experienced this in himself and knowing of it in others, called it the Noetic Quality. This quality is irrational and is not an increase in facts. Rather, it is in the nature of psychological insight.

The parallels between these research findings on the characteristics of persons close to their subjective selves and the independent research findings on creative people are most intriguing. Professor Frank Barron at the University of California recently published his data on the three traits that mark the highly creative person:

The first has to do with the relationships of complexity to simplicity, and of order to disorder. Creative individuals seem to be able to discern more true complexity in whatever it is they attend. This results in part from the fact that they are attracted to complexity and find it more challenging, so that indeed there is more complexity for them to discern. They prefer phenomena and visual displays not easily ordered, or those that present perplexing contradictions. When confronted with an ambiguous perceptual field, as in Rorschach's inkblot test they seek a synthesizing image that will unite many diverse elements.

A second trait of creative people in Barron's findings is perceptual openness, or resistance to premature closure. This may relate to the first, since such an attitude provides more opportunity for complexity to develop in the phenomenal field. A good measure of it derives from the theories of C. G. Jung, which contrast the perceptual attitude and the judgmental attitude. According to Jung, when a person faces an event, he performs either an act of perception (he becomes aware of something) or an act of judgment (he comes to a conclusion, often an evaluative conclusion, about something). If one of these action tendencies is strong in a person, the other is correspondingly weak. The judging attitude is said to lead to an orderly, prudently planned life, based on relatively closed principles, whereas the perceptual attitude leads to more openness to experience, including experience of the inner world of self. The perceptual attitude facilitates spontaneity and flexibility.

In Barron's studies, every group but scientists is predominantly perceptual rather than judgmental, and in every group, including scientists, the more creative individuals are more perceptually oriented and the less creative are more judgmentally oriented.

The third characteristic of creative persons according to Barron is reliance on intuition, hunches, and inexplicable feelings. They trust the irrational processes of their own mind. Intuition . . . is a greater awareness of deeper meanings and possibilities. Creative individuals are characteristically intuitive. Test results cited by Barron indicate that more than 90 percent of the creative individuals studied are predominantly intuitive. Experiments and interviews confirm the test scores.

Stated simply, recent theoretical innovations recognize that greater access to the subjective self is a cardinal feature of creative and other novel perceptual experiences. And creative or revelatory experiences including a temporary and voluntary breaking up of perceptual constancies, permitting one "to shake free from dead literalism, to recombine the old familiar elements into new, imaginative, amusing, or beautiful patterns."

A second significant parallel between the Barron work and that of others concerns the remarkable subjective and behavioral similarities of these experiences. Consistent findings in research on hypnotic and dream states, certain phases of the creative process, and sensory and dream deprivation indicate an almost complete overlap of major effects. Reported communalities include significant complexities in perception, dominance of intuition and imagery over verbal-associative thinking, and suspension of conventional judgments.

In a 1964 issue of *The American Psychologist*, an incisive paper by Holt, a well-known research psychologist, is entitled "Imagery: The Return of the Ostracised." After examining the traditional scientific and cultural resistances to such phenomena as pseudo-hallucinations, hypnogogic and dream images, extrasensory perception, and hypnosis, the author goes on to describe the current status in these fields. He points to a number of recent breakthroughs in a variety of research areas that signal the second phase of a psychological revolution. The first phase, covering the first half of this century, was characterized by the scientific extremism of psychoanalysis and behaviorism, movements that purged psychology of the unique and the private. While both psychoanalysis and behaviorism in their orthodox forms have made valuable contributions to our understanding of man, it seems evident now to Holt that these orientations can no longer exclude altered states of consciousness and novel perceptual experiences from the primary subject matter of a normal psychology.

Significantly, some of the leading exponents of both theories, such as B. F. Skinner and H. Hartmann, have recognized these omissions and indicated a need for revision. Consistent with theoretical developments, behavioristic research shows an increasing concern with internal processes, including sensations, images, and cognitions. Similarly, psychoanalytic studies focus more on normal or superior functioning and less on pathology. These trends are not surprising, since some of the most exciting developments during the past decade have occurred in experimental work with dream activity, sensory deprivation, creativity, and hypnosis. Viewing this rich array of research activity as occurring within a broader cultural context, one convergent finding seems of major significance; namely, that richness of imagination and so-called regressive experiences are not the exclusive privilege of madmen and artists. Instead, this work indicates quite conclusively that under favorable circumstances, most people can greatly expand their experiential horizons without sacrificing effectiveness in dealing with conventional reality.

The significant parallels among relatively independent lines of investigation are most striking. They all point to the idea that in the depths of human psyche there is an integrative center around which the whole person—not the ego only, but the shadow and the autonomous complexes also—can effectively form. The evidence for this subjective self has been principally in the field of religious experience. But anyone who uses one of the methods of approach developed by modern psychology is likely to make the discovery for himself. The subjective self is not a religious tenet but a psychological fact.

From this it would seem that, if this discovery of the subjective self (and of the whole person integrated around it) is to be effectively followed up, neither the psychotherapists (as such) nor the social scientists (as such) are likely to take a major part. So far as can be seen, it is in religion, in social service, in the humanities, and above all, in education, that the work must be done.

So far, social science has not taken seriously that lesson that the average man knows quite well. We could be much greater than we are if we really wanted it enough and insisted that those who have the resources to produce such growth would actually apply them where they could do the most good: not to the sick and crippled but to the healthy.

Aldous Huxley promises that when education takes the subjective self into account, ". . . from being an activity mainly concerned with symbols, education will be transformed into an activity concerned mainly with experience and intuition . . . an everyday mysticism underlying and giving significance to everyday rationality, everyday tasks and duties, everyday human relationships." Future man, he noted elsewhere, can be a Zen Buddhist electrical engineer.

In closing, I remember the story of Samuel Beckett's, who, after conducting his hero through a series of misadventures, puts him finally by the side of a road where the hero tries to get the attention of passing travellers. "I tried to groan—Help! Help!—" the hero laments, "but the tone that came out was that of polite conversation."

Readers, do not be heedless of my message, even though the tone is colloquial.

REFERENCES

1. Barron, Frank. "The Dream of Art and Poetry." *Psychology Today*, Dec. 1968.

2. Benoit, Hubert. *The Supreme Doctrine*, N.Y., Viking Press, 1959.

3. Boss, Medard, *A Psychiatrist Discovers India*, Chester Springs, Pa., DuFour, 1965.

4. Fromm, Erich, *The Sane Society*, N.Y., Holt, 1955.

5. Grof, Stanislav, *LSD—A Report on Czekoslovakian Research*, Esalen Recordings, Big Sur, California, 1968.

6. Kantor, Robert E., "The Mutability of Art Styles and Research in Perception," *Art Journal*, Spring, 1968, 27, No. 3, 279–283.

7. Laing, Ronald D., *The Politics of Experience*, N.Y., Pantheon Books, 1966.

8. Maslow, Abraham. *Toward a Psychology of Being*, Princeton, N.J., Van Nostrand, 1962.

9. Pahnke, Walter N., "The Contribution of the Psychology of Religion to the Therapeutic Use of the Psychedelic Substances," in *The Use of LSD in Psychotherapy and Alcoholism*. H. A. Abramson, ed., Indianapolis, Bobbs-Merrill, 1967, 629–652.

10. Stewart, Kilton. "Dream Theory in Malaya," *Complex*, 1951, No. 6. [Reprinted in *Altered States of Consciousness*, Charles Tart (ed), Doubleday, New York, 1969.]

11. Taft, Ronald, "Peak Experiences and Ego Permissiveness," *Acta Psychologica*, 1967.

"DO YOU HAVE YOUR DREAM FOR ENGLISH?" *

Rosemary Hayes

Dreaming, A Useful State. "Altered consciousness, meditation, and all that stuff is interesting, but if I ever did it in my room, I'd raise a few eyebrows, if not lose my job." Using transpersonal psychology in the classroom doesn't require a bizarre overhaul of current practices. In this article a teacher shows how she used one of our most common altered states, dreams, in her classroom. It's nice to know that this experienced teacher found this "the best first experience in poetry that I ever had," but from a larger perspective she demonstrated to her students that at least one altered state can be beneficial. Although we may waste our ability to dream, we have the possibility of using this state. And if the dreaming state can be used this way, how might we use it other ways? Could we use other altered states too?

One day last spring I gave my Creative Writing students the assignment of bringing in the next day dreams which they had had and which they could still remember quite well. I offered no further explanation. The assignment itself intrigued them. Even as they came into the room the next day, they were all still talking about the assignment. Over the usual level of talk I heard one student ask another, "Do you have your dream for English?"

As soon as the bell rang, I gave them an assignment sheet which read simply:

Write about your dream—
    What does the world of your dream look like?
    Who is in it?
    What happens?
Then, if you can, think of your dream as a "vision of truth," personal or otherwise. What do you think it means?

Their only additional instructions were simply to be very quiet and to try to crawl back inside the dream for about five minutes to "see" the way it was, and to recapture the feeling the dream had given them. Then, they were to write just as fast as they could without worrying about literary style or mechanics. Their purpose was to get as much of their dream as possible down on paper in vivid, sharp, detailed language.

We turned out the lights and pulled the drapes. The room became semi-dark and very, very still.

---

*"Do You Have Your Dream for English" was written especially for this book.

Dr. Hayes is Chairman of the Department of English, East Leyden High School, Franklin Park, Illinois.

I had expected some resistance or at least some embarrassed uneasiness, but there was none. Some students leaned back and stretched their legs out in front of them; others put their heads on their desks; some just sat with eyes closed. After about five minutes, one or two began to write. One by one in the next few minutes, they all began. No one broke the silence until a few seconds before the bell rang when I asked them to bring their papers (many of which were finished by this time) with them the next day.

At the beginning of the period the following day, I asked them to go through what they had written and to select the most vital parts of the dream and the most vivid wording. Using what they selected, they were to write a poem. (We had only begun to work with poetry, having spent two days of individual browsing/reading in poetry collections.) The only restrictions placed on the students were that they should not use rhyme and that they should "squeeze out" every excess word.

This is one of the first writings and the subsequent poem:

My dream world was real. It was my hotel room in Acapulco; then for awhile it was the beach; then a public bathroom.

The people in it were not any of my friends. The main lady was the waitress that served me and my friends at the club.

That lady came pounding on my hotel door, screaming and insisting that we ran out without paying for our drinks. I try to explain calmly that we only drank water and she told us it was free. We argue back and forth. She leaves.

Then I'm hanging clothes down at the beach. The same lady comes with a man. In Spanish she tells him, "There she is. She tried to beat me up. She wouldn't pay me my money. Arrest her."

I try to tell him I did no such thing, but he is Spanish and doesn't understand me. The jail, I guess, was a bathroom with some girls. One speaks English so we talk. She told me not to be sad because she has a plan. She puts her arms around me and wants to kiss me.

This dream could mean I felt guilty for not ordering any drinks, but the end could mean I was homesick for affection.

She came pounding on my door and woke me from my sleep.
She wanted my money for reasons unknown;
She went back on her word; the water was free.
She left but came again and not alone.
I wanted to explain. He only spoke Spanish and I was lost.
They put me away where I met a girl who spoke English.
I thought I was saved when she tried to kiss me.

—JoAnn LoCascio

One boy wrote almost nothing the first day, and the next day he came without even that. When he heard the poetry assignment, he said, "Good, I think I can get it down in a poem!" He wrote this:

Blackness
Flat without depth

Hot, suffocated of all light,
Deadly, fearful black.

Is there an edge?

I am tense, sweating with anxiety.

Will anything come?
Will it go on forever?
Or will it win?

My ears are ringing with the muted
soft, tiny whispering voice
of . . . the queen?

It grates on my nerves so that my mind must scream.
My body is dead, hanging dull and aching, senseless in limbo.

A thin white silver thread
Cuts through the top of the blackness,
Cutting downward like a missile.

My head ringing louder, a single howling note.

"Stop!"

But it does not stop.
It cuts down and disappears
As suddenly as the noise.

The whispers cry out to no one.
I try to answer but no words can leave my sandy throat.

The silver mercury thread army shoots toward the top,
My body too wary to stop them.
The blackness becomes a shattered pane of glass,
And so my mind.

—Cary Plettau

Another boy focused on the sensory aspects of his dream:

   I. scent of unseen woods
      far off the horizon,
      a crystalline edge
      on an aqua pond.
      bitter sweetness of grass
      and musky earth smell.
      soft and fluffy dirt,
      dry and powderlike,
      coursing through my fingers,
      ant-hill of crunchy
      grains of hollow dirt heaped.
      dark green prickle plant,
      leaf-like thorns and

partially opened flowers.
gnarled, old tree, twisted,
thick, big, untall,
rough, recessed bark,
concave, convex, concave.
scattered leaves and
seed casings shriveled and
dry in cream brown
sense of something horrible
to come soon
to break peace.

II. yellow squares, dissolving
from the outside.
poof, they pop
and disappear.
suddenly on the horizon looms
a giant monolith? or
monument? or building?
a great distance away
threatening and evil
demonishly interesting.
run toward it but
it never nears.
yellow and red slabs
continue to stay
heaped on the
horizon.
starting to get hazy
it blurs and wavers
and like a mirage
disappears.

Tom Zajac

After the students had written their poems, they did have some feeling that this wasn't poetry. We read "Kubla Khan" and discussed briefly the relationship between dreams and poetry and the suggestive quality of poetry.

The assignment, I felt, was a success for three major reasons: (1) Everyone had something to write about. (2) They were all fascinated by dreams and uninhibited about sharing them. (3) The vivid quality of dreams lends itself to poetic expression.

It was the best first experience in poetry that I have ever tried.

EXCERPTS FROM *THE NATURAL MIND**

Andrew Weil

Altered Consciousness, A Realm to Use. In Koestler's article we saw how several advanced scientific thinkers have used the altered state of reverie. If we recognize the drive for these states as part of human nature, then it is up to us to use that drive in beneficial ways, rather than to force it into the psychological underground, where it may erupt destructively. In some of the other articles in this section we see examples of how altered states have been beneficial and examples of how we might teach their proper use in schools. We have developed many abilities of our normal state, but we have almost ignored altered states. Instead of causing ourselves and our society problems by fighting human nature, we may be able to develop whole ranges of abilities in different altered states. Here is a new educational domain.

It is my belief that the desire to alter consciousness periodically is an innate, normal drive analogous to hunger or the sexual drive. Note that I do not say "desire to alter consciousness by means of chemical agents." Drugs are merely one means of satisfying this drive; there are many others, and I will discuss them in due course. In postulating an inborn drive of this sort, I am not advancing a proposition to be proved or disproved but simply a model to be tried out for usefulness in simplifying our understanding of our observations. The model I propose is consistent with observable evidence. In particular, the omnipresence of the phenomenon argues that we are dealing not with something socially or culturally based bur rather with a biological characteristic of the species. Furthermore, the need for periods of nonordinary consciousness begins to be expressed at ages far too young for it to have much to do with social conditioning. Anyone who watches very young children without revealing his presence will find them regularly practicing techniques that induce striking changes in mental states. Three- and four-year-olds, for example, commonly whirl themselves into vertiginous stupors. They hyperventilate and have other children squeeze them around the chest until they faint. They also choke each other to produce loss of consciousness.

To my knowledge these practices appear spontaneously among children of all societies, and I suspect they have done so throughout history as well. It is most interesting that children quickly learn to keep this sort of play out of sight of grown—ups, who instinctively try to stop them. The sight of a child being throttled into unconsciousness scares the parent, but the child seems to have a wonderful time; at least, he goes right off and

*From Andrew Weil, *The Natural Mind* (Boston: Houghton Mifflin Company, 1972), pp. 19–25, by permission of the publisher. Dr. Weil is a pioneer researcher on the behavilral effects of psychoactive drugs and has published widely in the field.

does it again. Psychologists have paid remarkably little attention to these activities of all children. Some Freudians have noted them and called them "sexual equivalents," suggesting that they are somehow related to the experience of orgasm. But merely labeling a phenomenon does not automatically increase our ability to describe, predict, or influence it; besides, our understanding of sexual experience is too primitive to help us much.

Growing children engage in extensive experimentation with mental states, usually in the direction of loss of waking consciousness. Many of them discover that the transition zone between waking and sleep offers many possibilities for unusual sensations, such as hallucinations and out-of-the-body experiences, and they look forward to this period each night. (And yet, falling asleep becomes suddenly frightening at a later age, possibly when the ego sense has developed more fully. We will return to this point in a moment.) It is only a matter of time before children find out that similar experiences may be obtained chemically; many of them learn it before the age of five. The most common route to this knowledge is the discovery that inhalation of the fumes of volatile solvents in household products induces experiences similar to those caused by whirling or fainting. An alternate route is introduction to general anesthesia in connection with a childhood operation—an experience that invariably becomes one of the most vivid early memories.

By the time most American children enter school they have already explored a variety of altered states of consciousness and usually know that chemical substances are one doorway to this fascinating realm. They also know that it is a forbidden realm in that grown—ups will always attempt to stop them from going there if they catch them at it. But, as I have said, the desire to repeat these experiences is not mere whim; it looks like a real drive arising from the neurophysiological structure of the human brain. What, then, happens to it as the child becomes more and more involved in the process of socialization? In most cases, it goes underground. Children learn very quickly that they must pursue antisocial behavior patterns if they wish to continue to alter consciousness regularly. Hence the secret meetings in cloakrooms, garages, and playground corners where they can continue to whirl, choke each other, and, perhaps, sniff cleaning fluids or gasoline.

As the growing child's sense of self is reinforced more and more by parents, school, and society at large, the drive to alter consciousness may go underground in the individual as well. That is, its indulgence becomes a very private matter, much like masturbation. Furthermore, in view of the overwhelming social pressure against such indulgence and the strangeness of the experiences from the point of view of normal, ego-centered consciousness, many children become quite frightened of episodes of nonordinary awareness and very unwilling to admit their occurrence. The development of this kind of fear may account for the change from looking forward to falling asleep to being afraid of it; in many cases it leads to repression of memories of the experiences.

Yet co-existing with these emotional attitudes is always the underlying need to satisfy an inner drive. In this regard, the Freudian analogy to sexual experience seems highly pertinent. Like the cyclic urge to relieve sexual tension (which probably begins to be felt at much lower ages than many think), the urge to suspend ordinary awareness arises spontaneously from within, builds to a peak, finds relief, and dissipates—all in accordance with its own intrinsic rhythm. The form of the appearance and course of this desire is identical to that of sexual desire. And the pleasure, in both cases, arises from relief of accumulated tension. Both experiences are thus self-validating; their worth is obvious in their own terms, and it is not necessary to justify them by reference to anything else. In other words, episodes of sexual release and episodes of suspension of ordinary consciousness feel good; they satisfy an inner need. Why they should feel good is another sort of question, which I will try to answer toward the end of this chapter. In the meantime, it will be useful to keep in mind the analogy between sexual experience and the experience of altered consciousness (and the possibility that the former is a special case of the latter rather than the reverse).

Despite the accompaniment of fear and guilt, experiences of nonordinary consciousness persist into adolescence and adult life, although awareness of them may diminish. If one takes the trouble to ask people if they have ever had strange experiences at the point of falling asleep, many adults will admit to hallucinations and feelings of being out of their bodies. Significantly, most will do this with a great sense of relief at being able to tell someone else about it, and at learning that such experiences do not mark them as psychologically disturbed. One woman who listened to a lecture I gave came up to me afterward and said, "I never knew other people had things like that. You don't know how much better I feel." The fear and guilt that reveal themselves in statements of this sort doubtless develop at early ages and probably are the source of the very social attitudes that engender more fear and guilt in the next generation. The process is curiously circular and self-perpetuating.

There is one more step in the development of adult attitudes toward consciousness alteration. At some point (rather late, I suspect), children learn that social support exists for one method of doing it—namely, the use of alcohol—and that if they are patient, they will be allowed to try it. Until recently, most persons who reached adulthood in our society were content to drink alcohol if they wished to continue to have experiences of this sort by means of chemicals. Now, however, many young people are discovering that other chemicals may be preferable. After all, this is what drug users themselves say: that certain illegal substances give better highs than alcohol.

At this point, I would like to summarize the main ideas I have presented so far and then illustrate them with personal examples. We seem to be born with a drive to experience episodes of altered consciousness. This drive expresses itself at very early ages in all children in activities designed to cause loss or major disturbance of ordinary awareness. To an outside adult observer these practices seem perverse and even dangerous, but in most cases adults have simply forgotten their own identical experiences as children. As children grow, they explore many ways of inducing similar changes in consciousness, and usually discover chemical methods before they enter school. Overwhelming social pressures against public indulgence of this need force children to pursue antisocial, secretive behavior patterns in their explorations of consciousness. In addition, the development of a strong ego sense in this social context often leads to fear and guilt about the desire for periods of altered awareness. Consequently, many youngsters come to indulge this desire in private or to repress it. Finally, older children come to understand that social support is available for chemical satisfaction of this need by means of alcohol. Today's youth, in their continuing experimentation with methods of changing awareness, have come across a variety of other chemicals, which they prefer to alcohol. Thus, use of illegal drugs is nothing more than a logical continuation of a developmental sequence going back to early childhood. It cannot be isolated as a unique phenomenon of adolescence, of contemporary America, of cities, or of any particular social or economic class.

I feel confident about this developmental scheme for two reasons. First, I have seen it clearly in the histories of many hundreds of drug users I have interviewed and known.* Second, I have experienced it myself. I was an avid whirler and could spend hours collapsed on the ground with the world spinning around—this despite the obvious unpleasant side effects of nausea, dizziness, and sheer exhaustion (the only aspects of the experience visible to grownups). From my point of view these effects were incidental to a state of consciousness that was extraordinarily fascinating—more interesting than any other state except the one I entered at the verge of sleep. I soon found out that my spinning made grownups upset; I learned to do it with other neighborhood children in out-of-the-way locations, and I kept it up until I was nine or ten. At about the age of four, like most members of my generation, I had my tonsils out, and the experience of ether anesthesia (administered by the old-fashioned open-drop method) remains one of my strongest memories of early life. It was frightening, intensely interesting, and intimately bound up with my thoughts about death. Some years later I discovered that a particular brand of cleaning fluid in the basement of my house gave me a similar experience, and I sniffed it many times, often in the company of others my age. I could not have explained what I was doing to anyone; the experience was interesting rather than pleasant, and I knew it was important to me to explore its territory.

*When I was a student at Harvard, many of my friends and associates used drugs and discussed them with me. I began to publish articles on drugs while still in college and became known as a drug expert before I entered medical school, which led other users to seek me out for advice. In 1968, I conducted formal interviews of users in the Boston area in an effort to recruit subjects for laboratory experiments on marihuana. Publicity surrounding publication of these experiments while I was an intern in San Francisco brought numbers of users to me as patients. As a volunteer physician at the Haight-Ashbury Medical Clinic, I saw many more users before finishing my clinical training. Since then I have continued to discuss drugs with persons who use them in a variety of settings. It has been my experience that users are delighted to talk about drugs with anyone willing to listen.

INTELLECTUAL GROWTH IN CHILDREN AND THE THEORY OF 'BIOPLASMIC FORCES' *

Earl J. Ogletree

A Transpersonal Theory of Development. This article and Andrew Weil's, which preceeds this one, illustrate how transpersonal interests can be used in developmental psychology. When we review our image of man, then our views of childhood change too. With its emphasis on a stage theory of development based on 'bioplasmic forces,' Ogletree's approach is similar to Erikson's stage theory based on psychosocial stages and Anna Freud's theory based on psychosexual stages. It also resembles Roberts's stages based on Maslow's needs-hierarchy, but is strongly at odds with Baer's learning theory approach. In this article Ogletree shows the transpersonal interest in a new form of energy (or psychological control of currently recognized forms). He also shows a characteristic activity of people working with a new paradigm: the reinterpreting of existing information to see whether it fits with the new way of looking at things. This article and Weil's demonstrate ways transpersonal interests can be used to help formulate a transpersonal theory of developmental psychology. The formulation and testing of such a theory remains to be accomplished by a new breed of developmental psychologists, those who can bring knowledge of transpersonal psychology to bear on developmental interests.

Certain studies in child and cognitive development suggest that academic learning before a child is maturationally ready will reduce his learning potential.[1] A new theory of energy forces in human growth and development seems to substantiate this suggestion. The purpose of this paper is to present this theory and discuss stages of cognitive development, school readiness, and environmental retardation.

In brief, the theory of energy forces indicates that schools are wasting the energy needed for growth during a child's formative years by forcing premature intellectual learning of school subjects which could be more readily and easily mastered at a later age. It has an important bearing on the question, What are the effects of premature schooling?

There is presently a drive for early schooling. Some of its promoters propose formal schooling as early as age 4. This "hurry-up-and-learn" philosophy has roots in the knowledge explosion and is furthered by concern for minority children whose home environment is inadequate. First, upper-grade subjects were pressed down into the lower grades. Now

*From Earl J. Ogletree, "Intellectual Growth in Children and the Theory of 'Bioplasmic Forces,' " *Phi Delta Kappan* (February, 1974), pp. 407–412, by permission of the author and publisher. Earl J. Ogletree is Associate Professor of Education at Chicago State University and editor of the forthcoming book *Education of the Spanish-Speaking Urban Child* (Springfield, Illinois: Charles C. Thomas, Publishers).

primary-grade subjects have become more intellectual and abstract. This has happened, for example, in the new math and science programs. But research in child development does not support the "hurry-up-and-learn" concept. It indicates that a child is not ready for academic or intellectual learning until age 7, 8, or sometimes 9.[2] The child's brain is not fully insulated or completely developed physically until age 8. Some psychologists put the age of readiness at 11, but Jean Piaget, the noted Swiss psychologist, has shown that a child does not have adequate control over his thinking until at least age 7 or 8. At this age there is a shift from the preoperational to the concrete operational level of thinking, and the child can then perform new cognitive operations.

Neither is the child's intersensory development—sight and hearing—fully developed until age 8 or later. For example, before age 7 a child has perceptual difficulties; he often cannot distinguish visually between *b* and *d* and *q* and *p*.[3] He cannot hear the difference between *b* and *p*; *m* and *n*; *g* and *k*; *s* and *z*, etc.[4] Few preschool programs have been effective in producing lasting gains in academic learning or intellectual development. Preschool academic and language training programs have generally been no more effective than the unstructured, play-type preschool programs in enhancing learning abilities.[5]

It is well known that forcing a child to learn a skill or master a subject before he is maturationally ready is inefficient and may be ineffective. It takes him longer to learn it, and the learning is less complete. Moreover, children who begin reading at age 6, one year ahead of their class peers, are often one year behind them in reading achievement at the end of the seventh grade.[6] Not only do later school beginners surpass those who started school at an earlier age, but the latter group seems to have greater emotional and social adjustment problems. Accelerated maturity in one area may cause immaturity in another area of development. The retention level of immature learners is much less than that of somewhat older learners. Forced learning can cause frustration, anxiety, alienation, and loss of interest in learning. The learning is not only inefficient or "pseudo-learning," but research indicates a resultant lowering of learning capacity. Forced learning may result in a permanent learning handicap—not only a distaste for a certain subject but permanent intellectual retardation.[7] Why is this so?

Until very recently, educators have spoken about school readiness in generalities, e.g., as "the amount of learning that can transfer to new learning," or, "the child must be mature in terms of physical, mental, and emotional growth and social maturity." However, none of these points of view really explains readiness or the possible damaging effects of early schooling.

As Arthur Jensen states, these "disagreements [regarding readiness] arise only when we try to explain readiness."[8] The reason for the disagreement as to when a child is or is not ready for schooling is that we lack a sound theory of human development. We do not understand the processes of physical and mental development and their relationship. We therefore have no agreed-upon concept of readiness.

Let me explain. At this time educators do not have a total or realistic theory of human development. Mental and physical development are two separate phenomena. Psychological and physiological development are thought to be two ways of viewing human development. The physiologist is primarily concerned with the organic, somatic, and physical aspects of man, whereas the psychologist is concerned with mental, psychological, and motivational aspects of development. In regard to offering a unifying or total theory of human development, the two fields have remained separate and impotent. Attempts have been made to develop a mental/physical conceptual model of human development using such theories as vitalism, mechanism, and the organismic and field theories.[9] These theories or models do not explain the relationship between physical and mental growth, mental maturation and readiness. One limitation of the theories was the attempt to apply concepts that explain the inorganic world to the organic world.[10] It is becoming increasingly evident that the forces operative in the inanimate world cannot explain the phenomenon of life. Therefore, I am offering a new theoretical model, based on the bioplasmic theory. Since bioplasmic forces are invisible, though their effects are recordable, a model is necessary.

What is meant by a model in this context? Models or hypotheses are merely perceptual aids to explain phenomenological relationships. In an effort to gain a fuller understanding, the model is refined and differentiated. It becomes the criterion by which we test and judge the accuracy of our reasoning and provide a sufficient comprehension of the subject to facilitate inquiry and possible validation of the model. Is this not a valid approach for a theory of human development based on invisible forces? After all, no one has ever seen magnetism, gravity, or electricity, only their results and effects. The same applies to the atomic theory; no one has seen an atom, electrons, etc. Nevertheless, we borrow a model from the macrocosmic world—the planets and galaxy—to explicate our physical/chemical world through the use of the atomic theory, which is a microcosmic model of the universe. These models or scientific theories become laws when they consistently explain physical phenomena.

What is the bioplasmic model? The bioplasmic forces theory is based on the concept that all living matter is made up of an energy body and a physical body, as concluded by Russian scientists and homeopathic and acupuncture physicians. Apart from the bioplasmic theory, biologists developed a term—"electrometabolic fields"—to explain the relationship between the electrical phenomenon and the metabolic processes in the body. The bioplasmic forces theory goes a step further; it is more comprehensive in its explanation of human development. Russian psychologists and scientists have recently discovered energy or "bioplasmic" forces to be the basis for human growth and development.

The Russian findings gave visible proof to the premises of the Chinese art of medicine, acupuncture, which works on the same principle, that there are energy-regenerative currents flowing throughout the body. This energy is spent on the vital jobs of growing into maturity and keeping the body chemistry and organs functioning properly. It changes the minerals of the body from an inert to an active state, facilitating the reproduction and regeneration of organs and body cells, etc. The energy used for maintaining bodily functions is measured as basal metabolism. The remainder is available for growth and activity. Basically, the source for this energy is food. However, other factors can affect it, such as physical health, emotional well-being, and the environment. Mental health can affect physical health and growth, just as physical health can affect our emotions, hence behavior. The reaction is cyclical.

Energy output varies with age. As we grow older we are less energetic and physically active, whereas the child has an abundance of energy. He expends much energy through growth, play, and other physical activity.

We have observed this phenomenon in daily life, in the organic world. Now Russian scientists have begun to explain it in new terms. They have actually photographed bioplasmic force. Sheila Ostrander and Lynn Schroeder, who visited research centers in Russia, report "a brand new concept in Soviet biology" in their book, *Psychic Discoveries Behind the Iron Curtain.*[11]

Russian experiments indicate that the energy body we are talking about is not just a chaotic system of particles but a unified body which acts as a holistic, structured, organized unit. Each organ of the body seems to have its own unified, specific etheric or bioplasmic forces. The forces are in continuous motion and metamorphosis. They are responsible for the maintenance of all the elements in the body to keep the organism going, and to keep it healthy.

Acupuncture, as a means of correcting bioplasmic imbalance, is based on energy levels or current flows, which sustain the development and replacement of cells in the body. Chinese physicians state that the skin, liver, kidneys, etc., are temporary deposits for a number of energy current flows which move at various rates throughout the body. Recent physiological studies have shown that the liver is changed in 10 days, the tongue in a longer period. The substance of the brain takes longer, while it is six months before new molecules are found in the bones. The hair and nails regenerate rapidly, whereas it takes seven years before all the skin cells have been replaced.

The basis of health, says the acupuncture physician, is the balance of energy currents in the body. "Good health is the free and unimpeded circulation of energy—the life forces—flowing from organ to organ along an invisible network of intercommunicating channels," which affects the flow of blood to the organs and tissues. Illness is then the blockage and imbalance of the flow of these bioplasmic currents. The insertion of needles in one or more of the energy centers or acupoints on the skin revitalizes and facilitates the energy current flow, putting the organism back in balance.[13]

It is worth mentioning that these bioplasmic forces account for the phenomenon called "the phantom limb." Persons who have a missing leg or arm as the result of a birth defect or an accident can sense the missing limb. A study by E. Weinstein and his associates has shown that among 101 children born with missing limbs, 18 had clear perception of phantom limbs.[14] George Von Arnim theorizes that the bioplasmic phantom limb is a phenomenon that accounts for the equal rate of body scheme acquisition by limbless, sightless, and normal children.[15] In other words, the bioplasmic forces contain the pattern or framework of the species, the dynamic processes or energy forces for growth. They facilitate the development of the physical limb when the physical material is present. The phantom or bioplasmic limb grows and develops just like the physical limb, except that it is nonmaterial, invisible. The Russian scientists who photographed the bioplasmic body state:

> [T]he energy body didn't merely seem to be a radiation of the physical body. The physical appeared somehow to mirror what was happening in the energy.[16]

Another characteristic of bioplasmic forces is their regenerative power in lower animals, e.g., the flatworm, cut in half, completely regenerates itself; the same is true of an amphibian's legs and the fins of a lungfish. However, higher animals, particularly man, do not have this regenerative power. Instead, the formative or bioplasmic forces are transmuted into the powers of cognition, the power or energy to control thinking.[17] This concept of growth forces transmuted into cognitive energy has been known in acupuncture and homeopathy for years.[18] Rudolf Steiner developed the concept over 50 years ago, and it is part of the learning theory and practices being used in the more than 100 Waldorf schools that he and his students founded.[19]

What does all this mean for the education of the child and readiness for schooling? As I have indicated, energy or bioplasmic forces are used for human growth and maintenance of the body as well as for motor, emotional, and thinking activities. All of these require the expenditure of energy in one form or another. Each person has a certain amount of energy available. The crux of my argument regarding the damage school does to children is that, as a result of an inappropriate curriculum, activities, and assignments, children's energy forces are displaced and atrophied prematurely, causing damage to their development.

How does this occur? As every teacher knows, the most formative years of childhood are the first seven. This is the age of imitation, play, and physical activity. It is also the period when the greatest growth rate occurs. It is the time when the energy level is high and the bioplasmic forces are concentrated mainly on physical growth. In a sense, the child grows from the head downward. He gains greater and greater voluntary control over his movements, speech organization, and thinking. This theme of voluntary control is very important to understanding the transformation of growth or energy forces.

The child at birth has no control over his chaotic eye, mouth, head, and neck movements. Movement control proceeds to the shoulders, arms, and hands; eye/hand coordination becomes possible. An infant is generally able to grasp objects by the third month. His speech changes from cooing to babbling. By the twelfth month he toddles and begins to walk. He has by this time developed a minimal level of control over his physical movements. Along with motor development comes speech development, which correlates better with motor development than it does with age. The child's speech development proceeds through the stages of cooing, babbling, saying (an expressing of inner needs and instincts—hunger, etc.— and the imitation of words), naming, talking. At the same time, speech could also be considered a finer form of motor movement (the lower jaw is a fifth limb, in a sense); the child gains greater mastery over his speech organization by use of the finer muscles of the mouth, tongue, lips, teeth, and larynx.

The rate of language development and vocabulary acquisition is slowed down when the child is struggling to master walking, running, skipping, hopping, etc. The rate increases when his mastery over locomotion reaches a plateau; for example, at age 2½ to 3, when he can jump with two feet, stand on one foot, tiptoe, and climb stairs using alternate feet, the child's vocabulary increases to 1,000 words, understanding increases considerably, and his utterances are fairly correct grammatically. As a result there is a displacement of energy from gross motor control to the finer motor control of speech.

Karl Konig has also worked out a descent of the development of grammar in children from the "head to the toe"—from nouns to the cognitive, adjectives to the affective, verbs to the psychomotor, as follows:

	Age	Nouns	Adjectives	Verbs
Cognitive	1.3	100%		
Affective	1.8	78%	22%	
Psychomotor	2.0	63%	14%	23%

Hence there seems to be a correlation between grammatical development and motor control.[20]

Physical and speech development are controlled motor movement—one gross, the other fine. Thinking, which is a form of control over one's mind, is also a much finer and more subtle form of movement.

Piaget has shown that all children's minds evolve through a series of intellectual stages as they progress from early childhood through adolescence. He has classified these as follows:

1. Sensory-Motor Stage (0–2 years)
2. Preoperational Stage (2–7 years)
3. Concrete Operational Stage (7–12 years)
4. Formal Operational Stage (12–15 years and over)

Each of these stages has its own particular characteristics. Studies demonstrate that children's thinking shifts from the sense-bound to the emotional to the rational forms of expression. The stages signify different centers of control. Piaget has devised tasks to determine the level of a child's thinking.

Before the shift from the preoperational to the concrete operational levels, the child "is involved in direct perceptual relationships with a minimum of reasoning or thinking." He is not able to distinguish between how things look and how they really are. If the form of an object is changed, he thinks the quantity is different. One experiment is the changing of one of two spherical clay balls of equal size into a sausage shape. The child does not understand that the sausage has the same quantity of clay as the ball from which it was rolled. The preoperational child will generally say the sausage shape is larger than the ball, even though he saw the experimenter roll the ball into a sausage. The child cannot conserve (retain a mental image of the two clay balls), nor reverse his thinking (compare the sausage with its prior ball shape, which should be retained as a mental picture if he is mature enough). The child who has attained the concrete operational level of thinking is able to perform this and smaller tasks successfully. I have devised an outline of the mental characteristics of the three major stages:

Preoperational (2–7 years)

1. Cannot conserve (hold mental images)
2. Thinking is perceptual or sense-bound
3. Thinking is nonreversible
4. Cannot deal with variables or changes
5. Has little control (voluntary) over thinking

Concrete Operational (7–12 or 14 years)

1. Can conserve (hold mental images)
2. Thinking is bound to emotional or affective life, but operational
3. Thinking is reversible
4. Has greater voluntary control over thinking
5. Thinking is pictorial
6. Needs concrete props to support problem solving
7. Can deal with one variable

Formal Operational (14 years and older)

1. Thinking is under voluntary control, i.e., it is operational
2. Thinking is relatively free of physical and emotional life, more objective
3. Can manipulate two or more variables
4. Thinking is more flexible
5. Predictive problem solving is possible without concrete props
6. Can manipulate symbols and concepts without outer perceptual props

As one examines these three stages in terms of their developmental sequence, it appears that the theme of increased voluntary control over thinking processes (movement) is just as applicable as it was to physical locomotion and speech development. However, in the Piaget stages, movement in cognition is more refined, sophisticated, and subtle. These transitional periods, from preoperational to concrete, and from concrete to formal, are marked by definite physiological and biological changes.

The terms used by Piaget are realistic; they accurately describe the thinking characteristics and abilities at each level. Preoperational means the child cannot operate (move) his thinking, joining mental image to mental image, concept to concept, idea to idea. The child has not matured enough to be able to control his own thinking; he cannot reason. His thinking is nonoperational, uncontrollable, to a certain extent. At the concrete level, the older child can retain mental images and reverse his thinking; in short, his thinking is operational. He has control over his mind but needs concrete objects to solve problems. The same pattern of voluntarily controlled movements applies to change from the concrete to the formal operational level of thinking. Here the youngster can solve problems and predict solutions by making an educated guess—hypothesizing. He no longer needs concrete props to solve problems. He can solve such symbolic problems with several variables, e.g., when A is greater than B and B is greater than C, what is the relationship between A and C? His thinking is symbolic.

Piaget states that for a child to learn and actually experience what he is learning, his thinking must act on it, transform it, modify it. In other words, operate on it. The level of operation is determined by the maturation of the organism—the development of the growing child.

I have advanced the theory that motor activity and the development of speech and thinking are dependent upon gaining voluntary control over these areas. The displacement and expenditure of energy are integral parts of the maturing process. Physical or organismic (total) maturation of the child is needed if he is to proceed through these stages at the proper rate.

The changes in thinking levels occur at about seven-year periods: preoperation (2–7), concrete operation (7–14), and formal operation (14 and older). The significance is that certain major physical changes or plateaus also occur in seven-year periods. These are the change of teeth (second dentition) at age 7 and puberty at approximately age 14. If we keep the theory of the transmutation of growth of bioplasmic forces in mind, it is no coincidence that at about age 7 (average age, 6.8 years), second teething occurs at the same time as the child's intellectual shift from the preoperational to the concrete operational level of thinking.

Francis Ilg and Louise Ames report the results of their study on second teething of 80 children in relation to school readiness.[21] Those children who were ahead of schedule in teething (96%) were definitely ready for, and could profit from, academic school experiences. Of those children who were behind schedule in teething, 54% should have repeated (22% of this group did repeat), and 40% would have profited by repetition. Of those children who were in-between—whether ahead or behind schedule in teething—64% would have benefited by repetition (14% of this group did repeat; 36% were hard workers, doing well). The study indicates that subsequent to teething the children seemed to have reached a higher level of mental development—the concrete operational level of thinking.

What does all this signify for our theory of maturation? It means that second teething is an indication of the culmination of physical growth of the head. The head has reached a plateau of physical maturation. The brain has reached 95% of its development, the head two-thirds of adult proportion. This signifies that the growth, energy, or bioplasmic forces have to a certain degree completed their task in the physical development of the head and brain. The growth forces are then released (gradually) from physical growth for the processes of thinking (subtle movement); this accounts for the transition from preoperational (noncontrollable) to concrete operational (controllable) thinking in the child. The child now has greater voluntary control over his thinking processes.

This same relationship applies to the onset of puberty and the child's change from the concrete operational to the formal operational level of thinking. J. D. Nisbet found that in England those adolescents who attained puberty scored higher on intellectual and academic achievement tests than those youngsters who were still at the prepuberty stage of development.[22] During this time there is a growth spurt; the teenager is reaching adult proportions. The energy or growth forces are then released to be used for the higher level of formal operational thinking. There has not been much research on this level. However, there are indications that there is a delay in the attainment of the formal operational level of thinking even after the attainment of puberty. Physical maturation seems to have raced ahead of mental development at this later stage. No one really knows the reason; further research is needed.

As we have indicated, the child is not fully mature and ready for learning until age 7 or 8. His brain is not fully developed, nor are his senses of hearing and sight. I hold that if the child has not reached the indicated levels of maturity and is forced or persuaded to do intellectual learning, there occurs a premature use of the bioplasmic or energy forces for thinking. The physical body is robbed of the growth forces needed to develop the brain (the head) to its fullest potential for physical growth. The difference in growth of the brain may be so subtle that it cannot yet be measured. But nevertheless it does occur. There is also an inefficient use of the energy forces. When the child is still at the preoperational stage, in no sense of the word can he be forced or coerced to a higher level of thinking. Therefore little is accomplished by trying. The learning is of a pseudo or partial nature, incomplete; furthermore, physical development as well as emotional development have been sacrificed as a result. A. Portman reports, "Whenever acceleration has occurred, there has been a noticeably increased susceptibility to certain diseases, especially those of psychological origin."[23]

Shortened processes of maturation cause later immaturity. This would account for the increased maladjustment of early school entrants found by Inez King.[24] Learning is hardly ever a purely cognitive process, particularly with children, but includes emotional involvement—interest, motivation, and preference. Children who are forced to learn subjects beyond their capacity and maturation develop anxiety and frustration; in short, they are "turned off." Emotional fatigue can cause physical fatigue, a dissipation of energy, mental and physical.

When Russian scientists photographed the energy or bioplasmic forces, they found that illness, emotions, fatigue, and particular thoughts and states of mind have a distinct effect on the flow of bioplasmic forces throughout the body. When a person is fatigued, tired, or emotionally overstrained, more energy appears to pour out of the body than when he is in a healthy mental state of mind. So it is with the child who is forced prematurely into learning. It follows that as a result of the state of unreadiness for learning, the resulting frustration and anxiety cause the bioplasmic forces to dissipate. The bioplasmic forces available for physical growth and activity are accordingly reduced. Retardation is the final result, for there are two factors working against the child: the depletion and ineffective use of the growth forces resulting from premature attempts at thinking (preoperational level), and the degradation of the growth forces resulting from frustration and anxiety.

The plasticity of intelligence decreases with age; forced learning accelerates this loss of plasticity because of premature dissipation of the bioplasmic forces. The child's intelligence and his learning capacity become differentiated and fixed; this, in turn, limits the quantity and quality of experiences he can have. His intellectual and learning potentials reach a plateau prematurely.

If premature educational pressures have these kinds of effects on normally reared or middle-class children, what must be the effect on children from socially and culturally deprived environments? The result is disastrous. It is well known that the public schools have never been able to educate the poor very successfully. Compensatory and Head Start programs have generally been a failure, despite enormous effort and the expenditure of considerable sums. As a result of poor environment, the deprived child begins school with a handicap. In short, he is environmentally retarded, which affects his mental and academic capacities. Here, too, the environment has depleted his bioplasmic growth forces. He therefore begins schooling with weakened and insufficient growth forces. Herbert Sieweke states:

> Any disturbance or change in the etheric (bioplasmic) forces during the formative years of childhood will have an impact on the emotional and intellectual constitution of the child. The metamorphosis of the etheric (bioplasmic)

forces from physical development to emotional-cognitive development can be accelerated or retarded. There is a delicate function between the two functions (physical and mental development) of the etheric forces.[25]

When the child matures enough to shift from a lower stage of mental development to a higher level (preoperational to concrete), he does not possess enough growth forces to be changed into forces for thinking to make the transition complete. He is neither out of the preoperational stage nor in the concrete operational stage. He hovers in between. His rate of development is retarded. When these developmental problems are compounded by forced premature learning, the result can only be further retardation, perhaps permanent retardation.

Therefore the popular educational approaches of today, with their intellectual heavy-handedness, will never allow children to develop and blossom naturally. They can only do damage, making children into premature, unhappy adults. Such approaches will never be able to serve children from different and less desirable economic environments. Education must begin looking at the dynamic needs of the growing child.

Our conventional approaches—pouring knowledge into the child, "fitting him into a curriculum" that is foreign to his nature—must cease. We must examine the needs of the child, *how* and *why* he develops as he does. Then what we need is to develop a curriculum and methods compatible with his unfolding and developing stages of growth. The bioplasmic or growth forces theory supports such an approach. It explains human growth, the development of thinking children, and the rationale for readiness. If the theory is correct, it implies that the educational process should help the child to sustain and develop his bioplasmic body, his forces of growth. A curriculum, extracurricular activities, etc., compatible with and supportive of these growth forces would have to be developed. The bioplasmic theory may be the key to human and child development. It may be the road back to humanism for education. It could very well revolutionize education.

NOTES

1. Raymond Moore, Robert Moon, and Dennis Moore, "The California Report: Early Schooling for All?" *Phi Delta Kappan*, June, 1972, pp. 617–19; and Arthur Jensen, *Understanding Readiness: An Occasional Paper* (Urbana: University of Illinois Press, 1969), pp. 12–15.

2. Moore, Moon, and Moore, op. cit., p. 617.

3. Luella Cole, *The Improvement of Reading with Special Reference to Remedial Instruction* (New York: Farrar and Rinehart, 1938), p. 284.

4. Ibid., p. 282.

5. Westinghouse and Ohio University, "The Import of Head Start: An Evaluation of the Effects of Head Start on Children's Cognitive and Affective Development," in *The Disadvantaged Child*, Joe L. Frost and Glen R. Hawkes, eds. (Boston: Houghton Mifflin, 1970), pp. 197–201.

6. Henry M. David, "Don't Push Your School Beginners," *Parent's Magazine*, October, 1952, pp. 140, 141; and Lowell B. Carter, "The Effects of Early School Entrance on the Scholastic Achievement of Elementary School Children in Austin Public Schools," *Journal of Educational Research*, October, 1956, pp. 91–103.

7. See Moore, Moon, and Moore, op. cit., for additional information and supportive evidence.

8. Jensen, op. cit., fn. 1, p. 1.

9. Morris L. Bigge and Maurice Hunt, *Psychological Foundations of Education* (New York: Harper & Row, 1964), pp. 60–64.

10. Ibid.

11. Sheila Ostrander and Lynn Schroeder, *Psychic Discoveries Behind the Iron Curtain* (Englewood Cliffs, N.J.: Prentice-Hall, 1971). Dr. William E. Tiller of Stanford University and private research foundations such as the Academy of Parapsychology and Medicine have been replicating the Russians' research and are also pioneering research on the bioplasmic body and acupuncture (see fn. 13).

12. Felix Mann, *Acupuncture: The Ancient Chinese Art of Healing and How It Works Scientifically* (New York: Random House, 1972), pp. 4–8.

13. Edward E. Tiller, *Energy Fields and the Human Body*, Parts I & II; A.R.E. Medical Symposium on "Mind/Body Relationship in the Disease Process," monograph, Phoenix, Ariz., January, 1972.

14. E. Winstein, R. Sersen, and A. Vetter, "Phantom and Somatic Sensations in Cases of Congenital Aphasia," *Cortex*, vol. 1, 1964, pp. 216–90.

15. George Von Arnim, "Imitation and the Body Scheme," *The Cresset*, October, 1967, pp. 21, 22.

16. Ostrander and Schroeder, op. cit.

17. Mann, op. cit.

18. Harry Coulter, *Homeopathic Medicine* (Washington, D.C.: American Institute of Homeopathy, 1973), pp. 3–10.

19. Rudolf Steiner, *The New Art of Education* (London: Anthroposophical Press, 1928).

20. Karl Konig, *The First Three Years of Childhood* (New York: Anthroposophical Press, 1969), p. 46.

21. Francis L. Ilg and Louise B. Ames, *School Readiness* (New York: Harper & Row, 1964), pp. 238, 239.

22. J. D. Nisbet, "Puberty and Test Performance," *British Journal of Educational Psychology*, June, 1964, pp. 202, 203.

23. A. Portman, "Umzuchtung des Menschen? Aspekte heutiger Biotechnic," *Universitas*, vol. 21, 1966, pp. 785–803.

24. Inez B. King, "Effects of School Entrance into Grade 1 upon Achievement in Elementary School," *Elementary School Journal*, February, 1955, pp. 331–36.

25. Herbert Sieweke, *Anthroposophic Medizin* (Dornach, Switzerland: Philosophisch–Anthroposophisches Verlag, 1959), pp. 142–44.

EDUCATION FOR TRANSCENDENCE*

Michael H. Murphy

The Step Beyond Self-Concept. In Freudian-based education we saw that one of the major goals is a strong ego. In humanistic education, a good self-concept is an objective. But what happens after these are achieved? Murphy says that surpassing the ego emerges as a goal. How can giving up one's selfhood result in anything good? Murphy points to several answers: peak experiences, those moments of extreme pleasure, are experienced as selfless; letting oneself go can become a rearrangement of personality elements into a healthier person; experiencing of mystical states or cosmic awareness opens the door to fuller understanding of much art and many religions; a new perspective on one's ordinary self can bring about a desire for improvement of that ordinary state; feeling oneself as part of everything else and everyone else is a basis for social responsibility; and having broadened one's experience to find there was more to life than one thought, the natural question arises, "Is there even more than I now know?" Besides these, more practical benefits are described in Koestler's article, and in the articles on Transcendental Meditation.

In America today there is widespread and growing interest in various psychophysical disciplines which evoke transcendent experience. Some of these disciplines, such as transcendental meditation or Zen training, are explicit about their transcendent aims. Others, such as techniques for increasing sensory and kinesthetic awareness or the various group encounter formats, describe their aims in terms of "personal growth," increased sensitivity and awareness, or some other psychological or physical outcome. But these latter disciplines regularly evoke ego-surpassing, often ecstatic experience which is identical in crucial ways to the experience sought by the more explicitly contemplative methods.[1]

EXPANSION OF PERSONAL BOUNDARIES

All of these disciplines—whether explicitly seeking transcendence or not—share certain salient features. They all focus attention upon unfamiliar aspects or possibilities of one's world; they all attempt to break perceptual constancies; they all require surrender at crucial moments to alien and formerly resisted perceptions or feelings; they all engender increased vitality and joy and a greater sense of meaning, freedom and power when their practice is successful. Common to the practitioners of all of them is the sense that a fuller reality has made itself known, that

*From Michael H. Murphy, "Education for Transcendence," *Journal of Transpersonal Psychology* 1, no. 1 (Spring, 1969): 21–32, by permission of the author. Michael H. Murphy is the founder of the Esalen Institute. He is the author of the book *Golf in the Kingdom* (New York: Dell Publishing Company, 1972).

438

something more has entered one's being, that a grace has been bestowed. In T-groups, sensory awakening sessions, psychodramas and Gestalt therapy, as well as in prayer or meditation, personal boundaries expand—often in ecstasy. This feeling of being entered—or entering upon—something greater is at the heart of the sense of transcendence.

WESTERN CULTURE DE-EMPHASIZES TRANSCENDENCE

One reason for the silence regarding the transcendent aspect of this kind of contemporary experience is that the jargon of psychotherapists, group dynamics experts and sensitivity trainers does not include categories to deal with it; modern psychology and sociology generally relegate transcendence to an inferior order of reality. Another reason for the silence is that most contemplative traditions, and the contemporary disciplines that derive from them, relegate many sensory and interpersonal illuminations to an inferior status, insisting that satori or union with God be achieved through a particular method, and be expressed in a particular way. The cults which have formed around such teachings are generally critical of any other path.[2] Narrowness on both sides keeps the picture incomplete.

But in spite of the inadequacies of modern psychological theory and traditional religious formulations, disciplines and centers are emerging all over the United States to stimulate and nurture self-transcending personal growth, and from these there are coalescing the beginnings of a contemporary education for transcendence. Severin Petersen, a research associate at Esalen Institute, has catalogued over 150 such disciplines, and in the past two years at least fourteen such centers have been organized. Theory to match this practice will emerge, I think, when transcendence is assigned a fundamental reality, and when it comes to be seen as multidimensional and inclusive of all man's parts rather than the specialized, ascetic phenomenon it has generally been conceived to be by traditional religious thought. Beginnings have been made toward such relevant and inclusive formulations, by Abraham Maslow (1962) and R. D. Laing (1967), for example, by Aldous Huxley in his last essays and novel *Island* (in which he outlined an education for man the "multiple amphibian"), and by Bishop John Robinson in *Exploration into God* (1967). Following Robert Bellah's suggestion, I think contemporary notions of transcendence must be democratic rather than hierarchical and authoritarian. The Net of Jewels in Hindu mythology, in which every facet of existence mirrors every other facet, is a better symbol for the consciousness of our times than the image of a three-story psyche to be climbed with a narrow ladder of perfection.[3]

In spite of these new beginnings, however, the still dominant intellectual attitude in the Western world does not esteem transcendence as other cultures have. Instead, recent Western culture has prized science, social order and control of the natural world. In America it seems that we would rather conquer the moon than explore the worlds of subjective experience and personal relationship.

Nowhere is this attitude more obvious than in our educational system.

On entering school, our children must adapt to the various demands of classroom efficiency. They are taught to behave "normally," to think rationally and objectively, to relate verbally and to control, rather than cultivate, their feelings. They may graduate as good citizens, well educated in the cognitive disciplines, well prepared to function as components in society, but be strikingly unaware of themselves or others.

BASIC CONCERN FOR ULTIMATE VALUES

Such is the price, some say, of our progress. Others, however, are now declaring that the price may not be worth paying. On college campuses throughout America, students are demanding that they be taught not only to think, but also to feel. Many of them are insisting that a basic concern for ultimate values be added to their curricula and are turning meanwhile to psychedelic drugs, Eastern philosophy and social action.

This new concern is paralleled by a growing interest in transcendental experience within the scientific community. In recent years, studies by Western psychologists have linked such experience with human growth and learning. Some educators and social scientists have begun to re-evaluate transcendence and to develop techniques which evoke and nurture it.

VOYAGES OF DISCOVERY

One of the significant efforts to re-evaluate transcendence has been that of psychoanalyst R. D. Laing of the Tavistock Clinic in London. In treating psychotic patients evidencing extreme ego loss, Dr. Laing discovered that many such patients were undergoing experiences similar to those described by mystics for centuries. He found that these psychotic breaks were guided by a "will towards health" and, if allowed to run their natural course, led to a positive reintegration in which patients attained great personal learning and improved functioning. Dr. Laing began to treat these psychoses as "voyages of discovery," and established "blow-out centers" in England where they could be experienced in a supportive and warm environment. His findings have since been supported by the independent research of two Americans, psychologist Julian Silverman of the National Institute of Mental Health in Bethesda, Maryland, and Dr. John Weir Perry of the University of California Medical Center in San Francisco. In his research, Dr. Silverman has found that certain acute, non-paranoid schizophrenic breaks lead to spontaneous recovery with a measurable increase in the patient's functioning (1967). Dr. Perry has similarly observed that a certain type of schizophrenia follows a course in which patients experience a common train of cosmic religious imagery and "emerge from their psychoses as deeper and broader personalities" (1962). Similar findings by psychiatrist Kazinierz Dabrowski and his colleagues in Warsaw have been described by Dabrowski (1964). Still another study of the healthful, often transcendent aspects of psychosis, is Anton Boisen's *The Exploration of the Inner World.*

The indications are, therefore, that certain forms of what is commonly called "madness" in our society are actually breaks from ordinary consciousness which lead to richer perception and fuller functioning. This new finding is explored by Dr. Laing (1967). He writes:

> Most people, most of the time, experience themselves and others in one or another way that I shall call "egoic." That is, centrally of peripherally, they experience the world and themselves in terms of a constant identity within a framwork of certain ground structures of space and time shared by other members of their society.
>
> However, religious ... philosophies have agreed that such egoic experience is a preliminary illusion, a veil, a film of maya—a dream to Heraclitus and to Lao Tze, the fundamental illusion of all Buddhism, a state of sleep, of death, of socially accepted madness, a womb state to which one has to die, from which one has to be born.
>
> The person going through ego-loss or transcendental experiences may or may not become in different ways confused. Then he might legitimately be regarded as mad. But to be mad is not necessarily to be ill, notwithstanding the fact that in our culture the two categories have become confused. The 'ego' is the instrument for living in this world. If the ego is broken up or destroyed (by the insurmountable contradictions of certain life situations, by toxins, chemicals, etc.) then the person may be exposed to other worlds, 'real' in different ways from the more familiar territory of dreams, imagination, perception or fantasy.
>
> True sanity entails in one way or another the dissolution of the normal ego, that false self competently adjusted to our alienated social reality; the emergence of the 'inner' archetypal meditators of divine power, and through this death a rebirth, and the eventual re-establishment of a new kind of ego functioning, the ego now being the servant of the divine, no longer its betrayer.

INNER NATURE AND TRANSCENDENCE

While Dr. Laing draws his conclusions from his experience with psychotic patients, contemporary studies of normal human beings indicate that the experience of transcendence is both a common phenomenon and an important factor in human learning. Abraham Maslow has advanced a theory of man's "inner" nature and the value of transcendental experience, which derives from studies of healthy, well-functioning people. As Dr. Maslow describes it (1962), man's inner nature seems not to be intrinsically evil, but rather either neutral or positively "good." Although this inner nature "is weak and delicate and subtle and easily overcome by habit, cultural pressures and wrong attitudes towards it," it consistently works toward fulfillment and makes any therapy or spontaneous recovery possible. In healthy persons, it constantly strives towards realization, or "self-actualization." Personal growth, according to Maslow, is catalyzed and illuminated by the "peak experiences" of life. These peak experiences are:

> ... felt as self-validating, self-justifying moments. There is a very characteristic disorientation in time and space. Perception is richer and tends strongly to be idiographic and non-classificatory. The experience, or object, tends to be seen as

a whole, as a complete unit, detached from relations, from possible usefulness, from expediency and from purpose ... many dichotomies, polarities and conflicts are fused, transcended or resolved.

Cognition during the peak experience is much more passive and receptive than active. The emotional reaction in the peak experience has a special flavor of wonder, of awe, of reverence, of humility and surrender before something great. Perception can be relatively ego-transcending, self-forgetful.

Peak experiences are seemingly egoless, beyond time and space, good and evil. They involve a giving up of self to receive inspiration and knowledge. Furthermore, Dr. Maslow notes, they are intense identity experiences in which the creator becomes one with the work being created, the mother feels one with her child. Attainment of integration, identity, autonomy, of selfhood is simultaneously a transcending of the ordinary sense of self.

In a recent study, Marghanita Laski (1961) found that the triggers that set off transcendent ecstasy in people from all walks of life include natural scenery, sexual love, child-birth, movement, religion, art, scientific or poetical knowledge, creative work, introspection and beauty. Like Dr. Laing, who links the experience of his patients with certain precipitate life situations, Mrs. Laski notes that "encounter with a trigger is almost always a necessary precondition for ecstasy, except where ecstatic states are deliberately induced by drugs or disciplines."

DISCIPLINES AND "TRIGGERS"

Of the disciplines to which Mrs. Laski refers, perhaps the most widely used is meditation, a mental exercise in which attention is focused on an object image or bodily process. The practitioner may be trained to watch, rather than direct, his thoughts, or to concentrate as in the training of Rinzai Zen on an intellectually unsolvable paradox. Through this activity, his attention bypasses ordinary cognitive functioning. The meditator becomes a passive witness of his own consciousness, then identifies with and becomes the true self, the source of consciousness.

In spite of its long history in Eastern societies, meditation has remained outside the interest of Western science until recent years, when psychologists began to examine the technique for its relation to the alteration of consciousness (Deikman, 1963, 1966a). Perhaps the most important innovation from this research has been achieved by Dr. Joe Kamiya of the Langley Porter Neuropsychiatric Institute in San Francisco. A research psychologist who has devoted much of his professional life to the study of dreaming, Dr. Kamiya has recently developed a method to train people to control their brain activity.

MEDITATION REEXAMINED

Dr. Kamiya's approach combines methods from experimental psychology, computer technology and physiology. In it, he feeds back electroencephalographic information ("brain waves") to trainees in the form of sound and light patterns, so that they can hear and see the course of their own brain activity, and discover for themselves how to change the sounds and lights by varying their moods and feelings. Dr. Kamiya first used this technique to train people to discern the alpha functions of their brains. Concurrently, the Japanese researchers Kasamatsu and Hirai discovered that a high, steady rate of alpha waves characterized the EEG records of Japanese Zen masters. Dr. Kamiya has since trained experienced meditators and has found that they can learn to control their alpha functions more readily than trainees selected at random. It is possible that he has accidentally hit upon a crucial index of successful meditation. His work to date suggests that he has found a way to lead people swiftly toward a state of brain activity achieved only after long years of practice.

Since the high alpha state is characterized as being serene and alert, Dr. Kamiya believes the initial application for his technique may be in alleviating human anxiety. But the broadest application may lie in the field of education. As Dr. Kamiya (1968) puts it:

> Education for both young and old has for perhaps too long focused on knowledge about the material and social world outside the learner, or on trained skills where externally observable performances are available. Little systematic effort appears to be devoted to the training of self discernment and self control of the more covert processes of mental activity. For example, events such as after-images, subjective color, heart beats, pains, thoughts, dreams, proprioceptive sensations, day dreams, visual illusions, etc., are not standard curriculum items in the early education of the child, even though they may constitute a substantial portion of the total range of his everyday experience.
>
> In this age of technological sophistication, there seems to be no good reason why a beginning cannot be made toward courses in 'physiological awareness,' in which students are taught the subjective feel of changes in heart rate, blood pressure, EEG waves, sleep stages, electrodermal changes accompanying social stimuli, gastric contractions, etc.
>
> The dictum 'Know Thyself" could be made easier to follow with techniques that make the covert internal processes of brain and body directly observable to the person ... When new methods of experiencing the world or self arises, they are eagerly tried. The response of people upon hearing of our laboratory experiments has been almost uniformly 'Can I be a subject?' If the research continues to provide further evidence of the relationship between the experiential and physiological, it is possible that a whole new method of exploring, modifying, and enriching our lives will emerge.

NEW METHODS—GROUP

While Dr. Kamiya's method and traditional meditation seek transcendence in rather solitary circumstances, several modern techniques do so within a group setting. One such technique is the T-group or encounter group, developed by psychologists during the past twenty years. This approach is an unstructured stress session, usually lasting twenty-four hours or longer, in which a small number of participants, often strangers at the outset, discuss and develop their feelings towards themselves and one another in a here and now setting. The group normally forbids excessive intellectual-ization and serves as a laboratory in which participants are encouraged to experience previously unfamiliar feelings, to attempt new patterns in their interpersonal relationships, and to attain new insights about themselves and their relations to others. As trust and support develop, once resisted feelings and perceptions often break through in this deliberately con-structed situation. The participants often describe such breakthroughs in specifically religious terms (Bugental, 1967, p. 253).

The encounter group has been modified by many psychologists in recent years, and several professional group leaders have integrated new techniques into the basic group format. Many of these techniques are exercises in physical sensitivity. Dr. William Schutz, for example, a psychologist at Esalen Institute, has combined elements of fantasy train-ing, psychodrama and body movement in his workshops, and has led many group participants through personally revealing, often ecstatic experiences.

NEW METHODS—SOLITARY

One such experience was recently reported in the *New York Times* by San Francisco novelist Leo Litwak (1967), who took part in one of Dr. Schutz's workshops at Big Sur. During the workshop, Litwak became aware that he had closed himself to certain feelings because of over-whelming wartime experiences. He asked Dr. Schutz to lead him on a fantasy excursion through his own body to locate the sources of his emotional coldness. As Litwak describes it, "the trip through my body lasted more than one hour. I found wounds everywhere. I remembered a wounded friend whimpering: 'help me, Leo,' which I did— a close friend, yet after he was hit no friend at all, not missed a second after I heard of his death, numb to him as I was to everyone else, preparing for losses by anesthetizing myself. And in the course of that trip through my body I started to feel again and discovered what I'd missed. I felt wide open, lightened, ready to meet others simply and directly."

Gestalt therapy, a pioneering form of existential psychotherapy, is practiced at Esalen Institute by psychiatrist Frederick Perls and his students. Dr. Perls believes that men stop growing, or expanding their consciousness, because of certain "catastrophic expectations" that chain them to a repetitive status quo. His technique is designed to help people transcend their "impasse points," or limited self boundaries.

In his workshops, Dr. Perls works with participants individually in a group setting that stimulates feeling and feedback. Participants present him with dreams, fantasies, or feelings, and he then asks them to play the several parts of their material, or to act out dialogues between the parts. These parts, Dr. Perls believes, are unintegrated facets of personality that must be unified if true growth is to occur.

As a participant gets further and further into these dialogues, he reaches an impasse point and flounders helplessly, actually and figuratively afraid to move. Using various techniques, such as shifting the participant's awareness from within to without his body, Dr. Perls tries to lead him through the impasse, freeing suppressed energies and establishing extended boundaries for awareness and behavior. When Perls is successful, participants often experience rushes of ecstatic feeling, gaining new insight and a sense of integration.

Perls believes that man's intellect often interferes with the vitality of his physical existence and, "like a computer, deprives us of the vivid immediacy of sensing and experiencing." He emphasizes the inseparability of mind and body, and considers his technique a method whereby people can bypass intellectual defenses and free the wisdom of the body. Dr. Perls's belief in the body's wisdom is shared by Dr. Alexander Lowen, a New York psychiatrist who has developed several physical exercises to remove obstacles that prevent the body from spontaneously releasing its tensions and thereby "curing itself." Like Perls, Dr. Lowen has based many of his techniques on the findings of Wilhelm Reich, a psychiatrist who first identified "character armor" in pathology. This "armor" includes physical musculature that people develop at an early age to hold back excitation and strong feeling. It serves the ego in denying feelings or unwanted wishes, but in so doing cripples or desensitizes the body, preventing spontaneous emotion and the possibility of transcendent experience (1963).

PRECONDITION OF TRANSCENDENCE

In his practice, Lowen combines his physical exercises with verbal therapy. In one such exercise, he has his patients arch their backs over a stool, stretching their back muscles and releasing tensions of the diaphragm. In other, they strike a couch with tennis rackets or kick their legs on a bed to activate pent-up anger. To develop a greater sense of identity, they may tighten the backs of their necks, thrust their jaws forward, and repeat the words "no" and "yes" until they invest more feeling in their articulation.

Such techniques allow people to regain their "infantile" capacity of expression, help them experience their muscular and personality rigidity and, once such rigidity is known, to break through the character armor that has stifled their full self-awareness. Once the armor is deeply felt, previously unknown or forgotten truths may become conscious, and the body is freed to effect its own cure.

Lowen (1967) links the high incidence of character armor and chronic tension in our society with our insistence on emotional control in place of healthy spontaneity. He argues that "civilization" is itself the cause of civilized man's problems:

> . . . the acquisition of knowledge transformed by the primitive view of reality. Civilized man discarded the idea of the supernatural; he overcame the awe with which the primitive viewed the unknown and, therefore, mysterious processes of the body and nature; and he replaced the primitive belief in spirits by a faith in

the mind and reason. Through its identification with the mind, the ego proclaimed its domination over the body. 'I think, therefore I am.' Finally, man became egoistic, objective, and detached, and lost the feeling of unity with nature.

As long as the ego dominates the individual, he cannot have the oceanic or transcendental experiences that make life meaningful. Since the ego recognizes only direct cause, it cannot admit the existence of forces beyond its comprehension. Thus, not until the ego bows down to a higher power (as in prayer, for instance) can the individual have a truly religious experience. Not until the ego surrenders to the body in sex can a person have an orgasmic experience. And only when the ego abdicates before the majesty of nature will a person have a mystical experience.

It is not my intention to attack the ego or negate the value of knowledge. My argument is that an ego dissociated from the body is weak and vulnerable, and that knowledge divorced from feeling is empty and meaningless. An education that is to be effective in preparing a child for life must take into account his emotional as well as mental development. The school should recognize that spontaneity and pleasure are as important as productivity and achievement.

In spite of this strong criticism from Dr. Lowen and many other psychologists, few schools in America today do concern themselves with a child's emotional development. Although the techniques described in the previous pages are being explored at such institutions as the Esalen Institute, the National Training Laboratories and the Western Behavioral Sciences Institute at La Jolla, California, they have certainly not been integrated into our society. Such integration, I believe, can only occur when they are included in the curriculum of our schools.

DEVELOPMENTS IN AFFECTIVE EDUCATION

The beginnings of such an integration is now occurring on some American college campuses. Drs. Schutz and Perls and several Esalen Resident Fellows are leading encounter groups, Gestalt therapy workshops and other sensitivity training programs at campuses in the San Francisco Bay Area and elsewhere. At Stanford University, for example, over one thousand students and faculty members have participated in Esalen activities.

Similar advances are also being made on the elementary and secondary school level. Educators are increasingly aware that life's important lessons are learned early in a child's development, and many teachers are trying to reach children with sensitivity training before their creativity and spontaneity are stifled entirely in the classroom. A pilot program for this new direction in education was launched by Esalen Institute last year with the financial assistance of the Ford Foundation. This project is led by Dr. George Brown, Professor of Education at the University of California at Santa Barbara. Dr. Brown is training elementary and secondary school teachers in several techniques derived from or related to those described in this paper, and the teachers themselves are experimenting with them in the classroom. Another such project in affective education is being conducted in the Philadelphia school system by Terry Borton, Norman

Newberg and others. At Stanford, techniques that trigger transcendent experience have been integrated into regular courses such as Design, Physical Education and Business Administration. Similar techniques could enhance the teaching of the arts, philosophy and psychology.

As the introduction of these techniques into education progresses, it becomes possible to envision a future in which transcendent disciplines for individuals, families and groups serve as an integral facet of Western culture. If, as many futurists predict, affluence and leisure increase and education becomes the *raison d'etre* for most of our lives, then the age-old quest for meaning will be forced upon us with new intensity. More than ever, we will need an education to match our hunger for transcendence.

NOTES

[1] Many group dynamics programs, in industry and elsewhere, are vehicles for religious joy—though the joy usually goes unnamed in the formal descriptions of these programs. For an exception see James V. Clark's chapter, "*Toward a theory and practice of religious experiencing,*" in Bugental (1967).

[2] Examples of such tradition-oriented groups with substantial followings are the Zen Center of San Francisco, the Transcendental Meditation Society of Mashesh Maharishi, the Krishna Consciousness Society of Swami Bhaktivedanta, and the various groups which have formed around the teachings of Sri Meher Baba, Gurdjieff and Ouspenski. The Transcendental Meditation Society claims to have more than 10,000 members in the United States.

[3] One reason perhaps for the wide usage of such terms as "personal growth" and "self-actualization" is their open-endedness and their freedom from the limiting connotations of older terms such as "spiritual development" or "mystical perfection."

REFERENCES

Boisen, A. *The exploration of the inner world: a study of mental disorder and religious experience.* Chicago: Willett, Clark & Co., 1936.

Bugental, J. *Challenges of humanistic psychology.* New York: McGraw-Hill, 1967.

Clark, J. Toward a theory and practice of religious experiencing. In J. Bugental (Ed.), *Challenges of humanistic psychology.* New York: McGraw-Hill, 1967.

Deikman, A. Experimental meditation. *J. merv. & ment. Dis.,* 1963, *136*, 4, 329–343.

Deikman, A. De-automatization and the mystic experience. *Psychiatry,* 1966a, 29, 4, 324–338.

Deikman, A. Implications of experimentally induced contemplative meditation. *J. nerv. & ment. Dis.,* 1966b, 142, 2, 101–116.

Dabrowski, K. *Positive disintegration.* Boston: Little, Brown & Co., 1964.

Hibai, T. & Kasamatsu, A. An EEG study on the Zen meditation (zazen). *Folia psychiatrica neurologica Japanica,* 1966, *20*, 315–336.

Kamiya, J. Conscious control of brain waves. *Psychology Today,* 1968, *1*, 11, 56–60.

Laing, R. D. *The politics of experience.* New York: Pantheon Books, 1967.

Laski, M. *Ecstasy; a study of some secular and religious experience.* Bloomington: Indiana Univ. Press, 1962.

Litwak, L. Joy is the prize. *The New York Times.* Dec. 31, 1967.

Lowen, A. *The betrayal of the body.* New York: Macmillan, 1967.

Maslow, A. *Toward a psychology of being.* New York: Van Nostrand, 1962.

Perry, J. W. Reconstitutive process in the psychopathology of the self. *Annals of the New York Academy of Science,* 1962.

Perry, J. W. *Lord of the four quarters; myths of the royal father.* New York: G. Braziller, 1966.

Reich, W. *Character analysis* (3rd Ed.). New York: Farrar, Strauss & Co., 1963.

Robinson, J. *Exploration into God.* Stanford, Calif.: Stanford Press, 1967.

Silverman, J. Shamans and acute schizophrenia. *Amer. Anthropologist,* 1967, 69, 1, 21–31.

Silverman, J. A paradigm for the study of altered states of consciousness. *The British J. of Psychiatry.* (In press).

AN OUTLINE OF TRANSPERSONAL PSYCHOLOGY: ITS MEANING AND RELEVANCE FOR EDUCATION *

Barry McWaters

More Than Is Dreamt Of In Our Philosophies. This article organizes a variety of ideas into a new typology of educational domains. McWaters starts with the observation that most transpersonal psychologists would agree with: there is more to human experience that we have been able to account for. They try to bring these realms into closer study by including them in the domain of psychology. This expands the content of psychology, and consequently, the field of educational psychology. McWaters's table of methods of self-development implies a possible explosion of our ideas of what education is, and can be. If we humans are capable of learning the variety of abilities that McWaters says we can, then any education of the whole man should include all parts of the whole. Suddenly, we see that our current curricula concentrate on only a small segment of our abilities. What we thought was the horizon of ability and learning turns out to be only the foreground.

We live in a time of alarmingly rapid change. Today, in contrast to more stable and conservative eras, almost every area of human interest is open to inquiry. As knowledge of external reality becomes increasingly profound, contemporary Western man is resuming his search into the depths of himself—the inner world of human being.

Within the past five years there has been a resurgence of both personal and empirical exploration of altered states of consciousness, that is, those states of consciousness in which the individual experiences himself as having transcended the limitations of his ordinary waking consciousness. Psychical phenomena, such as clairvoyance and astral projection, and religious phenomena, such as the speaking of tongues and mystical union, are examples of transpersonal experience. Throughout the country, individuals and groups, especially youth, are experimenting with a wide variety of methods for enhancing the capacity for transpersonal experience. These methods include such varied practices as drug induction, biofeedback, dance, and meditation.

Transpersonal psychology, which is now becoming a recognized fourth force in the field of psychology, begins, especially on the university level, to make inroads into the world of education. In 1969, the *Journal of Transpersonal Psychology* was first published, and in 1973, the Association for Transpersonal Psychology held its first conference in Menlo Park, California. In that same year the first conference on Transpersonal

---

*"An Outline of Transpersonal Psychology: Its Meaning and Relevance for Education," was written especially for this book. Barry McWaters is a clinical psychologist and humanistic growth consultant; he has edited the book *The Art and Science of Man*.

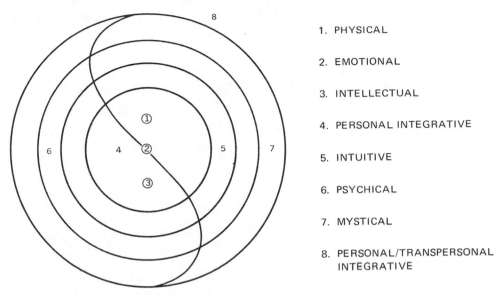

1. PHYSICAL

2. EMOTIONAL

3. INTELLECTUAL

4. PERSONAL INTEGRATIVE

5. INTUITIVE

6. PSYCHICAL

7. MYSTICAL

8. PERSONAL/TRANSPERSONAL
   INTEGRATIVE

Fig. 1. Levels of Human Function and Consciousness

Psychology and Education, held at Northern Illinois University, attracted educators from across the country.

TRANSPERSONAL VIEW OF THE HUMAN BEING

This trend toward exploring the transpersonal dimensions of the person reflects a larger trend in the study of human behavior—the exploration and development of the whole person, in all his complexity and dimension. In both psychology and education there is a growing realization that focus on simply the physical, emotional, or intellectual aspects of the person leaves much of his inner nature unexplored, and therefore unrealized. Figure 1 depicts a multidimensional view of the human being.

In this diagram: circle 1 represents the physical dimension of human energy; circle 2, the emotional; and circle 3, the intellectual. Circle 4 represents the integration of 1, 2, and 3 into a process of harmonious functioning on the personal level. Circle 5 represents the intuitional dimension, in which vague, fleeting (and often misunderstood) experiences of trans-sensory perception begin to come into waking awareness. Circle 6 then represents the psychical dimension in which the individual clearly experiences himself as having transcended sensory awareness, and, simultaneously realizes integration with larger energy fields, such as humanity or the mystical body of Christ. Circle 7 represents the highest mode of experience—mystical union or enlightenment, in which the self transcends duality and merges with all that is. Beyond the seven levels cited there is said to be a further level of potential development (personal/transpersonal integrative) in which all dimensions are experienced simultaneously.

Figure 2 relates the above discussed schema to a variety of methods

FIGURE 2.

Methods of Self Development: Personal and Transpersonal

Mode of Experience		Methods of Development
Title	*Description*	
1. Physical	The five senses	Sensory awareness, dance, diet, sport, massage, exercise, Rolfing, Polarity therapy, Hatha Yoga, Alexander technique
2. Emotional	Love, anger, sadness, joy, etc.	Psychotherapy, music, art, T.A., play therapy, bioenergetic, encounter, psychodrama, gestalt, co-counseling
3. Mental	Intellect, discursive thinking	Empirical research, scholarly research, math, language, philosophy
4. Personal Integrative	Capacity for fulfillment in outer life, the world	Psychoanalysis, psychosynthesis, Existential therapy, direct decision therapy, behavior modification
5. Intuitional	Empathy, vague ESP, imagery	Spontaneous imagery, visualization, analytic psychology, guided fantasy, dream analysis, self-hypnosis
6. Psychic	Parapsychological phenomena	Bio-feedback training, Scientology, psychedelics, directed meditation, yoga, psychic training, astrology, tarot
7. Mystical	Experience of Universal Oneness, Unity	Dance, asceticism, prayer, Bhakti yoga, Quiet meditation, meditation in action
8. Personal/Transpersonal Integrative	Simultaneous experience of all dimensions	Arica Training, Gurdjeiff method, Zen Analytic Psychology, Psychosynthesis, Yoga, Sufism, Buddhism

(Rows 1–4 grouped as *Personal*; rows 5–8 grouped as *Transpersonal*.)

which are being widely practiced today. Space unfortunately does not allow discussion of particular methods. For summary statements on these and other methods of self-development the reader is referred to *A Catalogue of the Ways People Grow* (Peterson, 1971).

This chart, of course, represents just one map of a largely unexplored territory. Hence correspondences are often loose and overlapping. Nonetheless, the thesis is evident: *Different methods tend to emphasize the development of different aspects of the human potential.* However, most often it is not clear in the literature of specific methods just what is offered to the potential student, other than the general direction of "growth." There are, however, many types of growth. My personal bias is that harmonious development of all functional levels is preferable to one-sided development of any single potential.

The chart is divided into two main categories: personal and transpersonal. Development on the personal level refers to the harmonization of energies and expansion of awareness within the individual as an entity separate from the rest of the universe—an other. I am weak, you are strong; I am man, it is a tree; I am real, it is unreal; etc. Most of Western psychology (when it has been concerned with humans) focused on this, the personal dimension of human being. In fact most of Western psychotherapy (notably the psychoanalytic and behavioristic schools) have relegated the transpersonal dimension to either fantasy or psychosis. Carl Jung, however, who could well be called the forefather of transpersonal psychology, went beyond the personality-limited framework and introduced into the field of psychology the concepts of archetype and the collective unconscious, which broadly speaking, refer to the worlds of transpersonal consciousness.

The transpersonal dimension, then, refers to those experiences of human being in which one progressively realizes his essential unity with all being.

RELEVANCE FOR EDUCATION

What relevance then for educators? Many influences have opened the eyes of today's youth to the vast depths of human potential—not the least of these influences has been the psychedelic drug experience. Young people are asking questions, and they seek honest and informed answers— answers that will lead toward their own transpersonal realization. If educators in the establishment do not have intelligent responses, we can be sure that students will turn their backs and look elsewhere. And rightly so: their life is at stake—their inner life of psychological and spiritual health.

Educators, therefore, are called upon to become informed of the general parameters of transpersonal psychology (*Journal of Transpersonal Psychology* and McWaters, 1972). However, in order to truly understand anything, first-hand experience is necessary. This is especially true of transpersonal experience. Hence educators who seek to be guidelights for youth will find rich rewards in the development of their own transpersonal potentials. In this way, the establishment may begin to produce true teachers and counselors in the traditional sense of leading the student toward the truth of himself and the Universe. This being so, education may become a significant influence in the realization of peace on earth and within ourselves.

REFERENCES AND SUGGESTED READING

Assagioli, Roberto. 1965. *Psychosynthesis*. New York: Viking Press.
Journal of Transpersonal Psychology. P.O. Box 4437, Palo Alto, California.

Jung, Carl G. 1963. *Memories, Dreams and Reflections*, trans. Richard and Clara Winston. New York: Pantheon Books.

Maslow, Abraham H. 1962. *Toward a Psychology of Being*. New York: D. Van Nostrand Company, Inc.

Maslow, Abraham H. 1971. *Farther Reaches of Human Nature*. New York, The Viking Press.

McWaters, Barry. 1972. *A Comparative Analysis of Diverse Schemata of Transpersonal Experience*. Unpublished Doctoral Dissertation, San Diego, United States International University.

Ouspensky, P. D. 1950. *In Search of the Miraculous*. London: Routledge, Kegan Paul Ltd.

Peterson, Severin. 1971 *A Catalogue of the Ways People Grow*. New York: Balantine Books.

Tart, Charles (ed.). 1969. *Altered States of Consciousness*. New York: John Weiley & Sons.

Weil, Andrew. 1972. *The Natural Mind*. Boston: Houghton Mifflin Company.

White, John. 1972. *The Highest State of Consciousness*. New York: Anchor Books.

SOME APPLICATIONS OF PSYCHOSYNTHESIS IN THE EDUCATIONAL FIELD*

Martha Crampton

A Humanistic-Transpersonal Bridge. Psychosynthesis combines humanistic and transpersonal views of man, and generally interprets humanistic personal growth as providing a base which leads to transpersonal growth. This article weaves together the personal elements of identity, self-knowledge, will, and social relationships with transpersonal elements such as "higher intuition," ultimate values, and the attempt to use and educate intuition. Some of the educational materials Crampton mentions have now been developed and are available from Canadian Institute of Psychosynthesis, Inc., 3496 Avenue Marlow, Montreal 260, Quebec. Information on psychosynthesis in the U.S. is available from two groups: Psychosynthesis Research Foundation, Room 1902, 40 East 49th St., New York, New York 10017, and from Psychosynthesis Institute, 150 Doherty Way, Redwood City, California 94062.

Tonight I'd like to talk to you a little bit about some of the projects I am involved in for the Quebec Ministry of Education working with some of the graduate students at Sir George Williams University in Montreal. The Quebec Government has decided in the last year to institute a new required course in the schools called "Formation de la personne" or "Personal and social education," to try to deal with the increasing problems of alienation among students and the obvious need to humanize the schools. The talk was announced as "Some Applications of Psychosynthesis in the Educational Field," but the topic is too vast to try to cover in a comprehensive manner, and we have only just begun to explore it ourselves. So I'd prefer to keep the formal talk fairly brief, sketching in some of the approaches we are using, and allowing ample time for discussion so that I can benefit from your own ideas on the subject. I will perhaps finish with an experiential exercise, if you are willing, which may help to bring the material more alive.

In attempting to develop a philosophy for psychosynthesis in education, the concept of integration has been central. We have been using the term "integrative education," which is also used by the Foundation for Integrative Education. The Foundation edits *Main Currents in Modern Thought*, though their emphasis is slightly different from and, I believe, complementary to our own. While their approach has been basically intellectual, seeking integration of the various disciplines through discovery of common underlying principles, our own work is more grounded in a

*From Martha Crampton, "Some Applications of Psychosynthesis in the Educational Field" mimeographed (Speech before Psychosynthesis Seminars, 1971–1972 Series), pp. 1–8, by permission of the author. Martha Crampton is Director of the Canadian Institute of Psychosynthesis, Inc. She is developing psychosynthesis-based instruction for the Quebec Ministry of Education.

psychological approach, taking the microcosm of the human psyche as the point of departure for relating to the various disciplines of the macrocosm.

We have preferred the term "integrative education" to the various other terms which are used to describe work in this field, such as "humanistic," "affective," or "psychological" educatio , as it seems more comprehensive and less limiting. The distinction between the cognitive and affective domains has always seemed artificial to me; our own conception is closer to that of George Brown in what he calls "confluent education" (to suggest the confluence of the cognitive and affective realms), though the word "integrative" has a more psychosynthetic feel to it as it suggests the synthesizing or integrative function of the self. It also implies, in our conception, various types and levels of integration.

First of all, there is integration of the different aspects or "bodies" of man—physical, emotional, mental and spiritual. Then there is the integration of the individual and his environments or ecologies—natural, social, and cosmic. And finally, we hope, through the exploration of fundamental psychological laws and principles, to provide a framework from which to reach out to the other disciplines, helping students to relate to them in a more personally meaningful way and to gain greater insight into their workings through the laws or correspondence or analogy.

Over the last few years, many of the concepts and methods developed in the human potential movement have been applied in the educational field. A new journal, *Humanizing Education*, put out by many of the leading figures in humanistic education, is just starting, and the AHP is now in process of organizing an educational network. A number of universities have or are developing programs in this field, the longest established being the School of Education at the University of Massachusetts, where Gerald Weinstein and his co-workers have been developing and testing affective curricula at all grade levels under a grant from the Ford Foundation.

The Esalen Institute has also sponsored a number of programs concerned with bringing humanistic ideas and methods into the schools, and has been working on another Ford Foundation grant along with George Brown's group in "confluent education" from the University of Santa Barbara to train teachers in affective methods so that they can develop their own curricula which integrate humanistic principles.

The approach in confluent education is not to develop a separate curriculum for the emotions, but rather to make a place for the emotions within the traditional curricula, helping children to understand themselves better through affective interaction with the subject matter, and deepening and enriching their understanding of the subject matter through feeling as well as thinking about it. I understand that the Browns have recently been studying with our colleagues, the Vargius, and have been including psychosynthetic approaches in some of their recent seminars, and I look forward very much to seeing how they will weave psychosynthesis into their own work in the educational field.

We have tried in our own work not to duplicate the fine accomplishments of others in the field of humanistic education, and to concentrate our efforts on aspects which have received less attention by other workers. We are involved at the present time in two projects: a unit on concentraton and meditation, and a unit on what we have called the "integrative qualities" (historically known as the "virtues"). We have started some preliminary field testing in a local high school, and will continue in a more systematic way next year in two junior colleges. My recent appointment as curriculum consultant to the Quebec Ministry of Education to develop a new program in "personal and social education" will give us an opportunity to bring our material directly into the school system—the course will be required in all schools in the near future—and it has stimulated me, through my responsibility for developing the "health" sector of this program, to develop some psychosynthetic approaches to education in this broader area.

Our choice of projects was motivated by a wish to complement existing approaches, and also by the need to develop curricula which could be readily accommodated within the existing educational structures. The integrative qualities material can fit very nicely into courses given under humanities departments, and the meditation course has appeal for many educators who see it as an alternative to drugs.

We have been concerned in our approach not primarily to educate the emotions as such, which is the focus of most humanistic curricula, but to help students to build bridges between the various aspects of their being: between their emotions and their intellect; between the higher abstract mind—the archetypal realm—and the realm of the concrete mind; between knowledge and action; between intuition and reason.

We are particularly interested from the research point of view in varying types of learning styles, in exploring approaches which can help those students who seem to need to approach cognitive learning through affective experience as well as those who function best by starting at the other end and who use new cognitive insights to evolve in the affective domain.

We do not yet know what approaches are most suited to different age and ability levels, though as a general principle it seems likely that learning takes place most readily with a strong affective component, particularly until the abstract mind begins to develop around the age of 14. It also seems likely that the brighter youngsters will be more able to "work down" from mental to emotional levels than the less gifted. The Vargius have mentioned that many of the gifted adolescents with whom they have been working show an unusual capacity to do just this, and that they can progress more rapidly than less gifted youngsters because they can work from the cognitive to the affective (from the higher vibratory level) instead of the other way around. It would seem the esoteric teaching that the mental "body" or aspect of man is at a higher vibratory level than the emotional body may have some relevance here.

In addition to working with the higher intuition, we will also be concerned with the cognitive domain, with the problems of identity and will, with linking knowledge and action. We will be using a graded series of exercises for disidentification and self-identification, starting with the 7th grade with simple exercises to help youngsters expand the boundaries of their identity to include other things and people, and working up to a more formal introduction to disidentification and self-identification in the 9th grade or about the age of 14 when questions of self identity are normally paramount. We have developed a series of cartoons to help get the idea across, showing a person's head up in the sky looking down at the various roles he plays on the stage of life, the various emotions he expresses, and many physical states he experiences, and the constantly changing flow of thoughts that go by.

It remains to be seen, however, to what extent and in what ways disidentification is really necessary in the generation of young people that has grown up on the psychedelic drugs. Many of them seem to have this awareness already, and are faced instead with the problem of re-entry, of how to relate what they have glimpsed in the transpersonal realm to their everyday lives.

Education of the will seems very necessary, though I suspect that we will have to find new ways of doing this to meet the challenge these young people present us. Certain facets of will development are covered by some of the humanistic education curriculum, especially such aspects as goal-setting and choosing between alternatives. These methods serve a function, probably particularly at the elementary and possibly junior high levels, though many students who have been through the drug scene seem to require another approach to the will which would involve a deeply experienced sense of meaning and purpose, and which would therefore draw on transpersonal levels.

Some of our more deliberate and rationalistic approaches which start at the personality level fail to inspire those who have experienced deeper levels of ecstasy and meaning. The units on meditation and the "integrative qualities" will attempt to meet this need to some extent by helping students to contact their own sources of inner guidance, and to relate this to their practical living in the world.

The "Integrative Qualities" curriculum started out with the germ of an idea provided by Dr. Assagioli in his technique of "Evocative Words." He here suggests that the psychological techniques of suggestion can be employed to evoke desirable qualities in people, just as they are misused in the hands of advertisers and the manipulators of public opinion. In addition to the use of evocative words for this purpose, he suggests the use of posters, suggestive phrases and slogans, pictures, musical themes and rhythmic movements to help inspire people to follow higher goals. The idea would be to build a corpus of material that would serve as an accumulator of energy related to the various qualities one might wish to develop.

Assagioli is not the only one to have advocated such an approach. John Wilson in his book, *Moral Education*, has suggested that a collection of quotations related to what used to be called the virtues and vices might be a good point of departure for teaching in this field. And there is a delightful section in the *Autobiography of Benjamin Franklin* in which he describes a project he conceived for "arriving at moral perfection." He selected a list of some 13 integrative qualities or virtues, as he called them—which are probably not ones which would be selected for a contemporary curriculum, as the list was largely made up of virtues with a strong puritanical tinge such as Temperance, Order, Frugality, Industry, Cleanliness, and Chastity, though the principle used is the same—and for each virtue he wrote an "evocative phrase" which he called a precept. He then proceeded in a systematic manner to cultivate these qualities, one at a time, making a daily examination of conscience concerning the particular virtue he was working on at the time, and entering any black marks in a little book he kept for this purpose. He took great pleasure in seeing the number of black marks diminish, and likened the process to weeding a garden.

Although this method may seem a bit heavy to many people today, he nevertheless felt that it had served him well, attributing to it much of his success and happiness in life, and he even hoped, had there been time, to have completed a book for the benefit of others which would have explained the value of possessing the various virtues and the mischiefs attending their opposite vice. His testimony about the experiences he had in using the method makes a fascinating psychological study, and is very moving from the human point of view because of his exceptional capacity for honesty with himself. I am sure that psychosynthesis and the growth psychologies generally would have a great deal to learn from study of the lives of the great geniuses in history, many of whom must have likewise devised methods of their own to accelerate psychological development.

In our own project, we wished to avoid the puritanical tone of words such as "virtue" and "vice," and after much thought hit upon the term "integrative qualities," though we are open to other ideas if someone has a better suggestion. To start off we chose the qualities of Openness, Centeredness, and Inclusiveness, with a further unit to be developed around those qualities concerned with Interrelatedness and Right Relationship. These were chosen on an a priori basis as they seemed to be qualities that people in the New Age are interested in developing, though we will have to find out by experiment what qualities are of greatest importance to people in the different age groups.

The qualities can be considered alone, but it is more interesting to consider them in relation to each other as, for example, the right relation between Openness and Centeredness or Inclusiveness and Centeredness. If Openness is not balanced by Centeredness, the individual risks becoming submerged in a flood of experience he cannot handle, some of which may actually be harmful. One aspect of being centered may be the capacity to distinguish those experiences which are beneficial and nourishing from those that retard growth, the capacity for insulation without isolation.

The analogy of the semi-permeable membrane of a cell might be appropriate here, as the cell takes in through osmosis those substances it requires for its own functions, rejecting, in general, those which are not useful. (We have tried in these curricula to draw on analogies from other disciplines, both for their value in elucidating psychological principles, and for the powerful stimulus they seem to provide to exploration in other fields.)

Each of the organizing concepts or qualities has a cluster of related qualities which it subsumes. Centeredness, for example, would be related to such qualities as Simplicity, Silence, Self-Acceptance, Positivity, Alignment with the Self, Sense of Rhythm, Serenity, and Objectivity. Inclusiveness would be related to such qualities as Empathy, Love, Service, and Oneness. And Openness would be related to such qualities as Sensitivity, Beauty, Wonder, Appreciation, Pattern Recognition, Acceptance, and so on.

We also plan to develop some materials related to corresponding non-integrative qualities or "vices," which will probably be called "Distortions" or "Glamours" or "Illusions." Again, any suggestions as to an appropriate term would be most welcome. The term "glamour," which has been used in this context in certain esoteric writings, has a certain appeal, as it expresses the fact that our emotional responses which are rooted in the illusory sense of ego are often very glamorous to us. In spite of the harm they bring us, we cling to such attitudes as self-pity, possessiveness, and pride, and are unwilling to let go of them. The word "glamour" is also very nice as it seems to derive from an old Anglo-Saxon word for "fog" or "miasma"—a symbol of what the Hindus call "Maya" or illusion—and, in fact, nonintegrative attitudes might be defined as those which are rooted in illusion of some kind.

We have not yet worked out the details on how to weave in the non-integrative qualities, and do not want to make them the major focus since the soundest approach, psychologically speaking, seems to be to place the emphasis on the positive or integrative qualities. We feel that it will be useful, however, to gather materials which will help people to realize the limiting and ultimately illusory nature of the non-integrative qualities, and which will make clear distinctions which need to be made. The quality of Centeredness, for example, can easily be distorted or misunderstood to become self-centeredness and it may be associated with the glamour of self-sufficiency. Or the quality of Inclusiveness may be distorted by possessiveness or confused with a regressive type of merging that results in loss of one's own center.

We are especially interested in finding materials which bring in an element of humor in dealing with the glamours. Young people are very responsive to comics and cartoons, and this approach helps to "make light of" and to gain a certain detachment from the quality in question. We found a wonderful illustration of the vice of Envy in a medieval fresco by Giotto in which a person is depicted with a long tongue going out like a snake which doubles back on itself to bite the envious person, reflecting the boomerang "law of karma." And we have a before and after picture from a Charles Atlas advertisement of a body-building course which should help to make graphically vivid the advantages of regular discipline and the development of the will.

Our accent will be on the positive and on helping people find techniques of transforming the energy bound up in the nonintegrative qualities.

In the "Integrative Qualities" project, we are collecting and producing materials of all kinds pertaining to the qualities which have been selected. We are gathering quotations and seed thoughts (short aphorisms and evocative phrases) which can be used as topics for discussion or meditation. We do not wish to limit ourselves, however, to the principle of suggestion and to what, from a certain point of view, could be considered the dehumanizing techniques of the advertisers, even when these techniques are used in the service of a worthy cause.

We hope to encourage deeper reflection on the concepts and qualities involved, and for this purpose will include provocative statements and paradoxes so that personal search is required to reconcile apparently contradictory statements. (Thus Kahlil Gibran's statement "My enemy said to me, 'Love your enemy' and I obeyed him and loved myself," or Emerson's statement "There is no wall like an idea," or the notion in the Tao Te Ching that "By letting it go it all gets done.")

We are also collecting myths, legends, and fables illustrative of the qualities chosen. The mythological notion of the axis mundi discussed by Eliade, for example, is a good one to relate to the concept of centering, and La Fontaine's fable about the oak tree and the reed can illustrate the fact that centeredness is not rigid, but must flow with the Tao. Thus, the oak tree which was unable to bend in the storm was uprooted, while the supple reed survived. Cultural materials of this kind provide valuable inputs for curricula in the humanities, and can be further supplemented by works of literature and biography.

We are also developing a variety of audio and visual materials to go into the "packages." This includes slides, photographs, drawings, transparencies, cartoons and audiotapes, and may include some filmstrips and videotapes. I'm also thinking of suggesting some films to the National Film Board, as we do not presently have resources for this sort of production. (Any ideas you may have would be most welcome.) One of our co-workers is presently working on a slide-tape presentation on centeredness, using excerpts from interviews with people about their own experience with this quality and visuals of everything from mandalas to potters' wheels.

We are also working on a variety of awareness exercises related to the various qualities, and plan to include many alternatives and suggestions so that a group working with the materials will not feel constrained by a rigid curriculum, but can choose those activities which seem best suited to its own needs and interests.

Always we are concerned with developing a creative attitude, with encouraging students to make up their own exercises, and to gather and create their own materials. We are trying to avoid the mistake of flooding people with too much external input, as we find that this can inhibit creativity, and we are still experimenting to find the right balance. Frank Haronian sent me a copy recently of an interesting article which appeared in the *N.Y. Times* by our colleague from Paris, Dr. Fretigny. He wrote of his theory that too much sensory bombardment through the visual media, providing people with predigested images, tends to cut them off from their own deeper sources of experience. This seems to be a precaution worth bearing in mind.

So we are trying to learn to use the media and curriculum with a light touch—to stimulate but not to stultify, to help bring forth what is within rather than to impose some external vision, however good it may seem. We are experimenting now with the use of various audio inputs to help enhance mental imagery and meditative experience, and are obtaining interesting results with such things as white noise and water sounds. We are also beginning to explore various background sounds in the alpha and theta frequency ranges to see what possibilities this may open up for enhancing intuitive awareness in a group setting.

The scope of the various projects in which we are involved is too broad to be able to give an overall picture in any depth; it might be best if I were to give a few concrete examples of one approach which we have found to be of particular value in linking the cognitive and affective domains, and which we have employed in several of the curriculum units; then we can do a practical exercise together.

This technique is the use of mental imagery to explore one's attitudes toward, and conceptions of, various things—both concrete and abstract. The method is basically that which is described in my paper on "Answers from the unconscious," a revised version of which will appear in the forthcoming book edited by Fadiman on *The Practice of Psychosynthesis*, the "questions" being more of a general conceptual nature rather than oriented toward strictly psychotherapeutic ends as when the method was originally developed.

This method is one of the approaches used in the Integrative Qualities unit as well as in the meditation course. After a preliminary stage of relaxation and alignment—basic training in imagery projection—subjects are asked to hold in their minds a concept such as "Joy," "Positivity," "Interrelatedness," "Synergy," or some philosophic theme, and to allow their insights concerning it to come through in the form of mental imagery—usually visual, but it may also be auditory or kinesthetic and occasionally even in the other sensory modalities. This imagery is written down, drawn, or expressed in movement, and the sharing is generally a very meaningful experience.

We also encourage articulation of the intuitions experienced in this manner in both poetic and abstract language, as this is a great aid to cognitive and creative development. The aphorisms, affirmations, questions, and paradoxes that emerge in this way help to anchor the knowledge gained, and help to prepare the next step in further refinement and clarification of one's ideas. The affirmations may also be used as seed thoughts for meditation and for positive suggestion in self-programming.

We have used other kinds of imagery techniques in the Health Education units I am preparing for the Quebec Ministry of Education's new course in Personal and Social Education. This material has not yet been field tested, but I am hoping it will help children to contact their own deeper values and to relate to conceptual material more meaningfully.

In a lesson on smoking, for example, the children will be asked to experience through imagery what it would be like if they were the lungs of a person who smokes. And the lesson in dental care will have them identify with a tooth which is being allowed to decay. This is really an exercise in expansion of consciousness in which self-identity is extended temporarily to become one with something outside its usual boundaries. It is intended to help children learn to empathize with their own bodies which they, along with many adults, often treat in a manner that they wouldn't treat a dog.

These techniques also show great promise not only for discussion and awareness sessions, but for fundamental scientific research. I have been working for a couple of years with creative people in a variety of fields using mental imagery techniques for problem-solving, and have been able to help people in fields as far removed from my own areas of competence as mathematics and engineering to get over hurdles in work on their theses.

The method lends itself equally well to work in fields such as the behavioral sciences, philosophy, and the creative arts. It is well known that many scientists have obtained their intuitional breakthroughs in the form of mental imagery (Einstein and Kekulé are perhaps the most famous examples), and there is tremendous potential in teaching people to voluntarily do what people such as these have happened upon spontaneously.

One of my most interesting experiences in working with the method was a meditation group held last summer with a group of friends for the purpose of exploring laws of psychological development. In focusing on fundamental issues in this field with the imagery techniques, we came across some fascinating patterns of psychic energy, which opened up many fruitful avenues of exploration. The drawings I have here will give you an example of the way in which it worked. These images were seen by different members of the group in reflecting on the theme of growth stages.

We had been talking about the fact that archetypal symbolism suggests that growth takes place not only as a continuous process but that it is also marked by discrete stages, analogous perhaps to the dual nature of light which manifests both as a continuous wave and as discrete particles or photons. This is reflected in ladder or step symbolism, the metaphor often employed by mystics of rooms in a mansion to be entered in succession, the Sufi notion of "stations" of wisdom, the concept of "initiation" (the Jungian analyst, Jos. Henderson has written a book on the archetype of initiation); and in nature it is found in the growth rings of a tree or the growth nodes of a bamboo plant.

In concentrating on the significance of the growth node concept, the group members saw a pattern in which energy seemed to come up through the central core of a cylinder following a rotary pattern of movement, spilling out at the top of the segment as though it were a fountain overflowing, and coming up through the center again, bringing with it strands of energy moving up from the segment below it. One idea that came out of this was the need for service—that when we reach a certain stage in our own development, there seems to be a law which requires us to share with others what we have gained before we can move on ourselves.

The similarity to the lines of force around a bar magnet is very interesting. Some of the energy does move on up, but much of it bends back to reenter the south pole. We found ourselves becoming very fascinated by analogies or correspondences between psychological laws and the laws of nature, many of us scurrying back to introductory physics books, and felt that an approach of this kind had great potential for involving students in exploring the physical and biological sciences. It is interesting to conceive of the possibility of research teams, with specialists from a variety of disciplines, working together on problems of this kind. Perhaps this is one future direction for psychosynthesis in the educational field.

THE INS AND OUTS OF MIND-BODY ENERGY*

Elmer E. Green and Alyce M. Green

Voluntary Body Control: Doorway to What? Does complete physical education mean more than learning to defeat someone else, more than the rules of badminton? Does it mean learning to use our bodies for our greater physical health, social happiness, and spiritual well-being? If so, then biofeedback presents a much higher realm of physical education, not just muscle development, but complete bodily control. As the later articles on meditation show, physical education can also be part of mental education. The implications of biofeedback training and the authors' associated investigations go far beyond p.e. How much *can* we learn to control our bodies? Do these abilities open doors which will lead us to a new vision of what it means to be human and to a new view of the universe? A new research frontier is developing in which physics, psychology, parapsychology, and medicine are blending to form "noetics," the science of consciousness and its transformations.

Seated in a chair in our laboratory at the Menninger Foundation in Topeka, Kans., a 45-year-old Indian yogi named Swami Rama performed an incredible feat. While seven of us watched, the Swami caused a 14-inch aluminum knitting needle, mounted horizontally on a vertical shaft 5 feet away from him, to rotate toward him through 10 degrees of arc. The Swami had been fitted with a plastic mask that covered his nose and mouth. He breathed through a foam-rubber insert which was covered by a plexiglass shield to deflect any "air currents" down to the sides. Even with this, one of the observers was convinced that the Swami had used some method that could be explained by some already known physical law.

We had warned the Swami that even if he succeeded in demonstrating this kind of phenomena not everyone would accept his explanation of how he had done it. He replied, "That's all right. Every man can have his own hypothesis, but he still has to account for the facts."

In science, facts have always been more sacred than theories. But a nonconforming fact usually becomes scientifically acceptable only when an enlarged theory is developed that rationally unites the nonconforming fact with the existing scientific data. Yet this does not always hold true, because the emotions of scientists get in the way. Some nonconforming facts are apparently too outrageous to be tolerated and some scientists ridicule them out of existence. They claim that the best explanation for

*From Elmer E. Green and Alyce M. Green, "The Ins and Outs of Mind-Body Energy," *Science Year, The World Book Science Annual*, © 1973 Field Enterprises Educational Corporation. Elmer Green is Director of the Voluntary Controls Program and head of the psychophysiology laboratory at the Menninger Foundation. Alyce Green is Associate Research Psychologist with the Voluntary Controls Program.

statistically validated parapsychological phenomena is trickery by the experimenters. Others who are intrigued by the nonconforming facts generally remain silent. Heresy can cost them their promotions and reputations. Eugene Condon, former head of the National Bureau of Standards, phrased the threat in this manner: "Flying saucers and astrology are not the only pseudosciences which have a considerable following among us. . . . There continues to be extrasensory perception, psychokinesis, and a host of others, . . . In my view, publishers who publish or teachers who teach any of the pseudosciences should, on being found guilty, be publicly horsewhipped and forever banned from further activity. . . ."

Nevertheless, some scientists have seriously investigated a host of "unexplainable" phenomena for about a century, and this field of study has grown rapidly in recent years. One of the most interesting and potentially useful areas is control of the autonomic nervous system, through which most psychosomatic (mind-body) diseases are developed. Physicians believe that from 50 to 80 percent of human diseases are psychosomatic, that is, they result from the body's unconscious reaction to psychological stress. Thus it is possible, in theory, to train patients to control 50 to 80 percent of their diseases, to handle other psychosomatic problems, and, hopefully, to decrease their dependence on drugs.

We once thought that the autonomic nervous system, which regulates the body's organs, could not be voluntarily, or consciously, controlled to any significant degree. But recent evidence indicates otherwise. Psychologist Neal E. Miller of Rockefeller University has used a system of rewards and punishments to demonstrate that animals can be conditioned to control autonomic processes, such as the flow of blood to various parts of the body. Human beings also can develop voluntary control of the autonomic nervous system—for example, lowering their blood pressure—apparently by learning to control normally unconscious parts of the mind. This kind of learning usually requires visual or audible feedback, such as a light that flashes or a buzzer that buzzes. These cues inform the subject of his success, telling him whether or not he is controlling what is happening in the normally unconscious domain inside the skin.

Although there is a line of separation between the conscious and the unconscious—the voluntary and involuntary nervous systems—this separation apparently can shift back and forth. For example, when we learn to drive a car we focus conscious attention on every detail of muscular behavior and visual feedback. In other words, we manipulate steering wheel, gas pedal, and brakes according to what we see on the road ahead of us. This tells us what we are doing and suggests corrections if, for example, the car heads toward a ditch. Through such feedback we learn conscious control of the striate, or voluntary, muscles. After much experience, driving becomes automatic. We then may drive through a long section of town while thinking about something else and then wonder if we stopped at all the traffic lights.

When this behavior occurs, processes normally controlled by the conscious have temporarily shifted—to the unconscious. When, through feedback, voluntary control is exerted over so-called involuntary processes, such as dilating and contracting the smooth muscles that control blood flow, the shift is to the conscious domain.

In 1964, we began a voluntary-controls research project at the Menninger Foundation to test this conscious control of the unconscious. We set up a laboratory in which we could monitor the physiological variables of our subjects while they practiced autogenic, or self-generated, techniques. Our equipment included an electroencephalograph (EEG) to measure brain waves, and electrocardiograph (EKG) to measure heart rates, galvanic skin response devices (GSP and GSR) to measure electrical potential and resistance of the skin, thermistors to measure skin temperature, and equipment to measure breathing rates and blood flow in the adjacent room so that we could collect, and later analyze, all the data.

In one series of tests, our subjects—a group of women from the Topeka area—attempted to raise the temperature of one hand by increasing the flow of blood into the hand. Through a technique called passive concentration, some of our subjects were able to raise their hand temperature by several degrees.

Observing this early work, psychologist Gardner Murphy, then head of the Menninger Foundation Research Department, felt that biofeedback might be useful. This meant connecting the monitoring equipment to visual or audible signaling devices. For example, when a thermistor was connected to a meter or a buzzer, the subject could tell if his attempt to change his skin temperature was succeeding by watching the meter needle or hearing the buzzer. When we combined biofeedback with autogenic training, we found that many people learned to control unconscious physiological functions more quickly than with either one alone. We called this combination of the two systems "autogenic feedback training." Autogenic training supplied a strong, suggestive imagery and biofeedback supplied immediate knowledge of the results. These are powerful factors in gaining voluntary control of involuntary processes, and are of great importance in our continuing research program.

In a few short years, voluntary-controls research throughout the United States has begun to show positive results in alleviating a number of medical complaints. One of these is relief from migraine headaches. Patients have learned to cause their hands to become warmer, an action that relaxes the autonomic nervous system, thereby relieving the migraine pain. Other human malfunctions that can be brought under some degree of self-reglulation include erratic heart rate, high blood pressure, Raynaud's disease (which involves deficient blood flow to the extremities), and unconscious muscle tension (responsible for or associated with many unpleasant symptoms).

How does all this take place? Perhaps as follows: According to neuroanatomists, the subcortex of the brain contains a neural network called

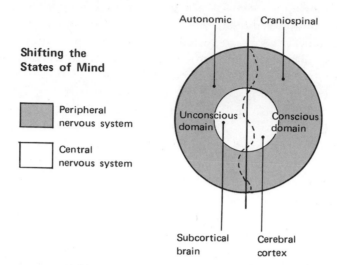

The large circle represents the entire nervous system; the small circle only the central nervous system—brain and spinal cord. A solid vertical line divides the system into the conscious domain, which includes all voluntary processes, and the unconscious domain, which includes all involuntary processes. The dotted line suggests that this division is not fixed; there is a continuous undulating separation between the conscious and the unconscious.

the limbic system that responds to emotions. Whenever we "have an emotion," the electrical activity of the limbic system changes. This system, however, is linked by many nerve fibers to other sections of the subcortex which contain the neural circuits that control most of the body's involuntary, or autonomic, functions. The exact neural pathways have not yet been traced, but this much seems certain: If we have a thought that is associated with a feeling (and few thoughts are not), the limbic system, through its connections with various control circuits, brings about unconscious changes in some of the body's involuntary functions.

Whatever the exact explanation, the important fact is that if we use a sensitive detector and visual and auditory displays to reveal minute physiological changes, we often can learn to control the sections of the involuntary system that regulate these changes. Theoretically, at least, we should be able to bring under control all our physiological processes with this technique.

This extension of conscious control over involuntary systems has far-reaching implications for psychology and medicine. It suggests that human beings are not biological robots, controlled entirely by genes and the conditioning of life experiences. Migraine, for example, tends to run in families and thus seems to be partly, at least, genetic in origin. When it is brought under voluntary control through autogenic feedback training, the patient is apparently overcoming a genetic predisposition. The freedom gained is not just physiological, however; it has an important psychological component. Many people who learn to control physiological problems find themselves relieved of some emotional and mental symptoms at the same time.

The self-regulation of mind-body energies by consciously controlling normally unconscious functions may, at first glance, seem to be little more than a simple medical advance, but the implications are "theory busting," to say the least. The investigation of voluntary or conscious control of mind-body energies has expanded to include two separate but related areas: Control by the mind of the energy inside the skin (Ins), the domain of psychology, physiology, and medicine; and control by the mind of the energy outside the skin (Outs), the domain again of psychology, but also of physics and parapsychology—the psychic phenomena. Furthermore, Ins and Outs energies are special parts of a general "field of mind" theory, which we will examine later. In a curious blend of Eastern theory and Western technology, a new "science of consciousness" seems to be developing.

Swami Rama, trained in the Himalaya in the discipline of yoga, is contributing to this blend. He came to the United States from India in 1969 and now lives in Palatine, Ill. His guru, or teacher, suggested that he could help bring Eastern and Western science closer together by working with psychologists and medical doctors who are studying mental and physical phenomena. Daniel Ferguson, a psychiatrist at the Veterans Administration Hospital at Fort Snelling, St. Paul, Minn., suggested that our Voluntary-Controls Project might want to study Swami Rama. It would be an opportunity to examine someone with extraordinary control over the autonomic system. In addition, because the Swami appears to have a measure of control over Outs energy as well as Ins, we could also study how the unconscious functions in the relationship between psychology and parapsychology.

Ferguson and the Swami first visited our laboratory in March, 1970. As with our other subjects, we wired up the Swami to record brain waves, heart behavior, respiration, skin resistance and potential, muscle tension, blood flow in hands, and hand temperature. He first made the temperature of the little-finger side of his right palm differ from the temperature of the thumb side by 10° F. He did this apparently by controlling the flow of blood in the large radial and ulnar arteries of his wrist. Without moving or using muscle tension, he "turned on" one of them and "turned off" the other. Later, he demonstrated that he could stop his heart from pumping blood, and could produce specific brain wave patterns on demand.

We asked the Swami how he controlled his heart and blood vessels, and how he consciously produced various kinds of brain waves at will. He explained that these phenomena were possible because, "All of the body is in the mind. But," he added, "not all of the mind is in the body." In other words, each part of the energy structure called the body is literally a part of the energy structure called the mind, although the reverse is not necessarily true.

In the raja yoga school of philosophy, two of the most interesting concepts relating to Ins energy are that every part of the body is

Controlling the Uncontrollable

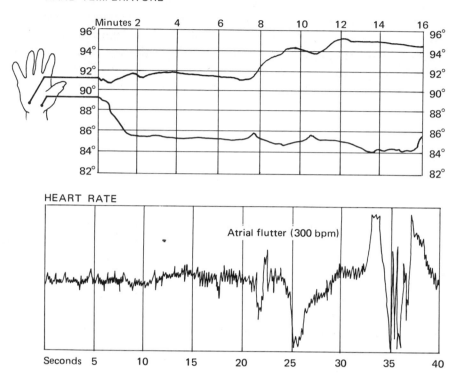

HAND TEMPERATURE

HEART RATE

The Swami demonstrated that he can control the temperature of areas of his palm. After 12 minutes he obtained a spread of 10 degrees between the thumb side and the little-finger side .The Swami's attempt to stop his heart caused an atrial flutter, raising the heartbeat from a normal reading of 70 to 300 beats per minute.

represented in the unconscious, and every part of the body also *represents* the unconscious. What potent ideas! They mean that when we extend conscious control over a specific part of the unconscious, as in autogenic feedback training, the associated physiological processes can be brought under voluntary control.

In yogic theory, the mind is not merely a person's perception of involuntary electrochemical changes in the body. On the contrary, the body is only the densest section of a "field of energy" that includes both body and mind. It is interesting to remember that our bodies, like everything else in the universe, are electromagnetic fields with swarms of particles as dense portions. We are almost entirely empty space, although we see ourselves and all nature as solid matter because that is the way we were constructed by evolution to see.

Yogis believe that, without exception, all body processes are mind processes. The mind handles Ins energy because it *is* Ins energy, even though that is not all it is. For mind is an energy structure, and all matter, whether physiological or nonphysiological, is a matrix of energy that is somehow related to mind. In every thought and in every cell, we are part of the general field, but we are normally unaware of this because we are not conscious of our own unconscious.

Swami Rama represents the classical tradition of Eastern philosophy, but Jack Schwarz, a member of our Western culture, demonstrated some of the same types of phenomena as the Swami. Schwarz, who now lives in Selma, Ore., came to the United States from Holland in 1957. Now in his late 40s, he first learned of his ability to control pain when he was a young child.

Schwarz first visited our laboratory in 1971. After we had wired him up in the same way we had the Swami, he produced a 6-inch darning needle that he first rolled in the dirt on the floor and then proceeded to push through the biceps of his left arm. The needle pierced skin, muscle, and a vein. After he pulled it out, the wound bled for almost 15 seconds. Then he said, "Now it stops." Two seconds later, the wound stopped bleeding. In a second demonstration, the wound did not bleed at all. At no time did he appear to be in pain.

The monitoring equipment provided intriguing information. The GSR showed that he was under no unusual stress. His heart rate remained essentially the same. But the thermistors attached to his fingers showed elevated temperature—a sign of relaxation. And his brain-wave patterns showed what we interpret as alert detachment.

In view of what we had learned from autogenic feedback research and from Swami Rama, it was interesting to hear Schwarz explain how he controls his body functions. Control, he says, depends on cooperation from the "subconscious." He does not force the phenomena to take place, but asks his subconscious if it is willing.

When Schwarz was asked to repeat the demonstration, there was a long pause before he said, "Okay." When we asked why he had paused, he said, "I had to ask the subconscious if it was willing to do it again. When it said yes, than I said 'okay.' " Schwarz also said that part of the delay was due to the fact that his "paraconscious" also considered the situation. He described this level of mind as "wiser" than either the conscious or subconscious. It acts as a kind of intuitional guide.

If we do not have conscious communication with our unconscious (what Schwarz calls the subconscious), it operates as an automaton. That is why a person with a psychosomatic disease cannot control the disease merely by knowing that it is psychosomatic. A certain kind of internal communication is necessary. Indirect control of the unconscious can be temporarily established in human beings by hypnosis, conditioning, or of course, drugs. But the ultimate value of any method of controlling psychosomatic diseases seems to depend on how truly voluntary it is.

So much data on Outs energy has been collected over the last 100 years that many scientists believe the subject can no longer be ignored. The American Association for the Advancement of Science, the American Psychological Association, and the American Psychiatric Association have begun to recognize the need for serious scientific inquiry by sponsoring panels for discussion of parapsychological research. Parapsychology is the study of several kinds of phenomena including *clairvoyance* (seeing without using the eyes), *clairaudience* (hearing without using the ears), *precognition* (knowing of future events with no known source of information), and *psychokinesis* (the movement of physical matter by mind alone).

Psychokinesis, which Swami Rama demonstrated with the knitting needle, is the area that seems most likely to yield scientific facts that are beyond the need for statistical support. One of the earliest scientific investigations was conducted in the early 1900s by Sir William Crookes, chemist, physicist, and a president of the Royal Society of London. After years of research, he announced that he had observed psychokinetic (and other) events under strict laboratory conditions. But he could not account for the facts and would have to learn more before attempting to explain them. Because Crookes could offer no suitable theory, and had no color movies, videotapes, or polygraphs to record information, the evidence he reported convinced only those who observed the events directly. Sir William's less-charitable colleagues thought he had lost his mind.

The next major effort to demonstrate psychokinetic effects took place in the laboratory of Joseph B. and Louisa Rhine at Duke University in the 1930s and 1940s. They first tested whether subjects could influence the roll of dice by thought. Subsequent experiments by the Rhines and other researchers have amassed statistical evidence showing that the probability that chance alone could account for experimental results is less than one in trillions.

Yet, without personal experience, people remain unconvinced. When presented without a rationale, the idea of Ins and Outs energy seems quite difficult to accept. Swami Rama and Jack Schwarz have a simple theory to explain these phenomena, although it may not be very easy to believe.

According to their theory, not only is all of the body in the mind, but all of nature is a "field of mind." Magnetic, electrostatic, electromagnetic, gravitational, and other fields surround the planet and are special parts of a general planetary field of energy. Human minds are part of this normally unconscious field, and Outs energies can be controlled when we become conscious of the Outs, or extrapersonal, extension of our unconscious. This is a generalization of the theory that explains voluntary control of Ins energy. In other words, we can control both Ins and Outs energies only after we become conscious of our unconscious. Psychokinesis, and all other parapsychological phenomena, as well as control of physiological processes, are included in this field of mind theory.

As far as we know, no one has yet been able to detect the "energy" associated with such psychokinetic phenomena. But it seems only a matter of time until a satisfactory energy detector is built and the field of psychokinesis will be opened for further studies of variables in mind and in matter.

Schwarz demonstrated what could be regarded as parapsychological phenomena—perhaps even psychokinetic—some years ago before physicians of the Los Angeles County medical and hypnosis associations. After the doctors examined his hands, Schwarz put them into a large brazier of burning coals, picked some up, and carried them arround the room. Subsequent examination of his hands showed no burns or other signs of heat.

Schwarz's explanation for this is much the same as Swami Rama's. Mind and matter are essentially the same. But we are normally unaware of this because at best we are only slightly aware of our own unconscious and the field of mind of which it is a part. As we become more aware, we can draw on the field of mind for specific powers. In this case, it provided for Schwarz some sort of extremely effective insulation against the hot coals.

Clearly, our capability to regulate our physiological processes has great potential for our well-being. But apart from satisfying our scientific curiosity, why do we bother with parapsychological matters? Partly because there is a potential for misuse of these abilities. As parapsychology becomes scientifically established, we must consider what will happen if human beings can learn to control the minds of other human beings. Evidence of such a possibility is already being seriously discussed by a number of scientists. In *Psychic Discoveries Behind the Iron Curtain*, published in 1970, authors Sheiler Ostrander and Lynn Schroeder discuss the possible use of parapsychological forces for espionage and sabotage. Thus parapsychology confronts us with a number of moral problems.

When the atomic bomb was developed, moral questions were discussed after-the-fact because of the secrecy required by national security. However, psychokinesis is not a secret, and we shall have time to develop rules to guide us in this field of scientific inquiry.

We tend to agree with the existential experts who maintain that the only good "measure and countermeasure" is knowledge and transpersonal awareness. This awareness of the mind operates from a center above or beyond our personal egotism. It transcends the extrapersonal awareness used in developing psychic abilities. According to the field of mind theory, the only dependable guide for the extrapersonal is the transpersonal. Thus it seems that we should support transpersonal research, if only for reasons of safety. If human beings destroy either themselves or their planet it will not be for lack of extrapersonal development, but for lack of transpersonal development.

Whatever else may be said, it seems clear that there are problems in using Outs energy wisely. By default, we have already allowed physical pollution to endanger the planet. There is a disturbing similarity between man's current abuse of nature and his possible exploitation of parapsychological forces for personal gain. Perhaps by serious scientific study of the field of mind, the "science of consciousness," we can avert "psychic" pollution.

FOR FURTHER READING

Aurobindo, *The Synthesis of Yoga*, Sri Aurobindo Ashram Press, 1955. (Available from the California Institute of Asian Studies, San Francisco, Calif.)

Barber, T. X., et al. (Eds.), *Biofeedback and Self-Control, 1970: An Aldine Annual*, Aldine-Atherton, Inc., 1971.

Green, E., Green, A., and Walters, E., "Voluntary Control of Internal States: Psychological and Physiological," *Journal of Transpersonal Psychology*, Volume II, 1970.

Rorvik, David M., "Jack Schwarz Feels No Pain," *Esquire*, December, 1972.

Schultz, J. H., and Luthe, W., *Autogenic Training: A Psychophysiologic Approach in Psychotherapy*, Grune and Stratton, 1959.

Stulman, Julius, *Fields Within Fields . . . Within Fields*, Volume 5, Number 1, 1972.

[Editor's note: A fascinating movie showing the Greens' research, including segments on Swami Rama, Jack Schwarz, and other people with unusual abilities is *Biofeedback: Yoga of the West,* Hartley Productions, Cos Cob, Conn., 1974. Including applications in education, medicine, and counseling, it is recommended for high school, college, and adult audiences.]

ATTENTION TRAINING: A PILOT PROGRAM IN THE DEVELOPMENT OF AUTONOMIC CONTROLS *

Michel P. Richard

Yoga, a Road To Self-discipline. Richard recommends Hatha Yoga and meditation to us because they can increase our control over our bodies and minds, and he envisions these as parts of current elementary and high school curricula. His recommendations in this article could be a first step toward enriching schools with new practices to match new times, and eventually toward a curriculum based on transpersonal views of man. Could these also be steps toward combining the best of the East and the West into a culture of hybrid vigor, and of better understanding? He, like the authors of "Voluntary Control of Internal States," may be pointing to a combined physical-mental-social education of the future. And as the authors of the articles on transcendental meditation point out, there may be current practical benefits as well as future possible benefits.

DIMENSIONS OF THE PROBLEM

There is room for disagreement regarding the goals of education and the nature of the learning process, but there is one principle which is beyond dispute. Teaching and learning cannot take place without some form of discipline. Although the term has punitive connotations, even A. S. Neill accords a place to it. Even in a permissive environment such as Summerhill a pupil who is persistently out of community faces the possibility of exclusion, for without respect for the rights of others and a modicum of restraint on the part of its members no institution can endure.

The ultimate objective, of course, is self-discipline. Without it the individual would be nothing more than a puppet, and the educational system would be forced to devote a disproportionate amount of time and energy to police functions. Perhaps this is already the case. Our schools have done a remarkable job in meeting the demand for mass education, but to the extent that children experience education as a ransom to the future our schools are failing to educate them properly. This is not necessarily the fault of teachers and administrators, since by and large they are conscientious and competent people. The problem is simply that there are few recognized techniques for training young people in the arts and sciences of self-discipline. As a result teachers are forced to rely on relatively ineffective verbal admonitions, appeals to parents, and occasional gold stars.

*From Michel Richard, "Attention Training: A Pilot Program in the Development of Autonomic Controls," *Contemporary Education* 43, no. 3 (January 1972): 57–60, by permission of the author, the publisher, and Indiana State University. Michel Richard is Associate Professor of Sociology, State University of New York, Geneseo, New York. He is author of the books *Exploring Social Space* (New York: The Free Press, 1973) and *Introduction to Sociology: A Values Approach* (Boston: Allyn & Bacon, 1974).

Children learn to placate their teachers and mask their feelings or drop out of the educational system. The unruly pupil becomes a listless undergraduate; then a plodding graduate student, and in the final metamorphis, a professional. Our young people learn the techniques of social and economic survival, but it is doubtful that they really learn self-discipline. They can survive without it, but they do not realize their full potentialities.

In periods of social turbulence students demand "freedom," and educators, like colonial administrators, may find it expedient to give ground. Unless the ground for liberation has been carefully prepared the transition will be wasteful and disorderly. If we are serious about resolving this dilemma we must be willing to seek solutions wherever we can find them, without undue concern for disciplinary boundaries or even cultural parameters. What is *terra incognita* to the cartographer may be someone else's familiar habitat.

There exists in every culture a powerful ethnocentric bias which blinds its members to the reality of other configurations. This bias is functional insofar as it promotes a sense of corporate identity. Civilization, however, is a product of diffusion. All great cultures have borrowed a variety of ideas and techniques from one another. There are no patents on man's most significant inventions. As Melko points out, even a religious system may find greater acceptance in another cultural context than in its place of origin, precisely because it is alien and offers something fresh which cannot be developed in a society enmeshed in its own traditions.[1] Both Christianity and Buddhism illustrate the point, and both testify to the vigor of cultural transplants. The statement that there are few recognized techniques for training individuals in self-discipline is true within our cultural context, but certain techniques which have been developed elsewhere are highly effective. Perhaps it is time to see if we can adapt them to fit our particular needs.

All forms of discipline have a common requirement: they must focus the individual's attention. In military organizations throughout the world this command over the individual's attention is employed fairly effectively for the penalties for disobedience are severe. In Aldous Huxley's fictional paradise entitled *Island* the command is repeated frequently by a nonhuman agent. When the mynah bird cries "Attention!" it is mindlessly voicing a command which all living things must obey. Attentiveness to the external world is part of the survival kit of every organism. Human beings carry this one step further: they have reflexive consciousness. In man, consciousness is aware of itself. Without training, however, this capacity for self-awareness cannot develop properly. Either it withers or it runs wild, as in the case of our drug sub-culture which has become a contraculture today.

Since the waning of the Middle Ages the consciousness of Western man has been turned outwards. In this respect Western man resembles an amoeba. His extroverted bent is manifest in the conquest of outer space; with pseudopods he has managed to embrace the moon. Inner space, if it exists, has been handed over to the hippies. They rely on pharmacology to explore this domain; ironically they too believe in "better living through chemistry."

They may be the astronauts of inner space, but their command module is out of control. They are marooned.

If we are to realize our potentialities for consciousness and freedom we must continue the exploration of inner space. But we must begin to do it with a greater measure of self-discipline. The problem is that we do not like discipline, because we associate it with punishment, discomfort and fear. We want to expand consciousness, but not consciousness of our responsibilities. We want to be "free," but we do not want to be deprived of our sophisticated distractions. In short, we are locked into the predicament of Western man. It is for this reason that we are beginning to turn elsewhere for a solution.

STEPS TOWARD A SOLUTION

None of the major religions of mankind originated in the Western world. By the same token, the most sophisticated techniques of autonomic control are of Eastern provenience. These methods of internal discipline have been perfected during the course of many centuries, and they rest on solidly empirical foundations which have nothing to do with what we call "mysticism." Although the idiom employed by their practitioners is alien to us, their effects can be verified by any competent observer. Students of Hatha Yoga, for example, have demonstrated remarkable control over physiological functions. The effects of meditation are more difficult to measure under laboratory conditions, but recent studies of alpha-wave activity are promising.[2]

Hatha Yoga consists of certain breathing exercises and various static and dynamic postures, called "asanas." These exercises are designed not only to increase muscular tones but also to train the will and clear the mind. The exercises are graded according to difficulty so that the student can set his own pace and measure his own progress. Although novices are advised to work with an accomplished teacher, illustrated instructions for the exercises are available in a variety of published sources.[3] Unlike competitive sports which tend to exclude the person of average ability, Hatha Yoga is recommended for any normal individual. In terms of my own experience, even young children take readily to this discipline and show surprising persistence. One is led to wonder how far they might go if this activity were built into the curriculum of our elementary and secondary schools.

Meditation also employs certain breathing exercises, but only one of the asanas. In the cross-legged position or the more advanced lotus position the upper body is balanced and erect, and one feels self-reliant and receptive. In the Japanese tradition a kneeling posture is substituted for the lotus position. These positions are somewhat uncomfortable for the average Western adult, but tolerance develops rapidly.

As an activity, meditation has been described in various ways: it is a way of centering the self, or dissolving the ego; a way of "gathering the light and letting it flow," and so on. To the casual observer it resembles a form of deep passivity, but anyone who tries it soon discovers that it is hard work. It is different from other forms of mental activity, for in meditation the critical and analytic faculties are suspended. Under these conditions one would normally doze off or daydream, but in meditation one practices the art of tensionless concentration, and develops an immunity to both inner and outer distractions. In this state the individual may have the experience of transcending various problems which confront him in everyday life, rather than solving them on the level at which they were initially stated.

IMPLEMENTATION

As indicated earlier, there appears to be no reason why Hatha Yoga should not be incorporated in the elementary grades. Meditation, however, is probably best postponed until adolescence. At this time physiological changes are contributing to the child's altered self-perception, and life-goals are beginning to take on serious importance. Meditation, then, should be introduced into the curriculum at the 7th or 8th grade level. Whether or not it will be effective at this level is an empirical question to be determined by the pilot program. Although we know that average college students are receptive to meditation, in the case of younger children we are simply making educated guesses on the basis of very limited observations.[4]

Where would Hatha Yoga and meditation fit in the curriculum? Short of building new time blocks into already crowded programs, the most feasible plan would be to introduce meditation during homeroom period (i.e., before 1st period) starting at grade levels 7, 8, or 9, and Hatha Yoga during gym period at grade levels 2, 3, or 4.

Who would teach meditation and Hatha Yoga? There are several alternatives. One possibility would be to secure the services of accomplished practitioners on a consulting basis, if per diem funds can be provided by the schools participating in the pilot program. Another possibility would be to send interested teachers to existing training centers, if stipends can be provided for this purpose.

How will the results of the program be evaluated? The duration of the project could be a full year or less; this remains to be determined. The effectiveness of the training program could be assessed in terms of the following criteria:

1) Self-evaluation (verbal and essay reports written by pupils)
2) Comments by teachers (e.g., changes in deportment, study habits, task performance, attitudes, and cooperative or "helping behavior)
3) Other measures to be developed (e.g., measures of attention span; changes in attitudes toward drug use as determined by anonymous questionnaires, etc.)[5]

One contingency which must be anticipated is that of parental and community reaction. Along with other public relations approaches, it might be a good idea to enlist local PTA support. It will also be helpful to secure endorsements for the program from persons of established reputation in the field of education and from local administrators and officials. However, a certain amount of opposition to any new program must be expected. Hatha

Yoga may be less controversial if it is incorporated into the health education program; after all, other alien forms of physical culture (particularly the arts of self-defense such as Judo, Karate, and Aikido) have already been assimilated in the popular culture. Meditation, however, will pose some problems, insofar as it is associated with introspection. Perhaps the problem is basically a semantic one. Our teacher suggested that we title the activity self-concept. I have chosen, however, to refer to it as attention training.

As the field of awareness expands, there may be accompanying changes in familiar sense perceptions. Colors become intensified; objects appear to radiate light, or take on a two-dimensional appearance. If the exercise is performed with the eyes closed, there may be flashes of visual imagery. Frequently there are changes in the ordinary perception of time: the present moment is experienced as eternity, or as the stillness of absolute motion. One may also hear a ringing sound of very high pitch. Other physical sensations may include a feeling of warmth and changes in respiration. One emerges from the experience with a sense of physical well being, emotional balance, and mental clarity. Returning to ordinary life tasks, it is as if a hidden battery had been recharged, and interpersonal relationships seem less complicated and abrasive.

Although this description of the effects of meditation may sound analogous to accounts of drug experience, there are crucial differences. First, none of these psychedelic effects are experienced as ends in themselves. Rather, they provide a form of autonomic feed-back, because they are indications that something is happening. Secondly, in meditation the individual is in complete control of his own inner experience; not in the sense that he deliberately produces these psychic phenomena, but in the sense that he is able to open or shut the doors of perception at any desired moment. For this reason, there is no such thing as a "bad trip" in meditation.

NOTES

[1] Matthew Melko, "The Interaction of Civilizations," *Journal of World History*, XI (1969), 565.

[2] See "An Electroencephalographic Study on the Zen Meditation" by Akira Kasamatsu and Tomio Hirai in *Altered States of Consciousness* edited by Charles T. Tart (New York: John Wiley & Sons, 1969), pp. 489–501.

[3] The most advanced exercises aim at purging the body of impurities and cannot be mastered without expert supervision. Such practices go far beyond the Westerner's conception of cleanliness, and they are also outside the scope of this proposal.

[4] See "Meditation" by Edward Maupin in *Ways of Growth* edited by Herbert Otto and John Mann (New York: Grossman, 1968), pp. 189–198; also *Experimental Introduction to Social Science* by Michel P. Richard and John Mann (New York: The Free Press, in press).

[5] In line with earlier comments, our hypothesis would be that involvement in Hatha Yoga and meditation will be associated with declining interest in drug experimentation.

PARAPSYCHOLOGY AND EDUCATION *

Stanley Krippner and Gardner Murphy

ESP-pedagogy? Krippner and Murphy tend to see parapsychological abilities as associated with humanistic psychology and to see them as among the more unusual human potentials. The four kinds of ESP (telepathy, clairvoyance, precognition, and psychokinesis) frequently are associated with various altered states of consciousness. As we learn to control our consciousness, will we then be able to learn to control ESP too? The articles by Koestler, the Greens, Targ, and Weil suggest that our restricted beliefs about what it is possible to do limit our abilities to our expectations. When we expand those expectations, the possibilities enlarge, and a new domain of education opens.

A number of parapsychological experiments indicate that successful teaching may have a psi component. For example, M. L. Anderson and R. A. White (1958) found that students who liked their teachers scored higher on ESP [extra-sensory perception] card-guessing tests (and received better grades) than students who did not like their teachers.

Humanistic psychologists stress experiential education which could well have a psi component. Instead of scoffing at a student who reports on an out-of-the-body experience or a telepathic dream, the teacher could deal with the report openly and authentically, using it to help the student enrich his knowledge of self. It would not even be necessary to pass judgment on the validity of the report initially.

The elicitation of extraordinary life episodes by teachers is vital if children are to recognize and appreciate "peak experiences." Maslow (1971) notes, "It looks as if any experience of real excellence, of real perfection, of any moving toward the perfect justice or toward perfect values tends to produce a peak experience [pp. 170–177]." As examples, he cites "peak experiences" obtained through music, mathematics, personal relationships, and childbirth. He concludes, "We may be able to use them as a model by which to reevaluate history teaching or any other kind of teaching (p. 178)." To Maslow, learning one's identity is an essential part of the educational process. If education fails at this task, it is without significant merit.

The well-documented case studies (e.g., Heywood, 1961; L. E. Rhine, 1961) appearing in the parapsychological literature often demonstrate how

*From Stanley Krippner and Gardner Murphy, "Humanistic Psychology and Parapsychology," *The Journal of Humanistic Psychology* 13, no. 4 (Fall, 1973): 17–20 with selected references, by permission of the authors. Stanley Krippner is Director of the Maimonides Dream Laboratory, 1974–5 President of the Association for Humanistic Psychology, Director of Research for the New York Institute for Child Development, and co-author of *Dream Telepathy* and *The Kirlian Aura*. Gardner Murphy is past President of the American Psychological Association and the Society for Psychical Research. He was Director of Research at the Menninger Foundation, and is now Professor of Psychology at George Washington University.

ESP or PK [extra-sensory perception or psychokinesis] occurrences have assisted an individual's developing self-concept. Sometimes this was fostered by a teacher, as in the case of Malcolm Bessent who studied with the eminent English medium, Douglas Johnson, at the College of Psychic Studies in London. Bessent learned to incorporate his rapidly developing paranormal abilities into his self-concept rather than avoid coming to terms with them. He went on to participate in several successful laboratory experiments involving both telepathy (e.g., Krippner, Honorton, & Ullman, in press) and precognition (e.g., Honorton, 1971; Krippner, Ullman, & Honorton, 1971).

The world view adopted by many psychic sensitives is one which places the self firmly within the environmental matrix. It is the world view implicit in the writings of Eastern philosophers, mystics, psychic sensitives, prophets, and some theoretical physicists (Le Shan, 1969). Alan W. Watts (1940) has described this world view as follows:

> Thus the free man has the feeling of an unchanging center in himself—a center which is not exactly in his ego and not exactly in life, nature, or the unconscious as independent of the ego. It is the middle of the dance, the point around which the two partners revolve and in which they realize union.

An increasing number of scientists are becoming involved in research which demonstrates one's interaction with environmental forces. One approach is taken by both Y. A. Kholodov (1966) and A. S. Presman (1970) who have investigated the body's electromagnetic and electrostatic fields from the vantage point of information theory. This direction has influenced parapsychological research in the Soviet Union, especially as regards experiments in telepathy at a distance (Vasiliev, 1965), electromagnetic and electrostatic concomitants of PK (Adamenko, 1972; Naumov, 1968), and photographic techniques which reportedly record the body's fields (Iniushin, 1971; Sergeyev, 1971). In a way, these research efforts mirror the world view stated by F. A. Brown (1967): "Man is unquestionably and inextricably linked by many threads with the rest of the universe."

Le Shan (1968, pp. 129-131), reflecting the viewpoint of humanistic psychology, takes issue with the assumption that the "unaltered" state of unconsciousness is a normal, nonpathological one which provides the most valid picture of reality. Instead, Le Shan suggests that "unaltered" consciousness is "a provincial artifact of Western mechanized civilization" and only one of several types of consciousness to which a culture can educate its individuals. As the impact of humanistic psychology upon education increases (e.g., Krippner & Blickenstaff, 1970), children may undergo subtle changes in consciousness that will increase the likelihood of paranormal events. If so, their teachers must be prepared to understand these occurrences and assist their students to make sense of them. R. A. McConnell (1971) has prepared a curriculum guide in psychical research to assist both teachers and students in this quest.

At the same time, Western science must come to terms with psychic phenomena. Maslow's (1966) reconceptualization of scientific methods and goals presents a humanistic science well-equipped to encompass ESP, PK, and any number of other unusual phenomena which are too important to ignore and too blatantly apparent to overlook. Murphy (1963) points out, "The people who are asking questions beyond operationalism or logical positivism are asking the most profound questions about the limits of knowledge and particularly of knowledge of human personality [p. 63]."

E. M. Segal and Roy Lachman (1972) raise additional questions concerning the adequacy of current scientific paradigms in the study of higher mental processes and conclude that,

> The justification for the domination of psychology by neobehaviorism has eroded, as has the domination itself not only by way of the physical instruments he has invented, but also by way of the amazing sensitivities of his own living substance.

This world view is similar to that found in many preliterate societies in which ESP and PK are accepted as basic facts of life. Although little parapsychological work has been done in these societies, a number of studies (e.g., Stevenson, 1966) suggest these cultures would be fertile grounds for parapsychologists.

The encouragement of self-exploration in education by humanistic psychologists is one of the most important areas in which the parapsychological literature can be helpful. Young people who grow up in a milieu where unique experiences are accepted and openly discussed are more liable to become what Aldous Huxley (1962) has called "full-blown human beings" than students whose self-expression is criticized and repressed. As humanistic psychologists search for the ultimate parameters of human nature, they cannot help but encounter parapsychology. It is to be hoped that the encounter will be meaningful and mutually enriching for both disciplines.

REFERENCES

Adamenko, V. Objects moved at a distance by means of a controlled bioelectric field. Paper prepared for the World Congress of Psychology, Tokyo, Japan, 1972.

Anderson, M. L., & White, R. A. ESP score level in relation to students' attitude toward teacher-agents acting simultaneously. *Journal of Parapsychology*, 1958, 22, 20–28,.

Brown, F. Foreword to *The cosmic clocks* by Michel Gauquelin. New York: Regnery, 1967.

Heywood, R. *Beyond the reach of sense*. New York. Dutton, 1961.

Honorton, C. Automated forced-choice precognition tests with a "sensitive." *Journal of the American Society for Psychical Research*, 1971, 65, 476–481.

Huxley, A. *Island*. New York: Harper & Row, 1962.

Iniushin, V. Biological plasma of human and animal organisms. In Zdenek Rejdak (Ed.), *Symposium of Psychotronics*, Wiltshire, England: Paraphysical Laboratory, 1971.

Kholodov, Y. *The effect of electromagnetic and magnetic fields on the central nervous system*. Moscow: Institute of Higher Nervous Activity and Neurophysiology, Academy of Sciences, 1966.

Krippner, S., & Blickenstaff, R. The development of self-concept as part of an arts workshop for the gifted. *Gifted Child Quarterly*, 1970, 14, 163–166.

Krippner, S., Honorton, C., & Ullman, M. A long-distance study of ESP in dreams using multiple agents. *Journal of the American Society of Psychosymatic Dentistry and Medicine*, in press.

Krippner, S., Ullman, M., & Honorton, C. A precognitive dream study with a single subject. *Journal of the American Society for Psychial Research*, 1971, 65, 192–203.

Le Shan, L. Psi and altered states of consciousness. In Roberto Cavanna & Montague Ullmann (Eds.), *Psi and altered states of consciousness*. New York: Parapsychology Foundation, 1969.

McConnell, R. *ESP curriculum guide*. New York: Simon & Schuster, 1971.

Maslow, A. Defense and growth. *Merrill-Palmer Quarterly*, 1956, 3, 36–47.

Maslow, A. The psychology of science: A reconnaisance. New York: Harper & Row, 1966.

Maslow, A. *The farther reaches of human nature*. New York: Viking, 1971.

Murphy, G. Parapsychology. In Norman L. Faberow (Ed.), *Taboo Topics*. New York: Atherton Press, 1963.

Naumov, E. From telepathy to telekinesis. *Journal of Paraphysics*, 1968, 2, 39–49.

Presman, A. *Electromagnetic fields and life*. New York: Plenum, 1970.

Rhine, L. *Hidden channels of the mind*. New York: Sloane, 1961.

Segal, E., & Lachman, R. Complex behavior or higher mental process: Is there a paradigm shift? *American Psychologist*, 1972, 27, 46–55.

Sergeyev, G. KNIS phenomenon. In Zdnek Rejdak (Ed.), *Symposium of Psychotrnoics*. Wiltshire, England: Paraphysical Laboratory, 1971.

Stevenson, I. *Twenty cases suggestive of reincarnation*. New York: American Society for Psychical Research, 1966.

Vasiliev, L. *Mysterious phenomena of the human psyche*. New Hyde Park, N.Y.: University Books, 1965.

Watts, A. *The meaning of happiness*. New York: Harper & Row, 1940.

USE OF AN AUTOMATIC STIMULUS GENERATOR TO TEACH EXTRA SENSORY PERCEPTION*

Russell Targ and David B. Hurt

Dad, Will You Help Me With My ESP Assignment? If we change our view of human nature to include ESP, then the question arises: Can we teach people to do it, or is it a gift that only a few lucky people possess? Targ and Hurt start with the assumption that ESP exists, and go on to see whether practice improves performance, as it does with other human abilities. Are ESP abilities distributed normally throughout the population, so that various people have it to varying amounts? Scientists in the USSR assume that everyone can learn ESP, although only some people have developed the ability. This is described more fully in *Psychic Discoveries Behind the Iron Curtain.*

Abstract

Feedback reinforcement techniques have been used in an effort to teach extra sensory perception. A machine which randomly selects among four targets, provides immediate feedback indicating correctness of subjects' determination of the machine chosen target. The machine can make its choice either before or after the subject has made his determination, with some evidence for learning in both cases.

The research reported here describes an apparatus for increasing extra sensory perception (ESP) of some subjects by means of an ESP teaching machine. At the present time, there is a substantial body of literature, describing carefully conducted experiments to demonstrate the existence of ESP.[1-3] It is not our purpose to add just another demonstration of the statistical appearance of ESP, but rather to show that learning can take place.

The apparatus used in this work was designed with the goal of enhancing the ESP ability which may be a more or less latent capacity to some extent in all people.[4] Our hypothesis is that enhancement can be accomplished by allowing the user of the machine to become consciously aware of his own mental state at those times when he is most successfully employing his extra sensory faculties. With increased conscious awareness of this mental state, we believe that he is then able to bring his otherwise intermittent faculties under his volitional control.

The teaching machine we used randomly selects one of four targets on each trial. These targets are chosen by the machine and are not presented to the subject until he has indicated to the machine what he believes the target

*From Russell Targ and David B. Hurt, "Use of an Automatic Stimulus Generator to Teach Extra Sensory Perception," (Invited paper presented at the International Institute of Electrical and Electronics Engineers, January, 1972), pp. 37–47, by permission of the authors. Abridged by the editor. Russell Targ and David B. Hurt are associated with Stanford Research Institute.

to be. The targets are 35 mm color transparencies of San Francisco and the subject's task is to select the one the machine has chosen by means of its random target generator.

An important feature of the machine is that the choice *per se* of a target is not forced. That is, the subject may press a PASS button on the machine when he wishes not to guess. Thus, with practice, the subject can learn to recognize those states of mind in which he can correctly choose the target. He does not have to guess at targets when he does not feel that he "knows" which to choose.

When the PASS button is pushed the machine indicates what its choice was, and neither a hit nor a trial is scored by the machine which then goes on to make its next selection. We consider this elimination of forced choice to be a significant condition for learning ESP.

When the user of the machine indicates his choice to the machine, he is immediately and automatically informed of the correct answer. The machine described here is being used to enhance clairvoyant perception in which experimenter and the subject both remain ignorant of the machine's state until the subject has made his choice.

Because the user obtains immediate information feedback as to the correct answer, he may be able to recognize his mental state at those times when he has made a correct response. If the information feedback to the user were not immediate, we believe as much learning would not take place and less or no enhancement would be achieved.

The machine has the following general properties:

It generates random targets automatically and rapidly, with the rate determined by the user. It automatically records and scores both the user's responses and the targets generated, and it displays for the user the current number of trials and hits (correct guesses). The all solid state machine has no moving parts and provides no sensory cue to the user as to its internal state. Its randomness has also been carefully investigated.[5] The machine has four stable internal states. The machine passes through each of its four states at a rate of 250,000 times per second. Once the machine is in a fixed state (not scaling), the user indicates his choice as to which state he thinks the machine is in by pressing a button on the machine under the color slide of his choice. The correct slide will then be illuminated. The correct answer for the next choice is determined by the length of time the choice button was depressed in making the selection. There is no way for the user to control the final state of the machine since his reaction time is four orders of magnitude too slow for this. In addition to the reward of having pushed the button under the slide which lights, a bell rings to indicate that a correct answer choice was made, and four lights carrying messages of encouragement are lit sequentially as the subject obtains 8, 10, 12 and 14 hits.

In the course of this work we have encountered three general classes of subjects. The majority of the 12 subjects working with the machine in this study did not show any significant improvement in their ESP ability. The subjects in this study were not pre-screened, but were chosen from the community at large, on the basis of their interest in the investigation. They ranged in age from 8 to 35 years old, with the younger subjects achieving higher scores, though not necessarily greater learning. Three of the subjects gave indirect evidence of increased ESP by guessing at targets in a manner to cause their score distribution to become bimodal. Whereas chance scores should give a skewed binominal distribution, with the probability of a hit at each trial equal to 1/4, we observe that several subjects show an increasing deviation from this distribution. That is, they generate a disproportaionte number of high and low hits per run of 24. This variance of scoring patterns has been noted in the ESP literature.[6] Among these subjects a particularly high score such as 12 out of 24 is often followed by a particularly low score such as 2 out of 24. We interpret this variance pattern as an indication of ESP although it is not an effect which we set out to cultivate.

In the group indicating some improvement, one subject has shown an exceptional increase in ESP scores through more than 1600 trials. This subject has apparently learned to perceive the state of the machine clairvoyantly, to an extent providing a significant deviation from chance expectation. The hypothesis that this might be a psychokinetic effect will be the subject of a future investigation.

The protocol for the experiment was for the subject to make four runs of 24 trials. This was followed by a rest period, and four more runs of 24.

The most successful subject in this experiment eventually reached a scoring level where on three occasions she scored more than 40 hits out of 96 trials in one of these sets of four runs, where only 24 hits would be expected. From the null hypothesis (no ESP), the probability of 40 or more hits out of 96 trials is less than 10^{-3}, (CR – 3.77). This subject made a total of 64 runs of 24 trials with a mean score of 8.6 hits per run.[7] (CR = 9.81, P for the whole series is approximately 10^{-15}.)

On the basis of the outcome of this work, we sought to determine if another phenomena in the ESP realm could be similarly enhanced.

The machine was altered so that the target was not chosen by the machine until after the subject indicated his choice. The time delay was approximately 0.2 second, which is to say that subjects were asked to make a perception of an event which was to occur 0.2 second in the future. We chose this short delay time because we believe that the accuracy of precognition will be found to vary inversely with the temporal distance separating the perceiver from the event.

The single subject, graduated to the precognitive experiment, reported at the beginning of her first run, "I don't feel anything anymore," about which picture would light, and moreover that she was "just guessing." This was borne out in her early scores in the precognition experiment. However, in the course of 672 trials, her performance increased to a level approaching her scores in the clairvoyant test; e.g., she obtained 19 hits out of her first 96 trials and 38 hits out of her last 96 trials. The results of the 28 precognitive runs of 24 trials each were subjected to a linear regression analysis and are plotted in blocks of 96, corresponding to experimental protocol.[8] The grouped data for all precognitive trials are shown below, and give a best fit to a line with positive slope 2.24 hits per run of 96, and a Y intercept of 20.0. The correlation coefficient is 0.51 using the data from the 28 runs separately, giving P < 0.005 one tailed.[9] This is strongly suggestive that learning has taken place.

We conclude from this work that it may be possible to teach and enhance ESP phenomena through techniques of feedback and reward in much the same way as visceral and glandular functions are brought under volitional control.[10] Additional experiments will shortly be undertaken to determine the relationship between accuracy of precognition and the temporal distance from the event.[11] Our overall goal is to achieve an understanding of the functional relationship of ESP to the various physical and psychological variables which control it.

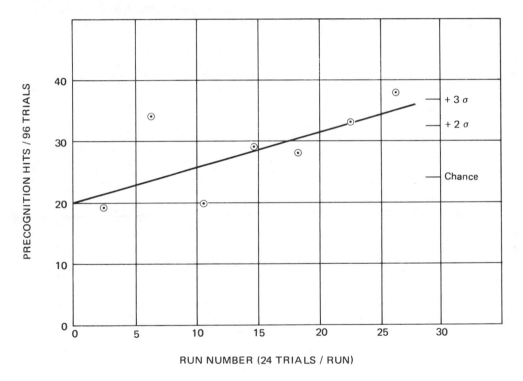

Fig. 1. Precognition Experiment showing number of hits/run of 96 trials vs. average trial number. Linear regression analysis of the data is also shown. 672 trials, P < 0.005.

NOTES

1. J. Pratt, J. B. Rhine, C. Stuart and J. Greenwood, *Extra Sensory Perception After Sixty Years*, New York, Henry Holt, 1940.

2. S. Soal and F. Bateman, *Modern Experiments in Telepathy*, London, Faber and Faber, 1954.

3. L. L. Vasilliev, *Experiments in Mental Suggestion*, Hampshire, England, ISMI Publications, 1963.

4. C. Tart, J. American Soc. Psychical Res., 60, 46 (1966).

5. The distribution of targets with regard to singles, consecutive doubles, consecutive tripeles and sequential runs was analyzed for 2400 trials, and was found to lie within one standard deviation of the expected value.

6. D. P. Rodgers, J. Parapsychology 30, 151 (1966); J. C. Carpenter, J. Parapsychology 30, 73 (1966).

Clairvoyance data showing hits per run of 24 trials for 64 runs.

9,9,8,8: 3,10,12,9: 6,8,9,8: 10,9,8,8:

10,9,10,9: 7,6,9,3: 9,9,10,10: 10,9,7,10:

12,9,10,8: 10,10,11,10: 10,9,8,6: 5, 7, 7, 13:

1,6,8,5: 16,10,4,12: 3,16,12,13: 3,3,8,7:

8. Precognition data showing hits per run of 24 trials for 28 runs. The machine was damaged at this point, causing the experiment to be terminated.

3,5,3,8: 9,9,8,8: 3,6,5,6: 6,8,6,9: 7,5,8,8: 7,8,9,9: 13,9,5,11:

9. Biometrika Tables, Table 13, edited by E. S. Pearson and H. O. Hartley, Cambridge at the University Press, England, 1962.

10. N. E. Miller, Science, 1963, 434 (1969).

11. We hypothesize that significant events create a perturbation in the space-time in which they occur, and that this disturbance propagates forward, and to a small degree, backward in time. Since precognitive phenomena are quite rare, the disturbance evidently dies out extremely rapidly in the −t direction.

12. This work was supported by a grant from the Parapsychology Foundation.

[Editor's Note: For more recent information about research on telepathy at Stanford Research Institute, see: Russell Targ and Harold E. Puthoff, "Information Transmission Under Conditions of Sensory Shielding," *Nature*, Vol. 251, No. 5476, 602-607, October, 1974.]

ARTIFICIAL REINCARNATION *

Shiela Ostrander and Lynn Schroeder

Hypnosis, Are We Already Doing It? Hypnosis is another altered state (or range of states) which has implications for education. In this chapter the authors explore one use. Are they describing a more advanced level of self-control of the type that Richard advocated in "Attention Training"? Although we cannot hypnotise our students, we can help them to relax, to concentrate on what they are doing, and to believe in their abilities. In fact, isn't this what many good teachers already do? In their classes the students feel less anxiety, pay close attention, and have self-confidence. Perhaps hypnosis is an intensification of a good classroom "atmosphere" as the Freudians and humanistic educators would describe it. (See the articles by Tyler, Tenebaum, and Webb.) I know of some teachers who start classes by relaxation and calming, rather than by increasing the stimulation. They say this puts the class in a more receptive mood. Could they be onto something?

Recently, in a large sunlit studio in Moscow, a cluster of art students eyed their model intently. Each deep in his own vision of the girl, they glanced up and down checking the curves of the model against the figure growing on their sketch pads. Not one head turned when their instructor, Dr. Vladimir L. Raikov, entered the room and circled around them talking with a visitor.

"I want you to meet one of my best students," Raikov said. A young girl in her early twenties stood up, rather grudgingly it seemed. But then, as if coming to herself, she turned quickly to the visitor and extended her hand. "I am Raphael of Urbino," she said.

The visitor wasn't as surprised at the name as he was at the nonchalant way this seemingly normal, wide-awake girl tried to pass herself off as the great Renaissance painter.

"Could you tell me, by any chance, what year it is?" he asked.

"Why, 1505, of course."

Needing a moment to order his thoughts, the guest stepped back to focus his camera on the pretty young student. Instructor Raikov asked, "Do you know what he has there?"

"No!"

"Well, have you ever seen anything at all similar to it?"

"Never. I've never seen anything like it in my life."

After clicking a few shots, the visitor began talking again about cameras, jets, sputniks, and—as the girl grew more adamant in her denials—about anything that came into his head concerning 1966, the year they were living in.

*From Sheila Ostrander and Lynn Schroeder, *Psychic Discoveries Behind the Iron Curtain* (Englewood Cliffs, N.J.: Prentice-Hall, Inc., 1970), pp. 146–159, by permission of the authors and publisher. Copyright 1970 by Sheila Ostrander and Lynn Schroeder. Their most recent book is Handbook of PSI Discoveries (New York; Putnam, 1974).

"Phantasmagoria! It's all foolishness. You're bothering me with nonsense!" the girl cried angrily.

"All right, thank you for letting us talk to you," her instructor said. "Go back to work now. Draw! Draw to the very best of your ability, Maestro Raphael."

"That is an example," said Dr. Raikov to his guest, a writer from *Komsomolskaya Pravda*, "of what we call reincarnation."

This reincarnation of Raphael in Ira, a young science student, has not sent psychiatrist Raikov on a hunt through cobwebs and crumbling churchyard records to corroborate the girl's tale of a glorious past life. Raikov, who works with the Popov parapsychologists, knows how this Raphael became reincarnated—just as he knows how the other three Raphaels in the class came into the flesh again. Raikov called them into being. He is a master hypnotist.

With his dynamic brand of reincarnation, Raikov is trying to evoke the birth of talent, perhaps even genius, in his students. We're not giving people something from the outside with reincarnation, something they don't have, the Soviets say. But few people, if any, realize the extraordinary powers they do possess.

"I am able to evoke this phenomenon of reincarnation only when the subject is in exceedingly deep trance," Raikov reports. "It is a new form of active trance." Action is the dominant beat in Raikov's reincarnation. Alla is a high-ranking physics student at Moscow University. Art really didn't interest her much. She felt she had no talent in drawing. Alla's sketches, when she volunteered for Raikov's experiments, bore out her opinion, showing only a little more feeling than stick figures.

"You are Ilya Repin," Dr. Raikov insisted to the deeply entranced Alla. Repin, a great Russian painter at the turn of the century, is still vigorously studied in the Soviet Union. "You think like Repin. You *see* like Repin. You have the abilities of Repin. You *are* Repin. Consequently, the talent of Repin is yours to command."

After a few reincarnation sessions, anyone could see that Alla sketched much better. She began, after ten afternoons as Repin, to want to draw on her own time and took to carrying a sketch pad. In three months, when Raikov brought her to the end of her twenty-five lesson course, Alla drew like a professional—not like Repin or Raphael, two of her many reincarnations, but as well as a competent magazine illustrator. Her new talent exploded so vibrantly in Alla that she's seriously considering chucking her physics theorems and letting loose at the easel full time.

"Alla could not learn how to do this in the usual state of deep hypnosis, which is passive," Raikov explains. Raikov, one of the new breed of young Soviet mind explorers, is thoroughly experienced in passive trance where his word is will to the subject. Raikov has displayed his powers with the Popov group in most of their telepathic sleep-wake experiments, and he has delivered scientific papers on his work in eliciting psychic phenomena under hypnosis. He can easily put Alla into passive trance. He commanded her to "perform" in this state for one visitor. At Raikov's hypnotic word, Alla, her eyes shut, moved around the room with the underwater motions of a sleep-walker. Raikov handed her an invisible glass of apple juice. She gulped down the "juice." "Thank you," she said, "that makes me feel much better."

In reincarnation, Alla is her own person—even if the person happens to be Maestro Raphael. She is alert, extraordinarily wide awake. She sees her model, her pencil, her sketch pad. She consciously composes her own drawing, pours her own feeling into the lines. Not a Svengali-turned-painter, Raikov is offstage as far as Alla is concerned. He is an observer—simply the man who turns the switch.

"Reincarnation brought the girl to a state in which she submits to new laws that have been very little researched. The elaboration of these unknown laws is the goal of my work," Raikov states. "Reincarnation is important for itself. It opens before us the unexplored side of man's psyche."

Dr. Vasiliev, the pioneer parapsychologist, agreed about the importance of the unexplored psyche. Shortly before his death, Vasiliev, writing his thoughts on the arts and creative inspiration, said, "With progress in para-psychology we come closer to unraveling the mysteries of creativity. We now know that man's psychic and creative faculties have much in common."

Parapsychologists and critics of the arts generally recognize that creativity and inspiration are shot through with the force that latter-day scientists have termed ESP.

But—"You too can learn to draw in twenty easy lessons?" The unveiling of Alla the artist seems a little too easy. And it would be, the Soviets agree, by any of the usual modes of instruction. But, they say, reincarnation lets the mind become supercreative, because it allows the mind to operate on new, almost "magical" laws. These laws bear stable gifts. Alla, it appears, didn't come down from her artistic high after she was cut off from Raikov. Neither did his other subjects.

Dr. Raikov and his collaborators ran initial tests with twenty young (late teens, early twenties) unartistic but intelligent students. Raikov gave each of them five to twenty reincarnation experiences. After their final incarnation as a genius some drew better than others, but everyone improved markedly and Raikov has the pictures to prove it. Everyone wound up, in his own opinion, with a newfound talent.

Your activity as a reincarnated master leaves no snatch of memory. Not surprisingly, in their unreincarnated state these students at first refused to believe they'd drawn the pictures shown them—and they probably didn't want to believe they'd signed "Repin" or "Raphael" with a nice flourish at the bottom. As the sessions progressed, however, the drawing skill acquired as Repin began to filter through into their own conscious personalities. Contrary to all previous experience, students found that they could draw after all. "By the tenth session," Naumov told us, "the new talent is stabilized and part of the conscious equipment of the student. What they've acquired stays with them."

Raikov explains, "The student is thinking, forming relationships and judgments, acquiring his own experience during reincarnation. Consequently the creative potential he develops, draws out, becomes his own."

Another scientist, Dr. Milan Ryzl, working in Prague early in the 1960s, devised a hypnotic system to evoke psychic rather than artistic talent in people. Some of Ryzl's subjects also found that the ESP talent that bloomed under hypnosis stabilized as a new, consciously controlled ability in everyday life.

Asked if he weren't just transplanting something into students in a receptive state, Raikov remarked, "As a hypnotist, I simply get them to this state of super wakefulness, but after that I'm not imposing anything on them; sometimes it is very much to the contrary."

Raikov remembers one girl he reincarnated not as an artist, but as a famous English queen. "We desire to hold a ball," the sudden queen announced. "You," she said to Raikov, "be off and take care of the arrangements. It is my command!" she said in the best grand manner when the usually commanding Raikov hesitated.

Raikov reincarnated another student, Volodnya, as a nineteenth-century Russian artist listed simply as "N." Volodnya as "N" considered Raikov his personal model. He dedicated his pictures to "my best model and friend, 1883." While drawing, "N" liked to expound his theories of art. "Would you like to publish them?" model Raikov asked. "Of course," the boy sighed, "but they would never pass the censor."

At this juncture, another psychiatrist came into the room. "Ah," said Raikov, "here's our censor now. I'd like you to meet him, please."

The censor-doctor extended his hand. Volodnya jumped up, putting his own hand behind his back. "Never! Never shall I take the hand of a tsarist censor!" Pacing around them glowering, he shouted to Raikov. "Friend of mine, drive out of here all censors!"

Raikov couldn't resist trying to introduce the high-passioned Volodnya to another student, Elena, also reincarnated for the moment as the famous "N."

"N is, of course, only one person. And *I* am, of course, that person. Now this lady . . . she is a false face," Volodnya observed to Raikov.

Volodnya, like the others, felt he had acquired artistic talent in compressed time. As one Soviet writer put it, "The students feel as if all the spadework is behind them. They feel they've learned all the techniques of drawing while reincarnated as a procession of masters—Repin, Raphael, Matisse and others. Now they're ready to synthesise and develop their own style." Raikov's instruction is similar to traditional art teaching, in which the student would sit with a sketch pad in a museum before the paintings of great artists—except that Raikov's reincarnation encapsulates days into hours, years into months. Alla flipped through her sketch pad, from semi-stick figures to a respectable portrait in three months. Her sudden opening up to art through reincarnation only took her a few hours each week.

Raikov has presented students with wider perspectives than "seeing" through the eyes of famous painters. He hypnotically regressed his student Luba so she could see the world with the eyes of a child. But she didn't see it again as a younger Luba; she was reincarnated as another person called Olga, at ages five, eight, ten, and fourteen. Next Raikov provided her with an even wider storehouse of experience. He reincarnated her as a boy named Ilya with the same age shifts bringing her up to seventeen, Luba's age at the time. Her drawings reflected the various stops on her reincarnation route. The pictures done as a girl showed "more plasticity and softness."

Raikov gave an adult an even stranger dose of widened experience. In this case he departed from his mainline effort to evoke creativity, unless you consider self-healing a possible and creative act. As a psychiatrist, Raikov confronted the problem of Boris, a middle-aged, well-educated chronic alcoholic. The man appeared spasmodically for treatment at the psychiatric clinic. He kept drinking, bouts of d.t.'s followed, and his weary family was about to give up and leave. "O was some Pow'r the giftie gie us, to see oursels as ithers see us!" Robert Burns wrote. Dr. Raikov thought he knew of one such power. He decided to reincarnate Boris's relatives in him. The psychiatrist started with the man's mother, whom he regarded with "warmth and love."

"Who are you?"

"I'm Tatyana Nikolaevna," said Boris, pronouncing his mother's name. Raikov told the man reincarnated as his own mother that "her" son was lying on the couch in a drunken stupor. "He's turned blue, it's sickening, things are really bad." Raikov laid it on.

The patient with his eyes wide open threw himself on the couch and gave "her" son artificial respiration, splashed imaginary water on him, spooned out invisible medicine, and implored the doctors for first aid. "Oh how could you drink like that," lamented the reincarnated mother. "You're dying of alcohol. Your wife is leaving you, your daughter won't love you."

Raikov made a gurgling sound with a bottle of water. "Tatyana Nikolaevna, your son seems to be drinking again," he called. "Tatyana," he faced creased with repugnance, tried to grab the bottle from her invisible "son" and smash it.

Later Raikov reincarnated Boris's daughter in him. "Papa," Boris said in a quiet, soft voice, similar to his daughter's, "Papa, why have you been drinking again? What's the matter with you? It's terrible for me." Tears streamed down the face of Boris reincarnated as his own daughter.

Eventually Raikov evoked the man's wife and other members of his family on him. Boris remembered nothing of these emotion-charged moments as his own family. Then, one day, he told his psychiatrist, Dr. Raikov, that he suddenly had begun thinking how his family felt toward him. He almost physically seemed to feel their anger and disgust, "I began to see all the loathsomeness of my drunkenness through their eyes. It's horrifying."

According to Raikov, this medical reincarnation, playing on Boris's strongest ties with life, gradually helped him form a critical attitude toward his behavior. "A type of reincarnation," Raikov says, "can be an excellent addition to psychotherapeutic treatment." It could also be used for rehabilitation of criminals.

Raikov's medical experiments sound promising, yet his project to force creative talent into bloom in his reincarnation hothouse is even more exciting and fertile. It could be used not only for talents, but also for business and industrial retraining, for headstart programs.

As a Soviet psychiatrist, Raikov is naturally interested in the physiological side of this reincarnation that permits even people like a medical student who said not only that she couldn't draw, but also that she disliked art, to quickly develop facility at sketching. Connecting the usual monitoring devices, Raikov confirmed the supposition that the trance of reincarnation is a new thing, is different in kind from the usual passive trance of deep hypnosis, in which the EEG shows the alpha rest rhythm. In reincarnation the alpha disappears completely and the EEG shows a pattern like that normally recorded in high wakefulness. During a student's whirl as Raphael, physiologically she seems to be super awake. Intense concentration shows in the brain, with distraction leveled out. It's as if the entire being was pulled up into one unwavering floodlight. Reincarnation is, in many ways, the antithesis of sleep. Yet reincarnation has affinities with regular trance. Students fall into a deep sleep before snapping back to themselves. Even though Raikov doesn't suggest amnesia, they never remember a pulse of their lives as another person. According to the Soviets, only a widely adept hypnotist can steer people into the freedom of reincarnation. Not every subject can be lulled into the first step, deep trance. And even Raikov has failed to jog some people from this trance to a burst of reincarnation.

Raikov uses a brand-new and highly unusual instrument invented by a talented twenty-nine-year-old physicist, Victor Adamenko, to check his work. This machine registers energy flow in the body using as check points for its electrodes, interestingly enough, the acupuncture treatment points of traditional Chinese medicine. The ancient Chinese inserted long needles at specific points on the skin to cure disease. Physicist Adamenko attaches his wires to the same spots on the skin and picks up changes in body energy caused by alterations of consciousness and varying emotional states.

In Raikov's laboratory Adamenko carefully attached his machine, called the CCAP (Conductivity of the Channels of Acupuncture Points), to test volunteers and control groups. Then Raikov took over. He put subjects into passive hypnosis. Completely in his sway, they saw rose gardens he conjured for them; they gestured like sleepwalkers. He also put subjects into reincarnation hypnosis. Like the student "Raphaels" and "Repins," they were completely on their own in trance.

At the end of many sessions, Raikov and Adamenko checked the graphs of the CCAP. They found a pronounced difference between the different forms of hypnosis Raikov had tried. "With the CCAP we can chart objectively the psychical activity of the mind in states of somnambulism and various levels of hypnosis," the two reported in the 1968 *Journal of Neuro-*

pathology and Psychiatry, of the Sechenov Medical Institute. They'd come up with a new way to see into the mind, to chart consciousness. "These states are very hard to measure by any other method," they said. Raikov and Adamenko found there was even more activity in the mind during reincarnation than there is when a person is wide awake. This corroborates the EEG findings that reincarnation is a state of "super wakefulness" and that it is a very different animal than regular, passive hypnosis.

The CCAP registers changes in bodily energy as emotion and consciousness vary. It provides a clear, scientific way of showing how thought actually affects us. Parapsychologists eventually tried to see if the CCAP could pick up any bodily effect of thought at a distance. American science doesn't seem to have made use of the CCAP yet. But Adamenko and Raikov's careful reports published by the prestigious Sechenov Medical Institute certainly imply that the CCAP—a new way of looking inside and catching the subtle interplay between thought and body, psyche and soma—will have much wider use than charting the mental states of reincarnated artists.

Musical ability as well as artistic talent has been enhanced by Raikov. He reincarnated the master violinist, Fritz Kreisler, in a student at the Moscow Conservatory of Music. Believing himself to be Kreisler, the boy began to play in the manner of Kreisler. This ability became consolidated in his conscious state.

Raikov states that reincarnation can be used in artistic, musical, and scientific training. His quick leap from discovery to application reflects the Soviet preoccupation with searching out new, radical teaching methods. *The Other Side of the Mind*, by business leader and writer W. Clement Stone and journalist Norma Lee Browning, mentioned the first stirrings of renewed ESP research in Russia in the early 1960s. Sensitive to the global competition of the USSR and the USA and to the great, often neglected, resource of nations—mind power—Stone went to Washington, where he arranged an interview with Oliver Caldwell, then Acting Commissioner for International Education with the Department of Health, Education, and Welfare. Caldwell, an expert on Russian matters, told Stone and Browning, "I am amazed at the skepticism and sometimes hostility which I encounter when I try to tell Americans about some of the experimentation which is taking place in the USSR in parapsychology and related fields. I find this strange because there is available documentation in translation which substantiates most of the things I saw in the USSR. I am really disturbed, because if the United States does not make a serious effort to move forward on this new frontier, in another ten years it may be too late."

Caldwell spoke of many bold and exciting avenues the Soviets were exploring in their push to open up man's intellectual capacities. He told of a conversation he'd had with the late Lev Landau, one of the two or three top physicists in Russia, about the coming possibility of tuning one mind to another telepathically. Landau told him, "When this happens, the teacher can teach a student beyond the normal capacity of his mind by broadcasting over the defense mechanism into the normally empty 90 percent of the brain."

As a stimulant to creativity and to the use of the dormant part of the brain in pure science, Raikov and his colleagues reincarnated a European mathematical genius in a college math student. What enhances the super concentration of reincarnation is the student's belief that he too is a genius, Raikov says. The boy is supremely confident, no inhibitions block the creative flow. He uses "reserves" in his work that usually lie for a lifetime untapped. The experience gained by this student in his hours as a reincarnated mathematical genius also reflected in his waking life. His grades rose sharply. But if you think you'd like to try reincarnation as a quick cram course, don't. Raikov is explicit about the very real dangers in it. No one, he states, except a completely experienced psychiatric hypnotist should ever attempt to evoke separate personalities in another person (or in himself). All of Raikov's own students survived reincarnation with gusto. They felt "good," "rested" after their sessions. Reportedly, they automatically mastered the technique of self-hypnosis in the process, helping them to achieve greater strength of will and memory.

The imaginative Raikov tried an ingenious experiment with an aeronautics engineer—reincarnation in the future, which most Westerners would call precognition.

"You are a great inventor of the future," Raikov told the engineer. "With your knowledge you can easily design a method of taking photos of cosmic rockets." The "man of the future" agreed and quickly set to work. "We put the designs away in a safe place to see if they ever prove correct," Raikov says.

Raikov's published research on artificial reincarnation ignited interest in professionals from many different fields. One of the most popular Soviet psychologists, Dr. K. K. Platonov, commented. "Developing drawing ability is only a partial example of more general laws. There is much talk here about studying the latent powers of man's psyche, which science has demonstrated are unusually great."

Said an outstanding neurophysiologist, Dr. F. Bassin, "Using hypnosis, Raikov is influencing personal characteristics of a person, trying to open up secrets of intellectual abilities and the possibility of training them. This is a new approach in teaching. It demands attention."

Dr. E. Shorokova, Vice President of the Society of Psychologists of the USSR, said, "One must hail these attempts to penetrate deeply into so personal and complex a process as creativity." An exciting new popular film, "Seven Steps Beyond the Horizon," produced by Kiev Films in 1969, probes still further into Raikov's brand of artificial reincarntation.

Creativity, inspiration, that sudden dazzling, that sudden processing of a power that one does not normally have, has been courted immemorially. Raikov moved the courtship into the laboratory by trying to develop at least one pragmatic way of breaking the inspiration barrier. Creativity with its psychic coloring is not essentially a laboratory creature. Charisma, presence— every great performer radiates "it" when he's "on." Raikov remarks that

Russian actors and actresses often tell him they have become different people, drawing on different powers than those they usually display.

The triumph of creativity flowing, and the struggle to bring it on happens privately in the other arts. One of Russia's most brilliant composers, Sergei Rachmaninoff, created a precedent of sorts for Raikov's work. Rachmaninoff's First Symphony was performed in St. Petersburg to unanimous catcalls. The composer was devastated. He collapsed and determined to give up composing. Over the next few years any music that might have moved in him was blocked. Rachmaninoff felt as though he were wearing mental earmuffs. His friends, fearing he would never compose again, finally convinced him to go to a hypnotist, Dr. Dahl.

"You have great talent. And you have the ability to express it," Dahl suggested to the composer. "Inspiration flows freely in you, nothing can block it." After some training in autosuggestion, music surged back to Rachmaninoff. He wrote down this magnificent, powerful music that flooded like spring through the frozen Russian land. Today it is counted among the world's greatest. It was the famous Second Pinao Concerto in C Minor. Rachmaninoff dedicated the concerto to his hypnotist, Dr. Dahl.

Having overcome his mental block, Rachmaninoff later described how his creative gift would seize him. He would often walk in the country and suddenly, as he looked at rain-soaked foliage or a sunset, the music would swirl to him: "All the voices at once. Not a bit here, a bit there. All. The whole grows. Whence it came, how it began, how can I say? It came up within me, was entertained, written down . . ."

Muses and goddesses, spirits and second selves, genies—ever since writers began ordering words they've talked of that *outside* something that comes bearing gifts. The contemporary Soviet poet Andrei Voznesensky describes this feeling better than most: "The poet is two people. One is an insignificant person, leading the most insignificant of lives. But behind him, like an echo, is the other person who writes poetry. . . . Often the real man has no idea what path or what action the other will take. That other man is the prophet who is in every poet."

There is hardly a writer even half-alive who hasn't said, "It came to me. It was like taking dictation."

Creativity isn't bundled into separate fields, as is shown by the career of America's brightest renaissance man, Buckminster Fuller, engineer, cosmogonist, architect (the geodesic dome), mathematician, poet *ad infinitum*. Fuller thinks the age of telepathy is just about to begin and that it will have a profound effect on life. Considering inspiration-intuition, Fuller told writer Walter McGraw, "I've had mathematical discoveries . . . really flash ones . . . and I've had a most extraordinary sense of a sort of intellectual mustiness— that this idea was known before." Stories are legion of scientists who see their great discovery whole, in a nutshell, and then spend a decade or so drawing plans, making formulae to get the kernel out of the shell to show other people. Many great Russian scientists—Metchnikov, Butlerov, Mendeleyev—have experienced this sudden full flush. D. I. Mendeleyev, the famous chemist, saw his entire periodic table of elements one night in a well-lit dream.

The great mediums have affinities with artists. They too at times seem to have access to knowledge and powers not in their everyday selves. Like the artists with their second selves and muses, mediums have their larger selves and, sometimes, control personalities. It's almost as if an artist directs the power into the medium of words, notes, paint, and plastics, while in the psychic arts, the medium is the medium.

The way in which gifted people can turn on their inspiration interested parapsychologist Vasiliev. The "magic charm" he found was personal and subjective in the extreme. Some people, like Rachmaninoff, take a walk in the country, others lie down with their heads pointing north. You might put on a special smock, pray, read a book, drink, hold your breath, crystal gaze, swim, sharpen pencils, rub a ring. Vasiliev thought that all the infinite antics people go through serve to click off a highly individualized conditioned response. At some point in the past you experienced a burst of inspiration. The mind casts about for something that "caused" it, Vasiliev theorized. You light on something that was probably not really a cause. But it becomes a "cause" if it is ritually repeated every time inspiration is desired. According to Vasiliev, Schiller always kept rotting apples in his desk. He maintained he couldn't write without smelling them. Vasiliev believed Schiller must have conceived or written a brilliant passage one day in the autumn when apples lay doing to seed on the ground. The tangy-musty smell became a spring to Schiller's inspiration.

Raikov explains his reincarnation route to inspiration in the same way. "The word 'Repin' or 'Raphael' is only a symbol which helps the hypnotist penetrate into the mystery of man's abilities to reach to the reserves of the organism which are not utilized in the awakened state." By using the word "Repin," Raikov says, the doctor breaks through the "crust" of those centers of the brain that are awake during hypnosis, thereby creating high excitement in other areas of the brain. All of this is then focused solely to creative work: to draw, draw, draw, like Repin.

Dr. Raikov thinks that reincarnation allows the student to connect with some part of the 90 percent of his brain cells that usually lie dormant. A Westerner familiar with Jungian psychology might say that the symbol "Repin" allows the student to connect with and draw on the collective unconscious. There are a lot of theories on what is happening and a lot of semantics to go with them, but the key point is the circumference of the everyday you, the definition of self. Whatever connects in the moment of inspiration is beyond that circle of "you." One of the aims of Communist parapsychologists is to increase the circumference of you: to plug into that waiting part of being, turn on the lights, set more life in motion. The idea is to increase range and power, like the step-up from ukulele to electric guitar.

What about a more long-term form of increase—reincarnation in the traditional meaning? Western parapsychologists, notably Dr. Ian Stevenson of the

University of Virginia, have begun scientific investigations of alleged cases of reincarnation. In Iron Curtain countries, other than Russia, that we visited, we found active interest in the idea. Given the political philosophy of the Soviet Union, it would be too sticky a subject to investigate scientifically yet there. Perhaps the last Russian word on reincarnation should be spoken by a man they still read and revere, Tolstoy. In the early twentieth century Tolstoy wrote, "Our whole life is a dream. The dreams of our present life are the environment in which we work out the impressions, thoughts, feelings, of a former life. As we live through thousands of dreams in our present life, so is our present life only one of thousands of such lives which we enter from the other, more real life—and then return to after death. Our life is but one of the dreams of that more real life.

I believe in it. I know it. I see it without a doubt."

FANTASY AND IMAGINATION*

Frances Clark

Tuning in the Mind's Weaker Signals. Some of the most readily adaptable trans-personal techniques are these that Clark proposes. She has used these in a variety of classes, and they fit in smoothly with current practices since they do not require an intense change of consciousness or other unusual behavior. Often in schools we neglect these abilities, or punish them right out of existence. From a transpersonal point of view, it would be better to develop self-control over one's mind, so that we can choose the kind of thinking that is best for the task at hand, Einstein's selection of a non-verbal cognitive mode referred to in Koestler's article is an example of such a process. Can we teach more people to tune in to these weak but valuable signals coming up from beyond our ordinary consciousness? Can we teach people to select the right mental state for various tasks? Clark is taking us some steps in that direction. Imagine what could happen if you were to read this article in a state of mental and physical relaxation, with enough time to tune in to your mind's imaginings.

Transpersonal psychology in education is primarily concerned with the optimum development of human consciousness. Affirming man's capacity for intentional self-realization and self-transcendence, transpersonal psychology focuses on intra-personal experience as the means of awakening self-consciousness. Attention is directed to the inner self rather than the personality, and although the change process may be described as learning, it cannot be taught in traditional ways.

The contention that intrapersonal experience is an important aspect of education is based in part on recognition of the fact that willed introversion is a classic device of creative genius (Campbell: 1949). Intentional focusing on inner experience not only reveals repressed aspects of the personality, but also provides the key to self-knowledge and creative expression. By descending through the depths of his own psyche, the individual may also experience the deepest layer of transpersonal consciousness, from which every particularized ego consciousness is derived (Newmann: 1954). Moreover, it is in learning to experience his own inner being that the individual may come to understand the meaning of his life (Jung: 1958).

The training for self-awareness discussed in this chapter is intended to facilitate the discovery of meaning and connectedness in the depths of the psyche. Progoff (1959) has observed that the personality unfolds by means

*From Frances V. Clark, "Approaching Transpersonal Consciousness through Affective Imagery in Higher Education." (Doctoral dissertation, California School of Professional Psychology), No. 73-19777 (Ann Arbor, Mich.: University Microfilms, 1973), by permission of the author. Frances Clark is a Research Associate with the Transpersonal Institute, Palo Alto, California, and is a therapist in San Anselmo, California. She is co-author of *Transpersonal Psychology in Education* (Fastback series, Phi Delta Kappa: Bloomington, 1975).

of images, and by increasing awareness of this pre-verbal level of subjective experience, a student can learn to move through the layers of his personal unconscious into transpersonal consciousness.

When a person becomes aware of the possibility of transcending environmental determinants as well as self-image, he may increasingly assume responsibility for making significant choices in his life. In learning to transcend self-imposed limitations and expectations in the inner world, the individual learns to actualize his potential, and frequently reports a sense of transcending personal separateness. In a time when illusions of separateness have brought us to the brink of extinction, the importance of recognizing our ecological interdependence on this planet cannot be overestimated. Subjective validation of the connective levels of consciousness afforded by transpersonal experience may be of central significance in determining our future as a species.

In transpersonal psychology, attention of students and teachers alike is directed to the psychological processes which control internal states and thereby determine personal growth. Learning is not geared to the acquisition or transmission of information, but to participation in the process of unfolding from within. Techniques devised for eliciting transpersonal experience do not automatically lead to the awakening of transpersonal awareness. The process is one of allowing it, rather than making it happen, of getting out of the way, rather than directing or instructing. It is important to remember that since the truth we are seeking is to be discovered within, all the teacher can do is create the appropriate situation. The sharing of subjective experience with others is the means of developing oneself. Learning takes place through continuing exchange, and teaching and learning become indistinguishable. Since the subject matter is the self, the material never runs out, and no one who opens himself to participation is bored (Trungpa: 1970).

One of the problems in developing a framework for awakening transpersonal consciousness in education is that attempts to structure experience frequently result in the stifling of creative expression. Many elaborately structured religious rituals have been designed to induce spiritual experience, awaken love, and inspire faith. Regardless of whether the structure is provided by secular or religious institutions, efforts to awaken a particular predetermined response inevitably stifle spontaneous discovery. In discussing methods for developing transpersonal consciousness, it is necessary to remember that we are talking about experience, and as such we cannot make it, give it, earn it, or take it. However, the fact that experiences of love, faith, insight or unitive consciousness cannot be produced on demand does not diminish their subjective validity or the importance of their effects on our lives.

Methods outlined in this article may be of some help to those attempting to explore their own inner resources, but any map of inner space is necessarily limited, and studying the map cannot be compared to crossing the terrain. In the application of transpersonal psychology, we are continually challenged to expand our own capacity for transpersonal experience, without which the exercises become an empty form rather than an experience of living reality. Teacher and student are not exchanging information, but participating in a level of experience which is subjectively self-validating. A teacher cannot convey or understand the meaning of transpersonal experience unless he has access to it. Likewise, the student cannot be required to comprehend the experience; he can only be invited to participate.

THE LANGUAGE OF IMAGERY

As soon as a person turns his attention inward and begins to explore his inner world, he enters a realm of images, in which imagination and reality may at times become indistinguishable. The emotional, physiological and behavioral effects of imagery are often significant, and sometimes disturbing. However, our primary concern here is not with the effects of imagery, but with learning to understand the language of spontaneous imagery as it occurs in both sleep and waking states. As the student gains familiarity with his own symbolic imagery, he is in fact learning a universal language (Fromm: 1951). Jung (1964) characterized symbolic imagery as the language of the unconscious, to which we have access through dreams, fantasy and various meditative techniques. Symbolic imagery may occur in visual, auditory or kinesthetic form. Intentional use of the language of imagery in the process of self-exploration not only facilitates the process of learning to understand imagery as a metaphor of inner experience, but also gives access to levels of awareness which are not otherwise accessible to consciousness. Understanding of creativity, intuition, and primary thought processes is also enhanced in learning the language of affective imagery.

Practical application of educational techniques involving affective imagery may begin with experiential training in the use of imagery as language. Students may be asked to express how they feel at the moment by verbalizing a poetic image. Subjective identification with a particular object, animal or an aspect of nature which suits the mood of the moment can be shared easily without explanation. Although specific sequence in the use of imagery is not necessary, initial resistance to sharing affective imagery may be reduced by discouraging interpretations, and stressing the importance of letting the image speak for itself.

DREAMS

Classroom discussion of dreams may include a discussion of traditional and contemporary methods of dream interpretation. However, it is important to recognize the fact that *any* interpretation is likely to inhibit sharing of dream material. Students may be reluctant to share material which is highly charged emotionally, yet be eager to learn more about the significance of their own dreams. Questions regarding the importance of dreams, how we can remember dreams, and other matters of practical value in learning to work with dreams may be discussed with reference to current research on dreams (Faraday: 1972; Krippner: 1970; Perls: 1969; Rossi: 1972; Stewart: 1969; Tart: 1969). Students should be encouraged to pay attention to their own dreams, keep a record of their dreams, and regard them as important vehicles for expanding consciousness.

The following suggestions may be helpful in facilitating dream recall: lying quietly upon waking and reviewing dream fragments which may be accessible prior to active engagement in the routines of the day; setting an alarm in order to awaken during the night at different intervals during the regular ninety-minute dream-sleep cycle; asking a friend to observe the eyes and awaken the dreamer during REM (rapid eye movement) sleep, which indicates dreaming; keeping a tape recorder or a paper and pencil next to the bed in order to record dreams immediately. Students may also be encouraged to record expressions of affect accompanying a dream, since the emotional impact frequently fades as waking consciouness displaces dream consciousness. Dreams are remembered more easily when the dreamer is awakened in the middle of a dream, and a sudden awakening, as with a loud alarm, is more conducive to recall than a slow, gentle or spontaneous awakening (Farady: 1972).

The powerful impact of affective imagery is nowhere more evident than in dreams. According to Rossi (1972), the essence of being human is manifested in the original psychological experience of the dream, and optimal psychological development requires maximizing original experience and learning to share it with others. Heightened sensitivity to dream experience, which increases awareness of the processes of spontaneous psychological transformation, is also essential in recognizing and assimilating new patterns of perception and identity.

Gestalt dreamwork, in which the subject is asked to become various figures in a dream through symbolic identification and dramatize the various parts of the dream, is a useful method for learning to expand awareness of the personality. However, the technique is powerful, and may generate emotional stress. In the absence of a therapist, it should be used with caution. The use of active imagination, in which the subject continues a dream in fantasy beyond the actual end of the dream, is also a valuable technique for getting in touch with unknown aspects of the self; here again, however, the subject himself must be responsible for the extent to which he probes the unknown.

Arbitrary interpretation of dream material should be discouraged in the interest of learning to listen to the language of imagery, and allowing the symbols to speak for themselves. Obvious interpretations may only inhibit the discovery of deeper meaning both for the dreamer and for those who are sharing subjective responses to the dream.

A transpersonal approach to dreams is unique in that it calls for group participation in a dream experience rather than objective analysis. When a student volunteers to share a dream, he is asked to close his eyes and recount the dream in present tense, as if he were in it at the moment. The rest of the class is asked to close their eyes also, and identify with the dreamer, in order to experience the dream as if it were their experience. The key words *as if* allow various degrees of participation. When resistance is high, the "as if" experience may be superficial, but this does not make it invalid. Each student participates only to the degree that he is willing. Classroom techniques thus differ from psychotherapy in that resistance is respected, and each person is invited to share his inner life only to the degree that he is comfortable doing so. This approach is not likely to lead to dramatic breakthroughs which frequently result from dreamwork in psychotherapy, but the objective is also different. As long as the teacher is not assuming the responsibilities of a therapist, he must rely on the individual's own judgment of what he can undertake, and allow each participant to proceed at his own rate. The role of the teacher, and the role of the group, is one of offering support rather than leading or interpreting. When a person is willing to share a dream and risk exposing himself in a new way, the power of his experience may be either affirmed or destroyed by those to whom he entrusts the experience. His own resistance to change in self image, whether positive or negative, is likely to be encountered as soon as he begins to explore his symbolic imagery, and resistance is heightened when others seek to impose interpretations. Subjective responses to the dream may be encouraged on condition that the person responding be willing to own his response; i.e., to preface his remarks by saying, "If that were my dream, I would . . ." The sharing of dream material in class is not designed to be therapy, except in the broad sense of being growth enhancing. Its value is primarily in the area of affirmation. The lesson is simply that we can learn a lot about ourselves by paying attention to our dreams. The process is one of learning to listen to our own and other peoples' dreams and allowing them to speak for themselves.

Although there may be some risk of emotional disturbance in the process of bringing unconscious material to consciousness, it is evident that the risk of remaining unconscious is far greater. The teacher need not be an expert in dream interpretation, but he must know how to listen and maintain a nonjudgmental attitude. He must also be willing to acknowledge his own ignorance. For example, in any discussion of precognitive dreams, it is necessary to recognize that our knowledge is extremely limited and we simply do not know how to explain them satisfactorily in accordance with scientific methodology. Our inability to explain certain phenomena, however, does not justify ignoring it or pretending it is unimportant. The systematic exploration of transpersonal dimensions of consciousness is just beginning, and current knowledge is very limited.

Interest in dreams may evoke interest in the development of dream control and lucid dreams; i.e., those in which the dreamer knows that he is dreaming. Suggestions for the development of dream control and deliberate, conscious action in the dream state include self-hypnotic suggestion just prior to going to sleep, listening to dreams, learning the language of dreams, reading the literature on dreams, and learning to shift from an active to a receptive mode of consciousness at will. Whatever the method, as a person becomes more conscious of his dreams, he is also likely to become more conscious in his dreams, and a change in the quality of dream life may also be observed. Students have reported increased incidence of lucid and precognitive dreams as a result of classroom discussion on dreams, keeping a written dream journal, and experiential Gestalt dreamwork.

Students may be encouraged to keep dream journals, writing down their dreams in whatever way seems appropriate to them. Some may wish to record all dreams, including dream fragments, others may wish to record only those dreams which seem to be particularly significant. It is useful to give special attention to recurring dreams and note any changes which take place as a result of increased attention to dream life. One appealing method for recording dreams is that of recording dreams as poems, allowing greater freedom in the juxtaposition of images, associations and emotions than prose, in which there is a greater tendency to impose logical order. The poetic image, conveying as it does a depth of perception linking inner experience to the external world, is particularly well-suited to the articulation of imagistic impressions.

Hypnagogic and hypnopompic imagery may be treated similarly to dreams. Here we have unbidden imagery finding its way to consciousness on the threshold of the sleep state. It usually appears totally irrational, but may also provide a key to self-understanding if its symbolic nature is explored. Furthermore, hypnagogic imagery is associated with creativity, as demonstrated by current research in psychophysiological training for creativity (Green, Green and Walters: 1970). Biofeedback training seems to be particularly promising in the exploration of this level of imagery.

However, investigation of hypnagogic imagery may also be carried out simply by waking oneself up just on the point of falling asleep by such simple methods as holding one arm in a vertical position, holding the head erect, and recording impressions immediately upon jolting back to waking consciousness when the arm or the head drop to one side. Short daytime naps are particularly useful for the investigation of this kind of imagery, and a student may also wish to try setting an alarm at brief intervals. All of these experiments may be carried out outside the classroom, while the class itself can serve as a forum for discussion and sharing of experience.

FANTASY

Active imagination, fantasy and guided daydreams all serve as excellent methods of introduction to the imaginal worlds of inner space. Guidance may be specific and detailed, as when subjects are given continuing instructions to visualize a sequence of events, or it may be minimal, as when the guide gives preliminary instructions and allows subjects to go their own way.

Every exercise in guided fantasy should be preceded by a brief period of relaxation and instructions to focus attention on the present, letting go of thoughts and feelings associated with past and future. Attention may be focused on breathing, for simple observation, with no attempt to change it. An attitude of non-interfering, non-judgmental awareness is thus encouraged. Participants should also be instructed to suspend attempts at interpretation of images until a later time. Emphasis should be on learning to develop inner vision, and learning to listen to what emerges, rather than trying to consciously fabricate images. Introductory work with imagery, however, should be quite specific, until the participants become familiar with their own capacity for using imagination as a tool of self-discovery, and recognize the uniqueness of their own imagery. A simple exercise such as the following can help participants recognize their own capacity for vivid imagery which is frequently accompanied by noticeable physiological effects.

> Imagine that you are standing in front of a blank screen, and on the screen you see a picture of a lemon. As you look at the lemon, it becomes three dimensional and you are able to hold it in your hand. Notice the texture of the skin, all the little dots on the surface, the bump at one end and the place where it was attached to the tree at the other end. Smell the lemon and put it down on a table. Now pick up a knife and, very slowly, cut the lemon, noticing every movement. When the lemon is cut, look at the inside of it, noticing the white part, the sections inside, and the texture of each part. Now squeeze one part slightly and taste it. (Pause) When you are ready, open your eyes.

Sensations of salivation which may be experienced during this exercise are tangible effects which affirm participants' belief in their own capacity for vivid imaginary experience. Questions regarding the relative reality of imaginary experience, and the effects of fantasy thinking on everyday life should be discussed as they arise, but such theoretical issues tend to reinforce critical analysis of the experience and may therefore be more appropriately discussed in didactic sessions after the experiential portion of the session is complete. An important part of the experiential session is the sharing of experience. Here again, it is important to maintain an attitude of acceptance and receptive listening. Interpretation is frequently threatening, and although it is a useful adjunct, it is not always necessary. In an introductory exercise such as the one described above, interpretation is obviously irrelevant, which makes it easy for participants to learn to listen without being judgmental. Even in a simple exercise such as this, important individual differences may be reported, helping each participant to notice the uniqueness of his own experience, in addition to participating in a common experience with others in the group. In more advanced exercises, this sense of common experience is an important connective bond which develops among participants, and may be the first step toward a conscious realization of transpersonal dimensions of experience.

Resistances which may arise from time to time among participants should be respected. Normally the psyche will block material which it is not prepared to handle, but threatening imagery which does emerge should not be disregarded. A participant may wish to explore it further in the context of a one-to-one counseling relationship, or he may be able to regard it as he would a dream image. Imagery emerging in fantasy is likely to have the same irrational quality as dream imagery, and it is up to the individual participant to decide when, where and how he wants to explore it in depth. Suggestions for dealing with negative, threatening images may include engaging the image in dialogue, examining it closely and describing it in detail, feeding it, bathing it, leading it up to a place of light, transforming it with the use of a magic wand, and finally, identifying with it.

The possibility of introducing transpersonal symbols, i.e. symbols of awakening, illumination, transformation, death and rebirth, and liberation, into a guided fantasy makes it particularly suitable to the development of transpersonal consciousness. However, since a person is likely to be more responsive to an image which emerges spontaneously from his own unconscious than to one which someone else suggests to him, the transformative power of such symbols may be diluted when they are introduced by a guide. Moreover, when a subject discovers his own unique connection to the transpersonal through his symbolic imagery, the spontaneity of the process reinforces the subject's faith in his own inner resources.

Following are a series of exercises in guided fantasy which may elicit transpersonal imagery and are appropriate for classroom use:

1. Imagine yourself as a seed in the earth which begins to germinate and grow. What kind of plant are you? How do you experience each of the seasons as the growth process continues? How do you experience being the roots of this plant? The stem? The flower or the leaves? What does the sunlight feel like? The rain? The wind? Imagine that as this plant you are sensitive to everything in your environment.

2. You are standing before a closed door. Over the door is written a word. (The guide may suggest a specific word or let the subject imagine his own.) Someone you know brings you a key. You open the door and go in.

3. You are at the foot of a mountain which you are prepared to climb. The ascent is difficult but you are able to overcome the various obstacles which you encounter on the way. Take your time and keep going until you reach the top of the mountain.

4. You are walking up a mountain path and you see a cave. You enter the cave and see a fire glowing deep within. As you approach the fire, you see a very old person seated by the fire. This person is very wise and will answer any question you ask, and will give you a significant object to bring back with you.

5. You are standing at a crossroads. There is a sign at the crossroads. You read the sign and choose to follow one of the roads. Notice what you are taking with you on this journey. Follow the road of your choice and see where it leads.

6. You are in a meadow. Explore the meadow and get to know it. Notice the size of the meadow and the weather. Someone is going to come into your meadow. When that person is with you, imagine that you become him or her

and see yourself and the meadow through his eyes. Experience as fully as you can what it would be like to be the other person's body. Become yourself again, and say goodbye to the other person.

7. Imagine that you are a body of water. Choose a body of water which symbolizes the way you feel at this time. Experience the cycles of light and dark and be aware of any life forms existing within you. Imagine the process of evaporation as the sun warms you, and the process of cooling and precipitation.

8. Imagine that you are going on a journey into space. As you move away from the earth your perception of time and space is altered, allowing you to perceive reality in a totally new way. As you continue to move out through avenues of stars your wisdom and understanding increases. When you return to your localized awareness you will remember the insight you gained from this perspective.

9. You are entering a room of mirrors. Every surface reflects a different image of you. Look at each one and get to know it.

10. Imagine that you are a very young infant. Notice your surroundings, and how it feels to be where you are. You do not have to rely on memory. Simply imagine what it is like to be a very small child. Going forward in time, imagine what it is like to be five years old. How do you experience the world at the age of five? How does it feel to be five? Going on to the age of twelve now, what is it like to be twelve years old? How do you see the world at age twelve? Going on now to age twenty-five, how does it feel to be you at twenty-five? How do you experience the world at twenty-five? Going on now to age forty, how does it feel to be you at forty? How do you feel about yourself and the world at forty? Now imagine that you are sixty-five years old. How do you see your life from the point of view of sixty-five years? Imagine now that you are very, very old. Soon you will die. Allow yourself to imagine your own death, and rest a while after that experience. Imagine now that you can be reborn as anything you choose. When you feel ready to open your eyes, imagine that you are seeing the world for the first time.

It is evident that certain suggestions are more likely to evoke threatening imagery than others. For example, an exploration of the depths of the ocean is likely to be scary if it is not superficial. While the deliberate confrontation of fearful images may be useful in therapy, it is not recommended for introductory classroom experience. Relatively simple, non-threatening suggestions can serve the purpose of putting participants in touch with meaningful inner experience without being frightening. In time the group itself will determine the depth and intensity of experience it is willing to explore.

Any fantasy introduction may be changed, adapted or invented by any group member to suit a particular situation. Exercises with the detailed instructions are best suited to groups with little or no experience in this type of work. With practice, however, as the student learns to concentrate his attention on the flow of imagery which unfolds from within with very little effort; detailed instructions may be an annoying interference.

Many guided fantasies are adaptable to working with partners or in small groups. For example, students may be instructed to find a partner they do not know, spend a few minutes looking at each other until they have a clear image of each other with eyes closed, and then proceed to carry out a fantasy experience in which they are doing something together. Suggestions for climbing a mountain, or being marooned on an island together are well-suited to working with one or two other people. During the course of the exercise, everyone should remain silent, and share experiences only after the exercise is complete. It is interesting to note the similarities and differences in the imagery which arises among different partners or groups.

Another way of working with fantasy in pairs is to have one person serve as a guide and ask the other to fantasize and verbalize the fantasy in progress. Those serving as guides should be instructed to interfere as little as possible, giving only minimum prompting to their partners. If the person fantasizing lapses into a long silence, the guide may inquire about what is happening, and may remind the subject from time to time that in fantasy anything is possible, therefore any obstacle can be overcome. In working with many pairs in one room, music may be used as background to prevent distraction from hearing one another, but the type of music selected will certainly affect the experience of those participating. In a totally unstructured fantasy experience, music can be programmed for the evocation of transpersonal experience. Experimental work with this kind of programming is currently in progress (Bonny: 1972).

MEDITATION

Meditation is the royal road to transpersonal experience. The student may experience considerable difficulty in selecting a particular school of meditation, since many offer apparently contradictory paths to enlightenment. Naranjo (1971) has described in detail three basic approaches to meditation: the way of concentration, the way of emptiness, and the way of surrender or self-expression. Each one may be introduced in the classroom. Basic instructions for any meditation exercises are simply to sit quietly, keeping the spine straight.

The way of concentration is also called the way of forms, or absorptive meditation. This is essentially the type of meditation which has been adapted by Assagioli (1965) to the process of psychosynthesis. Its relevance to education is self-evident, since it is geared to developing the will and powers of concentration. The experience of becoming one with the object of meditation which is frequently reported as a result of this type of practice (Deikman: 1969) may give the student immediate experiential validation of transpersonal consciousness. When the boundaries between subject and object are experientially transcended, albeit momentarily, the experience is self-validating. While these effects of meditation are usually the result of persistent, consistent practice, classroom participation in introductory exercises may be sufficient incentive for some students to continue practice on their own.

Initially, concentration meditation is facilitated by focusing on an external object. A candle flame, a pinpoint of light on a screen, a mandala, or a yantra are suitable objects for visual meditation. Concentration may also be aided by auditory stimuli, such as repetition of a mantra, or a tape loop with a single repeating word, such as *cogitate* (Lilly: 1972). One introductory concentration meditation expeience which tends to stimulate considerable response among participants is the "third eye meditation." In this exercise, participants work in pairs, facing each other and looking at a point between and slightly above the eyes of the partner. Instructions are to concentrate on this point, imagining that you are looking out of your own third eye, for a period of ten to thirty minutes. This exercise frequently leads to visual distortions and a flow of unbidden imagery. The period of time may be varied, but ten minutes is sufficient for an introductory experience.

Concentration meditation may also be practiced with eyes closed, in which case emphasis is on the development of inner vision. A simple introductory exercise is one in which participants are asked to visualize a white dot inside a white circle on a black background for four minutes, then a white plus sign on a black background for four minutes, and then a white triangle on a black background for four minutes. Initial attempts are usually discouraging. Participants are likely to be surprised by how little control they have over their imagery and how difficult the exercise is. It is useful in demonstrating the ineffectiveness of the will, and is used in psychosynthesis as an exercise for the development of will. Experimental research on the effects of this exercise is currently in progress (Gerard: 1972). Students may be encouraged to experiment with the effects of daily practice over a period of several months.

Other forms of concentration meditation which do not involve external aids include concentration on a word, on an ideal, on a color, on a scene from nature, or any appropriate symbol. One excellent introductory meditative exercise involves simple concentration on breathing. The student may be instructed to simply observe each breath, or he may be instructed to count his breaths from one to ten and then start again, and continue the process of counting breaths from one to ten for a period of ten to twenty minutes. Initially, a short period of meditation such as ten minutes may seem long, but as practice continues the period of time may be lengthened to forty-five minutes, according to what is appropriate to the situation.

The type of meditation defined as the way of emptiness is easy to explain, but difficult to practice. Instruction for this type of meditation is, simply, sit, and do nothing. Sensations, thoughts, feelings or images are discouraged and, where present, disregarded. The objective is emptiness, and the way is not-doing. In psychological terms it is the way of disidentification and self-denial. Naranjo (1971) has called it the negative way. The disidentification exercises outlined by Assagioli (1965) may be used as an introduction to this particular discipline. Initially, the question, "Who are you?" may be repeated over and over again for a period of five to ten minutes, until every form of self-identification is recognized. Each one may then be discarded as a mask or aspect of the persona. Subsequently, the student may continue the process of disidentification by meditating on the following phrases: "I have a body, but I am not my body. I have emotions, but I am not my emotions. I have a mind, but I am not my mind." This exercise is useful in awakening some awareness of a transpersonal self, as a point of pure consciousness, but it should be used with discretion as premature emphasis on disidentification may exacerbate psychological problems of disassociation and lead to pseudo-spiritual schizophrenic disorders. However, the question, "Who are you?" is an appropriate starting point for any introductory course dealing with self-discovery, and is particularly helpful in demonstrating the difference between psychological work pertaining to the personality and transpersonal work pertaining to the continuing self.

The third type of meditation, or the way of self-expression, is also well suited to an educational setting. The focus is on becoming fully aware of whatever is. Instructions may be limited to directing attention to self observation as a continuing process. In sitting, no attempt is made to suppress thoughts or images. Whatever emerges is observed non-judgmentally. Everything, including imagination and conceptualization, is accepted as useful in the development of conscious awareness. Psychic forces manifested as symbolic images are considered real rather than illusory, and only insofar as consciousness begins to detach itself from its contents are these forces considered relatively real (Jung: 1962). In this way, consciousness is expanded through the conscious assimilation of projected unconscious material. The transformation of apparently destructive forces into constructive energy through creative expression is an important aspect of this approach to self-discovery. Naranjo (1971) has characterized this as the way of surrender, in which the creative process unfolds without conscious interference. The transformation of energy into an emotionally expressive form, e.g., poetry, painting, dance, or music is an integral part of this approach.

The expressive arts have always had their place in the educational system, but in the context of transpersonal psychology they are not judged according to traditional standards. Creative expression is frequently stifled by critical evaluation in formal training in the arts, and only those with exceptional talents survive the competitive struggle for recognition. In this context, the objective of artistic expression is not the production of an objectively valuable work of art, but increased self-awareness and original experience. The value is in the process rather than the product. A teacher does not need to be an expert in order to create a climate of acceptance and encouragement for individual effort. He should, however, have some personal experience with risk-taking in self-expression using unfamiliar media. The importance of venturing into a new form of self-expression, using art media as a vehicle for the communication of inner experience, must not be underestimated. Expectations of failure and critical judgment can be a major obstacle to self-discovery. The ego must learn to stand aside in order to let imagery flow, and judgment must be suspended when attempts are made to give form to images which emerge from the depths of the psyche. We need to be patient with ourselves and others in any attempt to delve into the inner world. A flow of personal imagery which seems trite and inconsequential need not be discouraging. In the process of exploring the inner world, it is sometimes necessary to work through layers of personal psychic debris, before encountering images of a transpersonal nature. For this reason, work in a classroom may best be described as an *approach* to transpersonal consciousness. There is no guarantee that anyone will find himself in contact with transpersonal levels of awareness as a result of any of these exercises, but all of them, including intellectual discussions of the science of transpersonal psychology, can serve as approaches.

An exercise which lends itself well to expressive techniques through art media is one which is used in psychosynthesis for the integration of feelings and mind. Instructions are as follows: Close your eyes and visualize an image of your mind. When the image is clear, draw the image with colored crayons or chalk. When this portion of the exercise is complete, instructions are given in the same way for visualizing and drawing an image of feelings. The exercise may then be continued as a guided fantasy in which each participant interacts with his own symbolic images, asking them what they want, what he can do for them and what they can do for each other.

A similar exercise involving self-portraits is also a way of eliciting meaningful symbolic imagery. Instructions to draw an abstract or symbolic self-portrait are less threatening than instructions to draw a realistic self-portrait which lends itself more readily to amateur psychoanalytic interpretation. In working with symbolic imagery elicited in this type of exercise, no less than in working with dreams and fantasy, it is important to avoid interpretation in the classroom situation. Responses should be shared as personal feelings, not as clinical diagnoses. The focus remains on gaining insight into oneself rather than others. The underlying assumption is that in order to truly know others, one must first know oneself, and only by touching transpersonal depths within can one really understand and connect with those dimensions in another.

INTUITION

Intuitive perception, frequently associated with creative genius, is an important field of study in transpersonal psychology. Metaphysical systems in both eastern and western traditions regard intuitive mind as a level of consciousness which transcends sensation, emotion, and rational thinking, and is capable of direct apprehension of truth. Furthermore, intuition is often associated with dreaming, meditation, and other receptive modes of consciousness. Most of the time intuitive flashes are experienced as spontaneous and transient, and disregarded as hunches of questionable validity.

Despite the fact that the greatest advances in man's understanding of reality are made by intuitive leaps of the imagination, and only subsequently verified in rational terms, our educational system continues to operate on the assumption that training of the intellect is developing man's highest potential. According to Weil (1972) wise men throughout history have repeatedly told us there exists within us a source of direct information about reality, and all we need to do in order to get in touch with it is to suspend our ordinary mental activity. Relaxation and concentration are the methods whereby we can learn to disengage our awareness from ego consciousness and allow intuitive knowledge to emerge. It is a matter of opening the door to an immeasurable storehouse of knowledge available to each of us in the depths of the psyche which is usually unconscious.

As the language of the unconscious, imagery can also unlock the door to intuitive knowledge. Learning the language of imagery is an essential part of making intuitive perception comprehensible in intellectual terms. Moreover, it is a way of training and developing the intuitive function which is operative in both artistic creation and scientific discovery. While the classroom itself may be a detriment rather than an asset to intuitive learning, for the present we are concerned with the possibility of making better use of the existing system for the development of the highest human potentials, and training in receptivity to intuitive imagery is easily adapted to a traditional educational setting.

Practical training in the development of intuition may begin with the following exercise (Gerard: 1972):

> Choose a partner whom you do not know, and sit facing each other. Allow a few moments to relax and quiet your mind. In silence notice any sensations, feelings or thoughts that may come to your awareness as you focus your attention on your partner. Do not try to interpret them or make sense out of them. Simply notice them. Notice any imagery that comes to you, visual, auditory or kinesthetic. The flow of imagery may be activated by asking yourself such questions as: If this person were an animal or a plant, what kind would it be? If this person were a light, what intensity or color would it be? What type of sound would this person be? If this person were any part of nature, what would his qualities be?

Following a period of quiet, non-interfering observation of images associated with the partner, the two people can discuss their impressions of each other. Each must be willing to risk being wrong, thus learning to distinguish between projection and symbolic perception. As in working with dreams and fantasy, working with the imagery of intuition is facilitated by an attitude of non-judgmental acceptance of whatever emerges. Learning to interpret the language of imagery is important to the total process of developing the reliability and usefulness of intuition, but it also tends to inhibit the spontaneous flow of imagery through which we can learn to listen to the unconscious. Interpretation therefore remains a secondary process, which should not be unduly emphasized in the beginning.

In any didactic discussion of intuition, it is useful to distinguish between intuition based on sensory clues, and what may be called pure intuition, which does not depend on clues at all. Experiential recognition of this distinction is simply a matter of subjective differentiation. A person who is aware of a physical sensation such as tension associated with particular individuals or situations, may depend on this type of clue to determine his actions. Another person may have a clear sense of when he is drawn to something and when he feels aversion, and may choose to act on these feelings, or to ignore them. Training oneself to listen to sensory and emotional clues in everyday experience not only sensitizes one to intuitive perceptions which may otherwise remain below the threshold of consciousness, but is also a means of increasing self-awareness. Awareness does not imply that one must act on these perceptions. On the contrary, as awareness increases, choices can be made more deliberately. Deliberate choice implies freedom, but does not necessarily imply rationality. An acceptance of irrational elements in the psyche which may be experienced as powerful forces beyond our control, is a necessary concommitment to the development of psychic potentials which transcend reason. As Jung (1933) has pointed out, intuition is not necessarily in conflict with reason, but goes beyond it.

Pure intuition does not appear to depend on clues at all. At this level, intuition may be defined as the ability to see into the nature of things, as a way of knowing that transcends the boundaries of time and space, and apprehends reality directly on a transpersonal level. Assagioli (1965) has discussed the function of intuition as a psychological experience which needs no explanation or demonstration. It does, however, need affirmation and cultivation if it is to be more fully developed as the most far-reaching function of human consciousness.

SUMMARY AND CONCLUSIONS

Transpersonal psychology, with its holistic view of man, offers us the possibility of making all experience conscious and voluntary. By legitimizing the scientific study of man's inner states and his transcendent potentials, it offers a totally new perspective on the educational dictum "Know thyself." Imagery, as the language of the unconscious, offers easy access to the depths of intrapsychic experience in which transpersonal consciousness is grounded. Many techniques for the use of imagery as a vehicle of self-discovery are well-suited to classroom use, and may easily be introduced in the existing educational system. Knowledge of truth is the goal, and an extension of consciousness the means of attaining it. According to Campbell (1949), every failure to cope with a life situation must be laid in the end to a restriction of consciousness. Our survival as a species depends, not only on increased ecological awareness of our external interdependence with the environment, but also on increased awareness of the transpersonal nature of our innermost being.

REFERENCES

Assagioli, R. *Psychosynthesis*. New York: Hobbs, Dorman, 1965.

Bonny, H. "A New Way To Music: Therapeutic and Transpersonal Implications." Paper presented at the annual meeting of the Association for Humanistic Psychology, Squaw Valley, September, 1972.

Campbell, J. *The Hero With a Thousand Faces*. New York: Pantheon, 1949.

Deikman, A. "Deautomatization and the Mystic Experience," in Tart, C. (ed.) *Altered States of Consciousness*. New York: John Wiley, 1969.

Fromm, E. *The Forgotten Language: An Introduction to the Understanding of Dreams, Fairytales and Myths*. New York: Holt, Rinehart and Winston, 1951.

Faraday, A. *Dream Power*. New York: Coward, McCann and Geohegan, 1972.

Gerard, R. Workshop notes. "Professional Training in Psychosynthesis; Intuitive Awareness." October 6–8, 1972.

Green, E., Green A. and Walters, D. "Psychophysical Training for Creativity." Paper presented at the 1971 meeting of the American Psychological Association, Washington, D.C.: 1971.

Jung, C. *Psychological Types*. New York: Harcourt, 1933.

Jung, C. *The Undiscovered Self*. New York: New American Library, 1958.

Jung, C. *The Secret of the Golden Flower*. (Ref. ed.) New York: Harcourt, 1962.

Jung, C. *Man and His Symbols*. Garden City, New York: Doubleday, 1964.

Krippner, S. and Hughes, W. Dreams and Human Potential. *Journal of Humanistic Psychology*. 1970, 10 (1), 1–20.

Lilly, J. "Meditative Exercises." Big Sur recordings, 1972.

Naranjo, C. and Ornstein, R. *Psychology of Meditation*. New York: Viking Press, 1971.

Neumann, E. *The Origins and History of Consciousness*. New York: Pantheon, 1954.

Perls, F. *Gestalt Therapy Verbatim*. Lafayette, California: Real People Press, 1969.

Progoff, I. *Depth Psychology and Modern Man*. New York: Julian Press, 1959.

Rossi, L. *Dreams and the Growth of Personality*. Elmsford, New York: Pergamon Press, 1972.

Stewart, K. Dream Theory in Malaya, in Tart, C. (ed.) *Altered States of Consciousness*. New York: John Wiley, 1969.

Weil, A. *The Natural Mind*. Boston: Houghton Mifflin, as reprinted in *Psychology Today*, October, 1972.

TRANSCENDENTAL MEDITATION
AND ITS POTENTIAL USES FOR SCHOOLS*

Al E. Rubottom

> I wonder whether the yoga discipline may not be, after all, in all its phases
> simply a methodical way of waking up deeper levels of will power than are
> habitually used, and thereby increasing the individual's vital tone and energy. I
> have no doubt whatever that most people live, whether physically,
> intellectually or morally, in a very restricted circle of their potential being.
> They make use of a very small portion of their possible consciousness, and of
> their soul's resources in general, much like a man who, out of his whole
> bodily organism, should get into a habit of using and moving only his little
> finger. . . . May the yoga practices not be, after all, methods of getting at our
> deeper functional levels?
>
> —William James [1]

James's intuitions about yoga have been borne out nearly three-quarters of
a century later. Today's technologies in the sciences of psychophysiology,
biochemistry and electroencephalography have enabled researchers to
measure empirically in the laboratory the changes produced by meditational techniques such as yoga, Zen, and transcendental meditation. Transcendental meditation, or TM, is by far the most widespread of these
practices in America and throughout the world; over 250,000 people
worldwide have begun the practice of TM; most of these in America
within the past five years. Recent studies have verified that during the
practice of TM profound changes occur in metabolic activity, blood
chemistry and brain functioning which suggest that TM may have practical
value for those applications James described: "increasing the individual's
vital tone and energy . . . [and] getting at our deeper functional levels."

Nearly three years ago R. Keith Wallace published the findings of his
U.C.L.A. doctoral researches on TM's physiological effects in *Science*.[2] At
about the same time Dr. Herbert Benson, a cardiologist at Harvard Medical
School, began to investigate TM in his work on methods of lowering blood
pressure. Wallace and Benson now work together at Harvard, and they
reported their latest findings in the February, 1972, issue of *Scientific
American* :

> To sum up, our subjects during the practice of transcendental meditation mani-
> fested the physiological signs of what we describe as a "wakeful, hypometabolic"
> state: reductions in oxygen consumption, carbon dioxide elimination and

*From Al E. Rubottom, "Transcendental Meditation and Its Potential Uses for Schools," *Social
Education* (December, 1972), pp. 851–857, by permission of the author and publisher. Al E.
Rubottom is a teacher of Transcendental Meditation and a student of Chinese; he has written articles
for the *Yale Alumni Magazine* and Connecticut magazine.

the rate and volume of respiration; a slight increase in the acidity of arterial blood; a marked decrease in the blood-lactate level; a slowing of the heartbeat; a considerable increase in skin resistance, and an electroencephalogram pattern of intensification of slow alpha waves with occasional theta-wave activity. These physiological modifications, in people who were practicing the easily learned technique of transcendental meditation, were very similar to those that have been observed in highly trained experts in yoga and in Zen monks who have had 15 to 20 years of experience in meditation. (3a)

The reduction in oxygen consumption, a prime measure of metabolic rate, was a 16% drop in 20 to 30 minutes of TM, as compared with about an 8% decrease occurring slowly after six hours of sleep; "meditation brings twice the reduction in a fraction of the time. No significant change occurs under hypnosis."[3b] The arterial concentration of lactate, a chemical correlated with anxiety, dropped "four times faster than the rate of decrease in people normally resting in a supine position or in the subjects themselves during their premeditation period."[3c] Skin resistance, a measure of relaxation, "increased markedly, in some cases more than fourfold."[3d] The recordings of brain-waves "disclosed a marked intensification of alpha waves in all the subjects."[3e] Changes in relaxed states of sleep and hypnosis bear little resemblance. Moreover, the practice of TM produces this integrated pattern of changes in a way that operant conditioning, now popularized as "biofeedback" training to control alpha-waves, heart rate, blood pressure, and other functions, simply cannot. While such "conditioning is limited to producing specific responses and depends on a stimulus and feedback of a reinforcer, meditation is independent of such assistance and produces not a single specific response but a complex of responses that marks a highly relaxed state."[3f] Like an opposite counterpart to the well-known "fight or flight" defense alarm reaction which is triggered in animals and human reflexively, TM is a reliable method of activating an inborn capability of gaining deepest relaxation at will.

During the past six years, TM, as taught by Maharishi Mahesh Yogi, has been offered on nearly every college campus in the country through the Students' International Meditation Society (SIMS), a federally tax-exempt, nonprofit educational organization. Of the approximately 150,000 Americans who have begun the practice to date, most are students and young adults. However, with the publication of scientific studies confirming TM's validity, many adults have learned the practice. TM is popular among many businessmen and professionals. The practice has been used by organizations such as Kaiser Aluminum Co., by the Strategic Air Command, and by scientists at the Houston Space Center, including an astronaut. *The Wall Street Journal* reported on TM's adherents among brokerage firm partners, Army generals, and even a State Department China expert who accompanied Kissinger to Peking.[4] To offer instruction in TM more publicly than the primarily campus-based SIMS, the International Meditation Society (IMS) was formed as an affiliate of SIMS.

THE SCIENCE OF CREATIVE INTELLIGENCE

To account for the experience of increased energy, creativity and happiness that meditators report, a coherent theoretical structure became necessary. In response to student demand at Stanford University, an accredited course in "The Science of Creative Intelligence," treating the principles underlying the practice of TM, was offered in 1970. Since then numerous other colleges and universities have offered similar courses in the science of creative intelligence (SCI), usually as an interdisciplinary survey and synthesis of philosophical and psychophysiological speculations and findings about human potential.[5] During the past year Maharishi has formulated a comprehensive syllabus for the teaching of SCI in junior and senior high schools. Last August 130 high school teachers attended a one-month SCI Teacher Training course at Humboldt State University in Arcata, California, for graduate credit. About half received scholarship stipends from a $21,000 Department of Health, Education, and Welfare grant. Many of these teachers have taught SCI at their schools this fall as an elective or extracurricular offering, in conjunction with a course of instruction in the practice of TM provided by SIMS.

The science of Creative Intelligence may be described as a practical inquiry into the sources and uses of intelligence and creativity. Intelligence is defined as the ability to perceive order and to make appropriate choices. Creativity is defined as the agency which accomplishes appropriate change. The unified and multiple flow of energy (creativity) and directedness (intelligence) is called creative intelligence. A science is taken to be a systematic investigation by means of a repeatable experiment to gain useful and testable knowledge. The Science of Creative Intelligence is the theoretical and applied study of the nature, origin and development of creative intelligence. This science arose from the discovery that there exists in every human being a constant source of energy, intelligence, and happiness. This source can be easily drawn upon by anyone for spontaneous use in everyday life, bringing personal integration and a harmoniously productive relationship with others and the world. Like any other science, SCI has its theoretical and applied aspects. The conceptual delineation of the principles of SCI can be derived from an examination of laws in other sciences:

> The Science of Creative Intelligence has its beginning in the observation of the phenomenal world. Closely examining a phenomenon reveals laws which are then found to have application and use in other fields according to their range and influence. Just like any other science, the Science of Creative Intelligence is advanced by close observation and study, and what it observes and studies is how one creates.
>
> Since the physical properties of phenomena differ, the study of the physical nature of things alone can never present a common basis for all knowledge. A common basis can only be found in something which is the same in all phenomena and in every study. Order in nature and man's power of ordering show that intelligence is at the core of every physical existence and every human mind. The study of the nature of intelligence, therefore, can be the common

ground of all knowledge. Thus it is creative intelligence which is the dynamic of interdisciplinary study and through which its goal can be achieved. Established on this foundation of all knowledge, everyone will feel at home in every field of investigation and achieve maximum efficiency in thought and action.[6]

Due to the divergent nature of life different disciplines have arisen, with the purpose of presenting the knowledge of each separate field. With specialization, education impels an individual to recognize his continually increasing lack of familiarity with and knowledge of other fields; the more we come to know, it is said, the more we realize how much we don't know. Historically, great thinkers in every age have recognized that no single branch of learning can fulfill man's physical, intellectual and spiritual needs. Because of the tendency of our "knowledge explosion" to isolate each branch of learning from every other, educators have sought to integrate all branches of learning. The aim of interdisciplinary study is to forge the links that connect each discipline. The purpose of SCI in education is to provide this common connection between disciplines in order to lay a permanent foundation for knowledge in all fields and to bring fulfillment to the aspirations of education.

The practical application of SCI is found in the practice of TM, the systematic procedure for directly experiencing the nature, origin and development of creative intelligence. TM is an effortless technique which allows the mind to experience finer, more fundamental levels of a thought until it arrives at the finest state of a thought and transcends it, reaching the source of thought, awareness without thought, the field of pure intelligence as pure consciousness. The process is one of direct perception, not of intellectual analysis.* During the practice an individual sits quietly and, using a technique learned through personal instruction, allows the activity of his mind to be reduced until he gains a state of extreme restful alertness, a state in which his mind is most quiet yet at the same time at its maximum potential of alertness. Although psychologists have long recognized that man does not utilize his innate potentialities fully, until very recently, with the advent of TM, scientists had found no repeatable procedure for reliably contacting and exploring the latent resources of the mind. Efforts to unfold mental potential in psychiatry and psychotherapy have been largely unsuccessful, due to the lack of a reproducible method. With the practice of TM, however, a universally applicable technique is available for making man's oft-acknowledged but seldom uncovered resources accessible.

Just as physics has shown that matter is structured in levels ranging from galaxies to sub-atomic particles, so SCI demonstrates that thought ranges in perceptibility from the more obvious to the less obvious. Moreover, physics has proven that direct contact with more fundamental levels of matter yields greater energy. Similarly, the experiential contact with more fundamental levels of thought yields greater energies within the thinking process and its applications. Furthermore, quantum field theory reveals how the structure present at sub-atomic levels of existence offers the most comprehensive explanation for all physical phenomena. Likewise, conscious contact with the sub-structure of thinking, the field of pure intelligence, engenders increasingly coherent insight into the full range of thought and its potential for human life. The significance of SCI is that it consists of a systematic program combining intellectual inquiry and direct experience which simultaneously benefits every aspect of the personality. Instead of merely developing specific values of intelligence in localized areas of life, the subjective experience of restful alertness (the wakeful hypometabolic state), when supplemented by a program of intellectual inquiry into the principles involved, develops the physiology, the emotions and the intellect in a holistic manner.

THE NEED FOR SCI IN EDUCATION TODAY

> There have been countless attempts to improve the quality of education in America, which have resulted in many important changes, innovations and improvements. Yet the billions of dollars spent by private foundations and public agencies in the last twenty-five years appear to leave a great many teachers and students unfulfilled. Teachers as well as students find themselves overwhelmed with a mass of information, knowledge, and thoughts for which they can find no connections. SCI suggests that the unifying process exists within each individual, and that each person can learn how to be in touch with that process within himself. Thus SCI seems able to provide a missing ingredient that can give focus and meaning to so much that is worthwhile in education.[7]

These remarks of Dr. Sidney Reisberg, Associate Dean and Director of Prototype Teaching Programs at State University of New York in Albany, reflect the widespread recognition among educators that fundamental change is a crucial need in our schools. The notion of a unifying process through which both teaching and learning can be integrated is a salient feature of nearly all educational theories. However, the various styles and methodologies used in both established institutions and the educational avant-garde still consist essentially in modifying teaching in order to enhance learning. Clearly what is needed is not merely newer or different teaching, but a way to support the development of individual learning potential to its maximum. In writing about one popular trend in teaching styles, the affective education movement, Douglas H. Heath, professor of psychology at Haverford College, researcher on student development, and author of *Explorations of Maturity, Growing Up in College*, and *Humanizing Schools*, described the basis for the kind of educability we should foster in our students:

> My understanding of man tells me the deepest source of the creative-aesthetic impulse is in our less conscious and more primitive inner world, and that we make contact with it through a receptive meditative attitude. Not until we learn how to reach and touch, and then channel and witness our inner voices, will we be truly educable. If a youth learns how to develop such accessibility to his inner powers and integrates such forces and insights with more social modes of communication, then I have no fear for him. He will have developed a capacity

for resiliency and autonomy that will enable him to cure his estrangements and create his own adaptations to his unknown society of the future. He will come into control of his growth. ... Within a few years, schools and colleges will be offering courses on meditation. Fanciful? Not at all. One of the exciting frontiers of psychological research is the demonstration that man can secure much greater access to and control over his consciouness through meditation than most of us have thought possible.[8]

Heath's prescription for the integration of creative intelligence in each individual student's consciousness through meditation is precisely what is accomplished through the implementation of the applied and theoretical aspects of SCI. Upon a strong foundation of "educability" true learning becomes a reality for both student and teacher. Dr. Dean Brown, Director of Educational Technology Project, Stanford Research Institute, summarized his experiences in developing computer-teaching programs for UNESCO in Africa, Spain and Yugoslavia as follows:

> We have worked with so many different types of children in our laboratory that to find really useful applications we've had to find a common denominator definition of teaching that was really worth making an effort to put into the computers and videos. ... After cultivating a curriculum of basic educational material, it's becoming obvious that we're converting on the Science of Creative Intelligence. I believe now that the Science of Creative Intelligence is this common denominator of teaching, which applies in all geographic areas, all cultural areas; in all knowledge of past, present and the future; and throughout all the changes that a man experiences in a healthy life.[9]

Psychological and educational theory have become intensely concerned with "all the changes that a man experiences in a healthy life" in the past few years. As Heath writes, "Educators have not really confronted seriously the implications that an increasingly affluent, leisure-oriented, interdependent, impersonal society have for the way we should educate. ... Increasingly, our almost exclusive mode of didactic teaching, that is, reliance on verbal abstract symbolic manipulation, is out of phase with the emerging needs of youth. ... The basic principle of growth we have violated is that a person grows as an organism, not just as a head."[10] The most pertinent theory on human development to be considered here is the notion of unfoldment of full potential as described by Maharishi. His ideas are very strongly supported by the thought of Abraham Maslow, author of *Toward a Psychology of Being*, in his "hieararchy of needs." Maslow postulates that as one fulfills the basic sustenance needs—safety, belonging, love—the higher needs—self-esteem and self-actualization—gain increasing importance to the individual. Self-actualization is roughly synonymous with the other growth theories in psychology, such as those of Fromm, Jung, Horney, and Rogers. Maharishi categorically states that through the practice of TM the human nervous system is normalized so completely that the style of functioning of the nervous system, the machinery of experience, is refined and integrated to maintain continuous conscious contact with the field of pure intelligence—to realize or "actualize" one's innermost self.

Studies on personality development using the Personality Orientation Inventory and tests measuring determinants of happiness indicate that subjects practicing TM do become more self-actualized, using the characteristics of self-actualized persons as summarized by Maslow. Those are increased acceptance of self, of others and of nature; increased ability to enjoy social interaction and to enjoy solitude; greater freshness of appreciation and emotional richness; increased autonomy and firm identity; improved interpersonal relationships; greater creativity; superior perception of reality; increased integration, wholeness and unity of person; increased spontaneity, expressiveness and liveliness.[11] Although such psychological effects of TM are more difficult to verify with empirical precision than the physiological changes, they are far more interesting in terms of their importance to the quality of one's life. There is, however, an intimate and direct interrelation between the physiological findings and the psychological values that result from the regular practice of TM. Numerous studies have already succeeded in quantifying specific parameters of known relevance which suggest that the entire constellation of psychological and physiological mechanisms involved in perception and activity are involved in and are affected by the practice of TM in an integrated fashion. For instance, improved reaction time, though purely a measure of heightened physical efficiency in responding to a cue, shows that the coordination of mind and body in perception and performance of an action is refreshed markedly.[12] Likewise, improvement of auditory ability in a test of frequency and amplitude discrimination reflects increased clarity and refinement of perception[13] which necessarily has a profound influence on how one's mind is capable of reacting to the environment. In a study on TM's effects on autonomic stability, as measured in a test on meditators' and non-meditators' habituation in response to a repeated stressful stimulus, Dr. D. W. Orme-Johnson reported that meditators recover from stress more quickly than do non-meditators, meaning that meditators have more resistance to environmental stress, psychosomatic disease and behavioral instability:

> The practice of TM, then, appears to increase the proportion of rapid habituators, indicating that meditation results in rapid recovery of homeostatic balance under auditory stress and suggesting that the physiological and behavioral attributes correlated with rapid habituation, cortical maturity and dominance and emotional stability may also be advantages derived from the practice of Transcendental Meditation.[14]

In a complex perceptual motor test, meditators performed three times faster than non-meditators, suggesting greater perceptual awareness and flexibility and enhanced neuromuscular integration.[15]Meditators also perform better on recall tests, learn more quickly and show significantly better results on difficult material than do non-meditators, meaning that TM improves memory recall and learning ability.[16]

TM is also being investigated for its clinical usefulness. At Stanford Research Institute an 18-month study has confirmed that subjects who were not predisposed to learn TM previously were easily taught the technique and successfully practice it. In a survey of 570 subjects substantial reductions in the use of prescribed and non-prescribed drugs were reported.[17] In addition, significant psychological benefits were measured, but the findings were not available as of this writing. At the Institute of Living, a private psychiatric hospital in Hartford, Connecticut, a three-year study of TM's potential therapeutic applications has been in progress for several months. Dr. Bernard Glueck, Jr., Director of Research, is interested in the value of TM as "perhaps the most effective technique of deep relaxation presently available."[18] TM will be compared by means of computer-analyzed data with alpha conditioning and other therapies. Studies at over thirty other colleges, universities, medical schools, and research centers in America and abroad either are in progress or have reported data on TM's effects.

As for those needs we may find important in the future, Maynard Shelly, professor of psychology and business at University of Kansas, has gathered data that indicate that TM taps inner resources that are crucial in meeting the demands man will encounter in post-industrial society. "Meditators have increased personal resources," writes Shelly. "As we move from the industrialized society (one in which mass production became possible) to the postindustrialized society (one in which computers take over much of production and decision-making), we shall encounter many problems, and many people will find it more difficult to live a happy life. Evidence indicates that TM may be one method which will help people to adjust to this emerging postindustrial society. . . . We've trained the brain for generations to solve problems; we should train the brain now to appreciate living. I think TM will be the final step to eliminate alienation."[19] Shelly has devised tests to measure what he terms "personal resources"—less dependence on external surroundings for happiness—and meditators have more than non-meditators.

During the past several months, the Eastchester Public Schools, Eastchester, New York, have facilitated bringing to its junior and senior high school students The Science of Creative Intelligence, more popularly known as the technique of Transcendental Meditation. Our concern for bringing this unique and distinctive type of educational experience to our youngsters was motivated as the result of our becoming acquainted with the growing accumulation of evidence which appears to support the following:
1. Students improve their grades.
2. Students get along better with teachers.
3. Students get along better with parents.
4. Students get along better with other students.
5. Evidence of lessening use of drugs.

Our experience with this program has been as successful with our adult population and faculty members as it has been with our students.

As a statement of endorsement concerning the acceptance of this technique of Transendental Meditation, this autumn of 1971, The Science of Creative Intelligence will become a regular course as part of our overall instructional program.

Francis G. Driscoll, Superintendent of Schools

Eastchester, New York

Transcendental meditation is the only thing I'm aware of aside from the "don't-do-it" lectures that offers promise in the mounting drug abuse problem . . . . Transcendental meditation has done a lot for me personally. My friends and colleagues and my wife say it has improved by disposition, and my doctor says it's knocked my blood pressure down ten points.

Major General Franklin B. Davis, Commandant

U.S. Army War College

The best-documented result of TM is the voluntary elimination and reduction of drug use. In a survey of 1,862 subjects, Benson and Wallace found that 79% had smoked marijuana before starting TM; after six months of practice, only 37% continued to smoke, and after 21 months only 12% remained smokers, and of these 83% smoked less than three times a month. Use of all other drugs, including LSD, other hallucinogens, narcotics, amphetamines, barbiturates, liquor and nicotine decreased even more markedly. In addition, 96% of those involved in selling drugs stopped selling after beginning TM, and over 95% of all subjects discouraged others from abusing drugs after starting TM. Dr. Benson is now engaged in a study of 10,000 randomly selected high school juniors, representing a fairly cohesive group for a year. Voluntary confidential questionnaires assessed drug use or non-use, as well as some psychological traits. Half of the subjects were offered TM through introductory lectures. After three, six and nine months another survey of the original sample will net data about patterns of drug use or non-use in relation to the practice of TM. The parents and faculty were informed of the study in meetings with the researchers and were offered the opportunity to learn TM. Two Massachusetts school districts are currently offering courses in TM to their students; three more have approved the program as of this writing. Paul J. Andrews, Project Director for Drug Education of the Massachusetts Department of Education, has written, "We are very enthusiastic about it, and feel that it is worthy of further investigation as a non-chemical alternative to drug abuse."[20]

As we all know, drug users are very knowledgeable about the undesirable effects of drug abuse. In general, most drug users do not find it difficult to stop using drugs. Most drugs commonly used are not addictive. The problem lies in getting them to want to stop. Curiosity, rebellion, "kicks," and the more philosophical, inner-directed quests for self-exploration and "expansion of consciousness" are among the more obvious motives for drug use. Everyone concerned with this very significant social problem agrees that what is needed is not more education about drugs, but a non-chemical alternative to drug use. Official recognition of the benefits and effectiveness of the TM and SCI programs was expressed in the form of a House Resolution adopted by the Illinois State General Assembly last May, in which implementation of these programs in state educational and mental health institutions and drug abuse sections is recommended.

The Science of Creative Intelligence, through its applied practice of Transcendental Meditation, has the potential of fulfilling the aspirations of each individual in our society. The global acceptance and success of TM's values for people everywhere attest to the universal practicality of the technique for everyday use. Scientific studies on TM continue to verify its effectiveness in all applications. The need for SCI in education has been recognized; steps are now being taken to make SCI as widely available as possible. The response to the SCI courses that have been offered in schools and colleges has been unanimously enthusiastic. At the college level, SCI students find a unifying basis for the diverse studies to which they are exposed, and are better able to integrate their experience and understanding. The lab work of this program is invariably TM, which is taught through on-campus SIMS chapters at over 1,000 colleges and universities.

In the junior and senior high school syllabus, the SCI course begins with instruction in the practice of TM, provided by SIMS. On the basis of experiential contact—the applied aspect of SCI—the students inductively analyze their experience with TM and in their lives to generate and substantiate fundamental premises that can be shown to have universal applicability. The connections drawn between all disciplines clarify the theoretical principles of SCI on a level which gives the notion of interdisciplinary studies a new relevance—familiarity based on direct experience with the source and goal of all knowledge. Programs will soon become available for elementary school students. The possibility of making education most effective in promoting individual evolution is now providing a uniquely unifying experience for many thousands of our youth.

NOTES

[1] William James, in *William James in Psychical Research*, Murphy G. and Ballou, R. V. (eds.), New York, Viking Press, 1963.

[2] "The Physiological Effects of Transcendental Meditation," Robert Keith Wallace, *Science*, March 27, 1970.

[3a] "The Physiology of Meditation," R. Keith Wallace and Herbert Benson, *Scientific American*, February, 1972 (Vol. 226, No. 2).

[3b] *Ibid.*

[3c] *Ibid.*

[3d] *Ibid.*

[3e] *Ibid.*

[3f] *Ibid.*

[4] "Transcendent Trend," Ellen Graham, *The Wall Street Journal*, August 31, 1972.

[5]SCI courses have been offered at Yale University, New York University, the Universities of California, Colorado, Connecticut, and Wisconsin, and York University in Toronto, and many others. Approximately 75 colleges will offer SCI courses this academic year, as of this writing.

[6]Maharishi Mahesh Yogi, excerpt from his inaugural address, First International Symposium on the Science of Creative Intelligence, University of Massachusetts, July 18, 1971. Proceedings in press.

*The technique of TM is easily learned by anyone, regardless of intellectual ability or cultural background. No concentration, contemplation, or mental or physical control is involved. No belief or faith is required for the practice to work. There are no moral tenets involved; TM is not a religion or a philosophy and there is no conflict with one's existing affiliations. No changes need be made in diet, posture or personal preference. Instruction requires only four two-hour sessions, one each day for four days. After personal instruction in a private appointment, three meetings for verification of correct practice and further instruction are conducted, with a follow-up program available as needed.

[7]Dr. Sidney Reisberg, personal communication to the author.

[8]"Affective Education," Douglas H. Heath, *School Review*, May, 1972 (Vol. 80, No. 3), University of Chicago.

[9]Dr. Dean Brown, *International Symposium on the Science of Creative Intelligence*, December, 1971, MIU Press.

[10]Heath, *op. cit.*

[11]Seeman, Nidich and Banta, *Journal of Counseling Psychology*, May-June 1972.

[12]Shaw and Kolb, University of Texas, Austin, 1971, cited in *Scientific Research on Transcendental Meditation*, MIU Press.

[13]Graham, University of Sussex, 1971.

[14]Orme-Johnson, *Psychosomatic Medicine.*

[15]Blasdell, U.C.L.A., 1971.

[16]Abrams, U.C. Berkeley, 1972.

[17]Otis, Stanford Research Institute, 1972.

[18]Dr. Bernard Glueck, Jr., personal communication with the author.

[19]Maynard Shelly, *Meaningful Leisure*, in press.

[20]TM—What Is It?, Mitchell J. Posner, *The Massachusetts Teacher,* May/June 1972.

TM AS A SECONDARY SCHOOL SUBJECT *

Francis Driscoll

Meditation in School: Practical Approach, Positive Response. This article is important in two ways. First, Driscoll, as a school superintendent, has a positive evaluation of TM for social as well as intellectual reasons. Second, he outlines how he and the TM teachers prepared the ground for this innovation in his schools by involving and educating the teachers, parents, and community. In research since this article was written, the benefits of TM have generally been confirmed; although one report from Stanford Research Institute indicates that TM may be useful as a growth experience for those who are basically healthy, but not as a therapy, particularly not for people with previous, serious psychosomatic symptoms. Other information, including a bibliography of research on TM, is available from SIMS, 1015 Gayley Avenue, Los Angeles, California 90024.

The Eastchester Public Schools became interested in transcendental meditation when a trained meditator visited my office in the autumn of 1970. The meditator had requested an opportunity to present the TM concept to me and to the high school principal and his assistant. During the presentation it became apparent that the practice of meditation possessed considerable promise for students of high school age. We were particularly impressed by the research completed at that time, limited though it was, indicating that students involved in meditation were completely free of drug usage or drug experimentation. This information was very dramatic and elevated our interest in TM as another possibility for diminishing the drug abuse menace for our students. In addition, the teacher of transcendental meditation reported research revealing that students participating in TM began to achieve better scholastic grades and improved relations with their teachers, parents, and peers.

There was no doubt in the minds of the school administrators present that TM could be useful. Our problem was one of comprehending exactly and precisely the meaning, nature, and technique of transcendental meditation. Thus the representative arranged to visit with us again within a week or two, accompanied by a national director from the Students' International Meditation Society.

On the occasion of the second visit we were better prepared, for we had examined descriptive literature left with us. The second meeting gave us an in-depth understanding of the "science of creative intelligence" or transcendental meditation. We understood that it was not a religion or even a

*From Francis Driscoll, "TM as a Secondary School Subject," *Phi Delta Kappan* 54, no. 4 (December, 1972): 236–237, by permission of the author. Francis Driscoll is Superintendent of Public Schools, Eastchester, New York.

philosophy but rather a thought process to teach people how to meditate and achieve what is now recognized as a "fourth state of consciousness."

At this juncture we agreed not only that transcendental meditation possessed considerable potential for our secondary school students but was administratively feasible; it involved no religious or philosophic conflict. However, we perceived that preparing and educating the community might present some difficulties. We began a public information program. News releases recapitulated the administrative meetings held with the meditators from the New York Students' International Meditation Society. Also, I announced at public meetings of the board of education that these meetings had been conducted, and presented a summary of each.

Next, trained meditators from the New York City SIMS office were requested to speak at local Rotary, Lions, and Kiwanis meetings to explain transcendental meditation. In addition, meetings with local PTA groups were arranged. A private meeting between the board of education and a national SIMS representative was set up so that board members could get authoritative answers to their many questions. Most significantly, parents of secondary school students were urged to attend an introductory lecture on transcendental meditation. Each of the aforementioned meetings was highly publicized throughout the community. It appeared to our administrative team that it was absolutely vital for the community, and for parents of secondary school children in particular, to be fully aware of TM and to develop an understanding of it before we suggested a program of instruction for our secondary school students. The program of community and parent information covered a period of approximately six months.

In January of 1971 an introductory lecture on TM was presented to the student body of the Eastchester Senior High School. Following the assembly, which was attended by the entire student body, four trained meditators were available to individual students throughout the day. Thus interested students obtained answers to their questions on an intimate, one-to-one basis. An introductory lecture on TM was also delivered to our faculty and their spouses. The response was very impressively favorable. In a relatively short period approximately 12% of the faculty were participating in transcendental meditation.

Following the introductory lecture, students who wished to pursue TM or SCI further were able to sign up for the explanatory lectures leading to meditation. These lectures were conducted outside of the school day but on school premises. Classrooms were made available to New York City SIMS personnel for this purpose.

In February of 1971, transcendental meditation was introduced into our local adult education program. It was an immediate success.

The policy of offering TM to our students and adult citizens has continued and, so far as I can see now, will not be dropped. Our schools are open during all school vacation periods for programs of interest to the community. Consequently, it is standard practice for the Students' International Meditation Society to conduct lectures in our facilities throughout the year.

Reflecting upon our modest success, we feel that it is attributable to the great potential for student welfare that the practice of transcendental meditation offers. Another vital factor in the success of our program was the well thought-out, comprehensive community and parent information program carried out in the autumn and early winter of 1971 before we introduced TM to the student population.

Finally, we believe that transcendental meditation has been of direct and positive help to students in our secondary school who have begun to meditate. Students, parents, and teachers report similar findings. Scholastic grades improve, relationships with family, teachers, and peers are better, and, very significantly, drug abuse disappears or does not begin.

EXPERIENCING EDUCATION WITH *est* *

Benjamin S. Westheimer

Preparing the Transpersonal Teacher. Westheimer's description of *est* and how some teachers have adapted the *est* techniques to their classrooms and themselves illustrates several characteristics of transpersonal education. First, the field is wide open for future educational researchers. In this article most of the research is at the anecdotal and descriptive stages, with a beginning of more careful empirical verification. Transpersonal educational psychology and *est* are both intriguing because of their possibilities; yet one should be careful about claims until further, more exact investigation is completed. Second, there is a need for new theories and new views of human psychology to account for the results. Third, open-mindedness to experimenting with new teaching techniques is exemplified; although some of these "processes" come from outside the usual resources for educational practices, these teachers tried new activities and altered them for their own classes. Fourth, the ideas of relaxation and awareness of one's inner experience pick up the transpersonal assumption that there is a realm of "weak signals" which we can perceive by reducing outside stimulation and by focusing on what is going on inside us. The fine tuning of oneself is also shown in the Greens' article on biofeedback, Richard's "Attention Training," and Clark's "Fantasy and Imagination."

The purpose of this paper is to examine the means and results of applying Erhard Seminars Training (referred to here as *est*) to the classroom. *Est* is one of the many forms of transpersonal/humanistic education that has flourished during the last two decades. *Est* was developed by Werner Erhard in 1971 "for the purpose of serving people by bringing them to a greater realization of themselves, their automaticities, and their own aliveness." The training consists of two weekends of lecture, training experiences (called processes), and communication. *Est* costs two hundred dollars and is offered in San Francisco, New York, Hawaii, Aspen, and Los Angeles. At the time the pilot study was begun, 8,000 people had taken the *est* training; of these 8,000, over 400 were teachers.

Forty-five teachers were interviewed intensively about their applications and uses of *est*, and the transcripts of the interviews were compared. All of the quotations in this paper are from those interviews. While there is much quantitative work yet to be done with the *est* teachers, my objective was to examine what was being done and what was happening as observed by the teachers. The *est* teachers ranged in age from 24 to 62 years old, were predominately female and white, and taught pre-school through university level in both public and private schools.

Est takes many of its forms from Zen, Gestalt, sensory awareness,

*"Experiencing Education With *est*" was written especially for this book. An *est* graduate, Benjamin Westheimer is Director of Youth Services, Gladman Memorial Hospital, Oakland, California, and a Vice President of the Mental Health Association of Alameda County, California.

Scientology, Maslow, Subud, and other less classical forms of self-improvement, self-actualization, transcendence, and communication. *Est* accomplishes its objective in an almost alarmingly successful manner. Virtually every one of the teachers whom I interviewed stated that her (or his) ability to communicate and rate of personal success have grown rapidly. It appears that this is also indicated for each of the other 13,000 *est* graduates. Recent outside testing of persons taking *est* by the Behaviordyne Corporation tends to support these observations.(1) Behaviordyne noted that the ability of *est* graduates to cope with everyday concerns was significantly strengthened. Additionally, *est* graduates had an improved self-image, fewer guilts and fears, a greater sense of self, and a lessening of psychophysiologic reactions.

The teachers began to show interest in applying *est* to their classroom situations even before their trainings ended. It seemed that the revolution that is coming to education is one in which teachers realize that the content they have to teach is relatively easy to learn, and given the means to teach effectively, teachers will have a great deal of excess time in which to humanize the classroom and raise the consciousness of students. Teachers intuitively know what experiments like Summerhill have pointed out: a student can learn several years of subject matter in less than one year if that is what the student wants to do. Repeatedly during the interviews, teachers expressed the desire to let the students grow and develop, and to discover their own values and means of self-actualization—something which the school systems avoid and which some school administrators specifically forbid, "as the school system is traditionally concerned with control and regimentation of the student so that he will learn skills, traits, and values deemed necessary for society."

During the period that the initial interviews took place, California's Stull Act went into effect. This legislation effectively stifled experimentation in many classrooms after September of 1972 by creating district-wide criteria for teacher evaluation. In spite of a more conservative tenor seen in most school districts, the *est* teachers did apply their *est* experience to their classrooms. The majority of the teachers used techniques that had to do with relaxation, communication, confrontation, fantasy journey, and mental imagery. (2)

School administrators often saw this radical departure from normal curricula as suspect. Yet the teachers overwhelmingly reported positive results that seemed to both them and their principals totally out of proportion with what was done in the classroom.

> My principal was highly suspect of my using confrontation techniques with my students, who are all behavioral problem kinds. But every time he came to visit the class there was order, and learning was taking place ... this was finally demonstrated when my students placed above average for the school-wide tests at the end of the year.

The techniques that this teacher used were ones in which each student had an opportunity to experience what he or she was putting in the way of communicating with the rest of the class. These 12-to-15-year-old students had five minutes of confrontation each week. One by one they would stand in front of the class while everyone was silent and attentive. They were instructed to, "Simply stand in a relaxed manner and be aware of everything you do to make it easier for you to be up there." The students also had five minutes of a self-awareness exercise each week. This sharing exercise involved both students, first, in an active role, and then a passive, or listening, role. The listening partner was instructed to listen actively without interrupting the other student unless there was a lapse in the communication, in which case he would only ask enough questions to get the other person talking again.

Judith, a 34-year-old high school English teacher pointed out, "Having a quiet class doesn't mean a thing to anyone, except my principal. If he sees your class is quiet, he'll let you do almost anything . . . even have the class lie flat on its back for an hour English class every week." Judging from the proportion of teachers involved in the language-oriented subjects, it seems that many of the techniques are best suited to creative writing, drama, English, poetry, and literature classes. However, the following teacher speaks for the substantial number of non-language teachers who were equally enthusiastic with the results they had achieved by using *est* processes.

> I would start each Monday with a guided fantasy journey. It sounds silly, I mean to take them on an imaginary walk through a foreign country, or to a beach, or into a color when I teach math to junior high age students. But they responded. They settled down, seemed more intent . . . and damnit, they just did better math. The class average shot up 30% in about six weeks.

This same teacher was a homeroom teacher and would do a fantasy journey with those students who wanted to participate each week.

> . . . two things happened. First, I had practically every kid in school trying to get into my homeroom after the word got out, and that had never happened to me before. Anyway, I don't think they view me as being the nicest teacher in the school. Secondly, the kids began to tell me that on the days when we would do a fantasy journey their whole day would go better. I mean, they'd come back and thank me later in the day for some little trick I'd taught them . . . like Mary really began to use some of the relaxation techniques we did before the fantasy journey before she took her tests, and her grades went way up. She said, "It [taking tests] is like playing a game now, and before it was for real, like with everyone looking." What do I care what she thinks about taking tests, when she can do so well when she wants to, and she can do it all by herself without our interfering or helping her.

Many of the concepts that seem to predominate in the humanistic and transpersonal growth movements occur as specific agreements and statements during the training. These can be immediately adapted by the teachers. These concepts include; a) accepting responsibility not only for yourself and your immediate actions, but also for what happens to you and to others; b) learning to identify alternatives and to choose on the basis of ethical objectivity; c) learning to be objective about oneself and the events in one's own universe; d) and being in the here-and-now. Interestingly, the application of this last concept may have accounted for the lessening of daydreaming, window-watching, and other nonproductive activity that many teachers noted.

A commonly used technique already adapted to many workshops and seminars is now being adapted to the classroom. Simply stated, it is a body awareness process similar to breath relaxation and other types of 'letting go' or 'clearing' exercises done by many disciplines. *Est* uses the body awareness process, and it seems to be a memorable one, for almost all of the teachers I talked with had immediately adapted it to the classroom. Judging from a few remarkable instances, this simple technique is extremely powerful and has many uses for the learning process. It consists of having the person(s) assume a comfortable and relaxing position, lying down or sitting in a chair. The students were then directed to allow their awareness (some teachers use alternative words such as: breath, light, energy, etc.) to move slowly and systematically through their bodies. Most of the teachers felt that a complete description and "run-through" of the technique should be given before doing it so that there would be no surprises, and they all gave their students the chance not to participate in the exercise. Time spent doing the exercise varied from 15 to 90 minutes.

There does not seem to be very much difference in the teachers' nor the students' attitudes correlated to the time spent with the relaxation exercises.

Many of the teachers had had no experience with this type of exercise in a classroom. The only time that they had experienced the procedure was during the *est* training. Some of the reports I received were from non-*est* teachers whose only contact with the procedure was during one of my presentations; yet they adapted it to their classroom situations with remarkable success. Since experimentation is still encouraged with mentally retarded and educationally handicapped classes, and since marked change and development can be so easily seen with these types of classes, many of the teachers who attempted to use this technique on the basis of a one-time presentation were involved with the MR and EH [mentally retarded and educationally handicapped] classes. One teacher of MR students led them in an imaginary journey through their bodies. After eight sessions over a two-week period, their drawings of themselves showed body details such as ankles, knees, and chins, and clothing details such as pants, belt-buckles, and necklines. Previously they had drawn only childlike blobs with arms sticking out to the sides. Also, their pictures occupied most of the papers instead of being crowded down in a corner or off to one side.

While these teachers are not teaching *est*, they are using several of its forms and concepts. One concept that virtually every teacher related was seeing *est* in terms of learning to communicate in the most effective manner. Almost universally, the teachers felt that their ability to communicate had been opened up through the training, and that the results they were getting in the classroom were due to this increased level of communication. Much of this appears to come from centering techniques similar to ones used in meditation, Zen, and sensory awareness.

Sharon, a highly self-analytical pre-school teacher, remarked that many of the day's incidents take the form of problems, and that she had felt "barely able to cope with them all before the training," but that she had made some major changes in how she managed after taking *est*:

> My ground of being is different. I feel centered, and I know that I am able to handle whatever needs to be done, and I have no hesitancy to do so—like when it is necessary to take a child to the office and explain his alternatives to him. For example, he wants to play with a toy that another child is using. He will say, "I want this (toy)." I explain that he can either play with the other toy or he can go outside, and that he cannot take the toy away from the other child. He will come back with, "I want it." I will say, "I know you want it and you are stuck with that idea, aren't you? Do you want the toy?" He will say, "Yes." I say, "What is it that you can do?" And he comes back with "Go outside or play with other toys." He chose to go outside.
>
> I don't know why he got what was going on. He's only four years old. But I don't hassle, cajole, threaten, or anything else that looks negative to me. ... I treat them like I treat everyone else; I know they are toally capable, and all I really have to do is get out of the way ... they are going to make it with me or without me. I can participate in their growth and their life, and I really am not so damned important.

Many teachers commented that their directions seemed clearer and that they had to repeat themselves less often. Even though they had not changed the content of their lessons, they reported that what they had to say had been communicated clearly as a result of learning to be "on purpose" with what was to be communicated.

Another aspect of teaching that most teachers reported to be changing was their ability to deal with student behavior in more rewarding and less frustrating ways. A twenty-eight-year-old high school drama teacher, Judy, remarked:

> I am able to confront a student's act by just letting him run it in front of me. Sometimes I have him repeat it verbatim or even exaggerate it. I don't explain anything, I don't engage him in meaningful dialogue, and I don't belittle him or challenge the rightness of his act. I just let him experience it.
>
> I know that they all think my behavior is a bit weird, but they start to drop the whole "I am a high school teenager who can't stand school" bit and become real live human beings with me. That's been the real change in my teaching since I took the training.

Much of the fear and uncertainty that the teachers said they used to feel about "facing" their classes seem to have disappeared after the *est* training. Many of them expressed the sentiment that now it did not matter how many students passed, failed, or dropped out of their classes; and now they felt they could get on with the business of teaching.

Commonly, the teachers stated that their classroom communications were "so clear, powerful, and ethical" that they had no trouble making themselves understood: The responses they elicited, moreover, were fast becoming as clear as their own. Bob, a junior high school teacher for eight years, stated:

> If before [*est*] I had three good classes and two disasters, it was the best I could hope for. Suddenly, I have five fantastic classes. I am confident, able to joke in class—a major change for me: I am at ease and able to do what I want to do in class without regard for the class's reactions . . . and they respond by doing three, four, sometimes five times the amount of work—all of it of better quality. And all of this gets done after I use maybe a quarter or a third of the class time on some fantasy journey into a marshmallow or a potato chip.

One teacher reported that the most important aspect of the *est* training had to do with learning what she was not, and under what circumstances she was able to survive major upsets. She translated this to the classroom both in terms of her instructions and agreements with her students at the start of the semester, and in terms of her in-class confrontation with the students. Several teachers commented that their previous ideas of how far you could challenge a student were very limited. They commented that their new willingness to challenge their students came from their own experience of being challenged by the training's "unreasonable attitude toward everything . . . all with an eye towards producing a result." Many teachers spoke of adopting this same point of view in their classrooms.

> I am now very expectation-oriented right at the start of the year . . . I am totally unreasonable with the pupil in terms of my expectations. I have changed, though. I am not arbitrary. If they want to do something, no matter how unusual, outside of the area of my expectations (attendance, deadlines, and quality), that is all right. I am not a victim in my classroom anymore. I am in control and let it happen and develop into a learning experience rather than prearrange it. But they must stay within the boundaries of my expectations and rules, or they fail. I do not get excited, or lecture, or plead, or wonder where I went wrong; I simply fail them. They know this from the start, and they elect to play along with me or not. I have a higher degree of tolerance for their actions, but this does not extend to license when I can see a clearly destructive outcome from their actions. By the way, I have yet to fail anyone . . . though about five percent of my first day students drop out before the deadline.

The teachers spoke of having images or improved intuition of what was motivating their student's behavior, success/failure, or attitude. They could quickly create an atmosphere of trust and openness in which the student could talk. An important part of this process that was referred to repeatedly was an increasing awareness of how to talk to others without making the other person wrong for what he was thinking. Although *est* does use techniques for practicing this aspect of interpersonal communication, most teachers commented that the training enabled them to look objectively at what they were saying and at what they wanted to accomplish, and then to determine if what they did produced the desired result or not. While this sounds simplistic, most of the teachers related many examples of how they had taught from a system of beliefs that was not producing results and which they had never bothered to look at until they had taken *est*.

Many teachers also adapted these principles into the classroom as exercises for their students. One teacher has each student stand in front of the room for one minute silently and then read a short story of poem he has written. The class then asks critically what the purpose or each important line or phrase is. This teacher feels that allowing the student to rework the composition and present it again the next day directs more awareness to the student's responsibility for creating the piece.

Another teacher has her students begin each class with five minute (non-verbal) greeting exercises. These are followed by a five minute relaxation process, after which the class breaks into discussion groups to deal with the homework. She says that all the lessons are done at home, and that this is a very radical departure for this non-extraordinary class. It is also a radical change from the way she had been teaching eighth graders for the past twenty-seven years. She does hasten to mention that she has become aware that her students are far more capable of doing, "anything at all than I had ever imagined . . . I was even trained that to relinquish any control of the class would spell disaster."

One biology teacher, junior college level, says that he puts his classes through a simple relaxation process about once a week and then, "because I am able to perceive exactly what my purpose is in the class, I simply create in my head what I want them to get and they get it." This teacher also expressed surprise at how much more willing he was to put every student completely on his own responsibility for attending class, for dealing with the course, getting assignments done, passing and failing. He said that he now devotes full time to teaching. And his willingness to accept a high dropout rate is being met with a lower dropout rate as well as better student performance and comprehension.

While the results that the teachers achieved from applying *est* to the classroom seem to be out of proportion to the amount of time and effort expended, several teachers who had not actively applied *est* to their classes asked how they might "sneak it into the school without becoming suspect, losing respect, or being fired." None of the more active *est* teachers has been fired, but many said that they relied on the side effects of the processes they did in the classroom. For example, a teacher who does fantasy journeys to produce better comprehension of a biology dissection may find that the classroom behavior improves. Many teachers said that this one result so impressed their administrators that they were allowed to depart from the approved, normal methods of teaching. Or they found ways to circumvent administrative direction to end their activities. One teacher, warned to cease "meditation-like practices in school since these are of a religious nature," simply instructed his students to do them as homework. This appears to have worked as well as if they had done them in class.

Most of the teachers said that their greatest benefit came not from what they did in class, but rather from how they approached the whole matter of teaching. They felt they were better teachers and that their students' performance demonstrated this, and that this was not due to any specific classroom action.

While it is not clear why this is so, nor how it comes about as a result of the training, it seems that the feelings of being centered or grounded are at the heart of this change. Of course, this type of change comes to the classroom in the form of a teacher and will not have to be "sneaked" into the school.

As a summary of the areas in which *est* appears most useful in the classroom, I have listed those points that are repeatedly seen in the transcripts of the interviews. *Est*:

1) is a means of bettering the student-teacher relationship.
2) enhances the teacher's level of communication.
3) enhances the class performance level.
4) improves in-class behavior and attitude.
5) "processes" appear to give the student a sense of integration between the teacher and the subject and himself.
6) adds a dimension of control to the learning process in the classroom. Learning seems less haphazard.
7) humanizes the classroom.

While this pilot study was not intended to quantify nor to predict the value of *est* in the school system, it seems obvious that *est* can be a tremendous resource for teachers who wish to improve their teaching situations. While the training is designed for the general population, and is not aimed specifically at teachers, it is readily adapted to the classroom. *est* is aware of its benefits to teachers, and special seminars and trainings have been held to enable teachers to use *est* better.

Recently the *est* training was offered to a fifth grade class in the Watts district in Los Angeles. It was taught by the regular teacher during four school days in November of 1973. She reports the most significant changes are that the students are no longer as great a discipline problem, that they follow instructions more easily, and that they now understand and use the principles of agreement. She also reports that she "looks forward to Mondays now" which is a change for her since last year she was sick 30 days and decided to resign twice. Her principal was very supportive and wants to continue this type of transpersonal education at his school. It appears that the *est* training may directly become a valuable addition to the education process.

Learning and teaching can be enhanced by some of the techniques *est* uses. And since the "processes" themselves are the most tangible adaptations of *est*, they become the most observable. More important is the *est* philosophy, which is based on the principle that the individual is ultimately responsible. *Est* presents this philosophy in a way which allows the individual to experience his own responsibility. If teachers are grounded in this concept, they can communicate it to their students by allowing the students to experience being responsible. They do not make responsibility a duty and thereby create resistance to it.

School should supposedly prepare students for life beyond school. To this end, a current myth is found at all levels of our society: the more education one has, the better a person he will become. Teachers who are grounded in the principles of *est* communicate not only subject matter and skills, but do so in a way that communicates responsibility. They will be contributing to the overall development of their students directly and will not just be fulfilling the duties of the modern teacher, which one teacher characterized as being a combination of encyclopedia and babysitter. Students who have learned to be independent, responsible human beings are going to continue to learn long after they have left school.

REFERENCES

1. "The Behaviordyne Report on Psychological Changes Measured After Taking the Erhard Seminars Training," privately published, May 1973, San Francisco. Copies available from *est*, 1750 Union St., San Francisco, Calif. 94123.

2. See "Fantasy and Imagination" by Frances Clark for a fuller explanation of these techniques.

*[This paper is drawn from research now in progress concerning *est* and its uses in the classroom. The pilot project results were presented at the Conference on Transpersonal Psychology Applied to Education held at Northern Illinois University in May 1973].

ZEN MEDITATION AND THE DEVELOPMENT OF EMPATHY IN COUNSELORS *

Terry V. Lesh

A Psychological Hybrid. Lesh combines the transpersonal element of altered consciousness through meditation with the humanistic elements of self-actualization and interpersonal relations, and brings in the Freudian idea of regression-in-service-of-the-ego. These share the quality of sensitivity to one's self. The theme that self-knowledge, or inner-knowledge, has exterior, or social, effects runs through these psychologies and through this article. By showing how these three psychologies can complement each other, Lesh may exemplify an approach to the educational psychology of the future ... a multiparadigm psychology, which looks for convergence of findings, theories, methods, and instrumentation from several separate psychologies.

BACKGROUND AND RATIONALE

The experience of counseling supervisors and researchers of the counseling process has suggested that student counselors, as well as experienced counselors, frequently do not demonstrate adequate sensitivity to the client's feelings (Rogers *et al.*, 1967). Yet these same counselors often are quite sophisticated in psychological and counseling theory. If it is true that the ability of the counselor to demonstrate his sense of what the client is communicating through his feelings is an important dimension of the counseling relationship, then it is necessary to look deeper at what constitutes the more subtle nuances between human beings.

While the studies that have been done on empathy do show its importance in the counseling process, there still exists some debate on the exact meaning of this concept.

While the studies cited above have shown the importance of the counselor's ability to empathize with the client, there has been little success in increasing this ability in counselors (Matthes, 1967; Albright, 1967; Mellow, 1964). Some studies have shown that graduate students in counseling do not demonstrate any more empathic ability than a random selection of high school students (Truax & Carkhuff, 1963). Why do counselors in training programs gain little or nothing in their empathic capacities? What are the psychological processes within an individual that allow him to be empathic or open to the feelings of another? It is necessary to turn to another conceptual framework in order to answer some of these questions.

*From Terry V. Lesh, "Zen Meditation and the Development of Empathy in Counselors," *Journal of Humanistic Psychology* 10, no. 1 (Spring, 1970): 39–74, by permission of the author. Abridged by the editor. Terry V. Lesh is author of the forthcoming book *From Where I Sit: Meditational Infusion.*

The concept of *regression-in-the-service-of-the-ego* (hereinafter called "adaptive regression") may aid in understanding the deeper intrapsychic processes involved in the human capacity for relating. Shafter (1954) considers adaptive regression to be the essential process, insofar as it is adaptive, involved in direct interpersonal relations such as empathy, intimacy, orgasm, therapeutic understanding, and communication. He suggests that adaptive regression depends on certain facilitative conditions. These conditions are very much like those we would hold for the growth-producing counseling relationship (Shafer, 1954; Mellow, 1964; Rogers, 1958).

If the capacity to be empathic is related to adaptive regression, how is a person taught to utilize this deeper potentiality, to "regress in the service of his ego?" How do we teach someone (counselor, therapist, etc.) to "modify his level of psychic awareness and functioning to more basic primary processes within himself?"

The underlying assumption in this study is that a form of Zen meditation, *zazen*, is a way an individual learns to control and to be aware of these internal psychic processes.

Operational Definitions.

Empathy. Through [the] maze of attempts to define, operationalize, and measure accurate empathy, one realizes that: (1) It is an important concept in human interaction, and as such has been the subject of extensive research; and (2) rather than being a simple single component, accurate empathy is a complex process of interaction between human beings involving at least six major components. These could be described as: (1) The *perception* of two levels of feeling in the client, those that are stated or conscious and those that are not stated but are present—preconscious; (2) the *identification* of the feelings of the client; (3) the *differentiation* between the client's feelings and the counselor's feelings; (4) the *objectification* or separation of the client's feelings; (5) the *interpretation* of the client's feelings; and (6) the *articulation* of the client's feelings, both stated and preconscious.

The disagreement and lack of reliability resulting from attempts to measure this process reflect the substantial subjective judgment required to rate samples of client-counselor interactions which occur at different phases of the process. This study, therefore, will attempt measurement of only the first phase of the empathic process; that is, ". . . the ability to detect (perceive) and describe the immediate affective state of another . . . (Kagan, 1967, p. 463)." In terms of communication theory this is ". . . the ability to receive and decode affective communication (Kagan, Krathwohl, & Farquhar, 1965)." This definition of empathy is called "affective sensitivity."

Zen Meditation or Zazen. Zazen means sitting Zen meditation. "The student [of Zen] sets aside a portion of the day to sit motionless and concentrate" (Maupin, 1962). The object of the concentration is one's own breathing. The aim of this concentration is to suspend the flow of ordinary thoughts without falling asleep or going into a trance.

Essentially *zazen* is the conscious attempt to loosen oneself from all the thoughts one has about oneself in the past and in the future. To free oneself from the past and the future (in thought), and to enter the present fully, is the aim of Zen in terms of its attentional dimension. To be "in the present," or to be aware or conscious of all that is "present" in the present includes the awareness of what is "inside" one's mind (Berger, 1962). The attentional process of *zazen* is one of allowing one's conscious attention to open inward to one's own mental processes.

Kubie (1967) describes how education has served to overemphasize the conscious control of thinking which acts to inhibit one's capacity for "fully functioning" thinking. This in turn inhibits preconscious processes. Kubie continues with some suggestions for the direction research in mental functioning might take:

> This premature introduction of conscious sampling, through the repetitive emphasis on drill and grill, is precisely what makes jailers out of the processes of conscious sampling and conscious symbolic representation. Conscious processes thereby become inhibiting and paralyzing forces which restrict the free play of preconscious function. Therefore the goal of basic research in education must be to find better substitutes, to find better ways of tapping what is going on, and finding out what is being taken in subliminally and what is being processed preconsciously. We must find out how to dip a tin cup into the rushing preconscious stream without damming it up or diverting it [Kubie, 1967, p. 88].

This taking of larger samples of the "other than conscious processes" is precisely what *zazen* is. The attentional aspects of *zazen* may be considered (for the purpose of describing the conscious *process* of meditation) as directional. Starting with the assumption that "other than conscious processes" lie underneath (e.g., subliminal = below awareness) normal waking thought, the attention is turned (or opened) to the next most immediate level of awareness, the preconscious processes. Continuing with the intense concentration, the attention is opened to the next level of consciousness underlying the preconscious, the unconscious processes.

The object of *zazen* is the allowing of all these processes to surface to one's awareness until there is no splitting-up of consciousness. There is no cognition, no dreaming, no hallucinations, no data input (via normal sensory modalities), no information processing, no conscious activity at all, just full waking attention.

Adaptive Regression or Regression in the Service of the Ego. The meditation process, as outlined above, parallels Maupin's suggestion (1962) that "meditation brings about a sequence of more or less regressive states." This is taken to mean a conscious regression of attention to more primitive mental processes than one is normally aware of in the daily waking state. In his study of individual differences in response to Zen meditation, Maupin found a significant (tau = .49, P = H.001) correlation between responses to meditation and adaptive regression as measured by the Rorschach, and a test of visual imagery in free association. In psychoanalytic terms (Kris, 1952), "regression-in-the-service-of-the-ego" is synonymous with adaptive regression. As Maupin reported in his study, "structurally the process implies suspension of some ego functions such as defensive or logical functions and sometimes emphasis on genetically primitive mechanisms."

Shafer (1958) has expanded on the concept of regression in the service of the ego to account for the ability of individuals to make use of increased access to preconscious mental content, and its organization, without being overwhelmed by this preconscious material. The enlarged concept has been used to promote understanding of sleeping, dreaming, empathy, capacity for orgastic experience, hypnosis, free association, etc. The preconscious refers to "material, which though at the moment unconscious, is available and ready to become conscious; also topographically of a region, as it were, in the mind, intermediate between consciousness and the unconsciousness as such (Drever, 1952, p. 215)."

Moving then, from the concept of adaptive regression, focusing primarily on the oscillation between secondary and primary thought processes, to the concept of openness to experience, it can be seen that openness to experience includes inner experiences as well as outer experiences. From the standpoint of research it will be much easier to discriminate among those who are open to experience and those who are not, than to discriminate on the basis of "regression in the service of the ego" in terms of primary and secondary process operation.

Hypotheses. The purpose of this study is to determine if there is a relationship between the practice of *zazen* and the development of empathy in counseling students.

Hypothesis 1. Counselors who practice *zazen* regularly over a prescribed length of time will develop a higher degree of empathy as measured by the Affective Sensitivity Scale than counselors who do not practice *zazen* over the same time span.

Hypothesis 2. There will be a positive correlation between the individual response to meditation and scores on the Affective Sensitivity Scale.

Hypothesis 3. Response to meditation will be positively correlated with openness to experience as measured by the Experience Inquiry.

Hypothesis 4. Individual scores in openness to experience will be positively correlated with individual scores in affective sensitivity (from low to high).

Hypothesis 5. Those individuals scoring high in affective sensitivity will score high in each of 12 categories of the Personal Orientation Inventory (Shostrom, 1966):

DESIGN AND SAMPLE

The resulting design was of a three-group nature. The first group (N = 16) were those students in the Master's degree program (regardless of level) who volunteered to participate in the study and who actually did the meditation.

The second group (N = 12) were all Master's degree students *taking* counseling courses, but who were not necessarily in the counseling department. This group volunteered to do the meditation, but, in fact, did not actually do it. This group served as the first control group.

The third group (N = 11) were again Master's degree students taking counseling courses, but were not necessarily students under the counseling department. Again all levels of progress in the degree program were represented. These were people who definitely were against participating in the meditation exercise, but did complete all of the criterion measures, as did groups one and two.

Procedures. All of the subjects in the three groups were given a pretest (on the same day) for empathy or affective sensitivity, openness to experience (for adaptive regression), and a measure of self-actualization. Exactly 4 weeks later, at the same time during the day, all the subjects in all three groups were given the same measures again.

In the intervening 4 weeks, the people in all groups continued with their regular studies in the counseling program. The subjects in the experimental group, however, participated in the meditation exercise. The other two groups did not. A room was selected in the music listening section of the library where all the subjects could do the meditation together. They practiced the meditation exercise for 30 minutes each week day for 4 weeks, from 12:30 to 1:00 p.m.

Instructions for meditation exercise. Keep your back straight and erect; your hands in your lap, the left hand palm facing inward on the right palm, with the tips of the thumbs touching. Your head too is erect, the ears on the plane of the shoulders, and the nose in line with the navel. You may keep your eyes closed or open as you prefer. If you have them open fix them, unfocused, on the floor at a point about two or three feet in front of you. Now raise your whole body slowly and quietly, move it repeatedly to the left and to the right, forward and around, until you feel the best position.

Breathe through your nose, inhaling as much as you need, letting the air come in by distending the diaphragm. Don't draw it in, rather let it come to you. Exhale slowly and completely, getting all the air out of your lungs. As you exhale slowly, count "one." Now inhale again, then exhale to the count of "two." And so on up to ten. Then start over again with "one" and repeat up to ten again, etc.

You will find the counting difficult as your mind will wander. Keep at it though, keep bringing your mind back to the process of counting your breath. As you become able to do the counting with reasonable success start playing the following game with the counting. As you count "one" and are slowly exhaling, pretend that the "one" is going down, down, down, into your stomach. Then think of its being down there as you inhale, and begin to count "two." As you exhale bring the "two" down and place it in your stomach beside the "one." Eventually you will find that your mind itself, so to speak, will descend into your stomach. Gradually it will become possible for you to concentrate with more and more success on the numbers. Your mind will wander, and you will find yourself carried away on trains of thought, but it will become easier and easier to bring your mind back to the counting of your breath. Don't try to keep the "alien" thoughts out. Instead just try to concentrate on the counting. You may take note of the thoughts as they come in, if necessary, and then return to the counting. Get rid of the thoughts not by pushing them out of your mind, but by concentrating on the counting.

You may find that you become anxious or uncomfortable. This is because sitting still and concentrating like this restricts the usual ways we have of avoiding discomfort. If you feel uncomfortable, just accept it. If you feel pleasant, accept that with the same indifference. Eventually you will be able to be quiet in both body and mind [adapted from Wienpahl (1964) and Maupin, 1962].

The tape then ran silently for exactly 30 minutes, after which the experimenter's voice again became audible: "OK, the time is up, now without talking to anyone, please record your experience."

Criterion Measures.

Affective Sensitivity Scale. This instrument is a situational test designed to measure that aspect of empathy called affective sensitivity.

According to the authors of this test:

> The test is made up of video taped sequences from actual counseling sessions accompanied by items which describe various affective states which the client may be expressing. The procedure requires that the subject [empathizer] be able to detect and identify the feelings experienced by the client.

Experience Inquiry. The Experience Inquiry was developed (Fitzgerald, 1966) to measure adaptive regression by tapping the subjects' openness to inner and outer experience. This test samples the person's experience with life in terms of the way he approaches, perceives, and experiences life. A total score is obtained that gives an overall openness to experience rating. The test is made up of items designed to tap each of the following categories: Tolerance for Regressive Experience; Tolerance for Logical Inconsistencies; Constructive Use of Regression; Capacity for Regressive Experiences; Altered States; Peak Experiences; Tolerance for the Irrational.

. . . Schachtel's (1959) description of the person who is open to experience fits the characteristics of those subjects who scored highly on the Experience Inquiry. Namely, that they are not bound by the conventional modes of thought, memory and perception; they are sensitive to the possibilities and subtle nuances of experience which elude others; they are at home in the midst of conceptual disorder and complexity; and that they seek change and novelty.

Personal Orientation Inventory (POI). This inventory attempts to measure, by the use of 12 subscales, the individual's degree of self-actualization. The subscales are titled: time competence, inner support, self-actualizing value, existentiality, feeling reactivity, spontaneity, self-regard, self-acceptance, nature of man, synergy, acceptance of aggression, and capacity for intimate contact.

RESULTS

Table 1 shows the increases in ASS scores for the experimental group after the meditation experience. After adjustment of means within and between the groups for variability, the experimental group shows a net mean gain of 7.23—significant beyond the .001 level.

TABLE 1.

Changes in ASS Mean Difference (MD) Scores
After Meditation

Group	Post Treatment MD	Adjusted MD*	Adjusted S_EMD	Adjusted t**
Experimental	+6.000	+8.5894	1.0870	7.23***
Control 1	+1.667	+0.3459	1.0618	0.29†
Control 2	+0.500	−2.3711	1.2794	−1.82†

*After analysis of covariance[3]
**Required t's; df = 35; .001 = 3.291
***P = < .001; † nonsignificant

The hypothesis that the practice of *zazen* is an effective means of increasing empathy *is confirmed*.

The second hypothesis is: There will be a positive correlation between the individual response to meditation and scores on the Affective Sensitivity Scale. Correlations between the subjects' meditation responses in the experimental group and their scores on the ASS are Tau = .034 at pretest and .086 at posttest. *The hypothesis is rejected.*

The third hypothesis is: Response to meditation will be positively correlated with openness to experience as measured by the Experience Inquiry. Correlations between the subjects' meditation responses in the experimental group and their scores on the Experience Inquiry are: Tau =

.560 at pretest (significant at the .01 level) and Tau = .412 at posttest (significant at the .05 level). *The hypothesis is confirmed.*

The fourth hypothesis, that individual scores in openness to experience will be positively correlated with individual scores in Affective Sensitivity, *is also confirmed.* [When] the groups are combined and the data are treated in a manner allowing the testing of this hypothesis across all groups, the relationship between openness to experience and affective sensitivity is highly significant.

The fifth and last hypothesis [that those individuals scoring high in Affective Sensitivity will score high in self-actualization, as measured by the Personal Orientation Inventory (Shostrom, 1966)], *is also confirmed.* [When] the data for all three groups are combined a highly significant relationship exists between self-actualization and affective sensitivity.

DISCUSSION

Zazen and Counselor Empathy. The interpretation of the data in support of the first hypothesis (a highly positive relationship between the practice of *zazen* and the development of empathy or affective sensitivity) is still a limited one. The least we can say is that with this group of counselor trainees, the practice of *zazen* did, in fact, seem to contribute significantly to an increase in their ability to accurately detect and describe the affective states of others under less than ideal conditions.

The criticism might be raised that the experimental group was indeed an exceptional group of people, in that they volunteered for such an unusual experiment in the first place. This is a cogent argument since the pretest scores for the experimental group on tests measuring openness to experience and self-actualization are significantly higher than for either of the control groups. The same is true for the scores on the ASS at pretest. That is, the experimental group was significantly higher in empathy before the experiment had even begun.

Further analysis of the data reveals that the experimental group increased in openness to experience after the meditation, but not significantly so. Control group one apparently decreased on the dimension of openness to experience, but again not significantly so. However, control group two decreased in openness to experience between pre-and post-testing ... which is significant at the .01 level. The experimental group did not have any significant decreases. In view of the fact that all of these people were actively engaged in a primarily didactic counseling program during the experiment, the data suggest that, as the term wore on, the rational intellect took a firmer and firmer hold on these people, and tolerance for nonrational or affective experience generally decreased; that is, *except* for the people who were doing the meditation.

For the writer, the above findings emphasize a point made by Kubie:

Psychologists, psychiatrists, neurologists, neurophysiologists have erred together in their undue emphasis on the conscious components of mentation. This has led the educator into neglecting the *preconscious* instrument of learning, which is the effective instrument of recording, processing and of creating [Kubie, 1967, p. 78].

This is particularly relevant to a counselor training program. Are counselors being trained to "go into their heads," and "get uptight?" Is the result of a heavily didactic program that a "trained" counselor has no tolerance for the irrational and illogical in his client?

Level of Concentration and Empathy. The rejection of the second hypothesis (the predicted relationship between the *individual's* response to the meditation experience and his affective sensitivity scores) seems to indicate that the levels of concentration one achieves in meditation appears not to have any effect on an increase or decrease in empathic ability. This is contrary to what would have been expected. The only speculation that can be offered here is that with the instrument used to detect an individual's empathic ability, and under the conditions it was administered, the scores achieved by the experimental group began to approach the maximum possible, and further score changes could not be detectable.

Zazen and Openness to Experience. The testing of the third hypothesis was found to confirm the idea that response to meditation is related to openness to experience. The interpretation here is that people who are normally open to experience will be interested in meditation and have significant experience in the practice of it. The kind of experiences one encounters in the practice of *zazen* ranges from extreme difficulty in even sitting still, through dreamlike stages, to experiences that border on the religious, mystical and parapsychological.

An example of the kind of difficulties encountered in *zazen* is conveyed by excerpts from comments written by some meditators immediately after their sessions.

> I feel like a real failure as far as meditating goes. My mind is awash with thoughts—I am holding in, holding on, holding out; and there is no change. I hated sitting still, and had to force myself to concentrate. I'm confused about my goal because I think what I was doing for meditation earlier is not right for me now. I still feel too vulnerable to let go.

It's clear that the form of concentration required in *zazen* quickly reveals to one how unrelated people usually are to their innermost thoughts, fears, feelings, and desires. All forms of resistance to facing oneself emerge during such intense concentration.

Meditation apparently precipitates an acute awareness first of one's immediate outer environment (provided one can concentrate at all), then an awareness of one's immediate innermost environment, and then an awareness of something beyond any of these.

> I was anxious when I started this time, but soon fell into a pattern of breathing. Then the breathing fell into the background, and there began a building up of anxieties with reference to sexual capabilities and all associated with a client I was working with. I felt alone and inside of myself and a tremendous feeling of awareness of things within me.

Resistance seems to occur at three main points in the practice of *zazen*: first at the point of even sitting still and facing oneself, secondly at the point of allowing into one's consciousness the inner conflicts that are going on, and thirdly at the point of realizing one is a part of something "not self."

On the other hand, a few people managed to break through all these barriers and "see" further.

> I hate to try and put this into words—it's mine and I don't feel like sharing it. But I'll try. I had cotton in my ears and my breathing was loud in my head. I stayed in my head—seemed as if I flipped my eyeballs backward and up. Kind of a big void—then it seemed like I was looking in a long tunnel with a pinpoint of light at the very end. My eyelids were flickering, trying to pull open, but I kept pulling them shut because I didn't want to lose whatever I was drawn to. I felt like I was one with God—I was aware I was crying—I felt like I'd come home at last—an end to all loneliness and struggle—and I wanted to stay there forever. I didn't but kept going back *up* into my head anytime I felt anything intruding—all the while my breathing was kind of a comforting background rhythm. My head stayed erect—time went quickly—I fell very peaceful and quiet inside.

There were a number of unusual phenomena that occurred during the meditation sessions. An incident was described by a subject who said during the meditation he felt like the back of his head was burning and moving. He then got an image of the man behind him getting up and coming over to say something to him; he couldn't remember what it was the other subject wanted to say. (Most of the subjects went through the meditation exercise with their eyes closed.) The subject sitting immediately behind the one mentioned above, reported during this same session that he had an image of this man getting up and coming over to say something to him. It seems unusual that two separate persons sitting relatively near each other would have comparable images and sensations. It's difficult to accept this type of thing as being merely coincidental. After the study these two subjects were asked if they had been talking together prior to the session, or in any way felt they had any unresolved conflicts between each other. Neither one had seen each other that day, or within the previous week, except during the time they came for the meditation. Neither felt they had had any previous unresolved feelings about the other, except the man in front felt he was a bit self-conscious around the one sitting behind him.

The explanation of these phenomena is difficult without going over into the area of extra-sensory perception, or at least budding beginnings of it (Barron and Mordkoff, 1968). It's quite likely, in the opinion of the author, that very highly developed empathy touches on extrasensory perception of a sort. It appears as though one person can sense from another his feelings, even though the other person has not mentioned them. The transference of images between individuals without using language is suggested in the incidences such as the one above. Just how far accurate empathy reaches, or what the human potential for empathy may be, are unexplored questions. It appears to offer extremely interesting possibilities.

Adaptive regression is a potential mode of functioning innate in everyone, but only some people have learned to use it. However, it may be more correct to say that it is an ability that they have been able to maintain, whereas most people lose it through education's overemphasis on the rational process. Meditation may act more as a means of maintaining this ability in people who already have it than developing or recovering it in people who have lost it.

Openness to Experience and Empathy. The acceptance of the fourth hypothesis (that there is a relationship between openness to experience and empathic ability) lends support to the idea that in order for one to be able to sense or feel what another person is experiencing he must be open to what is going on in himself as well. Openness to experience, as measured by the Experience Inquiry, means that the person is open to both his inner and outer experiences. Openness to experience means that one is able to enter into many different situations, and allow himself to experience these situations without placing any judgment on the experience. It might be said that such a person understands because he *feels* what it is like. Much of human experience, especially at the deeper levels of feeling and emotion, is irrational and nonlogical. These experiences cannot be denied just because they don't make sense to us. The client's experience of what he is trying to communicate to us cannot be denied because it doesn't make any sense to us.

Zen meditation may be looked upon as an exercise in learning to listen to one's own inner experience. Reference to the quotes of the meditators' experiences show how difficult this really is. The therapeutic process is one wherein the people involved flow and move in each others' and their own experience of life and the immediate relationship they are in. Blindness and judgment come when one person says something of an emotional nature to another that sets up in him an emotional reaction that he does not recognize or cannot deal with in himself. An example might be a situation wherein the counselor has not dealt openly with his fears of his own sexuality. This counselor is suceptible to seductive actions on the part of the client. He is not able to see through to the person who is using this seduction. He therefore is apt to be judgmental, never really allowing the client to work through the meaning of this behavior.

Going over the responses given on the ASS show that all of the wrong answers given by the subjects are judgments about what the client was trying to say, rather than an accurate perception and understanding of what the client was saying and feeling. Knowing what one's own experience is or at least being somehow secure enough in one's self not to deny experience in others is crucial for empathic understanding. The deeper levels of Zen meditation are those wherein experiences can occur, but their occurrence requires no action on the part of the experiencer.

This degree of inner peace and quiet allows the therapist to experience the deepest and strongest emotions that human beings have without becoming fearful or feeling he must do something about the thing he is experiencing. This is the level at which B-Love occurs between human beings, and the level at which healing may begin (Maslow, 1962).

Self-actualization and Empathy. The fifth hypothesis (that there is a relationship between self-actualization and affective sensitivity) was accepted. Generally, the acceptance of this hypothesis means that people who are more self-actualizing, who have realized their own potentials more than others, are also more able to exercise greater empathic understanding for others.

These findings indicate that apparently the most important personal characteristics required in empathic ability are: a high personal self regard, a value system that sees developing one's own potential as important, a high degree of awareness and acceptance of one's feelings, a sense of personal freedom and willingness to be one's self, and a high degree of *acting* out of one's own feelings rather than *reacting* to others.

Examining the data for individual scores shows that those people who went down in empathic ability also went down in the above areas, but they also went down in their ability to express and receive negative feelings such as anger.

CONCLUSIONS AND SUGGESTIONS FOR FURTHER RESEARCH

The primary conclusion the experimenter has reached as a result of the present study is that Zen meditation holds far more potential for personal growth and scientific investigation than we have previously supposed. Meditation does appear to have a significant effect in the psychological and interpersonal domains of our experience. The psychic dynamics of the mind during the concentration required by *zazen* holds almost unlimited potential for investigation and further understanding of the functioning of consciousness.

The writer has long held that there is more hope for discovery in anomalous experience than there is in the already known and accepted. If there are questions about the meaning of our existence, the place to look for the answers seems to be in those odd and infrequent experiences that exist but cannot be explained. What we call mystical, cultish, and parapsychological, are no doubt just unexplored and undeveloped areas of our own potential. The taboo of exploring these areas, of experiencing them, is a holdover from the times of witch-burning. Fear and superstition about things that seem to be supernatural are understandable in the sense that we all fear knowing something new about ourselves.

Perception is a function of belief and need as well as a function of how we utilize our neurophysiological systems. There is enough evidence now accumulated (Deikman, 1966; Platt, 1969; Asimov, 1966) to substantiate the fact that there is a reality of time, space, and matter beyond that which has been thought real and fixed. The suggestion is that the way we perceive our world and its objects is morphologically bound. That is, we cannot see through solid objects because our mass is unable to move through them. Under different physical properties of our own existence, undoubtedly our perception of the environment would also be different. Even though our present mode of perceiving the world is physiologically functional (though perhaps increasingly less psychologically functional), we do have the potential of seeing greater aspects of reality.

Along with such studies should come work that would help the understanding of how to utilize this new knowledge in aiding the development of potentials, and to help people overcome difficulties in their lives. Frequently it is the gifted person (i.e., that person who, for whatever reasons yet to be understood, seems to have talents or abilities or senses that others do not seem to understand) who has the most trouble living an unburdened life. In his review of the mystical literature, and after having worked with several "unusual" people, William James (1963) concluded that unexplainable experiences do happen, that they are valid, they are real, they are frequently ineffable, and they are unpredictable. However, he also concluded that these experiences seem to happen to people who are in some kind of conflict, or who might be called more neurotic than most.

The writer is coming to the conclusion that this is an intrapsychical conflict that arises out of the person's inability to understand his gift or potential, and to integrate the use of his potential with what the culture calls a normal life. It is not that the neurosis causes unusual experiences, but that the different way of seeing things seems unacceptable to the culture, and the person comes to feel as if the way he feels about life is so unacceptable that he must be wrong. He therefore "puts himself down," becomes inhibited, tense, closed to experience, judgmental, unhappy, etc.

To apply the findings of this study to everyday life and the educational process, one could use Zen meditation in a counseling training program. Practice must be done daily, and the students should be required to keep a log of the experiences. The ideal condition would be that they also meet in encounter groups to discuss their experiences with the meditation as well as their experiences in life. This combination of "getting with oneself," and then being able to manifest the self in relation to others, may be the most potent catalyst for growth yet discovered.

REFERENCES

Albright, D. R. An application of a theory of process in client-centered psychotherapy in counseling. Unpublished doctoral dissertation, Indiana University, 1967.

Asimov, I. *The universe: From flat earth to quasar.* New York: Walker & Co., 1966.

Barron, F. & Mordkoff, A. M. An attempt to relate creativity to possible extrasensory empathy as measured by physiological arousal in identical twins. *Journal of the American Society for Psychical Research,* 1968, *62* (1), 73–79.

Berger, E. Zen Buddhism, general psychology and counseling psychology. *Journal of Counseling Psychology,* 1962, *9* (2), 122–127.

Deikman, A. J. Implications of experimentally induced contemplative meditation. *The Journal of Nervous and Mental Disease, 142* (2), 1966.

Drever, J. *A dictionary of psychology.* Baltimore: Penguin Books Ltd., 1952.

Fenichel, O. *The psychoanalytic theory of neurosis.* New York: W. W. Norton, 1945.

Fitzgerald, E. T. The measurement of openness to experience: A study of regression in the service of the ego. Unpublished doctoral dissertation, University of California, 1966.

James, W. The varieties of religious experience. In W. P. Alston, *Religious beliefs and philosophical thought.* New York: Harcourt, Brace & World, Inc., 1963.

Kagan, N. & Krathwohl, D. R. *et al. Studies in human interaction.* Educational Publication Services: Michigan State University, Lansing, Mich. Project No. 5-0800) 1967.

Katan, N., Krathwohl, D. R. & Farquhar, W. W. Developing a scale to measure affective sensitivity. *Educational Research Series,* March 1965, Michigan State University, No. 30.

Kris, E. *Psychoanalytic explorations in art.* New York: International Universities Press, 1952.

Kubie, L. S. Research in protecting preconscious functions in education. In R. M. Jones (Ed.), *Contemporary educational psychology.* New York: Harper Torch Books, 1967.

Maslow, A. H. *Toward a psychology of being.* Princeton: D. Van Nostrand Company, Inc., 1962.

Matthes, W. A. The relationship between conditions in counseling and selected outcome variables. Unpublished doctoral dissertation, Indiana University, 1967.

Maupin, E. W. An exploratory study of individual differences in response to a Zen meditation exercise. Unpublished doctoral dissertation, University of Michigan, 1962.

Mellow, R. A. Accurate empathy and counselor effectiveness. Unpublished doctoral dissertation, The University of Florida, 1964.

Platt, J. R. The two faces of perception. In B. Rothblatt (Ed.), *Changing perspectives on man.* Chicago: University of Chicago Press, 1969.

Rogers, C. R. The characteristics of a helping relationship. *The Personnel and Guidance Journal,* 37 (1), 1958.

Rogers, C. R., Gendlin, E. T., Kiesler, D. & Truax, C. G. *The therapeutic relationship and its impact: A study of psychotherapy with schizophrenics.* Madison: University of Wisconsin Press, 1967.

Schachtel, E. *Metamorphosis.* New York: Basic Books, Inc., 1959.

Shafer, R. *Psychoanalytic interpretation in Rorschach testing.* New York: Grune and Stratton, 1954.

Shafer, R. Regression in the service of the ego: The relevance of a psychoanalytic concept for personality assessment. In G. Lindzey (Ed.), *Assessment of human motives.* New York: Rinehart, 1958.

Shostrom, E. L. *Manual, personal orientation inventory.* San Diego: Educational and Industrial Testing Service, 1966.

Truax, C. B. & Carkhuff, R. R. For better or worse. The process of psychotherapeutic personality change. In *Recent advances in the study of behavior change.* Montreal: McGill University Press, 1963.

Wienpahl, P. *The matter of zen: A brief account of zazen.* New York: New York University Press, 1964.

*Based on a doctoral dissertation submitted to the University of Oregon. The author wishes to express his special appreciation to his wife Patricia, Barton E. Clements, Gordon A. Dudley and Philip Runkle.

Appendix

A GUIDE TO RESOURCES IN HUMANISTIC AND TRANSPERSONAL EDUCATION*

John T. Canfield and Mark Phillips

In Massachusetts, a student stops a teacher in the hall and asks, "Why are you only running our 'experimental class' for three weeks?" "I assume from your question, Patti, that you've enjoyed the class." "Well," she responds, "It's the only time in school that I've ever really liked myself; the only time when I've really felt happy. I also made a friend, or discovered one that I didn't know I had."

In Philadelphia, as part of an exercise in improvisational theater, a self-conscious seventeen-year-old girl is asked to create an object out of the space in front of her. Hesitant at first, she slowly begins to assume the shape of a cat with graceful and spontaneous movements. Completing the exercise she laughs and cries out, "I did it! I *did* it!"

In California, a first grade teacher writes in her log: "Jay and Jerry are sitting together working on a writing assignment. Jay was not able to trust anybody or give much warmth or affection all year. Yet here they sit, arm in arm, heads together, working together, and I realize that something has happened to him."

In New York, a student writes in her journal after a class in humanistic education, "To begin with, I've found that there is no one else like me, anywhere, like snowflakes. No one else feels completely the way I do. No one else sees things in the same scope as I do. So my first discovery about myself is that I'm me."

Classroom incidents like these are the result of many educators beginning to focus more and more attention on the nonacademic aspects of the child's growth in school. Working with psychologists on the frontier of the human potential movement, these educators are beginning to introduce new courses and activities into the schools—courses and activities that address themselves primarily to the psychological growth of the students. At present these include efforts to enhance positive self-concept, increase achievement motivation, promote creative thinking and behavior, enhance self-awareness, clarify values and promote better human relations. Intrinsic to all of these approaches is an effort to increase self-understanding and to enable students to relate that self to others more effectively.

Until recently, few schools treated the emotional growth of students as a distinct process, worthy of considerable time and energy; in most schools this neglect has actually retarded emotional growth. In the past ten years psychologists such as Carl Rogers, Abraham Maslow, Fritz Perls, and Arthur Combs have begun to turn their attention away from the

*John T. Canfield is Director of the New England Center for Personal and Organizational Development. He is author of the forthcoming books *100 Ways to Enhance Self Concept in the Classroom* (with Harold Wells) and *A Guide to Methods and Resources in Humanistic Education.*

medical mode of "curing the sick," and have begun to focus their energies upon *preventing* mental illness from occurring and upon helping normal, healthy individuals develop to their full potential.

Many educators have responded to this new thrust and centers for the development of classroom approaches to deal with the emotional growth of students have begun to spring up all across the nation. While most people working in these centers agree on the same basic assumptions and goals, the approaches that are being developed are widely divergent. The field of activity ranges from those interested only in improving the teacher's communication skills to those involved in developing highly sophisticated and complex psychological curricula and to those involved in reshaping the classroom climates and organizational structures of our educational institutions.

A clearer sense of what directions are being taken can be obtained by briefly examining three approaches currently being undertaken in the development of affective curricula. While the three approaches described all attempt to help students to accept and express their feelings, to become more aware of themselves and their potential, to guide their own growth as human beings, and to incorporate the processes needed to continue to grow after they leave school, they differ in their methods of implementation.

At the Center for Humanistic Education at the University of Massachusetts School of Education, Gerald Weinstein is directing a project to develop what he calls "Psychological Curriculum"—curriculum in which the subject matter becomes the student's psychological concerns over identity ("Who am I?" "Why am I black?" "What does it mean to be a girl today?"); connectedness ("Who are my friends?" "How do I get into a group?" "What are my values?" "To whom do I owe allegiance?"); and power ("What's the use of trying? You can't fight City Hall!" "I'm Hercules; I can do anything!"). By having students explore their unique responses to a series of structured self-confrontations, one is able to enhance the student's ability to perceive and act upon his true feelings and thoughts; thus increasing his sense of his own identity, increasing his ability to relate to others, and increasing his control over the course of his own life. This approach calls for separate classes devoted specifically to the teaching of psychological curriculum.

The Center for Development and Research in Confluent Education at the University of California at Santa Barbara, under the direction of George I. Brown, is involved in developing and implementing "Confluent Education," which Brown defines as the integration or flowing together of the affective and cognitive elements in education. Attempting to introduce affective techniques into conventional classrooms, the DRICE staff is developing classroom strategies to integrate affective learning experience with curriculum content, thus allowing reading, math, humanities, science and social science teachers to attend to the emotional lives of their students. The two questions the teachers are encouraged to ask themselves are: (1) What possible relevance does this content material have to the *present* lives of my students? (2) How do my students feel about this content or material? Using these questions as a starter, every teacher, no matter what his overall style, should be able to begin to introduce affective components into the classroom.

In Philadelphia, the Affective Education Development Project, under the direction of Terry Borton and Norman Newberg, is involved in developing curriculum and training teachers in what they call "Process Education." While their focus is again on the affective development of the students, their particular emphasis is on teaching students the processes needed for them to continue to direct their own personal growth and development.

In addition to the trends in psychological education that we have just described, a fourth movement has begun to emerge in the past several years—transpersonal education. People working in the areas of transpersonal psychology and education have been focusing on yet another neglected aspect of the total person—one's spiritual development. It is doubtful that schools will begin to respond to this area of personal growth until they first accept the emotional domain as legitimate for concentrated attention; however, there are isolated groups working successfully in the area, most notably Martha Crampton's curriculum development project at the Canadian Institute for Psychosynthesis in Montreal, Quebec. For this reason we have devoted a special section to Transpersonal Education at the end of the Guide.

As in most movements in education, there has been a quick response to the new "trends," and publishers are beginning to publish books, curricula, learning kits, films, tapes, etc. to meet the newly-created demand.

This guide is an attempt to provide teachers and administrators who are interested in learning more with information regarding what is available, whom to look to for help and where to go next, and hopefully includes some help in making selections from the vast number of available resources.

No guide of this sort can ever be complete. At best it is a working bibliography-in-progress. Every day new books are being written, new curricula being published, new courses offered, and new projects begun. While this is anxiety-producing for compilers of bibliographies, it is nevertheless reassuring to those of us who are struggling to make schools more totally human places for students and teachers.

BOOKS

Interest in affective education grows, and the publishers follow close behind, meeting the demand with a continually increasing flood of books related to the subject. We have attempted to select those books which we have found most useful in our own work, which colleagues have lauded, and which teachers beginning to work in this area have found most helpful.

The first section, providing a *Basic Library* of books, is the logical place for newcomers to the field to begin, and for school libraries to use in making initial purchases. These are the books we would choose to give to teachers to introduce them to humanistic education. Section two focuses on *Humanistic Psychology*, and includes a list of books designed to provide teachers with a fundamental knowledge of the psychological theory and processes which relate most closely to this educational movement. The third section, *Related Classics*, includes those books which most educators are already familiar with, which are primarily child-centered, and which are humanistic in the broadest sense. The final section, *General Books*, might also be called a "Secondary Library." It contains books related to humanistic education which we consider non-essential but highly recommended. In a sense, it is a catchall for the many books we like but couldn't find a place for in the other three categories.

Basic Library. *Anger and the Rocking Chair: Gestalt Awareness with Children* by Janet Lederman with photographs by Lillian R. Cutler. (New York: McGraw-Hill, 1969) 276 pages, $4.95.

This book is a dramatic, visual account of Gestalt methods with so-called "difficult" or "disturbed" children in elementary school. Rather than suppressing students' rebellion and anger, Miss Lederman helps her pupils transform these powerful impulses into constructive attitudes and behavior.

Fantasy and Feeling in Education by Richard M. Jones. (New York: New York University Press, 1968) 276 pages, $6.95.

One of the few books in humanistic education written from the viewpoint of a Freudian-oriented psychoanalyst. Jones begins with a perceptive critique of EDC's curriculum, "Man: A Course of Study," and goes on to point out the limitations of Jerome Bruner's work, the importance of fantasy and creative thinking in education, explores the implications of Erick Erickson's theories, and makes specific recommendations for new approaches to affective education. Tough to read at times, but it is worth the effort.

Freedom to Learn by Carl Rogers (Columbus, Ohio: Charles E. Merrill, 1969) 355 pages, $3.95.

This is an excellent book which explains in considerable detail how and why classrooms should be organized to free students to learn. Rogers clearly points the direction of education in the years to come.

Learning to Feel—Feeling to Learn by Harold C. Lyon, Jr. (Columbus, Ohio: Charles Merrill, 1971) 321 pages, $3.95.

This is a disjointed but comprehensive survey of the people, places, and ideas in the field of affective education. The sections on "Humanistic Education Techniques" and "Applying Humanistic to Classroom Situations" are particularly valuable. This book is the next logical step after reading this guide.

Human Teaching for Human Learning: An Introduction to Confluent

Education by George Brown (New York: The Viking Press, 1971) 298 pages, $8.50.

George Brown has been working with both the University of California at Santa Barbara and the Esalen Institute as part of a Ford Foundation project in affective education.

This book contains a statement of the purposes of the project, extensive examples of affective techniques and their classroom applications, and a series of personal commentaries by teachers involved in the project.

Perceiving, Behaving and Becoming by the Association for Supervision and Curriculum Development (1201—16th Street, N.W., Washington, D.C.: 1962) $4.50. Edited by Arthur Combs, this book presents a series of articles by the leading educational theorists in perception, self-concept and self-actualization. Included are statements by Carl Rogers, Abraham Maslow, and Earl Kelly. *Toward Humanistic Education.* Edited by Gerald Weinstein and Mario Fantini. (New York: Praeger Publishers, 1970) 228 pages, $7.00.

The outgrowth of the Elementary School Teaching Project of the Ford Foundation, this book outlines a model for curriculum and instruction based on pupils' concerns and feelings rather than on purely cognitive goals. The book contains many new ideas that can be immediately applied by the classroom teachers. *Reach, Touch and Teach* by Terry Borton (New York: McGraw-Hill, 1970) 213 pages, $3.95.

A readable, provocative, and informative introduction to process education for student concerns. Borton believes that major emphasis should be placed on helping children to understand the process of change, to give students practice in using it, and "to instill confidence in the student so that he can go about the business of changing himself in his own time and as he sees fit." The book explores the theoretical basis for Borton's work, presents numerous examples of its application in Philadelphia, and discusses a number of related projects in other parts of the country.

Values and Teaching: Working with Values in the Classroom by Louis E. Raths, Merrill Harmin and Sidney B. Simon (Columbus: Charles E. Merrill, 1966) 275 pages, $3.95.

This book outlines a theory of values and a classroom methodology for the clarification of values. It contains many practical classroom activities that teachers can employ to help students clarify their values.

Values Clarification: A Handbook of Practical Strategies for Teachers and Students by Sidney B. Simon, Leland W. Howe, Howard Kirschenbaum (New York: Hart Publishing Company, 1972) 397 pages, $3.95.

This extremely practical and valuable book contains seventy-nine classroom exercises designed to help students clarify their values. Each exercise is clearly written and contains many examples of ways in which it can be used. This book promises to become a classic in humanistic education. It belongs in your basic library!

Will the Real Teacher Please Stand Up?: A Primer in Humanistic

Education by Mary Greer and Bonnie Rubenstein (Pacific Palisades, Calif.: Goodyear Publishing Company, 1972) 236 pages.

Charles Weingartner writes: "It's about kids and how fragile and vulnerable they are—like seedlings. (Kids are seedlings.) And it's about how they need to be nurtured to help them in the process of growing and becoming so that they can develop and flower rather than be broken, and get stunted and withered. And, in a wistful way, it's about the little kid somewhere inside each of us. And it's about how sad it is when little kids (inside or outside of us) are squashed or denied . . . It is full of smart stuff by smart people who think and feel deeply about educating kids. It's full of stuff that makes you think about yourself, and stuff that makes you wistful, and stuff that makes you smile."

Humanistic Psychology. *Challenges of Humanistic Psychology.* Edited by James Bugental. (New York: McGraw-Hill, 1967) 362 pages, $4.95.

Readings in Humanistic Psychology. Edited by Anthony Sutich and Miles Vich. (New York: The Free Press, 1969) 440 pages, $3.95.

Both of the books provide a good overview of the field of humanistic psychology, through a selection of essays by leading psychologists, including Rollo May, Abraham Maslow, Carl Rogers, and Sidney Jourard.

Gestalt Therapy by Frederick Perls, Ralph Hefferline, and Paul Goodman. (New York: Delta Books, 1951) 470 pages, $2.65.

The first part of this book provides an experimental introduction to the basic tenets of Gestalt therapy through a series of experiments designed for the reader. The second part is highly theoretical and abstract, and is likely to interest only the professionals and the devotees of Gestalt.

Gestalt Therapy Verbatim by Frederick Perls. (LaFayette, California: Real People Press, 1969) 279 pages, $3.50.

Fritz Perls was the founder of modern Gestalt therapy. He was also a man of incredible insight and great wit. This book, composed of verbatim transcripts of complete Gestalt therapy sessions, reflects both his wit and his widsom.

Gestalt Therapy Integrated: Contours of Theory and Practice by Erving and Miriam Polster (New York: Brunner/Mazel, 1973) 329 pages, $12.50.

We feel that this is the most lucid book written to date on the theory and techniques of Gestalt therapy. The Polster's poetic view of life and the world brings a human quality to the book that makes it valuable and enjoyable reading. The insights drawn from therapy relate directly to the process of education.

Here Comes Everybody by William C. Schutz. (New York: Harper & Row, 1971) $6.95

In his book Schutz attempts to describe what he calls the "encounter culture." Central to his discussion is a new awareness of the intimate connections between bodily expression and how we think.

Psychosynthesis: A Manual of Principles and Techniques by Roberto Assagioli (New York: Hobbs, Dorman and Company, 1965; paper, New York: Viking Press, 1970)

Psychosynthesis is a way of pulling it all together. It is an approach which fosters the balanced development and integration of the body, feelings, mind, and spirit around a unifying center of being and awareness—the Transpersonal Self. The best introduction to this approach is Assagioli's book.

Related Classics. *Education and Ecstasy* by George Leonard. (New York: Delta, 1968) 237 pages, $2.95.

This was the first book to effectively relate the human potential movement to education. If some of Leonard's thinking now seems somewhat dated, it is a mark of how far we have come (at least in writing!) in three years.

New Priorities in the Curriculum by Louise Berman (Columbus, Ohio: Charles Merrill, 1968) 241 pages, $6.00.

In many respects this book presents the most important new approach to curriculum development. Designed to provide a framework for developing process-curriculum, it will probably be most valuable as a guidebook for schools which wish to move in that direction. Starting from the premise that the major emphasis in education should be on developing process-oriented persons, the book discusses eight processes and possible ways of centering curriculum on these processes. The processes discussed are: perceiving, communicating, loving, knowing, desicion-making, patterning, creating, and valuing.

The Open Classroom by Herbert Kohl (New York: Vintage Books, 1969) 116 pages, $1.65.

This is a short, but extremely vital book detailing the author's experiences in opening up his elementary classroom in Berkeley, California. There is much to be learned from his insights and suggestions.

Schools Without Failure by William Glasser (New York: Harper & Row, 1969) 235 pages, $4.95.

This book details the shortcomings of current educational practices and proposes a daring new approach to reduce school failures—an approach based on personal involvement, relevance, and thinking. He demonstrates how to reach negatively oriented, failure-conscious students and how to help them to aim for positive goal-setting, personal achievement and individual responsibility.

Teaching Achievement Motivation by Alfred Alschuler, Diane Tabor, and James McIntyre (Middletown, Conn.: Educational Ventures, Inc., 1970) 217 pages, $4.00.

Alschuler's work has been directed toward providing opportunities for students to achieve goals they set for themselves. This book outlines the theory behind achievement motivation and provides the basic framework for using the approach with both teachers and students.

General Books in Affective Education. *Encouraging Creativity in the Classroom* by E. Paul Torrance, 133 pages; *Expanding the Self: Personal*

Growth for Teachers by Angelo Boy and Geralk Pine, 127 pages; *Group Processes in the Classroom* by Richard and Patricia Schmuck, 156 pages. (All published by William C. Brown in Dubuque, Iowa in 1971, and all are $3.95.)

Three books in a new series entitled "Issues and Innovations in Education." All provide excellent introductions to the specific subjects and are likely to be particularly useful for teachers who are beginning to introduce humanistic education into their classrooms and for administrators who want to introduce humanistic processes to their staffs.

Improving Educational Assessment and An Inventory of Measures of Affective Behavior edited by Walcott H. Beatty. (Available from the Association for Supervision and Curriculum Development, 1201 16th Street, N.W. Washington, D.C., 20036) $3.00

A very useful starting point for looking at the problems and process of evaluating growth in the affective domain.

New Directions in Psychological Education. Edited by Alfred Alschuler. (Educational Opportunities Forum. June 1969, Albany, New York: N.Y. State Department of Education)

An excellent collection of articles dealing with varied approaches to humanistic education in the schools. Among the topics covered are: achievement motivation, process courses, value clarification, sensitivity training, strength training for teachers, and creativity training. The volume is scheduled to be published by Educational Ventures, Inc., in Middletown, Connecticut for broader distribution.

Self Concept and School Achievement by William W. Purkey (Englewood Cliffs, New Jersey: Prentice-Hall, 1970) $2.50

Explores the growing emphasis on the student's subjective and personal evaluation of himself as a dominant influence on his success or failure in school. It explains how the self-concept develops in social-interaction and what happens to it in school. It also suggests ways for the teacher to reinforce positive and realistic self-concepts in students.

WAD-JA-GET? The Grading Game in American Education by Howard A. Kirschenbaum, Sidney Simon, and Rodney W. Napier (New York: Hart Publishing Co., 1971) 315 pages, $1.95. If schools are to emphasize the psychological development of children and are to place a major emphasis on feelings, creativity, communication, etc., the issue of grades becomes a vital one. The authors of this book present their case against grades in the form of a fictional account of one teacher and one class who decide to challenge the system. The book's appendices, a compilation of alternative grading systems and an annotated bibliography of research on grading, are, by themselves, worth the price of the book.

What Do I Do Monday? by John Holt, (New York: E. P. Dutton, 1970) 318 pages, $6.95.

In this book Holt combines his theories of education—the idea of learning as a growth process, a moving and expanding of the child into the world around him; a belief that we learn best when we feel the wholeness and the openness of the world around us, and our freedom and power and competence in it—with practical, easy to use ideas and exercises in reading, writing, and mathematics.

SIMULATIONS

It has been our experience that the use of games and simulations introduces many humanizing influences into a classroom. Every simulation game is different in its assumptions and goals, but the intrinsic process of simulation may, in and of itself, positively effect the environment in which learning takes place, thus leading to greater personal growth in the students. We tend to agree with the following "hunches" about simulation games that were compiled by Project Simile at the Western Behavioral Sciences Institute.

(1) *Maybe simulations affect attitudes.* Maybe they gain empathy for real-life decision makers, maybe they get a feeling that life is much more complicated than they ever imagined, maybe they get a feeling that they can do something important about affecting their personal lives, their nation or the world. (2) *Maybe the main importance of simulations is their effect on the social setting in which learning takes place.* Maybe their physical format alone, which demands a significant departure from the usual setup of a classroom (chair shuffling, grouping, possibly room dividers, etc.) produces a more relaxed, natural exchange between teachers and students later on. Since simulations are student-run exercises, maybe they move "control" of the classroom from the teacher to the structure of the simulation, and thereby allow for better student-teacher relations. (3) *Maybe simulations lead to personal growth.* The high degree of involvement may provide some of the outcomes hoped for from T-groups, sensitivity training, basic encounter groups, etc.

The games and simulations that are listed below relate specifically to the affective domain; they focus directly on the psychological concerns and processes of the students. The great number of simulation games available warrant their own bibliography and are too numerous to annotate here. For more information on over 400 games and simulations see *The Guide to Simulation Games for Education and Training* by David W. Zuckerman and Robert E. Horn. It is available for $15 from Information Resources, Inc., 1675 Massachusetts Avenue, Cambridge, Massachusetts, 02138. *(Also see, Media and Methods, October, 1970).*

Body Talk (Psychology Today Games, Del Mar, California, 92014, $5.95)/A game designed to help people communicate more effectively without words and to enable them to more effectively understand the non-verbal communication of others. Players express emotions provided on cards, and others must try to accurately determine these emotions. Can be used on all age levels with as many as ten players.

Hang Up—The Game of Empathy (Synectics Education Systems, 121 Brattle Street, Cambridge, Massachusetts, 02138, $15)/Designed to develop empathetic insight, *Hang Up* is a board game in which participants assume make-believe personalities with hang ups they must successfully act out in a conflict confrontation between their game personality and the Stress Situations of the game. The game has been used in grades 3 through 12.

Group Therapy (Park Plastics, Linden, New Jersey, 07036, $8.50) Individuals are asked to perform various verbal or physical tasks and are rated by the others as either being "with it" or a "cop out." The game is designed to push individuals toward greater openness, greater honesty, and self-disclosure to others. It should be used only with the most mature individuals, is infinitely more potentially damaging both to individuals and to the process of humanistic education than almost any of the curriculum materials being developed in the field. Group therapy in the hands of amateurs could be destructive. If you use it at all, even with colleagues, use it with caution.

Insight (Games Research, Inc., 48 Wareham Street, Boston, Mass., 02118, $8.00) Each participant examines a series of cards which provide him with choices. (In which of these settings would you be happiest? Which of these books would you take with you to a desert island?) He marks his own choices and also predicts the choices each of the other participants will make. The game is useful in helping individuals learn more about themselves, about the others, and in increasing interpersonal communication. Most importantly it is also fun and has a low risk level. Can be used with 2 to 20 players.

Micro-Society, developed by Dennis Dobbs, Carol Goodell and Robert Hill (Real World Learning Corporation, 134 Sunnydale Road, San Carlos, California, 94070) This stimulation restructures the entire class into a miniature society with all the economic, political and social problems that are inherent with any emerging society. It is the most all-encompassing simulation we know of. Be sure to write for their brochure.

Sensitivity (Sensitivity Games, Inc., 9 Newbury St., Boston, Mass., $10.00) A game of psychodrama or role playing which is designed to help individuals learn more about themselves, how they relate to others, and how they identify with others. Players assume the roles of individuals involved in personal crisis and improvise and act out these individual's responses. Useful with older and more mature adolescents, but teachers might try developing their own versions for younger students.

The Value Game. (Herder and Herder, 232 Madison Avenue, New York, New York, $7.95 for the game plus $.75 for student readings to accompany the game) The game consists of ten to twenty situations requiring decisions and is designed to help demonstrate the inadequacy of a moral system which is based on absolute right and wrong. Can be used with 5 to 35 players.

Classroom Exercises

Awareness by John O. Stevens (Real People Press, Box F, Moab, Utah 84532, 1971) 275 pages, $3.50

This is an excellent book combining theory and over 100 exercises drawn from Gestalt awareness training, almost all of which can be used in the classroom. The exercises include personal awareness, communication with others, fantasy journeys, exercises for couples and groups, exercises utilizing art, movement, and sound, and a special section entitled "To the Group Leader or Teacher." Highly recommended!

Born to Win: Transactional Analysis with Gestalt Experiments by Muriel James and Dorothy Jongeward (Reading, Mass.: Addison-Wesley, 1971) 297 pages.

This book is valuable in many ways. It contains a clearcut statement of the theory of transactional analysis and its applications of everyday life, as well as Gestalt-oriented experiments to help people discover the many parts of their personality, to help them integrate them, and to help them develop an inner core of self-confidence.

Composition for Personal Growth: Values Clarification through Writing by Sidney B. Simon, Robert C. Hawley, and David D. Britton (New York: Hant, 1974)

This useful manual contains a variety of self-awareness exercises that lead to creative writing and greater self-identity. A large part of the work is based on the value clarification exercises developed by Sid Simon.

The Gestalt Art Experience by Janie Rhyne (Belmont, California: Brooks/Cole Publishing Co., 1973) $12.50.

Describes ways to use art media for discovering and exploring unique personal qualities in oneself and others. In addition to the many useful exercises described, the book contains a wealth of ideas about the nature of human growth that are helpful to the teacher.

A Handbook of Personal Growth Activities for Classroom Use by Robert C. Hawley and Isabel L. Hawley (Available for $5.00 from Education Research Associates, Box 767, Amherst, Massachusetts 01002)

Contains a wealth of activities in such areas as achievement motivation, effective communication, creativity, decision-making, brainstorming, value clarification, fantasy work, and enhancing positive self-concepts.

A Handbook of Structured Experiences for Human Relations Training, Volumes I, II, III, and IV. (University Associates Press, P.O. Box 615, Iowa City, Iowa, 52240, $3.00 per volume).

These handbooks are compilations of techniques, ideas, and forms useful in a variety of human relations training designs. They range from exercises requiring little or no training in human relations work to ones used by facilitators with extensive behavioral science background. These are incredibly useful books and should be in your basic library.

Learning Discussion Skills Through Games, by Gene Stanford and Barbara Dobbs Stanford. (New York: Citation Press, 1969, $2.25.)

Drawing ideas from the encounter-group movement, group dynamics, and their own experiences in the classroom, the authors suggest a sequence of activities to help students get acquainted, organize their group for effective action, overcome reluctance to participate, listen in depth to other members, draw others out rather than argue, and arrive at a consensus.

Joy: Expanding Human Awareness, by William Schutz. (New York: Grove Press, 1967)

This popular book contains a useful discussion of the theory underlying encounter groups, as well as many exercises that can be adapted for use in the classroom.

100 Ways to Enhance Self-Concept in the Classroom, (In preparation.), by John T. Canfield and Harold Wells. Write New England Center, Box 575, Amherst, Mass. 01002 for information.

Contains 100 classroom activities for kindergarten through college, designed to enhance the positive self-concept of students.

Sense Relaxation Below Your Mind, by Bernard Gunther. (New York: Macmillan Company, 1968)

A beautiful book with accompanying pictures for each exercise. Gunther details exercises which help a person wake up his senses.

The Magic If: Stanislavski for Children by Elizabeth Y. Kelly (Baltimore, Maryland: National Educational Press, 1973) 169 pages, $7.95

Starting with the "magic question" that awakens the imagination, "What would I do *if* I were king or queen, rich man, poor man, beggar man, or thief?" Kelly leads her students to enter into the hearts and minds of others and at the same time, through acting out thoughts and feelings carefully observed, to experience their own thoughts and feelings more keenly. The exercises contained in her book are readily usable by any teacher.

Teaching Human Beings: 101 Subversive Activities for the Classroom by Jeffrey Schrank (Boston: Beacon Press, 1972) 192 pages, $3.45

A wealth of material and activities utilizing encounter techniques, self awareness exercises, simulation games, and the use of books and films that rarely appear in traditional classrooms.

Ten Interaction Exercises for the Classroom. (NTL Institute Publications, 1201 16th Street N.W., Washington, D.C., 20036, $2.50)

The second NTL Institute's series of training exercise packets (the first was "10 Exercises for Trainers"), adapts to exercise format a selection of "Interaction Briefs," a continuing feature of *Today's Education*, the journal of the National Education Association. "Interaction Briefs" are designed to bring human interaction exercise material to the teacher at the elementary and secondary school level.

Toward Self-Understanding: Group Techniques in Self-Confrontation, by Daniel Malamud and S. Machover, (Springfield, Illinois: Charles C. Thomas, 1965).

This very useful book provides the rationale and exercises for a course in self-understanding that the authors conducted at New York University.

What To Do Until the Messiah Comes, by Bernard Gunther. (New York: Collier Books, 1971).

This is the second of Gunther's books outlining more methods to relax and awaken our bodies. Again the graphics are strikingly beautiful.

Improvisation for the Theater, by Viola Spolin. 397 pages. (Evanston, Illinois: Northwestern University Press, $6.95). This is the most popular text on theater games and is written primarily for the teacher. It contains more than 200 games and exercises in manual form, almost all of which are designed to help develop spontaneity and release creativity. The book has served as a primary reference for almost all of the educators who are developing and implementing humanistic classroom approaches.

CURRICULA AND STUDENT MATERIALS

About Life by the Center for Learning, Box 910, Villa Maria, Pennsylvania 16155, is a sixteen unit values program for junior and senior high school students currently being developed. Nine week units now available are Try to Remember, The Personality Puzzle, Awakening of a Social Conscience, The Spirit of Man and His Future. The units are heavily influenced by the Values Clarification work of Sid Simon.

About Me: A Curriculum for a Developing Self by Harold Wells and John T. Canfield. (Encyclopedia Britannica Educational Corporation, 425 North Michigan Avenue, Chicago, Illinois 60611) This inexpensive curriculum is designed to help children in grades 4–6 develop positive self-concepts. Lessons include I Know Who I Am, I Know My Strengths, I Can Set and Achieve Goals, I Try to Be Myself, and I Am in Charge of Becoming Myself.

Achievement Competence Training (ACT!) by Russell A. Hill and the staff of the Humanizing Learning Program of Research for Better Schools, Inc. (Research for Better Schools, Suite 1700, 1700 Market Street, Philadelphia, Pennsylvania 19103) ACT is a comprehensive learning package designed to teach students a variety of strategies for setting and reaching their goals. Hill and his colleagues have developed a really solid program to enhance students' self motivation, self confidence and self actualization. The program is a bit expensive but well worth checking into.

Achievement Motivation Materials, by Alfred Alschuler, Diane Table, and James McIntyre. (Education Ventures, Inc., 209 Court Street, Middletown, Connecticut, 06457). The materials were adapted for ninth grade use from those developed by the Achievement Motivation Development Project at Harvard University. Brief teacher's guides accompany these materials and suggest variations of their use:

Choose Life: Value Education for the Young Adult, by Patricia Kennedy Arlin. (Argus Communications, 3505 North Ashland Avenue, Chicago, Illinois, 60657). This is an amazing curriculum, to say the least. Not only are the booklets, tapes and filmstrips useful in promoting self-awareness, they are a model of communication in graphics. The package includes teacher resource materials and teacher training materials.

The Coping with Books, by Gilbert Wreen and Shirley Schwarzock. (American Guidance Service, Publishers' Building, Circle Pines, Minnesota, 55014). A really exciting series of books for teenagers, dealing with their problems, interests and concerns. Some of the 17 titles in this series are:

Coping with Cliques, Living with Loneliness, To Like and Be Liked, Easing the Scene, Can You Talk With Someone Else?, and Some Common Crutches.

Developing Understanding of Self and Others, by Don Dinkmeyer. (American Guidance Service, Inc., Dept. EL-4, Publishers' Building, Circle Pines, Minnesota, 55014). A program designed to help elementary children understand themselves and those around them. The DUSO kits provide a wide variety of experiences designed to reach children with unique learning styles through varied media and modes.

Dimensions of Personality Series, by Walter J. Limbacher. (George A. Pflaum, Publisher, 38 West Fifth Street, Dayton, Ohio, 45402). This series is based on the belief that the classroom teacher can be an enormously successful partner in helping youngsters live useful and happy lives. The program is experiential and discussion-centered, built around a book of very good readings for each grade level. The books are *Here I Am* (grade 4), *I'm Not Alone* (grade 5), and *Becoming Myself*, (grade 6).

Effective Communication, by Jeffrey Schrank. (Argus Communications, 3505 N. Ashland Avenue, Chicago, Illinois, 60657, $27.50). A 4-tape series with spirit masters for student materials. The tapes cover listening, reflective listening, identifying and expressing feelings, brainstorming, non-verbal communication, and feedback mechanism.

Experiences in Being, edited by Bernice Marshall. (Brooks/Cole Publishing Company, 10 David Drive, Belmont, California, 94002). A book of readings applicable to any high school or college course in English, social studies, psychology, or human relations. The book provides a good overview of humanistic psychology.

Focus on Self Development, by Judith L. Anderson, Carole J. Lang and Virginia R. Scott. (Science Research Associates, 259 East Erie Street, Chicago, Illinois, 60611). This is a developmental affective educational program for grades one through three. The overall objectives are to lead the child toward an understanding of self, an understanding of others and an understanding of the environment and its effects. It includes filmstrips, records, photoboards, pupil activity books and a teacher's guide.

Gateway English, by Marjorie B. Smiley and others. (The Macmillan Company, 866 Third Avenue, New York, New York, 10022). A junior high and high school Literature and Language Arts Program developed in Hunter College's Project English. The books are concerned with many significant human themes, as shown by the titles in the series: *Who Am I, Coping, A Family Is A Way of Feeling, Striving, Two Roads to Greatness* (Abraham Lincoln and Frederick Douglass), *Creatures in Verse* and *A Western Sampler*.

Hello People, by Judith O'Connell and Janet Cosmos. (Argus Communications, 3505 North Ashland Avenue, Chicago, Illinois, 60657). A multimedia, multi-ethnic social studies program for 6–9 year olds, which focuses directly on the growth of the child's self-concept and teaches him to relate to others in a humane way. The program's emphasis on social integration meets an important need of the child in coping with today's complex society.

The Human Development Program, by Dr. Uvaldo Palmoares and Dr. Harold Bessell. (Human Development Training Institute, 4455 Twain Avenue, Suite H, San Diego, California, 92120). This program is designed to facilitate learning in the affective domain, thereby improving motivation and achievement in all areas of education. The strategy is to employ cumulative, sequential activities on a daily basis as outlined in the lesson guides. One of the best we've reviewed!

I Have Feelings, by Terry Berger. (Behavioral Publications, 2852 Broadway, New York, New York, 10025). Covering seventeen different feelings, both good and bad, and the situations that precipitated each one, the book is geared for children ages 4–9.

Impact Series, by C. Brooks and I. Trout. (Holt, Rinehart and Winston, 383 Madison Avenue, New York, New York, 10017). The series contains several books on key themes, *I've Got A Name, At Your Own Risk, Cities* and *Larger Than Life*.

Kindle Series (Unit One: Who Am I?), by Inside-Out Productions. (Scholastic Magazines, 900 Sylvan Avenue, Englewood Cliffs, New Jersey, 07632). This series concerns itself with the special world of small children in their own social environment. The primary aim is to help the early primary and preprimary child understand himself, and feel good about himself.

Making It Strange, by Synectics, Inc., (Published by Harper and Row, 49 East 33rd Street, New York, New York, 10016). A four book series with a teacher's manual designed to teach children to be more creative.

Merrill Mainstream Books, by Charles G. Spiegler and Helen H. Johnson. (Charles E. Merrill Publishing Company, Columbus, Ohio, 43216). Each book in this junior and senior high series contains a collection of short stories, poems and quotations pertaining to the theme of the book. The series includes: *In New Directions*, dealing with the problems of "coming of age" of a number of people; *Against the Odds*, portraying people who took a risk, fought against all the odds and won; *They were First*, covering trailblazers in several fields; *Courage Under Fire*, about people who have made choices and, once having chosen, have had the courage to stand by their decision; and *People Like You*, stories about people who have problems and frustrations "just like you." Reading about other people's problems, students may find it easier to understand and cope with their own.

Motivation Advance Program, by Audrey J. Peterson. (Combined Motivation Education Systems, 6300 River Road, Rosemont, Illinois, 60018). This program provides experiences and information to assist youth in expanding their attitudes toward self-acceptance as worthwhile, unique individuals. Designed for junior high and high school, the program includes establishing group rapport, analyzing achievement patterns, identifying untapped personal resources, clarifying values, setting goals and managing conflict.

Self-Enhancing Education: A Program To Motivate Learners, by Norma Randolph and William Howe. (Stanford Press, Palo Alto, California.) This book describes a program which teachers may use to help their students grow in self-esteem through practical and effective processes.

Social Science Laboratory Units, by Ronald Lippitt, Robert Fox, and Lucille Schible. (Science Research Associates, 259 East Erie Street, Chicago, Illinois, 60611). An intermediate-grade social studies curriculum providing a modified laboratory approach to learning. The classroom becomes a laboratory for guided inquiries into the causes and effects of human behavior.

Unfinished Stores. (Color; Doubleday and Company, Inc., 277 Park Avenue, Garden City, New York, 10017.) This is a series of short films primarily designed for junior high school students. Each film portrays a conflict of conscience and then leaves it up to the students to decide what they should do. (Printed versions of the stories are available from the NEA Publications Sales Division, 1201 16th Street, N.W., Washington, D.C., 20036).

Value Formation and Change, by Dr. Brian Hall. (Argus Communications, 3505 N. Ashland Avenue, Chicago, Illinois, 60657.) This is an in-service teacher kit to develop humanistic skills for good teacher-student rapport, and a high school classroom program for direct student-teacher exploration of change and values.

Values in Action: Role-Playing Problem Situations for the Intermediate Grades, by Fannie and George Shaftel. (Hold, Rinehart and Winston, 383 Madison Avenue, New York, New York, 10017, $99.00.) This program of filmstrips and recordings for role-playing and discussion depicts personal conflicts involving cliquing, group pressure, and individual responsibilities in terms that will arouse the immediate concern and empathy of preadolescents. Each problem story stops precisely where a value decision must be made.

Words and Actions: Role Playing Photo-Problems for Young Children, by Fannie Shaftel and George Shaftel. (Holt, Rinehart and Winston Company, 383 Madison Avenue, New York, New York, 10017.) A series of urban-oriented photographs with accompanying role-plays focused around such problems as disagreement with parents over shoe styles, a fight over blocks and spilled groceries, to help children recognize and deal with their feelings.

CREATIVITY

Thinking creatively is an intrinsic part of developing one's repertoire for responding to a wide variety of emotional and cognitive conflicts and confrontations. We wish to thank Doris J. Shallcross for her contribution to this section.

Creative Education Foundation (Bishop Hall, State University College, 1300 Elmwood Ave., Buffalo, New York, 14222).

This nonprofit organization promotes creative education in all fields. In addition to running the annual Creative Problem-Solving Institute (new in its eighteenth year), the Foundation publishes *The Journal of Creative Behavior*, the only completely interdisciplinary professional journal available. Write to C.E.F. for information about its activities, The Journal, the Institute, and for its "Available Materials" catalogue, from which things can be purchased at cost.

The Creative Process, by Brewster Ghiselin (New York: The New American Library, 1955).

An oldy, but a "must" for anyone investigating the whole area of creative behavior. Ghiselin's excellent introduction is an attempt to define the elements in a creative process by examining processes of people deemed highly creative in a variety of fields. The remainder of the book is a series of essays by well-known artists describing their own processes.

Creativity: Its Educational Implications, by Demos Gowan and E. Paul Torrance. (New York: Wiley & Sons, Inc., 1967).

A superb collection of articles by practicing educators, pointing out significant research in creative behavior and its practical applications to education.

Applied Imagination, by Alex F. Osborn. (New York: Scribner's, 1963.)

The late Dr. Osborn's motto, "Keep it simple," is well illustrated in this straightforward guide to increasing the use of one's creative potential. The book includes numerous examples, exercises, and techniques that one can utilize individually or with a group.

Creative Behavior Guidebook, by Sidney J. Parnes. (New York: Scribner's, 1967). This book is designed for anyone who wants to delve into the "whys" as well as the "hows" of nurturing creative talent. Part I provides a solid foundation in the philosophy and psychology of creative behavior, and Part II is a detailed instructional program for cultivating creative behavior. A valuable guide, including both theory and practice.

Synectics Education Systems, (121 Brattle Street, Cambridge, Massachusetts, 02138).

Synectics' Theory is based on the hypothesis that learning and creativity are grounded in the use of analogy and metaphors. Synectics' technique, therefore, consists of methods for using metaphors and analogies to help students visualize substantive material. In addition to W. J. J. Gordon's introductory book on the subject, *Synectics* (New York: Harper & Row, 1961), you might be interested in the following materials available from SES:

The Metaphorical Way of Learning and Knowing, by W. J. J. Gordon. This book serves as an excellent introduction to Synectics' theory as it is applied to elementary and secondary education.

The Art of the Possible is a social studies workbook for grades 7-10. These materials are designed to bring out in students new depths and sensitivities about such abstract concepts as freedom, pleasure, violence, and morality. Attitude change in such areas as self-concept is focused upon. (For example, in the second section students are shown how some people can invent their way out of the private prisons.) Included are readings about such people as Helen Keller, Claude Brown, and Kamala, the "Wolf-girl," who were or were not able to invent ways to transcend their environment.

Making It Whole is a course designed for grades 4 through 10. In an attempt to foster integrated learning, the exercises show students how one subject area is understood in terms of the metaphors and analogies drawn from another. Students are urged to make metaphorical connections between their experience/feelings and the facts of substantive knowledge.

Strange and Familiar is a workbook for grades K through 10. It is designed to draw students into the practice of creative thinking in general.

Teaching Is Learning to Listen is a programmed teacher-training course for individual use. It is designed to help teachers develop their classroom teaching techniques and listening skills.

Making It Strange is another source of student material based on the Synectics' approach to creative thinking. This is a series of language arts workbooks concentrating on helping students develop the creative thinking that forms the basis for good writing. Available from Harper and Row, Evanston, Illinois, 60201.

HUMANISTIC EDUCATION ORGANIZATIONS

Adirondack Mountain Humanistic Education Center, Upper Jay, New York, 12987. In addition to conducting seminars in humanistic education and value clarification, the Center has available reprints of many books and articles in the area of values by Sidney B. Simon, Merrill Harmin, Louis Raths and Howard Kirschenbaum.

Affective Education Development Project, Room 323, Philadelphia Board of Education, Twenty-first and the Parkway, Philadelphia, Pennsylvania, 12103. (Norman Newberg and Terry Borton, Directors). This project has been developing curricula and providing in-service teacher training for what the directors term "process education." The theory and application of this curriculum is explored in Borton's book, *Reach, Touch and Teach*.

Association for Humanistic Psychology, 325 Ninth Street, San Francisco, California, 94103, is a tremendously useful organization to belong to. In addition to publishing a monthly newsletter and *Journal of Humanistic Psychology*, AHP holds an annual conference that is unparalleled in bringing together a wide variety of people working in the area. At the 1973 conference there were nineteen sessions devoted specifically to humanistic education. The association also publishes the *Paper Dragon*, a vehicle for circulating ideas on humanistic education.

AHP Education Network, 325 Ninth Street, San Francisco, California, 94103, is a network of psychologists and educators attempting to compile and share their experiences, humanistically oriented materials, lesson plans, etc. for classroom use. There is a newsletter (c/o Dr. Norm Leer, Department of English, Roosevelt University, 430 South Michigan Avenue, Chicago, Illinois 60605), a series of "Paper Dragons" (reprinted articles and other materials), and a book planned. The Network has also been collecting studies empirically validating humanistic-affective-confluent (whatever term you use) educational procedures in the classroom. If you are in need of such data, write the network in San Francisco.

The Center for Curriculum Design, 823 Foster Street, Evanston, Illinois, 60204 (Noel McInnis, Director), is involved in developing humanistically-oriented curricula for the future. Recently they have been engaged in work in the human potential movement, ecology, alternative life styles and futuristics.

The Center for Humanistic Education, University of Massachusetts, Amherst, Massachusetts, 01002 (Gerald Weinstein, Director). Offers graduate and undergraduate courses in Education of the Self, Value Clarification, Humanistic Curriculum Development, Theory of Psychological Education, Race Relations, and Strength Training. The Center is currently involved in a curriculum development project, funded by the Ford Foundation, to produce and implement psychological curriculum that deals with the concerns of identity, interpersonal relationships, and personal power.

Center for Humanistic Education, Norman Hall, University of Florida, Gainesville, Florida 32061 (William W. Purkey, Director) was recently begun to "assist school districts (and other institutions) in finding practical solutions to dehumanizing problems, to disseminate information on humanistic education, to conduct research in developing and substantiating the theory and practice of humanizing approaches to education."

Center for Learning, Box 910, Villa Maria, Pennsylvania 16155, has been developing a sixteen unit Values Program for junior and senior high school entitled *About Life*, which contains nine-week units on personality, human growth, social awareness, futurology, etc. They also conduct training workshops for teachers wishing to use the materials. Write to the Center for a description of the materials durrently available.

Center for Theatre Techniques in Education, American Shakespeare Festival Theatre, Stratford, Connecticut, 06497. Under the direction of Mary Hunter Wolf, the Center has been in existence for three years developing techniques for innovative education. The foundation of the techniques employed is the use of improvisations and theatre games to build better communication, quicker response and creative interactions in the classroom community in a manner derived from learning processes used in theatre rehearsals. The Center provides workshops and allied services to schools, school districts, area service centers and teachers.

Development and Research in Confluent Education, Department of Education, University of California, Santa Barbara, California, 93106 (George I. Brown, Director), is developing curricula and training teachers in the area of confluent education. Their aim is to integrate the knowledge and activities of the human potential movement with the traditional classroom curriculum, thus creating a more total or holistic learning situation for students. The basic work of DRICE is reported in Brown's book *Human Teaching for Human Learning.*

Education Research Associates, Box 767, Amherst, Massachusetts 01002, provides workshops, consultation and publications in the area of "teaching for personal and social growth." For a list of workshops and publications, write ERA for a brochure.

Education Ventures, Inc., 209 Court Street, Middletown, Connecticut, 06457. In addition to publishing materials to teach achievement motivation, EVI conducts a series of summer workshops in achievement motivation and humanistic education. It's a good idea to get your name on their mailing list.

Educator Training Center, 2140 West Olympic Blvd., Los Angeles, California, 90006. The Center was created by Dr. William Glasser to research ideas and develop methods for combating school failure. Building primarily on a process called the "classroom discussion," ETC has developed a practical inservice program which any elementary school can use to help eliminate failure by building the self-worth of the students through effective communication and motivation. Seminars are also offered for credit through La Verne College in La Verne, California.

Effectiveness Training Association, 110 East Euclid, Pasadena, California, 91101. Under the direction of Dr. Thomas Gordon, ETA is an organization whose object is "to provide educational experience for people who want to learn the specific skills required to develop and foster effective human relationships in which people can fulfill their own potential, help others to fulfill theirs and resolve their conflicts in a spirit of mutual respect, in friendship, and in peace." After a 5-day intensive training workshop, ETA Associates are able to offer three basic courses in their own communities: Parent Effectiveness Training, Teacher Effectiveness Training, and Leader Effectiveness Training.

The Earth Science Educational Program, originally located in Boulder, Colorado, was an extensive project dedicated to help students and teachers move "toward a heightened awareness of self and learning through environmental study." It was one of the most exciting educational projects in the country. Funded by the National Science Foundation, ESEP operated three interrelated programs: the *Environmental Studies Project*, the *Earth Science Teacher Preparation Project*, and the *Earth Science Curriculum Project*. The materials that have been produced by the projects include the *Environmental Studies Kit* ($20.00) which consists of 75 assignment cards which are investigation strategies to be applied to particular aspects of self and the environment, a *Poster Packet* of ten colorful posters dealing with the human side of education ($4.00), and two volumes of *The Cutting Edges . . . or How to Innovate and Survive*, which record how some people in the colleges and secondary schools are creating conditions where learners are looked at as real people ($3.00). They also published a lively and useful newsletter entitled *Sensorsheet*.

In the summer of 1973, the project directors decied to leave Boulder and set up offices in several other places. So here's how it looks now:

The Environmental Studies Project, now called ESSENTIA, is located at Evergreen State College, Olympia, Washington 98505 (Bob Sluss and Bob Samples, Directors). They work with teachers, administrators and parents to give them a clear picture of their new roles in the open, humane environments encouraged by the ESP materials. They also are continuing the publication of *Sensorsheet*.

Earth Science Teacher Preparation Project, under the direction of John Thompson, is now located at the Research-Learning Center, Clarion State College, Clarion, Pennsylvania 16214, where it operates a "limited program" to coordinate the implementation of experimental programs in alternative, humanistic education in undergraduate earth science. The major work in that area is now being taken over by seven regional centers. The regional contact people are:

> *Bob Hanss, Department of Geology, St. Mary's University, 2700 Cincinnati Avenue, San Antonio, Texas 78228,
>
> *Eric Clausen, Director, Experimental College, Minot State College, Minot, North Dakota 58701,
>
> *Tom Bridge, Department of Physical Science, Kansas State Teachers College, Emporia, Kansas 66801,
>
> *Dick Dietz, Department of Earth Sciences, University of Northern Colorado, Greeley, Colorado 80631,
>
> *John Rusch, School of Geology and Geophysics, The University of Oklahoma, Norman, Oklahoma 73069,
>
> *Bill Elberty, Department of Geology and Geography, St. Lawrence University, Canton, New York 13617, and
>
> *John Carpenter, Department of Geology, University of South Carolina, Columbia, South Carolina 29208.

The National Center for Humanistic Environments, Box 4612, Boulder, Colorado 80302 (Bob Lepper and Gail Griffith, Directors), a third spin-off of the ESEP project, offers "General consultation in the areas of humanistic education, open education, rich learning environments, communication skills, organization of creativity (synectics) groups in institutions, and direction of creativity workshops to facilitate the development of creative potential and problem solving skills."

The Hill, Old Walpole Road, Walpole, New Hampshire 03608 (Audrey Beste and Nancy Stuart, Directors) is a Center for the study of Psychosynthesis in education. The Center conducts training workshops and provides individual and group consultations. The directors are especially interested in the gifted and creative child, and they were both recently elected to the National and International Coordinating Councils of Gifted and Talented Children. (In that regard, you might also want to write to the Gifted Children Research Institute, Suite 4-W, 300 West 55th Street, New York, New York 10019.)

Institute for Consciousness and Music, 721 St. John's Road, Baltimore, Maryland 21210 (Helen Bonny and Louis Savary, Directors) offers workshops, leadership training, books and tapes in the area of the use of music to attain altered states of consciousness. The books available include *Passages: A Guide for Pilgrims of the Mind* by Andersen and Savary, and *Music and Your Mind* by Bonny and Savary. Write for a newsletter containing a list of upcoming workshops and a list of tapes and book available from the Institute.

Institute for Humanistic Education of the New England Center, Box 575, Amherst, Massachusetts 01002 (Jack Canfield, Director) conducts workshops, offers consulting services and distributes publications in the area of humanistic education. This includes self concept, values clarification, the Human Development Program, gestalt awareness training, psychosynthesis, and transactional analysis. Write for a brochure.

Institute for Humanistic Education, 535 St. Paul Place, Baltimore, Maryland 21202 (Barbara Raines, Director) is involved in training teachers to implement humanistic education. They are also involved in helping teachers form support groups for mutually exploring more humanistic ways of teaching. Michael Glaser is also preparing a bibliography of humanistic-affective materials and resources.

Institute for the Personal Effectiveness of Children, P.O. Box 20233, San Diego, California, 92120 (Uvaldo Palomares, President), is a non-profit organization formed to promote character and emotional development of children through effective interpersonal communication. IPEC offers preservice and in-service training programs for techniques used in the Human Development Program, a program designed to develop children's self-awareness, self-confidence and human relationships. (See curriculum section.) Write for a brochure listing times and places of their workshops.

NEXTEP Fellowship Program, Southern Illinois University, Edwardsville, Illinois, 62025 (Merrill Harmin, Director), is involved in discovering ways to humanize classroom learning environments. The NEXTEP approach is one of the most comprehensive efforts in the field.

Teacher Drop-Out Center, Box 521, Amherst, Massachusetts, 01002, has identified schools at all levels that have a relatively high degree of student-centered learning and a low-pressure, humane atmosphere where students can develop self-respect and a sense of dignity. The Center acts as a clearinghouse of information and a specialized placement service for teachers finding it difficult to function in traditional schools.

Temple University's Center for the Study of Psychoeducational Processes, Suite 802, Stauffer Hall, Temple University, Philadelphia, Pennsylvania 19122 (Dr. Leland Howe is the best contact person there) offers graduate degree programs and shorter term workshops in the areas of humanistic education, human relations training and organizational development. Write for more information.

Values Associates, P.O. Box 43, Amherst, Massachusetts 01002, is a team of educational consultants directed by Dr. Sidney B. Simon (Co-author of *Values and Teaching* and *Values Clarification*) who have spent many years working with teachers, students, parents, and churches in the area of values clarification. Send for a brochure describing their weekend, and summer workshops, as well as their consulting services.

Youth Research Foundation, 122 West Franklin Avenue, Minneapolis, Minnesota 55404, has long been involved in designing and conducting programs for youth, teachers and parents in the areas of value clarification, positive self-actualization and human relations training. They also operate as a Center for Thomas Gordon's Parent Effectiveness Program.

GROWTH CENTERS

Almost any experience by teachers, counselors and administrators at any growth center can be beneficial to the advancement of humanistic education. Personal growth experiences help the teacher become more aware of his own emotional life and the effect of his behavior on others (including students). They also promote the teacher's self-actualization, thus allowing him to be more in touch with his own feelings and those of his students.

Above and beyond the general workshops in encounter, sensory awareness, gestalt, massage, theater games, psychodrama, movement, psychosynthesis and bio-energetics, many Growth Centers are now conducting programs specifically for educators. For a list of over 145 growth centers across the country, write AHP, 325 Ninth St., San Francisco, California, 94103, and ask for their Growth Center List.

We have listed below several of the Growth Centers that have addressed themselves most directly to humanistic education. We suggest you write for their future brochures.

Associates for Human Resources, P.O. Box 727, Concord, Massachusetts, 01742. Wendy Wyatt, Bob and Niela Horn and Jack Marvin have all been conducting workshops in humanistic education for the past several years.

Cambridge House, 1900 N. Cambridge Avenue, Milwaukee, Wisconsin, 53202, always includes several workshops focusing on the personal growth of teachers in its programs.

Center for the Studies of the Person, 1125 Torrey Pines Road, La Jolla, California 92037, is the Center originally founded by Carl Rogers. The Center is involved in several projects to implement humanistic education in the schools.

Esalen Institute, 1776 Union Street, San Francisco, California, 94123, is the first Growth Center established in America. It always has several top-flight workshops for educators, most of them being run by George I. Brown, Aaron Hillman and other staff of the Ford/Esalen Project in Confluent Education.

Gestalt Institute of Cleveland, 12921 Euclid Avenue, Cleveland, Ohio 44112, conducts several weekend workshops and a professional training series for educators in the use of gestalt methods in education. The

Institute has also developed an experimental course for undergraduate college students who are already enrolled in a college program. The twelve-week course includes Gestalt group work and the theory as well as a field placement experience.

Human Dimensions Institute, 4380 Main Street, Buffalo, New York 14226, is a center primarily concerned with transpersonal growth and has worked extensively in this area with teachers in and around Buffalo.

National Center for the Exploration of Human Potential, 976 Chalcedony Street, San Diego, California 92109, is very involved in both training and research in the area of humanistic education. For a description of one of their more interesting projects write to Arleen Lorrance at the Center for a report on Project Love.

New England Center, Box 575, Amherst, Massachusetts 01002, is a personal growth center dedicated to helping people expand their personal, interpersonal and transpersonal potential through the sponsorship of weekend, weeklong and ongoing workshops in such areas as Gestalt, bioenergetics, psychosynthesis, meditation, yoga, etc. The Center is especially interested in fostering the expansion of human potential in the schools and has recently established an Institute for Humanistic Education, which offers personal growth and professional training for educators.

NTL Institute of Applied Behavioral Science, 1201 16th Street, N.W., Washington, D.C. 20036, conducts seminars for educators at its many centers around the country. Seminars include those in Student Involvement in Learning, Change Agents in Education and Educational Leadership, as well as the Basic and Advanced Labs in Personal Growth.

OASIS, 6 West Ontario Street, Chicago, Illinois 60610, is the major growth center in the Midwest. In addition to a wide range of programs in personal growth, they sponsor occasional workshops in humanistic, affective and confluent education.

Psychosynthesis Institute, 150 Doherty Way, Redwood City, California 94062, sponsors workshops and training programs in psychosynthesis for educators and other mental health professionals. George Brown, Tom Yeomans and several others from the DRICE Confluent Education project have been greatly influenced by their work with Jim and Susan Vargiu at the Institute.

Quest Center for Human Growth, 4933 Auburn Avenue, Bethesda, Maryland 20014, has been sponsoring workshops in humanistic education with Hal Lyon, author of *Learning to Feel—Feeling to Learn*.

JOURNALS AND NEWSLETTERS

AHP Newsletter (free to members), and the *Journal of Humanistic Psychology* ($6.50 to nonmembers; $5.50 to members), are both publications of the Association for Humanistic Psychology, 325 Ninth St., San Francisco, California 94103. They both contain mountains of useful information for those trying to humanize education.

Alternatives in Religious Education, 3206 South St. Paul Street, Denver, Colorado 80210, started as a very helpful magazine offering humanistic approaches to the teaching of Jewish religious education, and has expanded into a full-fledged educational corporation offering curriculum materials, workshops, consultation, and in-service training for teachers. For more information, write Audrey Friedman at the above address. The cost of the magazine is $6.00 per year.

Confluent Education Newsletter, c/o Confluent Education Program, Box 219, Minnedosa, Manitoba, Canada, is published periodically by the Confluent Education Project in Manitoba. They also run workshops on confluent education and have several demonstration schools set up. Write for more information.

Humanistic Education Quarterly, Adirondack Mountain Humanistic Education Center, Upper Jay, New York 12987, is one of the best compilations of new techniques, new materials, book reviews, articles, interviews, and listings of upcoming events in the area of humanistic education to be found. It is totally devoted to the discussion of the affective development of students. The $2.00 per year subscription price is one of the few real bargains still left around. Don't pass it up!

Journal of Applied Behavioral Science, NTL Institute for Applied Behavioral Science, 1201 16th Street, N.W., Washington, D.C. 20036. Contains articles, research reports and book reviews on group dynamics, laboratory training, organizational development and education.

Journal of Creative Behavior, Creative Education Foundation, State University College, 1300 Elmwood Avenue, Buffalo, New York 14222 ($9.00). Articles, research reports and book reviews on creativity and education.

Journal of Transpersonal Psychology, P.O. Box 4437, Stanford, California 94305 ($7.50 per year), is a journal of theoretical and applied research in peak experience, self-transcendence, ultimate values, ecstasy, wonder, B-values, transcendental phenomena and related concepts, experiences and activities.

Learning Magazine, 1255 Portland Place, Boulder, Colorado 80302, is consistently the best major magazine in education that we read each month. It is full of useful articles on new approaches to teaching, new materials available, and new ways of conceptualizing the teaching-learning process. In a recent publicity piece they described themselves as a magazine that "simply gives you a good *feeling*—about yourself, your kids and the job you're trying so hard to do for them." We think they stated what they do very well. The $8.00 a year is well worth it.

Media and Methods, 134 N. 13th Street, Philadelphia, Pennsylvania 19107, is $6.00 per year. It always contains its fair share of articles about humanizing the learning process. M&M is of special interest to teachers of English and teachers using film and movies in their teaching.

People-Watching: Curriculum and Techniques for Teaching the Behavioral Sciences in the Classroom. Behavioral Publications, 2852 Broadway,

New York, N.Y. 10025. This is a new quarterly publication featuring articles, techniques, reviews, and programs which deal with aspects of the behavioral sciences and their application in the school curriculum. Subscriptions are $5.00 per year.

Teachers and Writers Collaborative Newsletter, Pratt Center for Community Improvement, 244 Vanderbilt Avenue, Brooklyn, New York 11205. The Collaborative brings together writers, teachers, and students for the purpose of creating a curriculum that is relevant to the lives of children, and which can therefore make the study of language a living process. Much of what is found here can be used to provide students with new ways of emotional expression. ($3.00 per year)

TRANSPERSONAL PSYCHOLOGY AND EDUCATION

Journal of Transpersonal Psychology, P.O. Box 4437, Stanford, California 94305 ($7.50 per year) is concerned with the publication of "articles and studies in metaneeds, ultimate values, unitive consciousness, peak experiences, ecstasy, mystical experience, B values, essence, bliss, awe, wonder, self-actualization, ultimate meaning, transcendence of the self, spirit ... oneness, cosmic awareness, cosmic play, individual and species-wide synergy, maximal interpersonal encounter, transcendental phenomena, maximal sensory awareness, responsiveness and expression, and related concepts, experiences and activities." Believe it or not, they do all that, and what's more, they do it in issues that elicit cover-to-cover reading each time!

Altered States of Consciousness edited by Charles Tart (New York: John Wiley & Sons, 1969; paperback, Garden City, New York: Doubleday Anchor Books, 1972) 589 pages, $4.95 in paper. This classic book is the first major serious treatment of the subject of altered states of consciousness to appear. Tart has collected articles from a wide range of sources to show the scientific dimensions of the subject. The book covers the effects of drugs, yoga, self-hypnosis, mutual hypnosis, meditation, brain wave feedback, and dream consciousness.

The One Quest by Claudio Naranjo (New York: Viking Press, 1972; paperback, New York: Ballantine Books, 1973) 245 pages, $1.50 in paper. This book has been the single most useful book in our reading in terms of helping us see the universal pattern in both humanistic psychology and in transpersonal psychology of man's search for self-realization. Naranjo helped us see the similarities between gestalt therapy and Karen Horney's theories *and* such traditional transpersonal paths as Taoism, Buddhism, meditation and mysticism. We highly recommend this book for humanistic educators who are trying to find the bridge between what they are doing now and the newer transpersonal approaches which are gaining popularity.

The Crack in the Cosmic Egg: Challenging Constructs of Mind and Reality by Joseph Chilton Pearce (New York: Julian Press, 1971; paperback, New York: Pocket Books, 1973) 219 pages, $1.25 in paperback.

John Lilly has written that a belief is a limit to be overcome. In this book Pearce has overcome quite a few of our more common beliefs about the nature of reality. A basic reading for those attempting to develop cognitive maps for their transpersonal experiences.

The Master Game: Pathways to Higher Consciousness Beyond the Drug Experience by Robert S. DeRopp (New York: Dell Publishing Co., 1968, paperback) 252 pages, $2.25. A useful exploration of the human psyche and of the specific techniques of "Creative Psychology" through which man can achieve higher levels of consciousness. Provides a helpful overall perspective of the transpersonal movement.

The Farther Reaches of Human Nature by Abraham H. Maslow (New York: Viking Press, 1972) 423 pages, $2.95 in paperback. A posthumous collection of Maslow's most important papers, including three on education: "Knower and Known," "Education and Peak Experiences," and "Goals and Implications of Humanistic Education."

The Natural Mind by Andrew Weil (Boston: Houghton Mifflin, 1972) 229 pages, $5.95, also available in paperback. Weil posits that altered states of consciousness are a natural drive in human beings and that drugs are not the best way to achieve them, but prefers paths such as yoga and meditation. Weil's perspective on drug use is useful to anyone pursuing transpersonal psychology as an alternative to drug abuse for their students.

The Center of the Cyclone: An Autobiography of Inner Space by John C. Lilly, M.D. (New York: Julian Press, 1972) 222 pages, $6.95. A helpful book in that through his own personal experiences with LSD, the Arica training of Oscar Ichazo, and other transpersonal methods, Lilly outlines a possible map of higher states of consciousness.

On the Psychology of Meditation by Claudio Naranjo and Robert Ornstein (New York: Viking Press, 1971) Available in paper, also, at $2.25. These two eminent psychologists examine the spiritual ground of meditation and the implications of meditation for modern psychology, incorporating insights from new experimental work in the nature of consciousness.

The Psychology of Consciousness by Robert F. Ornstein (New York: Viking Press, 1973) Ornstein attempts to reconcile the two forms of consciousness which he terms "linear" or rational with "nonlinear" or intuitive. The attempt is an illuminating work on the nature of consciousness.

Mind Games: The Guide to Inner Space by Robert Masters and Jean Houston (New York: Viking Press, 1972) 246 pages, $7.95, also available in paperback. A handbook of exercises for altering, exploring and regulating human consciousness. In addition to the 64 mind expanding exercises, there is a section on how to be a guide for taking others through the uncharted spaces that these games open the door to. A useful guide for teachers planning to work with altered states of consciousness in any organized way. Especially valuable for teachers and counselors seeking to provide students with alternatives to drug induced highs.

Passages: A Guide for Pilgrims of the Mind by Marianne S. Andersen and Louis M. Savary (New York: Harper and Row, 1972) 221 pages, $4.95. This is a beautiful book combining photography, theory, inspirational and insightful quotations, and 43 exercises designed to help us journey farther into our own higher states of consciousness. Extremely useful reading and helpful exercises. Highly recommended!

You are Not the Target by Laura Huxley (North Hollywood, California: Wilshire Book Company, 1972 paperback) 289 pages, $2.00. Contains 32 "recipes" for living and loving. The basis of the recipes is the "transformation of energy," which is discussed in detail in the beginning of the book. The recipes have great merit for your own personal growth as well as for use with students.

Psychosynthesis: A Manual of Principles and Techniques by Roberto Assagioli (New York: Hobbs, Dorman, and Company, 1965; paperback, New York: Viking Press, 1970) This book is the best introduction to psychosynthesis, which has been gaining in its impact on affective educators across the country. Psychosynthesis provides a theory and an approach to a balanced and integrative development of the mind, the emotions, the body and the spirit, all around a unifying center of being and awareness called the "Transpersonal Self."

The Act of Will by Roberto Assagioli (New York: Viking Press, 1973) 278 pages, $10.00. In this book Assagioli attempts to bring the long neglected human will back into its rightful perspective in psychology and education. The old conception of the harsh and repressive "will power" has been replaced with a more comprehensive notion of a "skillful will," and beyond that, the notion of a "transpersonal will." Valuable reading!

If you find that we have omitted resources that have been of value to you and/or that you feel might be of value to others, we hope that you will send us information about them so that we may include them in our forthcoming book *Toward a Guide to Humanistic Education*, which will include annotated listings of all the books, curricula, media, projects, people, places and ideas that are in any way related to the process of humanizing the teaching-learning process both inside and outside of our schools. Information should be sent to John T. Canfield, New England Center, Box 575, Amherst, Massachusetts 01002.

Index